Lecture Notes in Computer Science 7939

Commenced Publication in 1973
Founding and Former Series Editors:
Gerhard Goos, Juris Hartmanis, and Jan van Leeuwen

Jan vom Brocke   Riitta Hekkala
Sudha Ram   Matti Rossi (Eds.)

Design Science at the Intersection of Physical and Virtual Design

8th International Conference, DESRIST 2013
Helsinki, Finland, June 11-12, 2013
Proceedings

 Springer

Volume Editors

Jan vom Brocke
University of Liechtenstein
9490 Vaduz, Liechtenstein
E-mail: jan.vom.brocke@uni.li

Riitta Hekkala
Matti Rossi
Aalto University
00076 Aalto, Finland
E-mail:{riitta.hekkala, matti.rossi}@aalto.fi

Sudha Ram
University of Arizona
Tucson, AZ 85721, USA
E-mail: ram@eller.arizona.edu

ISSN 0302-9743   e-ISSN 1611-3349
ISBN 978-3-642-38826-2   e-ISBN 978-3-642-38827-9
DOI 10.1007/978-3-642-38827-9
Springer Heidelberg Dordrecht London New York

Library of Congress Control Number: 2013939725

CR Subject Classification (1998): H.1, H.5, H.4, J.1, D.2, K.6, H.3

LNCS Sublibrary: SL 3 – Information Systems and Application, incl. Internet/Web
and HCI

Typesetting: Camera-ready by author, data conversion by Scientific Publishing Services, Chennai, India

Printed on acid-free paper

Springer is part of Springer Science+Business Media (www.springer.com)

Preface

The Second European DESRIST Conference continued the tradition of advancing design research within the information systems discipline. As in previous years, scholars and design practitioners from many areas such as information systems, computer science, industrial design, medical informatics, and software engineering came together to solve human problems through the innovative use of information technology and applications. The outputs of DESRIST, new and innovative constructs, models, methods, processes, and systems provide the basis for novel solutions to design problems in many fields.

The eighth DESRIST conference, DESRIST 2013, held in Helsinki built on the tradition and foundation of seven prior highly successful international conferences held in Claremont, Pasadena, Atlanta, Philadelphia, St. Gallen, Milwaukee, and Las Vegas.

The title of this volume, *Design Science at the Intersection of Physical and Virtual Design*, reflects the idea that much of the current design combines virtual and physical aspects of environment, examples of this being new applications for saving energy and for aiding in health care. The accepted papers are evenly distributed between exemplars of design and theory development. As in previous years, a substantial majority of the submitted papers described the application of design science research to real-world design problems in both industry and government.

A record number of 93 papers were submitted to the conference for review. Each paper was reviewed by at least two referees. The reviews were double blind, meaning that each of the two groups – authors and referees – remained anonymous to one another. In all, 25 full papers, eight research-in-progress papers, 12 short papers describing prototype demonstrations, and eight poster abstracts were accepted. The program also contained two panels and two industrial keynotes.

We thank the authors, who submitted papers to DESRIST 2013, and trust the readers will find the papers as interesting and informative as we did. We would like to thank the members of the Program Committee as well as the additional referees, who took the time to provide detailed and constructive reviews for the authors. We would also like to thank other members of the Organizing Committee, as well as the volunteers, whose dedication and effort helped bring about another successful conference. We believe the papers in the DESRIST 2013 proceedings provide several interesting and valuable insights into the theory and practice of design science, and they open up new and exciting possibilities for research in the discipline.

June 2013

Jan vom Brocke
Riitta Hekkala
Sudha Ram
Matti Rossi

Organization

General Chairs

Ken Peffers — University of Nevada Las Vegas, USA
Marcus Rothenberger — University of Nevada Las Vegas, USA
Samir Chatterjee — Claremont Graduate University, USA

Program Chairs

Jam vom Brocke — University of Liechtenstein, Liechtenstein
Sudha Ram — University of Arizona, USA
Matti Rossi — Aalto University, Finland

Proceedings Chair

Riitta Hekkala — Aalto University, Finland

Local Arrangements Chair

Virpi Kristiina Tuunainen — Aalto University, Finland

Doctoral Consortium Chairs

Kari Smolander — Lappeenranta University of Technology, Finland
Stefan Seidel — University of Liechtenstein, Liechtenstein
Jan Pries-Heje — Roskilde University, Denmark

Program Committee

Wil van der Aalst — Eindhoven University of Technology, The Netherlands
Frederik Ahlemann — University of Duisburg-Essen, Germany
Richard Baskerville — Georgia State University, USA
Jörg Becker — University of Münster, Germany
Sven Carlsson — Lund University, Sweden
Guoqing Chen — Tsinghua University, China
Roger Chiang — University of Cincinnati, USA

Table of Contents

System Integration and Design

How to Prevent Reinventing the Wheel? – Design Principles for Project
Knowledge Management Systems 1
   Silvia Schacht and Alexander Mädche

Designing an Artifact for the Integration of Ubiquitous Information
Systems in an Enterprise Context 18
   Oliver Gaß, Alexander Mädche, Harald Biegel, and Mahei Li

Design Principles for Research Data Export: Lessons Learned in
e-Health Design Research 34
   Mudassir Imran Mustafa and Jonas Sjöström

Metaissues

What's the Best Bet? An Analysis of Design Scientists' Perceptions
of Receptivity and Impact of IS Journals 50
   Debra VanderMeer and Monica Chiarini Tremblay

Seeking Constructive Synergy: Design Science and the Constructive
Research Approach 59
   Kalle A. Piirainen and Rafael A. Gonzalez

Pattern-Based Design Research – An Iterative Research Method
Balancing Rigor and Relevance 73
   *Sabine Buckl, Florian Matthes, Alexander W. Schneider, and
   Christian M. Schweda*

Business Process Management and ERP

Patterns as an Artifact for Business Process Improvement - Insights
from a Case Study 88
   Thomas Falk, Philipp Griesberger, and Susanne Leist

ERP Event Log Preprocessing: Timestamps vs. Accounting Logic 105
   Niels Mueller-Wickop and Martin Schultz

Enriching Process Models for Business Process Compliance Checking
in ERP Environments 120
   Martin Schultz

Theory Development 1

Rethinking Design Theory in Information Systems 136
  John R. Venable

How to Generalize an Information Technology Case Study 150
  Rúben Pereira, Rafael Almeida, and Miguel Mira da Silva

Reconciling Theories with Design Choices in Design Science Research... 165
  Roman Lukyanenko and Jeffrey Parsons

Emerging Themes

Formidable Bracelet, Beautiful Lantern: Studying Multi-sensory User
Experience from a Semiotic Perspective 181
  Rebekah Rousi

Boundary Resources Dependency in Third-Party Development from
the Developer's Perspective 197
  Asma Rafiq, Pär J. Ågerfalk, and Jonas Sjöström

Organizational Design of Innovative Education – Insights from
a Combined Design and Action Research Project.................... 212
  Olivera Marjanovic

Theory Development 2

Don't Ignore the Iceberg: Timely Revelation of Justification in DSR 228
  Dirk S. Hovorka and Jan Pries-Heje

An Argumentative Approach of Conceptual Modelling and Model
Validation through Theory Building 242
  Sebastian Bittmann and Oliver Thomas

BWW Ontology as a Lens on IS Design Theory: Extending the Design
Science Research Roadmap.. 258
  Ahmad Alturki, Guy G. Gable, and Wasana Bandara

Green IS and Service Management

Towards an Innovative Service Development Process in the Electricity
Industry 278
  Yannic Domigall, Antonia Albani, and Robert Winter

Design Science in Practice: Designing an Electricity Demand Response
System 293
  Philipp Bodenbenner, Stefan Feuerriegel, and Dirk Neumann

A Decision Support Tool to Define Scope in IT Service Management
Process Assessment and Improvement 308
    Anup Shrestha, Aileen Cater-Steel, Mark Toleman, and Wui-Gee Tan

Green IS for GHG Emission Reporting on Product-Level? An Action
Design Research Project in the Meat Industry 324
    Hendrik Hilpert, Christoph Beckers, Lutz M. Kolbe, and
    Matthias Schumann

Method Engineering

Design Methodology for Construction of Mapping Applications 340
    Olusola Samuel-Ojo, Lorne Olfman, Linda A. Reinen,
    Arjuna Flenner, David D. Oglesby, and Gareth J. Funning

Cherry Picking with Meta-Models: A Systematic Approach for the
Organization-Specific Configuration of Maturity Models 353
    Janusch Patas, Jens Pöppelbuß, and Matthias Goeken

Towards a Domain-Specific Method for Multi-Perspective Hospital
Modelling – Motivation and Requirements 369
    Michael Heß

Products and Prototypes

The Service Meta Modeling Editor – Bottom-Up Integration of Service
Models 386
    Christoph Augenstein and André Ludwig

Icebricks: Business Process Modeling on the Basis of Semantic
Standardization... 394
    Jörg Becker, Nico Clever, Justus Holler, and Maria Shitkova

Estimating Operating System Process Energy Consumption in Real
Time 400
    Kaushik Dutta, Vivek Kumar Singh, and Debra VanderMeer

Cross-Platform Development of Business Apps with MD^2 405
    Henning Heitkötter and Tim A. Majchrzak

Context-Awareness in the Car: Prediction, Evaluation and Usage
of Route Trajectories 412
    Patrick Helmholz, Edgar Ziesmann, and Susanne Robra-Bissantz

Self-Service Management Support Systems—There's an App
for That 420
    Bernhard Krönke, Alexa Reinecke, Jörg Hans Mayer,
    Gotthard Tischner, Hannes Feistenauer, and Jörg Hauke

Designing a Web-Based Classroom Response System 425
Dennis Kundisch, Philipp Herrmann, Michael Whittaker,
Jürgen Neumann, Johannes Magenheim, Wolfgang Reinhardt,
Marc Beutner, and Andrea Zoyke

New-Generation Managers and Their IS Support—Getting It Right
with the Corporate Navigator 432
Jörg Hans Mayer and Robert Winter

MUSE: Implementation of a Design Theory for Systems that Support
Convergent and Divergent Thinking 438
Oliver Müller, Stefan Debortoli, and Stefan Seidel

Mini Smart Grid @ Copenhagen Business School: Prototype
Demonstration.. 446
Rasmus U. Pedersen, Szymon J. Furtak, Ivan Häuser,
Codrina Lauth, and Rob Van Kranenburg

preCEP: Facilitating Predictive Event-Driven Process Analytics........ 448
Bernd Schwegmann, Martin Matzner, and Christian Janiesch

Developing Creative Business Models – The OctoProz Tool............ 456
Matthias Voigt, Kevin Ortbach, Ralf Plattfaut, and Björn Niehaves

Work in Progress Papers

Using Empirical Knowledge and Studies in the Frame of Design Science
Research... 464
Ilia Bider, Paul Johannesson, and Erik Perjons

Towards a Reference Model for a Productivity-Optimized Delivery
of Technology Mediated Learning Services.......................... 471
Philipp Bitzer, Frank Weiß, and Jan Marco Leimeister

A Framework for Classifying Design Research Methods 479
Dan Harnesk and Devinder Thapa

Constructing Software-Intensive Methods: A Design Science Research
Process with Early Feedback Cycles 486
Robert Krawatzeck, Marcus Hofmann, Frieder Jacobi, and
Barbara Dinter

User Guidance for Document-Driven Processes in Enterprise Systems ... 494
Stefan Morana, Silvia Schacht, Ansgar Scherp, and
Alexander Mädche

Cooperative Games and Their Effect on Group Collaboration 502
Maaz Nasir, Kelly Lyons, Rock Leung, and Ali Moradian

Respondent Behavior Logging: An Opportunity for Online Survey
Design   511
    Jonas Sjöström, Mohammad Hafijur Rahman, Asma Rafiq,
    Ruth Lochan, and Pär J. Ågerfalk

Towards Design Principles for Pharmacist-Patient Health Information
Systems   519
    Dirk Volland, Klaus Korak, David Brückner, and Tobias Kowatsch

Author Index   527

How to Prevent Reinventing the Wheel? – Design Principles for Project Knowledge Management Systems

Silvia Schacht[1] and Alexander Mädche[1,2]

[1] Chair of Information Systems IV, University of Mannheim, Mannheim, Germany
{schacht,maedche}@es.uni-mannheim.de
[2] Institute for Enterprise Systems, University of Mannheim, Mannheim, Germany

Abstract. Today, many companies still struggle in documenting and reusing the knowledge gained by project teams. However, knowledge only creates value if it is applied. There exists a vast amount of research in the field of knowledge management focusing on documentation, storage and exchange of knowledge, but knowledge reuse is often omitted by researchers. The presented work aims to close this gap by developing a project knowledge management system enabling project teams to apply company-internal knowledge. We followed an action design research approach to explore meta-requirements in a case company, translate these requirements into design principles and test the design principles by evaluating an artifact of a project knowledge management system. By our work, the knowledge management research field can benefit since our design theory extends the existing body of knowledge. Furthermore, our research results are instantiated in a concrete artifact which can be directly transferred into practice.

Keywords: Project Knowledge Management System, Knowledge Reuse, Project Management, Action Design Research.

1 Introduction

A growing number of companies are organized in project-based structures [1] to translate their strategic targets into operative actions. Since projects are knowledge-intensive work [2], their management is not easy for several reasons. Most reasons are grounded in the definition of projects as *"... a temporary endeavor undertaken to create a unique product or service"* [3, p. 4]. Project teams are composed of different employees having different knowledge background and sets of skills. Because projects are of temporary nature, teams are set up for limited amount of time [4] resulting in members leaving the project within its duration. When leaving, they take their experiences with them, often without providing their key insights to a central knowledge base [5]. Another challenge of managing projects arises from the goal of creating unique products or services requiring a team having a broad field of expertise to cover the full range of required skills [1]. Consequently, knowledge produced and reused in one project many be valuable for another one. A special kind of projects is the information system (IS) project. IS projects have a high potential to benefit from

J. vom Brocke et al. (Eds.): DESRIST 2013, LNCS 7939, pp. 1–17, 2013.

previous project insights because a remarkable amount of IS project activities are similar to each other [6]. However, one reason why companies still struggle to perform IS projects in time and in budget is the lack of knowledge reuse. This results in repeating the same mistake, reinventing the wheel by finding already known solutions or performing redundant work [7].

In recent years many researchers examined the knowledge management (KM) field from different points of view like the supportive nature of modern technologies (e.g. [8-9]) or the role of social interactions (e.g. [5], [7]). Altogether, there exist vast amount of results in KM research. However, the knowledge reuse seems to be often omitted by researchers as valuable process phase of KM [10]. As Choi et al. [11] conclude in their work by stating *"... no matter how much knowledge is shared among team members, it cannot enhance team performance unless it is effectively applied."* [11, p. 866], we strongly belief that knowledge reuse is an important KM process phase being of interest for researchers and practitioners. Therefore, our overall research aims to answer the question on how KM activities in organizations can be structured in order to increase knowledge reuse across projects. Our research focuses on the social and technological subsystem of KM systems [12], since effective KM needs both appropriate technology and social interaction between individuals. While we will report on our research regarding the social subsystem of a project KM system in another article, the research presented in this article focuses on answering the following research question:

> *Which design principles of a project KM system increase individuals' intention to reuse existing, project-related knowledge?*

The remainder of this paper is structured as follows: In subsequent section 2, we describe the methodology of our research and provide an overview on our research phases. Section 3 presents the first stage of our research focusing on the problem definition of knowledge reuse in a case company. In section 4, we present the mockup design of the project KM system grounded on our design principles. Section 5 discusses the evaluation of this design based on the feedback provided by experts of the case company. Section 6 summarizes our findings and discusses the limitations of our work.

2   Methodology

Our research aims to develop an artifact-based solution for increasing the reuse of project knowledge among various projects. Therefore, our work bases on the framework of Sein et al. [13] along the paradigm of design science research (DSR). In their work, the researchers call this form of DSR action design research (ADR) because it draws on action research (AR). The combination of both research approaches is intensively discussed by many researchers (e.g. [13-16]) since both research streams possess some advantages and disadvantages. Today, DSR is generally accepted in the IS discipline as a rigorous method. However, some critics argue that DSR results in an imbalance between rigor and relevance [13]. On the contrary, AR has a long tradition in psychology and organizational science. AR is defined as the *"... combined generation of theory with changing the social system through the researcher acting on or in the social system"* [17, p. 586]. Unlike DSR, AR is strongly oriented toward collaboration between researchers and practitioners. Hence, AR addresses to solve current practical problems and to expand scientific knowledge simultaneously [18]. However, AR is often criticized for focusing too much on practical relevance on costs of methodological rigor. Often it is maligned as consultation projects [19] or *"... research with little action or action with little research ..."* [20, p. 131]. By combing DSR and AR typical risks of both methods will be accommodated. A key advantage of the conjunction is an improved problem understanding and evaluation. In line with this view, the entire work follows the four stage model as presented by Sein et al. [13].

The **first stage** focuses on the identification and definition of the problem in a case company. Subsequently, we capture a set of meta-requirements [21] on a project KM system and deduce appropriate design principles enabling practitioners and researchers to create further artifacts that belong to the same kind of systems [13, 21-22]. The **second stage** bases on the planning and conduction of interventions. These interventions are concrete design decisions inferred from the design principles. The **third stage** aims to evaluate the effects of the interventions. We divide the evaluation stage in two cycles: (1) we evaluate the mockup design of our project KM system based on the feedback of some experts employed in the case company, and (2) we refine the design of the artifact based on the provided feedback, realize it within the case company and evaluate the system by studying users' intention to use it. Finally, the **fourth stage** serves for reflecting the research in terms of practical and theoretical contributions.

3　　Stage 1: Problem Definition

The first stage of our research aims to get an overview on the awareness of challenges of project insights' reuse in companies and existing literature. We conducted an exploratory case study in a project-based company. Since IS projects seem to have a high potential to benefit from knowledge reuse [6], we focus on these projects. In the following subsections we describe our research activities within this first stage.

3.1　　Case Company Selection

Given the focus on project knowledge reuse and the special characteristics of IS projects, we purposefully selected a financial service provider as the subject of our studies. Today, this sector heavily relies on IS to acquire, process and deliver information to all relevant users. These service-related systems are developed in IS projects [23]. Because of the high number of IS projects conducted in financial service companies, we expect a high demand on knowledge reuse to gain high organizational performance. We conducted our study in an IS service department of a large German financial service provider. To ensure anonymity of our research subject, we name the financial service provider "GeFiS" and its IS service department

"IS@GeFiS". Today, GeFiS operates in over 70 countries and employs more than 100.000 employees. IS@GeFiS is organized in a project-based structure and recently engages about 180 employees regularly supported by external consultants.

3.2   Exploratory Interview Study

To get an overview on the IS@GeFiS' issues with knowledge reuse among IS projects, we conducted an exploratory interview study. As a preparation and to triangulate gathered data, we started by studying some documents regarding project insights of IS@GeFiS. All in all, 31 documents were provided by the company. The documents include guidelines for the collection and documentation of project insights called lessons learned, some exemplarily lessons learned, and role descriptions of various professionals. In the document study we realized that the provided documents show considerable differences in their appearance and content. In our view, this is reasoned by a missing consistency of the lessons learned process and according instructions. Based on the result of our document analysis we defined some working assumptions forming the groundwork of our interview study.

The sampling of the interviewees was coordinated by some employees of IS@GeFiS. In order to prevent a selection bias, we briefed the employees how to deploy a good sample. In sum, 27 interviewees were selected (14 project managers, 8 technical specialists, 2 functional analysts, 2 professional development managers, 1 department head) reflecting the distribution of roles in the entire department. The selection of interviewees can be described to be a purposeful sampling [24]. At the beginning of an interview, we provided some information to the interviewees regarding anonymity, purpose of the research study, and use of gathered data [25]. The interviews lasted between 20 and 50 minutes. All interviews were conducted by two researchers – one conducting the interview and one taking notes. The questions addressed a wide range of KM topics to cover all aspects regarding both, the social and technological subsystem of a project KM system. Depending on the information needed, we extended the guideline with additional questions within the particular interview. The interviews were recorded and afterwards transcribed as text files. The records and transcripts are stored anonymously and cannot be traced back to the participants.

Although we had some working assumptions, we used the inductive coding approach for the data analysis instead of the deductive approach as described by Thomas [26]. While the deductive approach aims to test consistencies with prior assumptions or hypotheses, the inductive approach facilitates us to extract themes that are mentioned by the interviewees frequently, dominantly or significantly. To discover the company's knowledge reuse issues, inductive coding approach seemed to be most adequate. In order to increase internal validity [27-28] two researchers coded the interviews whereas one of the researchers was not involved in any other aspects of the project. After transcribing the interview recordings, we started to read the text files carefully. In the next phase, we identified specific text segments related to the research objective, marked all these segments and labeled them with codes using MaxQDA – a software application especially intended for qualitative data analysis.

As a result from this coding process, we developed 51 categories. If codes were clustered in more than one category, we discussed the findings and agreed on one of the categories. Furthermore, synonyms were resolved. Consequently, we reduced the amount of categories to 20. Finally, we searched for subtopics and established clear connections between subtopics and categories.

Table 1. Meta-requirements of the technological subsystem of project KM systems

Subtopic	Meta-Requirement	Exemplarily Quote
Access	MR1: Full accessibility to project insight data base for all organization members	"I was out of the project. At some time, my account was cleared. That means I have no access to the [project] drive anymore."
	MR2: Central storage including consistent filing and search functionalities	"It must be somewhere central, so everybody can access it."
	MR3: Possibility to structure documents by indexing, categorizing and clustering	"This actually happens quite informally, either you know someone working on a project. Then you talk with him/her having a coffee, lunch, and so on, or sometimes if you want to know something about a specific topic, then you ask: How was your experiences?"
Structure	MR4: Full accessibility to project insight data base for all organization members	"Of course, it has to be structured and tagged so that you can pick key information to a certain topic."
	MR5: Pre-structured documents for easy completion	"You have to structure it in some way so that you can use it afterwards And also efficiently for future similar projects."
	MR6: Including sufficient free space for additional explanations	"... but I think every project is different. It should also contain a plenty of space to provide some free texts. Yes, of course, there are some aspects where I can tally: good, moderate, bad. But a lot of specifics of a project [...] cannot be pre-structured."
Feedback and Maintenance	MR7: Provide feedback on documented project insights	"... if anyone says to you: 'I read your lessons learned. Thank you for your presentation making the issue transparent for us [...].' I think this kind of recognitions is incentive enough – or should be incentive enough."
	MR8: Ensured maintenance of project insight documents	"It is a time exposure to maintain and manage it. I mean, information important in one project can later be invalid or outdated."

Considering the codes related to the technological subsystem, we identified three main subtopics: (1) *access* to project insights, (2) *structure* of effective project insight documentation, and (3) *feedback* provision on and *maintenance* of documented project insights. Within these three categories, we derived eight meta-requirements (out of 13 meta-requirements for both, the social and technological subsystem). The meta-requirements and some exemplarily quotes are summarized in Table 1.

3.3   Results of the Interview Study

Building on the identified meta-requirements, we derived three design principles covering the technological issues of project KM. In doing so, we consulted literature published in the project KM field to interrelate the meta-requirements with the knowledge base of existing research. The mapping of the meta-requirements to design principles is discussed in the following subsections.

Access to Experts and Expertise
Access to project knowledge can take place via both, information technology and social interaction. From a technological point of view, there exist many applications to file project insights. This may be traditional storage bins such as repositories or databases or modern technologies like wikis or blogs. Both forms of technologies are coming with some advantages and disadvantages. Repositories, for example, possess hierarchical structures forcing users to file the documents in only one location. This in turn forces organizations to provide a strict categorization of documents. Such a categorization makes it difficult for employees to decide where to file, manage, locate and share specific documents like project insights [29]. Furthermore, many researchers (e.g. [4-5], [30]) realized that repositories are used by individuals only sporadically. The situation is exacerbated if documents contain lessons learned. Lessons learned, by definition, are essential experiences of a project team gained during the course of the project. However, such experiences are often characterized as tacit and bound to people involved in the problem-solving process [31]. Since tacit knowledge is difficult to externalize – if not even impossible – not every insight gained in a project can be captured in a repository [32]. Looking at more modern technologies like wikis, we observe some improvements in storing project insights. Wikis ease the knowledge documentation process in terms of authoring, sharing and finding the knowledge due to their included functionalities such as content-to-page-mapping, indexing, hyperlinking, duplicate removing, searching, and using the power of the crowd [33]. The usage of wikis in organizational settings, however, is still low [34]. Although these technologies possess some drawbacks, companies rely on the documentation of knowledge and insights for continuous organizational learning [35]. Hence, the implementation of an adequate central storage medium adapted to the needs of organizations and their employees is a vital necessity (**MR2**). The access of employees to this central storage technology, however, is inevitable (**MR1**).

Project insights may contain information perceived by individuals as very sensitive, especially when they have to fear negative consequences or misleading others [36]. Thus, people prefer to document their findings anonymously resulting in cutting off the documents from the experts. Because nearly all employees of large companies like GeFiS have some project-related experiences, the search for a specific expert will be like looking for the needle in a haystack. The provision of multiple channels for knowledge exchange is important for large-scale companies [37]. Hence, the technological subsystem of an effective project KM system should enable knowledge seekers to search for project insights via two ways: (1) direct search of documented (externalized) knowledge by browsing storage locations, and (2) indirect search of internalized knowledge by contacting experts (**MR3**).

Following our findings collected in the interview study and our literature review, we identified access to both, documented knowledge and knowledge that resides in individuals as a design principle (DP) of project KM systems. Therefore, we reword Markus' call for providing *"... access to the detailed resumes of every employee's experience and area of expertise in addition to documents..."* [38, p. 75] to our first design principle, which is also formulated in this way by Petter and Vaishnavi [9].

DP1:   *Ensure access to both experts and expertise.*

Structure of Project Insights
Although project reviews are mostly documented at the end of projects [39], the capturing of insights in documents takes place only seldom [31]. Even if insights are collected and codified, they are often not valuable for others since its documentation often lacks on structure, degree of granularity, or context information [40-41]. One reason for such ill-structured documents is the high complexity of projects itself resulting in individuals' struggle in codification of their project insights [9]. For an efficient project KM, however, organizations have to structure and store the insights in a way that other employees can also use them, even if they were not part of the project team. Here, structuring the insights means that experiences have to be expressed, codified and prepared for an easy sharing [41].

Besides the structuring of insights, it is also important to organize the codified documents in a way that they can be found when needed [41]. Thus, a format supporting hyperlinking, indexing and search mechanisms are needed (**MR4**). In literature, many formats are discussed for project reviews. Often they are called postmortems. They are used to reflect what happened in projects aiming to improve future working practices [40]. These reviews focus on learning from success and failure instead of evaluating the project and its team. In general, there are three main perspectives on capturing and sharing knowledge of projects: reflective, formal, and narrative perspective. While the reflective perspective has mainly a subjective note and the formal perspective is highly objective, the narrative perspective focuses on telling a story to appeal to emotions [42]. Narratives are an easy-to-share and easy-to-remember format containing high amount of knowledge in a semi-structured format [9]. Compared to traditional postmortems they are easy-to-remember, but require a high effort in codification [40]. Thus, a well balanced mix of pre-structured documents to ease the documentation and retrieve lessons learned (**MR5**), and free-text fields to provide additional information (**MR6**) are needed. Resulting from the literature of existing research and the meta-requirements of our case study, we formulate our second design principle:

DP2:   *Provide contextual and packaged information in structured documents.*

Feedback and Maintenance

Providing incentives to employees for knowledge contribution is also an important factor influencing their willingness to share and reuse knowledge [9]. While the provisioning of incentives for motivating employees is part of our social subsystem of a project KM system, we identified feedback as another important part of the technological and social subsystem. There are many studies on intrinsic and extrinsic mechanisms motivating employees to share knowledge (e.g. [43-44]). Nevertheless, most of them realize that *"[...] knowledge self-efficacy is an important antecedent to employee knowledge sharing attitudes and intentions."* [44, p. 145] Thus, providing useful feedback (**MR7**) improves self-efficacy of individuals and increases their willingness to share knowledge. Documenting project insights facilitates managers to provide structured feedback and hence increase the performance of project teams [40]. In addition to feedback which can be provided by managers, feedback of colleagues is also valuable for an increased knowledge reuse [45]. Consequently, providing feedback is also a powerful method to incentivize individuals for sharing their project knowledge with others.

As King et al. [46] realized the currency of knowledge is also a challenge companies need to cope with in order to implement effective KM strategies [46]. One modern possibility to maintain project insights with regard to their currency and usefulness (**MR8**) is the implementation of rating functionalities. While rating is often used as feedback mechanisms for example in social networks (e.g. Facebook, Twitter, etc.) or online markets (e.g. eBay, Amazon), it can also be used in order to assess the project insights. Less rated insights are maybe of less interest for other projects because they are either outdated or not valuable. The usage of rating functionalities in order to assess a product or service is highly discussed in the research area of online markets (see [47]). From the findings of the interviews and the literature study, we thus formulate the following, third design principle:

DP3:   *Enable project insight maintenance based on feedback regarding usefulness and currency of project insights.*

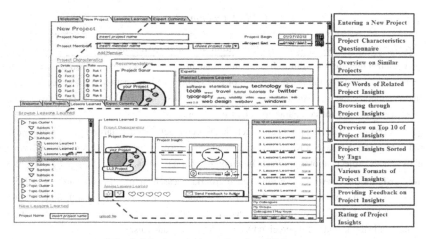

Fig. 1. Mockup design of project KM system

4   Stage 2 – Intervention

Based on the design principles DP1 to DP3, we designed an artifact of a project KM system. We translated our design principles into concrete design decisions again by consulting existing literature. Figure 1 presents two exemplarily mockups that include those functionalities that we perceive as adequate design decisions. Since most design decisions result from our discussed meta-requirements, we summarized the functionalities of the project KM system in Table 2.

Table 2. Design decisions derived from design principles

Design Decision	Source
DP1: Ensure access to both experts and expertise.	
• **Social networks and communities:** Knowledge communities are an instantiation of Communities of Practice (CoP). By implementing communities, companies promote informal knowledge exchange which facilitates knowledge reuse. Examples of technological implementations can be social networks, forums or chat rooms.	[4], [36]
• **Search functionality:** Today, many platforms come with semantic search functionality. This enables users, to find unstructured information captured in various documents or other formats of knowledge documentation.	[49]
• **Hyperlinking and tagging:** Hyperlinking and tagging are mechanisms that ease the documentation, search and retrieval of knowledge. Each time a document is stored at the platform, individuals provide some key words or links to related documents. This enables the development of an information network which eases to explore project insights.	[32-33]
• **Access control:** By implementing user authentication and authorization mechanisms, users of various roles may get different access rights to documents. Thus, project team members can share their knowledge in documents that are either open for all users of the project KM system or private only for the use of the project team members.	[50]

Table 2. (*continued*)

DP2: Provide contextual and packaged information in structured documents.

• **Project characteristic questionnaire:** A questionnaire on project characteristics is a structured way to enable the provisioning project's contextual information. Such a questionnaire supports the standardization of processes, is easy to complete and provides some metrics that ease the comparability of various projects.	Interview study
• **Project overview:** Using the project characterization conducted in the starting phase and stored at a central database, a KMS can be enriched by a project overview. This overview visually relates projects to other projects based on its characteristics.	Interview study
• **Project insights overview:** In addition to an appropriate search engine, the provision of an overview on that project insights that relate to another project ease the search and retrieval of knowledge. Here, the rating mechanism can be used in order to display those project insights that were perceived as most useful for other users.	Interview study
• **Variety of formats:** Various projects possess varying complexity. Thus a fully standardization of project insight documentations is not feasible. The more complex a project, the more individuals should be able to include additional information, for example, by providing additional formats of documentation (e.g. photos, videos, etc.).	[9], [42]

DP3:   Enable project insight maintenance based on feedback regarding usefulness and currency of project insights.

• **Rating:** Rating products or services is intensively used in electronic markets. Rating mechanisms summarize the opinion of users and provide for potential users a brief overview on the product or service. By implementing the rating functionality in the project KM system, knowledge seekers get a quick overview on the usefulness and applicability of documented project insights	[47]
• **Feedback provisioning:** If individuals receive constructive feedback on their work, they are more willing to share their knowledge. By implementing mechanisms enabling project teams to assess the received expertise or the experts who provided the knowledge, continuous learning due to regular up-dates of existing, organizational knowledge can be facilitated.	[9], [40], [45]
• **Automatically updating;** Using the assessment functionality, project insights can be ranked according to their usefulness and applicability. The resulting ranking enables the identification of project insights that are not used anymore because they are and not useful anymore.	[46], [47]

In order to bundle the functionalities in one system, we decided to develop the project KM system as an integrated platform. We perceive the platform design as appropriate, since platforms are defined as an *"... extensible codebase of a software-based system that provides core functionality shared by the modules that interoperate with it and the interfaces through which they interoperate."* [48, p. 676] The ease of extensibility is the key advantage of platforms resulting in the possibility of continuously improving the system by adding or removing modules.

5   Stage 3 – Evaluation

The resulting mockup design is evaluated via a workshop series within the case company. The **first workshop** aimed to get feedback from key decision makers of IS@GeFiS. Thus, we invited the department's head, one Professional Development Manager and one Project Manager as participants to the workshop. The entire session lasted 60 minutes and consisted of three parts: First, we presented the key findings of our interview study and literature review. We engaged the attention of department's management on typically challenges of knowledge reuse within IS@GeFiS. In the second part, we presented the meta-requirements, the resulting design principles and the mockup design of the project KM system we perceive as being effective in IS@GeFiS. After presenting the results and the mockup design, we opened a discussion round as the final part. Each participant was asked to provide feedback on the design. In order to motivate the participants to discuss the design very open, we decided to refrain from recording the session. Instead, the researchers took notes and collected these notes in a research field work journal. The key result of this first session can be summarized by one statement of the department's head: *"The design seems to be a good one. However, I think it makes more sense to evaluate the design by asking those people who will be supposed to use the system."*

In consequence of the workshop's key finding, we conducted a **second workshop** session aiming to get feedback from key players in IS@GeFiS' projects. In sum, we invited 10 participants possessing various roles within the department. However, only five participants were able to attend the workshop session. The workshop lasted 90 minutes. This workshop consisted of two parts: First, the presentation of the mockup design by one researcher. Second, we have obtained the participants' feedback on the design of the mockups. In order to get a structured feedback, we asked the participants to assess the design along the dimensions strengths, weaknesses, opportunities and threats (called SWOT-analysis). Finally, the participants were asked to brainstorm on key functionalities and their effect on an active knowledge reuse culture within the department. In order to motivate an open discussion, we decided once again to refrain from recording the statements. However, we took a photo protocol and summarized the key findings in our research field work journal. The key findings of the second workshop are displayed in Figure 3.

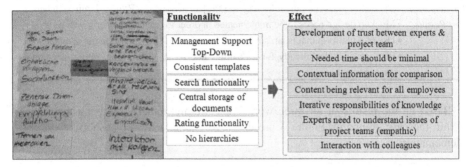

Fig. 2. Photo and translated results of workshop session 2

The left side of Figure 2 displays the photo documentation of the brainstorming session. Since the workshop is done in German, we present at the right side of Figure 3 a translation of the key results. At the end of the workshop, we collected five key points as feedback. The feedback of all workshop sessions and an overview on the sessions is provided in Table 3.

Since the participants of the second workshop were mainly project managers, we decided to conduct a **third workshop** session with project team members. Therefore, we invited eight project team members possessing different roles within a project. In coordination with some employees of IS@GeFiS we purposefully selected the participants of this third workshop. We selected employees as participants who were known for their attitude towards project in-sights. Thus, the group of participants consisted of some employees being skeptics of project insights collection methods and some having a positive attitude towards knowledge reuse. The third session lasted 60 minutes. After the presentation of the mockup design, the participants were asked to provide their feedback in an open feedback round. After a brief discussion, all participants agreed to implement at least the key functionalities of the mockup design in order to decide whether it is useful or not. Since the organization is already using a platform similar to Microsoft's SharePoint, the implementation of the functionalities seemed to be feasible with low effort.

Table 3. Evaluation of mockup design in three workshops

Workshop 1:	**Open Feedback**
Participants:	1 Head of IS@GeFiS, 1 Professional Development Manager, 1 Project Manager
Key Results:	• For better feedback ask those persons who are supposed to use the system

Workshop 2:	**SWOT-Analysis**
Participants:	1 Professional Development Manager, 1 Project Manager
Key Results:	• Documentation of the project insights requires a methodological toolbox as support
	• Templates would help to create consistent project insights
	• Project characteristics questionnaire needs some examples to support employees
	• Project comparison using the project characteristics questionnaire is still difficult
	• System needs some free text fields in order to include insights that are specialties

Workshop 3:	**Open Feedback**
Participants:	1 Professional Development Manager, 3 Project Manager, 4 Project Team Members
Key Results:	• Mockup design needs to be implemented in order to decide whether it will be used
	• Use of a platform that is already implemented and deployed within the company
	• Platform includes already functionalities like social networking, rating, document management, etc.

Based on the results of all three workshops, we are actually realizing the design within the case company. Figure 3 presents two exemplarily screenshots of the implementation.

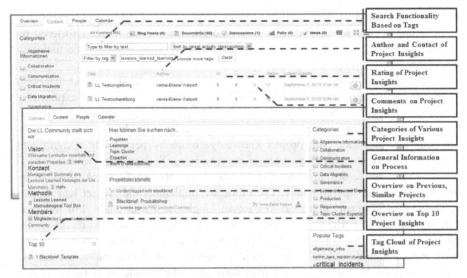

Fig. 3. Screenshots of implemented project KM system

6   Conclusion

The research presented in this paper presents our work on developing a project KM system. We provide a comprehensive overview on the entire process of our work beginning with the definition of problems related to knowledge reuse in a case company until the development of a project KM artifact within the company and its evaluation. The evaluation of our mockup design gave us first indication that the instantiation of a project KM system may increase knowledge reuse within and among projects. In particular, our work highlights the importance of providing individuals' access to both, experts and expertise. Many studies (e.g. [4-5], [9]) demonstrate that individuals prefer bilateral communications instead of writing down their project experiences in documents. Direct communication possesses advantages like the possibility of providing contextual information, foundation of trust between knowledge provider and knowledge seeker, or fast response to questions. In order to increase organizational learning, however, companies rely on the externalization of such experiences. While the project KM system presented in this article also provides some mechanisms for direct communication with experts (e.g. social networking sites, forums, chats), the design principles and decisions mainly focus on the externalization of knowledge, its storage, retrieval and reuse. Within our research we realized the importance of considering all phases of the KM process in order to encourage the reuse of existing project knowledge. The design principles as well as the derived design decisions therefore address all these phases: First, templates and the project characteristics questionnaire aim to ease and partially standardize the knowledge documentation phase. Second, implementing the project KM system as an integrated platform containing document management functionalities ensures the central storage of project insights. Third, functionalities like tagging, hyperlinking, search, and overview on projects and its characteristics enable employees to find project insights being most appropriate for their current issue. Fourth, knowledge reuse is fostered by the implementation of feedback and rating mechanisms, which enables the maintenance of documented project insights.

We are aware that our research has some limitations. First, our research bases on the results of studies within one company. Such single case studies are exposed by limited generalizability. Since the aim of our research is to develop (instead of testing) a design theory, we cope with the limited generalizability by conducting an in-depth analysis of issues with project knowledge reuse by performing a significant number of interviews with employees of varying roles. Second, the evaluation conducted to validate the design principles actually only bases on feedback provided by some experts of the case company. Therefore, we implement the project KM system within the case company and plan to conduct longitudinal user study. For this purpose, we decided to perform a quantitative user study based on unified theory of acceptance and use of technology (UTAUT) as described by Venkatesh et al. [51]. Third, our research described in this article focuses only on the technological subsystem of a project KM system. In order to achieve an active knowledge reuse in companies, the implementation of design principles regarding the social subsystem is also necessary. Thus, more research on the development of a process model as well as the definition of various roles in the knowledge reuse process is also needed.

Although, our research has some limitations, we perceive the presented work as valuable for both, researchers and practitioners. Since our design principles extend the existing body of knowledge on project knowledge reuse, researchers may build their work on our findings. Additional work is needed, for example, in testing the design theory by translating the design principles in other design decisions or in different contextual backgrounds. Furthermore, practitioners may benefit from our research, since we provide a set of activities that will increase the reuse of project knowledge and thus, may increase the performance of projects within companies.

Acknowledgement. This paper was written in the context of the research project WeChange (promotional reference 01HH11059) which is funded by the German Federal Ministry of Education and Research (BMBF).

References

1. Ajmal, M.M., Koskinen, K.U.: Knowledge transfer in project-based organizations: An organizational culture perspective. Project Management Journal 39(1), 7–15 (2008)
2. Hsu, J., Shih, S.-P., Chiang, J.C., Liu, J.: The impact of transactive memory systems on IS development teams' coordination, communication, and performance. International Journal of Project Management 30(3), 329–340 (2012)
3. PMI, IEEE Guide–Adoption of the Project Management Institute (PMI®) Standard A Guide to the Project Management Body of Knowledge (PMBOK® Guide), 4th edn., IEEE Std 1490-2011, 1-508 (2011),
   http://ieeexplore.ieee.org/xpl/mostRecentIssue.jsp?
   punumber=6086683

4. Julian, J.: How project management office leaders facilitate cross-project learning and continuous improvement. Project Management Journal 39(3), 43–58 (2008)
5. Petter, S., Randolph, A.B.: Developing soft skills to manage user expectations in IT projects: Knowledge reuse among IT project managers. Project Management Journal 40(4), 45–59 (2009)
6. Reich, B.H., Gemino, A., Sauer, C.: Modeling the knowledge perspective of IT projects. Project Management Journal 39, 4–14 (2008)
7. Eskerod, P., Skriver, H.J.: Organizational culture restraining in-house knowledge transfer between project managers-A case study. Project Management Journal 38(1), 110–122 (2007)
8. Yang, X., Hu, D., Davidson, R.M.: How microblog follower networks affect open source software project success. In: ICIS 2010 Proceedings. Paper 205 (2010)
9. Petter, S., Vaishnavi, V.: Facilitating experience reuse among software project managers. Information Sciences 178(7), 1783–1802 (2008)
10. Nesheim, T., Olsen, K.M., Tobiassen, A.E.: Knowledge communities in matrix-like organizations: managing knowledge towards application. Journal of Knowledge Management 15(5), 836–850 (2011)
11. Choi, S.Y., Lee, H., Yoo, Y.: The Impact of Information Technology and Transactive Memory Systems on Knowledge Sharing, Application, and Team Performance: A Field Study. MIS Quarterly 34(4), 855–870 (2010)
12. Bostrom, R.P., Gupta, S., Thomas, D.: A meta-theory for understanding information systems within sociotechnical systems. Journal of Management Information Systems 26(1), 17–48 (2009)
13. Sein, M.K., Henfridsson, O., Purao, S., Rossi, M., Rikard, L.: Action design research. MIS Quarterly 35(1), 37–56 (2011)
14. Baskerville, R., Pries-Heje, J., Venable, J.: Soft Design Science Research: Extending the Boundaries of Evaluation in Design Science Research. In: DESRIST 2007 Proceedings, pp. 18–38 (2007)
15. Iivari, J., Venable, J.R.: Action research and design science research-seemingly similar but decisively dissimilar. In: ECIS 2009 Proceedings (2009)
16. Järvinen, P.: Action Research is Similar to Design Science. Quality & Quantity 41(1), 37–54 (2007)
17. Susman, G.I., Evered, R.D.: An assessment of the scientific merits of action research. Administrative Science Quarterly 23(4), 582–603 (1978)
18. Baskerville, R., Myers, M.D.: Special issue on action research in information systems: Making IS research relevant to practice. MIS Quarterly 28(3), 329–335 (2004)
19. Davison, R., Martinsons, M.G., Kock, N.: Principles of canonical action re-search. Information Systems Journal 14(1), 65–86 (2004)
20. Dickens, L., Watkins, K.: Action Research: Rethinking Lewin. Management Learning 30(2), 127–140 (1999)
21. Walls, J.G., Widmeyer, G.R., El Sawy, O.: Information System Design Theory for Vigilant EIS. Information Systems Research 3(1), 36–60 (1992)
22. Markus, M.L., Majchrzak, A., Gasser, L.: A Design Theory for Systems That Support Emergent Knowledge Processes. MIS Quarterly 26(3), 179–212 (2002)
23. Tan, M., Teo, T.: Factors influencing the adoption of Internet banking. Journal of the AIS 1(5), 1–42 (2000)
24. Coyne, I.T.: Sampling in qualitative research. Purposeful and theoretical sampling; merging or clear boundaries? Journal of Advanced Nursing 26(3), 623–630 (1997)

25. Myers, M.D., Newman, M.: The qualitative interview in IS research: Examining the craft. Information and Organization 17(1), 2–26 (2007)
26. Thomas, D.R.: A general inductive approach for analyzing qualitative evaluation data. American Journal of Evaluation 27(2), 237–246 (2006)
27. Morse, J., Barrett, M., Mayan, M., Olson, K., Spiers, J.: Verification strategies for establishing reliability and validity in qualitative research. International Journal of Qualitative Methods 1(2), 13–22 (2002)
28. Rolfe, G.: Validity, trustworthiness and rigour: quality and the idea of qualitative research. Journal of Advanced Nursing 53(3), 304–310 (2006)
29. Dourish, P., Edwards, W.K., LaMarca, A., Lamping, J., Petersen, K., Salisbury, M., Terry, D.B., et al.: Extending document management systems with user-specific active properties. ACM Transactions on Information Systems 18(2), 140–170 (2000)
30. Koskinen, K.U., Pihlanto, P., Vanharanta, H.: Tacit knowledge acquisition and sharing in a project work context. International Journal of Project Management 21(4), 281–290 (2003)
31. Schindler, M., Eppler, M.J.: Harvesting project knowledge: a review of project learning methods and success factors. International Journal of Project Management 21, 219–228 (2003)
32. Sutton, D.: What is knowledge and can it be managed? European Journal of Information Systems 10(2), 80–88 (2001)
33. Wagner, C.: Wiki: A technology for conversational knowledge management and group collaboration. Communications of the Association for Information Systems 13(1), 265–289 (2004)
34. Arazy, O., Gellatly, I., Jang, S., Patterson, R.: Wiki Deployment in Corporate Settings. IEEE Technology and Society Magazine 28(2), 57–64 (2009)
35. Argote, L., McEvily, B., Reagans, R.: Managing knowledge in organizations: An integrative framework and review of emerging themes. Management Science 49(4), 571–582 (2003)
36. Ardichvili, A., Page, V., Wentling, T.: Motivation and barriers to participation in virtual knowledge-sharing communities of practice. Journal of Knowledge Management 7(1), 64–77 (2003)
37. Davenport, T.H., De Long, D.W., Beers, M.C.: Successful knowledge management projects. Sloan Management Review 39(2), 43–57 (1998)
38. Markus, M.L.: Toward a theory of knowledge reuse: Types of knowledge reuse situations and factors in reuse success. Journal of Management Information Systems 18(1), 57–93 (2001)
39. Newell, S.: Enhancing cross-project learning. Management 16(1), 12–20 (2004)
40. Desouza, K.C., Evaristo, J.R.: Managing knowledge in distributed projects. Communications of the ACM 47(4), 87–91 (2004)
41. Wu, J.-H.: A design methodology for form-based knowledge reuse and representation. Information & Management 46(7), 365–375 (2009)
42. Nielsen, L., Madsen, S.: Storytelling as method for sharing knowledge across IT projects. In: HICSS 2006 Proceedings (2006)
43. Hsu, M.-H., Ju, T.L., Yen, C.-H., Chang, C.-M.: Knowledge sharing behavior in virtual communities: The relationship between trust, self-efficacy, and outcome expectations. International Journal of Human-Computer Studies 65(2), 153–169 (2007)
44. Lin, H.-F.: Effects of extrinsic and intrinsic motivation on employee knowledge sharing intentions. Journal of Information Science 33(2), 135–149 (2007)

45. Bartsch, V., Ebers, M., Maurer, I.: Learning in project-based organizations: The role of project teams' social capital for overcoming barriers to learning. International Journal of Project Management 31(2), 239–251 (2013)
46. King, W., Marks Jr., P., McCoy, S.: The most important issues in knowledge management. Communications of the ACM 45(9), 93–97 (2002)
47. Dellarocas, C.: The Digitization of Word of Mouth: Promise and Challenges of Online Feedback Mechanisms. Management Science 49(10), 1407–1424 (2003)
48. Tiwana, A., Konsynski, B., Bush, A.A.: Research Commentary–Platform Evolution: Co-evolution of Platform Architecture, Governance, and Environmental Dynamics. Information Systems Research 21(4), 675–687 (2010)
49. Popov, B., Kiryakov, A., Ognyanoff, D., Manov, D., Kirilov, A.: KIM – a semantic platform for information extraction and retrieval. Natural Language Engineering 10, 375–392 (2004)
50. Tolone, W., Ahn, G., Pal, T., Hong, S.: Access Control in Collaborative Systems. ACM Computing Surveys 37(1), 29–41 (2005)
51. Venkatesh, V., Morris, M.G., Davis, G.B., Davis, F.D.: User acceptance of information technology: Toward a unified view. MIS Quarterly 27(3), 425–478 (2003)

Designing an Artifact for the Integration of Ubiquitous Information Systems in an Enterprise Context

Oliver Gaß[1], Alexander Mädche [1,2], Harald Biegel[1], and Mahei Li[1]

[1] University of Mannheim, Chair of Information Systems IV, Mannheim, Germany
{gass,maedche}@es.uni-mannheim.de,
harald.biegel@googlemail.com,
mali@mail.uni-mannheim.de
[2] University of Mannheim, Institute for Enterprise Systems, Mannheim, Germany

Abstract. In the past most IT innovations were initially introduced inside or-ganizations and it was there where individuals first came in contact with new technologies. Nowadays, also the private life has gained importance for the adoption of technologies. Not often, individuals acquire new IT innovations privately, before they realize their value for professional activities and start us-ing them for work. Their employers, however, struggle to integrate those inno-vations into their already heterogeneous organizational landscapes. The result is often an overly insufficient and ineffective use of private IT in organizations. In fact, previous integration research has provided various concepts to abate such negative effects, integrating the data and functionality of a few more private systems seems not a big deal. However, if one looks closer, it becomes apparent that private IT is autonomous from organizational control, rendering many common approaches inapplicable. Our research addresses this problem. Using the scenario of self-employed insurance brokers, we identify several characte-ristics of private IT ecosystems, here conceptualized as ubiquitous information systems (UIS), which prevent its productive use for professional activities. Based on these findings we suggest and instantiate a solution design which solves many issues of heterogeneity, but also accounts for the autonomy and distribution of the private UIS and its sub-systems. We conclude our research with a discussion of six propositions about the expected impact of our solution on individual performance.

Keywords: Ubiquitous Information System, Integration, Interoperability, Individual Performance, Activity Theory, Task-Technology-Fit.

1 Introduction

Not long ago, IT innovations were initially deployed inside organizations and it was there where employees first came in contact with these innovations [1]. Today, tech-nology adoption works also the other way around. Driven by a variety of technologi-cal developments and demographic changes, it is nowadays often the individual who adopts IT innovations first. The so called "individualization of IT" [2] has created a reality in which individuals employ extensive information systems that consist of

J. vom Brocke et al. (Eds.): DESRIST 2013, LNCS 7939, pp. 18–33, 2013.

countless sub-systems, such as software packages, cloud solutions and mobile services, but also numerous end-user devices including laptops, tablets, smartphones, desktops and peripherals. Previous research has coined such personal ecosystems ubiquitous information system [3] because its sub-systems have infiltrated almost every area of live of its owners. This applies in particular for the professional life, which is highly influenced by personal IT that employees bring to work and use for professional activities. From the perspective of an individual, the trend to use familiar and often more current private IT has the potential to increase individual performance and satisfaction [4]. From the perspective of an organization, satisfied and productive employees contribute to higher organizational performance. The adoption of individual IT innovations also increases the overall innovative capacity of the organization, resulting in more timeliness and cost-efficient adjustment to environmental changes [4]. However, the sole adoption of an UIS in the organizational context is not sufficient to realize those benefits [4, 5]. Equally important is the seamless integration of its functionality and data. Three characteristics of UIS are thereby major obstacles to their integration: first, UIS in general are characterized by a high degree of heterogeneity in functionality and information representation [6, 7]. Second, the sub-systems are usually physically distributed across various locations [6]. Third, individuals act autonomously and compose their UIS according to idiosyncratic needs and preferences, and seldom align them with organizational requirements [2, 6]. In addition, heterogeneity, distribution and autonomy constitute several fields of tension. Any attempt to resolve one of them may result in conflicts with the other two. For example, an integration approach may reduce heterogeneity, but may also violate the autonomy of each integrated UIS. At first, finding a solution appears merely a question of technical possibilities. However, the impact of a solution in a professional context is usually not measured in technical means, but in business relevant figures, e.g., individual productivity. The technical dimension alone is not sufficient to anticipate the business impact of a solution. Instead, previous research on UIS suggests three additional dimensions of consideration: first, the type of activities conducted, second the context of application and third idiosyncratic factors of its users [3].

In summary, finding a solution to integrate an UIS with its organizational context constitutes a complex socio-technical problem. Its solving requires a holistic research approach, combining empirical findings with theories and technical approaches, to synthesize a solution concept which leads to the intended business impact. In this paper, we follow this train of thought, and apply a design science approach to develop a solution which fosters the integration between the UIS and enterprise systems of the organizational context. Following Vodanovich et al. [3], we start with an empirical analysis of the problem space, captured by our first research question (RQ):

- **RQ1:** Which barriers prevent the efficient use of UIS for professional activities?

Building on these empirical findings, we derive a set of meta-requirements which should be addressed by a solution in order to increase individual performance in professional activities. The development of the solution design is the focus of the second research question:

- **RQ2:** Which design principles for an UIS (and its sub-systems) lead to an increase of individual performance in professional activities?

The solution builds on the explanatory power of existing IS theory and is formalized as normative design principles as key concepts behind our approach. Additionally, we put our concept into practice and show its instantiation on the architectural level in form of architectural design choice and also provide first details about an actual implementation as a Windows 8 prototype. Based on the applied theories, we derive and discuss six preliminary propositions about the predicted impact of the design on individual performance. We conclude our paper with a summary of our current contribution and provide an outlook on the next steps of our research.

2   Related Work

This section introduces previous theoretical work and summarizes existing technological solutions. From a theoretical point of view, we look at existing IS research conceptualizing individual performance and its antecedents, and research which focuses on the interaction of IS and their social context. The explanatory power of such kernel theories [8] is reflected by our solution design and respectively used to derive testable propositions about its impact on the dependent variable – individual performance.

The first relevant theory is the Technology-to-Performance Chain (TPC), which allows the study of the impact of technology and various social factors on individual performance [9]. The TPC names three factors that affect individual performance: technological characteristics, individual characteristics and task characteristics. Task characteristics, individual characteristics and technology characteristics influence individual performance in two different ways: first, a greater Task-Technology Fit (TTF) will result in a higher performance, because the system will more closely meet the task needs of the individual. TTF is thereby defined as the correspondence between task requirements, individual abilities, and the functionality of technology. Second, performance is influenced by the antecedents via the utilization of technology, because if technology is not used, it cannot create benefits [9]. TPC as part of this research serves as the main kernel theory, as our solution design attempts to increase individual performance directly by increasing TTF via a technological intervention. However, the TPC does not answer sufficiently why particular individual, task or technology characteristics lead to a higher TTF or not. This requires more kernel theories which offer additional explanatory power to inform the solution design. An important theory which is leveraged by our work is cognitive-load-theory (CLT). CLT provides a model to link individual cognitive capabilities to task and system complexity and predict their impact on individual performance [10]. The second branch of the TPC also indicates that technology must be used to create benefits. In the case of UIS this usage is strongly affected by the autonomy of each individual, which decides independently whether to adopt a particular (sub-) system or not. Following this trail of thought, any solution which attempts to create benefits must also encourage adoption and usage. Previous IS research on this topic has identified numerous factors which may influence the intention to use technology or lead to actual usage, e.g. TAM3 [11]. However, most research of this kind usually considers IT as one single entity that individuals adopt or use. Factors which may influence adoption under the availability of several competing alternatives are often faded out. One exception is Roger's diffusion of innovation theory (DOI) [12] which originates from management sciences, but has also found wide application for individual and organizational IT [13]. Roger names five attributes which are relevant in the adoption of innovations. First, the functionality must provide relative advantage compared to its alternatives. Second, it must be compatible with the existing values, needs and past of the adopter. Third, the innovation must not be perceived as too difficult to use. Fourth, the purpose of the innovations is clearly observable and fifth, individuals may have the possibility to try it out [12]. Another limitation of the TPC is the fact that it does not consider the influence of the contextual dimension [3] on individual performance [9]. In fact, the diversity of this dimension suggests numerous theories that may fill the gap here and explain the influence of particular contextual factors on individual performance systematically. However, the integration of all these theories with the TPC is rather difficult. Therefore, we fade out the direct influence and consider contextual factors solely as constraints which limit the possible solution space. A theory which provides structure to elicit these constraints systematically is activity theory (AT) [14]. Activity theory suggests that human activity is always directed towards and objective, for example, a particular goal. The activity is mediated by an artifact, e.g., the UIS used in the process, and also charged by the surrounding social context, characterized by a community, its rules and division of labor [15]. Even though AT does not allow predications about performance, it provides a structure to analyze the role of UIS in the interaction between individuals and their social context, including constraints which may result from this role.

From a practical point of view, we rely on design principles and pattern provided by previous research that has been carried out to address the tension between heterogeneity, autonomy and distribution technologically. Such research usually pursues the integration of entities on several abstraction-layers, for example, UI integration, functional integration or data integration [16], or targets different degrees of integration, such as compatibility, interoperability or full integration [17]. Of particular interest for the presented research are such findings which pursue integration under consideration of autonomy and distribution. Starting with research on database systems, relevant contributions include techniques for schema integration and ways to deal with schematic and representational heterogeneity. Two prominent design patterns have emerged from this research stream: First, the loosely-coupled architecture that provides for a more dynamic and flexible federation but also leads to a lower degree of data integration which in consequence requires more individual effort. Second, the tightly-coupled architecture that provides for more stable federation, resulting in a better integration of data across the different sub-systems but also requires the configuration by professionals [6]. Research in the middleware community addresses the consolidation of heterogeneous structures. Important design principles have been formulated in the context of Service-Orientated Architecture (SOA). SOA design principles foster interoperability within an architecture and enable the dynamic combination of business processes. Such design principles are loose coupling, discoverability, reusability, autonomy, abstraction, statelessness, composability, sub-systemization, modularity and encapsulation of functionality and data structures [18, 19]. A commonly used design pattern for SOA is the service encapsulation pattern to create interoperable applications across an enterprise. Further contributions originate from the Semantic Web movement [20] and the Web2.0 community [21]. Design principles which were identified to facilitate semantic interoperability in web applications and mashups are reusability [21], composability, statelessness [22] and extensibility and sub-systemization [23]. Two design patterns which have emerged on top of these principles and find particularly wide application in loosely-coupled architectures are the mediator pattern and the wrapper pattern [24]. Mediator-wrapper architectures consist of three layers: a source layer that contains different data sources from local systems, a wrapper layer that enables communication between the mediator and the local systems and the mediator layer that holds the mediator, which guarantees that the different data sources are all interoperable [25].

3   Methodology

Our research applies the design science approach to IS to address both research questions [26]. It follows the design research cycle methodology as introduced by Vaishnavi and Kuechler [27]. The methodology defines five sub processes of design research which are executed iteratively: (1) Awareness of problem, (2) suggestion of key concepts to address the problems, (3) development of a solution design, (4) the evaluation of the solution and (5) the conclusion to decide which elements of the solution to adopt.

In order to create awareness of the problem (phase 1), we conducted 15 exploratory interviews among self-employed insurance brokers. Self-employed insurance brokers are a type of sales agents which sell the insurance products of many different insurance corporations to their own customer base. Their case is characterized by a high diversity in the technical and non-technical dimensions. First, the insurance brokers are not bound to one particular organization. Instead, they act as legally independent entities collaborating with multiple organizational contexts. Second, they conduct a wide variety of professional activities. Third, the diversity of the environment requires a broad bandwidth of technological support, which leads to extensive UIS. Fourth, the weak link to an organizational context suggests a stronger importance of individual characteristics. This applies in particular for the composition of the UIS, since usually no standardized enterprise IT is provided by the organizational context. Our sample was drawn from the professional social network XING[1]. From the list of about 250 relevant subjects (self-employed and at least 2 years work experience); we randomly contacted subjects and on agreement conducted semi-structured interviews until we had collected the 15 data sets. The questions focused on the professional activities of brokers, the composition of the UIS they use, and the problems which occur in the process. The interviews, each about 90 minutes long, were transcribed and then analyzed in two rounds: the macro plane analysis focused on the interaction between

---

[1] http://www.xing.de

the insurance broker and their social context to determine the conditions under which the UIS is used. Therefore, we applied the theoretical lens of activity theory. The unit-of-analysis was an activity, for example "consulting a customer". We developed a coding framework based on the external structure of activity theory [15] to elicit the involved entities in each activity and the conditions applying. Assigned codes marked the subject acting, i.e., insurance broker, the expected outcome of the activity, the social community involved, applying rules and division of labor between the subject and its community, and most importantly, the tools, represented by a sub-system of the UIS or an enterprise system, used to conduct the activity. If the analysis suggested, either directly through negative comments, or indirectly through the resulting external structure, that an involved tools was the cause that an activity was executed inefficiently, we conducted a second, more detailed analysis of the prevailing conditions. In the micro plane analysis we applied the theoretical lens of the Technology-to-Performance Chain, i.e., we assumed that low TTF was the cause of low individual performance. Consequently, we applied a coding scheme based on the constructs of the TPC, to identify individual, task and technology characteristics which occurred in the corresponding activity. More importantly we focused on the negative effects which originate from their simultaneous presence.

Our reasoning during the suggestion (phase 2) and development (phase 3) of the solution design was guided by the assumption that each identified lack of TTF resulted from the manifestation of particular individual, task and technology characteristics in a given context. Since the solution design targets a solely technical intervention, an improvement in the dependent factor individual performance, here interpreted as time to complete a task / activity, can be achieved only if the technical intervention compensates particular individual or task characteristics and is consistent with contextual requirements. The solution design was developed on three abstraction layers: first, we derived abstract meta-requirements that define the overall solution space (4.2). Second, normative design principles were formulated, which outline the key concepts of our approach (4.3). Third, we developed a set of design choice (4.4) which describes the solution on the level of architecture, and leverages design patterns from computer science research as introduced in chapter 2.

4   Results

4.1   Awareness of Problems

The analysis of the qualitative data identified several factors which seem to affect the individual performance in the context of UIS. Usually those factors appear together and create a variety of barriers against the efficient use of UIS for professional activities: first, insufficient functional scope of the sub-systems causes additional effort which results in lower individual performance. Low experience with IT [28] is the first obstacle to the awareness that sufficient functionality is already installed and how to use it most efficiently. However, more commonly, sub-system designed for private purposes just lack the scope to support business tasks optimally. This applies, in particular, under high task complexity [29], which asks for dedicated functionality to process the larger amounts of required information in the most efficient way. UIS also lack the functional scope to support interdependent tasks [30] that involve more than one individual. The collaboration in teams, for example, is only supported by generic communication functionalities, sufficient for private purposes, but insufficient for the most efficient collaboration along business processes.

Second, negative effects are also caused by the inflexibility of available sub-systems to adapt to frequently changing requirements. Many sub-systems of the UIS were designed with respect to private activities. Private activities are usually conducted in a different environment, characterized by a smaller degree of task variety and interdependence [30]. Many electronic address books, for example, are sufficient to store information about friends, but are not flexible enough to store the constantly changing set of different entities (contacts, accounts, etc.) and their sub-types (key accounts, leads, prospects, etc.) involved in a business process.

Third, negative effects are a result of the general higher complexity of an UIS that is used for professional activities. UIS, especially when they are used to interact with multiple organizational contexts, are characterized by a high degree of heterogeneity on the technical side. Each involved organization, for example, provides a particular sub-system to support its variant of a sales process. If the degree of integration among these sub-systems and/or with corresponding systems of the organizational context is low, the results are media discontinuities, low data quality and lack of timeliness due to varying formats and the distribution of data across the UIS. This results in additional and often redundant activities to execute a business process [9]. In cases of high task complexity, the inefficiencies are even greater because the demand for information usually grows with complexity [29].

Fourth, negative effects are also caused by an overall incapability of individuals to compose and adjust an UIS according to the needs of professional activities. This can result from an individual's personality such as the lack of openness towards innovations [31] that prevents it from adopting better sub-systems. Low experience with IT [28] is another obstacle and causes additional problems when it is required to customize or configure a sub-system with regards to the rest of the UIS. Many agents, for example, manage their contacts simultaneously on their phone and a social network because they don't know how to use the available option to integrate both. Other individuals just do not trust [32] the organizational context they interact with. Hence, they do not use technology provided by this context to avoid creating a relation of dependency. This applies for social networks as well as business partners. The first one, have a bad reputation among some agents due to their allegedly careless handling of private data. The second group, in particular large insurance organizations, is suspected to steal customers. Hence, independent agents are rather reluctant to take technological measures which increase their efficiency, but also allow the organizational context to access their data more easily. This inadequate adjustment of the UIS causes a variety of performance related issues. First, the abundance of innovative, properly selected and configured solutions promotes the already mentioned lack of functional scope and missing flexibility. Second, the tendency to use allegedly proved and tested solutions causes additional effort to integrate legacy solutions with newer sub-systems. Third, the resulting UIS often show low system quality under varying environmental conditions [33]. Although proper functionality and data exists in the UIS, its usage is restricted to a particular device, e.g., the desktop computer in the office, or dependent on particular technical conditions, e.g., an available 3G network. In consequence, agents generally - not just in the problematic cases, fall back to rather inefficient but reliable solutions. Pen and paper forms, for example, still find wide application, even though they create additional effort afterwards.

4.2 Solution Suggestion: Meta-requirements

Starting with the first problem, UIS often do not provide the level of functional support to conduct professional tasks most efficiently. In other words, the available technologies result in a low Task-Technology-Fit and consequently lower individual performance. Following the reasoning of the TPC, a higher TTF can be achieved by providing better functionality for particular task types. However, task requirements may change over time, in conclusion; also the UIS has to evolve. An autonomous individual will not replace its complete UIS, but instead replace particular sub-systems only. Hence, the technological solution must allow the successive extension with task specific functionality (MR1). However, with an increasing degree of functionality comes also an increasing degree of complexity, resulting in lower individual performance. Cognitive load theory [10] offers an explanation of this matter. It suggests that the mental workload of an individual is divided into intrinsic load and extrinsic load. Intrinsic load is defined by the task and extrinsic load by the technological support system. In cases in which the technological system is characterized by a high degree of complexity, the extrinsic load is also high, resulting in an overall high mental workload of the individual and a lower performance, even though the UIS may achieve a high TTF. This implies that the design must achieve a high TTF by avoiding complexity at all costs. This leads us to two additional meta-requirements. First, in order to avoid adding new functionality, existing solutions must be flexible with respect to minor changes in the task requirements (MR2), and work reliable also under a high degree of environmental uncertainty (MR3). Second, if greater changes of the environment require additional functionality, then the extension of the UIS should be conducted with the highest degree of integration across the sub-systems to prevent information split (inside the UIS and with systems of the organizational context) (MR4). In addition, any extension should avoid media discontinuities that would require redundant activities (MR5). The TPC also states that individuals must use technology to create benefits [9]. The autonomy of the UIS limits the possibilities of enforcement; furthermore, the autonomous composition of UIS is also the vehicle for higher satisfaction and performance [4]. Thus, the technical solution should enable the self-determined adoption of professional functionality (MR6) and not prevent it. Also, with respect to issues of trust, individuals must always maintain control about the installed functionality and stored data on their UIS (MR7). However, the empirical data also indicates an incapability of many individuals to identify appropriate professional functionality or adjust it to their business needs. Therefore, the technological solution should guide individuals in the selection and adoption of adequate technology without restricting their autonomy (MR8).

4.3   Solution Suggestion: Design Principles

Having identified the meta-requirements, we turn to the suggestion of a solution design to answer our second research question.

The key concept is to leave the autonomous character of the UIS intact and provide individuals with the opportunity to augment it with functionality which provides dedicated support for professional activities. In order to allow extensibility (MR1), we suggest that organizations encapsulate such business functionality in modules. The module itself should provide guidance (MR8) for which business purpose it should be used. Following the DOI theory [34], we suggest that encapsulated functionality is of limited complexity and serves a clearly observable business purpose (DP1) to allow individuals to assess the value of each module independently. In order to avoid negative effects from heterogeneity (MR4 and MR5) the modules must be interoperable. Hence, they must be deployed in an integrated business environment in the realm of the individual. With regards to the adoption of the integrated business environment (DP2), it must ensure that the deployment of functionality is always self-determined and reversible (MR7). This is necessary to allow individuals to try out functionality, e.g., to identify a module which provides relative advantages, and to adjust the environments to its current values and need, e.g., privacy concerns. In order to make the deployed functionality more reliable (MR2, MR3), we suggest that each module builds on parameterized functionality to compensate minor environmental changes. In order to support individuals with low experience in configuration, the integrated environment should also allow the exchange of settings between individuals and/or the organizational context (DP3). The integration of data and functionality is a necessary remedy to reduce the negative impact of heterogeneity on individual performance. The autonomy of individuals and the distribution of functionality and data, however, require additional considerations: we suggest integrating data and functionality bottom-up. A bottom-up approach starts at the individual level and then proceeds up the organizational hierarchy. The degree of integration between data sources and functions should be the highest on the individual level and lower further up. This has the advantage that the UIS remains autonomous from entities further up the organizational hierarchy. It also limits the distribution of functionality and data by concentrating both at the individual level and thereby insuring functional integrity of the UIS also under difficult environmental conditions (MR3). In addition, it allows the individual to restrict the integration of its UIS (and content) (MR8) with enterprise systems without losing the benefit of an integrated personal work environment.

4.4   Solution Development: Design Choices

The design choices constitute an instantiation of our design principles mainly on the level of architecture. An overview of the connection to the design principles is illustrated in figure 1, the resulting architecture is visualized in figure 2.

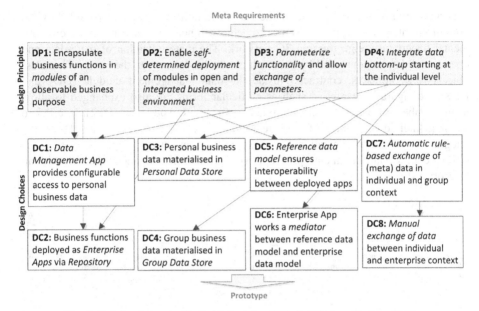

Fig. 1. Relation between Design Principles (DP) and Design Choices (DC)

The core element on the individual side is a central data management module (DD1) deployed on a device of the UIS. The data management module provides encapsulated functionality to manage business data (DP1). It serves as the central access point to business data materialized in the personal data store (DD3). The data management module encapsulates all functionality necessary to enter, browse and share business data. It also offers functionality to alter the data model of the personal data store, e.g., add custom fields. The provided data management functionality is configurable to ensure optimal support for a wide variety of tasks (DP3). Therefore, it allows composing forms to gather data, define views to browse / analyze data and apply reusable function blocks to automatize the processing of data before sharing. Additional enterprise modules that support dedicated business functions can be deployed from a central repository (DD2). To ensure interoperability between the additional enterprise modules and the data management module, we define a variety of standards for the integrated business environment on the device (DP2). In our case, each module has to comply with a domain-specific reference data model which covers a common denominator of fields common for the particular business domain. Each enterprise module can add extensions to the reference model to store app specific data. The enterprise modules employ the mediator design pattern to establish interoperability with the corresponding data models of the related enterprise systems (DD6). Given the limited IT experience of an individual, it is the responsibility of the organizational context to ensure interoperability between its provided modules and its enterprise systems. Exchange of data with other devices (of the same UIS) or the UIS of team members is established via a team data store (DD4). On connection, the data models of the personal data store and the team are synchronized, and user data is immediately materialized in both systems. The immediate materialization is thereby guided by the bottom-up integration approach (DP4) to achieve functional integrity under environmental uncertainty, e.g., missing 3G network. The materialization of meta-data and operational data is controlled by rules which can be defined on the basis of business objects (e.g., contacts, contracts) inside the data management module (DD7 and DD8). Configuration patterns, such as particular forms are also exchanged to allow team members to benefit from each other's effort and experience (DP2). In order to maintain individual control of the integration of personal business data (DP4), the integration with an organizational context must be manually triggered by the user (DD8), e.g., by starting an enterprise app which synchronizes data on the UIS with an enterprise system.

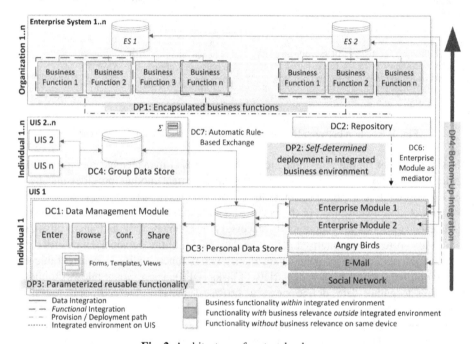

Fig. 2. Architecture of system landscape

4.5 Solution Development: Prototype Implementation and Setup of System landscape

The solution design was instantiated on the Windows 8 platform (see figure 3). We implemented the data management module (DD1) and developed several complementing enterprise modules in form of mobile apps. Each enterprise app supports a set of particular business functions (DP1) from the analyzed insurance broker case (e.g., life insurance consulting app, billing app, and contract management app). In addition, we installed and configured various apps from third party vendors that provide generic functionality useful for various business functions (e.g., social network and email app). The personal data store (DD3) was instantiated as a SQLite database on the mobile device, the team data store (DD4) was realized as a MSSQL database in the local network. The data model was designed to allow maximum flexibility and extensibility (indirectly required by DP3). Hence, we implemented a basic meta-data repository. Actual data is stored as chunks, referring to tuples of key and value that are linked to one type of meta-data. Records are realized as linked list of several keys. Access to both databases is abstracted by a .net wrapper (in C# and LinQ) which can be accessed by any app on the device familiar with the interface.

During the implementation we had to solve various technical problems that resulted from the newness of Windows 8 and the restrictions of Windows store apps and SQLite. Eventually, we had to developed many features ourselves that are considered commodities on other platforms. The user-interface (UI) was implemented in XAML. Since UI design was not in the focus of our research, we followed Microsoft's guidelines for Windows Store apps[2]. In order to simulate the interaction of our solution with an organizational context, we installed and configured two Salesforce.com Sales Cloud[3] instances, which exemplify the enterprise systems of affiliated insurances.

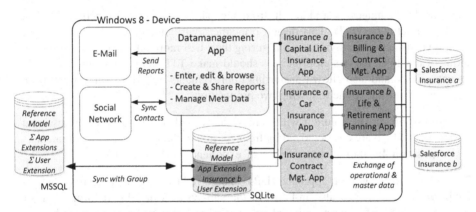

Fig. 3. Overview of implemented apps and instantiation of system landscape

5   Discussion

In the following we discuss the expected impact of our solution design based on the embodied kernel theories. The results of the discussion are condensed into six, yet unconfirmed, propositions which will be tested during the evaluation phase to determine the individual impact of each design principles.

The first design principle, the encapsulation of dedicated functionality in modules, promotes autonomy by enabling the flexible adoption of IT according to individual and task characteristics or contextual constraints. The deployment in an integrated

---

[2] http://msdn.microsoft.com/en-us/library/windows/apps/
     hh465424.aspx
[3] http://www.salesforce.com/de/sales-cloud/

business environment (DP2) should prevent negative effects from heterogeneity and distribution, such as media-discontinuities and information split in-between modules. If we express the expected impact of these two design principles in terms of the TPC, we arrive at the following two propositions. First, the deployment of dedicated functionality on the UIS (DP1) should cause a better alignment of technology with task requirements and thus result in higher TTF leading to higher performance [9].

- **Proposition 1:** The solution will increase the individual performance in professional activities if dedicated modules are available on the UIS.

Second, the deployment in an integrated business environment (DP2) helps to lower extrinsic load compared to monolithic solutions (e.g., non-integrated apps). This should pay off especially in tasks with higher complexity because they are characterized by an already high intrinsic load [29].

- **Proposition 2:** The increase of individual performance is higher in tasks characterized by a high complexity.

Additional advantages should result from the parameterizing of functionality and sharing of settings (DP3). This design principle contributes to the flexibility of the solution and supports individuals configuring their UIS more effectively. Expressed in terms of the TPC, the design principles should make TTF more robust to changes in its antecedents and also allow transferring improvements in TTF to other users. Both advantages translate to the following two propositions:

- **Proposition 3:** The solution will increase individual performance in professional activities which are characterized by frequent minor changes in task-requirements.
- **Proposition 4:** Individuals with low IT experience will benefit more.

The bottom-up integration approach (DP4) should reduce dependencies from the organizational context and also in-between the sub-systems of UIS. It forms a major vehicle to account for the negative effects on individual performance caused by distribution. In addition, it should relieve individuals of complicated and laborious integration tasks by leaving the responsibility with the vendors of enterprise apps (DD6). Both characteristics, distinguish our solution from related concepts, such as Platform-as-a-service (PaaS) [35] and middleware solutions. PaaS share similar characteristics in terms of encapsulation and composition of functionality, but may work less reliable under high environmental uncertainty. Middleware on the other hand may work independent from the environment, but often requires professional know how for configuration. Expressed in terms of the TPC this leads to the next proposition:

- **Proposition 5:** The solution will increase individual performance in professional activities which are characterized by high environmental uncertainty independent from individual IT experience.

DP4 should also improve the perceived degree of autonomy that users experience when applying their UIS for professional activities. Following the argumentation of the TPC, technology must be used in order to create benefits [9]. Increasing the control about the professional data on the UIS, should resolve some reservations towards using or configuring (sub-) systems that may violate autonomy, for example by integrating the UIS with organizational systems. This should ease some negative effects on performance caused by heterogeneity and thereby allow individuals to be more efficient in professional activities that are characterized by frequent interaction (e.g., exchange of master data) with the organizational context.

- **Proposition 6:** The solution will favor the adoption of (sub-) systems which decrease heterogeneity, eventually, resulting in higher individual performance in professional activities which involve an organizational context.

6   Conclusion and Future Work

Design Science Research must be relevant and rigorous [26]. Following these principles we have applied multiple methods to develop a solution design based on empirical findings and theory, which addresses the tension between heterogeneity, autonomy and distribution in current UIS holistically. The innovative thought behind our concept is to bring dedicated enterprise functionality directly to the UIS and deploy it in an integrated business environment on a mobile device. The integration with other entities is thereby conducted bottom up, controlled by the individual but supported by the organizational context. This improves performance by reducing heterogeneity and equally accounts for the negative effects caused by distribution and the constraints resulting from the autonomy of an UIS, its sub-systems and users.

The main limitation of our approach is that interoperability between the suggested modules requires an agreement on common standards. We tried to resolve this problem by introducing a static reference model (DD5), while fading out the question which entity is responsible for its definition, enforcement and evolution over time. In the latter case, more advanced solutions from computer science could be helpful. Governance questions, on the other hand, were outside the scope of our research. Another limitation is that the assumption that low degree of complexity and observable business purpose alone will lead to an adoption of the encapsulated functionality (DP1). This is however highly subjective and also not enough if a person lacks the knowledge or willingness to adopt the optimal solution.

Despite these limitations, we think our work has already made two major contributions to the field: the theoretical contribution is the application of the TPC in the context of UIS, in particular the identified barriers that prevent their efficient application for professional activities (RQ1). In addition, we have developed a technical response to those barriers, summarized in four design principles (RQ2). The design principles constitute four, yet unconfirmed, key guidelines for the development of solutions which address the autonomy, heterogeneity and distribution of current UIS and intend to increase individual performance in professional activities at the same time. The practical contribution comprises the design choices which provide an example for an instantiation of the design principles on the level of architecture. The design choices as well as the lessons learned during the implementation and setup of the prototypical system landscape may be helpful for the development of similar solutions in the field of independent sales agents, and on the Windows 8 platform. With regards to the remaining phases of the DSR cycle, our research will proceed with the evaluation based on the derived propositions in an experiment setup. The preliminary experiment setup strives to identify the individual impact of each design principle based on the developed prototype. Further generalization attempts will pursue transferability of our design principles to other domains of information work and should finally lead to a general applicable design theory [36] for the integration of UIS into multiple organizational contexts.

Acknowledgement. This paper was written in the context of the research project WeChange (promotional reference 01HH11059) which is funded by the German Federal Ministry of Education and Research (BMBF).

References

1. Andriole, S.J.: Managing Technology in a 2.0 World. IT Professional 14, 50–57 (2012)
2. Baskerville, R.: Individual Information Systems as a Research Arena. European Journal of Information Systems 20, 251–254 (2011)
3. Vodanovich, S., Sundaram, D., Myers, M.: Digital Natives and Ubiquitous Information Systems. Information Systems Research 21, 711–723 (2010)
4. Harris, J., Ives, B., Junglas, I.: IT Consumerization: When Gadgets turn into Enterprise IT Tools. MIS Quarterly Executive 11, 99–112 (2012)
5. Davies, N., Gellersen, H.W.: Beyond Prototypes: Challenges in deploying Ubiquitous Systems. IEEE Pervasive Computing 1, 26–35 (2002)
6. Sheth, A.: Changing Focus on Interoperability in Information Systems: From System, Syntax, Structure to Semantics. In: Goodchild, M.F., Egenhofer, M.J., Fegeas, R., Kottman, C.A. (eds.) Interoperating Geographic Information Systems, pp. 1–25. Kluwer (1998)
7. Ouksel, A.M., Sheth, A.: Semantic Interoperability in Global Information Systems. ACM Sigmod Record 28, 5–12 (1999)
8. Walls, J.G., Widmeyer, G.R., El Sawy, O.: Building an information system design theory for vigilant EIS. Information Systems Research 3, 36–59 (1992)
9. Goodhue, D.L.: Understanding User Evaluations of Information Systems. Management Science 41, 1827–1844 (1995)
10. Sweller, J.: Cognitive Technology: Some Procedures for facilitating Learning and Problem solving in Mathematics and Science. Journal of Educational Psychology 81, 457–466 (1989)
11. Venkatesh, V., Bala, H.: Technology Acceptance Model 3 and a Research Agenda on Interventions. Decision Sciences 39, 273–315 (2008)
12. Rogers, E.M.: Diffusion of Innovations. The Free Press, New York (1995)
13. Prescott, M., Conger, S.: Information technology innovations: a classification by IT locus of impact and research approach. ACM SIGMIS Database 26 (1995)
14. Vygotski, L., Cole, M.: Mind in society: The development of higher psychological processes (1978)
15. Kuutti, K.: The Concept of Activity as a basic Unit of Analysis for CSCW Research. In: Proceedings of the Second European Conference on Computer-Supported Cooperative Work, pp. 249–264 (1991)

16. Balasubramanian, K., Schmidt, D.C., Molnár, Z., Lédeczi, Á.: System Integration using Model-driven Engineering. Designing Software-intensive Systems: Methods and Principles, 474–504 (2008)
17. Panetto, H., Molina, A.: Enterprise integration and interoperability in manufacturing systems: Trends and issues. Computers in Industry 59, 641–646 (2008)
18. Mauro, C., Leimeister, J.M., Krcmar, H.: Service Oriented Device Integration - An Analysis of SOA Design Patterns. In: 43rd Hawaii International Conference on System Sciences, pp. 1–10. IEEE (2010)
19. Legner, C., Vogel, T.: Design Principles for B2B Services: An Evaluation of two alternative Service Designs. In: International Conference on Services Computing, pp. 372–379 (2007)
20. Berners-Lee, T., Hendler, J., Lassil, O.: The Semantic Web. Scientific American 284, 28–37 (2001)
21. Ankolekar, A., Krötzsch, M., Tran, T., Vrandečić, D.: The two Cultures: Mashing up Web 2.0 and the Semantic Web. Web Semantics: Science. Services and Agents on the World Wide Web 6, 70–75 (2008)
22. Rosenberg, F., Curbera, F.: Composing restful services and collaborative workflows: A lightweight approach. Internet Computing 12, 24–31 (2008)
23. Yu, J., Benatallah, B., Casati, F., Daniel, F.: Understanding mashup development. IEEE Internet Computing 12, 44–52 (2008)
24. Nachouki, G., Quafafou, M.: MashUp Web Data Sources and Services based on semantic Queries. Information Systems 36, 151–173 (2011)
25. Suwanmanee, S., Benslimane, D., Thiran, P.: OWL-Based Approach for Semantic Interoperability. In: 19th International Conference on Advanced Information Networking and Applications, pp. 145–150 (2005)
26. Hevner, A.R., March, S.T., Park, J., Ram, S.: Design Science in Information Systems Research. MIS Quarterly 28, 75–105 (2004)
27. Vaishnavi, V.K., Kuechler, W.: Design science research methods and patterns: innovating information and communication technology. Auerbach, New York (2007)
28. Dishaw, M.T., Strong, D.M.: Extending the Technology Acceptance Model with Task-Technology Fit Constructs. Information & Management 36, 9–21 (1999)
29. Campbell, D.J.: Task Complexity: A Review and Analysis. Academy of Management Review 13, 40–52 (1988)
30. Fry, L.W., Slocum, J.W.: Technology, Structure, and Workgroup Effectiveness: A Test of a Contingency Model. Academy of Management Journal 27, 221–246 (1984)
31. McCrae, R.R., John, O.P.: An Introduction to the Five Factor Model and its Applications. Journal of Personality 60, 175–215 (1992)
32. Gefen, D.: Reflections on the Dimensions of Trust and Trustworthiness among online Consumers. ACM SiGMiS Database 33, 38–53 (2002)
33. Gladstein, D.L.: Groups in Context: A Model of Task Group Effectiveness. Administrative Science Quarterly 29, 499–517 (1984)
34. Rogers, E.M.E.E.M.: Diffusion of Innovations. The Free Press, New York (1995)
35. Lv, C., Li, Q., Lei, Z., Peng, J., Zhang, W., Wang, T.: PaaS: A Revolution for Information Technology Platforms. In: International Conference on Educational and Network Technology, pp. 346–349 (2010)
36. Gregor, S., Jones, D.: The Anatomy of a Design Theory. Journal of the Association for Information Systems 8, 313–335 (2007)

Design Principles for Research Data Export: Lessons Learned in e-Health Design Research

Mudassir Imran Mustafa and Jonas Sjöström

Uppsala University, Kyrkogårdsg 10, Box 513, 751 20 Uppsala, Sweden
{mudassir.imran,jonas.sjostrom}@im.uu.se

Abstract. Information technology (IT) allows for large-scale data collection and data analysis, e.g. through logs of user behavior and online surveys. While the issue of structured access to data is extremely important, previous research has not sufficiently emphasized design of data export for research purposes. If researchers are to make their data accessible, they must be empowered to export data in a flexible manner. In this paper, we employ action design research to develop design principles for data export in an e-Health context. Design is informed by a sociomaterial world-view, object-oriented patterns and principles, and usability goals. Through three build-intervene-evaluate cycles in an empirical setting where randomized controlled trials are designed, we propose nine design principles and a conceptual architecture for data export. Implications for research and practice are discussed.

Keywords: Data export, e-health, mutability, action design research.

1   Introduction

Information systems (IS) play an important role in contemporary research. Information technology (IT) allows for large-scale data collection and data analysis, e.g. through logs of user behavior [1] and through data collection through online surveys [2]. The Internet and its emerging importance as a medium for business and social interaction is clearly important for research, both as a subject of study and as a tool to conduct research.

In IS and related disciplines, topics like data extraction, data migration, data warehousing, data mining and data analysis are well explored. However, there has been little emphasis on design of data export for research purposes. In almost all cases researchers only mentioned the availability of data export functionality without detailing design issues related to such functionality. The importance of data export is significant, not only for analysis purposes, but also in relation to the growing demand from research funders that data should be open, i.e. accessible by peers for validation or further analysis[3]. There is an increased interest among both policy-makers and researchers to make data openly available, to support innovation [4] as well as creating additional value to the scientific community [5]. Clearly, if researchers are to make their data accessible to others, they must be empowered to export data in a flexible manner.

J. vom Brocke et al. (Eds.): DESRIST 2013, LNCS 7939, pp. 34–49, 2013.

Data export is a class of problems that relates to software in general, and research-supporting software in particular. Given the heterogeneous and emergent character of software, data export needs to be based on both (i) an understanding of the needs of the people who wants to export data, and (ii) design principles and design patterns that promote data export design in a manner that complies with best practices in software design. This topic has hardly been studied in the IS literature. Practitioners (e.g., developers, database administrators) tend to export data directly from databases using database management systems (DBMS) features [6] such as the structured query language (SQL).

Researchers are prone to express that exported information needs to be imported into their analysis software, such as SAS, SPSS or Excel. However, it is hard for anyone to know and express their needs in detail. User needs (and their ability to express their needs) emerge over time. Appropriation of new technology may lead to ways of use that were not anticipated by designers. The idea of 'design in use' has been explained as drift [7], tailoring [8], adaptation [9], and appropriation [10, 11], to mention a few.

Software architecture and internal design affect the resources required to update software, as well as the robustness of software [12]. In essence, we conceive of mutability [13] as an ideal for data export design. Based on the troubles that may be caused by changing requirements, we argue that design knowledge concerning adaptive data export may add significant value to research-oriented software.

In this paper, we propose a set of principles for design of generic data export. The principles emerged through reflection and learning in three build-intervene-evaluate (BIE) cycles in an action design research initiative [14] in a clinical eHealth research context. In addition to the principles, we present a conceptual architecture from the software that emerged during the design process, i.e. an instantiation of an IT artifact that resonate with the proposed principles. In addition, implications for research are discussed.

2   Research Approach

The design principles proposed in this paper result from an action design research (ADR) project in the Swedish health sector. ADR is an interpretive research approach, based on the sociomaterial recognition that human practice evolves over time [15, 16]. While the ADR approach acknowledges the emergent character of the social world, it resonates with the need for 'mutable' IT artifacts [13, 17]. Our appropriation of ADR [14] is outlined below.

Stage 1: Problem Formulation. In the first ADR stage, research questions are formulated based on a problem; perceived in practice, anticipated by researchers or practitioners, encountered in existing technologies, or identified in prior research. The research problem is regarded as an instance of a class of problems (i.e. "designing data export"). Research should be inspired by practice and based on a sound theoretical base for design. The design context for our work is further described in section 3. In addition, the researcher should actively inscribe theoretical elements in the ensemble artifact, thus manifesting the theory 'in a socially recognizable form'. The theoretical influences in our work are outlined in section 4.

Stage 2: Building, Intervention and Evaluation. The second stage of ADR uses the problem exploration and theoretical premises adopted in stage one to carry out a change in the target organization. The preliminary design of the artifact is based on the outcomes of stage one. During the BIE (building, intervention and evaluation) stage the artifact is built (B), put into the organizational situation (I), and formatively evaluated (E) to meet the practitioners' needs. Our work in this paper is a case of IT-dominant BIE, in which artifact design is the primary source of innovation (Figure 1). In BIE, the artifact and the organization shape one another, practitioners and researchers influence each other, and evaluation is continuous and situated in practice. Our BIE cycles are presented in section 5.

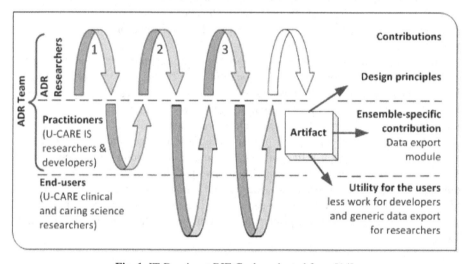

Fig. 1. IT-Dominant BIE Cycles adapted from [14]

Stage 3: Reflecting and Learning. Reflection and learning concern experiences and insights from the BIE cycles with respect to the problem formulated in the first stage. This stage is continuous and parallel to first two stages. This stage emphasizes that the ensemble artifact reflects not only the preliminary design but how it is shaped in organizational context. The guiding principle of this stage is guided emergence of the artifact, i.e. the emerging design of the artifact through the BIE cycles. Continual reflection and learning is explained as part of the BIE cycles in section 5.

Stage 4: Formalization of Learning. Despite of the situated nature of ADR, lessons learned in the organizational situation are developed into general solutions for a class of similar problems. In this stage the guiding principle is to generalize the outcome of BIE cycles. The formalized representation of our learning consists of the design principles presented in section 6, as well as in the concluding discussion.

3   Design Context and Problem Relevance

This research is part of the Uppsala University Psychosocial Care (U-CARE) research programme. The overarching goal of U-CARE is to promote psychosocial health among patients struck by somatic disease and their significant others, ideally at a low cost for individuals and society. Research is conducted in collaboration between research groups in psychology, information systems, caring sciences and health economics. Initial research activities are performed within the areas of paediatric oncology, adult oncology and cardiology, in close collaboration with clinicians at Uppsala University Hospital. Three randomized controlled trials (RCTs) are being designed, to study the efficacy and cost-effectiveness of Internet-based self-help and cognitive behavioural therapy (CBT) for the different patient groups. The role of IS researchers is to ingrain research with knowledge from the IS discipline and sibling disciplines (e.g. software engineering and interaction design). The IS researchers also contribute through the conceptual design and construction of actual software in the programme. The U-CARE design effort is thus a co-design of research, treatment protocols, and software to support both research and treatment via the Internet.

The design process was set up to resonate with agile values [18]. Development sprints lasted for 2–3 weeks, followed by sprint reviews where various stakeholders were exposed to the latest version of the platform. In addition, external specialists and patient groups were invited to explore the software, followed by workshops in which they provided feedback to the design team. In total, 40+ design workshops have been organized. IS researchers and other professionals were co-located; with the implication that many issues were discussed and resolved between meetings. The collaboration between researchers and other stakeholders promoted relevance, and practice informed and shaped design.

4   Knowledge Base

In this section, we outline our knowledge base: (1) A socio-material perspective, (2) design patterns for mutability, and (3) usability. Each aspect is elaborated below.

4.1   A Sociomaterial Perspective

IS researchers have increasingly recognized that conceptualizations in the IS field should acknowledge the emergent characteristics of the social world [19]. With such a world-view, the mutability of artifacts becomes important. IS design theory should encompass how the artifact can be adapted to a continuously changing use context and evolving technological infrastructures [13]. We need to conceive of the emergent properties of both technology and the social world, while also recognizing the complex interplay between them (e.g. [16, 20–22]).

We distinguish between (i) the need to relate design work to existing (and emerging) social and technological structures, and (ii) the socio-material insight that new (and existing) artifacts indeed transform the social world where they are put into play.

With respect to technological change, designers need to adapt technological solutions to an existing infrastructure. New technology is thus an artifact in a sense, but it is also a contribution to an evolving compound of technology. Technology, in our view, undergoes an evolution over time rather than being deliberately designed for a well-specified purpose known in advance. Gill & Hevner [17] suggest that "the fitness of a design artifact must be estimated using a utility function that considers the full range of characteristics that can impact the likelihood that the artifact will further be reproduced and evolve" (p. 247). While aiming at producing relevant and useful artifacts that impact society, it makes sense to factor in the likelihood of future use and evolution of the artifact, not only its aptness to solve a particular problem in a particular situation.

4.2   Design Patterns for Mutability

The notion of mutability is a core topic within the field of Software Engineering (SE), although SE discourse is different both in terms of knowledge interests and terminology. Developments in software design, such as modularization [23], abstract data types [24], and object orientation [25] reflect incrementally sophisticated solutions to developing mutable software. We have factored in a set of software engineering concepts for mutability into the design of data export, as elaborated below.

Separation of concerns [26] concerns the need to structure software for reduced complexity by delineating it into manageable parts. While separation of concerns is an overarching principle, there are several design patterns that provide detailed design advice to address specific problems. We adopt the model-view-controller (MVC) pattern. The *controller* (C) is the communication between the *model* (M) and *view* (V) objects [27]. The *model* is responsible for acting on logical conditions or rules by managing data from the application domain. It processes information according to the directions given by the *controller*. The *view* displays the *model*'s state in an appropriate format so that the users can easily understand. MVC was introduced by Reenskaug at Xerox Parc in the late 1970's. Today there are numerous available implementations of MVC (Wikipedia lists ~100 MVC implementations, covering all major development languages and platforms). The recognition of MVC among a large number of developers should allow developers to more quickly interpret code and make adaptations to it. *Domain-driven design* [28] is an approach to developing software for complex needs by connecting the implementation to an evolving model. MVC design is not sufficient, since *models* are subject to additional design decisions to allow for a good business logic API to evolve over time. A *domain-driven design* approach separates *application-specific logic* from *infrastructure logic* (data access), and business objects are separated into their own layer, making them re-usable across applications.

In data export, we are particularly interested in transfer of data between system parts. We draw on the concepts of data transfer objects (DTOs) and service data objects (SDOs) to manage data transfer. DTO is an ad hoc container object used to pass data between layers. The adoption of DTO adds flexibility to the business layer and subsequently to the design of the entire application [29]. When DTOs are employed, we also need a DTO adapter layer (an assembler) to adapt one or more entity objects to a different interface as required by the use case. A viable solution is the Assembler pattern, which creates DTOs from business objects and vice versa. Assembler is a specialized instance of the Mapper pattern. SDOs aim at unifying data from heterogeneous data sources (e.g. databases, XML data sources, web services, and enterprise information systems). SDOs require a data access service (DAS) to access its data source [30].

Metadata mapping – related to DTOs and SDOs - concerns how fields in a database correspond to fields in in-memory objects. There are two main methods for metadata mapping: code generation and reflective programming. Code generation depends on metadata to produce source code for classes. These classes are generated prior to compilation and deployed with the server code. It is a less dynamic approach, since changes require recompiling and redeploying. Instead we adopted a reflective programming approach, where changes can be done during runtime by just re-reading the metadata.

4.3   Usability

Preece, Rogers, & Sharp [31] state that one aim of interaction design is to build usable interactive products. Bevan, Kirakowski & Maissel [32] define usability in a simple but powerful manner, as the "user's view of software quality" (p. 4). However, usability is commonly conceived in a more specific manner. The ISO 9241 definition of usability presents the concept as the "… effectiveness, efficiency and satisfaction with which a specified set of users can achieve a specified set of goals in a particular environment". Effectiveness refers to users' ability to fulfill their goals through the use of the interactive product. Efficiency means that they should fulfill these goals with a minimum of effort. Satisfaction is a subjective measure, focusing the degree of satisfaction experienced by the user through their appropriating the artifact. In this work we find the ISO usability definition relevant, since data export resonates well with the task-solving design paradigm in which the ISO definition was developed.

Current technology facilitates storage and access of large amounts of data at virtually no cost. The main problem in current data-centric applications is how to use the collected raw data. The true value of data lies in our ability to use it. From a research perspective, to analyze it and to find interesting results, e.g. through the use of statistical analysis and inference or to apply qualitative analysis methods [33]. Researchers choose different software applications to analyze data. Software such as SAS and SPSS, as well as spreadsheet applications such as Microsoft Excel, are commonly used for statistical analysis. Our view is that data export has to permit export to different formats supported by common analytical tools. The formats we identified in the design process include CSV, XML and Excel. In addition, the trend towards open data formats requires a data export function to be adaptable to export into new (currently unknown) formats.

5   BIE Cycles

ADR cycles are characterized by a high degree of participation by various stakeholders (including, but not limited to, end-users) [14]. End users in U-CARE were committed to participating in the ADR process. The conceptual architecture for generic
data export emerged during the design process over the BIE cycles (Figure 2). The
conceptualization provides a holistic view on data export. In doing so, it partially
resembles prior work related to the domain [34–37].

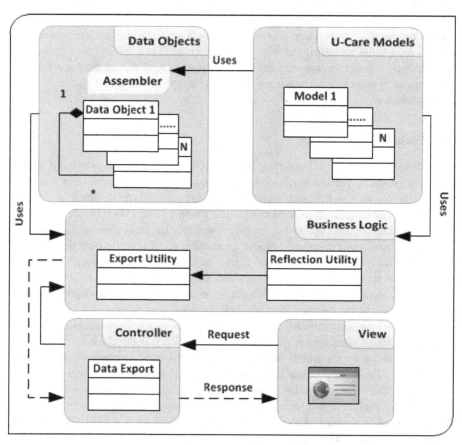

Fig. 2. Conceptual architecture for generic data export using MVC design pattern

The data object concept (DO) is merger of DTO and SDO concepts, and an implementation of the Adapter pattern. The DO constructors act as assemblers to populate
data from U-CARE (business) models. The reflection pattern was used to inspect
assemblies, types, and members of U-CARE data models (business objects). The
reflection utility read the DO and builds the user interface dynamically. The assembler uses reflection for both filtering and pivoting (converting rows to columns) of the

data. The export utility acts in its own layer that facilitates data export into different formats as well as persistent storage of user-defined export templates.

The data export feature that was developed was an evolutionary prototype. The involved stakeholders to support the actual data export following the U-CARE RCTs will appropriate it. We conceive of the design process as guided emergence. The role of IS researchers was to lead this process, establish mechanisms for feedback and conceptual reflection, and continually reflect about how additional theory could ingrain artifact design. Each cycle is detailed in the following subsections, by discussing the build activities, intervention activities, and evaluation activities. At the end of each cycle, we provide an account of the lessons learned.

5.1   BIE Cycle I - The 'Alpha' Prototype

Build. The initial challenge was to understand the problem domain. Part of this was to understand the existing software, from which data would be exported. The character of the existing software base was clearly important to factor into the design. In addition, design was influenced by practitioners with first-hand experience of the problem domain, the organizational setting, and projected future use of data export functionality. Prototype construction was highly influenced by the characteristics of the existing software base, and the challenges it implied.

The U-CARE software was a relatively large and complex system, built to satisfy user requirements from three different work packages conducting three RCTs. Therefore, it was decided that the alpha prototype would only support export of a subset of data (questionnaires and questionnaire results). Many aspects of the U-CARE software were designed for flexibility through a static model managing both data and metadata about various phenomena. The software provides generic solutions for designing questionnaires, themes, translations, RCT studies, patient indicators, treatment protocols *et cetera*. An implication was that the alpha prototype should be loosely coupled with the existing software through the use of interfaces (data objects), to minimize dependencies between the export feature and other parts of the software. While the software at hand offered plenty of configuration possibilities for end users, it made sense that the data export should also be configurable by the end users themselves. The main idea was that the software as a whole should be useful in a new context as-is, without further software development involved.

In addition to the study of the existing software and design literature, input from domain experts informed the design process. There were clear hierarchical structures in the data model, e.g. a workpackage including several studies. Each study includes several observation points, which in turn includes several questionnaires, consisting of multiple questions *et cetera*. The end users (researchers) were used to analyzing such data using cross-tabulations, i.e. getting all data about a participant in one row, where the answers to questions (and results of calculated expressions) would be put in columns. This forced the design to include pivoting (row-to-column transformation) features. The mutability was design both as (i) data objects (Figure 2) that adapted easily to a changing data model, and (ii) a GUI that adapted itself to the data objects (Figure 3).

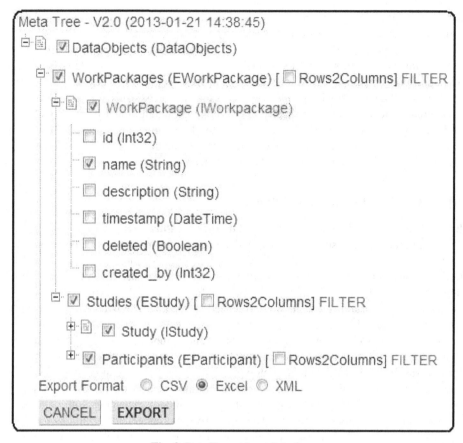

Fig. 3. Data Export Input Interface

Intervention and Evaluation. The emerging export feature was shown to and tested by domain experts in the ADR team in a series of meetings. The intervention and formative evaluation sessions were performed as a part of daily meetings between researchers, practitioners, and domain experts of clinical research. As stated by Venable, Pries-Heje, & Baskerville [38], formative evaluation is "in which an artifact still under development is evaluated to determine areas for improvement and refinement" (p. 426).

The process showed that practitioners appreciated the flexibility of the data export feature, allowing them to extract data in new ways independent of software developers. In addition, we learned that whenever the developers modified the U-CARE platform models, both the data objects and the data export GUI adapted automatically through the reflection pattern. The automatic adaptation frees resources to develop core features of the system without being concerned about dependencies to the export feature. Clearly, everything cannot adapt automatically. The addition of new models required a minor adaptation of the data object classes.

Learning and Reflections. During the evaluation, software developers suggested a series of performance improvements including: (i) User selections should be saved and during subsequent data export the same selection of fields or small variation can be exported efficiently with less clicks. (ii) Metadata should be generated only if the underneath models or data object tree structure is changed. (iii) Storing export module's data structures in database to allow users to reuse previous templates for data export. The main outcome of the evaluation was that reflection should not be used every time the data export module loads, and user selections should be possible to reuse at later stage. A first draft of design principles was phrased after this cycle.

5.2   BIE Cycle II - the 'Beta 1' Prototype

Build. The second cycle was oriented towards the organizational setting. Lessons learned from the first cycle were the basis to start work on the 'Beta 1' prototype. We continued the development with sketching, designing and implementing additional features.

The extensive use of reflection in the alpha version was addressed to develop a persistent structure of metadata (stored in database tables). The idea of the revision was to improve performance by only using reflection when a change is detected in the underlying data model. The second revision concerned the efficiency of data export from the user point-of-view. A new feature was added to manage 'data export packages' (templates). The design was revised so that users may create templates for data export. The user can then export data by activating the template and choosing a desired output format (e.g. Figure 4 illustrates data export in Excel format).

1 WORK PACKAGE NAME	2 USER NICK NAME	3 QUIZ NAME	4 QUESTION SERIAL	5 ANSWERS WEIGHT	.....	36 QUIZ RESULT NAME	37 QUIZ RESULT VALUE	....
WP2	Ucare9	HADS (WP2)	1	2	......	Ångestindex	14	....
WP2	Ucare8	HADS (WP2)	1	1	.....	Ångestindex	7	....
....	....	....	....	....	....	....	....	....
WP2	Ucare6	HADS (WP2)	1	3	.....	Ångestindex	17	....

Fig. 4. Data Export Output in Excel

Intervention and Evaluation. The beta prototype was integrated with U-CARE software and published on the U-CARE production server. Access to the data export feature was given to developers. At that time, the software was in beta-testing, and there was a substantive amount of test data available (provided by various stakeholders throughout the design process). A scenario-based evaluation [39] was conducted at a development meeting where researchers and managers were present. The participants represent different professions and different research work packages. The Beta 1 version was demonstrated and explained data from a rather excessive test study.

Learning and Reflections. Our overall interpretation is that all stakeholders appreciated the data export package. However, questions were raised about access to data export. The main outcome of the evaluation session was that the data export module should have restricted access regarding who is allowed to export data, which data and when, and that the anonymity of respondents is preserved. Another lesson learned during the cycle was the need for user-controlled row filtering when using a template for export. In the beta 1 version, only columns could be filtered. The design principles were revised to reflect the lessons learned.

5.3   BIE Cycle III - the 'Beta 2' Prototype

Build. The Beta 2 prototype was revised in accordance with the learning from BIE cycle 2. The new features were concerned with data access issues and row filtering. The data access issue was simple to address due to the existing support for role-based authentication and authorization in the U-CARE software. The issue of de-identified data was also managed. The existing software is based on a separation of collected data from personal data in two different databases. One database keeps the participants' identifiable data while other database keeps all study-related data (e.g. answers to questionnaires and logs of user behavior). Access to both databases would be needed to connect collected data to identified users. The data export module only has access to the de-identified data. In summary, there was a need for minor revisions of the data export software to fit the data access and privacy requirements from BIE cycle 2. However, in other contexts, there may be a need to revise the data export module to manage this issue.

New filters were design to support row filtering. A filter option was added to the GUI for every attribute provided by the data objects. The filter capabilities were designed to dynamically adapt to the underlying models.

Intervention and Evaluation. In this cycle, four semi-structured interviews with open-ended questions were carried out on-site. Each interview was immediately followed-up by an evaluation of the data export features in a controlled environment. Three respondents were researchers (i.e. domain experts on data analysis and presumptive users of the data export feature). The fourth respondent was a developer with an interest in the technical and conceptual qualities of the data export software.

Each interview started out with questions about the respondent's views on data export, their experience in use of data export tools, and their expectations on the beta 2 prototype. After that, we presented the data export feature, its intended use and its user interface. This was followed by a demonstration about how to use the features, using the same dataset as in the evaluation session in BIE cycle 2. After that, the respondent was asked to perform a number of data export tasks using the software. During their work and to follow-up their work, further questions were asked to learn more about the respondent's impressions. They were asked about both benefits and drawbacks. We queried them on what kind of information they were interested in exporting (e.g. data and/or metadata about an RCT) as well as usability-oriented issue (e.g. ease-of-use and reliability). The developer was asked different questions, focusing software design qualities such as compatibility, extensibility, fault-tolerance, maintainability, modularity, reliability, robustness, security and usability.

Learning and Reflections. The generic design of data export faced the design challenge that Sjöström et al. [1] explain as "...a trade-off situation between simplicity and mutability-in-use". Generic design of data export requires more training and usage. The data export displays all the fields/properties of the model including some fields that are stored to manage the logic, e.g. a timestamp, the user who created it et cetera. Due to this, the user interface become little complicated at first glance. This requires understanding of the field while exporting data. The main output of the intervention and evaluation was that there should not be too much customization and that the GUI should not present irrelevant data. Most of the end-users, however, were satisfied with the data export module. The design principles were revised into the version presented in the next section.

6 Design Principles for Generic Data Export

'*Formalization of learning*' is a discrete step in ADR. Although ADR postulates that reflection and learning occur continuously during ADR research, they conceptualize formalization of learning as an activity of its own. In practice, formalization of learning took place at the end of each BIE cycle (different versions of the set of design principles). In this paper - due to space limitations - we choose to present only the final version of the design principles, as shown in table 1.

Table 1. Design principles for generic data export

P1: The principle of simplicity. Data export features should be easy to use. Preferably, data export should be triggered by a single click, and the users should be guided to filter data according to their needs.
P2: The principle of developer independency. Data export features should be designed for end users (researchers) and should not require excessive technical knowledge. End users should be empowered to design their own export templates based on access to a view of exportable items.
P3: The principle of mutability (emergence). Data export should adapt itself or be easily adaptable to new data export requirements or changes in the software that hosts data.
P4: The principle of compatibility. Data export should render output in standardized or de facto formats (such as CSV, XML and Excel), to facilitate import by data analysis applications and statistical applications.

Table 1. (*continued*)

P5: The principle of easy development. The API for data export should be built in a way that minimizes the development resources required to add new export functionality. Developers should be able to develop core system features without continually addressing data export issues.
P6: The principle of export as a separate concern. Data export should require a minimum of development on every data export request. Insofar as possible, the data export software should be prepared for present and future data export requirements and adapt automatically to changes in the underlying data model. The data export layer needs to depend on the core features, but not the other way around.
P7: The principle of restricted data access. The access to data export features should be restricted to those who are allowed to export data. Authentication and authorization schemes should be applied so that only those who are permitted to retrieve data for analysis can access. Time restrictions may also apply to data export (e.g. 'only permitted after the trial is closed').
P8: The principle of anonymity. All data must be de-identified, so that a re-identification by use of different sets of published data or by linking exported data with other publicly available data sources should be impossible. The information needed to re-identify individuals should be separated from collected data insofar as possible.
P9: The principle of adequate customization. Customization should be afforded for end users, but it should not be too difficult. Only relevant information should be displayed. Customization options should be presented in semantic layers to allow basic features to all, while allowing advanced users more advanced options.

7   Concluding Discussion

In this paper, we have proposed a set of design principles to support the design of generic data export. The principles emerged through experiences gained from an action design research effort within a multi-disciplinary eHealth research programme in Sweden. The software design as a whole is designed for 'mutability', due to the anticipation that it will be used in different RCTs with using different treatment protocols. The export features were designed to support the complex and mutable character of the software as a whole. The ensemble artifact as well as the principles is ingrained with theories on mutability and usability. On basis of the theories adopted in the design work, we operate in a cumulative tradition [13]. The knowledge base in use supports the argument that the principles as well as the conceptual solution may be of value in a broader scope. The iterative character of ADR and the design context including stakeholders representing different RCTs is comparable to three different empirical contexts. This is coherent with the idea of abstracting our work from one case to another [40]. We thus argue that the principles are generalized outside a single case, although new cases would most certainly lead to an elaboration of the principles. The current principles state may however prove relevant and valuable outside the current empirical context. We do, however, realize that the word 'generic' is strong, and that any researcher or practitioner that implements the principles is responsible to use it wisely in the new situation. They constitute advice for designers rather than a solution that is transferrable 'as-is' into new design situations. The principles as such may be conceived of as a contribution to the IS knowledge base on designing data export. In addition, they are phrased in a way that should be meaningful for designers in practice.

The results of this research are currently biased towards software engineering and usability. Further research should draw more on quantitative data analysis, open standards, as well as research ethics, medical ethics, privacy and legal aspects. Such influences are likely lead to a revision of the principles, as well as entirely new principles.

We designed and implemented a software artifact that emerged in the ADR cycles. This artifact and its various representations in design models are not in focus in this paper. However, the conceptual architecture presented in Figure 2 is an additional contribution from our work. The architecture provides a conceptual solution that guides developers to operationalize the design principles into working software. Our plan is to release the entire software platform using some open source license, as an additional contribution both to practice and academia.

Finally, our work has emphasized a design domain that is becoming increasingly important in research. The current trend towards open data requires researchers to reflect about how to access and deliver their data to peers. Initiatives to develop research-centric software could benefit from the principles presented here, which (if appropriated in the development of new systems) provide researchers with an opportunity to access and export their data in flexible ways without the assistance of database experts.

Acknowledgements. This work was conducted as part of the Uppsala University Psychosocial Care Programme (U-CARE) at Uppsala University. U-CARE is a strategic research programme funded by the Swedish Government through the Swedish Research Council.

References

1. Sjöström, J., Ågerfalk, P.J., Lochan, A.R.: Mutability Matters: Baselining the Consequences of Design. In: Procedings of MCIS 2011, Limassol, Cyprus (2011)
2. Lumsden, J., Morgan, W.: Online-Questionnaire Design. Establishing Guidelines and Evaluating Existing Support (2005)
3. Peters, G.Y., Abraham, C., Crutzen, R.: Full disclosure: doing behavioural science necessitates sharing. The European Health Psychologist 14, 77–84 (2012)
4. Nature: Beta blockers? Nature 455, 708 (2008)
5. Murray-Rust, P.: Open data in science. Serials Review 34, 52–64 (2008)

6. Aspin, A.: Exporting Data from SQL server. SQL Server 2012 Data Integration Recipes: Solutions for Integration Services and Other ETL Tools, pp. 343–424. Apress, New York (2012)

7. Ciborra, C.U.: Groupware and Teamwork. Wiley & Sons, New York (1996)

8. Trigg, R.H., Bödker, S.: From implementation to design: tailoring and the emergence of systematization in CSCW. In: Procedings of CSCW 1994, pp. 45–54 (1994)

9. Majchrzak, A., Rice, R.E., Malhotra, A., King, N., Ba, S.: Technology adaption: the case of a computer-supported inter-organizational virtual team. MIS Quarterly 24, 569–600 (2000)

10. DeSanctis, G., Poole, M.S.: Capturing the complexity in advanced technology use: Adaptive structuration theory. Organization Science 5, 121–147 (1994)

11. Orlikowski, W.J.: Using technology and constituting structures: A practice lens for studying technology in organizations. Organization Science 11, 404–428 (2000)

12. McConnell, S.: Code complete. O'Reilly, Inc. (2009)

13. Gregor, S., Jonas, D.: The Anatomy of a Design Theory. Journal of the Association for Information Systems 8, 312–335 (2007)

14. Sein, M.K., Henfridsson, O., Purao, S., Rossi, M., Lindgren, R.: Action Design Research. Journal of the Association for Information Systems 35, 37–56 (2011)

15. Orlikowski, W.J.: The sociomateriality of organisational life: considering technology in management research. Cambridge Journal of Economics 34, 125–141 (2010)

16. Leonardi, P.M.: Materiality, Sociomateriality, and Socio-Technical Systems: What Do These Terms Mean? How Are They Related? Do We Need Them? In: Leonardi, P.M., Nardi, B.A., Kallinikos, J. (eds.) Materiality and Organizing: Social Interaction in a Technological World, pp. 25–48. Oxford University Press, Oxford (2012)

17. Gill, T.G., Hevner, A.R.: A fitness-utility model for design science research. In: Jain, H., Sinha, A.P., Vitharana, P. (eds.) DESRIST 2011. LNCS, vol. 6629, pp. 237–252. Springer, Heidelberg (2011)

18. Conboy, K.: Agility from first principles: Reconstructing the concept of agility in information systems development. Information Systems Research 20, 329–354 (2009)

19. Orlikowski, W.J., Iacono, C.S.: Research commentary: Desperately seeking "IT" in IT research - A call to theorizing the IT artifact. Information Systems Research 12, 121–134 (2001)

20. Orlikowski, W.J.: The Duality of Technology - Rethinking the Concept of Technology in Organizations. Organization Science 3, 398–427 (1992)

21. Orlikowski, W.J., Scott, S.V.: 10 Sociomateriality: Challenging the Separation of Technology, Work and Organization. The Academy of Management Annals 2, 433–474 (2008)

22. Walls, J., Widmeyer, G., El Sawy, O.: Assessing information system design theory in perspective: How useful was our 1992 initial rendition. Journal of Information Technology Theory and Application (JITTA) 6, 43–58 (2004)

23. Parnas, D.: On the criteria to be used in decomposing systems into modules. Communications of the ACM 15, 1053–1058 (1972)

24. Liskov, B., Zilles, S.: Programming with Abstract Data Types. In: Proceedings of ACM SIGPLAN Symposium on Very High Level Languages, Santa Monica, CA, pp. 50–59 (1974)

25. Rentsch, T.: Object Oriented Programming. ACM SIGPLAN Notices 17, 51–57 (1982)

26. Dijkstra, E.W.: On the Role of Scientific Thought. In: Dijkstra, E.W. (ed.) Selected Writings on Computing: A Personal Perspective. Springer (1982)

27. Gamma, E., Helm, R., Johnson, R., Vlissides, J.: Design Patterns: Elements of Reusable Object-Oriented Software. Addison-Wesley (1994)

28. Evans, E.: Domain-Driven Design, Tackling Complexity in the Heart of Software. Addison-Wesley (2003)
29. Fowler, M., Rice, D., Foemmel, M., Hieatt, E., Mee, R., Stafford, R.: Patterns of Enterprise Application Architecture. Addison-Wesley Longman Publishing Co., Inc., Boston (2002)
30. Portier, B., Budinsky, F.: Introduction to Service Data Objects, http://www.ibm.com/developerworks/java/library/j-sdo/
31. Preece, J., Rogers, Y., Sharp, H.: Interaction design: beyond human-computer interaction. John Wiley & Sons, Inc., New York (2002)
32. Bevan, N., Kirakowski, J., Maissel, J.: What is usability. In: Human Aspects in Computing: Design and Use of Interactive Systems with Terminals, pp. 651–655. Elsevier (1991)
33. Fayyad, U., Piatetsky-Shapiro, G., Smyth, P.: The KDD process for extracting useful knowledge from volumes of data. Communications of the ACM 39, 27–34 (1996)
34. Bennett, T.A., Bayrak, C.: Bridging the data integration gap: from theory to implementation. ACM SIGSOFT Software Engineering Notes 36 (2011)
35. Morris, H., Liao, H., Padmanabhan, S., Srinivasan, S., Lau, P., Shan, J., Wisnesky, R.: Bringing Business Objects into Extract-Transform-Load (ETL) Technology. In: IEEE International Conference on e-Business Engineering (ICEBE 2008), pp. 709–714 (2008)
36. Bordbar, B., Draheim, D., Horn, M., Schulz, I., Weber, G.: Integrated model-based software development, data access, and data migration. In: Briand, L.C., Williams, C. (eds.) MoDELS 2005. LNCS, vol. 3713, pp. 382–396. Springer, Heidelberg (2005)
37. Brandt, C.A., Morse, R., Matthews, K., Sun, K., Deshpande, A.M., Gadagkar, R., Cohen, D.B., Miller, P.L., Nadkarni, P.M.: Metadata-driven creation of data marts from an EAV-modeled clinical research database. International Journal of Medical Informatics 65, 225–241 (2002)
38. Venable, J., Pries-Heje, J., Baskerville, R.: A Comprehensive Framework for Evaluation in Design Science Research. In: Peffers, K., Rothenberger, M., Kuechler, B. (eds.) DESRIST 2012. LNCS, vol. 7286, pp. 423–438. Springer, Heidelberg (2012)
39. Hevner, A.R., Ram, S., March, S.T., Park, J.: Design science in information systems research. MIS Quarterly 28, 75–105 (2004)
40. Lee, A.S., Baskerville, R.L.: Generalizing Generalizability in Information Systems Research. Information Systems Research 14, 221–243 (2003)

What's the Best Bet? An Analysis of Design Scientists' Perceptions of Receptivity and Impact of IS Journals

Debra VanderMeer and Monica Chiarini Tremblay

College of Business, Florida International University, Miami, FL 33199
{vanderd,tremblay}@fiu.edu

Abstract. Design Science Research is now an accepted philosophy for Information Systems scholars, yet deciding where to publish is still enigmatic. Though several mainstream IS publications modified their editorial statements to welcome DSR manuscripts, their receptivity is uncertain. We survey the DSR community regarding individual researchers' experiences publishing DSR work in journals, and summarize our findings here. We identify journals that the DSR community perceives to be both receptive to DSR work and impactful to their careers. Our goal is to aid Design Science researchers in the selection of appropriate outlets for their future work, and possibly identify potential journal outlets they may not have considered.

Keywords: Journals, receptivity, impact.

1 Introduction

IS researchers have conducted Design Science Research (DSR) research for many years particularly outside the US [Wilde and Hess 2007; Winter 2008]. Hevner and his colleagues [2004] advanced DSR as a mainstream category of IS research with their conceptual framework and guidelines for performing design science research, published in information systems in one of IS's most recognized journals, MIS Quarterly. In recent years, several mainstream IS publications modified their editorial statements to welcome DSR manuscripts, and new generations of graduating IS scholars are being trained in depth in DSR methods. An important part of maintaining rigor in DS research involves communicating one's research results with the IS community [March and Smith 1995; Simon 1981], where a primary means of communicating one's research is to publish to journal outlets.

For DS researchers, the question of where to submit DSR manuscripts for possible publication arises. Every journal's mission and readership is different, and receptivity to DSR work will vary widely across journals. Given that timelines from submission to final decision can range from several months to several years, and tenure clocks impose a hard deadline, it is important that authors target their work carefully to achieve publication. This can be difficult, particularly for more junior researchers who may not have gained much exposure to specific journals' expectations.

In order to make better-informed decisions, it would be helpful to have some idea of the experience of other design science researchers in communicating their research

J. vom Brocke et al. (Eds.): DESRIST 2013, LNCS 7939, pp. 50–58, 2013.

through journal publication. In this work, we survey the DSR community regarding individual researchers' experiences publishing DSR work in journals, and summarize our findings here. We hope that these data points can help Design Science researchers select appropriate outlets for their work, and possibly identify potential journal outlets they have not considered previously. We note that our work here focuses exclusively on DSR research and does not address behavioral research in Information Systems.

2   Methodology

We take an approach similar to that of Le Rouge et al. [2010] and conduct a survey of members of the DSR community. In this survey, we ask participants to rate a set of 60 journals based on their perception of receptivity to DSR work, and to indicate journals to which they have submitted manuscripts, and where they have been successful in journal publication.

In selecting the journals for our survey, we aimed to include journals representing both the breadth of the Information Systems research area, as well as depth in terms of technically-oriented journals. For breadth across the field, we considered the list of MIS Journal Rankings (http://start.aisnet.org/?JournalRankings). To select the most relevant journals from this list, we retained any journal that was ranked by more than 50% of the 9 rankings considered. In terms of technically-oriented journals, we included all the journals listed in the "Design Science Research in Information Systems" page (http://desrist.org/design-research-in-information-systems/). The combination of these two sources yielded 60 journals.

We developed a set of four metrics to measure design science researchers' perceptions of these 60 journals: awareness, receptivity, impact, and respondent affiliation. Awareness is a measure of perceived relevance, i.e., the extent to which respondents believe the journal is relevant to their research. Receptivity is a measure of perceived acceptance, i.e., the extent to which respondents believe that journals will consider/accept their manuscripts for publication. Impact is a measure of perceived relative reward, i.e., the extent to which respondents believe that publication in a journal will have a beneficial impact on their career progress. Respondent affiliation asks about respondents' relationship(s) with a journal.

We designed a web-based survey instrument to measure each of these four metrics. The 60 journals were presented in groups of 15 journals at a time, for a total of four pages. Respondents were asked to consider awareness, receptivity, impact, and respondent affiliation for relevant journals. Journals were defined as relevant to the participants if they met one or more of these criteria: 1) the participant had published or aspired to publish in the journal, 2) the participant frequently read manuscripts published in the journal, 3) the participant frequently cited work published in the journal, the participant's unit or department considered the journal important for tenure & promotion, and/or 4) the participant considered the journal important for job placement. At the end of the survey, we gathered the following demographic data for each respondent: academic rank, whether current position is tenure track or not, highest degree earned, discipline of terminal degree, discipline of employment/study, and country of employment/study.

The survey was developed in Qualtrics and hosted on their servers. Qualtrics has the capability to post to social media sites such as LinkedIn, or send invitations via email. It also tracks IP addresses allowing respondents to begin a survey where they left off and disallowing multiple responses from one IP address. We piloted the survey with five design scientist volunteers to determine clarity of the survey and the length of time needed to complete the survey. A few small refinements, mainly for clarity, were made after the pilot. Because our survey was posted on the Internet, we decided to create a relatively complex web address to minimize the number of responses from individuals outside of the targeted sample. Only those who received an invitation were provided with the web address. The survey was disabled immediately after the close date. For a period of three months, several methods were used to invite participation. We repeated the requests once every month. In a request specifically targeting design science researchers, we created a post to the AISWorld general mailing list with a link to the survey. Additionally, we also posted a request and link to the survey to the LinkedIn Design Science Research in Information Systems and Technology (DESRIST) group. Finally, we obtained the mailing list for the program committees for Workshop on Information Technologies and Systems (WITS), DESRIST, and Conference on Information Systems and Technology (CIST) and created an e-mail list (after removing duplicate names). We e-mailed a request with the link to our survey.

3   Results

3.1   Demographics

We received a total of 138 responses. Not all responses contained sufficient data for inclusion in analysis. We found that respondents generally fell into two categories: either he/she rated several journals and provided demographic data, or she provided few (if any) journal ratings and no demographic data. The responses in the latter of these categories were not considered in our analysis. After removing non-responsive responses, we had 57 responses suitable for inclusion in our analysis (41% completion rate). A profile of the respondents by rank, degree and position type is provided in Table 1a, by terminal degree and area of employment in Table 1b, and by geographic location in Table 1c.

Table 1a. Respondents' Profile by Rank Degree Type and Position Type

Rank		Degree by Type	
Professor	46%	PhD	95%
Associate Professor	21%	Other	5%
Assistant Professor	29%	Type of Position	
Instructor/Lecturer	1%	Tenure Track	87%
Doctoral Student/ABD	1%	Non-Tenure Track	9%
		Not Faculty	4%

Table 1b. Respondents' Area of Terminal Degree and Area of Employment

	Terminal Degree	Employment
Computer Science / Electrical Engineering / Other Engineering	10%	2%
Management Information Systems	67%	82%
Management / Strategic Management	2%	
Operations Management / Industrial Engineering/ Decision Sciences	3%	2%
Other	18%	14%

Table 1c. Respondents' Geographic Location

Location	Percentage
Pacific/Asia	13%
Europe	30%
North America	58%

3.2   Summary of Responses

Figure 1 illustrates that we report awareness for a journal as a percentage of respondents who chose to rate the journal. On average, participants considered about 30 journals (and chose to provide information for each). Figure 1, which illustrates that most of our participants chose to rate more than 10 journals included on our list. One third of our participants rated at least 40 journals, a possible indication that our carefully selected list was accurate for this community.

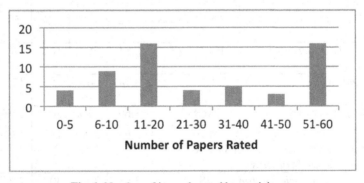

Fig. 1. Number of journals rated by participants

The survey allowed a respondent to choose to rate both receptivity and impact, receptivity alone, or impact alone for each journal. Thus, we have measures of awareness separately for both receptivity and impact. In practice, the difference between impact and receptivity awareness counts for any journal in our data set was never greater than one, so we report awareness as an average of these two counts. We report receptivity and impact as an average of the 5-point Likert scale ratings for each journal.

We report respondent affiliation as a percentage of respondents who checked the "submitted to," "published to," "reviewer for," and "editor for" each journal.

3.3   Journals

The following 15 journals showed the strongest indications of receptivity to design science research among our respondents (with receptivity higher than 3.6 on a 5 point Likert scale).

Table 2. Mean Receptivity of Journals

Journal Name	Abbreviation	Mean Receptivity	Awareness	Submitted	Published	Editor
ACM Transactions on Management Information Systems	ACM TMIS	4.44	56%	12%	9%	4%
Decision Support Systems	DSS	4.28	75%	33%	40%	9%
IEEE Transactions on Knowledge and Data Engineering	IEEE TKDE	4.09	56%	12%	12%	0%
ACM Transactions on Information Systems	ACM TOIS	4.06	56%	11%	7%	0%
Journal of Database Management	JDM	3.82	49%	12%	14%	9%
ACM Transactions on Database Systems	ACM TODS	3.82	49%	4%	5%	0%
IEEE Transactions on Software Engineering	IEEE TSE	3.81	56%	16%	16%	2%
Data and Knowledge Engineering	DKE	3.74	60%	9%	12%	0%
Communications of the ACM	CACM	3.69	84%	28%	39%	0%
IEEE Transactions on Systems, Man, and Cybernetics Part A: Systems and Humans	IEEE TSMCA	3.68	54%	12%	18%	2%
Journal of the Association for Information Systems	JAIS	3.68	70%	30%	21%	9%
Business and Information System Engineering	BISE	3.60	53%	14%	16%	7%
IEEE Transactions on Computers	IEEE TC	3.60	44%	4%	4%	0%

The following 17 journals showed the strongest indications of impact to our respondent's careers (with impact rated higher than 3.6 on a 5 point Likert scale).

Table 3. Mean Impact of Journals

Journal Name	Abbreviation	Mean Impact	Awareness	Submitted	Published	Editor
Information Systems Research	ISR	4.60	74%	30%	18%	4%
MIS Quarterly	MISQ	4.54	91%	42%	30%	7%
Journal of Management Information Systems	JMIS	4.38	74%	32%	23%	0%
Management Science	MS	4.24	58%	16%	12%	2%
Journal of the Association of Information Systems	JAIS	4.12	72%	30%	21%	9%
Decision Support Systems	DSS	4.02	75%	33%	40%	9%
European Journal of Information Systems	EJIS	3.96	81%	35%	26%	5%
Information Systems Journal	ISJ	3.89	49%	16%	14%	0%
Organization Science	OS	3.83	42%	5%	2%	0%
Decision Sciences	DS	3.82	60%	12%	12%	4%
Communications of the ACM	CACM	3.82	86%	28%	39%	0%
IEEE Transactions on Software Engineering	IEEE TSE	3.79	58%	16%	16%	2%
Harvard Business Review	HBR	3.73	53%	7%	0%	0%
ACM Transactions on Database Systems	ACM TODS	3.71	49%	4%	5%	0%
ACM Transactions on Management Information Systems	ACM TMIS	3.69	56%	12%	9%	4%
IEEE Transactions on Knowledge and Data Engineering	IEEE TKDE	3.69	56%	12%	12%	0%
ACM Transactions on Information Systems	ACM TOIS	3.64	58%	11%	7%	0%

In Figure 2, we take an intersection of these two tables to create a "magic quadrant" for design science research, where journals in the quadrant meet the 3.6 criteria for both receptivity and impact. We selected this cutoff because there was a natural gap for both axes when the data was displayed graphically. The x-axis represents mean receptivity, and the y-axis mean impact. The size of the circle indicates how many respondents published to these journals. This quadrant includes eight journals, listed alphabetically in Table 4.

Table 4. Magic Quadrant Journals

Journal	Mean Impact	Mean Receptivity	Published
ACM Transactions on Database Systems	3.71	3.82	3
ACM Transactions on Information Systems	3.64	4.06	4
ACM Transactions on Management Information Systems	3.69	4.44	5
Communications of the ACM	3.82	3.69	22
Decision Support Systems	4.02	4.28	23
IEEE Transactions on Knowledge and Data Engineering	3.69	4.09	7
IEEE Transactions on Software Engineering	3.79	3.81	9
Journal of the Association for Information Systems	4.12	3.68	12

3.4   Discussion of High Impact Journals Which Are Receptive to DSR Research

Our initial goal was to provide the DSR community with a consensus list that is both impactful and receptive. Fig 1 and Table 4 demonstrate clearly that there is a select set of journals that the DSR community perceives to be both highly receptive as well as highly impactful. This can help both junior and senior DSR researchers target their work, and perhaps look into journals they may not have previously considered. In some settings, departments or schools may have list-driven quality metrics that affect tenure and promotion decisions, and may be used as search criteria in the hiring process. It is our hope that the data points presented here can help with efforts to update these lists to ensure that they are inclusive of DSR work.

We note that some of the journals in the Senior Scholars' basket of journals (http://home.aisnet.org/displaycommon.cfm?an=1&subarticlenbr=346)   are   not represented in Figure 1. Our data show that these journals, while highly impactful (as shown in Table 3), are not perceived to be as receptive to DSR work, i.e., they did not receive an average receptivity rating of 3.0 or higher. For example, Information Systems Research was rated to have an average receptivity of 2.95, and Information Systems Journal was rated at 2.80.

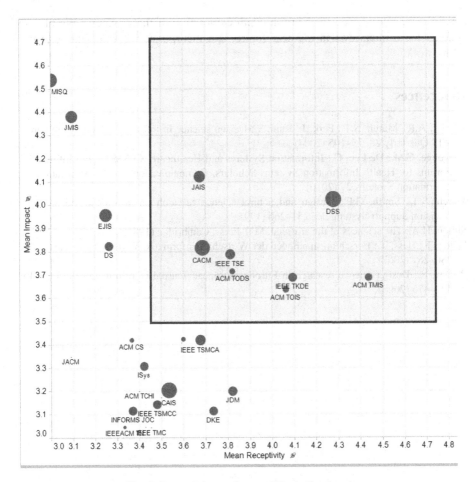

Fig. 2. Receptivity vs. Impact (Magic Quadrant)

4   Discussion and Future Work

In this work, we presented some initial results into our inquiry of perceptions of IS journal receptivity and impact for DS research. Our data includes information on where DS researchers have submitted, published, reviewed, and served in editorial capacities. We also have regional academic rank demographic, and field of degree and employment data, which can help us identify and compare differences between sub-groups. Further, our survey asked respondents whether they had ever changed their research methodology or context in order to publish to high-impact outlets, and to comment in general on IS journal receptivity, impact, and related topics. We are still in the process of analyzing this data, and plan to present the results of this analy-sis in future work. We have also identified a number of DS researchers who have agreed to be interviewed for more in-depth exploration of these issues. We plan to conduct these interviews in the near future, and incorporate those insights into our future work.

References

Hevner, A.R., March, S.T., Park, J., Ram, S.: Design science in information systems research. MIS Quarterly 28, 75–105 (2004)

Le Rouge, C.M., De Leo, G.: Information Systems and Healthcare XXXV: Health Informatics Forums for Health Information Systems Scholars. Communications of the Association for Information Systems 27 (2010)

March, S.T., Smith, G.F.: Design and natural science research on information technology. Decision Support Systems 15, 251–266 (1995)

Simon, H.A.: The sciences of the artificial. MIT Press, Cambridge (1981)

Wilde, T., Hess, T.: Forschungsmethoden der Wirtschaftsinformatik. Wirtschaftsinformatik 49, 280–287 (2007)

Winter, R.: Design science research in Europe. European Journal of Information Systems 17, 470–475 (2008)

Seeking Constructive Synergy: Design Science and the Constructive Research Approach

Kalle A. Piirainen[1] and Rafael A. Gonzalez[2]

[1] Lappeenranta University of Technology, Lappeenranta, Finland
kpii@r-m.com
[2] Javeriana University, Bogotá, Colombia
ragonzalez@javeriana.edu.co

Abstract. Information systems research and management science create knowledge which can be applied in organizations. Design science specifically aims at applying existing knowledge to solve interesting and relevant business problems and has been steadily gaining support in information systems research. However, design science is not the only design-oriented framework. Accordingly, this raises the question of whether it is possible to compare the results obtained from different brands of design-oriented research. This paper contributes to answering this question by comparing two research approaches, enabling mutual learning possibilities and suggesting improvements in transparency and rigor. The objective of this paper is to compare design science research with the constructive research approach. The conclusion is that the two approaches are compatible, save for details in practical requirements and partly underlying philosophical assumptions, but both have something to teach each other about how to define and execute design-oriented research in information systems and management science.

Keywords: design science research, constructive research approach, information systems, management science.

1 Introduction

Scholars in management science and information systems remind us every once in a while that rigorous research is a worthwhile effort, but that it should be able to deliver results which are applicable and relevant to practice as well (Holmström et al., 2009; van Aken, 2004). To reach a compromise and ground the abstract theoretical research to everyday activities and problems, it is generally conceded that information systems research (ISR) should generate new theoretical insights about the world and use them to solve (business) problems (e.g. Sein et al. 2010).

This demand had been recognized through the development of the action research approach and later through the proliferation of other "interventionist" research approaches (Jönsson and Lukka, 2007), such as the constructive research approach. The latter design-oriented tradition understands scientific activity as linked to the synthesis or construction of a new artifact to solve a problem. Recently, this research orientation has been labeled Design Science (DS). Through the work of Hevner et al. (2004), DS has received attention within ISR, while also gaining ground in the management field, especially through the efforts of van Aken (2004).

J. vom Brocke et al. (Eds.): DESRIST 2013, LNCS 7939, pp. 59–72, 2013.

The constructive research approach (CRA) has been a dominant design-oriented framework in Finnish and to some extent Scandinavian management literature (Jönsson and Lukka, 2007), while also receiving some attention within the information systems community (Gregor, 2006; Gregor and Jones, 2007). CRA was introduced, according to the authors, in 1986 (Kasanen et al., 1993). The international diffusion of CRA started with the English language follow-up in the Journal of Management Accounting Research (Kasanen et al., 1993). In brief, CRA aims to increase the relevance of management science research through putting theory to use by constructing or designing "constructions" (Kasanen et al., 1993; Lukka, 2006).

The goal shared by DS and CRA is using applicable theories, technical norms (e.g. Niiniluoto, 1993), or theories-in-use (Gregor, 2006), with high industrial relevance to design practical solutions. Thus, it seems that there are potentially two similar methodologies or research approaches applicable in similar problem situations. Despite increased awareness and adoption, there are some challenges that stem from the separate strands that apply the design-oriented research tradition. The first challenge is that different approaches and assumptions may inhibit understanding and comparison of results between domains. The second challenge is faced by the prospective design-oriented researcher who may be left baffled by the gamut of, often not easily comparable, approaches. The goal of this paper is to improve transparency and facilitate further adoption of design-oriented research approaches by discussing the ISR led DS approach, design science research (DSR), side-by-side with CRA from management science. Our guiding questions are: "what are the similarities and differences between DSR and CRA?" and "how can this comparison serve to improve design-oriented research?"

To answer the research questions, we analyze the literature on CRA as well as DSR critically and discuss whether the approaches have lessons to teach each other. In particular, our analysis underlines a problem previously surfaced by (Iivari 2007) who pointed out that design artifacts are often loosely coupled with the underlying theory they are supposedly built on. We will argue further, based on our analysis, that this loose coupling creates a rarely recognized challenge for DSR, as design-oriented research measures success based on utility and acceptance of artifacts, and the loose coupling may limit the theoretical contribution of DSR significantly. CRA may have something to teach DSR, at least from the critical realist perspective outlined by Carlsson (2007) who has called for a wider approach than the artifact-centered focus.

The rest of this paper is organized as follows: The second section will present an overview of the two research frameworks and a comparison between them. The third section compares CRA and DSR. The fourth section discusses the implications of our findings for design-oriented research. The fifth section concludes the paper and, and points out direction for further work.

2   Overview of the Design-Oriented Research Frameworks

2.1   Summary of the Constructive Research Approach

We base the bulk of our analysis of the constructive research approach (CRA), unless otherwise noted, on the most recent publications that we are aware of: Lukka (2006. CRA is "a methodology that creates innovative constructions to solve real world problems and thus contributes to the field of study where it is applied" (Lukka 2006 p. 112). It should be carefully noted that "construction" means here deliberate design of a thing, as opposed to emergent socially constructed phenomena and artifacts. The Finnish word "konstruktio" literally "a construction" includes all human-made artifacts, such as models, charts, plans and strategies, organizational structures, commercial products and information systems (Ibid.). To be clear, we will henceforth refer to "constructions" with the word artifact (as used in DSR) to avoid confusion. The basic conditions research classified as CRA are following: (Lukka 2006): (1) It focuses on real-life problems, which need solving; (2) It produces an innovative artifact, intended to solve the original real-life problem; (3) It includes an attempt to implement the artifact in order to test its applicability; (4) It includes intimate teamwork between the researcher and practitioners; (5) It is carefully linked to existing theoretical knowledge; (6) It pays special attention to creating a theoretical contribution.

CRA also has a clear-cut process which is elaborated by Lukka (2006). Figure 1 condenses the main activities in the process. The CRA process starts by finding or choosing a problem, which is scientifically relevant and interests practitioners. The second phase is to organize a project around the problem and to ensure the commitment of the stakeholders. The third phase then consists of analysis of the problem and review of relevant literature to gain holistic and thorough understanding of the problem space and the target organization. The fourth phase, the construction of the artifact, is described as an innovative and rather unstructured activity where little generic advice can be given. Kekäle (2001, p. 557) proposes that the researcher proposes a solution to the researched problem based on pre-understanding built in the previous phases of the process, practical experience or theory. In more practical terms Kasanen et al. (1993, p. 258) propose three guidelines for construction: 1) proceeding step-by-step following the chosen methodological and theoretical framework, 2) auditability and documentation of each consecutive step in the process of construction, and 3) the goal and criteria to be filled through the construction. After the synthesis, or construction, the process continues to implementation of the artifact in the fifth phase. Lukka (2006, p. 119) posits that the main and in fact only necessary test to validate the artifact is a "holistic market test", i.e. adoption and sustained use of the artifact in a business organization (Jönsson and Lukka, 2007, p. 385). Kasanen et al. (1993) discuss the spectrum of validation through a (holistic) market test from weak, through semi-strong, to strong market test (Kasanen et al 1993, p. 253):

- Weak market test: Has any manager responsible for the financial results of his/her business unit been willing to apply the [artifact] in question for his/her actual decision making?
- Semi-strong market test: Has the [artifact] become widely adopted by companies?
- Strong market test: Have the business units applying the [artifact] systematically produced better financial results than those which are not using it?

The CRA literature discusses generalizability in reference to the sixth phase of the process, where the researchers should map the scope of applicability of the artifact. Lukka and Kasanen (1995, p.85) have explicitly addressed "constructive generalizability" based on a pragmatist epistemology, according to which analysis of the problem and linking the solution to literature forms the basis for claiming that "a solution that has worked in a particular case can work in similar situations in other companies as well".

Fig. 1. The process outline and main activities in the constructive approach, adapted and rephrased from (Lukka, 2006)

Fig. 2. Process of DSR (adapted from Vaishnavi and Kuechler, 2004)

The seventh and last phase of the process is the identification of a theoretical contribution. Jönsson and Lukka (2007, p. 384) explain that generally the researcher compares the ex ante proposition that motivates the artifact with an ex post analysis of the intervention or instantiation, and identifies the causalities that lead to the observable outcome of the instantiation. This comparison gives rise to the theoretical contribution.. The sources of this contribution stem from the "positive relationships behind the [artifact]." (Lukka 2006, p. 119) This is to say that observation of these positive relationships or inferences enables the researcher to develop a new theory, or to test or refine an existing theory behind or embodied in the artifact.

2.2   Summary of the Design Science Approach

Design science research (DSR) seeks to create innovations that define the ideas, practices, technical capabilities, and products through which the analysis, design, implementation, management, and use of information systems can be effectively and efficiently accomplished (Hevner et al., 2004). As such, in information systems a DSR contribution requires identifying a relevant organizational information technology (IT) problem, developing an IT artifact that addresses this problem, rigorously evaluating the artifact, articulating the contribution to the IT knowledge-base and to practice, and explaining the implications for IT management and practice (March and Storey, 2008).

To condense the position presented in the core DS literature, Hevner et al. (2004) address the difference between routine design and DS by defining design as application of knowledge to solve a previously examined problem, while DS contributes to existing knowledge by seeking solutions to non-trivial problems in novel and innovative ways. Design science as an activity can be characterized as formulating design theories (Walls et al., 1992; Gregor and Jones, 2007), i.e. valid prescriptions on how to develop classes of artifacts, including constructs, models, methods, or instantiations (March and Smith, 1995), to fill certain problem spaces (Markus et al., 2002).

In terms of practical guidance, Hevner et al. (2004) describe a basic framework by explaining that IS research in general and DS research in particular, should be linked to both the surrounding (business) environment and the knowledge base built by previous research. They suggest that DSR builds and evaluates artifacts, and theories (Vaishnavi and Kuechler, 2004), using applicable knowledge from the knowledge base and business needs from the environment as input for design. Hevner et al. (2004) present guidelines similar to Lukka (above), arguing that DSR should: (1) produce a viable artifact (construct, model, method or instantiation); (2) develop (technological) solutions for important and relevant business problems; (3) demonstrate utility, quality and efficacy of the design rigorously; (4) provide a contribution (a) in the form of an artifact and/or instantiation and (b) to the foundations (knowledge base) of the design; (5) apply a rigorous methodology to construction and evaluation of the artifact; (6) search for means to attain the ends under the constrains of the environment; and (7) present the results to both technology and management-oriented audiences.

Vaishnavi and Kuechler (2004) were the first to introduce a concrete process description (Figure 2) to operationalize the DSR framework. Later, Peffers et al.

(2008) have modeled a DSR process and methodological framework, which fits into Vaishnavi and Kuechler's (2004) description. The first phase of the DSR process comprises finding a relevant problem and defining it. The second phase then concentrates on suggesting solutions to the problem defined in the proposal, where the knowledge base is accessed to find feasible solutions. The third phase is effectively the design phase. Here the researchers use the suggested solutions to develop or construct the artifact. After design and/or demonstration, the artifact moves into evaluation. The purpose of evaluation is to test how well the artifact contributes to the solution of the problem, through any reasonable empirical methodology as well as logical proof that the artifact solves the problem. For Hevner et al. (2004) such testing can follow established practices in IS research, including: observational (study of instantiations), analytical (structural and performance analysis), experimental (controlled or simulation experiments), testing (functional or structural) and descriptive (plausibility of the systems in use cases).

Vaishani and Kuechler (2004) and Peffers et al. (2008) argue that the process is not linear since evaluation may produce new insights for design and may lead to changes which call for new evaluations. Moreover, the design and evaluation may reveal an altogether different problem, which results in a completely new design cycle. For example, Markus et al. (2002) whose paper was outlined as a prime example in DSR by Hevner at al. (2004) developed essentially an agile process which resulted in iterative development and instant evaluation of the revisions. After the artifact is stable and satisfying, the process moves to the conclusion phase where the results are communicated.

3   Comparison between CRA and DSR

Starting from the definitions, we can note that the difference is that DSR literature seems to put more weight in applying previous knowledge through a specific kernel theory in the design, where CRA proposes a more soft or creative approach. Nevertheless, it would seem that CRA does not reject the use of a kernel theory. An example is presented by Kasanen et al. (1993, p. 247) where one of the authors developed a model for capital budgeting. The artifact was based on a rather clear kernel theory; it was tested with simulations and then implemented as an instantiation to verify the utility.

To underline the difference, we can make a simplification of the general definition of DSR (e.g. Hevner et al., 2004; Vaishnavi and Kuechler, 2004) and dress the difference in methodological terms: the basic logic of discovery in DSR is of a more deductive nature. Stereotypically one takes a previously unsolved problem and tries to find a kernel theory which can help solve the problem. In effect, the researcher takes a general causal inference (theory) and deducts an answer to a particular problem from the general abstract answer. The kernel (design) theory, thus, offers general principles that can be applied to the specific problem and, in doing so, ends up contributing to such theory either by providing further exemplary proofs of concept, or by extending the problem domain and thus the generalizability of the design principles.

In CRA the solution is based on deep knowledge of the problem and of existing theory and is found through a heuristic process (Lukka 2006). Even though CRA literature does not use the term "abductive" explicitly, comparing the description of the problem solving phase in the CRA process and the description of abductive reasoning we can draw a parallel between the two. Lukka (2006) proposes that the researcher should reflect upon the solution and seek general inferences revealed by the artifact's implementation, which seems to fit the description of inductive logic, in which the scientist observes a particular aspect of the world and inducts general inferences or explanations from the observations. In sum, the theory development process in CRA and DSR is contingent on when and where the knowledge contribution is sought. The early aim of extending or contributing to a kernel theory through the design of a new artifact in a new problem domain is different than the aim of finding generalizable principles through the reflection on an already designed artifact. Indeed, both paths seem to be possible in CRA as well as DSR, but the critical task for the researcher is a transparent and explicit choice in this respect.

Yet another analogy between CRA and DSR is that the definition and use of the word "construction" is quite similar to the "artifact" in the design science literature. When we compare March and Smith (1995) with Lukka (2006), the first paper articulated that products of DSR, the artifacts, include models, methods and constructs besides actual instantiations. The second paper by Lukka includes things such as models, charts, plans and strategies, organizational structures, commercial products and information systems.

Going from the abstract to the practical, the process in CRA and DSR for the most important parts is quite similar. If we compare the CRA process presented in Figure 1 to that of DSR presented in Figure 2, we can draw multiple parallels. Both processes go from developing problem awareness and definition to proposing solutions, developing artifacts and evaluating them. The process description of CRA puts more weight on the collaboration aspects, but the basic tasks are quite similar. The difference is that DSR places evaluation in a separate phase whereas in CRA the market test is included in the implementation phase. This is partly due to the design science claim that an artifact needs to be tested in the lab thoroughly before being "released" into practice (Hevner, 2007), but also to the more broad guidelines for DSR evaluation (Hevner et al., 2004). Another difference is that the conditions a research project has to fulfill in order to be considered CRA are stricter. When we compare the basic guidelines between Lukka (2006) and Hevner et al. (2004), there are restrictions in the basic guidelines for CRA with respect to DSR. More specifically, CRA guidelines 3 and 4, which require an instantiation to validate the artifact and require that the artifact is developed in close collaboration with the target organization. DSR literature does not prescribe a definitive process or mode of collaboration. DSR literature is also less unanimous about the instantiation, even though Hevner et al. (2004) prescribe that DSR should result in a viable artifact.

Another comparison can be made in terms of application context. DSR has been mostly prominent in the IS field, but has a bridge head in management and engineering (e.g. Peffers et al. 2008; van Aken, 2004). The most prominent examples of DSR seem to be IS-related projects such as systems development, e.g. Walls et al. (1992), Markus et al. (2002). There are also examples that can be positioned toward management science e.g. ontology for business models (Osterwalder, 2004) and a knowledge representation for knowledge dissemination and reuse (Wu, 2009). The examples given in CRA literature include a capital budgeting model (Kasanen et al.

1993), an accounting system (Hilmola, 2007) and a corporate real estate management framework (Lindholm, 2008). If we look at the projects from both disciplines, many projects (1) state a clear problem which is linked to real-world management, (2) solve the problem by developing a novel artifact and (3) may or may not use technology, such as information systems, as a part of the solution.

Overall, it seems that despite different backgrounds, there is more in common between the methodologies than what sets them apart. The main differences in the frameworks seem to be the slight difference in the logic and thus organization of the activities, and the evaluation, which is broader in DSR than CRA. To conclude the comparison, it seems to us that CRA projects could be regarded as DSR, with some reservations, as a project which fills the guidelines presented for CRA cannot be rejected as DSR. However, the other way round, we cannot conclude that at least all DSR satisfies the conditions for CRA in the form presented above. In this sense, if one will, CRA can be positioned as a subset of DSR but not the other way around. In writing this, we obviously have no pejorative intentions, but only the intent to facilitate scientific discussions and transparency of design oriented research. However, the generalization of CRA as a subset of DSR leaves certain differences between the background assumptions unaccounted for, which is the subject of the next section.

4 Discussion

Table 1 summarizes the main characteristics that surfaced from the previous comparison between CRA and DSR. Several findings show a common thread between the two approaches as a way to facilitate comparisons between published research, to provide entry points for sharing lessons learned and to make explicit the underpinnings where there might be possibilities for convergence or for pointing out potential differences. The characteristic in the table follow the material presented in the previous sections in terms of common concepts, guidelines, research process, and emphasizes the role of theory, underlying philosophy and evaluation / validation. The table also sets the stage for the final discussion and conclusions pointing at further research and opportunities for improvement of transparency and evaluation criteria.

Table 1. A side-by-side comparison of CRA and DSR

(Common) characteristic	CRA	DSR
Research mission or goal	Problem solving in real business environment (Kasanen et al., 1993; Lukka, 2006).	Problem solving in real business environment (Hevner et al, 2004).
Artifact	Konstruktio (Lukka, 2006): "all human made artifacts, such as models, charts, plans, action plans and strategies,	Artifact (March and Smith, 1995): constructs, models, methods or instantiations. See above for concrete examples

(Common) characteristic	CRA	DSR
	organizational structures, commercial products, and information systems". See above for concrete examples.	
Research guidelines	(Lukka 2006): - Focus on real problems - Produces innovative artifact that solves the problem - Includes implementation "attempt" to test practical applicability - Includes collaboration between researchers and practitioners - Linked to existing theoretical knowledge - Creates theoretical contribution.	(Hevner et al, 2004): - Produces viable technology-based artifact to solve a problem - Rigorously demonstrating utility, quality and efficacy of design - Contribution in the form of the artifact and to the knowledge base - Rigorous construction and evaluation methodology - Means-ends problem space searching - Present results to technology and management oriented audience.
Research process	Please refer to figures 1 and 2 in section 2.1	
Kernel theory	"Soft" support for a kernel theory. Examples: Kasanen (1993) model for capital budgeting (not explicit which kernel theory was employed), Lindholm (2008 uses a previously developed (grounded) theory to build a system, and Kekale (2001) supports kernel theory in general.	Support for a kernel theory when emphasis is placed on developing a design theory (Markus, 2002; Walls, 1992, 2004; Gregor and Jones 2007).
Logic of discovery	Abductive, according to Lukka (2003; 2006).	Deductive by looking at Cross, (1993); Hevner et al. (2004) and Vaishnavi and Kuechler (2004).
Domain of application	Management and some IS (GSS), examples included in section 3.1.	IS mostly but some management, examples included in section 3.1.

(Common) characteristic	CRA	DSR
Underlying philosophy	Pragmatism explicitly, e.g. Lindholm (2008).	Not explicit, could be pragmatism, interpretivism or positivism (Niehaves, 2007).
Evaluation	Utility-based market test, used in evaluation of the artifact and research process (Lindholm, 2008; Hilmola, 2007).	Utility-based (Hevner et al, 2003).

The side-by-side comparison indicates that DSR and CRA are compatible with each other in their main features. If, or when, it comes to choosing between the approaches, we hesitate to claim that one can be better than the other per se. Ultimately the choice is based on each researchers' epistemological assumptions, that is, what the researcher believes to be the best approach to get knowledge of the world, not to mention the traditions in each researchers' respective field and institution.. In this respect, CRA can be more helpful than DSR to researchers' who subscribe to the pragmatist assumptions, because it is more complete in its prescriptions. If we take CRA literature at face value, it has its own quite explicit philosophical basis and an established research process that is clear and relatively easy to follow. In contrast, DSR is more open to epistemological pluralism as argued by Niehaves (2007), so it can invite a wider audience. What have we learned from our analysis? Firstly, we found that the DSR literature is not unanimous on issues concerning the background epistemology. This feature is also an advantage, as it allows enveloping findings from other design-oriented research.

Second, we found CRS and DSR to be compatible. This is a contribution to ISR, mostly in a practical sense, as it enables recognition and framing of previous contributions in DSR terms, which makes them eligible for wider understanding and dissemination. It is, after all, well known that while DSR is still in its teens as a research tradition, there has been research that has had similar aims and form under different labels for a long time already (Winter, 2008). Potentially this openness improves transparency and allows wider dissemination of design oriented research from different backgrounds.

Besides finding the approaches compatible, we can see the CRA as a 'straw man' in a sense: by analyzing it rather critically at times we have learned something new about design oriented research in general. To recapitulate: CRA exhibits pragmatist research in quite a pure form in the sense that it directly seeks to solve a problem through design and draws conclusions about success and validity based on how well the design artifact was perceived to be useful in solving the problem. The same logic applies to DSR as well in many settings. However, our analysis underlines a seldom recognized feature in the (pragmatist) logic of measuring truthfulness or validity through utility. First, user acceptance as a proxy for utility and truth respectively is in fact quite a weak and relatively easily biased. Second, we recognize that the artifact itself is often conceptually quite weakly associated from the theoretical conjectures it is built on. These two findings lead us to the following methodological challenge: if the specific reasons for adoption and acceptance are not known, we cannot know whether the adoption is a consequence (in pragmatist terms) of our design and the underlying theoretical proposition that goes with it. Not to put too fine a point on it, we may have succeeded in getting a satisfied client, but at the same time we may have failed to gain new knowledge.

The implication of this latter finding for research is straightforward. Considering utility-based validation, a successful validation should then take the logical form of a classical syllogism, where the main line of argument is that, to solve problem X, we should take the course of action A, or a series of actions A1 to An, where A is the major premise, based on a theoretical proposition of inference between A and X. The minor premise to fill the syllogism form would be then that the instantiated action(-s) Ai instantiate or follow the theoretical proposition closely enough to say that the course of action followed the prescription. With these conditions, if the users are satisfied and problem X was solved, we can propose logically that the prescription was valid. This allows us not to abandon utility-based validation, but strengthens the argument, and following this form allows more convincing claims for theoretical contributions as well.

Additionally, the 'holistic market test' in CRA draws our attention to the issues discussed by Carlsson (2007), who proposes that in order to serve practical interests better, DSR would benefit from considering the implementation and use of the products of DSR. While we have presented potential shortcomings of the market test, the idea that the product of DSR should be accepted and useful is important. We would propose that rigor in validation or in seeking generalizability should not be at the expense of producing applicable design knowledge and solutions to practical problems. One solution for improving the chance of acceptance of the design might be combining collaborative design with explicit theorizing. While this need has been already recognized explicitly by Sein et al. (2010) who have proposed combining DSR and action research, the CRA tradition is itself already quite closely associated with AR (Jönsson and Lukka, 2007).

To close the discussion, we want to take our own medicine and be explicit about our own assumptions; we have conducted our analysis with a realist background and from a DSR perspective. This means that while trying to remain impartial, we have stronger background in DSR than CRA, which may have skewed our judgment inadvertently. Our philosophical background is in Popperian realism and interpretivism as understood in IS and positivism as understood in IS and management fields. These assumptions can be also outlined as the main limitations of our study. However, we propose that the utility-based validation issue stands regardless of the assumptions: there is no escape from not knowing what makes an artifact work or how it works.

5   Conclusions

Our research objective in this paper has been to examine the differences and similarities between the constructive research approach and the design science research framework. We would like to summarize our conclusions by proposing that both of the traditions have something to teach each other. On the surface, the greatest difference between design science and CRA is that DSR does not necessarily require an instantiation, but the default in CRA is that the validation is done through an instantiation. .CRA stresses practical relevance, applicability and development of an instantiation, but possibly at the expense of theory development and generalizable results. DSR on the other hand is a more open framework for design-oriented research and recognizes other levels of contribution besides an instantiation, as well as other forms of validation besides a market test. By conducting this analysis, we expect to have increased understanding of design oriented research approaches and to have added transparency and comparability between two existing research frameworks in this vein.

CRA and DSR have similar intentionality, problem domains and types of resulting artifacts. Within information systems, DSR is picking up pace and recognition, perhaps primarily by offering a suitable framework for research which is both rigorous and relevant. However, because it is still in the process of being adopted, several open issues include a clear underlying epistemology and evaluation / validation criteria. These are issues that are critical both from the point of view of the researcher(s) wishing to apply DSR and from the point of the view of the community that must evaluate or "accept" a DSR contribution (e.g. for publication). Our comparison contributes a set of categories from which to extract lessons learned from the CRA approach in order to contribute further arguments in favor of specific epistemological choices and validation criteria.

On the other hand, since some CRA projects (both past and future) can be framed as a contribution to the information systems field, it is also helpful to use those same categories (summarized in Table 1) as a potential source for presenting a CRA project as a DSR project. This would not only be an exercise in methodological pluralism or merging, but more importantly an extension of the domain, scope and audience (including publication outlets) of two fields that already have much in common. In fact, a potential extension of the present work would be to do precisely that by reframing published research in the CRA vein as DSR contributions. This should add more empirical content to our comparison framework and thus more exemplary material to construct a knowledge base of lessons learned that is common to both CRA and DSR.

References

1. van Aken, J.E.: Management Research Based on the Paradigm of the Design Sciences: The Quest for Field-tested and Grounded Technological Rules. Journal of Management Studies 41(2), 219–246 (2004)
2. Carlsson, S.A.: For Whom, What Type of Knowledge and How. Scandinavian Journal of Information Systems 19(2), 75–86 (2007)
3. Chang, W.L.: A value-based pricing system for strategic co-branding goods. Kybernetes 37(7), 978–996 (2008)
4. Gregor, S.: The Nature of Theory in Information Systems. MIS Quarterly 30(3), 611–642 (2006)

5. Gregor, S., Jones: The Anatomy of Design Theory. Journal of the Association for Information Systems 8(5), Article 2, 312–335 (2007)

6. Hevner, A.R., Ram, S., March, S.T., Park, J.: Design Science in Information Systems Research. MIS Quarterly 28(1), 75–105 (2004)

7. Hevner, A.R.: A Three Cycle View of Design Science Research. Scandinavian Journal of Information Systems 19(2), 39–64 (2007)

8. Hilmola, O.-P.: Building understanding from throughput accounting with productivity and price recovery: case analysis of electronics contract manufacturer. Int. J. Revenue Management 1(4), 346–367 (2007)

9. Holmström, J., Ketokivi, M., Hameri, A.-P.: Bridging Practice and Theory: A Design Science Approach. Decision Sciences 40(1), 65–87 (2009)

10. Iivari, J.: A Paradigmatic analysis of Information systems as a Design Science. Scandinavian Journal of Information Systems 19(2), 39–64 (2007)

11. Jönsson, S., Lukka, K.: There and Back Again: Doing Interventionist Research in Management Accounting. In: Chapman, C.S., Hopwood, A.G., Shields, H.G. (eds.) Handbook of Management Accounting Research, pp. 373–397. Elsevier (2007)

12. Kasanen, E.O., Lukka, K., Siitonen, A.: The Constructive Approach in Management Accounting Research. Journal of Management Accounting Research 5, 243–264 (1993)

13. Kekäle, T.: Construction and triangulation: weaponry for attempts to create and test theory. Management Decision 39(7), 556–563 (2001)

14. Lindholm, A.L.: A constructive study on creating core business relevant CREM strategy and performance measure. Facilities 20(7/8), 343–358 (2008)

15. Lukka, K.: Konstruktiivinen tutkimusote: luonne, prosessi ja arviointi. In: Rolin, K., Kakkuri-Knuutila, M.-L., Henttonen, E. (eds.) Soveltava Yhteiskuntatiede ja Filosofia, Gaudeamus, Helsinki, FI, pp. 111–133 (2006)

16. Lukka, K., Kasanen, E.: The problem of generalizability: anecdotes and evidence in accounting research. Accounting, Auditing & Accountability Journal 8(5), 71–90 (1995)

17. March, S.T., Smith, G.: Design and Natural Science Research on Information Technology. Decision Support Systems 15(4), 251–266 (1995)

18. March, S.T., Storey, V.C.: Design Science in the Information Systems Discipline: An Introduction to the Special Issue on Design Science Research. MIS Quarterly 32(4), 725–730 (2008)

19. Markus, M.L., Majchrzak, A., Gasser, L.: A Design Theory for Systems That Support Emergent Knowledge Processes. MIS Quarterly 26(3), 179–212 (2002)

20. Muntermann, J.: Towards ubiquitous information supply for individual investors: A decision support system design. Decision Support Systems 47(2), 82–92 (2009)

21. Niiniluoto, I.: The aim and structure of applied research. Erkenntnis 38(1), 1–21 (1993)

22. Niehaves, B.: On Epistemological Pluralism in Design Science. Scandinavian Journal of Information Systems 19(2), 99–110 (2007)

23. Osterwalder, A.: The Business Model Ontology: A Proposition in a design Science Approach, Ph.D. Thesis, Universite de Lausanne (2004)

24. Peffers, K., Tuunanen, T., Rothenbergerm, M.A., Chatterjee, S.: A Design Science Research Methodology for Information Systems Research. Journal of Management Information Systems 24(3), 45–77 (2008)

25. Sein, M.K., Henfridsson, O., Purao, S., Rossi, M., Lindgren, R.: Action Design Research. MIS Quarterly 35(2) (2010)

26. Vaishnavi, V., Kuechler, W.: Design Research in Information Systems. IS WorldNet (2004),
    `http://ais.affiniscape.com/displaycommon.cfm?an=1&subarticle`
    `nbr=279`
27. Walls, J.G., Widmeyer, G.R., El Sawy, O.A.: Building an Information Systems Design Theory for Vigilant EIS. Information Systems Research 3(1), 36–59 (1992)
28. Winter, R.: Design science research in Europe. European Journal of Information Systems 17, 470–475 (2008)
29. Wu, J.-H.: A design methodology for form-based knowledge reuse and representation. Information & Management 46(7), 365–375 (2009)

Pattern-Based Design Research – An Iterative Research Method Balancing Rigor and Relevance

Sabine Buckl[1], Florian Matthes[2], Alexander W. Schneider[2], and Christian M. Schweda[1]

[1] iteratec GmbH
Inselkammerstr. 4, 82008 München-Unterhaching, Germany
{sabine.buckl,christian.schweda}@iteratec.de
http://www.iteratec.de
[2] Technische Universität München (TUM)
Chair for Informatics 19 (sebis)
Boltzmannstr. 3, 85748 Garching bei München, Germany
{alexander.w.schneider,matthes}@in.tum.de
http://wwwmatthes.in.tum.de

Abstract. Researchers in the area of Information Systems (IS) applying the design science paradigm are confronted with the challenge to make theoretical contributions which also help to solve current and anticipated problems in practice. This is often referred to as the rigor and relevance challenge of design science research. To ensure relevance of the research outcome, research projects in IS are often conducted in close cooperation with one or more industry partners. This typically leads to a need for early results and a binding to the specific organizational context of the participating industry partner(s).

In this paper, we propose pattern-based design research (PDR), an iterative design research method consisting of four phases, to overcome this problem. We argue that patterns as early stage design artifacts enable researchers to build innovative artifacts that address current and anticipated problems of practitioners in an organizational context. Building on well-established concepts as patterns, design theories, and the design theory nexus, the proposed research method enables a researcher to theorize and learn from the intervention at the industry partner(s) while performing rigorous and relevant design science research. We illustrate the applicability of PDR by presenting a research project from the area of enterprise architecture management.

1   Rigor and Relevance in Practice-Driven Research

In the field of Information Systems (IS) research a pluralism of paradigms, methods, and research approaches is prevalent. While behavioral science traditionally plays a major role in IS research, the approach of design science is meanwhile also accepted by the scientific community. Design science approaches (cf. [1-3]) target the creation of a novel *artifact*, i.e., a solution to a relevant problem. Researchers designing an artifact need to account for two important criteria: *rigor* and *relevance* (cf. [3-5]). On the one hand, rigor can be achieved by applying sound methodologies [6]. On the

J. vom Brocke et al. (Eds.): DESRIST 2013, LNCS 7939, pp. 73–87, 2013.

other hand, relevance can be achieved by addressing the needs of using practitioners. Nevertheless, there is an on-going debate on the topic of rigor and relevance. Although many scientists agree that both rigor and relevance have to be achieved simultaneously [7, 3], another school of thought exists with the perception that rigor and relevance each compromise the other [8]. It, in this sense, remains challenging to account for both rigor and relevance [9].

Enterprise Architecture (EA) management is a field, susceptible to practice-driven resign research. While this field has been researched for more than 10 years [10], yet the diversity of the management challenges and the differing organizational contexts have hampered the development of single and embracing management approach. Moreover, the management function in general and modeling of the EA in particular has to be tailored to the concerns and context of the using organization [11]. With no well-established and sufficiently detailed management approach at hand and in the light of the diversity of the management concerns to be addressed, the development of an organization-specific EA management is far from a routine design activity. Especially, the design of the modeling languages is a challenge that is of interest for researchers and practitioners as well.

In a similar line as the aspect of relevance is gaining more and more importance for the field of IS research (cf. [5]), the number of research projects that are conducted in close cooperation with an industry partner or which even are industry-funded increases. Such cooperations on the one hand open the door for developing and extracting case studies (cf. [2, 12]) by employing an intrinsically motivated industry partner but on the other hand are typically subject to the partnering organization's pace. The demand for an early delivery of results and the methodological rigor required for academic contributions (cf. [13]) mirrors the tension between rigor and relevance. This leads to a situation in which researchers are challenged to ensure that their research does not degenerate into "routine design" that according to [3] must be distinguished from design science. In contrast, the close cooperation can be used to contribute to design by providing empirical evidence.

[14] coined the term *community determined output* to delineate that the expected level of abstraction in the research outcome is determined by the members of the participating community. This in particular applies to research performed in close cooperation with an industry partner. To address the different objectives of this community, consisting of practitioners – seeking for practical solutions – and academics – searching for theories – knowledge on different levels of abstraction has to be documented as research findings.

The situation in which scientists cooperate with industry can be described by further characteristics. In IS research often so called *wicked problems* (cf. [15, 16]) are tackled. Wicked problems occur, if the specific situations of different industry partners relate to asymmetric criteria determining the different solutions [17]. In order to increase the relevance of the developed design artifact in terms of importance and suitability (cf. [5]) often an iterative approach is applied. Thereby, each iteration – with a single or multiple industry partners – allows learning and accordingly the evolution of the designed artifact in order to provide a sustainable solution.

Findings originating from research projects that have been conducted in close co-operation with an industry partner should naturally account for the aspect of relevance. Therefore, we subsequently present the pattern-based design research (PDR) approach that addresses the aforementioned challenges accounting for the aspect of rigor in practice-driven research projects. It makes use of patterns, design theories, and a design theory nexus which are introduced in Section 2. By adding a dedicated phase for evaluation and learning to the existing methods an iterative approach – PDR – is created in Section 3. To illustrate the idea of PDR, a concrete example from the domain of Enterprise Architecture (EA) management is presented in Section 4. We use patterns for EA information models to show how they can be used to derive design theories and allow for a controlled nexus evolution by incorporating adjusted as well as new solutions to enhance the general design theories.

2   Contributing Perspectives and Approaches

The role of patterns for IS research is subject to controversies (cf. [18]). In other domains, like software engineering, patterns are well accepted artifacts. Similarly, the role of theories as artifacts for IS research is heavily discussed (cf. [19]). Patterns in contrast to design theories represent best practices that are bound to a specific context in which the provided solution has proven to work. Similarly a design theory nexus interlinks alternative design theories and details the context in which a specific design theory can be applied. The three concepts *pattern*, *design theory*, and *design theory nexus* are introduced in the following to prepare the presentation of PDR.

2.1   Patterns

[20] and [21] introduced the idea of patterns in the area of construction and urban planning. According thereto, a pattern documents a solution for a recurring problem given a specific context. [22] applied the pattern idea to document solutions within the domain of software engineering. They elicited a more explicit pattern structure extended with additional sections, namely *consequences, known uses*, and *related patterns*. The concept of patterns has also been used to document software architectures [23]. Accordingly, documenting good practice solutions to recurring problems in a specific context as patterns is a commonly accepted way to facilitate knowledge dissemination in design-intensives domains. The knowledge abstracted in these patterns is knowledge on operational principles in the sense of [14], i.e., is intended to be applied "as-is". If a solution to a single problem is too complex to be documented by a single pattern or the resulting pattern would be too specific, a pattern language can be used instead. A pattern language decomposes the complex problem/solution description into several self-contained patterns [24]. Since each pattern solves a specific problem within the shared context of the language references between the independent patterns are required. Such references according to [25] can be used to, e.g., identify a smaller pattern that is *used by* a larger pattern, define *variants* of patterns, or a *sequence of elaboration*, i.e. a sequence of patterns from the simple to the complex.

2.2   Design Theory

[26] were the first to introduce the notion of prescriptive theories in the field of IS research. The publications of [27-29], or [30] show, that prescriptive theories – also called *design theories* – generated special attention in the IS community. Such theories provide knowledge support to design activities. Hence, they are considered as "theorized practical knowledge" [31]. Accordingly, the development of design theories requires a close cooperation of scientists and practitioners. Figure 1 presents a conceptual framework for the activities of theorizing in design research according [29] and [32]. The two activities *observation* and *experimentation* call for research that is conducted in close cooperation with industry.

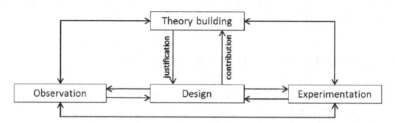

Fig. 1. Elements of theorizing in design research (Source: [32])

Different perspectives on the components of design theories have been taken by [26-27], and [28]. [30] presents a synthesized perspective, further influenced by the idea of pattern-based theory building. We adopt this perspective encompassing the components shown in Figure 2.

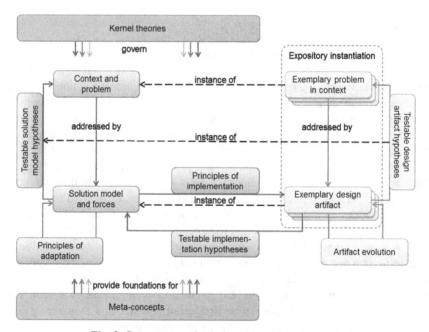

Fig. 2. Components of a design theory (Source: [30])

2.3   Design Theory Nexus

[17] presents the idea of a design theory nexus to address the challenge of wicked problems, i.e., of problems that are characterized by asymmetric criteria. In consequence, possible solutions can only be evaluated in terms of 'good' or 'bad'. A nexus connects these alternative solutions, i.e., design theories. Using the construct of a design theory nexus best practice solutions that evolve from research cooperation projects with industry can be combined to a knowledge base that helps "decision makers in choosing which of the theories are most suitable for their particular goals in their particular setting" [17]. Figure 3 gives an overview about the concept of a design theory nexus that connects different theories and defines the constraining goals and environmental contexts in which the different theories have proven to work good.

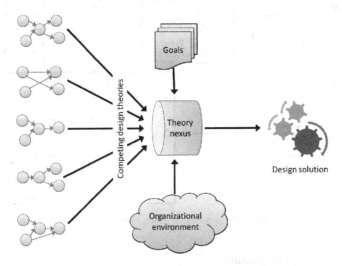

Fig. 3. Components of a design theory nexus [17]

To construct a design theory nexus, [17] detail a five step approach: (1) *identify approaches*, e.g. via a literature analysis, (2) *analyze approaches* to identify explicit or implicit conditions, i.e. context and problem descriptions, that must hold, (3) *formulate assertions* conditions are assessed for practical relevance and reformulated, (4) *develop decision making process* that builds on the assertions, and (5) *develop tool* that supports the evaluation regarding the fit for each design theory in a given situation.

3   Pattern-Based Design Research

Patterns can be understood as early stage design science artifacts observed in practice. Based on this understanding, we propose a pattern-based design research (PDR) method that outlines an approach to balance rigor and relevance in IS research. Following the *activity framework for design science research* as proposed by [33] our research method consists of four main activities: *observe & conceptualize* representing the problem diagnosis, *pattern-based theory building & nexus instantiation*, which enables the abstraction of observed solutions to better theories in terms of [14], *solution design & application*, representing the creation of an IS artifact, and *evaluation & learning* closing a direct feedback loop from practice to academia. Figure 4 gives an overview about our pattern-based design research method and illustrates the interplay between theory and practice.

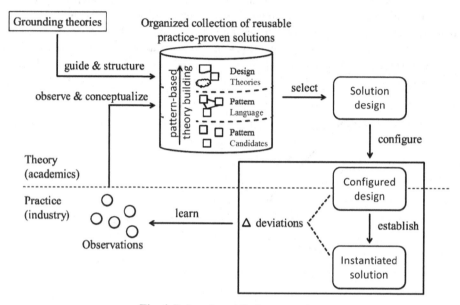

Fig. 4. Pattern-based design research

3.1   Observe and Conceptualize

Patterns are commonly accepted means to document good practice solutions to recurring problems in a specific context. Patterns are further accepted as way to facilitate knowledge abstraction and dissemination in design-intensive domains. Therein, patterns are operational knowledge in the sense of [14] gained from practice. Following this understanding, patterns are neither invented nor developed, but observed best practice solutions. *The rule of three*, established in [34], gives account to this fact: a documented pattern must provide reference to at least three known uses in practice to ensure the re-usability of the provided solution. The different patterns that have been published over the years, mostly follow a typical pattern format according to [23] consisting of a description of the addressed problem, the solution, and the intended application context for the solution. A pattern further identifies driving forces, denotes known usages as well as consequences, and makes relations to other patterns explicit.

In the *observe & conceptualize* activity of the PDR method, good practices from industry are observed and documented following a typical pattern structure. Thereby, the observer which can either be a researcher or practitioner describes at least the following concepts: *problem* to be addressed, *solution* that has proven to work good, *context* in which the solution can be applied, and *forces* that frame the solution space. Depending on the application domain, the conceptualization might be further detailed (see Section 4) by using grounding theories to elicit a pattern terminology for the application domain. The documentation of the pattern candidates is refined in cooperation with the industry partner during so-called pattern workshops. During the conceptualization and documentation of the pattern candidates, known patterns in the field are revisited for relevant terms. In particular, synonyms and homonyms used in the description are identified, and resolved, where possible. Unresolved terminological issues remain to be documented in the next phase via pattern relationships for linguistic compatibility.

3.2   Pattern-Based Theory Building and Nexus Instantiation

The *pattern-based theory building & nexus instantiation* activity of the PDR method describes how pattern candidates mature and evolve to competing design theories for a specific application domain that are interconnected in a design theory nexus. Patterns, which can be regarded as coherent and self-contained design entities describing a solution to a specific problem, can in line with [35] be understood as elementary design principles. In this sense, we interpret patterns as potential building blocks for a design theory. A design theory itself shows typical characteristics of a pattern, i.e. a design theory contains a context description in which the provided solution is applicable as well as the problem to which it can be applied (see Figure 2).

The construction of the design theory nexus from pattern candidates is a possible result from a research cooperation carried out between practice and academia. Thereby, a pattern candidate evolves over time to a pattern, a part of a pattern language, to a part of a design theory as illustrated in Figure 4 by the different levels of the organized collection. If a pattern candidate matures through three successful known uses in practice to a pattern, the researcher integrates the new pattern into the organized collection of patterns by defining relationships to the already existing patterns. Relationship types that can be used are the ones introduced in Section 2. Reflecting the inherent interdisciplinary of IS research, the researcher accounts for terminological compatibility by introducing two new types of relationships between patterns – *linguistically compatible* and *linguistically diverse* – to indicate that two patterns employ compatible or conflicting terminologies.

Building design theories from patterns might at a first glance be an easy to accomplish task, as some constituents of a design theory as introduced in Section 2.2 can be directly mapped to parts of the pattern description, e.g. *context and problem* as well as *solution model and forces*. Patterns however typically vary in respect to the level of granularity and abstraction on which they are described due to their observational nature. This in particular becomes obvious, when the patterns are to be composed into a design theory for a certain research field. The different relationship types of a pattern language support the researcher in addressing this problem and in doing so facilitate the construction of a design theory from a pattern language. Exemplifying this, we subsequently discuss selected relationship types and their roles in pattern-based theory development:

- **Used by** describes that and how a larger pattern employs another patter to solve a sub-problem of the larger pattern. Building on this relationship the researcher can aggregate solution building blocks into a comprehensive solution for a coarse grained problem.
- **Refined by** represents the inverse relationship of used by in which a refining pattern targets a similar problem and context as its "larger" pattern but provides a more detailed solution model or outlines a broader variety of forces to be balanced. Relationships of that can be used by the researcher to define *principles of adaptation* in the design theory as they sketch possible trajectories for refining the design artifact.
- **Variant** relates to a pattern with a similar or closely related problem and context as the initial pattern, providing a solution that only slightly differs from the original one. Relationships of that type may help the researcher to refine the context and problem description by both broadening the scope of the corresponding classes and by raising further dimensions of distinction.
- **Sequence of Elaboration** relates different patterns that describe more and more elaborate solutions for a similar problem and context. Patterns connected by that type of relationship may be understood as contribution to the *principles of adaptation* by providing possible ways to evolve the design artifact and to bring it to a more 'mature' level.

With the alternative or competing design theories developed from pattern-based theory building, the researcher has successfully processed step 1 and 3 of the construction process of a design theory nexus instantiation (see Section 2.3). The final steps 4 and 5 deal with the development of a decision making process and its implementation within a tool to support usability. The researcher is supported during these final steps by the common terminology established by the meta-conceptualization.

3.3   Solution Design and Application

The design theory nexus instantiation is applied in this activity of the PDR method by the researcher to construct a situated design artifact. Therefore, the *exemplary problem in context* is used as input to the decision making process whose output is the *exemplary design artifact*. Creating an expository instantiation, the researcher applies the principles of implementation in practice, i.e., in the environment of an organization willing to use the design theory nexus instantiation. Accounting for terminological aspects, the *solution design* must be configured and adapted to the terminology of the using organization. Finally the configured design is established as new solution in the organization under consideration.

3.4   Evaluation and Learning

While time passes, the instantiated solution may evolve and deviations from the originally configured design may arise in practice. These deviations represent the artifact evolution in terms of a design theory and can be ascribed to the ongoing change of environments, contexts, and goals of the using organization. Following the PDR approach these derivations observed by the practitioner can be used by the researcher to evolve the design theory nexus. Thereby two main types of deviations can be distinguished that result in different kinds of learning:

- Deviations in the instantiated solution that represent minor changes with respect to the configured design. These deviations can typically be traced back to the corresponding design theory, organizational context, or problem.
- Major changes in the instantiated solution that do not match a design theory, organizational context, or problem from the configured design. These deviations typically represent newly observed best practices.

To identify the above deviations a formal review process of the instantiated solution needs to be set up by the practitioner and researcher. If new best practices are observed they have to be documented as pattern candidates as described in the *observe & conceptualize* phase. Minor changes typically result in a rework of existing patterns in terms of changes with respect to context, problem, and solution interplay. Similarly, minor changes might also result in new relationships of the pattern language. In particular the relationships refined by, variant, and sequence elaboration are therefore used.

4   Pattern-Based Design Research Example _ BEAMS IBBs

The research described in this section is an *exemplary instantiation* of the pattern-based research design (PDR) method presented in the previous section. The example is based on previous research in the field of Enterprise Architecture (EA) management. EA management establishes a holistic perspective on all elements forming the architecture of an enterprise, e.g. business processes, applications, information, hardware, and their interrelations. For EA management, descriptions of the EA are created and used. A conceptual model, called "information model" or "meta-model", is usually used to define the structure of an EA description. Figure 5 shows an exemplary excerpt of such a model. Based on this perspective, the respective management function aims to increase transparency about the enterprise [36] and to control the enterprise evolution [37].

4.1   Observe and Conceptualize

In 2007 researchers from the Technische Universität München started to observe identical solutions to EA management problems during their various industry projects. With the idea of software design patterns [22] in mind, an extensive catalog of patterns for EA management has been published [38]. It includes patterns for EA management methods (M-pattern), patterns for EA management viewpoints (V-patterns), and patterns for information model fragments (I-patterns) [39].

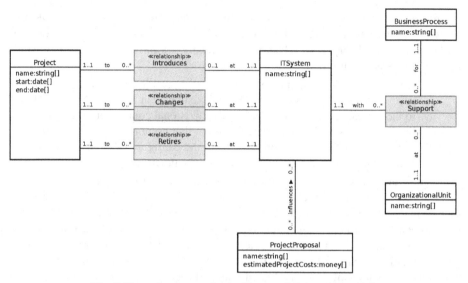

Fig. 5. Exemplary enterprise architecture information model

4.2   Pattern-Based Theory Building and Nexus Instantiation

Based on the context descriptions of the EA management patterns, the Building Blocks for Enterprise Architecture Management Solutions (BEAMS) [40, 41] demonstrated how patterns can be used to derive design theories for EA management. These theories were derived as reusable and configurable building blocks based on the initially observed patterns, for example as information model building blocks (IBBs). As outlined by [42] and visualized in Figure 3, a design theory nexus consists of goals, environment, theory nexus, and design solution. The five step process for a nexus construction suggested by [17] has been executed as follows.

1. The available approaches in the area under consideration, i.e. EA management, have been examined by pattern documentation.
2. Competing theories, i.e., patterns, have been investigated for explicit or implicit conditions, e.g. by determining their different goals.
3. Assertions based on prominent characteristics of competing approaches have been derived which resulted in the organizational context description of the nexus (environment). Centralized vs. decentralized IT organization is one of them.
4. Based on a fitting matrix including the identified EA management goals, the organizational context assumptions and the various solutions, a decision-making process for selecting one or more appropriate approaches for designing an EA management function has been developed. Therefore, these constraints, i.e., goals and organizational context, determine whether a competing EA management approach succeeds or fails.

5. A tool supporting the utilization of the presented nexus has been described by [43]. It begins with a characterization of the situation followed by a selection of building blocks and concludes with their assembly.

4.3   Solution Design and Application

With the characteristics of a specific organizational context and concrete problems as input, the introduced design theory nexus for EA management is able to design an EA meta-model suitable for a specific enterprise. Based on assembled building blocks, i.e the solution design, researchers and practitioners adapt the outcome to additional organization-specific requirements. This adaption includes, among others, the renaming of the general concepts provided by IBBs. Such renaming comprises, e.g. the adaptation of model element names to fit the terminology used by the implementing organization. The general concept of an *IT System*, as depicted in Figure 5, might be renamed to *Business Application* if this term is commonly accepted within the participating linguistic community. Another adaptation might extend or replace values of an enumeration to describe the organizational requirements in more detail. For example, if an IBB provides that a *Project Proposal* can either be in state *accepted* or *rejected*, another state *to be revised* could be added if necessary. As a result, this activity of PDR method provides an applicable EA meta-model which can be implemented by software tools and used for documenting an EA.

4.4   Evaluation and Learning

After the solution design and its organization specific adaption, the information model backing an EA management function is tailored to cover the concerns that are known at the time of its design. Changes in stakeholder composition, in the organizational context or the enterprise context, and the rising maturity of the enterprise-level management functions require EA management governance to take the adequate measures. Relevant measures given the perspective of pattern-based learning are measures that adapt the information model. Two kinds of such measures can be distinguished:

— Adaptations in which **new IBBs** are selected in response to changing concerns.
— Adaptations in which the information model is changed **without using IBBs**.

Adaptations of the latter kind in particular are sources for learning and for evolving the design theory nexus. To enable pattern-based learning, a minimum level of formality regarding the EA management governance (or the part of information model adaptations) is required: for each adaptation at least the responsible enterprise architect has to be documented. Additional information on the concern that caused the particular adaptation as well as on the stakeholders requiring the concern to be addressed is beneficial for the subsequent step of the learning-process, but not mandatory.

The different adaptations occurring in the information models of different industry partners are reviewed on a regular basis. A consulting company, the vendor of an EA management tool, or an organized body of practitioners can perform the necessary reviews. During these reviews, the group of reviewer groups and classifies singular adaptations, i.e., singular changes to an information model, into larger logic units of change. This grouping is performed either based on the documented concerns or based on the results of interviewing the responsible enterprise architects. The change units form "pattern candidates". For each of the pattern-candidates information following the structure proposed by [24] and the relationships to IBBs constituting the configuration previous to the adaptation are documented.

The mandatory elements (context, problem, solution, and related patterns) of describing an artifact of re-use do not only apply to newly identified pattern candidates, but are also applied to the validated artifacts, i.e., the patterns and the design theories. The mesh of relationships established by denoting related artifacts of re-use complement the perspective of the singular artifact to the whole of a pattern language in terms of [24], or a design theory nexus in terms of [17], respectively. The IBBs, i.e., the theories of the nexus, and the patterns and pattern candidates are thereby linked by two kinds of relationships:

— **Content-relationships** that express that an artifact of re-use (IBB, pattern or pattern candidate) depends on another artifact of re-use, being a prerequisite, a generalization or a foundation in another way. Content-relationships are the usual kind of relationships forming the core of a pattern language.
— **Learning-relationships** that express that an artifact of re-use has been learned from an artifact with lower formalization. A pattern for example is learned from at least one pattern candidate and provides the basis for learning at least one IBB. Learning-relationships are thereby used to document the evolution of the learning design theory nexus.

The conceptual model outlined in Figure 4 summarizes the understanding of pattern-based learning. On the more abstract level, the model describes the core structure of an organized library of re-usable artifacts, concretizing this structure to pattern candidates, patterns and design theories. On this concrete level, the different kinds of artifacts are understood as participating in a learning and formalization process.

5   Outlook

The pattern-based design research method is currently applied without dedicated tool support. The activities of pattern documentation and evolving the design theory nexus could well be supported by a tool. A related circumstance is already discussed by [26] and [17]. Tool support for the design phase of the PDR method, exemplified for the field of EA management, is further outlined in [43]. In this article, especially the need for tool support in comparing information models and in tracking model changes is highlighted.

Although we demonstrated a successful instantiation of a large part of the PDR method in the previous section including the first three phases at least the evaluation & learning phase still remains subject to evaluation in cooperation with practitioners. Such evaluation could benefit from available tool support. The evaluation of this phase nevertheless requires a longer-time span of research in order to be carried out. In the context of EA management a suitable time-span according to [44] would be five years. In addition, the PDR method needs still to be evaluated within IS disciplines other than EA management.

A researcher can assume different roles during the research activities carried out in cooperation with practitioners. Accounting for these roles, the PDR method can be further detailed. Especially during the application phase of PDR the participating researcher can inhabit different roles. Like in case studies, the researcher can act as an observer without intervening or like in action research the researcher can be an actor influencing the solution design instantiation. Furthermore, if design and evaluation are processed in parallel as suggested by [45] action design researchers are expected to share their knowledge of theory and technological advances. Accordingly, the appropriate degree of influence still needs to be found and may depend on the actual context.

References

1. Simon, H.A.: The Sciences of the Artificial, 2nd edn. MIT Press, Cambridge (1981)
2. Aken, J.: Management research based on the paradigm of the design sciences: The quest for field-tested and grounded technological rules. Journal of Management Studies 41(2), 219–246 (2004)
3. Hevner, A., March, S., Park, J., Ram, S.: Design science in information systems research. Management Information Systems Quarterly 28(1), 75–105 (2004)
4. King, J.L., Lyytinen, K.: The Future of the IS Field: Drawing Directions from Multiple Maps, pp. 345–354. John Wiley & Sons, West Sussex (2006)
5. Rosemann, M., Vessey, I.: Toward improving the relevance of information systems research to practice: the role of applicability checks. Management Information Systems Quarterly 32(1), 1–22 (2008)
6. Benbasat, I., Weber, R.: Rethinking 'diversity' in information systems research. Information Systems Research, 389–399 (1996)
7. Benbasad, I., Zmud, R.W.: Empirical research in information systems: The practice of relevance. Management Information Systems Quarterly 23(1), 3–16 (1999)
8. Davenport, T.H., Markus, L.M.: Rigor and relevance revisited: Response to benbasat and zmud. Management Information Systems Quarterly 23(1), 19–23 (1999)
9. Staw, B.M.: Repairs on the road to relevance and rigor: Some unexplored issues in publishing organizational research, pp. 85–97. Sage, London (1995)
10. Langenberg, K., Wegmann, A.: Enterprise architecture: What aspect is current research targeting? Technical report, Laboratory of Systemic Modeling, Ecole Polytechnique Fédérale de Lausanne, Lausanne, Switzerland (2004)
11. Aier, S., Kurpjuweit, S., Riege, C., Saat, J.: Stakeholderorientierte dokumentation und analyse der unternehmensarchitektur. GI Jahrestagung (2), 559–565 (2008)
12. Eisenhardt, K.M., Graebner, M.E.: Theory building from cases: Opportunities and challenges. Academy of Management Journal 50(1), 25–32 (2007)
13. Gallupe, R.B.: The tyranny of methodologies in information systems research. SIGMIS Database 38, 20–28 (2007)
14. Vaishnavi, V., Kuechler, W.: Design research in information systems (2004), http://desrist.org/design-research-ininformation-systems

15. Churchman, C.W.: Guest editorial: Wicked problems. Management Science 14(4), 141–142 (1967)
16. Rittel, H., Webber, M.: Dilemmas in a general theory of planning. Policy Sciences 4, 155–169 (1973)
17. Pries-Heje, J., Baskerville, R.: The design theory nexus. Management Information Systems Quarterly 32(4), 731–755 (2008)
18. Winter, R., vom Brocke, J., Fettke, P., Loos, P., Junginger, S., Moser, C., Keller, W., Matthes, F., Ernst, A.M.: Patterns in business and information systems engineering. Business & Information Systems Engineering, 468–474 (2009)
19. Straub, D.W.: Editor's comments: Does mis have native theories? MIS Quarterly (36), iii–xii (2012)
20. Alexander, C.: Notes on the Synthesis of Form. Harvard University Press, Cambridge (1972)
21. Alexander, C., Ishikawa, S., Silverstein, M., Jacobson, M., Fiksdahl-King, I., Angel, S.: A Pattern Language. Oxford University Press, New York (1977)
22. Gamma, E., Helm, R., Johnson, R., Vlissides., J.M.: Design Patterns: Elements of Reusable Object-Oriented Software. Addison-Wesley Professional (1994)
23. Buschmann, F., Meunier, R., Rohnert, H., Sommerlad, P., Stal, M.: Pattern-oriented software architecture: a system of patterns. John Wiley & Sons, Inc., New York (1996)
24. Meszaros, G., Doble, J.: A Pattern Language for Pattern Writing, pp. 529–574. Addison Wesley (1998)
25. Noble, J.: Classifying relationships between object-oriented design patterns. In: Australian Software Engineering Conference (ASWEC), pp. 98–107. IEEE Computer Society, Los Alamitos (1998)
26. Walls, J., Widmeyer, G., El Sawy, O.: Building an information system design theory for vigilant eis. Information Systems Research 3(1), 36–59 (1992)
27. Gregor, S., Jones, D.: The anatomy of a design theory. Journal of the Association of Information Systems 8(5), 312–335 (2007)
28. Schermann, M., Böhmann, T., Krcmar, H.: Fostering the evaluation of reference models: Application and extension of the concept of is design theories. Wirtschaftsinformatik 2, 181–198 (2007)
29. Gehlert, A., Schermann, M., Pohl, K., Krcmar, H.: Towards a research method for theory-driven design research. business services: Konzepte, technologien, anwendungen. In: 9. Internationale Tagung Wirtschaftsinformatik, pp. 441–450 (2009)
30. Buckl, S., Matthes, F., Schweda, C.M.: Utilizing patterns in developing design theories. In: 2010 International Conference on Information Systems, ICIS 2010 (2010)
31. Goldkuhl, G.: Design theories in information systems - a need for multi-grounding. Journal of Information Technology Theory and Application 6(2) (2004)
32. Nunamaker, J., Chen, M., Purdin, T.: Systems development in information systems research. Journal of Management Information Systems 7(3), 89–106 (1991)
33. Venable, J.R.: The role of theory and theorising in design science research. In: Design Science Research in Information Systems and Technology (2006)
34. Coplien, J.O.: Software Patterns: Management Briefs. Cambridge University Press, Cambridge (1996)
35. Markus, M.L., Majchrzak, A., Gasser, L.: A design theory for systems that support emergent knowledge processes. MIS Quaterly 26(3), 179–212 (2002)
36. Hanschke, I.: Strategic IT Management: A Toolkit for Enterprise Architecture Management. Springer (2009)
37. Murer, S., Bonati, B., Furrer, F.J.: Managed Evolution. Springer (2010)

38. Buckl, S., Ernst, A.M., Matthes, F.: Enterprise architecture management pattern catalog. Technical report, Technische Universität München, Munich, Germany (2008)
39. Buckl, S., Ernst, A.M., Lankes, J., Matthes, F., Schweda, C.M.: Enterprise architecture management patterns - exemplifying the approach. In: The 12th IEEE International EDOC Conference (EDOC 2008), München, pp. 393–402 (2008)
40. Buckl, S.M.: Developing Organization-Specific Enterprise Architecture Management Functions Using a Method Base. PhD thesis, Technische Universität München, München, Germany (2011)
41. Schweda, C.M.: Development of Organization-Specific Enterprise Architecture Modeling Languages Using Building Blocks. PhD thesis, Technische Universität München (2011)
42. Buckl, S., Matthes, F., Schweda, C.M.: A situated approach to enterprise architecture management. In: IEEE International Conference on Systems, Man and Cybernetics (SMC 2010), pp. 587–592. IEEE (2010)
43. Buckl, S., Matthes, F., Schweda, C.M.: A method base for enterprise architecture management. In: Ralyté, J., Mirbel, I., Deneckère, R. (eds.) ME 2011. IFIP AICT, vol. 351, pp. 34–48. Springer, Heidelberg (2011)
44. Ross, J.W., Beath, C.M.: Sustainable it outsourcing success: Let enterprise architecture be your guide. MIS Quarterly Executive 5(4), 181–192 (2006)
45. Sein, M.K., Henfridsson, O., Puraro, S., Rossi, M., Lindgren, R.: Action design research. MIS Quarterly (2) (2011)

Patterns as an Artifact for Business Process Improvement - Insights from a Case Study

Thomas Falk, Philipp Griesberger, and Susanne Leist

Chair of Business Engineering, University of Regensburg, Germany
{thomas.falk,philipp.griesberger,susanne.leist}@ur.de

Abstract. Several approaches were developed for business process improvement (BPI) (e.g. Six Sigma). However, it is often stated that these approaches do not provide sufficient support for the performers of a BPI initiative, especially concerning the phase where applicable measures that provoke improvement (act of improvement) are needed. In this paper, we suggest BPI patterns as a means to directly support the act of improvement. Even though the common concept of patterns had great success in other domains of information systems (IS), the concept has not been transferred to BPI so far. In this paper, the demonstration of BPI patterns in a case study is focused. The BPI patterns, which represent the artifact in this design science research, are derived on the basis of a previously developed metamodel. The results from the demonstration were discussed with the process owners to get a first evaluation of the developed BPI patterns.

Keywords: Patterns, Business Process Improvement, Case Study, Design Science Research.

1 Introduction

The intention of managing business processes is to make them more effective and efficient [1], which corresponds to Harrington's fundamental definition of BPI [2]. The improvement of business processes has been a core task in organizations (see [3]) and corresponding approaches are manifold [4]. We define BPI as changing the state of a business process with the state after the change exceeding the state before the change in such a way that the degree of accomplishing organizational goals is increased. Most attempts to optimize a business process are performed manually and do not involve a formal automated method [5]. But the use of structured methods, techniques or guidelines within improvement efforts is essential to enable BPI performers to reorganize their business activities and processes in an organization with regard to certain objectives [6]. Over the past decades, various methods including techniques and tools were developed that enable or support the general process of improving business processes or parts of it (see [7]). However, it is often stated that none of them adequately support the practitioner through all stages in an improvement project. Although instructions for practitioners exist for what improvement should be aimed at (e.g. reduce costs, shorten cycle-time etc.), actual instructions for the question of

J. vom Brocke et al. (Eds.): DESRIST 2013, LNCS 7939, pp. 88–104, 2013.

"how to do that" are very scarce and generic [8] (e.g. eliminating wasteful "redoing" or working on concurrent activities [9]). This very phase of process management, the transformation of a business process from its "as-is" to a desired "to-be" state, namely the "act of improvement", should get more attention, as there is consensus in literature that this major challenge within BPI is lacking sufficient guidance [5]. Thus, there are few publications that actually address what is to be done to implement improvement in an organization [10] by describing the necessary changes that have to take place [11]. To close this research gap, a pattern approach seems suitable. Patterns are reusable means which address a problem within a certain context by providing a solution [12]. This general approach has been adapted to many pattern-related research works. However, while pattern approaches have had seminal successes e.g. in the field of Software Development [13], the topic has so far barely been addressed neither in the general field of information systems (IS) [14] nor specifically in the field of BPI [15]. Previous research also states that the representation of existing process-related patterns is not adequately formal to directly be reused, e.g. for process modeling [16].

Summarizing, our research goal is to develop patterns that can be used in the context of BPI (artifact) and especially to support the act of improving business processes. These BPI patterns are described in a consistent notation format based on a metamodel and convey proven knowledge that directly supports the "act of improvement". In this paper, we lay the focus on the demonstration of the applicability and usefulness of BPI patterns in practice by means of a case study.

For our overall research goal, the research method of design science is suitable, as we strive to develop a new artifact (BPI patterns) which is represented in a structured form based on a metamodel and resolves a specific problem domain (no support for the act of improving business processes) (cf. [17]).

A design science research methodology (DSRM), according to Peffers et al., includes "conceptual principles to define what is meant by DS research, practice rules, and a process for carrying out and presenting the research" [18]. The latter is particularly important to ensure rigor and replicability of the research. There are several procedures available which are similar in form and content (e.g. [18], [19]). The research project presented in this paper follows the design science research methodology process (DSRM process) by Peffers et al. It comprises six steps: (1) identify problem & motivate, (2) define objectives of a solution, (3) design & development, (4) demonstration, (5) evaluation, and (6) communication of the results [18]. In addition to the clearly structured DSRM process, the seven "guidelines for design science in information systems" by Hevner et al. ([17]) were made an integral part of our research.

In sect. 1, we have already outlined the problem statement of our research (DSRM step 1). In sect. 2, we present relevant conceptual basics including a brief overview of patterns in general and a definition for BPI patterns along with the objectives of our solution in particular (DSRM step 2). Design and development of the BPI patterns (DSRM step 3) are described in sect. 3 which has already been the subject of a previously performed study where a metamodel for BPI patterns was developed (see [20]). This metamodel serves as a basis for the development and description of BPI patterns. The applicability of BPI patterns which is the focus of this study is subsequently demonstrated in a case study in sect. 4 (DSRM step 4). In addition, we present first indications regarding the evaluation of BPI patterns obtained from discussions with the process owners (DSRM step 5). Sect. 5 summarizes the findings of our research and outlines indications for further research. Finally, our paper partially represents step 6 of the DSRM process, the communication of our results.

2   Conceptual Basics

2.1   Business Process Management and Improvement

Business Process Management (BPM) is seen as a holistic approach for describing the way that organizations are managed, namely that they are organized according to their processes [21]. Thus, alignment of processes is required to take changes into consideration that e.g. result from corporate strategies or customer needs [21]. Recently, the growing number of possibilities to support the execution of business processes due to technological progress (e.g. by means of business process management systems) additionally strengthened the business process paradigm (see [22]). The BPM life cycle comprises eight steps: selection, definition, modeling (as-is), analysis, improvement (to-be), implementation, execution (to-do), and monitoring/controlling [23]. The main challenge is still the fifth step in the BPM-life cycle, namely the improvement of business processes and especially the "how to do that" [8] ("act of improvement").

Besides the evolutionary improvement-approach of BPI (see sect. 1.1), several other approaches have evolved within BPM which all have the superior goal of making processes more effective and efficient [24]. To mention but a few of these approaches, there are "Business Process Reengineering" [25, 26], "Process Innovation" [27], "Six Sigma" [28], "Business Restructuring" [29] or "Core Process Redesign" [30]. Highly prominent is the manifesto for business revolution by Hammer and Champy in which they coined the term business process reengineering (BPR) [26]. The commonly top-down focus of an organization's management of BPR lies on a radical redevelopment of an organization's business processes by abolishing current business processes and redeveloping them [31]. In contrast, the evolutionary approach of BPI which we focus is based on a bottom-up procedure emphasizing staff involvement and the maintaining of current business processes and the implementation of small changes [31].

2.2   Definition and Benefit of BPI Patterns

The understanding of the term "pattern" in the field of IS is strongly influenced by Alexander's work (see [12]). Alexander provides the fundamental definition of a pattern as "a three part rule, which expresses a relation between a certain context, a problem, and a solution" [32]. Software development was one of the first disciplines in IS that adopted and further developed the pattern approach (e.g. [13], [33]). The common basis of these works is that they all see patterns as abstract and therefore reusable components which describe the key aspects of a solution for a recurring problem in a certain context [13]. At the same time a pattern conveys existing, well-proven knowledge gained from experience [33]. In addition, patterns are "similar to but shorter and more structured than the case studies used to communicate knowledge" [19].

We define a BPI pattern as a reusable solution for a certain problem within a business process in a certain context. The overall goal is to transform a business process from an "as-is" to a desired "to-be" state (support of the "act of improvement"). The application of a BPI pattern results in some form of change, e.g. on the activities that constitute a business process or the required resources for its execution. The result-oriented perception of patterns (as in [13, 33, 34]) has to be distinguished from those patterns that characterize dynamic aspects of the occurring change by describing how to accomplish a desired output (procedure-oriented patterns as in [35-37]).

We argue that a systematic, structured, and reusable approach for improving business processes ultimately leads to improvement (see [38]). Furthermore, these structured guidelines support the creative skills of employees and therefore e.g. help to formalize improvement methods [39]. Accordingly, Barros states that a "common theme in the more recent business process literature is the search for approaches that allow to formalize domain knowledge into structures, patterns or frameworks which can be reused to facilitate process redesign" [34]. Hence, we focus the improvement of business processes by patterns because of the following reasons:

- First, as a pattern is defined as a reusable component that has proven itself in the past, it can be assumed that this solution can be helpful again [40]. This may also save time and work expense if a solution already exists and can be used [16].
- Second, alternative solution possibilities may exist if more than one pattern can be applied to solve a certain problem.
- Third, applying a pattern in BPI supports the involved employees with promising guidance, provided that the patterns are described properly.
- Fourth, the names of the patterns constitute a vocabulary which enhances the communication among participants [41].
- Fifth, generated patterns could also be integrated into BPM software for instant visualization of a pattern's impact on existing process models.
- Sixth, as patterns are well-proven and have succeeded elsewhere, they may help to bridge the resistance to change among employees (see [27]).

3   BPI Patterns

3.1   Metamodel of BPI Patterns

To define the structure of BPI patterns we developed a metamodel (see **Fig. 1**) (see [20]). Two basic requirements were considered as obligatory for the constitution of a BPI pattern. On the one hand, it must be possible to select a suitable pattern concerning a given problem situation (selection guide). On the other hand, a BPI pattern has to provide detailed guidelines for its application (instructions for use).

The metamodel was derived by means of a comprehensive literature review of pattern notation formats in fields of IS where patterns have proven to be successful (software development, enterprise application integration, workflow management, and business process modeling). This was performed in a previous study ([20]) and carried out as follows: In total, 21 notation formats from the different fields in IS were investigated according to their contained attributes, their similarities and differences. Thus, an initial list of 211 attributes resulted, which was gradually condensed by removing synonyms, homonyms, or different aggregation levels. This was based on the original description of the attributes and was performed in discussion groups consisting of the researchers. The final list of core attributes was analyzed against the background of requirements in BPI. Eventually, the necessary attributes for describing a BPI pattern were derived and additionally defined by means of a metamodel depicting their relationships (see **Fig. 1**), with the object types of the metamodel representing the attributes that are necessary to properly describe a BPI pattern.

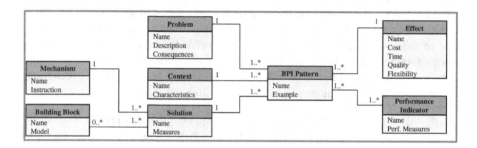

Fig. 1. Metamodel of a BPI Pattern

In the center of the metamodel, the object type *BPI pattern* is located which has (like every other object type) a *name* [34, 42] as its unique identifier to clearly distinguish BPI patterns. Further on, an *example* [13, 33] illustrates the application of a BPI pattern and provides the user with a primary impression. Every BPI pattern is specified by a single *problem*, a single *context*, and a single *solution*. This is reflected by the relationships between the *BPI pattern* type and the related *problem* type, the *context* type, and the *solution* type. The *problem* [33] statement represents the *description* of issues that have certain *consequences* and are meant to be solved by the use of a pattern. Due to the evolutionary nature of BPI, the description of a BPI pattern has to allow for an assessment of its applicability within a given situation and the suitability of the proposed problem-solving solution. These aspects specify the *context* [41, 43], which is represented by *characteristics* that implicate conditions for the applicability of a BPI pattern. The replicability of how to construct the *solution* [33, 44] based on a pattern is a crucial aspect. By providing detailed *measures* for its application, a pattern enables performers, experts as well as novices, to adapt a pattern within an individual situation. Therefore, the *solution* type is linked to the *mechanism* type as well as to the *building block* type, which means that every *solution* contains a single *mechanism* and optionally one (or more) *building block(s)*. For example, the elimination of activities, modifications of the control-flow, or the reduction of handovers represent *mechanisms* [36, 37] that can be used to improve a process. These *mechanisms* do not represent patterns as such, but unveil the way of proceeding and can be used within a pattern. *Building blocks* [13, 42] depict pre-built models for implementation that can be directly implemented within a process model. Summarizing, the object types *solution, mechanism,* and *building block* address the requirement of providing detailed instructions on how to change a business process or its elements to obtain an enhanced to-be status which corresponds to our definition of BPI (see sect. 1). The application of a BPI pattern is geared towards the reduction of e.g. costs or time, which is described with the object type *effect* [10, 39] and its corresponding attributes (*cost, time, quality,* and *flexibility*). A specification of these anticipated *effects* provides decision support for selecting patterns. In addition, the *performance indicator* [41] type depicts *performance measures* which capture the actual outcome of improvement. Thus, by means of *performance measures,* it can be verified if an improvement effort meets the desired objectives by measuring the resulting change.

3.2   Development of a BPI Pattern Catalog

In literature, related works in the field of BPI patterns could be identified. However, in these works, the derivation and representation of these reusable measures is approached rather differently:

- Forster aims at formalizing a framework for the classification of BPI patterns [39]. For the creation of these patterns, Forster notes that "relevant literature and real-case Business Process Improvement projects" can be used [39]. Forster states to have found over 50 BPI patterns which, however, are not published in his work except for four example patterns [39].
- Reijers/Limam Mansar provide 29 best practices for redesigning business processes and evaluate their impact on cost, time, quality, and flexibility [10]. They derive these best practices from a literature survey and supplement them with own experience [10].
- Barros develops business process patterns and frameworks that synthesize best practices from real process redesign projects which can be applied to improve a process [34]. As sources, Barros refers to the best practice literature, reported experiences, and direct observation of firms [34]. Additionally, he complements his patterns with own experience from various cases [34].
- Kim et al. provide an approach for managing process changes by means of recurrently occurring patterns [45]. Their patterns address the control-flow of business processes and are based on the workflow patterns by van der Aalst (see [42]).

Although these works aim at providing measures for the improvement of business processes, the description of these measures does not follow a consistent notation format which would facilitate the selection and proper application of the most suited measure. However, for the derivation of BPI patterns, the abovementioned works are used. Exemplarily, the provided best practices in Reijers/Limam Mansar are highly qualified as an input for BPI patterns. For example, one of their best practices proposes to divide a general task into two or more specialized tasks (solution) in order to better align to diverging characteristics of orders (problem) [10]. The anticipated effects are improvement of quality of a business process as well as cost and time advantages because of better resource utilization [10]. They also refer to cases in literature where this best practice has been applied (example) [10]. However, there is e.g. no further specification of context characteristics, i.e. in what situations this best practice is (not) applicable.

In addition to the abovementioned related work, patterns can also be derived from the general BPI literature. On the one hand, measures that were applied in successful BPI projects can serve as input. On the other hand, BPI methods and their associated techniques can be used as a basis to derive BPI patterns. For example, the technique "Process Cycle Time Reduction" is helpful when long cycle times prevent product delivery to customers and increase storage costs (problem) [2]. The solution is to focus on the activities of the process which slow down the process [2]. Then, several alternatives (e.g. parallelize activities, change activity sequence etc.) (mechanisms) can be examined to reduce the cycle time of a process (effect) [2]. For each mechanism, examples are given to illustrate their impact [2].

Based on the metamodel in sect. 3.1, it is possible to systematically integrate and record proven knowledge about the improvement of business processes from various sources in BPI literature. This is valid for all forms of reusable measures, whether in the form of patterns, best practices, or techniques, etc. Thus, recurring improvement actions in different cases become apparent and comparable, while gaps can be revealed where current BPI approaches have potential for improvement.

Summarizing, a collection of 20 BPI patterns has been derived so far which are described in detail following the notation format of the metamodel (see sect. 3.1). This collection is to be extended. The BPI patterns are stored in a structured pattern catalog which is intended to be used within a BPI initiative when actual measures for improvement are needed.

3.3   Procedure for the Selection of BPI Patterns

Having a collection of patterns stored in a catalog, several possibilities for selecting patterns are imaginable. First, an enumerative trial and error of all patterns could be considered to determine the most suitable pattern for a given situation. Naturally, this requires huge efforts depending on the size of the pattern catalog.

As all of our proposed patterns have the same notation format, i.e. they are described by means of the same attributes, the search for a suitable pattern can be performed in a much more structured way. For example, the problem statements of all patterns could be compared to the problem which is to be solved in a BPI initiative. Thus, only those patterns the problem statement of which is matching are to be regarded further. Alternatively, if a specific goal is pursued, the effects of a pattern provide a quick selection guide to finding appropriate patterns. Either way, both possibilities require the execution of both steps, i.e. if patterns are to be selected according to the problem statements, the next step is to filter the remaining patterns according to their effects and vice versa. In both cases, it has to be examined afterwards if there are prevailing conditions that hinder the application of a solution, which is determined by the context. Using a solution based on a wrong analogy may lead to unfavorable results (see [1]). Assuming that after this step several possible patterns remain, the most suited pattern has to be prioritized. Finally, the determined pattern can be applied.

4   Case Study

4.1   The Studying Process

Fig. 2 illustrates the studying process from the perspective of a registrar's office. We developed this process during a cooperation project with the administration department of a German university. The process is decomposed into several sub-processes to provide several levels of detail. The original sub-processes are simplified to increase clarity without deviating from the essential process flows. The studying process is triggered by a student candidate who wishes to go to university. After the successful application for the desired degree program, the candidate has to matriculate to become a student. During his or her studies, a student has to renew the matriculation by paying the semestral tuition fee. If the student does not pay the tuition fee or if s/he passes all of the exams, s/he will be exmatriculated thus finishing his or her studies.

4.2   Application of BPI Patterns

The usefulness of BPI patterns is demonstrated by means of a case study in which we describe a project to improve the processes of a registrar's office at a German university (see **Fig. 2**). The project pursues the clearly defined goal of reducing cycle time, thus we consider the search for patterns showing the desired effects as an ideal starting point. The first step of the procedure we suggest to select appropriate BPI patterns is to search the pattern catalog for those patterns whose resulting effects conform to the goal that is aimed at by the improvement initiative. In this case, the goal is to reduce the cycle times of three processes of the registrar's office (see **Fig. 2**) without affecting the levels of quality and cost. Therefore, each pattern from the catalog showing a positive effect on time and not having any negative effects on cost and quality is considered as a relevant candidate. Step 2 of the selection procedure consists of filtering those BPI patterns from all relevant candidates that are suitable to improve the processes at hand. For that purpose, the three processes which are objects for improvement are analyzed in respect of problems and weak points. Thus, all BPI patterns that are able to address the actual problems are identified. To accomplish this task, we used detailed process models of the studying process that were available for analysis. They enabled us to determine potential problems related to four process elements, namely control flow, activities, input/output, and resources, potentially having a negative impact on the process' performance measures. For example, in the current matriculation process we discovered that documents are issued in the first place, although they may prove unnecessary during subsequent activities. This is, more generally speaking, a matter of logical control flows regarding the sequence of the activities of a process.

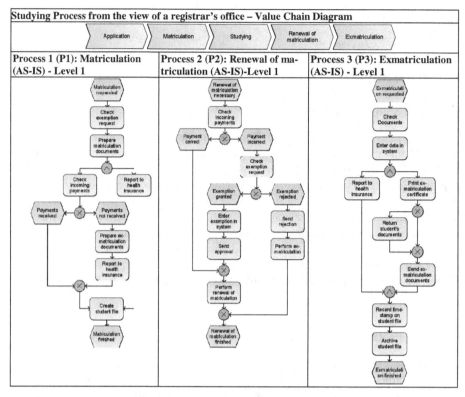

Fig. 2. Studying process (AS-IS-situation)

Other problems came up in personal interviews with the process owners and employees, e.g. the high workload during the weeks when the renewal of matriculation takes place twice a year. An overview of the problems that could be identified for the studying process is shown in **Tab. 1**.

Table 1. Problems identified for the studying process

Control flow	Activities
Implausible control flow: sequence of activities does not follow a logical order • Receipt of payment is checked too late • Documents issued before matriculation is confirmed	**Non-value-added activities:** activities are performed unnecessarily. • Report to health insurance must be corrected
Complex control flow: process contains a large number of decision points, loops and branches • Renewal of matriculation and exemption of tuition fees intertwine unfavorably	**Expensive activities:** activities consume high amounts of time and resources • Manual data entry of students' data
Input/Output	**Resources**
Waste: output is produced that is not needed • Matriculation documents must be recalled	**High workload:** personnel resources work to capacity • High workload in the context of the renewal of matriculation
Shortage: input is not available when needed • Information whether a student's fees are fully paid is missing when matriculation is due	

The analysis of as-is processes is an integral part of most of the existing BPM- or BPI-approaches and is supported by techniques such as value-added assessment [2] or cause and effect diagrams [46]. The results of this analysis phase provide valuable input for determining patterns suitable to solve the problems at hand.

In step 3, the selection of appropriate BPI patterns is further refined by comparing the context statement of each remaining pattern with the actual context that is in place with the process the improvement focuses on. Thereby it is verified if the solution part of a pattern is applicable in the given context, and only those patterns that show a match are considered as practicable candidates. In our case, we again used the process models and additional documents to determine the contextual factors. Further insights into the processes' contexts were gathered through personal interviews with the process owners. It should be noted that the regarded processes only focus on the process flow. Applying steps 1 to 3 of the selection procedure resulted in the following four BPI patterns that can be classified as relevant regarding the goals, suitable relating to the resolution of the problems at hand, and applicable in the given context:

- BPI Pattern 1: *Arrange activities based on their dependencies*
- BPI Pattern 2: *Divide complex processes into smaller sub-processes*
- BPI Pattern 3: *Automate decisions based on predefined rules*
- BPI Pattern 4: *Assign activities to external parties*

Step 4 of the selection procedure – prioritize patterns – is necessary e.g. if there is more than one BPI pattern that could be identified for the same purpose; it is also necessary if several patterns are in conflict with each other. During this step, additional information can be consulted to weigh the pros and cons of the individual patterns. In our case, all four patterns do not show any overlap or conflict and are therefore equally applicable for the improvement of the registrar's office's processes.

Finally, in step 5, the selected BPI patterns are applied to an existing business process. In the following, we demonstrate the application of a single BPI pattern and its outcome in more detail. For that purpose, we use the as-is process "Renewal of matriculation" which is shown on the left-hand side of **Fig. 3** and apply the BPI pattern 2: "Divide complex processes into smaller sub-processes". The outcome is two separate sub-processes as shown on the right-hand side of **Fig. 3**. This pattern addresses the problem of a complex control flow which may have a negative impact on cycle times and error rates. The solution part of the pattern suggests dividing a long and complex process into several sub-processes. To implement the pattern, we first clustered the activities which can be performed individually and independently as stated in the context section. For the "Renewal of matriculation" process, two separate tasks could be identified: check payment of tuition fees (comprising the activities check incoming payments, perform renewal of matriculation, and perform exmatriculation) and perform exemption of tuition fees (including the activities check exemption request, enter exemption in system, send approval, and send rejection). Following this, one sub-process for each task is constructed (see right-hand side of **Fig. 3**). The design of these sub-processes is straightforward and hence easier to understand and manage. The input/output that has to be exchanged between the two sub-processes is confined to a record that stores the amount each student has to pay as a tuition fee.

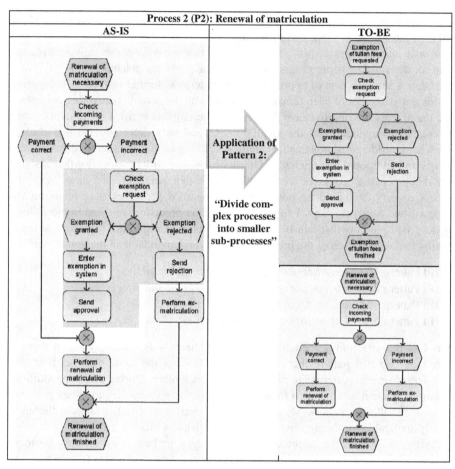

Fig. 3. Impact of the application of Pattern 2 "Divide complex processes into smaller sub-processes" on Process 2 "Renewal of matriculation"

Applying the pattern to the "Renewal of matriculation" process results in a number of desired positive effects. Since the receipt of payment can now be checked separately from processing requests for the exemption of tuition fees, waiting times are reduced. This effect is reinforced by the circumstance that requests for exemption can now be processed for a whole year while the checking of the payment receipt is bound to a specific date. An additional benefit is that the workload of the personnel is more equally distributed over the whole year avoiding peaks and idle times. Due to their straightforward design, the resulting sub-processes are less error-prone, and their ability to adapt to changing requirements is enhanced. The BPI pattern we described in detail in this section has already been implemented at the registrar's office and shows the desired effects. The specification of the BPI pattern "Divide complex processes into smaller sub-processes" itself, whose structure is determined by the metamodel, is shown in **Fig. 4**. The specifications of the remaining three patterns are included in the appendix (see [47]).

BPI PATTERN 2:   Divide complex processes into smaller sub-processes

Example:

Within the scope of an invoicing process, the additional tasks of billing working hours and material consumption as well as updating inventories are conducted. As numerous tasks are included in just one process, it is very difficult to manage, and many process instances that have been initialized are pending at a particular time. Since the invoicing process has to wait until all included tasks have been finished, its total cycle time from start to completion is quite long and the proportion of waiting time is extremely high.

PROBLEM:

Description:

Wide range of activities: One process deals with many different tasks and therefore contains a rather large number of activities that are only loosely connected regarding their underlying functions.

Complex control flow: The control flow is characterized by a large number of decision points, branches, and loops making it difficult to determine or follow the routing of a particular business case.

Various inputs: A plethora of inputs that have to be coordinated and provided in time, are required to correctly perform the activities of the process. Due to multiple dependencies, waiting times increase while the availability of necessary input is checked.

Consequences:

Since the process is inflated with activities that are merely loosely related to the process' central task, it becomes complex and difficult to manage. The flexibility of such a process, in the sense of its ability to adapt to changing requirements, is low, as simple change requests can escalate into unmanageable large projects. Because of the confusing process design and situations during a process run, error rates increase. Overall cycle times also increase because frequently making decisions or waiting for input that has to be provided by other activities delays the processing of a business case.

Cost	Time	Quality	Flexibility
neutral	negative	negative	negative
	Longer cycle time	High error rate	Low adaptability
	Long waiting time		

CONTEXT:

Characteristics:

Activities: There are activities within the process that can be performed individually and independently of each other; i.e. an activity A does not need any of the outputs produced by other activities within the process as an input.

Input/Output: The interfaces, regarding input-output-relationships, between the task that is a candidate for extraction and preceding or subsequent tasks are well-defined.

SOLUTION:

Measures:

Divide one long and complex process into several sub-processes in such a way that …

… each sub-process is short and straightforward regarding its design.

… exchange of e.g. material, information, etc. between the resulting sub-processes becomes minimal.

… organizational disruptions within each sub-process become minimal.

Mechanism: Modify control flow
Building Block: -

EFFECTS AND PERFORMANCE INDICATORS:

Applying the pattern splits a complex and overloaded process into smaller logical segments that are far easier to understand and manage. Compared to the original process, the cumulated cycle time of the new process segments is shorter because of fewer waiting times. Error rates decrease due to a clear process specification and a smaller number of dependencies that have to be considered during a process run. Since the interfaces between the sub-processes are minimal and well-defined, each interface can be managed and changed individually which enhances flexibility in regard to change requests.

Cost	Time	Quality	Flexibility
neutral	positive	positive	positive
Cost per process run	Cycle time	Error rate	Reaction time to change requests

Fig. 4. BPI Pattern "Divide complex processes into smaller sub-processes"

Fig. 5 shows the changed processes of the registrar's office resulting from the application of the four identified BPI patterns. Detailed descriptions of the BPI patterns 1, 3, and 4 are included in the appendix.

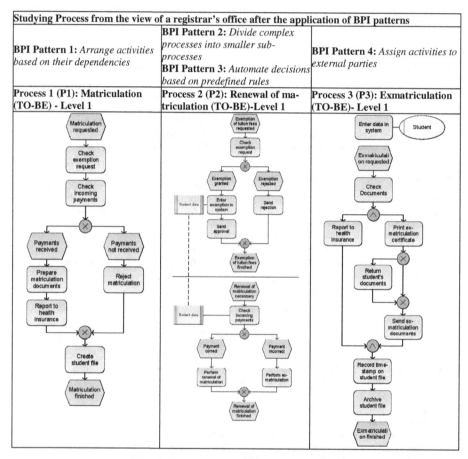

Fig. 5. Studying process (TO-BE-situation)

4.3   Discussion of the Results

As a first step for evaluating the BPI patterns we set up a workshop to discuss them with the process owners affected and directly involved in the execution of the processes who would decide about possible changes to be undertaken to improve these processes. Particular emphasis was laid on both the relevance and the comprehensibility of the selected BPI patterns for the investigated processes:

- The process owners approved of all the recommendations we suggested based on the selected BPI patterns as being useful. The basic principle of pattern 2 (Divide complex processes into smaller sub processes) had already been applied by the process owners on the process „renewal of matriculation", since in real-life checking the exemption of tuition fees before the renewal of the matriculation had already been in practice for quite some time – in compliance with our own previous suggestion. The long cycle times and the high commitment of resources mentioned as the prevailing shortcomings of processes by the process owners are addressed effectively by the selected BPI patterns.

- The pattern catalog was also regarded by the process owners to be useful for giving thought-provoking impulses in general, as it provides improvement measures that were useful in the past. Thereby, previously not considered alternatives for solving problems may be discovered.
- However, it turned out that the way of describing patterns is crucial as this e.g. determines their usability. Specifically, regarding their application, abstract descriptions of concrete issues may be problematic, e.g. describing the context of a pattern adequately. Thus, a thorough trade-off between describing patterns as abstract as possible and as specific as necessary will be of great importance when further developing our BPI pattern catalog. Additionally, the process owners recommended a tagging of all BPI patterns to facilitate their selection.

Summarizing, the process owners considered the BPI patterns as appropriate for being used within BPI initiatives. The proposed notation format for BPI patterns which is determined by the metamodel met with the process owner's approval in terms of effectiveness. This positive feedback from practitioners reflects the relevance of our research and confirms our intention to further develop the BPI pattern catalog.

5 Conclusion

In this paper, the use and benefit of patterns are shown as a promising approach for supporting the act of improvement within BPI. A metamodel, which was developed in a previous study (see [20]) denotes the structure of a BPI pattern. For our purposes, BPI patterns can be derived by analyzing BPI literature based on the question of "what has been done?" in successful BPI initiatives. Then, relevant sources can be systematically integrated into patterns which are stored in a structured pattern catalog and represent the artifact in our design science research project. As all of these patterns are described by means of the same attributes, which is determined by the metamodel, the selection of a most suited BPI pattern from the catalog for a BPI initiative is facilitated.

The applicability of the BPI pattern artifact is demonstrated by applying four patterns from the catalog on real-life processes. These processes comprise a studying process from the perspective of a registrar's office at a German university. The results from the application were discussed in a workshop with the process owners, which is, at the same time, a first step towards the evaluation of BPI patterns. The overall approach was considered as meaningful, the selected patterns as relevant, and their description as reasonable. An important result of the discussions was that the way in which the patterns are described must not be too abstract to ensure the pattern's usability. The findings presented in our paper also point to areas of further research: first, the adequate level of abstraction as well as a consistent vocabulary for the description of each pattern is of significant importance. Equally, the appropriate structuring of complex attributes such as problem or context must be given special attention. Second, the detailed evaluation (step 5 of the DSRM process) will have to be addressed.

The results from this paper are beneficial to both research and practitioners:

The pattern catalog represents a systematic integration of documented problems and the associated solutions that previously emerged in BPI. Thus, deriving BPI patterns on the basis of our metamodel reveals gaps and redundancies which exist in established BPI approaches. The catalog can be used in BPI methodologies where concrete improvement measures are needed.

The pattern catalog provides support to practitioners in the act of improving business processes. At this, the BPI patterns support the creative skills of the involved performers (as in [19]). The description of context characteristics for each pattern indicates requirements for their applicability.

References

1. Andersson, B., Bider, I., Johanesson, P., Perjons, E.: Towards a formal definition of goal-oriented business process patterns. BPMJ 11(6), 650–662 (2005)
2. Harrington, H.J.: Business Process Improvement - The breakthrough strategy for Total Quality, Productivity and Competitiveness. McGraw-Hill, New York (1991)
3. Gartner: Leading in Times of Transition: The 2010 CIO Agenda (2010)
4. Snee, R.: Lean Six Sigma – getting better all the time. International Journal of Lean Six Sigma 1(1), 9–29 (2010)
5. Vergidis, K., Tiwari, A., Majeed, B.: Business Process Improvement using multi-objective optimisation. BT Technology Journal 24(2), 229–235 (2006)
6. Valiris, G., Glykas, M.: Critical review of existing BPR methodologies. BPMJ 5(1), 65–86 (1999)
7. Doomun, R., Jungum, N.V.: Business process modelling, simulation and reengineering: call centres. BPMJ 14(6), 838–848 (2008)
8. Nwabueze, U.: Process improvement: the case of a drugs manufacturing company. BPMJ 18(4), 576–584 (2012)
9. Bhatt, G., Troutt, M.: Examining the relationship between business process improvement initiatives, information systems integration and customer focus: an empirical study. BPMJ 11(5), 532–558 (2005)
10. Reijers, H.A., Limam Mansar, S.: Best practices in business process redesign: an overview and qualitative evaluation of successful redesign heuristics. Omega 33(4), 283–306 (2005)
11. Povey, B.: The development of a best practice business process improvement methodology. Benchmarking for Quality Management & Technology 5(1), 27–44 (1998)
12. Alexander, C., Ishikawa, S., Silverstein, M., Jacobson, M., Fiksdahl-King, I., Angel, S.: A pattern language. Towns, Buildings, Construction. Oxford University Press, New York (1977)
13. Gamma, E., Helm, R., Johnson, R.E., Vlissides, J.: Design Patterns - Elements of Reusable Object-Oriented Software. Addison Wesley (1995)
14. Winter, R.: Patterns in Business and Information Systems Engineering. BISE 1(6), 468–474 (2009)

15. Pourshahid, A., Mussbacher, G., Amyot, D., Weiss, M.: An aspect-oriented framework for Business Process Improvement. In: Babin, G., Kropf, P., Weiss, M. (eds.) E-Technologies: Innovation in an Open World. LNBIP, vol. 26, pp. 290–305. Springer, Heidelberg (2009)

16. Tran, H.N., Coulette, B., Dong, B.T.: A UML-Based Process Meta-model Integrating a Rigorous Process Patterns Definition. In: Münch, J., Vierimaa, M. (eds.) PROFES 2006. LNCS, vol. 4034, pp. 429–434. Springer, Heidelberg (2006)

17. Hevner, A.R., March, S.T., Park, J., Ram, S.: Design Science in Information Systems Research. MIS Quarterly 28(1), 75–105 (2004)

18. Peffers, K., Tuunanen, T., Rothenberger, M., Chatterjee, S.: A Design Science Research Methodology for Information Systems Research. JMIS 24(3), 45–77 (2007)

19. Vaishnavi, V., Kuechler, W.: Design science research methods and patterns: innovating information and communication technology. Auerbach Publications, Boca Raton (2008)

20. Falk, T., Griesberger, P., Johannsen, F., Leist, S.: Patterns for Business Process Improvement - A First Approach. Universität Regensburg (2013)

21. Rosemann, M., de Bruin, T.: Application of a Holistic Model for Determining BPM Maturity. BPTrends, 1–21 (February 2005)

22. Smith, H., Fingar, P.: Business Process Management - The Third Wave. Meghan Kiffer Press (2003)

23. Rosemann, M.: Business Process Lifecycle Management. White Paper (April 2004)

24. Macdonald, J.: Together TQM and BPR are winners. The TQM Magazine 7(3), 21–25 (1995)

25. Hammer, M.: Reengineering Work: Don't automate, obliterate. HBR 68(4), 104–111 (1990)

26. Hammer, M., Champy, J.: Reengineering the corporation: a manifesto for business revolution. Harper Business, New York (1993)

27. Davenport, T.H.: Process Innovation - Reengineering work through Information Technology. Harvard Business School Press, Boston (1993)

28. Antony, J.: Six Sigma for service processes. BPMJ 12(2), 234–248 (2006)

29. Talwar, R.: Business Re-engineering - a strategy-driven approach. Long Range Planning 6(1), 22–40 (1993)

30. Kaplan, R.B., Murdock, L.: Core process redesign. The McKinsey Quarterly 28(2), 27–43 (1991)

31. Boerner, R., Moormann, J., Wang, M.: Staff training for business process improvement - The benefit of role-plays in the case of KreditSim. Journal of Workplace Learning 24(3), 200–225 (2012)

32. Alexander, C.: The timeless Way of Building. Oxford University Press, New York (1979)

33. Buschmann, F., Meunier, R., Rohnert, H., Sommerlad, P., Stal, M.: Pattern-Oriented Software Architecture: A System of Patterns. John Wiley&Sons, Chichester (1996)

34. Barros, O.: Business process patterns and frameworks. BPMJ 13(1), 47–69 (2007)

35. Gnatz, M., Marschall, F., Popp, G., Rausch, A., Schwerin, W.: Modular Process Patterns Supporting an Evolutionary Software Development Process. In: Bomarius, F., Komi-Sirviö, S. (eds.) PROFES 2001. LNCS, vol. 2188, pp. 326–340. Springer, Heidelberg (2001)

36. Hagen, M.: Definition einer Sprache zur Beschreibung von Prozessmustern zur Unterstützung agiler Softwareentwicklungsprozesse. University of Leipzig, Leipzig (2005)

37. Störrle, H.: Models of Software Architecture - Design and Analysis with UML and Petrinets. Books on Demand (2000)

38. Rohleder, T.R., Silver, E.A.: A tutorial on business process improvement. Journal of Operations Managament 15(2), 139–154 (1997)

39. Forster, F.: The Idea behind Business Process Improvement: Toward a Business Process Improvement Pattern Framework. BPTrends, 1–13 (April 2006)

40. Stephenson, C., Bandara, W.: Enhancing Best Practices in public health: Using process patterns for Business Process Management. In: ECIS 2007 Proceedings, St. Gallen (Switzerland), pp. 2123–2134 (2007)

41. Jung, J., Sprenger, J.: Muster für die Geschäftsprozessmodellierung. In: Schelp, J., Winter, R., Frank, U., Rieger, B., Turowski, K. (eds.) DW 2006: Integration, Informationslogistik und Architektur, pp. 189–204. Gesellschaft für Informatik, Friedrichshafen (2006)

42. van der Aalst, W.M.P., ter Hofstede, A.H.M., Kiepuszewski, B., Barros, A.P.: Workflow Patterns. Distributed and Parallel Databases 14(3), 5–51 (2003)

43. Manns, M.L., Rising, L.: Fearless Change - Patterns for Introducing New Ideas. Addison (2005)

44. Zimmermann, B.: Pattern-basierte Prozessbeschreibung und -unterstützung - Ein Werkzeug zur Unterstützung von Prozessen zur Anpassung von E-Learning-Materialien. TU Darmstadt (2008)

45. Kim, D., Kim, M., Kim, H.: Dynamic Business Process Management based on Process Change Patterns. In: ICCIT 2007, Gyeongju (Korea), pp. 1154–1161 (2007)

46. Pande, P.S., Neuman, R.P., Cavanagh, R.R.: The Six Sigma Way: How GE, Motorola, and other top companies are honing their performance. McGraw-Hill, New York (2000)

47. Falk, T., Griesberger, P., Leist, S.: Patterns for Business Process Improvement - Insights from a Case Study (Appendix) (2013), http://www-wiwi-cms.uni-regensburg.de/images/institute/winfo/leist/desrist_2013_appendix.pdf

ERP Event Log Preprocessing:
Timestamps vs. Accounting Logic

Niels Mueller-Wickop and Martin Schultz

Chair for Information Systems, University of Hamburg, Hamburg, Germany
{niels.mueller-wickop,martin.schultz}@wiso.uni-hamburg.de

Abstract. Process mining has been gaining significant attention in academia
and practice. A promising first step to apply process mining in the audit domain
was taken with the mining of process instances from accounting data. However,
the resulting process instances constitute graphs. Commonly, timestamp
oriented event log formats require a sequential list of activities and do not support graph structures. Thus, event log based process mining techniques cannot
readily be applied to accounting data. To close this gap, we present an algorithm that determines an activity sequence from accounting data. With this
algorithm, mined process instance graphs can be decomposed in a way they fit
into sequential event log formats. Event log based process mining techniques
can then be used to construct process models. A case study demonstrates the effectiveness of the presented approach. Results reveal that the preprocessing of
the event logs considerably improves the derived process models.

Keywords: Process Mining, Log File Preprocessing, Process Instances, ERP
Accounting Data.

1   Introduction

Today's business processes are extensively supported by information systems. Especially, enterprise resource planning (ERP) systems are widely used in companies and
highly integrated into business processes. Business process management (BPM) methods increasingly use process mining techniques as means to reconstruct the state of
affairs [14] [15]. Process mining has been adopted by a variety of research domains,
such as healthcare [18], the public sector [1], and audit [14]. Within the last domain
the accounting impact of process activities play a central role. Particularly in the
course of process audits, process mining techniques have gained academic attention
[3]. Likewise, the International Standards on Auditing (ISA) 315.81 require that "(...)
the auditor should obtain an understanding of the information system, including the
related business processes, relevant to financial reporting (...)" [13]. Until now, auditors have manually modeled audit-relevant business processes based on interviews
and information supplied by the client. This approach is error-prone and time-
consuming. Hence, applying process mining techniques in the domain of process
audits has the potential to increase the effectiveness and efficiency of auditors [15].

J. vom Brocke et al. (Eds.): DESRIST 2013, LNCS 7939, pp. 105–119, 2013.

As a result, manual modeling of processes becomes obsolete, and, as a consequence, saves time and improves accuracy. Auditors are interested in the data and functions of account modules of ERP systems and hence mainly focus on accounting-related processes. Therefore, this work addresses accounting-related data as a basis for process mining.

Auditors mainly use graphical representation in order to understand the business processes of their clients. An essential part of business process modeling is the sequence flow. The chronological order of executed activities is of great interest for auditors. For example, payments should be made after receiving an invoice. Hence, one of the main questions the auditor has to answer is how and in which order the activities of accounting related processes are executed in reality. We tested different process mining techniques with the objective of answering this question. It turns out that all of them use data fields, as for example timestamps, to define the sequence flow between activities. Using additional information besides timestamps is difficult as information in traditional event logs of information systems are not ordered in a logical manner, but rather in a chronological one. So far, not even the financial process mining (FPM) technique specifically developed for accounting data could determine a logically and chronologically correct order of activities [9]. Instead, mined process instances constitute graphs without sequence flow between activities. Activities are connected by their associated accounting items. Moreover, convergence and divergence frequently occur in accounting data. This poses a serious problem as conventional mining techniques require a sequential event log. The solution described in this paper is based on the open item accounting mechanism. It is used to put accounting activities in a logical order. Hence, this paper presents as one of two artifacts a method to transform process instances without directed sequence flows between activities into process instances resolving this problem. As a second artifact we present a method comprising four preprocessing steps that create an event log representing the logical order of events. In other words, based on the sequence flow, instance graphs can be decomposed into independent parts, which can be mapped into a sequential event log. A case study demonstrates that the process model derived from a preprocessed event log is superior to the model created from a purely timestamp-based event log for two reasons. First, due to the complex structure of accounting process instances common techniques cannot readily be used. Second, mined process models partly do not represent the de facto processes. By introducing the two before mentioned artifacts this paper opens up further research opportunities in the combination of process mining and compliance checking. The here set basis is a necessary step in order to establish process mining techniques as a basis for business process oriented compliance checking.

Contrary to most process mining techniques, FPM reconstructs process instances based on existing accounting data in ERP systems. Therefore, this technique is not dependent on switched-on logs as accounting data has to be recorded in any case. Moreover, due to double-entry bookkeeping, accounting software uses a worldwide standardized metadata structure, whereas log files are system specific and therefore need to be preprocessed with significant effort [14].

The following section describes related research and gives background information. This is followed by a description of the applied research method. Section 4 presents an algorithm for reconstructing the sequence flow of accounting activities. Section 5 presents an approach for the preprocessing of accounting-related data and the creation of a sequential event log. The approach is evaluated in a case study presented in section 6. The paper closes with a conclusion and implications for future research.

2   Background and Related Research

By now, process mining is a fairly well researched topic. The main goal is to "[...] discover, monitor and improve real processes (not assumed processes) by extracting knowledge from event logs readily available in today's (information) systems" [36]. A good overview until the year 2008 is given in [27].

Most of the early research was detached from practical application. This has rapidly changed in the last five years. There has been a considerable amount of research in the process mining area associated to specific domains [17] [1] [26]. As mentioned in the introduction, this paper especially focuses on the work of auditors and therefore the compliance domain. A good overview of process mining in the domain of compliance management is given in [24]. Moreover, in [16], a categorization of compliance analysis was proposed. Two central categories are identified: forward and backward compliance analysis. The first one aims at the execution time of processes, while the latter audits compliance in retro perspective.

One severe shortcoming was not tackled until 2005: the diverse event log formats. This problem was addressed by van Dongen and van der Aalst. They proposed a metadata model for event logs. The corresponding log-file format is called MXML [7]. However, extracting data from event logs stored in different kinds of information systems is still a persistent problem. Guenther describes the difficulties when extracting event log data from process-aware information systems (PAIS) [11]. With the introduction of ProM6 the XES file format was introduced providing an easier data transformation [29].

Yet another major challenge of business process mining on accounting data is the data structure of ERP systems. These systems represent one of the richest data sources for business process mining, but established ERP systems like SAP, Oracle JD Edwards or Microsoft Dynamics are not process-oriented even though they have built-in workflow engines. Data related to a particular process is stored across a multiplicity of tables without providing process-oriented linkages. Thus, extracting and preprocessing of process relevant data is not a trivial task [3]. So far, comparatively few attempts have been made to apply process mining in ERP environments. Lone van der Aalst et al. and Jans et al. describe different scenarios for process mining of data extracted from ERP systems especially focusing on auditors [3] [15] [14]. The latter uses an unique identifier (purchase order line item) to locate activities belonging to the same business process instance. The relevant database tables are determined based on a preselected list of activities. The process model is constructed with a timestamp based mining algorithm (fuzzy miner [10]). In this respect financial process mining (FPM) goes one step further: using the specific structure of accounting data, process instances are reconstructed without preselecting activities (see section 4.1) [9]. However, the resulting instances form graphs. Therefore, timestamp based mining algorithms cannot be readily applied. Addressing this gap, this paper proposes a preprocessing approach for accounting data in ERP environments. The presented approach facilitates the transfer of results from existing work on process mining to accounting data.

As the instances mined from accounting data constitute graphs, obviously graph based mining techniques can be applied. The main objective of graph based mining is to provide new principles and efficient algorithms to mine topological substructures embedded in graph data. Several methods are discussed in academic literature ranging from greedy search to inductive database approaches [30] [4]. Van Dongen and van der Aalst follow a similar approach with their work on multi-phase process mining. It focuses on the construction of instance graphs that can be seen as a model of a single process instance [8]. These instance graphs are aggregated to an overall model of the data set [2]. However, to our best knowledge these techniques have not been applied to accounting data.

3   Research Method

The underlying research approach is based on the design science approach. Both Hevner et al. and Peffers et al. emphasize that the artifact to be created should have a high relevance to the research domain addressed [12], [21]. In this work, the relevance is derived from the initially described necessity of auditors to gain an in depth understanding of their clients' business processes. The work presented by Österle et al. proposes four phases for the design science research cycle, namely analysis, design, evaluation, and diffusion [20]. The paper at hand follows this approach by first analyzing the requirements of stakeholders and pointing out a research gap. Secondly, an artifact is designed that aims at closing this gap.

Moreover, there is a consensus in literature that evaluation of a designed artifact is essential in design science research [22]. In this paper the evaluation method for the presented artifact is chosen based on the framework proposed by Venable et al.[28]. Having a socio-technical artifact potentially relevant for diverse stakeholders a naturalistic ex post evaluation strategy appears appropriate. Because of the availability of real-life data, a case study seems the method of choice. The effectiveness of the created artifact is evaluated and demonstrated in this work on the basis of this real-life data. As evaluation criteria the average connector degree for the mined process models is selected. The connector degree refers to the number of input and output arcs of a routing element. This factor influences the understandability of process models [19]. In the second step, both models are discussed with representatives from the case study company. This evaluation only constitutes a first step of a broader evaluation. However, it is easy to utilize and measure and therefore builds a valid starting point to gain first insides and results on this topic. Further investigation is certainly needed.

4   Logic Order of Accounting Processes

4.1   Structure of Accounting Entries

The structure of accounting data is highly standardized [25]. Each accounting entry consists of a document header and at least two associated document items, one credit and one debit. Each item refers to a specific account and contains a flag indicating whether the item is cleared or not. In case open item accounting is activated an item contains a reference (ClearingDocNo) to the document it was cleared by (clearing document) or does not refer to a document (item still open). For a graphical depiction of the data structure see Fig. 1.

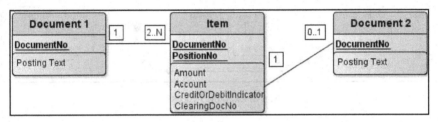

Fig. 1. Generalized data structure of an accounting entry using open item accounting

4.2   Reconstructing the Logical Order of Accounting Entries

The previously described data structure is now used to reconstruct a logical order of activities from graphs mined with FPM, whereby the clearing mechanism of open item accounting plays a central role. All associated items are marked starting from a random document header of the accounting data. These items are either cleared by items or clear items of other documents. The associated document is a logical predecessor or successor depending on whether they get cleared or clear other items. This induces the following two general definitions:

- Predecessor documents include items being cleared by items of the successor documents
  Rationale: following the accounting logic, a document with cleared items had to be posted before the clearing items could be posted.
- Successor documents include clearing items of the predecessor documents
  Rationale: a document can only include clearing items if the cleared items are booked beforehand.

An example depicted in Fig. 2 explains the approach. Let A and B be document headers each including one debit (A2, B2) and one credit item (A1, B1). The document items are posted by activity X (document A) and activity Y (document B). In consideration of the two definitions given above, document A must be a predecessor of Document B because item A2 was cleared by item B1. Therefore document B is set as clearing reference in item A2 (in Fig. 2 item A2 has "Doc B" as a reference). Also item B1 references Document B as clearing document. In this example item, A1 does not have a reference to any document because it is booked on an account not involved in open item accounting, whereas item B2 might either be booked on an account involved in open item accounting or not. As a result, the order of the corresponding activities can be determined. Activity X created document A and posted the items A1 and A2, activity Y created document B and posted the items B1 and B2. Since item B1 clears item A2, activity X (posted document A including items A1 and A2) must be a predecessor of activity Y (posted document B including B1 and B2). Therefore a directed sequence flow from activity X to activity Y can be modeled.

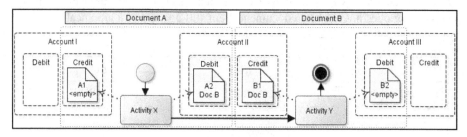

Fig. 2. Example Process

It should be noted that the created order of activities is not necessarily the chronological order: Let activity X be "goods receipt" and activity Y be "post invoice". Clearly, goods should be received before they are invoiced. However, in reality there are cases of goods being invoiced before they are received. Nevertheless, the accounting logic suggests a different order of activities. This mismatch is of great interest to the auditors.

The context described above results in the following algorithm depicted in pseudo code.

```
T = Set of all Document Header (SAP table: BKPF) of an
instance
I = Set of all Document Items (SAP table: BSEG) of an
instance
V_m =T
E_m ⊆ {(n_1, n_2) | (n_1 ∈ T ^ n_2 ∈ I) ∨ (n_1 ∈ I ^ n_2 ∈ T)}
G_m = (V_m, E_m) ≙ instance graph from FPM

function mapGraph(V_m, E_m)
  returns G_p =( V_p, E_p), V_p ⊆ T, E_p ⊆ V_p × V_p: {
  V_p = {}
  E_p = {}
  for (e_1 ∈ E_m) {
    for (e_2 ∈ E_m) {
      if (target_vertex(e_1) = source_vertex(e_2)) {
        V_p ← V_p U source_vertex(e_1)
        V_p ← V_p U target_vertex(e_2)
        Ep ← Ep U (source_vertex(e1), target_vertex(e2))
}}}} return (Vp, Ep)}
```

5   Event Log Preprocessing

5.1   Divergence and Convergence in Accounting Data

Through the principle of open item accounting, the concepts of convergence and divergence are present in the majority of process instances mined from accounting data. Multiple document items can be cleared by one single item. Also, one single activity is able to book not only on two accounts (one credit and one debit side), but on multiple accounts. Only the sums of debit and credit item amounts must be equal. Therefore, mined process instances constitute a directed graph rather than a sequentially ordered list of activities. This has substantial implications for the mining of process models based on this kind of process instances.

The following two sales process examples clarify the context. The first deals with the concept of convergence. Two activities X (e.g. "retro-billing") and Y (e.g. "create billing document") each posting an item (A2, B2) on the same account (e.g. "account trade receivables"). These two items are cleared by one item (C1) posted by activity Z (e.g. "post incoming payments"). The accounting logic proposes that activity Y and activity X are each followed by activity Z (see Fig. 3). Assumed item C2 is posted on an account involved in open item accounting, the item has not yet been cleared and therefore there can be no referenced clearing item.

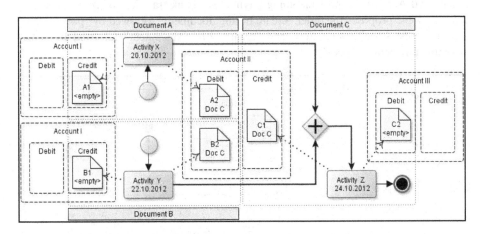

Fig. 3. Convergence example: sequence flow based on the accounting order

However, a chronological ordering of activities would change the sequence flow: In this case activity X "retro-billing" is followed by the activity Y "created billing document" before the activity "post incoming payment" is executed (see Fig. 4). Obviously this order of activities would not be executed in reality.

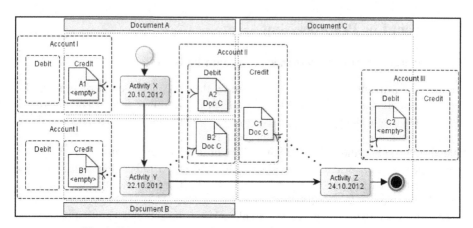

Fig. 4. Convergence example: sequence flow based on timestamps

The second example deals with the concept of divergence within a process instance (see Fig. 5). In this example, the first activity X (e.g. „create billing document") posts on three different accounts I, II and III, two of which are accounts receivable (e.g. "Debtor A" and "Debtor B"). The corresponding two items (A2 and A3) are cleared by items posted by different activities (e.g. Activity Y "post incoming payments - check" and Activity Z "post incoming payments – bank transaction"). Thus, the accounting logic proposes the order "create billing document" followed by "post incoming payments – back transaction" and "create billing document" followed by "post incoming payments – check".

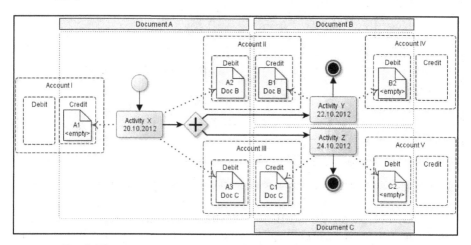

Fig. 5. Divergence example: sequence flow based on the accounting order

Again, the chronological order of activities and the logical accounting order fall apart. The proposed order in this case would be activity X "create billing document", activity Y "post incoming payments – check" followed by activity Z "post incoming payments – check". This obviously is not the case in standard business processes.

However, conventional mining algorithms are based on event log formats that are designed to store sequentially ordered lists of activities. The concepts of divergence and convergence are not taken into account on a process instance level. Regular process mining techniques deduct this semantics from comparing multiple instances of one process. Therefore, preprocessing is necessary to apply these mining algorithms to accounting data.

5.2   Event Log Preprocessing

Fig. 6 illustrates the concepts of divergence and especially convergence by showing a purchase process instance mined with the FPM algorithm based on the case study data (see section 6). Several goods receipts are depicted on the verge of the right instance part (SAP transaction code MIGO - "Goods Receipt"). These are linked to 1-n invoices (SAP transaction code MIRO - "Enter Incoming Invoice") with a n:m relation. Subsequently, a payment run clears n invoices (SAP transaction code F110 – "Automatic Payment"). Six payment runs surround the center of the instance on the right side of Fig. 6. The outgoing payments are posted to a bank clearing account. After receiving the bank statement, these items get cleared in a single step (SAP transaction code FB05 - "Post with Clearing"). The same linkages are present on the left side of the process instance. Particularly noteworthy are the highlighted documents "connecting" the two parts of the process instance. This is an item of goods receipt (MIGO - "Goods Receipt") that was cleared by different invoices (MIRO "Enter Incoming Invoice"). These invoices itself were paid in different payment runs (F110 – "Automatic Payment").

The example shows that several independent documents can be linked in a single process instance in accounting-related processes. The documents are represented as paths of activities converging into a single activity. In the example described above, this is caused by the clearing of several invoices by the same payment run. Considering these process instances as a sequentially ordered list of activities - as conventional process mining techniques would do - interferes with a reasonable representation of process models based on accounting data. Activities of independent process sequences may overlay each other due to their timestamps. This may cause an "incorrect" order of activities resulting in additional edges in the constructed process model. Therefore, this paper proposes the following preprocessing steps for process instances mined from accounting data and their representation in a sequential event log format:

1. **Step:** Mine the source data with the FPM algorithm. *Result:* Process instances represented as graphs including document headers and document items.
2. **Step:** Transform these graphs to directed activity graphs by applying the method described earlier in order to reconstruct the logical order of accounting activities. *Result:* Process instances represented as directed graphs.
3. **Step:** Enumerate all possible paths (precisely all open directed paths). The following properties of a path need to be considered: A path does not revisit nodes. A directed path is a path in a directed graph where the directions of edges match the directions of edges in the directed graph. *Result:* List of paths representing sub sequences of the mined process instances.

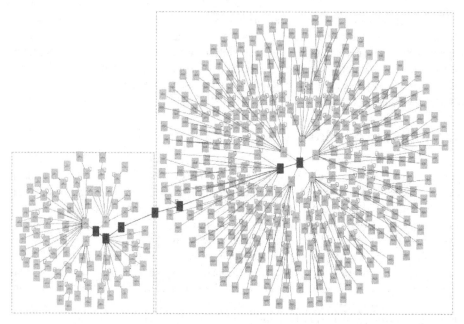

Fig. 6. Process instance example

4. **Step:** Store all paths in an event log (e.g. MXML format), where each path is a case and the corresponding nodes are the events of this case. Adjust the timestamp of each event to reflect the order of the path. *Result:* Event log representing the logical order of events.

These steps are implemented in a prototype used to derive process models from the data received in the subsequently described case study.

6   Evaluation: Accounting Logic vs. Timestamp Order

The presented case study is based on data from a big news-agency that uses SAP ECC 6.0. Accounting-relevant data is extracted (e.g. goods receipt, invoices, and payments) for the fiscal year 2011. To keep this case study as clear as possible, it only considers instances that are booked on a predefined balance sheet account (1604000 – "accounts payable"). This reflects the approach of external auditors who set their audit scope based on the materiality of accounts. This extracted subset of data encompasses 32,521 accounting documents. Out of this data, the FPM algorithm generates 1,873 instances. Each accounting document represents an activity with corresponding items. The number of activities per instance ranges from 1 to 1,206. The events are solely labeled with the SAP transaction code they were created with.

As described in section 1 the case study shows that the preprocessing leads to improved process models when using conventional process mining techniques. Therefore we create – as an object of comparison - an event log that represents the chronological order of activities of 1,873 process instances. For this end, the event log utilizes the timestamp information stored in the source data. The procedure follows the proposed approach by the used tool ProM6 (for further information, please refer to http://www.promtools.org/prom6/). Fig. 7 (a) depicts a profile of events per instance for this event log.

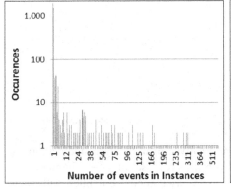 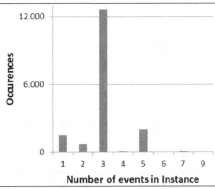

Fig. 7.   (a) Timestamp based Event Log   (b) Preprocessed Event Log

To facilitate comparison, we preprocess the 1,873 instances according to the listed steps in section 5.2 and create a second event log reflecting the logical order of events. Fig. 7 (b) depicts the profile of activities per instance for this event log. The number of instances in the event log increases to 17,115 whereas the maximum number of events per instance decreased considerably to 9. This is caused by the decomposition of instances (see section 5.2) into distinct paths of activities. The total number of activities in the event log increased from 32,521 to 52,229 as each activity included in two or more paths will be stored as many times in the event log. These numbers underline the frequent occurrence of convergence and divergence in instances of accounting-related processes.

As a next step, ProM6 is used to create process models of both event logs [29]. The fuzzy miner algorithm is deployed with standard settings [10]. Process models generated by the fuzzy miner indicate how often an activity is followed by another one by adjusting the thickness of the linking edge. Fig. 8 depicts the resulting models for both event logs. Due to the fact that the evaluation is based on real company data, we were obliged to anonymize the resulting models. However, the general structure as well as the number of activities and arcs is still recognizable.

The analysis reveals that both models contain the same nodes. However, the model based on the preprocessed event log has considerably fewer edges – the number of edges is reduced from 57 to 30 (53%). It is particularly noteworthy that the number of self-loops (nodes referring to themselves) could be reduced from 19 to 8 (42%). The average connector degree of nodes is reduced in the accounting logic-based model from 4,3 to 2,6 (median from 4 to 2). As discussed in section 3 "research method" this has a positive impact on the understandability of a process model [19].

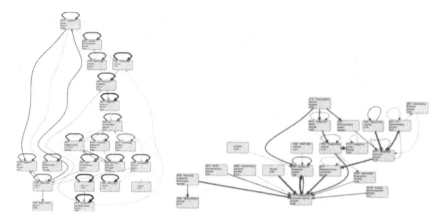

Fig. 8.   (a) Model based on timestamps   (b) Model based on accounting logic

In the second step, both models with representatives from the case study company are discussed. The representatives familiar with the processes and their implementation in SAP state that only the accounting logic-based model complies with their expectations for three reasons: 1). The timestamp based model encloses process sequences that – according to the best knowledge of the representatives – do not occur in their business transactions. For several unexpected sequences, representatives of the company investigated the underlying source data. Furthermore, they inquired with the personnel involved in the process. It is apparent that these sequences are derived from a chronologically ordered list of events not belonging to the same path in the directed graph of the process instance. This underlines the expectation: Activities of independent paths may overlay each other when ordered chronologically – resulting in "incorrect" edges in the process model. 2) The expected and most prevalent process flow (MIGO - "Goods Receipt" → MIRO - "Enter Incoming Invoice"→ F110 – "Automatic Payment" → FB05 - "Post with Clearing") could only be identified in the accounting logic-based process model. 3) The central role of F110 "Automatic Payment" as the final step of most business transactions in the purchase process is solely evident in the new process model.

The results of the evaluation strengthen the assumption that the presented approach for preprocessing ERP data is a valuable contribution for the process mining of accounting-related processes.

7   Conclusion and Future Research

Over the past years, increasing weight has been put on process audits by internal and external auditors. Process auditors have relied on manually modeled processes based on interviews and additional information supplied by the client until now. This is error-prone and time-consuming. A promising approach to increasing the effectiveness and efficiency of such audits is process mining. However, process mining has not yet been widely applied in the audit domain for several reasons. First, relevant data for process audits is largely related to accounting data stored in ERP systems. As a rule, these systems do not store the data in a process-oriented way, but in a distributed manner across several tables. The extraction and linkage of data from different tables causes remarkable effort. Second, conventional process mining algorithms are not able to mine accounting data. The application of FPM remedies this deficiency. Nevertheless, resulting process instances form graphs containing divergence and convergence of independent sequences due to the accounting-immanent data structure. Conventional mining algorithms cannot be applied to these instance graphs as they need an event log with a sequentially ordered list of activities.

Introducing an approach for the reconstruction of a logical order eliminates this shortcoming. By adding a directed sequence flow between activities of instance graphs, the decomposition into distinct sequences becomes possible. These sequences can be mapped to common event log formats. Analyses based on the comparison of the chronological with the logical order of activities are additional benefits of the presented approach.

The contribution of this paper is threefold: First, it presents an algorithm to reconstruct a logical order of activities in process instance graphs resulting from process mining based on accounting data. Second, mined process instance graphs can be decomposed and used as a basis for conventional process mining techniques based on the logical order. Third, a comparison and analysis of chronological and logical order of activities within the limits of the audit domain is enabled by the presented approach.

There are several opportunities for further research work. So far, FPM is restricted to accounting data and related processes. A combination with other data sources and existing process mining techniques would widen its range of application. Especially the integrated analysis of accounting data with corresponding activity logs (e.g. changes to accounting documents and master data) might be a useful next step. Moreover, graph based mining techniques have been neglected in this paper. Future research will include the application of graph based mining techniques on accounting data. Since mined process instances with FPM already form graphs, this approach is especially promising.

References

1. Van der Aalst, W.M.P.: Business Process Mining: An Industrial Application 32(5), 713–732 (2007)
2. Van der Aalst, W.M.P., Van Dongen, B.F.: Multi-Phase Process Mining: Aggregating Instance Graphs into EPCs and Petri Nets. Gehalten auf der ICATPN (2005)
3. Van der Aalst, W.M.P.: Auditing 2.0: Using Process Mining to Support Tomorrow's Auditor. Computer 43(3), 90–93 (2010)
4. Aggarwal, C.C., Wang, H.: Managing and mining graph data. Springer, Berlin (2010)
5. Cook, J.E., Wolf, A.L.: Automating process discovery through event-data analysis. In: Proceedings of the 17th International Conference on Software Engineering, pp. 73–82. ACM, New York (1995)

6. van Dongen, B.F., de Medeiros, A.K.A., Verbeek, H.M.W(E.), Weijters, A.J.M.M.T., van der Aalst, W.M.P.: The prom framework: a new era in process mining tool support. In: Ciardo, G., Darondeau, P. (eds.) ICATPN 2005. LNCS, vol. 3536, pp. 444–454. Springer, Heidelberg (2005)

7. Van Dongen, B.F., Van der Aalst, W.M.P.: A Meta Model for Process Mining Data. In: Proceedings of the CAiSE Workshops, pp. 309–320 (2005)

8. van Dongen, B.F., van der Aalst, W.M.P.: Multi-phase Process mining: Building Instance Graphs. In: Atzeni, P., Chu, W., Lu, H., Zhou, S., Ling, T.-W. (eds.) ER 2004. LNCS, vol. 3288, pp. 362–376. Springer, Heidelberg (2004)

9. Gehrke, N., Mueller-Wickop, N.: Basic Principles of Financial Process Mining A Journey through Financial Data in Accounting Information Systems. In: AMCIS 2010 Proceedings (2010)

10. Günther, C.W., van der Aalst, W.M.P.: Fuzzy Mining – Adaptive Process Simplification Based on Multi-perspective Metrics. In: Alonso, G., Dadam, P., Rosemann, M. (eds.) BPM 2007. LNCS, vol. 4714, pp. 328–343. Springer, Heidelberg (2007)

11. Günther, C.W., van der Aalst, W.M.P.: A Generic Import Framework For Process Event Logs. In: Eder, J., Dustdar, S. (eds.) BPM Workshops 2006. LNCS, vol. 4103, pp. 81–92. Springer, Heidelberg (2006)

12. Hevner, A.R.: Design science in information systems research. MIS Quarterly 1, 75–105 (2004)

13. International Federation of Accountants (IFAC): Handbook of International Quality Control, Auditing, Review, Other Assurance, and Related Services Pronouncements (2010)

14. Jans, M.: Process mining of event logs in auditing: Opportunities and challenges. In: International Symposium on Accounting Information Systems, Orlando (2010)

15. Jans, M.: Process Mining of Event Logs in Internal Auditing: A Case Study. In: 2nd International Symposium on Accounting Information Systems, Rome (2011)

16. Kharbili, M.E.: Business Process Compliance Checking: Current State and Future Challenges. Gehalten auf der MobIS (2008)

17. Mans, R.S.: Process mining techniques: an application to stroke care. Studies in Health Technology and Informatics 136, 573–578 (2008)

18. Mans, R.S., Schonenberg, M.H., Song, M., van der Aalst, W.M.P., Bakker, P.J.M.: Application of Process Mining in Healthcare - A Case Study in a Dutch Hospital. In: Fred, A., Filipe, J., Gamboa, H. (eds.) BIOSTEC 2008. CCIS, pp. 425–438. Springer, Heidelberg (2009)

19. Mendling, J., Reijers, H.A., Cardoso, J.: What Makes Process Models Understandable? In: Alonso, G., Dadam, P., Rosemann, M. (eds.) BPM 2007. LNCS, vol. 4714, pp. 48–63. Springer, Heidelberg (2007)

20. Österle, H.: Memorandum on design-oriented information systems research. European Journal of Information Systems 20(1), 7–10 (2010)

21. Peffers, K.: A Design Science Research Methodology for Information Systems Research. J. Manage. Inf. Syst. 24(3), 45–77 (2007)

22. Peffers, K., Rothenberger, M., Tuunanen, T., Vaezi, R.: Design science research evaluation. In: Peffers, K., Rothenberger, M., Kuechler, B. (eds.) DESRIST 2012. LNCS, vol. 7286, pp. 398–410. Springer, Heidelberg (2012)

23. Pries-Heje, J.: Strategies for Design Science Research Evaluation. In: ECIS 2008 Proceedings (2008)

24. Ramezani, E., Fahland, D., van der Aalst, W.M.P.: Where Did I Misbehave? Diagnostic Information in Compliance Checking. In: Barros, A., Gal, A., Kindler, E. (eds.) BPM 2012. LNCS, vol. 7481, pp. 262–278. Springer, Heidelberg (2012)

25. Romney, M.B., Steinbart, P.J.: Accounting Information Systems. Prentice Hall (2008)
26. Rubin, V., Günther, C.W., van der Aalst, W.M.P., Kindler, E., van Dongen, B.F., Schäfer, W.: Process Mining Framework for Software Processes. In: Wang, Q., Pfahl, D., Raffo, D.M. (eds.) ICSP 2007. LNCS, vol. 4470, pp. 169–181. Springer, Heidelberg (2007)
27. Tiwari, A.: A review of business process mining: state-of-the-art and future trends. Business Process Management Journal 14(1), 5–22 (2008)
28. Venable, J., Pries-Heje, J., Baskerville, R.: A Comprehensive Framework for Evaluation in Design Science Research. In: Peffers, K., Rothenberger, M., Kuechler, B. (eds.) DESRIST 2012. LNCS, vol. 7286, pp. 423–438. Springer, Heidelberg (2012)
29. Verbeek, E.: ProM 6: the process mining toolkit (2010), http://repository.tue.nl/729150
30. Washio, T., Motoda, H.: State of the art of graph-based data mining. SIGKDD Explor. Newsl. 5(1), 59–68 (2003)

Enriching Process Models for Business Process Compliance Checking in ERP Environments

Martin Schultz

Chair for Information Systems, University of Hamburg, Hamburg, Germany
martin.schultz@wiso.uni-hamburg.de

Abstract. In enterprise resource planning (ERP) environments the audit of business process compliance is a complex task as audit relevant context information about the ERP system like application controls (ACs) need to be considered to derive comprehensive audit results. Current compliance checking approaches neglect such information as it is not readily available in process models. Even if ACs are automatically analysed with audit software, the results still need to be linked to related processes. By now, this linking is not methodically supported. To address this gap this paper presents a method to automatically enrich process models with audit relevant information about ACs. The method consists of three phases: process model construction, automated analysis of ACs, and model enrichment. It utilizes two existing artefacts and combines them to provide a comprehensive basis for compliance checking. Moreover, the enriched process models can support auditors in conducting process audits in ERP environments.

Keywords: Compliance Checking, Application Controls, BPM, ERP.

1 Introduction

Since recent financial scandals (Enron 2001, MCI WorldCom 2002, Parmalat 2003, Satyam 2009, HRE 2011 or Olympus 2011) organisations face the challenge to manage compliance to a steadily increasing number of rules and regulations in their everyday business operations. The rules they have to comply with range from voluntary norms and standards (e.g. ISO 9000, COBIT) to directives imposed by active legislations (Sarbanes-Oxley Act, 8th EU directive). For instance, Lickel (2007) counted over 118,000 new rules in the USA since 1981 [1]. There are regulations that are relevant for specific industries or sectors (e.g. pharmaceutical, utilities, financial sector) and others - including regulations for financial reporting – that apply to all companies. All these compliance rules significantly influence the way organisations design and execute their business processes [2]. They constitute boundaries and an organisation has to ensure that its business processes stay within these boundaries [3]. Not surprisingly, practitioners and researchers dealing with business process management (BPM) pay growing attention to compliance aspects [2].

Nowadays, organisations extensively rely on information systems (IS) to support and automate their business processes. Especially enterprise resource planning (ERP)

J. vom Brocke et al. (Eds.): DESRIST 2013, LNCS 7939, pp. 120–135, 2013.

systems and accounting information systems (AIS) are widely used to process and store thousands and millions of business transactions each day. In this environment, embedding controls in the underlying IS is a reasonable approach to enforce compliance during the enactment of business processes [4], [5], [6]. Today's ERP and AIS offer diverse customizing settings to configure such automated controls, termed application controls (ACs) [7]. For example, particular process steps like approvals of business transactions can be enforced during process execution or automated checks are implemented to prevent duplicate entering of invoices. These ACs allow organisations to comprehensively control their business processes and ensure compliance to several regulations in a cost-effective way [8], [9].

ERP systems can be customized to such an extent that almost no deviation from a designed process is possible [10], [7]. But, configuring ERP systems in a strict way impairs process flexibility that companies need in today's competitive markets [11]. At worst, "over-controlled" systems lead to "shadow processes" or "feral systems" circumventing existing controls [7], [12]. However, less-strictly configured ERP systems allow undesired behaviour that deviating from the designed process. Therefore, processes need to be constantly monitored whether they comply with defined rules. This monitoring activity is related to the audit domain [3]. For audits of business processes compliance the ERP system of an organisation plays a key role: 1) It stores audit relevant data (transactional data, master data, change logs) and make it electronically accessible to the auditor. 2) Relevant system settings can be reviewed providing insights to what extent the system configuration already enforces a compliant enactment of business processes.

Auditing of business processes in an ERP environment is a complex task as not only the process flow itself has to be considered but also the underlying ERP system constituting the context in which a process is executed [13], [5], [14]. Auditors have to combine expertise from both worlds: a fundamental understanding of business processes and profound knowledge of ERP systems. This is a major challenge in current audit practice especially regarding ACs. They are considered as an important aspect of business process compliance but are not are not explicitly modelled in process models. Against this background, the method presented in this paper aims at automatically enriching process models with audit relevant information about ACs configured in the ERP system supporting the business process under audit. The method combines two already existing IS artefacts. In a first step a process model is reconstructed based on accounting data stored in an ERP system [15]. Secondly, relevant customizing settings are automatically extracted from the ERP system and interpreted in terms of ACs. These ACs are linked to the before constructed process model. This enriched process model constitutes an improved data basis for automated compliance checking techniques as it considers relevant context information about the ERP environment. By now, existing compliance checking approaches neglect this context information as it is not readily available in process models. Moreover, it supports auditors in conducting process audits in ERP environments.

The remainder of this paper is structured as follows. The next section describes the related research work regarding BPM and compliance, auditing of process compliance, and process mining. Section 3 explains the applied research method. In section

4 the developed method is presented in detail. The evaluation of the approach is outlined in section 5. The utility of our method is evaluated in a case study together with an organisation using SAP ERP. The paper closes with a conclusion and implications for future research work.

2   Related Work

2.1   Business Process Management and Compliance

Today's organisations strive for a comprehensively formalizing and automating their business processes to cope with their complex and competitive environment. Hence, many organisations show growing interest in BPM as it provides methods to model, automate, optimize and monitor business processes [2], [16]. For example, organisations increasingly make use of business process modelling languages (e.g. EPC, BPMN) to design and document their business processes [16]. As regulatory requirements directly impact business process modelling, practitioners and researchers from the BPM domain increasingly take compliance aspects into account in recent years [2]. Ensuring compliance of business processes is a challenging task: the number and complexity of regulations is increasing and the rules are subject to constant change. This calls for a holistic approach to manage compliance. Becker et al. (2012) define business process compliance management (BPCM) as "[...] the steady modelling, refinement, and analysis of business processes regarding the fulfilment of regulatory compliance" [16]. Ramezani et al. (2012) outline the interdependencies between BPM and Compliance Management (CM) and describes CM as a "[...] methodology to elicit, specify and formalize, implement, check and analyse, and optimize compliance requirements in organizations" [4].

However, considering compliance of business processes is not a new topic, especially not in the auditing and risk management domain. Here compliance is closely linked with the internal control system of an organization. According to COSO, internal control is broadly defined as a process designed to provide reasonable assurance regarding the achievement of objectives in three categories: 1) effectiveness and efficiency of operations, 2) reliability of financial reporting, and 3) compliance with applicable laws and regulations [17]. It is a system of integrated elements like people, organisational structure, processes, and procedures and covers procedural (e.g. business processes, auditing, and monitoring) as well as structural aspects (e.g. policies, organisational structures/ roles) [18, p. 248], [19]. In this context key concepts are *control objectives* and *control means*. A control objective describes a desired state of an organisation or a process and is associated with a recommended course of action that should be taken (control means) to ensure that a control objective is achieved [19]. Control means may involve policies, procedures, practices as well as organisational structures. They are either process independent or directly integrated into a particular business process [20], [19], [21]. For business processes supported by IS application controls are of high importance. ACs are the subset of internal controls related to business processes that are directly embedded in IS [9], [22], [5]. They are activated and configured via customizing and can be categorized into input, processing, and output controls [7], [9], [23, p. 126]. Objective of this type of controls is to ensure complete-ness, accuracy, validity, and authorisation of transaction and data processing within an IS. Common examples include automated reconciliations, data entry validations and logical access controls. ACs provide an effective and efficient means to enforce com-pliance rules in business processes as they are in general less prone to error (especially human error) and more reliable than manual controls [9], [22]. Moreover, they only need to be configured once - hence the cost of control does not depend on the number of transactions checked [5]. Not surprisingly, calculations of business cases show that ACs are more cost-effective in the long-term leading to an increasing tendency to re-place manual with automated controls [8], [7].

2.2   Auditing Compliance of Business Processes

The audit of an organisation's regulatory compliance is usually a legal requirement, e.g. annual audits of the financial statements. As audit standards enforce an in-depth analysis of the organization's operation, business processes constitute a central audit object [24]. Thereby, the auditor focuses on the system of internal controls the organi-zation has implemented for their processes ("The auditor shall obtain an understand-ing of internal control relevant to the audit [...]" [24]). This approach is based on the assumption that well-designed and controlled business processes lead to regulatory compliance of an organisation, e.g. fairly presented financial statements [25], [26]. Accordingly, all big audit firms consider process audits as an integral part of their audit approach [27], [25].

The vast number of compliance rules and the complexity of business processes in today's organisations call for an automated support for audit tasks [16], [7]. Hence, IS researchers have developed (semi-) automated, model-based compliance checking approaches: compliance rules are formally defined and applied to business process models and instances in order to determine whether they comply with the rules or not [16]. These approaches can be subdivided into two categories: forward and backward compliance checking. Forward compliance checking techniques proactively verify compliance rules at design and/ or execution time of a process. Backward compliance checking techniques retrospectively detect non-compliant behaviour in process in-stances [28]. Becker et al. (2012) present a comprehensive overview of forward com-pliance checking approaches [16]. For a review of backward compliance checking techniques please refer to [28].

However, compliance checking techniques mainly focus on the control flow of process models and/ or instances neglecting potentially relevant context information e.g. about related IS [3], [29], [30]. In general, the context a process is embedded in is "[...] the combination of all situational circumstances that impact process design and execution [...]" [31]. Rosemann et al. (2008) differentiate four types of context: an immediate, internal, external, and environmental. IS are on the immediate layer as they directly facilitate the enactment of a process [13]. It is agreed, that many compliance rules can only be comprehensively checked by taking such pertinent context informa-tion into account [3], [29]. There are a few approaches that consider the context of a process for compliance checking. Fundamental requirements for a comprehensive support of semantic constraints in process management systems are discussed in Ly et al. (2012) and a framework for compliance support over the process life cycle is proposed [29]. Van der Werf et al. (2012) link an event log of a process to its context that has to be described in a data model beforehand [3]. Approaches that consider the data flow of a process for checking business/ compliance rules are presented in [32] and [33]. The verification of access control properties based on a security annotated process model is outlined in Wolter et al. (2009) [34]. However, these approaches do not comprehensively consider relevant context information about the IS the process is supported by. As ACs are executed inherently through the IS these controls are in general not explicitly modelled in a process model at design time and do not generate an entry in the event log of an IS. Therefore, AC-related information is not readily available on process model level and cannot be considered by compliance checking techniques. To close this gap the method presented in this paper automatically analysis ACs and enriches process models with the derived information.

For automatically analysing the system settings of a SAP ERP system in terms of ACs, Alles et al. (2006) describe an approach in the context of continuous auditing (CA) [35]. Our method presented here utilises a similar IS artefact presented in [5]. It is a software prototype (ERP AuditLab) that enables an automated evaluation of ACs for audit purposes. However, both approaches do not link the gained audit results (e.g. status of AC) to the affected business processes.

From an auditor's point of view, considering context information about ACs in process models unfolds its full potential especially when the underlying process model is also derived with a retrospective view on data stored in an information system. Therefore, our method utilizes process mining to determine such a model. This fits to general audit practices as process compliance is mainly checked ex post, e.g. during financial audit. However, the here presented method to enrich process models can also be applied to already existing process models.

2.3   Process Mining in Auditing

Process mining is a research area combining data mining with process modelling and process analysis. The main goal is to "[...] discover, monitor and improve real processes (not assumed processes) by extracting knowledge from event logs readily available in today's (information) systems" [36]. Among others, it encompasses process discovery, conformance checking, organizational mining, model extension and repair [36]. The data source for process mining is an event log containing a series of events recorded in an IS. Each event can be linked to a well-defined activity in a process and is related to a particular process instance/ case [37], [36]. Process mining is a fairly well researched topic and associated techniques have matured over the last decade resulting in increasing interest from practice [36]. More and more software tools are available, and process mining is applied in diverse industry sectors. For an overview of process mining techniques until 2008 please refer to [38].

Also internal and external auditors working in an ERP environment can benefit from the capabilities process mining offers. Process mining facilitates full audits (instead of sample based) of business processes in an effective way based on data recorded independently of the auditee [39]. However, applying process mining techniques to data stored in ERP systems is still a challenge. Common ERP systems (e.g. SAP, Oracle, and Microsoft) are not process-oriented even though they have built-in workflow engines. Data related to a particular process instance is stored across several tables without readily providing a process-oriented linkage or case identifier. Thus, selecting, extracting, and pre-processing of relevant data is not a trivial task [37]. Van der Aalst et al. (2010) and Jans et al. (2010, 2011) describe different scenarios for process mining in an ERP environment from an audit perspective [37], [40], [10]. The latter uses a preselected list of process activities to determine tables including relevant data. In contrast, financial process mining (FPM) – which the here presented method utilises – takes advantage of the specific structure of accounting data for reconstructing process instances of financial processes without preselecting relevant activities [15]. Section 4.1 describes the approach in more detail.

3   Research Method

The research presented in this paper follows the design science approach [41], [42], [43]. The artefact is a method to automatically derive and enrich a process model with information about ACs based on ERP data. The relevance of the artefact results from the fact that it addresses a gap between process audits and IS audits prevalent in today's audit practices. It combines information from both audit areas in a structured way to enable a more comprehensive audit of business process compliance.

There is a consensus in literature that evaluating the designed artefact is an essential step in design science research [44]. Based on the framework presented in [45] a case study is selected as evaluation method [46]. The artefact is applied to data from a productive system of an organisation to demonstrate that it feasibly works in a real setting. To evaluate the utility of the presented method from a stakeholder perspective, a group of six auditors reviews the enriched process model.

4   Integrating Process Models and Application Controls

The here presented method consists of three phases: 1) A model of an accounting related process is automatically constructed from transactional data stored in an ERP system (section 4.1). 2) Audit relevant information about ACs is extracted from the ERP system (section 4.2) and 3) embedded in the process model (section 4.3).

4.1   Financial Process Mining (FPM)

Today's ERP systems use a largely uniform data structure to store accounting data [47]. An accounting document consists of a header and at least two associated items (debit and credit). In case open item accounting is used, each document item refers to the document header it was cleared by, e.g. a vendor invoice line item is linked to the corresponding payment document header. Using this data structure, FPM reconstructs the document flow representing the control flow of a particular process instance [15].

Such document references ERP systems are not limited to financial accounting. Also other processes can be covered, e.g. purchasing.

Fig. 1 (a) illustrates an instance of a purchase to pay process. Each document contains an activity name, the SAP transaction code, a document number and a user id. This instance consists of four vendor invoices (DocNo 28017, 29991, 28038, 28037) that are cleared by three different payment documents. These payments refer to the same document settling open items on the bank clearing account. Only one invoice (DocNo 28017) relates to a goods receipt (DocNo 28016), a corresponding purchase order, and a purchase requisition document. Another invoice (DocNo 28037) is at least linked to a purchase order whereas the two remaining invoices (DocNo 29991, 28038) are just entered and paid without upstream purchasing activities. In contrast to this fairly simple example, other process instances can become rather complex. Fig. 1 (b) depicts an instance with 1,996 documents.

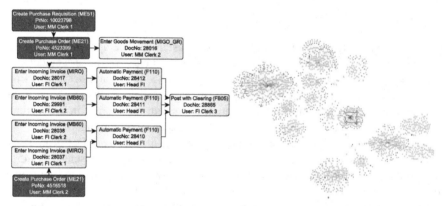

Fig. 1. (a) Instance of a Purchasing Process   (b) Complex Instance of a Purchasing Process

These process instances serve as a data basis to derive a process model by applying process mining techniques. A pre-processing of the instances is necessary to apply conventional process mining algorithms because they expect a sequential, timestamp-based event log as input. The instances constructed with FPM are graphs and therefore need to be mapped to a sequential event log structure, e.g. MXML [48].

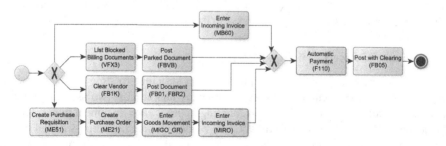

Fig. 2. Simplified process model for transactions of the "Trade Payable Domestic" account

Fig. 2 depicts a process model in the business process modelling notation (BPMN) created with the fuzzy miner [49]. The model is derived from all process instances that have posted to a particular balance sheet account (1650100 – "Trade Payables Domestic") in the organisation of the case study throughout one financial year. The instance in Fig. 1 (a) is covered by the process model as all activities and links are included. Such models are enriched by our method with information about ACs.

4.2   Extracting Information about Application Controls

As explained earlier, ACs are directly embedded in IS and configured by customizing settings. From an audit perspective there are two aspects that need to be considered during an audit of this type of controls. In a first step, it needs to be reviewed whether the AC is appropriately configured. The auditor checks this by reviewing the corresponding customizing settings. This audit step has to be done only once unless there are changes to the settings [22]. However, this check does not reveal subsequent changes of relevant settings throughout the time period under audit [10]. Hence, in a second step the auditor needs to review the change log of the customizing settings for non-compliant changes [35]. As the customizing settings and the change log are electronically stored in database tables in the ERP system, an analysis software like the ERP AuditLab presented in [5] can facilitate the audit of ACs. It uses the remote function call mechanism (RFC) provided by the ERP system. Based on the extracted tables it constructs so called data objects, each representing the current settings of a particular AC. With the help of pre-defined rules and default values the settings are evaluated from an audit perspective and an audit result is automatically derived. For a detailed description refer to [5]. Extending this technique to the audit trail of the customizing tables allows reconstructing not only the current status of an AC but also previous settings throughout the audit period. Doing so, the same rules and default values can be applied for the evaluation of former states.

4.3   Enriching Process Models with Application Controls

As described in section 2.1, controls can be process independent or directly integrated into a particular business process [20], [19], [21]. Process inherent application controls refer to the input, processing and output of a process. Process independent application controls do not relate to a specific processing phase in the IS but rather enclose the process as a whole and ensure that information is accurately and completely sent/received and protected from unauthorised access, e.g. reconciliations of data transfer between IS, segregation of duties (SoD) [22]. In the audit domain, process inherent controls are considered as a specific type of process activity when it comes to process modelling [50], [19]. However, as ACs are provided inherently through the IS these controls are in general not explicitly modelled as activities in a process model at design time. So they are not subject to forward compliance checking. At the same time, the execution of an AC itself do not generate an entry in the event log of the IS. Hence, considering this kind of controls in backward compliance checking and process mining is not possible. To close this gap three modelling patterns for process inherent ACs are designed. These patterns are based on the control pattern presented in [51] and the point in time a control is performed. Within these patterns ACs are modelled as new activities to reflect the understanding of ACs in the audit domain and to make them available to control flow based compliance checking techniques:

- **Preventive Control Pattern:** The control ensures that a check routine is automatically executed in conjunction with a certain process activity. Only in case the check routine passes successfully, the activity can be completed. The check routine refers either to the processing logic of the activity or processed data objects.
  Example: On entering an invoice a check is executed indicating potential double invoices.
- **Detective Control Pattern:** The control ensures that a check is executed after a certain process activity is completed. If the check routine identifies an exception, a corrective action is taken. The check refers to data objects created or modified by the activity.
  Example: After processing a batch of invoices for payment the totals of invoice and payment amounts are compared.
- **Required Activity Pattern:** The control ensures that a certain activity (conditionally) occurs (or is absent) if an activity has been performed in the business process.
  Example: On entering a purchase order an approval step can be configured as a mandatory step depending on the value of the purchase order.

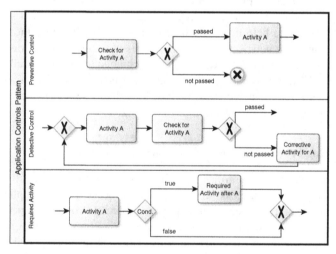

Fig. 3. Process fragments for process inherent application controls

Fig. 3 presents these patterns modelled as process fragments in BPMN. Process fragments are reusable process structures or building blocks that can be inserted into an existing process model [52]. To enable reuse the fragment needs to be specified on an abstract level. Preventive and detective control patterns are modelled as new activities (*Check for Activity A*). In case of a preventive AC the activity is added prior to the activity it refers to (*Activity A*). The process stops if the check is not successfully passed (*Cancel End Event*) and activity A is not completed. A detective AC is invoked after completing the activity it refers to (*Activity A*). Depending on the result of the check a corrective action is taken (*Corrective Activity for A*) or the next activity succeeding activity A in the original process model is executed. An application control complying with the required activity pattern adds an activity (*Required Activity after A*) directly succeeding the activity it refers to (*Activity A*). If applicable for the AC a condition can be added.

These patterns and corresponding process fragments are now used to enrich an existing process model. Input for this enrichment is – besides a given process model – a repository of ACs provided by the IS under audit. Software like the ERP AuditLab described in section 4.2 can provide such a repository. For each AC a list of activities (functionalities of the IS) is maintained that invoke the particular AC. Additionally, the abstract pattern to which an AC corresponds is added to the AC repository. Auditors/ software suppliers can provide both details. SAP ERP provides among many others following three ACs. Similar ACs are also available in other ERP systems:

1. **Double Invoice Check:** Application Controls Pattern: Preventive Control
   Invoked by: *Enter Incoming Invoice (MB60), Enter Incoming Invoice (MIRO), (...)*
2. **3-Way-Match:** Application Controls Pattern: Preventive Control
   Invoked by: *Enter Incoming Invoice (MIRO), (...)*
3. **Approval for Purchase Orders:** Application Controls Pattern: Required Activity
   Invoked by: *Create Purchase Order (ME21), (...)*

Following steps are performed for a given process model and AC repository:

- For each activity in the process model related ACs are derived.
- For each identified AC a compliance check is performed as described in section 4.2. All ACs that are not appropriately configured are disregarded.
- For each remaining activity-application control combination the corresponding abstract process fragment is instantiated with concrete values of the ACs (e.g. *Check for A* is replaced by *Double Invoice Check*) and added to the given process model. In case two or more ACs refer to the same process activity, the fragments are sequentially linked. In case an AC refers to more the one activity in the process, the fragment is added multiple times.

Fig. 4 illustrates the resulting process model after applying these steps to the process model of the "Trade Payable Domestic" account given in Fig. 2. Based on such an enriched process model a more comprehensive automated compliance checking can be performed, especially regarding compliance rules validating the existence or absence of certain activities, e.g. *"purchase orders have to be approved"* (for an overview of control flow oriented compliance rules refer to [30]).

To facilitate the interpretation of the process model by human auditors an annotation can be added to process fragments containing additional audit relevant information. Exemplarily, in Fig. 4 the date is added since when the AC is configured appropriately. This information is derived from the change log of the customizing settings.

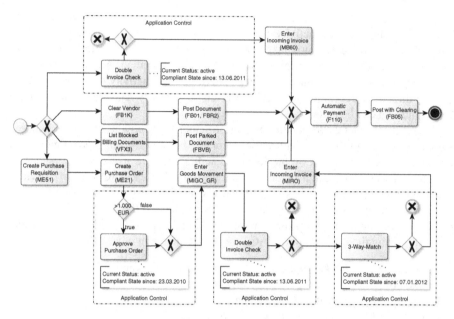

Fig. 4. Enriched process model for transactions of the "Trade Payable Domestic" account

In the paper a process model derived with process mining techniques is used as a basis. However, the method to enrich process models can obviously also be applied to already available process models.

5   Evaluation with a Case Study

The evaluation of the presented method is based on data from a big news-agency that uses SAP ECC 6.0 for its accounting and purchasing function. Transactional data related to both functions (e.g. purchase requisitions, purchase orders, goods receipt, invoices, and payments) for the fiscal year 2011 is extracted. Furthermore the customizing tables for 30 AC tests implemented in the ERP AuditLab (see section 4.2) and the corresponding change log are stored. To keep the case as clear as possible, only process instances are considered that relate to a predefined balance sheet account (1650100 – "Trade Payables Domestic"). This reflects the approach of auditors who define their audit scope based on balance sheet accounts. In total, the extracted data includes 3,412 accounting and 409 purchasing documents. Based on this data, the FPM algorithm generates 1,533 process instances. To facilitate comprehensibility the case only includes the three ACs listed in section 4.3 (Double Invoice Check, 3-Way-Match, Purchase Order Approval).

In terms of artefact evaluation Peffers et al. (2007) distinguish between two activities: demonstration and evaluation [53]. The first activity aims at demonstrating that the designed artefact solves an instance of the addressed problem and achieves its purpose. The demonstration for our artefact is outlined in section 4 by applying the method in a real life setting. In the second step it should be evaluated "[...] how well the artefact supports a solution to the problem" [53]. As the method focuses on auditors as main stakeholders, five external and one internal auditor are independently interviewed to evaluate the utility of the designed method. All auditors are knowledgeable about process audits and audits of IS. At first, a short description of the case, the process model depicted in Fig. 2, and the report for the three ACs produced by the ERP AuditLab are provided. The auditors are asked to outline their audit plan for the given process as part of an annual audit. In a second step, the auditors receive the enriched process model presented in Fig. 4. They were asked to compare both documentations and describe to what extent they would adjust their audit plan. For both steps a think-aloud protocol was recorded [46]. Following main statements are derived from the auditors:

- Both documentations provide an improved basis for process audits in an ERP environment compared to rather manual methods prevalent in current audit practice.
- Both documentations facilitate to focus on areas with higher risks when preparing an audit plan. All auditors agreed that they would mainly focus on the process sequences *Clear Vendor (FB1K)* → *Post Document (FB01, FBR2)* → *Automatic Payment (F110)* and *List Blocked Billing Documents (VFX3)* → *Post Parked Document (FBVB)* → *Automatic Payment (F110)* as they represent unusual resp. unexpected transactions.
- The definition of an audit scope is better supported by the enriched process model as it also intuitively indicates less controlled process sequences.
- The auditors stated that in practice reviews of ACs and process audits are performed by different auditors (process auditor and IS auditor). Against this background the enriched process model helps process auditors to abstract from technical aspects of ACs. In this context, the annotation of ACs was highlighted as valuable for process audits (e.g. date of last change of an application control).
- As main disadvantage all auditors mention the increased complexity of the enriched process model although only three ACs are added. They suggest presenting ACs related information on different detail levels. Besides, adding ACs is only one aspect in order to facilitate a comprehensive process audit. Manual controls need to be included as well.

6   Conclusion and Future Research

In today's complex and fast changing markets auditors play a crucial role for enhancing mutual trust between organizations. Due to comprehensive support of business processes with IS the amount of audit relevant information is steadily increasing. However, current audit practice encompasses predominately manual procedures. Against this background, many research endeavours have been undertaken to provide IS support for auditors. Developed solutions mostly focus on individual audit tasks. Up to now, an integrated view on interrelated audit tasks has not yet been taken. For example, several approaches for compliance checking of business processes or customizing of IS are discussed in literature. Nonetheless, the former approaches neglect audit relevant information about underlying IS constituting the context in which the process is executed. The later do not link the results to affected business processes.

To address this gap this paper has outlined a method that aims at automatically enriching process models with audit relevant information about ACs configured in an ERP system. The method consists of three phases. In a first step, a process model is automatically constructed based transactional data stored in an ERP system. Secondly relevant ACs are evaluated from an audit perspective. These results are then embedded in the before constructed process model. The method utilizes two already existing IS artefacts and combines them to provide a more comprehensive data basis for automated compliance checking approaches. Furthermore, the evaluation reveals that the enriched process models are a valuable support for auditors to conduct process audits in ERP environments.

There are several opportunities for further research work. The presented method is limited to electronically available data stored in ERP systems. As already mentioned by the auditors in the evaluation phase, methods for the integration of manual controls could be a valuable contribution. Current research activities are already addressing this topic [54]. The same applies to ACs that are process independent. Furthermore, the interrelation between process inherent controls and general controls related to the ERP system (e.g. change management controls, configuration of logging mechanisms) could be considered for a more comprehensive audit support. As the evaluation reveals, the appropriate presentation of audit relevant data in the context of process audits for the targeted audience (e.g. level of detail) is a reasonable research area. However, based on the evaluation results the author believes that the presented method is a useful step towards a comprehensive IS support for process audits.

References

1. Lickel, C.W.: Introduction. IBM Systems Journal 46, 1 (2007)
2. Liu, Y., Muller, S., Xu, K.: A static compliance-checking framework for business process models. IBM Systems Journal 46, 335–361 (2007)
3. van der Werf, J.M.E.M., Verbeek, H.M.W., van der Aalst, W.M.P.: Context-Aware Compliance Checking. In: Barros, A., Gal, A., Kindler, E. (eds.) BPM 2012. LNCS, vol. 7481, pp. 98–113. Springer, Heidelberg (2012)
4. Ramezani, E., Fahland, D., van der Werf, J.M., Mattheis, P.: Separating Compliance Management and Business Process Management. In: Daniel, F., Barkaoui, K., Dustdar, S. (eds.) BPM Workshops 2011, Part II. LNBIP, vol. 100, pp. 459–464. Springer, Heidelberg (2012)
5. Gehrke, N.: The ERP Auditlab - A Prototypical Framework for Evaluating Enterprise Resource Planning System Assurance. In: 43rd Hawaii International Conference on System Sciences (HICSS), pp. 1–9 (2010)
6. Van der Aalst, W., van Hee, K., van der Werf, J.M., Kumar, A., Verdonk, M.: Conceptual model for online auditing. Decision Support Systems 50, 636–647 (2011)
7. Asprion, P., Knolmayer, G.: Compliance und ERP-Systeme: Eine bivalente Beziehung. Controlling & Management 53, 40–47 (2009)

8. IT Governance Institute (ITGI): IT control objectives for Sarbanes-Oxley: the role of IT in the design and implementation of internal control over financial reporting. IT Governance Institute, Rolling Meadows, IL (2006)

9. Bellino, C., Wells, J., Hunt, S.: Global Technology Audit Guide (GTAG) 8: Auditing Application Controls (2007)

10. Jans, M., Alles, M., Vasarhelyi, M.: Process mining of event logs in auditing: Opportunities and challenges. In: International Symposium on Accounting Information Systems, Orlando (2010)

11. Caron, F., Vanthienen, J.: Applications of Business Process Analytics and Mining for Internal Control. ISACA Journal 4 (2012)

12. Kerr, D., Houghton, L., Burgess, K.: Power Relationships that lead to the Development of Feral Systems. Australasian Journal of Information Systems 14, 141–152 (2007)

13. Rosemann, M., Recker, J., Flender, C.: Contextualisation of business processes. International Journal of Business Process Integration and Management 3, 47–60 (2008)

14. Kuhn Jr., J.R., Sutton, S.G.: Continuous auditing in ERP system environments: The current state and future directions. Journal of Information Systems 24, 91–112 (2010)

15. Gehrke, N., Mueller-Wickop, N.: Basic Principles of Financial Process Mining A Journey through Financial Data in Accounting Information Systems. In: AMCIS 2010 Proceedings (2010)

16. Becker, J., Delfmann, P., Eggert, M., Schwittay, S.: Generalizability and Applicability of Model-Based Business Process Compliance-Checking Approaches – A State-of-the-Art Analysis and Research Roadmap. BuR - Business Research 5, 221–247 (2012)

17. Committee of Sponsoring Organizations of the Treadway Commission, C.: Internal Control - Integrated Framework (1992), http://www.coso.org

18. Gelinas, U.: Business processes and information technology. Thomson/South-Western, Mason Ohio (2004)

19. Strecker, S., Heise, D., Frank, U.: Prolegomena of a modelling method in support of audit risk assessment - Outline of a domain-specific modelling language for internal controls and internal control systems. Enterprise Modelling and Information Systems Architectures 6, 5–24 (2011)

20. Institut der Wirtschaftsprüfer in Deutschland e.V (IDW): PS 261 Feststellung und Beurteilung von Fehlerrisiken und Reaktionen des Abschlussprüfers auf die beurteilten Fehlerrisiken (2009)

21. Elder, R.J., Beasley, M.S., Arens, A.A.: Auditing and assurance services: an integrated approach. Pearson, Boston (2010)

22. Information Systems Audit and Control Association (ISACA): COBIT and Application Controls: A Management Guide (2009), http://www.isaca.org/Knowledge-Center/Research/ResearchDeliverables/Pages/COBIT-and-Application-Controls-A-Management-Guide.aspx

23. Bodnar, G.H., Hopwood, W.S.: Accounting information systems. Pearson, Upper Saddle River (2012)

24. International Auditing and Assurance Standards Board (IAASB): ISA 315 - Identifying and Assessing the risks of Material Misstatement through Understanding the Entity and its Environment (2009)

25. Bell, T.: Auditing Organizations Through a Strategic-Systems Lens: The KPMG Business Measurement Process. University of Illinois Press, Urbana Ill (1997)

26. Ruhnke, K.: Business Risk Audits: State of the Art und Entwicklungsperspektiven. Journal für Betriebswirtschaft 56, 189–218 (2006)

27. Stuart, I.C.: Auditing and assurance services: an applied approach. McGraw-Hill Irwin, New York (2012)
28. El Kharbili, M., De Medeiros, A.A., Stein, S., van Der Aalst, W.M.P.: Business process compliance checking: Current state and future challenges. In: Loos, P. (ed.) Modelling Business Information Systems (MoBIS 2008), pp. 107–113 (2008)
29. Ly, L.T., Rinderle-Ma, S., Göser, K., Dadam, P.: On enabling integrated process compliance with semantic constraints in process management systems. Inf. Syst. Front. 14, 195–219 (2012)
30. Ramezani, E., Fahland, D., van der Aalst, W.M.P.: Where Did I Misbehave? Diagnostic Information in Compliance Checking. In: Barros, A., Gal, A., Kindler, E. (eds.) BPM 2012. LNCS, vol. 7481, pp. 262–278. Springer, Heidelberg (2012)
31. Rosemann, M., Recker, J.C.: Context-aware process design: Exploring the extrinsic drivers for process flexibility. In: The 18th International Conference on Advanced Information Systems Engineering. Proceedings of Workshops and Doctoral Consortium, pp. 149–158 (2006)
32. Monakova, G., Kopp, O., Leymann, F., Moser, S., Schäfers, K.: Verifying Business Rules Using an SMT Solver for BPEL Processes. In: Business Process and Services Computing Conference, BPSC 2009 (2009)
33. Knuplesch, D., Ly, L.T., Rinderle-Ma, S., Pfeifer, H., Dadam, P.: On Enabling Data-Aware Compliance Checking of Business Process Models. In: Parsons, J., Saeki, M., Shoval, P., Woo, C., Wand, Y. (eds.) ER 2010. LNCS, vol. 6412, pp. 332–346. Springer, Heidelberg (2010)
34. Wolter, C., Miseldine, P., Meinel, C.: Verification of Business Process Entailment Constraints Using SPIN. In: Massacci, F., Redwine Jr., S.T., Zannone, N. (eds.) ESSoS 2009. LNCS, vol. 5429, pp. 1–15. Springer, Heidelberg (2009)
35. Alles, M., Brennan, G., Kogan, A., Vasarhelyi, M.A.: Continuous monitoring of business process controls: A pilot implementation of a continuous auditing system at Siemens. International Journal of Accounting Information Systems 7, 137–161 (2006)
36. van der Aalst, W.M.P., et al.: Process Mining Manifesto. In: Daniel, F., Barkaoui, K., Dustdar, S. (eds.) BPM Workshops 2011, Part I. Lecture Notes in Business Information Processing, vol. 99, pp. 169–194. Springer, Heidelberg (2012)
37. Van der Aalst, W.M.P., van Hee, K.M., van Werf, J.M., Verdonk, M.: Auditing 2.0: Using Process Mining to Support Tomorrow's Auditor. Computer 43, 90–93 (2010)
38. Tiwari, A., Turner, C.J., Majeed, B.: A review of business process mining: state-of-the-art and future trends. Business Process Management Journal 14, 5–22 (2008)
39. Jans, M., Alles, M., Vasarhelyi, M.: The case for process mining in auditing: Sources of value added and areas of application. International Journal of Accounting Information Systems 14, 1–20 (2013)
40. Jans, M., Alles, M., Vasarhelyi, M.: Process Mining of Event Logs in Internal Auditing: A Case Study. In: 2nd International Symposium on Accounting Information Systems, Rome (2011)
41. March, S.T., Smith, G.F.: Design and natural science research on information technology. Decis. Support Syst. 15, 251–266 (1995)
42. Hevner, A.R., March, S.T., Park, J., Ram, S.: Design science in information systems research. MIS Quarterly 28, 75–105 (2004)
43. Österle, H., Becker, J., Frank, U., Hess, T., Karagiannis, D., Krcmar, H., Loos, P., Mertens, P., Oberweis, A., Sinz, E.J.: Memorandum zur gestaltungsorientierten Wirtschaftsinformatik. Schmalenbachs Zeitschrift für Betriebswirtschaftliche Forschung 62, 662–672 (2010)

44. Peffers, K., Rothenberger, M., Tuunanen, T., Vaezi, R.: Design science research evaluation. In: Peffers, K., Rothenberger, M., Kuechler, B. (eds.) DESRIST 2012. LNCS, vol. 7286, pp. 398–410. Springer, Heidelberg (2012)
45. Venable, J., Pries-Heje, J., Baskerville, R.: A Comprehensive Framework for Evaluation in Design Science Research. In: Peffers, K., Rothenberger, M., Kuechler, B. (eds.) DESRIST 2012. LNCS, vol. 7286, pp. 423–438. Springer, Heidelberg (2012)
46. Yin, R.K.: Case study research: design and methods. Sage Publications, Los Angeles (2009)
47. Romney, M.B., Steinbart, P.J.: Accounting Information Systems. Prentice Hall (2008)
48. Van Dongen, B., van der Aalst, W.M.P.: A Meta Model for Process Mining Data. In: Conference on Advanced Information Systems Engineering (2005)
49. Günther, C.W., van der Aalst, W.M.P.: Fuzzy Mining – Adaptive Process Simplification Based on Multi-perspective Metrics. In: Alonso, G., Dadam, P., Rosemann, M. (eds.) BPM 2007. LNCS, vol. 4714, pp. 328–343. Springer, Heidelberg (2007)
50. Schultz, M., Müller-Wickop, N., Nüttgens, M.: Key Information Requirements for Process Audits - an Expert Perspective. In: EMISA, pp. 137–150 (2012)
51. Namiri, K., Stojanovic, N.: Pattern-Based Design and Validation of Business Process Compliance. In: Meersman, R., Tari, Z. (eds.) OTM 2007, Part I. LNCS, vol. 4803, pp. 59–76. Springer, Heidelberg (2007)
52. Schumm, D., Turetken, O., Kokash, N., Elgammal, A., Leymann, F., van den Heuvel, W.-J.: Business Process Compliance through Reusable Units of Compliant Processes. In: Daniel, F., Facca, F.M. (eds.) ICWE 2010. LNCS, vol. 6385, pp. 325–337. Springer, Heidelberg (2010)
53. Peffers, K., Tuunanen, T., Rothenberger, M.A., Chatterjee, S.: A Design Science Research Methodology for Information Systems Research. Journal of Management Information Systems 24, 45–77 (2007)
54. Leist, S., Lichtenegger, W.: Integration automatisch generierter und manuell konstruierter Prozessmodelle. In: Engels, G., Karagiannis, D., Mayer, H.C. (eds.) Modellierung 2010, Klagenfurt, March 24-26. LNI, vol. 161, pp. 99–116. Ges. für Informatik, Bonn (2010)

Rethinking Design Theory in Information Systems

John R. Venable

Curtin University, School of Information Systems, Perth, Western Australia, Australia
j.venable@curtin.edu.au

Abstract. Design Theory has been written about extensively in Information Systems (IS), but remains heavily problematic. Some researchers explicitly exclude design theory as an outcome of Design Science Research (DSR), others disagree about the form and purpose of design theories, many consider design theories to be too complicated to construct, some journal editors and researchers give low priority to design theory, and very few DSR publications propose design theories.

This paper reviews and critically examines the IS literature on design theories, the nature of technological design artefacts compared to phenomena in the natural, biological, and social domains, and whether design theory is 'prescriptive' or 'explanatory'.

Using a DSR approach, the paper makes recommendations concerning the form and use of design theory, in order to move toward a resolution of the disagreements about design theory and progress the development of clearer and more useful formalisations of knowledge for practical use.

Keywords: Design Theory, Design Science Research, Utility Theory, Information System.

1 Introduction

Over the past 20 years and with gathering momentum, the field of Information Systems (IS) has discussed and developed Design Science Research (DSR) [1-3] as an alternative research paradigm to positivist, interpretive, and critical research [4-5]. As described in the Information Systems literature, DSR is concerned with the development of new ways (or artefacts) to solve problems and make improvements [1-3]. Venable and Baskerville [5] have given one of the few definitions of DSR, which they define as "Research that invents a new purposeful artefact to address a generalised type of problem and evaluates its utility for solving problems of that type".

A Design Theory (DT) is a formalised statement of the knowledge that has been created through DSR. Since theory is a key output of rigorous academic research, one would expect the production of DT to be a key element of DSR [6]. The Information Systems field has written extensively about DT [1], [6-14]. In Gregor's [9] classification of theory in Information Systems, Design Theories are Type V theories: Theories for Design and Action.

However, Design Theory remains hugely problematic and controversial in DSR, with fundamental unresolved disagreements that significantly hinder its progress and

J. vom Brocke et al. (Eds.): DESRIST 2013, LNCS 7939, pp. 136–149, 2013.

practice. Key DSR exponents explicitly state that theory is not an outcome of DSR [2] and one of the most cited IS papers ever in our most prestigious journal, MIS Quarterly, Hevner et al [1] omit design theory as a research output. Hooker [15] asks whether design theory is possible and takes a rather pessimistic position, providing a few suggestions that bear little or no relation to other formulations of DT. Even when the existence and appropriateness of DT is agreed, there is disagreement about the form and purpose of design theories, with Walls et al [13] and Gregor and Jones [9-10] asserting that it is prescriptive, Venable [6] asserting that it is not prescriptive, but rather should formulate a utility theory, and Baskerville and Pries-Heje [7] asserting that it should be explanatory. Also, a recent survey on opinions about standards of Design Science Research found that journal editors and DSR practitioners gave very low priority to the production of design theories as an outcome of DSR and pointed out the opinion of some DSR researchers that design theories are too complicated to construct, providing a further disincentive to their use [16].

Most importantly, DT is only rarely an output of DSR. Walls et al [14] revisited their proposal for Information Systems Design Theory (ISDT) 12 years earlier ([13]) to examine how well their ideas had been taken up by the IS field. They found only 26 articles that had referenced their 1992 paper [13]. Of those 26, only four "used the ISDT concept extensively". Of those four, two formulated design theories were substantially incomplete and only two papers, by Markus et al. [12] and Hall et al. [17], substantially used all parts of their formulation of ISDTs. More recently, of the five papers in the MISQ special issue on DSR (2008), only one paper explicitly produced a design theory.

To summarise, the above discussion points out that (at least) four important problems remain concerning design theories in the IS field that inhibit their effective use in DSR.

1. There is fundamental disagreement about whether design theory is actually theory at all or should be an output of DSR.
2. There is disagreement about the purpose, nature, content and form design theories (assuming they are theories) should have.
3. IS journal editors and DSR practitioners give design theories low priority.
4. There is disturbingly low usage of design theory concepts and development of design theories in IS DSR publications.

The first two problems likely cause the latter two and the third problem certainly contributes to the final one.

This paper attempts to address these problems by reconsidering the nature and formulation of design theories in a way that will facilitate clearer understanding of their nature and what would make a good design theory. The paper attempts to answer the following research question.

"What understanding of the nature, properties, and formulation of a design theory would resolve the above problems and more effectively achieve the purpose of design theory?"

The next section critiques the literature on design theory, pointing out specific issues. Following that, section 3 adopts a DSR approach to make some proposals for an alternative formulation of design theories. Finally, the last section briefly summarises the paper's findings and proposes areas for further research and community action.

2   Critique of the Design Theory Literature

As highlighted above, the IS literature on Design Theory has many contradictions. This section critically reviews the DT literature and the nature of design theory to help resolve the contradictions and to clear up some misunderstandings that may get in the way of formulating a clearer conception of DT and a formulation that is more suitable for the developers and users of DT.

2.1   Design Theory vs. Theory in the Natural and Behavioural Sciences

March and Smith [2] assert that Design Science (Research) does not produce theory; only natural and behavioural sciences produce theory. This can be illustrated with several quotes. "Natural science is concerned with explaining how and why things are. Design science is concerned with 'devising artifacts to attain goals'" (p. 253, quoting Simon, 2nd edition, p. 133). "Rather than producing general theoretical knowledge, design scientists produce and apply knowledge of tasks or situations in order to create effective artifacts" (p. 253). For March and Smith [2], theory is not part of Design Science; theories are "deep, principled explanations of phenomena" (p. 253), which are developed by Natural Science. In summary, according to March and Smith [2], while design artefacts are evaluated for their utility in Design Science, explaining that utility (or lack of it) through theorising and justification is the province of Natural Science.

But why shouldn't theorising and theory justification be the province of DSR as well as natural and behavioural sciences? One possible explanation for March and Smith's position is the dynamic, temporal nature of the utility of technological artefacts. Despite the dynamic nature of the world, natural and behavioural science theories are expected to be timeless in nature. The way physics or chemistry works doesn't change over time. The way the human brain works and people behave individually or in groups don't change over time. Of course our *understanding* of physics, chemistry, psychology, sociology, etc., as formulated in theories, does change over time, but it is not the phenomena themselves as described or explained by the theories that change. Should a natural or behavioural science theory become invalid, it is because of better research, not because the phenomena they describe have changed.

In contrast, design theories cannot be timeless because their appropriateness and truth depend upon the state of the world, which is in a constant state of flux. First, new artefacts are invented that supplement or replace existing artefacts, thereby invalidating or requiring modification of corresponding design theories that assert an artefact should be used to achieve a given purpose. Second, the appropriateness of design theories often depends on many unstated assumptions about the nature and content of the social world in which they and the artefacts they describe exist. Organisational contexts constantly change as people come and go, departments and divisions are reorganised, new work processes come into being and older ones are modified or discarded, or organisations merge or fail and their existence ends. People's expectations of what they want and what they expect change as well. Culture itself undergoes somewhat slower change, but new generations often seem to change quite dramatically (as seen from the outside, generally not from the inside!).

Importantly, design theories must keep up with these changes. A design theory that is true and suggests or recommends one solution to a set of circumstances today, may become false and inappropriate tomorrow, depending on what changes in the world.

For example, consider that back only a couple of hundred years ago, if you wanted to communicate fast to someone at a long distance, say a hundred miles or more (a purpose and scope or general requirements), a prescriptive design theory might have stated that you should use a carrier pigeon. Of course, one must further specify in the scope of the general requirements that the communication could only be of a certain size and weight, or that the meta-design or general design should include ways to write very small and on very lightweight paper or the like.

Alternatively, one could have organised something like the American Pony Express, in which riders rode very fast, carried mail over shorter distances, and regularly changed horses and/or handed over the mail to other riders. Of course, such a design theory would need to include in its scope the constraint that such an approach could not be used over water or through enemy territory (unlike the carrier pigeon).

Later, a new technology became available – the telegraph. The telegraph allowed new design theories to join the field and compete with other design theories. Note that one could still use carrier pigeons or signal fires, but there was less benefit in doing so, particularly as the accessibility of telegraph service increased and the cost decreased. Note that these last two factors are more social in nature rather than being about the technology per se.

Later still, the telephone with voice communication became possible and even later widely accessible, again adding to the space of design theories and changing the balance of what was accepted and useful. At the outset, many people resented the imposition of a telephone in their home – how dare people phone when we're having dinner? Indeed many people still resent it, which is why answering machines and caller ID have become so popular.

Still later, wireless communication became possible, first wireless Morse code, then wireless voice, then television, then email, then satellite communication, then … Facebook. One wonders if it will ever end.

The point is that for each of these technological changes and improvements, there are new possibilities in the solution space of competing design theories. Moreover, for each of them, there are somewhat slower, but nevertheless present changes in the problem space, as expectations and the culture change. Many in the younger generations today only rarely use email and only if forced to do so by us fuddy duddies in the older generation!

All of this can be modelled using something like the flux of events and ideas unfolding over time, as described by Peter Checkland [18]. Each new technology artefact creates a change to the life world of the set of extant design theories, which influences the perceptions of others in the world, including both the design scientists and the practitioners that build new technologies and new design theories, as well as the practitioners who use the design theories. In doing so, culture and expectations also change, with somewhat of a lag and at a slower, but sometimes fairly fast, pace.

Design theories (using currently accepted formulations) may gradually (or even quickly) become invalid in the face of such change. As usually formulated, DTs therefore cannot be timeless in the way that natural and behavioural science theories are in the face of changes in technologies, organisational purposes, and cultural expectations, and their truth is therefore more transitory or even ephemeral. Such a difference may explain why some researchers do not consider design theories to be theory at all or to be a sensible output of DSR.

Importantly, the above discussion relates to the idea of a 'prescriptive' design theory, as discussed in the next section.

The lack of timelessness of design theory, in comparison to theories in the natural and behavioural sciences, can be addressed by changing the definition and formulation of design theory, as will be shown in section 3, which will help address the difference of opinion about whether design theories are appropriate at all.

2.2   Design Theory Is Not Prescriptive

Major works describing design theory, including Walls et al [13] and Gregor and Jones [10], assert that design theories are prescriptive. Baskerville and Pries-Heje [7] note that "design theory is assumed by many to be prescriptive" and do not contradict this. In contrast, Venable [6] asserts that design theories are not prescriptive, but should instead be of the nature and in the form of utility theories.

There are (at least) five reasons why design theories should not and cannot be prescriptive.

First, the online Oxford dictionary [19] defines prescriptive as "relating to the imposition or enforcement of a rule or method". Similar definitions can be found in any English language dictionary. Consulting a thesaurus [20], synonyms for prescriptive include dictatorial, rigid, authoritarian, legislating, dogmatic, and didactic, none of which seem to suit the nature of design theories. The authors of a design theory have no power to impose or enforce the design theory. Professional bodies might have such a power, but in most if not all fields (including the IS field), this is not the case. Therefore, a design theory cannot be prescriptive. Some may argue that 'prescriptive' means something less restrictive in the case of design theory, but this has not been adequately explained and also conflicts with the common meaning of the term, even though other terms may be more appropriate and meaningfully correct.

Second, while stating that design theories are prescriptive in their paper setting out their original formulation and explanation of design theories, Walls et al. [14] describe DTs in a way that indicates that they are not prescriptive. They state that "a design theory is a prescriptive theory based on theoretical underpinnings which says how a design process can be carried out in a way which is both effective and feasible" ([13], emphasis added). "Can" be carried out is very different from "must" be carried out, which indicates that Walls et al. [13] don't actually consider a design theory to be prescriptive in the sense described above.

Third, Herbert Simon [21] argued that "So called 'figures of merit' [which are measures of utility] permit comparison between designs in terms of 'better' and 'worse' but seldom provide a judgment of 'best'" (p. 119).

Fourth, and perhaps most importantly, prescriptions are (or should) only be made for specific instances of a problem by a practitioner, based on their judgment, not applied in all instances. Instead, a design theory is (potentially) relevant to a class of problems (or to a set of instances of that class of problem), but may not be suitable for a specific instance of a problem. Furthermore, any particular design theory competes with other design theories that might be followed. There are better and worse matches of the different design theories to the particular circumstances motivating action. Moreover, the particular action(s) taken need to be in accord with other constraints and requirements that may not be addressed in the design theory.

For example, a doctor may have several different treatments to choose from to treat pain, as described in the medical literature and product descriptions (which constitute at least partial design theories, even if not stated as such). However, various aspects not considered in the design theory may come into play, such as drug availability and cost to the patient, which influence the doctor's decision. Certainly not all relevant design theories for the treatment of pain would or should be followed, therefore design theories are not prescriptive.

Fifth and finally, the idea of a prescriptive theory setting out *the one, best artefact* or way to address a problem or reach a goal is inconsistent with the dynamic nature of the state of the art in DSR as described in the previous section. The more prescriptive the nature of a design theory is touted to be, the more subject to becoming outdated it will be.

Instead of being prescriptive, a design theory should only recommend or suggest a *possible* action (from among many possible actions). This distinction is important, as will be shown in section 3 of this paper.

2.3   Design Theory Is Not Explanatory

An alternative to prescriptive theory is provided by Baskerville and Pries-Heje [7], who assert that, in their "explanatory design theory", the relationship between the general requirements and the general design is one of explanation. They state that "The definitions of general requirements and general components must be circular. Requirements specify (and explain) the reasons for components. Components are justified by requirements." (p. 274). Later they assert that "The explanatory design theory explains why a component is being constructed into an artefact." (p. 275).

However, the author of this paper fails to see how merely connecting two things with a binary association (see figure 3-15 in [7]) is explanatory in the ordinary sense of the word or in the sense of Type II Theory in IS: Theory for Explanation or Type IV Theory: Theory for Explanation and Prediction [9]. In the ordinary sense of the word, explanation of "the reasons for components" should include a line of reasoning as to why including a particular component or set of components (and how they combine) is effective or efficient in solving a problem or achieving a goal, not simply that it does solve the problem or achieve the goal. In line with the ordinary sense of explanation, Gregor [9] states that "Explanation is closely linked to human understanding, as an explanation can be provided with the intent of inducing a subjective state of understanding in an individual." (p. 617). She goes on to say that "The theory provides an explanation of how, why, and when things happened, relying on varying views of causality and methods for argumentation." (p. 619). This statement further supports the above notion of the need for a line of reasoning for explanation, not simply a binary link. The statement further indicates that explanatory theory explains ex post, whereas the purpose of design theory should be to advise practitioners ex ante about potential courses of action. Ultimately Gregor states that a theory for explanation "provides explanations but does not aim to predict with any precision. There are no testable propositions." (p. 620). The infeasibility of testable propositions in an explanatory theory is in direct contradiction to their inclusion in the formulations of design theory by Walls et al. [13] as well as by Gregor and Jones [10].

Hovorka et al. [22] identify four kinds of explanation in information systems theory. Among them, they identify functional explanation, which is the closest to Gregor's teleological causal analysis in type II and type IV explanatory theory [9] and to explanatory design theory [7]. However, like explanatory theory, functional explanation is used ex post to postulate the ends upon which means were chosen to indicate why something was done, which is not the intention of design theory.

Considering the issue further, "general components" in Baskerville and Pries-Heje's [7] formulation of explanatory design theory constitute the means to achieve the ends described in their "general requirements". If we substitute the terms "means" for "general components" and "ends" for "general requirements", then we could restate this design theory formulation as "The ends explain the means.", which doesn't make sense. According to the description in Baskerville and Pries-Heje [7], the meaning of the arrow in the opposite direction would be that "The means are justified by the ends.", but this also does not make sense. While explanation and justification are desirable, this relationship doesn't seem to provide either explanation or justification, which instead require a line of reasoning or argumentation. Such a connection simply asserts that the means may be appropriately chosen to achieve the ends, but it does not explain why the choice is a good one or why the means will achieve the end – i.e. how they work to achieve that end.

Rather than describing design theory as containing a relationship that is explanatory, this paper will propose that the relationship in design theory should instead be an assertion of utility, as will be described in section 3.

2.4   Design Theory Is Unnecessarily Complex and Cumbersome

The main, accepted formulations of design theory ([10], [13]) can be (and have been) criticised as being unnecessarily complex and cumbersome. The Walls et al. [13] formulation of ISDT has seven parts as shown in figure 1 below, while the Gregor and Jones [10] formulation has eight parts as shown in table 1 below (ten if one considers two kinds of kernel theory and two kinds of testable propositions). They add three new core (mandatory) theory components – constructs, principles of form and function, and artefact mutability – as well as two additional (optional) design theory components – principles of implementation and expository instantiation to the Walls et al. [13] formulation.

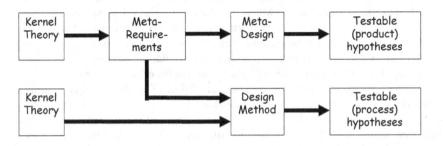

Fig. 1. Formulation of IS Design Theory [13]

Table 1. Formulation of IS Design Theory [10]

Gregor and Jones ISDT Construct	Analogous Walls et al ISDT Construct
Purpose and scope	Meta-Requirements
Constructs	Meta-Requirements, Meta-Design
Principles of form and function	Meta-Design
Artifact mutability	Meta-Design
Testable propositions	Testable product and method hypotheses
Justificatory knowledge	Kernel theories
Principles of implementation	Meta-design, Design Method
An expository instantiation	None

Several authors have criticised the complexity and difficulty of using these two formulations of design theories. Walls et al. [14], in their review of the usage of ISDTs, stated that "Some scholars appear to have some gripes with how cumbersome ISDT can be and identify some of its omissions that would facilitate usability." (p. 55)

Venable [6] criticised the complexity of ISDTs as formulated by Walls et al. [13]. He noted that kernel theories, while being helpful for providing an explanation of why a design theory should work, are sometimes unavailable and peripheral to the core of the design theory. Similarly, testable hypotheses are also peripheral and external to a theory. Finally, he noted that a design method was also unnecessary to a design theory, as a design method is itself a meta-design, but one with different meta-requirements (the need to effectively instantiate a meta-design). Instead, Venable [6] asserted that the meta-design (which he called the solution space), the meta-requirements (which he called the problem space), and the relationship between them (which he called a utility relationship) were the core of a design theory (which he termed a 'utility theory') and that such a simpler formulation was desirable.

Venable [16] later surveyed the editors (at all levels) of the IS Scholars' basket of eight journals, program committee members of DESRIST conferences, and authors of DESRIST papers concerning their opinions about standards, guidelines, and their expectations concerning DSR. One survey area concerned design theory. His study found that design theory rated lower in importance than other areas, such as the Hevner et al. [1] criteria and evaluation, as areas that should be addressed in DSR work. Concerning the components of design theory, specifying meta-requirements and meta-design (the core of design theory identified by Venable [6]) were the parts rated as most important, followed by kernel theories about the meta-requirements, then the design method, then kernel theories about the design method, and lastly the two testable hypotheses components of IDSTs being rated lowest. More importantly, there was extensive disagreement by respondents, with high standard deviations and ratings of these components by individual respondents ranging from a minimum of zero to a maximum of ten for all seven components of IDSTs.

Like Venable [6], Baskerville and Pries-Heje [7] were concerned with the complexity of design theory, stating that "the specific characteristics of design theory seem rather elaborate and overly complicated." (p. 271). Their "explanatory design theory" has only two main constructs, general requirements and general components and "their embodied relationships that explain the solution" (p. 274). While their use of "explanatory" has been criticised above, the terms "general requirements" and "general components" (being generalisations on specific, situated requirements and on specific designs for a specific solution) seem more appropriate than the terms meta-requirements and meta-design (which should literally mean requirements for requirements or design of a design). The simplicity of their design theory formulation is also commendable. However, as discussed in section 2.3 above, the use of an explanatory relationship is inappropriate.

The next section will take a DSR perspective on the design of design theory in order to reduce the complexity of design theory to a more manageable form, as well as address the concerns raised in sections 2.1-2.3.

3   A Design Science View of Design Theory

Theory, including design theory, like methods, including research methods, is a designed artefact [5]. Walls et al. [14] identified the need to improve the usability of ISDTs and propose four ways to improve their usability, including articulation strategies, tool-kit strategies, augmenting the structure of ISDTs, and ISDT evangelism. Only the third of these addresses the actual composition of ISDTs, while the others represent ancillary tools and practices. However, all of the four proposed strategies would extend the ISDT artefact as a way of improving it. As such, they apply a DSR approach to ISDTs (and ancillary tools and practices), even though the details are not worked out nor are the proposals evaluated in practice (i.e. through use in DSR).

In previous sections, this paper debated the suitability and desirable meaning, format and content of design theory. In this section, the paper applies a DSR approach to set out the meta-design [13], principles of form and function [10], solution space [6], or general design [7] for an improved version of design theories that addresses the problem discussed earlier and could be instantiated for all design theories. From a Design Science Research (DSR) perspective, one should consider what the meta-requirement [13], purpose and scope [10], problem space [6] or general requirements [7] for a design for a design theory are or should be before designing a solution.

To do so, we can first consider the question "Who are the stakeholders in and users of design theories, from whose perspective should we determine requirements?" There are (at least) two different kinds of stakeholders in design theories, practitioners, who use design theory to inform the conduct of design processes, and design science researchers, who review earlier design theories and generate new design theories (see figure 3 in [14], p. 48).

Second, we can consider the question "What is (are) the purpose(s) of design theories?" Design theories exist for several purposes. To some extent, the purpose of design theories depends on what stakeholder role a person is in. Among the relevant purposes for design theories are the following:

- Help people (practitioners) to identify *different possibilities* (candidate options) for what they might do to achieve some given purpose
- Help people (practitioners) to make better decisions about *what* they should do to achieve some given purpose, such as understanding the purpose, solving a problem, or making an improvement
- Help people (practitioners) to make better decisions about *how* they should do something to achieve some given purpose
- Help people (researchers) to understand, investigate, evaluate, and improve the truth and utility to practitioners of the design theory

Having set out some meta-requirements at a high level, some questions we could consider then would be "What are the desired properties of a design theory to achieve the above purposes?" and "What would give a design theory utility in achieving the above purposes?" We can identify several properties that would give a design theory utility for practitioners and design science researchers:

- Actionable – Design Theories should be in a form that a practitioner can use to take action.
  - Clear, understandable, and informative – The concepts and ideas of the general requirements as well as the general design must be well defined and explained and tell practitioners what they need to know. Clear names for the design theory components (e.g. "general requirements" and "general design") may be helpful.

- — Complete – All constraints and aspects of the general requirements should be included, as should all the things needed for the general solution.
- — Parsimonious – The design theory must be simple enough to understand, but not so simple that important aspects that could (seriously) affect outcomes are overlooked or omitted. Balancing this against completeness may be difficult.
- — Comparable – The design theory should be easy to compare to other design theories that attempt to achieve the same or a similar purpose. Design theorists should use language similar to that used in extant design theories whenever possible.
- Non-prescriptive – Design theories should not prescribe a particular solution, but only indicate that it is one of different possible choices, with different advantages and disadvantages with choice dependent on a number of contingent factors in the general requirements and the preferences of the practitioner or user of the design theory. This would improve the timelessness of a design theory and lessen its likelihood of obsolescence.
- Rigorously evaluated and true – The utility of the design to achieve its stated purpose should not be misrepresented. It should not give bad advice. To obtain this, the solutions in the design need to be evaluated for efficacy (benefit accrues from its use, not something else), effectiveness (practical to use in real contexts) and efficiency (resource consumption to instantiate and operate).
- Tolerant of the dynamic nature of reality – Being non-prescriptive, but concerned instead with different aspects of utility, will help make design theories somewhat more timeless, as new artefacts may have more utility, but not necessarily reduce the utility of existing artefacts to obsolescence. However, as the environment of artefact use changes, design theories will still need to be re-evaluated and possibly updated.

To meet these general requirements for design theories, this paper suggests that design theories be simplified, rather than extended as suggested by Walls et al. [14] and Gregor and Jones [10], and that the prescriptive or explanatory purposes of design theory should be replaced with a less strict statement of utility.

Herbert Simon [21] clearly considered utility to be the key relationship between the 'outer environment' (meta-requirements or generalized requirements) and the 'inner environment' (meta-design or generalized design), as measured by a utility function. Design decisions (e.g. choosing between different artefacts that have utility to achieve a purpose) require either maximizing the expected value of the relevant utility function or satisficing, i.e. choosing an artifact with an acceptable or satisfactory utility (Simon, 1996). Being able to compare different utilities for achieving the same purpose would facilitate design decisions at a high level (overall approach to achieve the purpose), while retaining a more timeless nature than a prescriptive theory.

This paper proposes a simpler design theory formulation, consisting of two main components – general requirements and general design (in line with the terminology in Baskerville and Pries-Heje [7]) together with utility relationships (in line with Venable [6]) should suffice for use in practice. The utility relationship should perhaps focus on efficacy, effectiveness, and efficiency. Note that multiple goals (general requirements) may be sought by an artefact, perhaps including secondary characteristics (e.g. security or reliability). Note as well that the need for a design method to instantiate the general design can be addressed by an additional design theory as described earlier. This has the advantage that design researchers might work to create new and better methods for designing and instantiating a particular general design.

Having identified this simpler formulation, guidance is still needed on how to clearly state the general requirement and general design. General requirements, for example, should state any constraints, as these reduce the scope of the situations for which the general design has utility. Furthermore, the general design part of the design theory formulation may be similarly expanded with concepts drawn from Gregor and Jones [10] to clarify the general design, e.g., principles of form and function or artefact mutability. Figure 2 below shows this simplified form of design theory. The bullet points provided in each box and relationship, while seemingly more complex, simply provide more detail of what is expected for each than is provided by the earlier figure from Walls et al. [13] and where aspects borrowed from Gregor and Jones [10] would fit.

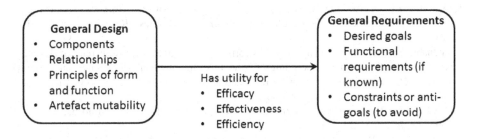

Fig. 2.   Proposed Simplified Design Theory formulation

Importantly, concepts mooted in other work that are not included in figure 2 include kernel theory/justificatory knowledge, testable hypotheses/propositions, constructs (which in any event are the terms used in the general requirement and general design), principles of implementation (which would be included in an additional design theory concerning the method for design and instantiation), and an expository instantiation. Of course any or all of these could additionally be provided, especially for purposes of academia, not practice, but would unnecessarily complicate the design theory formulation, so should be considered only as optional addenda to the core design theory described in figure 2.

4   Summary

This paper has discussed the nature and requirements of good design theory. It has critiqued the weaknesses of existing approaches. Using a DSR approach, it has examined the general requirements for a design theory and asserted the characteristics of what would make a good design theory. It has further proposed an initial, simplified general design for design theory. The simplified formulation has only two main components and one relationship, but describes what kinds of details might make up each of them. Further work needs to be done to flesh out this design for design theory and to evaluate it, using a DSR approach. Nonetheless, the work in this paper should reinvigorate the discussion on design theory and hopefully help move DSR practice to more workable and regular use and creation of design theory.

References

1. Hevner, A., March, S.T., Park, J., Ram, S.: Design Science in Information Systems Research. MIS Quarterly 28, 75–105 (2004)
2. March, S.T., Smith, G.F.: Design and natural science research on information technology. Decision Support Systems 15, 251–266 (1995)
3. Vaishnavi, V., Kuechler, W.: Design Research in Information Systems, http://www.isworld.org/Researchdesign/drisISworld.htm
4. Orlikowski, W.J., Baroudi, J.J.: Studying Information Technology in Organizations: Research Approaches and Assumptions. Information Systems Research 2, 1–28 (1991)
5. Venable, J.R., Baskerville, R.: Eating Our Own Cooking: Toward a More Rigorous Design Science of Research Methods. Electronic Journal of Business Research Methods 10, 141–153 (2012)
6. Venable, J.R.: The Role of Theory and Theorising in Design Science Research. In: Hevner, A., Chatterjee, S. (eds.) Proceedings of the First International Conference on Design Science Research in Information Systems and Technology (DESRIST 2006). Claremont Graduate University, Claremont (2006)
7. Baskerville, R., Pries-Heje, J.: Explanatory Design Theory. Business & Information Systems Engineering, 271-282 (2010)
8. Goldkuhl, G.: Design Theories in Information Systems - a Need for Multi-Grounding. JITTA: Journal of Information Technology Theory and Application 6, 59–72 (2004)
9. Gregor, S.: The Nature of Theory in Information Systems. MIS Quarterly 30, 611–642 (2006)
10. Gregor, S., Jones, D.: The Anatomy of a Design Theory. Journal of the Association for Information Systems 8, 312–335 (2007)
11. Kuechler, W., Vaishnavi, V.: On Theory Development in Design Science Research: Anatomy of a Research Project. European Journal Information Systems 17, 489–504 (2008)
12. Markus, M.L., Majchrzak, A., Gasser, L.: A design theory for systems that support emergent knowledge processes. MIS Quarterly 26, 179–212 (2002)
13. Walls, J.G., Widmeyer, G.R., El Sawy, O.A.: Building an information system design theory for vigilant EIS. Information Systems Research 3, 36–59 (1992)
14. Walls, J.G., Widmeyer, G.R., El Sawy, O.A.: Assessing Information System Design Theory in Perspective: How Useful Was Our 1992 Initial Rendition? JITTA: Journal of Information Technology Theory and Application 6, 43–58 (2004)
15. Hooker, J.N.: Is design theory possible? Journal of Information Technology Theory and Application 5, 73–82 (2004)
16. Venable, J.R.: Design Science Research Post Hevner et al.: Criteria, Standards, Guidelines, and Expectations. In: Winter, R., Zhao, J.L., Aier, S. (eds.) DESRIST 2010. LNCS, vol. 6105, pp. 109–123. Springer, Heidelberg (2010)

17. Hall, D., Paradice, D., Courtney, J.: Building a Theoretical Foundation for a Learning-Oriented Management System. JITTA:Journal of Information Technology Theory and Application 5, 63–85 (2003)
18. Checkland, P., Scholes, J.: Soft Systems Methodology in Action: A 30-Year Retrospective. Wiley, Chichester (1999)
19. Oxford Dictionary (online), http://oxforddictionaries.com/definition/prescriptive
20. Collins Thesaurus of the English Language – Complete and Unabridged 2nd Edition. HarperCollins Publishers, New York (2002)
21. Simon, H.A.: The Sciences of the Artificial, 3rd edn. MIT Press, Cambridge (1996)
22. Hovorka, D.S., Germonprez, M., Larsen, K.R.: Explanation in Information Systems. Information Systems Journal 18, 23–43 (2008)

How to Generalize an Information Technology Case Study

Rúben Pereira, Rafael Almeida, and Miguel Mira da Silva

Department of Computer Science, Instituto Superior Técnico, Lisbon, Portugal
{rubenfspereira,rafael.d.almeida,mms} @ist.utl.pt

Abstract. Case studies are a valuable way to look at the world around us and have been gaining special importance in the last years in the information technology area. However, some problems, as for example the lack of rigor or the dependency of a single case exploration, preclude case study generalization. Therefore, we propose to perform an extensive literature review about case study methodology, specifically in information technology domain, in order to leverage critical information about organizations, which should be present in all information technology case studies to enable their generalization and pattern matching. We end our research with limitations, contributions and future work.

Keywords: IT, Cast Study, IS, Organizational Context, Patterns, Generalization.

1 Introduction

Case studies are a valuable way of looking at the world around us [1][2]. Past literature reveals the application of the case study (CS) method in many areas and disciplines [3] where the researchers gain an "in-depth" understanding of complex issues, like the phenomena in a "real-life" setting [4].

In practice oriented fields of research, such as architecture, planning or even information technology (IT), the CS has a special importance [5] and different types have been used in a variety of ways in information systems (IS) research [6]. Indeed, a tremendous progress of interpretive research happened in the last 30 years in the IS community [7].

However, CSs are often accused of lack of rigor [3] making it difficult to reach a generalizing conclusion [8]. Lee [9] also pointed generalizability as a main CS problem. Another common pitfall associated with CS is that there is a tendency for researchers to attempt to answer a question that is too broad or a topic with too many goals for one study. In order to avoid this problem, several authors including Yin [10] and Stake [11] have suggested placing boundaries on a case to keep your study reasonably in scope. Plus, selecting the wrong CSs may result in a lack of theoretical generalizations [12]. Therefore, developing in-depth knowledge of theoretical and empirical literature to justify choices made is advisable.

Given such problems around CS in IT field, this article intends to contribute with the elicitation of the IT variables that should be present in any IT CS to enable the generalization. Our proposal can be used by IT CS researchers in order to add rigor to their research.

J. vom Brocke et al. (Eds.): DESRIST 2013, LNCS 7939, pp. 150–164, 2013.

2   Research Method

The research methodology that will be used in this research is Design Science Research (DSR). Toward the end of the 1990s it began growing in popularity for use in scholarly investigations in IS. DSR methodology is conducted in two complementary phases: build and evaluate. In contrast to behavior research, design-oriented research builds a "to-be" conception and then seeks to build the system according to the defined model taking into account restrictions and limitations [13]. Design science addresses research through the building and evaluation of artifacts designed to meet the identified business needs [14], instead of analyzing existing IS in order to identify causal relations [13].

In this article we build and evaluate new and innovative artifacts following the design research paradigm [14]. Based on the four design artifacts produced by design science research in IS (constructs, models, methods and instantiations), we will focus on constructs and models. Constructs are necessary to describe certain aspects of a problem domain and allow the development of the research project's terminology [15] while models use constructs to represent a real world situation, the design problem and the solution space [16]. The constructs we propose will be the IT/IS domain definition. The models will be the CS conceptual map and the identification of the IT CS variables.

As advisable by [17] the research methodology applied is divided according to the two processes of design science research in IS; build and evaluate. The build process is composed by two stages whereas the evaluation process is comprised by only one (Table 1).

Table 1. Research Methodology

BUILD		EVALUATE
Constructs Definition	**Model Construction**	**Evaluation**
- IT/IS Domain definition - CS Domain definition	- Based on the constructs produce a CS conceptual model - Main IT CS variables identification	- IT CS analysis and comparison

In this article the present artifacts were evaluated through the IT CSs analysis and comparison. In addition, by submitting these research results to respected international conferences, we have also used the appraisal of the scientific community as evaluation criteria. The diagram of the research process can be seen at Figure 1.

In order to elicit our constructs and models, a review of prior relevant literature is essential. The approach used in this paper follows the concept-centric methodology of IS literature reviews (LR) as outlined in Webster and Watson [18].

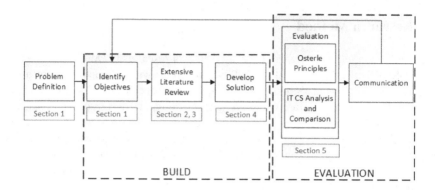

Fig. 1. Research Methodology

3   Case Study Literature Review

Past literature reveals the application of the CS method in many areas and disciplines. A CS is about the particular rather than the general [19] that can be used by researchers when: the focus of the study is to answer "how" and "why" questions [1][10]; they want to describe a theory development, in which it is used to provide evidence for hypothesis generation and for exploration of a phenomenon or process not yet theoretically understood [4][20]; they cannot manipulate the behavior of those involved in the study [10]; they want to test a certain theory [20]; they intend to explore and investigate contemporary real-life phenomenon through detailed contextual analysis of a limited number of events or conditions, and their relationships [3][21]; the boundaries are not clear between the phenomenon and context [10]; they want to describe a process or the effects of an event or an intervention, especially when such events affect many different parties [21]; or they intend to explain a complex phenomenon [21]. However, some topics about CS research are still under discussion among IT CS literature and in the next section we intend to clarify them.

The definition of CS is quite consensual among the literature [1][2][3][4][22][23]. The most used definition is provided by Yin [10], a CS is: "An empirical and holistic inquiry that investigates a contemporary phenomena within its real life context especially when the boundaries between phenomenon and context are not clearly evident". To better understand the previous CS definition it is important to go deeper into some concepts. A holistic inquiry may involve a collection of in-depth and detailed data that are rich in content and involve multiple sources of information as documents, interviews, etc. [2]. A phenomenon can be many things: a program, an event, an activity, a problem, or an individual. By real life context we mean the context within which the phenomenon appears. Context is included because contextual conditions are considered highly pertinent to the phenomenon being studied either because many factors in the setting impinge on the phenomenon or because the separation between the phenomenon and the context is not clearly evident [2].

Theory, for example, is another interesting concept about CS method. There are different perspectives for the use of theory in CSs. Stake [11] argued that theory can be absent from studies which focus on describing the case and its issues. On the contrary, Yin [10] stated that theory can be used to guide the CS in an exploratory way since it gives direction and structure to the initial set of questions the researcher asks [2]. In addition, Creswell [24] argued that theory is employed toward the end of the study providing a "theory-after" perspective in which other theories are compared and contrasted with the one developed in the CS.

However, in some cases a particular theoretical perspective can blind researchers to other perspectives at its moment of application [4][25]. The practical difficulty is that even if attempts are made to keep the initial theory as unbiased and open as possible the data collected cannot emerge independently of the researcher's personal ideological and theoretical stance [4]. If the empirical findings support either the theory, or a rival theory, theory development progresses [22].

Four types of theory usage should be considered. First, the study can be absent from any theory. An example is grounded theory, which suggests pre-defined theory has the potential to contaminate research and therefore, the theory should be allowed to "emerge" from the data [4]. Second, the single theory approach. An example is provided by Alvesson [26] who suggests the theory in use be "entrenched in the interpreter's person and his or her political-ethical position". Third, the multiple theory approach. Walsham [25] suggests this theory should be used as a "scaffold", to be discarded when no longer needed, which suggests there is no such thing as best theory, only different ways of seeing the world. Last but not least, the context dependent use of theory. This essentially realistic perspective argues that the selection of theory should be based on the "reality" of the research situation [4].

The appropriately developed theory is the level at which the generalization of the CS results will occur (usually called analytical generalization and different from statistical generalization) [19]. We will detail both analytical and statistical generalization in the next section.

Much concern, confusion and criticism of CS methods revolves around their representativeness and the ability to generalize findings beyond the actual case [22]. From a theory and the facts of a case, generalizations are drawn concerning the domain of the theory [5]. Findings are generalized to that theoretical base according to the degree of support they provide to the original propositions [22].

In the IS field, generalizations should, therefore, be seen as explanations of particular phenomena derived from empirical research [25]. Plus, the researcher should consider what generalizations are hoped for [27]. Kohn [21] noted that greater heterogeneity among the cases may enhance generalizability.

Generalization of a CS so that it contributes to theory is important but it can only be performed if the CS design has been appropriately informed by theory, and can thus be seen to add to the established theory. The method of generalization for CSs is not statistical [5], but analytical generalization in which a previously developed theory is used as a template with which to compare the empirical results of the CS [1].

Statistical generalization (as surveys, for example) is usually based on empirical data collected from a sample of the population. However, in analytical generalization (as CSs) a previously developed theory is used as a template with which to compare the empirical results of the CS and when two or more cases are shown to support the same theory, replication should be claimed. Empirical results could be even more potent if two or more cases support the same theory [19].

Another relevant concern is which steps we should have into consideration when performing a CS. In Table 2 we can see the final set of the steps elicited from the literature. We excluded all steps with less than one reference supporting them.

Table 2. IT Case Study Main Steps

N°	Step	References
1	Organization context	[6][27]
2	Research questions	[1][6][22][23][27]
3	Select the case	[1][6] [21][22][23][27]
4	Define the propositions	[1][23][27]
5	Data collection	[1][6][22][23][27]
6	Data analysis	[1][6] [21][22][23][27]
7	Reporting	[1][21][22][27]

Due to space limitation we are not able to provide detailed description about how we elicited such steps and what each step consists on. Nevertheless, more information about each step can be found in the correspondent references.

4   Proposal

As aforementioned, our contributions rely on two things: the conceptual map of CS domain, and the variables that should be present in each IT CS in order to promote the generalization.

Indeed, our proposal should be seen as a first step to promote the generalization of IT CSs which of course should be continued in future research in order to able to be adopted as a standard by IT CSs researchers.

4.1   CS Domain Conceptual Map

A conceptual model is typically a graphical representation so it can provide limited vocabulary [15]. Plus, conceptual models are a prerequisite for successfully planning and designing complex systems [28] and must be used to systematize knowledge, provide guiding research and map a portion of reality [29].

For space limitation we were not able to detail all the main issues of CS domain in Section 3. However, we developed a conceptual map where the issues approached in Section 3 may be seen as well as other relevant issues. In Figure 2 we can see the CS domain conceptual model.

It should be noted that some items are marked in red. Red colored items and connections represent the part of the CS domain that we intend to further explore and produce contributions to in this article, as we will see in Section 4.2.

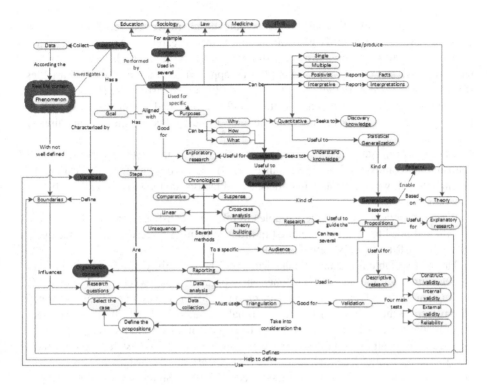

Fig. 2. CS Domain Conceptual Map

A brief explanation of why were these items chosen must be provided. As previously stated, the focus of this article is to help researchers doing CS research in IT domain, which self-explains the top red items in Figure 2. We have also already made clear that we intend to contribute with a new artifact to help the generalization and that is why the Generalization item is marked in red. However, the LR is straightforward about the most appropriate kind of generalization in CSs and that is why we marked the "Analytical Generalization". Finally, generalization usually leads to pattern elicitation, which in its turn uses variables that define the organizational context of the phenomenon under study. Such variables are not described among the literature and we intend to contribute to it in the next section.

4.2   IT CS Variables

Grounded in both IT and CS domain definitions (our constructs) provided in previous sections we are now able to elicit the most suitable variables (model) to be used by IT CS researchers in order to promote generalization. In DSR, models are used to represent real world situation, we argue that the variables that the authors will elicit may work as a way to enable the IT CS researchers to represent the real world organization that they are study.

The authors believe that any IT CS should be characterized according to some common variables to simplify generalization by other researchers. After a deep LR we believe the factors (culture, structure, strategy, maturity, regional differences, industry, size, trust, and ethic) proposed in [30] are appropriate to use as possible variables since it is a very recent study and it was made by an extensive LR. However, other variables can be used since generalization could be provided. In this case the authors believe that these factors are the most suitable to be applied by the reasons already described.

Since our proposal focuses on IT domain as well as on the IT CSs performed in organizational context and IT governance (ITG) is responsible for the business/IT alignment [31], we also believe that the selected factors are the most suitable to be our variables.

We have already selected the variables to take into consideration, but they are too general and need to be deeper detailed in order to be used by researchers. Once again we will use LR to detail possible variables.

The first variable is organizational structure. The possibility of effective ITG is also determined by the way the IT function is organized and where the IT decision-making authority is located in the organization. A lot of research has been performed with regard to the location of the decision-making authority [32][33] and some models of modes are developed, such as centralized, decentralized and federal [34].

In general, centralization leads to greater specialization, consistency, and standardized controls while decentralization provides local control, ownership, greater responsiveness and flexibility to business needs [35][36]. Some studies, for example, also indicate that a federal structure (i.e., a hybrid design of centralized infrastructure control and decentralized application control) is the dominant model in many contemporary enterprises since it tries to achieve the 'best of both worlds' [33][37].

Another hypothesis to define the structure of an organization was proposed by Weill and Ross [38] who used six archetypes to define the organizational structure. Nevertheless, we believe the first hypothesis is more suitable and simple to be adopted by CS researchers. Plus, each Weil and Ross [39] archetypes can be mapped into the Centralized, Federal and Decentralized perspective. We believe that for each CS the authors should point in which of these modes (centralized, decentralized, or federal) the organization under study is included.

The second variable is organizational culture. In fact, organizational culture is not just an important factor of an organization, it is the central driver of superior business performance [40]. Therefore, firms with strong culture are supposed to have policies for preserving that culture, the organization and making the most of its cultural benefits. A culture can be considered strong if norms and values are widely shared and held throughout the organization [41].

The dimensions that distinguished countries from each other could be grouped statistically into four clusters: Power Distance, Individualism versus Collectivism, Masculinity versus Femininity and Uncertainty Avoidance. A fifth and a sixth have already been added to the four dimensions: Long-Term Orientation and Indulgence versus Restraint [42]. Usually Hofstede maps these dimensions in implicit models.

According to Hofstede [43] there are three factors that determined employees' behavior in the workplace: national culture, organizational culture and occupational culture. The later will not be considered in our proposal. However, Hofstedes' dimensions of national cultures cannot be used by comparing organizations' cultures within the same country as the two models describe different layers of our reality [42]. Hofstede defines several implicit models of organizations taking into account the national and organizational culture. Due to space limitations we cannot define each dimension, but more information can be found in [42]. We argue that IT CS researchers should classify both national and organizational culture according to Hofstede's [43] definition.

The third variable is strategy. The purpose of IT strategy is that enterprises can enhance organizational level of IS, based on modern IT, and provide better services for the management strategy [34]. Plus, business/IT strategy should always be aligned.

Given this, we believe that the approach proposed by Sabherwal and Chan [44] should be used by the organization to characterize their IT strategy. The authors tried to define IT strategies that best map specific business strategies. Those business strategies were defined based on the Miles and Snow typology [45], which identifies different types of business strategies. The identified IT strategies are: "IT for efficiency", which is oriented toward internal and inter-organizational efficiencies and long-term decision-making, and maps well on the defender's business strategy; "IT for flexibility" that focuses on market flexibility and quick strategic decisions, which map the prospector's business strategy; and "IT for comprehensiveness" that enables comprehensive decisions and quick responses through knowledge of other organizations, which complies with the analyzer's business strategy [46][47].

Another possibility involves using the primary IT values drivers defined by Peterson [33]: Service Delivery, Solution Integration and Strategic Innovation. However, we believe that the first hypothesis is suitable since it provides more detailed definitions and is already linked to business strategy. We argue that IT CS researchers should make references to the strategy being applied by the organization under study.

The fourth variable is the maturity. The linkage between business and IT strategies and goals can be very helpful when an organization strives for a more mature strategic alignment process. Achieving alignment is evolutionary and dynamic [46]. To be able to measure its maturity, organizations can use a maturity model that offers an easy-to-understand way to determine the "as-is" and the "to-be" position and enables the organization to benchmark itself against best practices and standard guidelines [47]. This way, gaps can be identified and specific actions can be defined to move towards the desired level of strategic alignment maturity [48][49]. Nowadays, there are several maturity models and we argue that IT CS's researchers should be explicit if the organization uses any or even if it reaches a certain maturity level.

The fifth variable is regional differences. Some studies have been made about regional differences on ITG implementations. For example, [50] pointed out the importance of aspects, such as language, local laws and national information infrastructures. Another study performed by [51] made a cross-country comparative study where they found different ITG implementations, while [52] performed some regional CSs in different countries. We contend that the industry under which the CS is being performed should be stated in the CS's main document.

The sixth factor is the industry. IT has a wide range of applicability across almost all industries [53] and has different meanings in distinct industries, which is obvious by the different regulations that have been developed and by the different legislative documents [54]. We argue that in each CS the researchers should explicitly say the industry in which the organization under the CS is included.

The seventh variable is size. Some studies have attempted to discover the effect of organization size on ITG [46][55]. Sambamurthy and Zmud [32] state the size of a firm influences the ITG mode through its effect on the mode of corporate governance. Normally, small and medium enterprises are defined jointly as small and medium-sized enterprises (SMEs). There is no single globally accepted definition of SME. Countries use different definitions for a variety of reasons. In addition, we argue that in each IT CS the researchers should be explicit about the number of employees in the organizations where the CS is being performed as well as in the IT, allowing more accurate conclusions to be further elicited.

The eighth variable is trust. Trust is expressed in three levels: individual, group and system level. At an individual level, trust is based on interpersonal interaction [56] while in organizations trust refers to the global evaluation of an organization's trust-worthiness as perceived by the employees. Employees continually observe the organizational environment when they consider whether or not to trust their organization [57].

According to some researchers, managers play a central role in determining the overall level of trust within organizations. For example, managers design reward and control systems that are visible displays of basic levels of trust or mistrust within the organization as a whole. The beliefs and actions of managers also directly and indirectly influence trust in organizations [58]. We argue that an IT CS should be clear about the trust level within the organization. Related mechanisms like rewards for example may also be pointed out if existent.

The last variable is ethic. Nowadays, with high-profile business scandals, much attention focuses on the role that top executives play in setting the ethical tone of their organizations. Research studies have shown the importance of top management commitment in fostering ethical business practices within an organization. However, employees are often influenced the most by those closest to them—people they work with every day [59]. Implicit in most governance legislation and regulation is the need for prudent governance of the organizations' IT functions [60].

Organizations have adopted various efforts to implement programs aimed at fostering ethical behavior in their members [61]. These "ethical infrastructures" [62] contain both formal and informal elements: ethics codes and policies, communications, training, monitoring systems, sanctions, and rewards on the formal side, and attention to ethical environment and organizational cultures on the informal side.

We argue that if the organization under study has implemented an ethic mechanism, then it must be present in the IT CS.

5   Evaluation

To illustrate our proposal's application, we have selected five IT Governance CS articles among the IT literature from journals/conferences/books [14][63][64][65] [66]. Our goal is not to propose a critical evaluation of the quality of the research contributions, but rather to shed some light on our proposal. This kind of evaluation has been applied in other studies [67]. The CSs analysis is in Table 3.

Table 3. IT Case Studies Analysis

Variables		First Case	Second Case	Third Case	Fourth Case	Fifth Case
Regional Differences		Gulf	Belgian, AGF	Australia	Not Present	Germany. BMW
Industry		Airline Industry	Insurance	Higher education	Automotive Suppliers	Automotive Industry
Size		20% of the airline's $1.37 billion net profit	Over 1200 employees	Over 3,000 staff members	One of the top 100 companies in its headquarters country.	Not Present
Structure		Not Present	Centralized	Federal	Federal	Federal
Culture	National	The pyramidal organization	The solar system	The contest model	Not Present	The well-oiled machine
	Organizational	Not Present	Not Present	Not Present	Not Present	Not Present
Strategy		Not Present	IT for efficiency	IT for efficiency IT for flexibility	IT for efficiency IT for flexibility	IT for efficiency IT for flexibility
Ethic		Not Present	Not Present	Not Present	Not Present	Not Present
Maturity		Not Present	Not Present	Not Present	Not Present	Not Present
Trust		Not Present	Not Present	Not Present	Not Present	Not Present

After the analysis of the CSs, we will try to generalize which IT Governance mechanisms are more suitable for each organization's context.

6   Discussion

After analyzing the selected CSs, we concluded they lack a lot of crucial information regarding the proposed variables. As a result, it is clear that some CSs are more detailed than others.

Another particularity is that not all information was clear. For instance, about maturity there are some statements as in CS three: "...in the last two years IT has shown considerable maturity in project management..." or "...P-CMM is used as the standard of the IT staff management and development...". Such statements indicate that maturity may be a concern in the organization and was measured. However, we filled the cell of Table 3 with "No" because there is no information about the level achieved or even the framework(s) used.

Another example is the organizational culture. The national culture could be easily drawn since almost all the CSs provide the country of the organization under study so we just need to look in Hofstede´s theory, which indicates a specific culture to each country. Notwithstanding, to draw conclusions about organizational culture more information was needed in the CSs about what kind of practices and beliefs are being followed and performed by the organization, but this information is missing.

As stated by [10], when two or more cases support the same theory, generalization must be claimed. As we can see in Table 3, the possibilities of generalization are: size (CS 1,2,3,4), structure (CS 3,4,5), Strategy (CS 3,4,5), and any possible combination of this factors.

After analyzing all the possibilities only one generalization can be drawn. Big organizations (size) with federal structure and adopting "IT for efficiency" and "IT for flexibility" as strategy have two mechanisms in common: "Business/IT alignment model" and "Project tracking".

7   Conclusion

Only 50% of the information regarding the selected CSs was properly described to be elicited, as can be seen in Table 3 with 24 cells filled with "Not Present" from 50 possible cells. Not all the information was useful to generalize but we proved that when information is well presented, it is easier to formulate theories as for example that big organizations with federal structure and adopting "IT for efficiency" and "IT for flexibility" as strategy have the IT governance mechanisms "Business/IT alignment model" and "Project tracking" in common.

The main contributions of this research are the definition and characterization of the variables that should be used to define the organizational context of the IT CS and promote the generalization. The authors argue that once adopted the artifact proposed in this research by the IT CS researchers, more rigor is added to their researches.

Moreover, unlike quantitative analysis, which observes patterns in data at the macro level on the basis of the frequency of occurrence of the phenomena being observed [5], qualitative CS approach provides the opportunity to ask penetrating questions and to capture the richness of organizational behavior [12]. However, all the researchers noted that the analytic focus on CSs is on the overall pattern of variables within a case, looking at the parts in relation to the whole and then, if there are multiple cases, looking across them [21].

Finally, since CS takes into account the context, it encompasses many variables and qualities [3], variables that characterize the specific context need to be well-defined. Moreover, our proposal enables those who follow our variables and guidelines to achieve a set of qualitative IT CS patterns.

Nevertheless, this research also has some limitations. The proposed variables are not intended to be static, but more variables may be searched for and proposed in the future. We also admit that further detailed options to characterize each variable may still exist, especially regarding less evolved ones as ethic or trust. Finally, despite the undeniable value of Hofstede's study, the dimensions may not be the most updated ones and not all countries are contemplated in his book so further and more recent approaches may be considered in the future.

Future research should focus on strengthening the proposed artefacts as well as in the expansion of such generalization approach for areas as management CSs or business CSs.

References

1. Rowley, J.: Using case studies in research. Management Research News 25(1), 16–27 (2002)
2. Harling, K.: An Overview of Case Study. Technical report, Wilfrid Laurier University (2002)
3. Zainal, Z.: Case study as a research method. Jurnal Kemanusiaan 9, 1–6 (2007)
4. Dobson, P.J.: Approaches to Theory Use In Interpretive Case Studies – a Critical Realist Perspective. In: 10th Australasian Conference on Information Systems, pp. 259–270. AIS Press (1999)
5. Johansson, R.: Case Study Methodology. In: International Conference "Methodologies in Housing Research". Royal Institute of Technology in cooperation with the International Association of People–Environment Studies (2003)
6. Kaplan, B., Duchon, D.: Combining qualitative and quantitative methods information systems research: a case study. Management Information Systems Quarterly 12(4), 571–586 (1988)
7. Fernandez, W.D.: The Grounded Theory Method and Case Study Data in IS Research: Issues and Design. In: Information Systems Foundations Workshop: Constructing and Criticising, pp. 43–59. Australian National University EPress, Canberra (2004)
8. Tellis, W.: Introduction to Case Study. The Qualitative Report 3(2) (1997)
9. Lee, A.S.: A Scientific Methodology for MIS Case Studies. Management Information Systems Quarterly 13(1), 32–50 (1989)
10. Yin, R.K.: Case Study Research: Design and Method, 4th edn. Sage Publications, London (2009)
11. Stake, R.E.: The art of case study research. Sage Publications, London (1995)
12. Gable, G.G.: Integrating Case Study and Survey Research Methods: An Examples in Information Systems. European Journal of Information Systems 3(2), 112–126 (1994)
13. Osterle, H., Becker, J., Frank, U., Hess, T., Karagiannis, D., Krcmar, H., Loos, P., Mertens, P., Oberweis, A., Sinz, E.J.: Memorandum on Design-Oriented Information Systems Research. European Journal of Information Systems 20, 7–10 (2011)
14. Broadbent, M., Weill, P.: Effective IT Governance. Exp Premier, Gartner (2003)
15. Schermann, M., Böhmann, T., Krcmar, H.: Explicating Design Theories with Conceptual Models: Towards a Theoretical Role of Reference Models. In: Becker, J., Krcmar, H., Niehaves, B. (eds.) Wissenschaftstheorie und gestaltung-sorientierte Wirtschaftsinformatik, pp. 175–194. Physica-Verlag, Heidelberg (2009)
16. Simon, H.A.: The Sciences of the Artificial. MIT Press, Cambridge (1996)
17. March, S., Smith, G.: Design and Natural Science Research on Information Technology. Decision Support Systems 15, 251–266 (1995)
18. Webster, J., Watson, R.T.: Analyzing the past to prepare for the future: Writing a Literature Review. Management Information Systems Quarterly 26(2), xiii–xxiii (2002)

19. Thomas, G.: How to do your case study. Sage Publications, London (2011)
20. Blonk, H.: Writing case studies in information systems research. Journal of Information Technology 18, 45–52 (2003)
21. Kohn, L.T.: Methods in Case Study Analysis. Technical report, The Center for Studying Health System Change (1997)
22. Crosthwaite, J., MacLeod, N., Malcolm, B.: Case Studies: Theory and Practice in Natural Resource Management. In: Australian Association for Social Research Conference (1997)
23. Baxter, P., Jack, S.: Qualitative Case Study Methodology: Study Design and Implementation for Novice Researchers. The Qualitative Report 13(4), 544–559 (2008)
24. Creswell, J.W.: Research Design: Qualitative, Quantitative, and mixed methods approaches, 2nd edn. Sage Publications, California (2002)
25. Walsham, G.: Interpretive case studies in IS research: nature and method. European Journal of Information Systems 4, 74–81 (1995)
26. Alvesson, M.: Communications, Power and Organization. Walter de Gruyter, Berlin (1996)
27. Benbassat, I., Goldstein, D.K., Mead, M.: The case research strategy in studies of Information Systems. Management Information Systems Quarterly 11(3), 369–386 (1987)
28. Moody, D.L., Shanks, G.G.: Improving the Quality of Data Models: Empirical Validation of a Quality Management Framework. International Journal of Information Systems 28(6), 619–650 (2003)
29. Järvelin, K., Wilson, T.D.: On Conceptual Models for Information Seeking and Retrieval Research. Information Research 9(1), paper 163 (2003)
30. Pereira, R., Mira da Silva, M.: Towards an Integrated IT Governance and IT Management Framework. In: 16th Enterprise Distributed Object Computing Conference, pp. 191–200. IEEE Press, New York (2012)
31. Pereira, R., Mira da Silva, M.: Designing a new Integrated IT Governance and IT Management Framework Based on Both Scientific and Practitioner Viewpoint. International Journal of Enterprise Information Systems 8(4), 1–43 (2012)
32. Sambamurthy, V., Zmud, R.W.: Arrangements for Information Technology Governance: A Theory of Multiple Contingencies. Management Information Systems Quarterly 23(2), 261–290 (1999)
33. Peterson, R.R.: Information strategies and tactics for information technology governance. In: Van Grembergen, W. (ed.) Strategies for information technology governance, pp. 37–80. Idea Group Publishing, Hershey (2003)
34. Van Grembergen, W., De Haes, S., Guldentops, E.: Structures, Processes and Relational Mechanisms for IT Governance. In: Van Grembergen, W. (ed.) Strategies for information technology governance, pp. 1–36. Idea Group Publishing, Hershey (2003)
35. Brown, C.V., Magill, S.L.: Reconceptualizing the Context-Design Issue for the IS Function. Organization Science 9(2), 176–194 (1998)
36. Rockart, J.F., Earl, M.J., Ross, J.W.: Eight Imperatives for the new IT Organization. Sloan Management Review 38(1), 43–55 (1996)
37. Ribbers, P., Peterson, R., Parker, M.: Designing Information Technology Governance Processes: Diagnosing Contemporary Practices and Competing Theories. In: 35th Hawaii International Conference on System Sciences, pp. 3143–3154. IEEE Press, New York (2002)
38. Weill, P., Ross, J.: IT Governance: How Top Performers Manage It Decision Rights for Superior Results. Harvard Business Press, Boston (2004)
39. Weill, P., Ross, J.: IT Governance On One Page. MIT Sloan Working Paper 4517 (2004)

40. Gallagher, S., Brown, C., Brown, L.: A Strong Market Culture Drives Organizational Performance and Success. Employment Relations Today 35(1), 25–31 (2008)
41. O'Reilly, C., Chatman, J.A.: Culture as social control: Corporations, cults, and commitment. Research in Organizational Behavior 18, 157–200 (1996)
42. Hofstede, G., Hofstede, G.J., Minkov, M.: Cultures and Organizations: Software of the mind, 3rd edn. McGraw-Hill, New York (2010)
43. Hofstede, G.: Culture's Consequences: International Differences in Work-Related Values. Sage Publications, California (1980)
44. Sabherwal, R., Chan, Y.: Alignment between Business and IS Strategies: a study of prospectors, analyzers, defenders. Information Systems Research 12(1), 11–33 (2001)
45. Miles, R.E., Snow, C.C.: Organizational Strategy, Structure, and Process. McGraw-Hill, New York (1978)
46. Van Grembergen, W., De Haes, S.: Implementing IT Governance: Models, Practices, and Cases. Idea Group Publishing, Hershey (2008)
47. Van Grembergen, W., De Haes, S.: Enterprise Governance of IT: Achieving Strategic Alignment and Value. Springer Science, New York (2009)
48. Guldentops, E., Van Grembergen, W., De Haes, S.: Control and governance maturity survey: establishing a reference benchmark and a self-assessment tool. Information Systems Control Journal 6 (2002)
49. Information Technology Governance Institute: Board briefing on IT Governance (2005), http://www.itgi.org
50. Weisinger, J.Y., Trauth, E.M.: The Importance of Situating Culture in Cross-Cultural IT Management. IEEE Transactions on Engineering Management 50(1), 26–30 (2003)
51. Aagesen, G., van Veenstra, A.F., Janssen, M., Krogstie, J.: The Entanglement of Enterprise Architecture and IT-Governance: The Cases of Norway and the Netherlands. In: 44th Hawaii International Conference on System Sciences, pp. 1–10. IEEE Press, New York (2011)
52. Fink, K., Ploder, K.: Decision Support Framework for the Implementation of IT-Governance. In: 41st Hawaii International Conference on System Sciences, p. 432. IEEE Press, New York (2008)
53. Tanriverdi, H.: Performance Effects of Information Technology Synergies in Multibusiness Firms. Management Information Systems Quarterly 30(1), 57–77 (2006)
54. Webb, P., Pollard, C., Ridley, G.: Attempting to Define IT Governance: Wisdom or Folly? In: 39th Hawaii International Conference on System Sciences, p. 194a. IEEE Press, New York (2006)
55. Brown, A.E., Grant, G.G.: Framing the Frameworks: A Review of IT Governance Research. Communications of the Association for Information Systems 15, 696–712 (2005)
56. Atkinson, S., Butcher, D.: Trust in Managerial Relationships. Journal of Managerial Psychology 18(4), 282–304 (2003)
57. Tan, H.H., Tan, C.S.F.: Toward the Differentiation of Trust in Supervisor and Trust in Organization. Social, and General Psychology Monographs 126(2), 241–260 (2000)
58. Creed, D.R., Miles, R.E.: Trust in organizations: A conceptual framework linking organizational forms, managerial philosophies, and the opportunity costs of controls. In: Kramer, R.M., Tyler, T.R. (eds.) Trust in Organizations: Frontiers of Theory and Research, pp. 16–38. Sage, California (1996)
59. Weaver, G.R., Trevino, L.K., Agle, B.: Somebody I look up to: Ethical role models in organizations. Organizational Dynamics 34(4), 313–330 (2005)

60. Ali, S., Green, P., Parent, M.: The Role of a Culture of Compliance in Information Technology Governance. In: 2nd International Workshop on Governance, Risk and Compliance, pp. 1–14. CEUR Workshop Proceedings (2009)
61. Weaver, G.R., Treviño, L.K., Cochran, P.L.: Corporate ethics practices in the mid-1990s: An Empirical Study of the Fortune 1000. Journal of Business Ethics 18(3), 283–294 (1999)
62. Tenbrunsel, A.E., Smith-Crowe, K., Umphress, E.E.: Building houses on rocks: The role of ethical infrastructure in the ethical effectiveness of organizations. Social Justice Research 16, 285–307 (2003)
63. Iskandar, M., Akma, N., Salleh, M.: IT Governance in Airline Industry: A Multiple Case Study. International Journal of Digital Society 1(4), 308–313 (2010)
64. Van Grembergen, W., De Haes, S.: Information Technology Governance: Models, Practices, and Cases. Idea Group Publishing, Hershey (2008)
65. Bhattacharjya, J., Chang, V.: Evolving IT Governance Practices for IT and Business Alignment – A Case Study in an Australian Institution of Higher Education. Journal of Information Science and Technology 4(1) (2007)
66. Wittenburg, A., Matthes, F.: Building an integrated IT governance platform at the BMW Group. International Journal Business Process Integration and Management 2(4), 327–337 (2007)
67. Hevner, A.R., March, S.T., Park, J., Ram, S.: Design Science in Information Systems Research. Management Information Systems Quarterly 28(1), 75–105 (2004)

Reconciling Theories with Design Choices in Design Science Research

Roman Lukyanenko and Jeffrey Parsons

Faculty of Business Administration, Memorial University of Newfoundland
St. John's, NL Canada
{roman.lukyanenko,jeffreyp}@mun.ca

Abstract. Despite increased acceptance of design science research, concerns about rigor and relevance permeate the research community. One way to increase rigor is by codifying design knowledge into design theories. While this idea is gaining popularity, it is unclear how to approach design theorizing in a scientifically rigorous, yet practically relevant, way. In this paper, we address one particularly murky issue in design science research: reconciling theoretical abstractness with practicality. Since many design theories are moderately abstract, a gap exists between theoretical propositions and concrete issues faced in practice. We present a case study of real information system (IS) development where these issues become evident. Based on the identified issues we provide four theory-driven recommendations including specification of transformational rules, developing or imagining a real IS artifact, specification of boundary conditions and over-specification of the theoretical core. The consequences of these recommendations for design science theorizing are discussed.

Keywords: design science research, design theory, conceptual modeling, database design, rigor, relevance, information quality, data quality, citizen science.

1 Introduction

Design science research (DSR) has gained acceptance as a major component of the Information Systems (IS) discipline [1, 2]. The contribution of DSR includes constructs, models, methods, implementations [3, 4]. In addition, calls continue to codify design knowledge into design theories (DT) that specify properties of the designed artifact or prescribe processes of artifact development [5-7].

Despite the increased attention to DSR, it is still unclear what rigorous design science research is and how to codify design knowledge in a way most relevant to practice [8-13]. Establishing principles of rigor can help delineate design science research from, for example, theory-informed IS practice, Computer Science or Software Engineering [8]. Principles of relevance and rigor can also be used to advance and evaluate knowledge developed through artifact design.

This paper responds to calls to increase rigor and relevance in DSR by addressing an important, but not well-understood, aspect of design theorizing – the question of

J. vom Brocke et al. (Eds.): DESRIST 2013, LNCS 7939, pp. 165–180, 2013.

whether specific design choices used to instantiate a design theory should be considered and accounted for in the design theory.

It is widely contended that many IS theories (including design theories) are mid-range theories [14-17]. Merton [18] defines mid-range theories as theories that are moderately abstract (i.e., they do not purport to explain everything) but "close enough to observed data to be incorporated in propositions that permit empirical testing" (p. 39). Indeed, Kuechler and Vaishnavi [14] argue the middle is the most common level in IS theorizing given the discipline's applied focus and historical reliance on general theories from other disciplines.[1]

Mid-range theories may not be explicit about how to make specific design decisions (e.g., user interface choices, ways to organize application file structure). As a result, there may be ambiguity when instantiating a design theory (i.e., creating an artifact). Practitioners may wonder which of the possible instantiations are more suitable to solve a problem that a design theory purports to address. In the absence of explicit guidance, the connection from theoretical propositions to actual design may be made using tacit knowledge, prior experience, trial-and-error, or gut feeling of developers. Naturally, not all design choices lead to desirable outcomes.

Here, many fundamental questions arise, including: (How) Can mostly mid-range design theories account for specific implementation options? To what extent should design theory be cognizant of tools, technologies, and practices available to practitioners now (and in the near future)? How should abstract theoretical propositions be reconciled with technical, and often mundane, problems faced when developing IS artifacts? How much of design should be prescribed and guided and how much "artistic" freedom should be allowed? These questions touch on fundamental concerns about the role of DSR in guiding and being relevant to IS practice. It is generally accepted that the mandate of DSR is to make IS practice more effective and efficient by reducing development uncertainty [8, 19, 20]. At the same time, it is also contended that DSR is more than just generating "technological recipes" and should emphasize important classes of problems rather than micromanage development [7, 13].

The conventional wisdom in the design science literature is to promote generality. This is assumed to foster research rigor and make theories relevant to a (broad) class of problems and future practice [3, 7, 8, 13, 21]. At the same time, leaving considerations of design alternatives outside the scope of design theories may deny practitioners important guidance. There is a general tradeoff between generality of a theory and its ability to account for specific issues [22, 23]. In design science, this means higher levels of theoretical abstraction engender ambiguities of implementation. As the number of alternatives increases, different choices can trigger vastly different project outcomes. This issue is even more concerning since much of DSR is conceived and evaluated in a laboratory [3, 8, 21]. It is thus removed from challenges and contingencies of real organizational settings; hence the impact of different design alternatives may never become apparent to design science theorists.

---

[1] Some examples of mid-range theories in IS include theories of fit [59], technology acceptance [60], trust and online shopping [61], and information modeling [62].

In this paper we explore whether it is desirable and possible to reconcile theoretical generality with many alternative manifestations. We use a case of real IS development and theories in other disciplines (psychology, linguistics and management) to demonstrate the value and feasibility of prescribing specific design choices while maintaining theoretical abstractness. We provide four concrete recommendations that design theorists can use to reconcile theoretical generality with different design alternatives.

The remainder of the paper is organized as follows. We first set the issue of reconciling design theories with design alternatives in the context of active discourse on rigor and relevance in DSR. We then present a case study of IS development where the difficulty of reconciling design theories with design alternatives is evident. Based on the identified challenges we survey psychology, linguistics and management and derive four recommendations that we hope can guide future design science theorizing. We conclude with a discussion and outlook to future research.

2   Reconciling Theories with Design Choices in IS Literature

The issue of whether design theories should account for specific design choices is part of the debate on how to foster relevance and rigor [3, 5, 8]. Recently there is a growing consensus that both relevance and rigor in DSR can be promoted by systematic codification of design knowledge into design theories [5, 6, 10, 13, 14]. Using design theory increases transparency of DSR while generating useful knowledge for practice. At the same time, unlike explanatory and predictive theories in natural sciences, the primary goal of a design theory is to provide useful guidance for building systems [6, 13]. It is still not settled, however, what form a design theory should take and how to engage in effective design theorizing.

With the increased recognition of design theories, efforts are growing to better structure and formalize design theorizing. Notably, Gregor and Jones [5] identified constituent components of design theories. Venable [13] advances design science utility theory arguing that a design theory should focus on predicting outcomes of artifact implementation. Similarly, Hovorka and Gregor [11] stress the importance of specifying causal mechanisms imbued in artifacts. The general thrust is providing mechanisms for greater transparency and formality in design science theorizing [9, 10]. A related concern is improving alignment (e.g., mapping of constructs) between kernel and design science theories [5, 14, 24]. In reality, kernel theories can rarely be taken "as-is" "primarily because the scope and granularity of the generic kernel theory are often inadequate for guiding design" [24]. Bridging the gap between kernel theories and design science theorizing remains a major challenge [24]. With this paper, we explore a related, but less understood, problem: the extent to which design theories should address specific design choices.

While it is not clear how to reconcile generality of theories and specific choices, the issue itself is not new. Indeed, many authors note this problem with the general preference towards generality. Presenting design science knowledge abstractly promotes artistic freedom and accommodates organizational contingencies and emergent technologies. Gregor and Jones [5] suggest that principles of form and practice can be represented as an 'abstract "blueprint"' or as a design method showing "in a generalized form the shape and features" proposed. Walls et al. [7] recommend addressing "a class of problems" rather than "the design of a specific artifact" (p. 42). Considering this issue, Venable [13] concludes (p. 12):

> to weigh all possible alternative meta-designs would be quite difficult, if not impossible. Furthermore, such a prescription would be complicated in that what can be said to be the "best" meta-design (that with the best utility) will change over time...

Hevner et al. [3] consider "generalizability of the artifact" to be a component of rigor. Foundational disciplines, such as psychology, economics, and engineering, are generally focused on problems distinct from those of IS [25, 26]. As noted by Arazy et al. [24] and Kuechler and Vaishnavi [14] the generality of kernel theories may preclude straightforward mapping between constructs of a kernel and a design theory. One way to improve such mapping is to increase generality of design theories.

Despite the preference for generality, the limitations of this approach have been noted in prior studies. First, a general form may ignore some of the actual challenges faced by practitioners. Thus, Hevner et al. [3] caution that overemphasis on generalizability can come at the expense of relevance calling for balance between the objectives. Second, by abstracting from rich particulars of real artifacts some potentially useful problems, challenges and novel opportunities resident in specific instantiations may fail to be uncovered and disseminated. Hence, studying specific features of successful artifacts may prove valuable. For example, Iivari [8] credits the relational data model and object-oriented principles with facilitating solutions to problems that became apparent only after the inception and close scrutiny of these artifacts.

In summary, the prevailing wisdom in design science favors theoretical abstractness. Below, we present a case of real IS development that motivates accounting for at least some design alternatives in design theorizing.

3   A Case of Reconciling Design Theories with Design Choices

3.1   Background and Motivation

This case is based on the authors' involvement in the development of a natural history citizen science project, NL Nature. The objective of the project was to map biodiversity of a region in North America (a territory of over 150,000 square miles) using sightings of plants and animals by ordinary people. Citizen science is a kind of crowdsourcing in which scientists enlist ordinary people to perform tasks that support some research agenda [27]. Citizen science is increasingly looked upon to reduce information acquisition costs and facilitate discoveries [28]. The promise of citizen science increasingly motivates the design science community to address many socio-technological issues arising in this domain [29-32].

Typical to other design science research, this case was triggered by a real-world problem [3]. One of the major challenges in citizen science is accommodating diverse user views while ensuring that contributor-supplied information is of acceptable quality for scientific research [33, 34]. In this domain a trade-off between quality and participation emerged, as forcing contributors to adhere to scientific standards (e.g., biological taxonomy) can exclude many potential contributors (i.e., non-expert members of general public) unfamiliar with these standards.

3.2 Phase I: Development Following 'Traditional' Approaches (2009-2011)

In Phase I, the design strategy to improve information quality and participation was informed by prevailing practices in online citizen science. Consistent with similar projects (e.g., www.eBird.org, www.iSpot.org.uk), the objective of data collection was positive identification of species (e.g., American robin). To promote participation by non-expert users, project sponsors suggested a mixed convention of biological nomenclature and general knowledge ("folksonomy") to organize entities about which information was to be collected. Conceptual modeling followed the prevailing approach of class-based modeling, such as Entity-Relationship (E-R) grammar or UML (see Fig. 1) [35, 36]. A relational database was designed based on the conceptual model [36]; the same model informed menu items and the options in the data collection interface (see Fig. 1). To improve information quality (IQ), users were allowed to collaborate and assist each other in identifying species in a social-networking style (e.g., post comments, exchange emails). Additionally, verification mechanisms (e.g., geocoordinate analysis and expert verification) were implemented. In summary, solutions to the quality/participation tradeoff were informed by several contributions of DSR, including class-based conceptual modeling [35], relational database design [37], and emergent statistical and social networking solutions [38, 39].

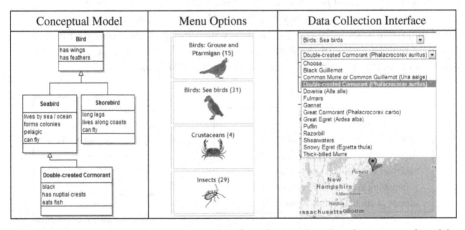

Fig. 1. Sample conceptual model and user interface elements based on the conceptual model

3.3 Evaluation of Phase I Information Quality and Participation

Once the project was launched, assessments of IQ were performed (including analysis of contributions, comments from users, and benchmark comparison with parallel scientific sampling). The authors of this paper in tandem with the biologists (i.e., project sponsors) determined that quality and level of participation were below expectations. Consistent with predictions by Parsons et al. [33], we identified the prevailing class-based approach to information modeling as a detriment to both quality and participation. The analysis of user comments suggested that some users, when unsure how to classify unfamiliar organisms, made guesses (to satisfy the requirement to classify organisms). Additionally, in several cases, the organisms could not be fully described using attributes of the correctly chosen species-level class (e.g., morph foxes had additional attributes not deducible from the class *Red fox*). Finally, the authors believed that many observations were not reported because of the incongruence between the conceptual model and user views (e.g., *Double-crested cormorants* may be considered by non-experts as *shorebirds*, rather than *seabirds,* due to the strong association with shore areas).

3.4   Phase II: Development Following Instance-Based Paradigm (2012-2013). Issues of Reconciling Design Theory and Design Choices

Based on the identified threats to IQ and user engagement, the project sponsors decided to redesign the project following an instance-based approach to citizen science proposed in [29, 40, 41]. Under the instance-based data model [42], users are not forced to classify instances using predefined classes (such as biological species), which relaxes the constraint for non-experts to understand and conform to a chosen taxonomy. Using attributes makes it then possible to capture individual variations of organisms (addressing the issue of storing unique insights of contributors). The attributes can be queried *post hoc* to infer classes of interest (e.g., species).

According to the design theory in [29, 40, 41], adopting an attribute and instance-based approach leads to increase in accuracy and user participation (see Fig. 2 for a graphical representation of the theory). Considering the objectives, it became unclear which of the many specific design decisions would be suitable.

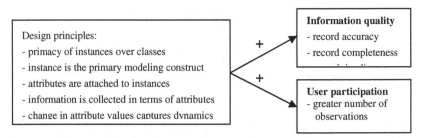

Fig. 2. Theoretical model based on [29, 40, 41]

When designing Phase II of the project, much of the previous experience with class-based conceptual modeling, database normalization, and user interface design, could no longer be leveraged. This meant that each development task in Phase II received more scrutiny and elaboration compared to Phase I. Implementing novel principles led to a critical introspection into issues of reconciling design science theories with design choices.

The initial realization was of a general nature: concomitant to broader DSR [11], the kernel theories of Bunge's ontology and cognition were developed outside the context of IS and, more specifically, online citizen science. As a result, neither theory operated with notions of, for example, web servers, programming languages (e.g., HTML, JavaScript, C#), Internet connection speeds, or client device types. These seemingly mundane choices were also not included in the general design science principles in [29, 40, 41]. Below we provide some examples of these issues.

Traditionally, surface elements of a system (such as a user interface, navigational structure, and menu choices) conform to structural assumptions at the deep (i.e., conceptual) level [43]. Since the underlying information model is instance-based, it follows that surface elements should follow the instance-based principles. At the same time, no strategy for mapping the principles in Fig. 2 into specific design objects is provided in the reference design theory. This means that answers to a number of questions cannot be justified based on theoretical prescriptions. For example, what should the first (landing) and subsequent pages look like? Do the landing page and other pages need to behave differently each time? Does the file structure become dynamic and personalized for each user? Furthermore, personalization is possible once users' profiles are known, suggesting that, at least for new users, some of the dynamic elements should be initially static. Then, at what point in user interaction should the switch to personalized content occur? In summary, while the instance-based design theory supports flexible design, it is unclear to what degree and what elements should be made dynamic *to ensure that IQ and user participation are increased.*

Similar ambiguity arose when building an information collection interface. The instance-based approach involves storing information about instances in terms of attributes. Here, a practical question is how to choose interface elements compliant with the instance-based theory. For example, a website can present attributes as a list allowing users to select/check off applicable attributes. This means all applicable attributes should be modeled in advance. Alternatively, attributes can be entered in a free-form manner – where any attribute is accepted even if it is not found in the existing attribute base. A variation on the free-form collection is guided free-form collection, where any attribute is accepted, but a prompt dynamically makes recommendations based on the string being typed (see, e.g., Fig. 3). In turn, this decision leads to additional questions. For example, if a guided free-form is chosen, should some (e.g., more common) attributes be cached for better performance? Alternatively, the prompt may be based on an active list of user-created attributes or a static authoritative list. In each case, there are also multiple ways to compute similarity (e.g., as a literal string match, or using a similarity algorithm).

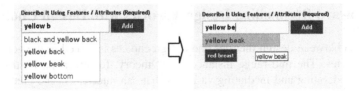

Fig. 3. Example of free-form guided attribute collection in Phase II

Considering the many design alternatives, it was not clear which options agree with the proposed principles (and thus achieve the predicted impact on the dependent variables). In addition, it was unclear if different decisions were better suited to other objectives and constraints of the project. For example, performance and aesthetics were important: the project sponsors feared that a slow and unattractive system could dissuade some uncommitted online users from contributing.

There was also an objective to make the project available in as many different user environments as possible (e.g., mobile devices, desktop systems). This meant that design solutions had to be tailored to these different environments. Subsequently, it was not obvious if some interface choices mentioned above were more appropriate for mobile use. For instance, a constrained-choice attribute collection appeared to be more suitable for mobile devices, while free-from guided interface seemed more appropriate for desktop clients. These decisions involved interpretation and fitting the referent design theory with other theories (e.g., of mobile computing).

The Phase II development demonstrates that there are many design decisions to be made during implementation and it is often unclear which ones are more consistent with the chosen design theory. The analysis of the case supports at least two arguments in favor of providing specific guidance to practice.

First, specific design choices are the concrete challenges faced by practitioners looking to reify theoretical prescriptions. With the growing diversity of development options, there appear few obvious (or optimal) implementation trajectories. Narrowing down the space of specific design decisions is of substantial practical value.

Second, different implementations may interfere with the predictions made by a design theory. For example, the instance-based principles purport to remove the constraints that traditional class-based modeling places on IQ and participation. When implementing the instance-based principles, however, it became apparent that different implementations engender additional constraints on quality and participation. There is increasing evidence that small screens on mobile devices make it difficult to present information and impede user interaction [44]. This means that presenting a large number of attributes on a mobile platform may negatively impact user engagement. A free-form attribute collection thus becomes difficult to use as it would entail typing on a small (real or virtual) keypad. This means that an instance-based theory agnostic of physical limitations (or affordances) of client devices may inadvertently support implementations that will result in negative impact on the dependent variables (in our case, IQ and participation).

4   Toward Reconciling Design Theories with Design Choices

The tension between design theories and design choices is rooted in the generality of design theories. The mid-range instance-based theory, for example, abstracts many potential moderating and mediating variables that can interfere in the predicted relationship. From the case above, it is evident that the omitted (i.e., abstracted away) constructs engender design ambiguity (graphically this is depicted in Fig. 4). For example, device types (e.g., mobile vs. desktop) may moderate the impact on participation since different modes of data entry may improve or hamper user-system interaction. Likewise, perceived ease of use or aesthetics may partially mediate the impact of the design principles on user participation. In a design science theory predictor variables translate to design principles and, hence, reduce development uncertainty.

Mid-range design theories strategically exclude some variables to achieve moderate abstractness. In the case of NL Nature, however, we demonstrated that the theoretical abstractness leads to practical ambiguity. Consequently, the question becomes: Assuming that many IS design theories are mid-range theories, is it possible to account for specific development trajectories while preserving the desired level of theoretical abstractness?

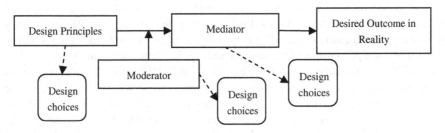

Fig. 4. Relationship between design theories and design choices (solid lines indicate causal impact; dashed lines indicate reduction of development uncertainty)

Here we turn to discourse in other disciplines where the problem of reconciling general form with many (possibly unlimited) specific manifestations has been considered in the past. Based on a survey of cognitive psychology, linguistics and organizational management[2], we propose four recommendations for IS design theorizing.

4.1   Specify Transformational Rules

This recommendation originates in linguistics. Human language offers a potent metaphor for building and thinking about IS artifacts [45]. In particular, languages are *productive* to the extent that finite grammatical rules can be used to produce in principle infinite unique forms. According to Chomsky [46] the gist of a sentence is termed *deep structure* (or abstract representation of a sentence) while the variable form constitutes *surface structure*. For example, the sentences "Ron Weber won the LEO Award" and "The LEO Award was won by Ron Weber!" convey the same idea in different ways. Chomsky proposed to derive surface structure from the underlying meaning using *transformational rules* that transform deep structure to produce surface

---

[2] The choice of the disciplines is informed by authors' familiarity with these disciplines and their proven status as theoretical foundations of IS research. Our objective is not to provide a comprehensive survey of theories and generate exhaustive list of recommendations, but rather to catalyze future thinking in IS design science research on the issues raised here.

structures such that the core meaning is preserved, but the forms are altered to better suit the situation (e.g., adding passive voice, a question mark, or an inflection).

Transformational rules can be incorporated in design science theorizing. In addition to theoretical propositions, a theorist can produce transformational rules or *lawful* principles by which different specific design forms can be produced infinitely many times. In other words, the role of a transformational rule is to show how or under what principles concrete physical objects (e.g., HTML tags, CSS styles, or server-side scripts) are derived from abstract propositions.

For example, a transformational rule can specify how entering attributes is handled on the interface side. One such rule can propose a principle by which any technological implementation is acceptable (i.e., in any user environment, or using any surface object) as long as a user is not *a priori* exposed to attribute choices. Alternatively, a rule can state that any technological implementation is acceptable as long as a user is not constrained by attribute choices. Each rule may be reflective of different underlying theoretical arguments and will likely produce different outcomes for the dependent variables. Specifying a particular rule reduces implementation ambiguity.

Notably, transformational rules are already used in DSR. For example, researchers proposed transformations from conceptual grammars to logical models [36], or rules for reverse engineering from logical to conceptual models [47] – in each case the rules were proposed after the respective theories/methods/artifacts became popular. Including transformational rules in design theorizing can better capture the original intent of a theorist and also help early adopters avoid implementation pitfalls.

4.2   Develop or Imagine a Real Application

Before formulating the recommendation that potentially involves development of a real IS artifact, we briefly consider different approaches to this issue in the research community. Whether DSR should be based in practice and focus on real development is an unresolved issue. On the one hand, Iivari [8] recommends "that artifacts developed in design science should first be tested in laboratory and experimental situations as far as possible. One should not start with testing in the real situations, except perhaps in very exceptional, special situations" (p. 54). In contrast, Sein et al. [48], Cole et al. [49], Figueiredo and Cunha [50], Jarvinen [51] argue that conducting design science in organizational setting increases relevance of DSR and promotes cross-pollination of ideas between theory and practice. Using design science research as an intervention is coined *action design research* [21, 52]. Nevertheless, laboratory-based DSR remains prevalent. Hevner et al. [3] note, "artifacts constructed in design-science research are rarely full-grown information systems that are used in practice" (p. 83).

Considering the real vs. lab debate, we advance a two-fold proposition: while developing a real artifact can reveal the tension between design theory and design choices, authentic development is not always possible. Therefore, we encourage researchers to engage in *disciplined imagination* that simulates authentic settings.

A real-world implementation with contingencies, conflicts, and unexpected challenges may improve a design theory by making it *contextually grounded*. Context theorizing – development and refinement of a mid-range theory by accounting for top-down and bottom-up forces is a growing trend in management research [53]. The context is increasingly regarded as a *tool* of theoretical development: "context as a sensitizing device ... makes us more aware of the potential situational and temporal boundary conditions to our theories" [53].

Indeed, before Phase II the authors contended that extending the instance-based data collection interface to mobile platforms would be seamless and unproblematic. Only upon immersion in development did the difficulties of implementation in a mobile environment become apparent. Various interpretations of the chosen design theory have yet to yield satisfying answers. In short, authentic development amounts to context theorizing that reveals firsthand how particular implementations and organizational contingencies bear upon predictions made by a design theory.

As real development may not take place for various reasons, we encourage researchers working in laboratory settings to engage in *disciplined imagination* that to the extent possible simulates authentic development. The concept of *disciplined imagination* is proposed by Weick [54, 55] as a method of increasing "usefulness" (i.e., relevance) of scientific theories. According to Weick [54], disciplined imagination should be central to any theorizing and involves "consistent application of selection criteria to trial-and-error thinking" (i.e., the disciplined part) and "deliberate diversity introduced into problem statements, thought trials, and selection criteria that comprise that thinking" (i.e., the imagination part) (p. 516).

With disciplined imagination it should be possible, for example, to imagine the impact of a design theory on search engine optimization (a variable unlikely to be of interest to laboratory settings, but that is of great interest to project proponents). Considering real challenges may lead to uncovering and specifying implementation traps that would otherwise threaten successful application of design theories in practice.

4.3   Explore the Invariables

Whether developing a real system or imagining one, it may not be possible to consider all manifestations of a design theory [13]. IS design theorizing has to account for complex interactions between organizations, people and technology. It is difficult to consider relevant variables and their interaction effects because each IS implementation is unique [56].

We argue theorists should consider to the extent possible the invariables of the environment – things that should not change at least for some time. Here, we suggest turning to fundamental theories for guidance. For example, committing to a realist ontology presumes an objective reality of mind-independent entities. This assumption can be embedded in the core principles of a design theory thus anchoring these principles into assumed stability of the basic paradigmatic assumptions. The primacy of instances over classes embedded in the nature of the instance-based data model [42] is a type of paradigmatic assumption.

Another source of invariance is theories of human psychology that aim to uncover basic principles of perception, memory, and thinking. Following these theories makes it easier to specify implementations that interact with a user in more predictable ways. For example, cognitive theories of similarity investigate fundamental principles by which humans perceive two objects to be similar [57]. Using findings from similarity theories can identify potentially implementation-invariant principles, such as those used in computer-aided schema matching or Extract, Transform, and Load (ETL) tools [58]. Analyzing these principles can also help identify specific design choices that would be proscribed on the basis of limitations to human cognitive, biological, and socio-behavioral capabilities. For example, considering ways a human can communicate information (e.g., gesticulation, speech, typing, handwriting, texting) can support a conclusion that an unconstrained list of attributes is unsuitable for use on devices with limited text-entry functionality.

4.4   Over-Specify the Core

In light of the proposed recommendations, an important question is: to what part(s) of the theory should the recommendations be applied? While any design theory proposition should be amenable to these principles, pragmatically not every proposition may be subjected to equally rigorous scrutiny with respect to specific design choices.

Our recommendation is to over-specify those constructs that constitute the *core* of a design theory. Following the discussion on causality in Hovorka and Gregor [11], we propose *core elements* of a design science theory to be the *necessary conditions* for the outcome predicted by the theory. For example, the core in the instance-based approach can be taken as representations that are consistent with the ontological postulate of the primacy of instances over classes. It may be argued that as long as an implementation is faithful to this core principle, the IQ-participation tradeoff is (or should) be avoided. The researcher can then consider or implement reasonable forms this core principle may produce (e.g., constrained-choice attributes collection, prompt-guided attributes collection, free-form unconstrained attributes collection). In each case, the outcomes can be noted in form of contingencies, such as if <design option A> then <likely outcome B>. The forms that yield desired outcomes (with respect to dependent variables of interest) may be further examined to uncover any underlying regularities they may share. In turn, this may serve as a basis for formulating more insightful transformational rules.

5   Discussion and Outlook for Future Research

One way to increase rigor and relevance of DSR is by codifying design knowledge into design theories. Accepting this premise, questions emerge about how to approach design theorizing. In this paper we explored a murky issue of design theorizing: reconciling theoretical abstractness with many potential design alternatives. As most IS design theories are mid-range theories, the natural gap exists between theoretical propositions and concrete issues faced in practice. In many cases, this may lead to atheoretical choices and unfulfilled expectations from DSR. A survey of psychology, linguistics and management literature identified several promising approaches with potential to redress this issue. In all cases, the tradeoff between generality and specificity of choices appears to be circumvented allowing design theorists to pursue both.

The notion of transformational rules extended from linguistics directly addresses many individual forms emanating from an abstract core. We are hopeful that future research will leverage this idea and begin specifying different implementation trajectories. In this sense, the recommendations to develop or consider real IS, identify invariables, and over-specify the core become sensitizing devices used to generate transformational rules. The identification of the core should help focus on the most critical areas of design theories and maximize likelihood of desired changes in dependent variables. In the same vein, the building or consideration of a real application is a process by which potential moderating variables and subsequent design choices can surface (see Fig. 4). DSR is argued to be effective at refining kernel theories [17]. Likewise, building or considering a real artifact may lead to better understanding of the impact of a design theory on design choices.

Note that the four proposed recommendations are not meant to be definitive or exhaustive. Rather the overarching objective is to examine whether and how researchers could consider different ways practitioners may instantiate design theories. Design theory is different in many ways from predictive-explanatory theories of natural sciences; it is also a less mature theory type [6]. Much is left for future research to investigate and refine. For example, more recommendations akin to those developed here can be proposed in future studies. Future work can examine other theoretical foundations (e.g., engineering, architecture, medicine, law or even art), where general vs. specific tension is likely to be present. The new disciples can led to novel guidelines or refinement of the existing ones.

The issues raised in this paper can pave the way to interesting questions future research can tackle. An important question is whether focusing on design alternatives can lead to better design science theorizing and more effective practice. Future research can also evaluate the guidelines empirically and investigate, for example, the relative impact of different approaches to design theorizing on the effectiveness and efficiency of IS development.

In conclusion, the prevailing wisdom in design science theorizing is to focus on generality of theories. In this paper we pose the question of whether it is possible to reconcile theoretical generality with many alternative incarnations. Based on the broad survey of disciplines that grapple with a similar problem, we identified four recommendations that in principle account for specific design alternatives without forcing design science to descend to micro-level theorizing. Considering the potential pitfalls of ignoring these concerns, we conclude that theorists should, to the extent possible, consider specific design alternatives when building design theories.

Acknowledgements. The authors thank Joerg Evermann for several useful comments on this paper.

This research was supported by funding from the Natural Sciences and Engineering Council of Canada.

References

1. Gregor, S., Hevner, A.R.: Introduction to the Special Issue on Design Science. Information Systems & e-Business Management 9, 1–9 (2011)
2. Lee, A., Chasson, M., Alter, S., Kremar, H.: Long Live Design Science Research! .... and Remind Me again about Whether it is a New Research Paradigm Or a Rationale of Last Resort for Worthwhile Research that Doesn't Fit Under any Other Umbrella. In: ICIS 2012 (2012)
3. Hevner, A., March, S., Park, J., Ram, S.: Design Science in Information Systems Research. MIS Quarterly 28, 75–105 (2004)
4. March, S.T., Smith, G.F.: Design and Natural Science Research on Information Technology. Decision Support Systems 15, 251–266 (1995)
5. Gregor, S., Jones, D.: The Anatomy of Design Theory. Journal of the Association for Information Systems 8, 312–335 (2007)
6. Gregor, S.: The Nature of Theory in Information Systems. MIS Quarterly 30, 611–642 (2006)
7. Walls, J.G., Widmeyer, G.R., El Sawy, O.A.: Building an Information System Design Theory for Vigilant EIS. Information Systems Research 3, 36–59 (1992)
8. Iivari, J.: A Paradigmatic Analysis of Information Systems as a Design Science. Scandinavian Journal of Information Systems, 39–64 (2007)
9. Gleasure, B., Feller, J., O'Flaherty, B.: Procedurally Transparent Design Science Research: A Design Process Model. In: ICIS 2012, pp. 1–19 (2012)
10. Piirainen, K.A., Briggs, R.O.: Design Theory in Practice – Making Design Science Research More Transparent. In: Jain, H., Sinha, A.P., Vitharana, P. (eds.) DESRIST 2011. LNCS, vol. 6629, pp. 47–61. Springer, Heidelberg (2011)
11. Hovorka, D., Gregor, S.: Untangling Causality in Design Science Theorizing. In: 5th Biennial ANU Workshop on Information Systems Foundations: Theory Building in Information Systems (2010)
12. Gregor, S., Hovorka, D.S.: Causality: The Elephant in the Room in Information Systems Epistemology. In: ECIS 2011 (2011)
13. Venable, J.: The Role of Theory and Theorising in Design Science Research. In: DESRIST 2006, pp. 1–18 (2006)
14. Kuechler, W., Vaishnavi, V.: A Framework for Theory Development in Design Science Research: Multiple Perspectives. Journal of the Association for Information Systems 13, 395–423 (2012)
15. Weber, R.: Evaluating and Developing Theories in the Information Systems Discipline. Journal of the Association for Information Systems 13, 2 (2012)
16. Moody, D.L., Iacob, M., Amrit, C. In: Search of Paradigms: Identifying the Theoretical Foundations of the Information System Field. In: ECIS 2010, pp. 1–15 (2010)
17. Kuechler, B., Vaishnavi, V.: On Theory Development in Design Science Research: Anatomy of a Research Project. European Journal of Information Systems 17, 489–504 (2008)
18. Merton, R.: On Sociological Theories of the Middle Range. In: Merton, R. (ed.) Social Theory and Social Structure, pp. 39–53. Simon & Schuster, New York (1949)
19. Venable, J.: Incorporating Design Science Research and Critical Research into an Introductory Business Research Methods Course. Electronic Journal of Business Research Methods 9 (2011)
20. Peffers, K., Tuunanen, T., Gengler, C.E., Rossi, M., Hui, W., Virtanen, V., Bragge, J.: The Design Science Research Process: A Model for Producing and Presenting Information Systems Research. In: DESRIST 2006, pp. 83–106 (2006)

21. Iivari, J.: Nothing is as Clear as Unclear. Scandinavian Journal of Information Systems 19, 111–117 (2007)
22. Sutton, R.I., Staw, B.M.: What Theory is Not. Administrative Science Quarterly, 371–384 (1995)
23. Weick, K.E.: Theory Construction as Disciplined Reflexivity: Tradeoffs in the 90s. Academy of Management Review 24, 797–806 (1999)
24. Arazy, O., Kumar, N., Shapira, B.: A Theory-Driven Design Framework for Social Recommender Systems. Journal of the Association for Information Systems 11, 455–490 (2010)
25. Benbasat, I., Weber, R.: Research Commentary: Rethinking "diversity" in Information Systems Research. Information Systems Research 7, 389–399 (1996)
26. Hirschheim, R.A., Klein, H.K.: Crisis in the IS Field? A Critical Reflection on the State of the Discipline. Journal of the Association for Information Systems 4, 237–293 (2003)
27. Silvertown, J.: A New Dawn for Citizen Science. Trends in Ecology & Evolution 24, 467–471 (2009)
28. Hand, E.: People Power. Nature 466, 685–687 (2010)
29. Lukyanenko, R., Parsons, J., Wiersma, Y.: Citizen Science 2.0: Data Management Principles to Harness the Power of the Crowd. In: Jain, H., Sinha, A.P., Vitharana, P. (eds.) DESRIST 2011. LNCS, vol. 6629, pp. 465–473. Springer, Heidelberg (2011)
30. Fortson, L., Masters, K., Nichol, R., Borne, K., Edmondson, E., Lintott, C., Raddick, J., Schawinski, K., Wallin, J.: Galaxy Zoo: Morphological Classification and Citizen Science. In: Advances in Machine Learning and Data Mining for Astronomy, pp. 1–11 (2011)
31. Prestopnik, N.R., Crowston, K.: Gaming for (Citizen) Science: Exploring Motivation and Data Quality in the Context of Crowdsourced Science through the Design and Evaluation of a Social-Computational System. In: "Computing for Citizen Science" Workshop at the IEEE eScience Conference, pp. 1–28 (2011)
32. Antelio, M., Esteves, M.G.P., Schneider, D., de Souza, J.M.: Qualitocracy: A Data Quality Collaborative Framework Applied to Citizen Science. In: 2012 IEEE International Conference on Systems, Man, and Cybernetics, pp. 931–936 (2012)
33. Parsons, J., Lukyanenko, R., Wiersma, Y.: Easier Citizen Science is Better. Nature 471, 37–37 (2011)
34. Rowland, K.: Citizen Science Goes 'Extreme'. Nature (2012)
35. Chen, P.: The Entity-Relationship Model - Toward a Unified View of Data. ACM Transactions on Database Systems 1, 9–36 (1976)
36. Teorey, T.J., Yang, D., Fry, J.P.: A Logical Design Methodology for Relational Data-bases using the Extended Entity-Relationship Model. ACM Computing Surveys 18, 197–222 (1986)
37. Codd, E.F.: Relational Database: A Practical Foundation for Productivity. Communications of the ACM 25, 109–117 (1982)
38. Hochachka, W.M., Fink, D., Hutchinson, R.A., Sheldon, D., Wong, W., Kelling, S.: Data-Intensive Science Applied to Broad-Scale Citizen Science. Trends in Ecology & Evolution 27, 130–137 (2012)
39. Silvertown, J.: Taxonomy: Include Social Networking. Nature 467, 788–788 (2010)
40. Lukyanenko, R., Parsons, J.: Conceptual Modeling Principles for Crowdsourcing. In: Proceedings of the 1st International Workshop on Multimodal Crowd Sensing, pp. 3–6 (2012)
41. Lukyanenko, R., Parsons, J.: Rethinking Data Quality as an Outcome of Conceptual Modeling Choices. In: 16th International Conference on Information Quality, pp. 1–16 (2011)

42. Parsons, J., Wand, Y.: Emancipating Instances from the Tyranny of Classes in Information Modeling. ACM Transactions on Database Systems 25, 228–268 (2000)
43. Wand, Y., Weber, R.: On the Deep Structure of Information Systems. Information Systems Journal 5, 203–223 (2008)
44. Ghose, A., Goldfarb, A., Han, S.: How is the Mobile Internet Different? Search Costs and Local Activities. Information Systems Research, pp. 1–19 (forthcoming)
45. Gredler, M., Shields, C.: Does no One Read Vygotsky's Words? Commentary on Glassman. Educational Researcher 33, 21–25 (2004)
46. Chomsky, N.: The minimalist program. MIT Press (1995)
47. Chiang, R.H.L., Barron, T.M., Storey, V.C.: Reverse Engineering of Relational Databases: Extraction of an EER Model from a Relational Database. Data & Knowledge Engineering 12, 107–142 (1994)
48. Sein, M.K., Rossi, M., Purao, S.: Exploring the Limits of the Possible. Scandinavian Journal of Information Systems 19, 105–110 (2007)
49. Cole, R., Purao, S., Rossi, M., Sein, M.: Being Rigorously Relevant: Design Research and Action Research in Information Systems. In: ICIS 2005, pp. 325–336 (2005)
50. Figueiredo, A., Cunha, P.: Action Research and design in Information Systems. In: Kock, N. (ed.) Information Systems Action Research, pp. 61–96. Springer (2007)
51. Järvinen, P.: Mapping Research Questions to Research Methods. In: Avison, D., Kasper, G.M., Pernici, B., Ramos, I., Roode, D. (eds.) Advances in Information Systems Research, Education and Practice. IFIP, vol. 274, pp. 29–41. Springer, Boston (2008)
52. Sein, M., Henfridsson, O., Purao, S., Rossi, M., Lindgren, R.: Action Design Research. MIS Quarterly 35, 37 (2011)
53. Bamberger, P.: From the Editors Beyond Contextualization: Using Context Theories to Narrow the Micro-Macro Gap in Management Research. Academy of Management Journal 51, 839–846 (2008)
54. Weick, K.E.: Theory Construction as Disciplined Imagination. Academy of Management Review, 516–531 (1989)
55. Weick, K.E.: What Theory is Not, Theorizing is. Administrative Science Quarterly 40, 385–390 (1995)
56. Lee, A.S.: A Scientific Methodology for MIS Case Studies. MIS Quarterly, 33–50 (1989)
57. Tversky, A.: Features of Similarity. Psychological Review 84, 327–352 (1977)
58. Evermann, J.: Applying Cognitive Principles of Similarity to Data Integration–the Case of SIAM. In: AMCIS 2012 (2012)
59. Te'eni, D.: Designs That Fit: An Overview of Fit Conceptualizations in HCI. In: Zhang, P., Galletta, D. (eds.) Human-Computer Interaction and Management Information Systems: Foundations, pp. 205–223. M.E. Sharpe (2006)
60. Venkatesh, V., Morris, M.G., Davis, G.B., Davis, F.D.: User Acceptance of Information Technology: Toward a Unified View. MIS Quarterly, 425–478 (2003)
61. Gefen, D., Karahanna, E., Straub, D.W.: Trust and TAM in Online Shopping: An Integrated Model. MIS Quarterly 27, 51–90 (2003)
62. Parsons, J., Wand, Y.: Using Cognitive Principles to Guide Classification in Information Systems Modeling. MIS Quarterly 32, 839–868 (2008)

Formidable Bracelet, Beautiful Lantern

Studying Multi-sensory User Experience from a Semiotic Perspective

Rebekah Rousi

Department of Computer Science and Information Systems, University of Jyväskylä, Finland
rebekah.rousi@jyu.fi

Abstract. We live in an experience economy. The more saturated the global market becomes with products offering the same functions, services and quality, the more companies are wanting to appeal to the intangible needs and desires of consumers. To achieve this, designers and researchers are turning inwards to investigate the psychological factors affecting peoples' relationships and reactions towards design properties. For this reason, design semantics studies on user experience have been advancing all the time. Much emphasis has been placed on visual product experience, as well as the relationship between brand perception and user experience. These are important steps, which are referred to in this paper. However, experience is multi-sensory, that is, our mental impressions and representations are constantly stimulated and informed by what we see, hear, taste, smell and touch. This paper explains user experience from a semiotic perspective. It then introduces a cognitive semiotic model, the C-model, of user experience and describes its application in an empirical study. Findings of the study suggest that while people favor what is perceived through sight in contrast to what is perceived through touch. However, the sense of touch inspires imaginative interpretation of form and associations with visual properties such as color.

Keywords: user experience, multi-sensory, semiotic, design, psychology.

1   Introduction

The global market is saturated with products which offer the same functions, quality and services. For a while now it has been known that 'something more' is required in order for a product to stand out from the rest. It is for this reason that the past few decades have been focused on examining not only what the product can do, or even say (social articulation), but how the product makes a user feel [1-2]. It was Pine and Gilmore [1] who suggested that we live in an experience economy. Experience is psychological [3-7]. Experience does not exist within a design. Design cannot induce a precise experience within a user. Further, we can never know exactly what another person experiences – how their thoughts (mental contents) combine to create specific impressions. Studies have been undertaken in relation to matters such as empathy [8-9] and HCI. Methods such as scenario-building and experience prototyping have been

J. vom Brocke et al. (Eds.): DESRIST 2013, LNCS 7939, pp. 181–196, 2013.

used as tools for understanding how people perceive, make sense of and react to particular interaction situations [10]. In terms of considering the potential user's emotions and conditions of thought when perceiving a product, these theories and analytical techniques are undoubtedly invaluable. However, empathy only explains our ability to understand how and why another person feels the way they do. As designers and researchers we are still limited to our own psychological boundaries of interpretation. These limitations have been explained in discussions on qualia and consciousness, whereby we can know what factors contribute to UX, but we cannot know *how* these emotions and thoughts are experienced [11-13]. What we can do is look at the readily available information that is presented to us via the qualitative material users provide when describing their interactions. We can see how (tangible) information contents contribute to the formation of the experience, and in what order, or priority these contents come to the fore.

Further, what is also known is that in order to experience, human beings are stimulated by information that is acquired through the senses: sight, touch, taste, smell, sound (even the mind has been considered an extra sense) [3], [14]. Design products always appeal to multiple senses [3], whether through touch and sight, sight and sound – even olfactory (smell) senses are constantly at work whether it is intended or not. Accordingly, design is moving in a direction towards inspiring user experiences (UXs) through not just one but several of these senses. Presently, a shift is occurring in the (information technology) design world. Focus is moving away from designing for ocular sensory experience, such as that seen in relation to graphic user interface (GUI) and web design, towards system designs which encourage multi-modal experience [3] (see studies on augmented or mixed-reality [15-16]).

This investigation concentrates on how people make sense of the designs they perceive through alternate senses (via touch and sight). Of interest here are the types of mental impressions that are formed when people encounter material and formal design elements through touch and sight. The empirical investigation focuses on how people qualitatively represent their experiences. The title of this paper "Formidable bracelet, beautiful lantern" reflects the findings of this study. It shows the mismatch of congruity between what was experienced through touch and sight. Touch opened the boundaries of imagination and lead participants to speculate on form, purpose, color, while also instilling a sense of caution, particularly if the touch sensation was unpleasant. Sight united the semiotic information obtained from the object and drew a sense of conclusiveness to what was perceived.

The paper proceeds by first drawing on previous studies regarding experience, UX and design semantics [2], [14], [17-26]. Multi-sensory experience is illustrated in the same section, by discussing research on the senses and design aesthetics [3], [27]. This is followed by an introduction to the working theory of this study - the cognitive semiotic model (C-model). The C-model was developed by the author as a theory and framework of empirical investigation to explain the semiotic process of UX, which relies not simply on user-artifact interaction itself but the signifying systems of how UX is represented through user feedback (representations) in response to designer representations (the products). Application of the C-model is exemplified in the instance of the empirical study – which investigates the momentary UX of three design objects via the senses of touch and sight. The concluding discussion throws light on some of the major findings of this study. It also suggests ways in which the C-model can be applied to investigating multi-sensory UX in the instance of human-computer interaction (HCI).

2   Semiotics and Multi-sensory UX

This paper refers to previous studies on design semantics [18] and experience [2], [14], [19-21] as well as design aesthetics [3], [27]. Charles Peirce's [28-29] basic semiotic model is used as a base for interpreting the user-design semantic sign systems. Peirce's basic semiotic model comprised three main elements: the object (that which is signified), the sign/symbol (or signifying element) and the interpretant (the mental understanding of the sign). In Peirce's work and re-works, there is mention of the elements which are crucial to the operation of the sign [28]. These elements are both formal in their signifying nature and causal. In other words, symbols or signs function due to associations made by those who interpret them as the result of habits and agreements which are socially, culturally and psychologically established. Thus, context and the user are the key players in establishing meaning.

As Krippendorff and Butter [18] point out, design objects are highly symbolic in nature. They constantly refer to either other objects or phenomena and draw on social and cultural codes such as values, hierarchies, traditions etc. Moreover, in UX research the design products under investigation may not simply be viewed as objects. Rather, they are dynamic objects [28] or symbolic mechanisms in themselves. In turn when encountered, these dynamic objects trigger chains of meaningful symbolism relating to, e.g. purpose, action, values etc. Of interest here, is how the material and formal qualities of the designs as perceived through touch and sight, generate these symbolic associations [30-32]. Ultimately, the objects of analysis at the end of the experimental process are the qualitative representations – interpretants – of the signification process. That is, this investigating looks at the way that a participant expresses their multi-sensory experience of a design. In turn, this expression or qualitative representation is a sign of not simply the object or the sign, but the mental impression induced by the experience.

This semiotic process is not limited to visual signs. Every mode of sensory input contributes to an understanding of a thing or phenomenon. Hekkert [3] argues that aesthetics or sensory perception is only part of an experience, and that cognition and emotion should be conceptually separated. On evolutionary and cognitive psychological grounds Hekkert [3] postulates that sensory aesthetics are used by the human mind as indicators, i.e. of that which is good or bad for us [27]. In turn, aesthetic response can be seen as an evolutionary alert mechanism designed to induce appropriate cognitive and/or emotional responses. In other words, our experiences are created through the dynamic multi-modal processing of sensory input, forming an aesthetic impression, generating cognitive response and emotional reaction.

3   The Cognitive Semiotic Model (C-model) of UX

With all the effort that has been placed into explaining the semiotic relationship between design semantics and UX, it seems fitting that a simplified model exemplifying
the experiential semiotic process is illustrated. Vihma [32] is critical of models that
position designers and users at opposite ends of the design and signification process.
The cognitive semiotic model of UX, or C-model, is proposed here as a theory which
exemplifies the relationship between symbolic representations. It does not position the
designer and user at a distance from one another. Rather, it illustrates the process of
signification from one articulation of ideas (the designer's or corporate's), to the articulation of impressions (the user's). The C-model can be seen in Fig. 1:

Fig. 1. Cognitive semiotic model (C-model) of UX

The C-model has been influenced by Krippendorff and Butter [18], as well as
Warell [2], [14], [23-24] in particular. The 'C', standing for cognitive, also serves to
exemplify the circular signification process. Krippendorff and Butter's [18] theory
comprises a circular process model for approaching product semantics. They state the
nature of a design form in that it: 1) articulates something about itself; 2) says something about the broader use context; and 3) generates a conceptual connection in the
mind of the user/consumer. Krippendorff and Butter suggest that the design does not
'say' what it is, but rather, the object is what it communicates to the user. Thus, the
meaning of the object, or its definition, is housed within the mind of the user based on
how they contextually interpret the form's features and application. Based on this
perspective experience – as meaning – is dynamic and ephemeral [6]. Things become
meaningful in interaction [3], [17], [19], [33-34]. This view on the semiotic relationship between product and consumer, or object and perceiver (and subsequently
interpretant) follows Peirce's [28] understanding that a sign is only a sign if it is understood as a sign. Or in other words, while the materialization of thoughts and ideas
takes place in product design and user feedback expression, the signification in itself

only takes place within the mind. Thus, the 'C' or the circle represents the continuous flow of thoughts and symbols in consciousness.

More practically, Warell [2], [14] [26] proposes the perceptual (or visual) product experience (PPE) model. PPE draws on Peirce's [46] theorization of presentation and representation. Warell states that where presentation can be viewed as the hedonic and pleasurable component of experience [19-22], [35-36], representation can be seen as the meaningful component. Thus, representation is the way in which the presentation is mentally and socially re-presented (or re-composed). Warell's [2], [14], [26] models comprise three non-linear modes: presentation, experience and representation. Each of these modes is accompanied by three psychological sub-modes. Presentation is attached to impression, appreciation and emotion. Experience is attached to sensory, cognitive and affective. Finally, representation is accompanied by recognition, association and comprehension.

When looking at PPE a separation can be seen in terms of the sensory, cognitive and affective factors of experience. This follows the conceptual separation of components of experience - the aesthetic, cognitive and emotional – [3]. As a model, PPE is quite comprehensive and incorporates multi-sensory perception. However, as experience is psychological these modes and sub-modes cannot be neatly categorized. The concepts of presentation and representation, or the re-presentation (re-telling) of the presentation are straight forward. In accordance with Peirce's semiotic model, presentation does not mean an original or tangible object in and of itself. The presentation is rather the stimulus of the chain of experiential interactions (mental and social). The object or thing that is presented can also be seen to re-present and draw reference to things other than itself [19], [28]. Thus, if we focus on the nature of the design product as the materialization of a designer's and corporate ideas [25], [32], it too is a re-presentation.

The C-model gives a basic illustration of this complex process. The idea is to highlight the main areas of analysis in a cognitive semiotic approach to UX. The symbolic representations offered by the user in their qualitative accounts of design experience are analyzed in light of their relationship to formal qualities and material characteristics of designs (representations). In other words, by placing the word "symbol" in the gap of the 'C', we are referring to ongoing representation stimulated by symbolism. Ideas behind design products do not simply originate from designers and the companies they design for, but are established and exist within specific contexts (temporal and spatial) and socio-cultural conditions (economic, hierarchies, values, traditions and beliefs etc.). Attached to each design decision, are strings of associations made as a result of the interaction between designer/company, its surroundings and agenda. Likewise, the user (and use situation) exists within a context (or set of contexts) and socio-cultural conditions. The string of symbolic associations is never the same, neither between designer/company and user, nor between two users. Added to the experiential process of forming mental impressions of designs and interactions (seen in the curve of the 'C' – user mental processing), are psychological conditions – prior experiences, pre-interaction impressions (i.e. through advertising or word-of-mouth), moods, usage and ownership goals etc. Designers can only hope to create a design which inspires certain types of interactions and experiences [18].

As humans are embodied multi-sensory beings, design interactions are always experienced through multiple senses. When interacting with a website for example, there is always (unless visually impaired) the most obvious senses of sight and maybe sound (intrinsic to the design). In addition, there is the sensation of touch through keypad or touch screen, the possible extrinsic sound of keypad feedback and other environmental noises, and the smell of the technological devices (plastic, warm electric residue). Based on Gestalt theory, the human mind has a tendency to draw connections between phenomena or features in order to establish an interpretive whole [37]. In other words, to process information the mind needs to make sense of things by constructing what it perceives as the entire picture at any given time. This makes studying the momentary UX of design forms from a multi-sensory perspective extremely interesting, as when something is perceived through one sense – i.e. sight or touch – the mind tends to fill in the other sensory gaps [38-39]. The next section outlines the empirical study. The focus of the empirical study was to examine how people qualitatively represented their experiences based on information obtained from isolated sensory perception of the design forms.

4   Method

4.1   Participants

This was an experimental study, designed to test a compact qualitative data collection technique to be implemented in future cross-cultural multi-sensory UX research. Participants (N = 35) represented a range of cultural backgrounds: 16 Finnish, three American (US), three Austrian, three Chinese, two Greek, two German and six from other nationalities (Pakistani, Tanzanian, Hungarian, Chilean, Nigerian and Polish). Ages ranged from 22 to 62 years old (mean age = 30,26; median = 29). Twenty-one females and 14 males participated.

4.2   Stimuli

The stimuli of this study were three home décor design objects chosen for their scale, form and material. The objects were: *White Peppermill* (Antonio Citterio, 2000); *Barn Owl* (Oiva Toikka, 1972) – a decoration; and *Fire* (Nathalie Lahdenmäki, 2002) – a candle lantern (seen in Fig. 2). The *White Peppermill* was chosen for its metallic material and cylindrical form. It is a utilitarian object for grinding pepper in food preparation. The *Barn Owl* is a decorative object chosen for its heavier weight, smooth ceramic surface and asymmetric form. Finally, *Fire* was chosen for its porous material, light weight and ambivalent utilitarian nature (the base was not included in the study). The stimuli were selected because they: 1) differ in form, semantic nature and use purpose; yet 2) are related in terms of use context (in the home), and are developed under the same brand – thus conforming with the same design strategy [23]. While this was not a comparative study of brands, the element of semantic recognition in strategic design practice is an interesting component in studying UX from a semiotic perspective [2], [14], [25]. More discussion about this will take place in a future paper.

Fig. 2. White *Peppermill* (left); *Barn Owl* (centre); *Fire* (right)

4.3   Material

The three design objects were placed in plain white boxes with hand-sized holes in the front, to prevent participants from seeing the objects. To feel the objects participants were asked to reach inside the boxes. Participants were presented with information sheets regarding the procedure and purpose of the experiments and were asked to sign a consent form. Participants were also asked to fill in a background information form asking: year of birth, gender, highest level of education obtained, professional field, nationality, native language, level of interest in design products and processes (Likert-scale: 1=not at all, 5=extremely interested), and types of designs of interest (i.e. architecture, web, fashion, home décor etc.). This information will be used for future between-subject and between-group analysis.

The main experiment material was a questionnaire form comprising two parts. The first part was for touch and the second for sight. In each of these parts, five blank rows were provided for each object (15 rows in total per part, and 30 overall). In these rows, participants were asked to provide the first five words or phrases that came to mind when perceiving the objects. Underneath the blank rows, participants were asked to rate the attractiveness of the objects (based on either touch or sight) on a Likert-scale of one to five. This paper concentrates on discussing the qualitative results.

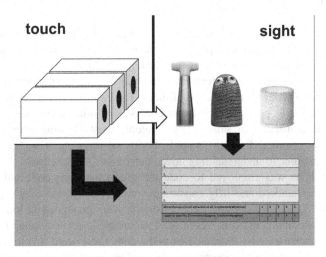

Fig. 3. Overview of materials

Fig. 3 shows an overview of the materials used in the experiment. The boxes were placed side by side so that once the experiments commenced, participants only needed to: place their hands in the holes (one-by-one), feel the objects, write the words/phrases (constructs) in the rows provided in response to the object they were feeling, rate it, then move on to the next hole (object) and repeat the procedure. In the sight part of the experiment the objects were revealed one-by-one – and were only observed one per time. The same writing and rating procedure was performed for each object in the sight part, as was completed during the touch part.

4.4   Procedure

Upon entering the experiment situation participants were given an information sheet explaining the experiment purpose and procedure, and a verbal introduction was given by the researcher. Participants were told that the experiment would take approximately 15 minutes to complete. Firstly, the information sheets and consent forms were read and signed. This was followed by completion of the background information forms. Participants were then directed to reach into the first box, feel the object, and write down the first things that came to mind (words or phrases) in response to what they were touching. Participants were told that they did not have a time limit and could feel the objects as much as they wanted, but they were encouraged to write the very first things that came to mind. The words/phrases could be anything (not everyone thinks in adjectives). The object was then quantitatively rated in terms of attractiveness and willingness to own. The entire procedure was repeated until all three objects had been felt. In the sight part of the experience, the objects were then revealed one at a time. The same procedure of writing the first five words that came to mind and quantitatively rating the objects was repeated.

5   Results

In line with Personal Construct Theory [40-41], the qualitative data was analyzed via content analysis. The words and phrases were treated as constructs of information representing the mental experiences of the participants. There are internal and external versions of constructs. The internal are the way we mentally construct, or package, phenomena in order to make sense of them. The external construct, is the way in which people frame or package their experience so that other people can make sense of them. These constructs of information contents exist in some communicational form, i.e. words, phrases, drawings, sounds, bodily gestures etc. They are the closest way that we can come to understanding how a person has made sense of the situation.

Content analysis was employed to code the qualitative data collected in the experiments. Three-hundred and fifty constructs were generated for each object by the 35 participants. One thousand and fifty constructs were generated in total. The data was carefully read and constructs were coded according to related content categories. Over all nine categories were extracted from the data, these were: 1) physical characteristics (actual); 2) shapes; 3) metaphors and analogies; 4) colours; 5) emotions and aesthetic response; 6) physical sensation (subjective); 7) formal and stylistic judgments; 8) utility; and 9) added value. The following sub-section focuses on explaining the construct categories and their relationship to the design forms. Then, descriptive statistics are used to briefly outline the results of the quantitative evaluations and frequencies of constructs in relation to the touch and sight experiences of the objects.

5.1   Content Categories

The following table explains the construct categories extracted from the qualitative data via content analysis. Words were placed in construct categories according to similarities in description types based on the criteria of what the words/phrases were describing and how they were described. There is no strict order of the construct categories, but the contents can be seen to represent the design-innate characteristics in the first half of the list, and then the user-innate descriptions in the second half of the list.

Table 1. Qualitative Content Construct Categories

Physical Characteristics (actual)	Refers to the words/phrases regarding the actual physicality and materiality of the objects. Constructs included: metal, ceramic, plastic, plaster of Paris, jagged edges, hollow, holes etc. These constructs referred to features that were physically tangible within the forms.
Shapes	Related to the physical characteristics, refers to constructs directly describing the shape of the objects. These constructs included: round, t-shaped, cylinder, oval, skewed etc.
Metaphors	Referring to associations made to objects and phenomena. These constructs included: bunny, weapon, fruit, jewel, bracelet, kaleidoscope, sailing boat, running pigs, hammer, trophy etc.
Colors	Constructs included: "It feels brown"; "The plastic feels red"; "The plastic feels black"; "This one (the owl) feels blue"; "This should have been orange"; "It is white but it feels beige".
Emotions & Aesthetic Response	Refers to aesthetically-based descriptions used to convey emotional content towards the designs in question. Constructs included: fun, beautiful, mysterious, dangerous, meaningful, romantic, ugly, interesting etc.
Physical Sensations (subjective)	Constructs subjectively (relatively) describing the physicality of the forms. Constructs included: cold, moist, warm, rough, durable, tickling, wide, light, pointy etc.
Formal & Stylistic Judgment	Content which judged the form and style of the objects. Constructs included: quality, timeless, technical, modern, outdated, shabby, fashionable, technical, every day, masculine, sterile, atmospheric and unique etc.

Table 1. (*continued*)

Utility	Constructs describing the utility/non-utility of the objects. Constructs included: usable, useful, useless, decorative, purposeless, functionless, play music, to hit, baking, food preparation, seasoning, cooking etc.
Added Value	Refers to the intangible element of value – cultural and social. Constructs included: brand, Finnish design, Iittala (a Finnish design company), design, well-designed, craft, art, and crème de la crème.

5.2   Frequencies of Construct Categories

Frequency analysis was performed in IBM SPSS of the construct categories. This analysis revealed the frequency in which certain types of constructs were used in relation to the objects, via both touch and right. Further, the analysis was also utilized to determine the order in which particular types of qualitative constructs were used. As the data is extremely large, pie charts have been used to summarize the construct distributions, and in which order the constructs were used. The colors featured in the pie charts represent the following construct categories: red = physical characteristics; blue = shapes; green = metaphors; light blue = colors; beige = emotions and aesthetic response; purple = physical sensations; yellow = formal and stylistic judgment; grey = utility; and puce = added value. Figs. 6-8 represent the objects. The top rows of the diagrams show the frequency of construct categories for the touch part of the experiment. The bottom rows show the frequency of construct categories for the sight part of the experiment. The numbers one to five represent the order in which the words/phrases were given (i.e. from first word/phrase to fifth word/phrase). These combined results give an idea of the type of thought content that first came to mind when perceiving the objects, and in which order the content occurred.

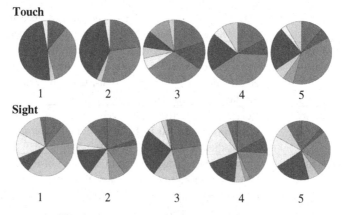

Fig. 4. White *Peppermill* construct frequencies

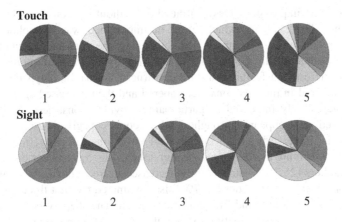

Fig. 5. Barn *Owl* construct frequencies

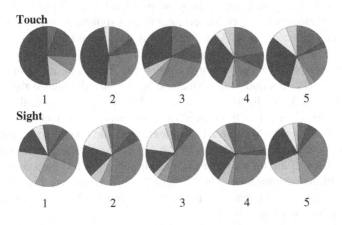

Fig. 6. Fire construct frequencies

Physical sensations (48.6%) dominated the very first impressions of experiencing the *White Peppermill* through touch (Fig.4). This continued when participants provided the second construct (40%), but was overtaken by metaphors (34.3%) when it was time to write the third construct. Thus, metaphors dominated the ways in which participants represented their experiences of touching the peppermill for the rest of the constructs (three through to five). Interestingly, it can be seen that physical sensations began to grow in importance again in relation to the fourth and fifth constructs. Other first impressions of touch included shapes (11.4%), which did not appear in the second construct, but were used again in the third through to fifth constructs. Then there was formal and stylistic judgment appearing somewhat through all construct positions and emotional aesthetic response. Utility began to be thought of by the third construct (2.9%) and increased in prominence with the fourth and fifth constructs. Also, colors (5.7%) came to mind by the third construct and were also used in the fifth. In the case of sight, the emotions and aesthetic response category (22.9%)

dominated the first impression. This continued throughout the constructs but became less important. The category which grew in importance was metaphors. Utility (14.3%) featured in the first constructs, then tapered by the third and began increasing again in the fourth and fifth. Color (14.3%) was also among the first impressions and decreased in interest (not featured in third construct). Formal and stylistic judgment (8.6%) was featured in the first construct, tapered and then increased again. Physical sensations interestingly increased as participants provided constructs. And associations with added value appeared throughout all the constructs given based on sight.

There was an increase in use of the physical sensations category (from 25.7% to 37.1%) when perceiving the *Barn Owl* through touch (Fig. 5). Another dominant category is metaphors (25.7%) which slightly decreased in frequency as constructs were given. The physical characteristics (25.7%) also dominated the first three impressions and decreased by the fourth and fifth constructs given. The shape was another dominant factor participants paid attention to, and after the first impression people started speculating about its (non)utility. Emotional and aesthetic responses were given in the first impressions, disappeared and then grew in importance. Colors, although few, featured almost throughout the constructs, and formal stylistic judgments were made in the second to fifth constructs. Added value was mentioned in the second and fifth constructs relating to touch. In response to seeing the object, people's responses were dominated by metaphors (57.1%) through reference to the owl or other things (nature, hangovers etc.). The Emotions and aesthetic category also dominated the constructs given, increasing to 34.3% by the fifth construct. Mention of the physical characteristics and colors were consistent throughout the constructs. Yet, colors grew in interest from the second to fourth construct positions. Stylistic judgment is represented throughout the constructs and mention of the object's (non)utility is almost always present. The shape of the object was mentioned in the second to third constructs and physical sensations were mentioned in the second to fifth constructs. From the third to fifth constructs there is reference to added value through identifying the design as belonging to a Finnish design brand.

In the case of the *Fire* candle lantern, physical sensations (51.4%) dominate the first impressions, as well as the rest of the constructs (Fig. 6). Attention was given to shape (20%) but decreased in frequency by the fifth construct. Emotional and aesthetic responses (14.3%) were also almost always present, and reference to the physical characteristics increased by the third to fifth constructs. Likewise, metaphors grew in importance particularly by the third construct (28.6%). Interestingly, although this was the touch component, colors were mentioned in the second to fifth constructs. Formal and stylistic judgment was given in the second, fourth and fifth constructs, and possible utility was mentioned in the fourth and fifth constructs. The colors (25.7%) were among the first things people paid attention to when viewing *Fire*. These were mainly in response to mismatched expectations based on the colors imagined during the touch part. Metaphors were also prominent throughout the constructs, particularly in third construct position (42.9%). Emotions and aesthetic responses were given throughout, but especially in the first and fifth construct positions (20%). The physical sensations category was prominent throughout, and formal-stylistic judgments were consistently made. Physical characteristics were constantly referred to, and the possible utility of the object was mentioned in the second to fifth constructs. Further, added value related to design was mentioned in the first to fourth constructs.

6   Concluding Discussion

In the scope of this paper, UX has been outlined in relation to psychological notions of experience, and multi-sensory perception. Here, the cognitive semiotic model (C-model) of UX has also been introduced and defined in light of previous theoretical understandings of semiotics and design. The C-model is intended to be an efficient and effective alternative for gathering qualitative material based on succinct first impressions gained through momentary UX. Where interviews, video data and subsequent methods such as protocol analysis demand ample time to transcribe, code and interpret, this method aims at gathering key constructs directly from participants. The current study has provided the ground work, whereby key construct categories have been extracted from the qualitative material. These categories can thus be used as an analytical framework for semiotic UX studies in the future – particularly in cross-cultural studies where greater structure provides more clarity into topics for comparison. Furthermore, where in traditional approaches to qualitative data collection (such as interviews and focus groups) sample sizes have been limited. This compact method allows for larger samples. In fact, the more participants the better the idea of what construct categories dominate people's impressions when experiencing design forms via multiple senses. Additionally, with more time devoted to interpretation of the results, richer insight into deep thought contents may be gained. Undoubtedly, the question that may be on many readers' minds might be: what about the actual content and meanings of the qualitative responses? As in the case of interviews, this takes time to interpret, but would reveal more detail regarding the relationship between how people perceive design elements and how they make sense of what they perceive.

The C-model may even be used to compliment other methods such as PPE, whereby qualitative constructs provided by the participants themselves, may be compared to semantic relationships drawn between user perceptions and e.g. design/marketing goals. In this instance, the designer/researcher could examine the connection between design/marketing terminology, design syntactics and user vocabulary. From the qualitative data gained in this study, numerous repetitions occurred whereby people reported colors when touching the objects. They associated the colors with specific material and surface qualities. For example, some participants had stated that plastic either felt "black" or "red", and were surprised to see that the object's (*White Peppermill*) plastic component was white. Others reported that the porous quality of the *Fire* candle lantern gave it a beige, brown or orange feel. Others claimed that the *Barn Owl* felt blue because of its cool, smooth texture. Thus, regarding multi-sensory information technology (such as augmented reality) designers may establish elements of surprise by manipulating the relationships between e.g. visual characteristics and tactile qualities.

Another interesting observation of these results shows how people quite often rely on metaphors to explain what they are thinking. Metaphors are noted as stylistic devices which operate as vehicles to communicate things which are difficult to articulate in words [3]. Through referring to things other than the source (or object in question) a string of meaning can be mapped out regarding what is being experienced [42]. In fact, the largest construct category of this study was that of metaphors. This was particularly so when people were able to connect what they perceived with some other form or phenomenon they were familiar with: for example, a sportsman associated the peppermill with a trophy, both through touch and sight; and a student who had been on exchange abroad associated the porous qualities of the *Fire* candle lantern and its shape, with piglets running around on a patch of dirt.

Brand and quality were also referred to by those either familiar with the forms in question, or with the company – thus, having connected the syntactic features to the company's design strategy. This is an extremely important factor to investigate in future studies, both in terms of what representations are produced in response to and in connection with brand associations, as well as what sensory input occurs when interacting with objects of particular brands. On this note, when designing technological applications that appeal to multiple senses it should be remembered that humans are embodied beings. Sight, when enabled, is a highly powerful tool for information collection. Yet, the other senses, such as touch, remind us we that have a body, providing a basis for experience itself [3]. The process of examining the semiotic relationship between designs, experience and sensory input is complicated. It is however hoped that the C-model can be viewed as a practical and logical tool for analyzing how UX is represented by the user.

Acknowledgements. Thank you Iittala for providing the stimuli for my research, Nokia and the University of Jyväskylä for funding my PhD research, and my supervisor Prof. Pertti Saariluoma for all his ideas and inspiration.

References

1. Pine, B.J., Gilmore, J.H.: The Experience Economy. Harvard Business School Press, Boston (1999)
2. Warell, A.: Visual Experience of Brand-Specific Automobile Design: Studying appreciation, emotion and comprehension using the VPE framework. In: 1st European Conference on Affective Design and Kansei (Emotion) Engineering, Lund University (2007), http://www.ep.liu.se/ecp/026/116/ecp0726116.pdf
3. Hekkert, P.: Design Aesthetics: principles of pleasure in design. J. Psych. Sci. 48, 157–172 (2006)
4. Dewey, J.: Art as Experience. Perigee, New York (1980)
5. Forlizzi, J., Battarbee, K.: Understanding Experience in Interactive Systems. In: Designing Interactive Systems: Processes, Practices, Methods, and Techniques, pp. 261–268. Human-Computer Interaction Institute, Cambridge (2004), http://repository.cmu.edu/hcii/46
6. McCarthy, J., Wright, P.: Technology as Experience. In: Interactions, vol. 11(5), pp. 42–43. ACM, New York (2004), doi:10.1145/1015530.1015549

7. Roto, V., Law, E., Vermeeren, A., Hoonhout, J.: User Experience White Paper – bringing clarity to the concept of user experience. Report, Dagstuhl Seminar on Demarcating User Experience (2011), http://www.allaboutux.org/files/UX-WhitePaper.pdf
8. Kohut, H.: Introspection, Empathy, and Psychoanalysis – an examination of the relationship between mode of observation and theory. JAPA 7, 459–483 (1959)
9. Lakoff, G.: Don't Think of an Elephant: Know Your Values and Frame the Debate: The Essential Guide for Progressives. Chelsea Green Publishing, White River Junction (2004)
10. Carroll, J.: Making Use: scenario-based design of human-computer interactions. MIT Press, Cambridge (2000)
11. Kerkow, D.: Don't have to know what it is like to be a Bat to Build a Radar Reflector – functionalism in UX. In: Towards a UX Manifesto, pp. 19–25 (2007), http://141.115.28.2/cost294/upload/506.pdf
12. Jackson, F.: Epiphenomenal Qualia. Phil. Q. 32, 127–136 (1982)
13. Revonsuo, A.: Consciousness: the science of subjectivity. Psychology Press, New York (2010)
14. Warell, A.: Multi-Modal Visual Experience of Brand-Specific Automobile Design. J. TQM 20(4), 356–371 (2008), http://dx.doi.org/10.1108/17542730810881348
15. Feiner, S., Macintyre, B., Seligmann, D.: Knowledge-Based Augmented Reality. In: Cohen, J. (ed.) Communications of the ACM Special Issue on Computer Augmented Environments: Back to the Real World, vol. 36(7), pp. 53–62. ACM, New York (1993)
16. Haller, M., Billinghurst, M., Thomas, B.: Emerging Technologies of Augmented Reality: Interfaces and Design. Idea Group Publishing, Hersey (2007)
17. Csikszentmihalyi, M., Rochberg-Halton, E.: The Meaning of Things: Domestic Symbols and the Self. Cambridge University Press, Cambridge (1981)
18. Krippendorff, K., Butter, R.: Product Semantics: exploring the symbolic qualities of form. In: IDSA (1984)
19. Vihma, S.: Products as Representations: a semiotic and aesthetic study of design products. Doctoral thesis, University of Art and Design, Helsinki (1995)
20. Monö, R.: Design for Product Understanding. Liber AB, Stockholm (1997)
21. Muller, W.: Order and Meaning in Design. Lemma Publishers, Utrecht (2001)
22. Van Breemen, E.J.J., Sudijono, S.: The Role of Shape in Communicating Designers' Aesthetic Intents. In: 1999 ASME Design Engineering Technical Conferences, Las Vegas (1999)
23. Warell, A.: Design Syntactics – a functional approach to visual product form. Doctoral thesis, Chalmers University of Technology, Gothenburg (2001)
24. Warell, A.: Towards a Theory-Based Method for Evaluation of Visual Form Syntactics. In: TMCE 2004, Tools and Methods of Competitive Engineering, Lausanne (2004)
25. Karjalainen, T.-M.: Semantic Transformation in Design – communicating strategic brand identity through product design references, Gummerus Kirjapaino Oy, Jyväskylä (2004)
26. Warell, A.: Modelling perceptual product experience – towards a cohesive framework of presentation and representation in design. Paper for Design and Emotion Conference (2008), http://www.designandemotion.org/library/page/viewDoc/207
27. Hekkert, P.L., Desmet, P.M.: The Basis of Product Emotions. In: Green, W., Jordan, P. (eds.) Pleasure with Products, Beyond Usability, pp. 60–68. Taylor & Francis, London (2002)

28. Peirce, C.S.: Collected Papers of Charles Sanders Peirce. In: Hartshorne, C., Weiss, P., Burks, A.W. (eds.), vol. 1-8, Harvard University Press, Cambridge (1931-1966)
29. Atkin, A.: Peirce's Theory of Signs. In: Stanford Encyclopedia of Philosophy (2010), http://plato.stanford.edu/entries/peirce-semiotics/
30. Govers, P.C.M., Schoormans, J.P.L.: Intangible Product Attributes of Watches. In: EMAC 2000, Rotterdam (2000)
31. Govers, P.C.M., Hekkert, P.L., Schoormans, J.P.L.: Happy, Cute and Tough: Can Designers Create a Product Personality that Consumers Understand? In: McDonagh, D., Hekkert, P., Van Erp, J., Gyi, D. (eds.) Design and Emotion: The Experience of Everyday Things, pp. 345–349. Taylor & Francis, London (2003)
32. Vihma, S.: Design Semantics and Aesthetics. In: the basic PARADOX - foundations for a groundless discipline (2003), http://home.snafu.de/jonasw/PARADOXVihmaE.html
33. Kuniavsky, M.: Observing the User Experience: a practitioner's guide to user research. Morgan Kaufmann Publishers, San Francisco (2003)
34. Kuniavsky, M.: User Experience and HCI (draft). In: HCI Handbook (2007), http://www.orangecone.com/hci_UX_chapter_0.7a.pdf
35. Akner-Koler, C.: Form and Formlessness. Chalmers University of Technology, Gothenburg (2007)
36. Hirschman, E.C., Holbrook, M.B.: Hedonic Consumption: emerging concepts, methods and propositions. J. Marketing 46(3), 92–101 (1982), http://www.jstor.org/stable/1251707
37. Graham, L.: Gestalt Theory in Interactive Media Design. J. Humanities & Social Sciences 2(1) (2008), http://www.scientificjournals.org/journals2008/articles/1288.pdf
38. Wertheimer, M.: Gestalt Theory. In: Ellis, W.D. (ed.) A Source Book of Gestalt Psychology. Harcourt Brace & Co., New York (1938)
39. Ijsselsteijn, W., Riva, G.: Being There: the experience of presence in mediated environments. In: Riva, G., Davide, F., IJsselsteijn, W. (eds.) Being There: Concepts, Effects and Measurement of User Presence in Synthetic Environments, vol. 2(1), IOS Press, Amsterdam (2003), http://www8.informatik.umu.se/~jwworth/4_01RIVA.pdf
40. Kelly, G.: The Psychology of Personal Constructs. Norton, New York (1955)
41. Green, B.: Personal Construct Psychology and Content Analysis. Personal Construct Theory and Practice 1, 82–91 (2004), http://www.pcp-net.org/journal/pctp04/green04.pdf
42. Forceville, C., Hekkert, P., Tan, E.: The Adaptive Value of Metaphors. In: Klein, U., Mellman, K., Metzger, S. (eds.) Heuristiken der Literaturwissenschaft. Einladung zu disziplinexternen Perspektiven auf Literatur, Mentis, Paderborn (2006)

Boundary Resources Dependency in Third-Party Development from the Developer's Perspective

Asma Rafiq, Pär J. Ågerfalk, and Jonas Sjöström

Department of Informatics and Media, Uppsala University, Kyrkogårdsg. 10
Box 513, 751 20 Uppsala, Sweden
{Asma.Rafiq,Par.Agerfalk,Jonas.Sjostrom}@im.uu.com

Abstract. The purpose of this paper is to explore issues pertaining to the development of third-party applications aimed to be hosted at software platforms. While prior research has addressed design challenges in platform design, and suggested a boundary resources model to understand such design, we argue that the application developers' perspective has not yet been scrutinized. Drawing on design experiences from application development for the Facebook platform, we suggest further elaboration of the boundary resources model for software platforms. Our results show that the developers and applications are highly affected by the unpredictability of software platforms. Based on an empirically justified account of experience with boundary resources dependencies, we propose a set of implications for third-party development as well as platform development and maintenance. The study should be helpful in determining the influence of boundary resources on third-party developers and applications whilst planning for application development on such platforms. It should also be useful to platform owners involved in the development and maintenance of boundary resources for third-party development.

Keywords: Third-party Development, Software Platforms, Boundary Resources, Facebook.

1   Introduction

In less than two decades, the Internet and the World Wide Web have emerged into a tool to harness collective intelligence [1]. This type of creativity is typically leveraged by the availability of propriety software platforms for the development of third-party applications. While software platform owners have recognized the importance of third-party applications for creating and sustaining innovation [2, 3] they still need to stay in control over unique, hard-to-recreate data sources. The platforms depend on their communities, which constitute online social networks from which valuable data (such as user profiling based on user behavior) may transpire, particularly if and when they reach a critical mass. Third-party applications play a significant role in attracting users to software platforms [2].

Information systems researchers have recently shown increased interest in online social networks [4, 5]. In May 2007, Facebook launched its platform at the first

J. vom Brocke et al. (Eds.): DESRIST 2013, LNCS 7939, pp. 197–211, 2013.
© Springer-Verlag Berlin Heidelberg 2013

developer conference, f8. Facebook Newsroom[1] states that Facebook is close to reaching a one billion user-base with access to more than nine million applications and websites integrated with Facebook by the end of March 2012. Facebook and other software platforms provide an increasingly important channel that has major impacts on individuals, businesses, and society as a whole.

In this paper, we draw on existing knowledge of platform boundary resources, as well as experiences from designing a Facebook application that recommends music based on user profiles. The aim of the research is to understand the boundary resources involved and their implications for development from the developers' perspective. In the paper, we introduce the concept of boundary resources dependency, and a set of tentative design principles for third-party application development.

2   Related Research

In the past literature, it has been suggested that web-based application development is different from other types of software development [6]. Application development for the web entails many inherent challenges such as inadequate document-centric and ad-hoc development approaches, error-prone and technology-dependent application development, unreliability, etc. [7]. We argue that third-party application development is even more complicated, due to the dependencies on boundary resources, controlled by the platform vendor. It has been reported[2] that third-party applications tend to crash frequently and this is not only (if at all) because of poor third-party development competence. Previous theoretical contributions concerning platform boundary resources explicitly adopt a platform vendor (or owner) perspective [2, 17]. There is clearly a need to complement this line of research with research aimed at investigating the complexities faced by the third party application developers using boundary resources of software platforms and explore the usefulness of the boundary resources model (BRM) [17] to explain development experience and to capture the third-party developer perspective.

3   Software Platform Boundary Resources

As mentioned above, this study investigates the concept of platform boundary resources and how it affects third-party development. The primary theoretical foundation is the BRM (see Fig.1). In the BRM a boundary resource is conceived of as the interface between a software platform and its third-party applications. Tiwana et al. (cited in [17]) define software platform as "the extensible codebase of a software-based system that provides core functionality shared by the modules that interoperate with it and the interfaces through which they operate."

---

[1]   http://newsroom.fb.com/Platform (Accessed on 12.01.2012).
[2]   http://www.huffingtonpost.com/2010/07/13/facebook-iphone-app-crash_n_645378.html (Accessed on 12.01.2012).

Drawing on the notion of boundary objects [8], boundary resources facilitate the interaction between platform and third-party applications and are "plastic enough to adapt to local needs and constraints of the several parties employing them, yet robust enough to maintain a common identity across sites." As such, they are designed in a way that although construed in a particular context they are useful in various contexts that may not even yet exist. In fact, boundary resources are designed so as to facilitate the development of new contexts defined by innovative third-party applications. Examples of boundary resources include application programming interfaces (APIs), documentation, and legal documents.

According to the BRM, proprietary platform owners design and make available boundary resources to facilitate development and use of third-party applications, and at the same time employ various strategies to maintain control of these resources in order to secure their interests in the platform. Third party applications are defined as the "executable pieces of software that are offered as applications, services, or systems to end-users of the platform" [17].

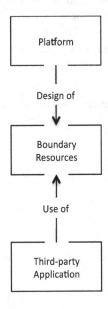

Fig. 1. The Boundary Resources Model adapted from [17]

4   Research Design

The research approach adopted can be characterized as a context initiated design research approach [9]. Existing artifacts in the form of boundary resources were the starting point for the formalization of learning. We studied the implementation process of a novel application that used the boundary resources provided by Facebook. Data collection was based on first-hand participation in the software development by the first author and consisted of system specifications, produced code, development notes and user feedback from the project. By designing and implementing a third-party application, a number of, what we refer to as boundary resources breakdowns (BRBs) were identified and described in detail. Each BRB consisted of an issue, or hurdle, in relation to boundary resources that arose during development and that were beyond the control of the developer. Based on the identified BRBs, a set of design principles was arrived at. Keeping the analysis open-ended, we allowed for principles related to both boundary resources design and third-party application to emerge.

While the initial research interest was oriented towards music recommendations based on user behaviors in a community of users, the design process clearly revealed the strong dependency on boundary resources in the design process. Essentially, the interpretation of experiences resembles an action design research (ADR) approach [18]. The breakdowns can be compared to cycles in ADR, through which new knowledge was gained. The re-interpretation of these experiences based on the boundary resources model and the formulation of design principles presented in this paper (see Section 6) correspond to the formalization of learning in ADR.

Fig. 2 provides a conceptual overview of the research approach. In addition to summarizing the above presentation, Fig. 2 also shows, by means of dashed boxes and lines, the aspects of the design context that are beyond the control of the third-party developers (i.e. the researchers in this study).

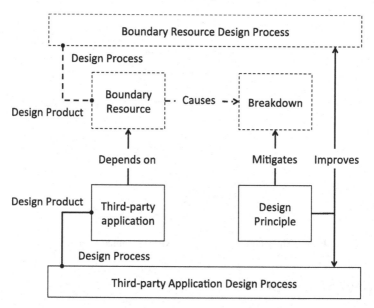

Fig. 2. Boundary Resources Dependency in third-party application development

Each identified BRB was described based on an adaptation of the framework suggested in [10]. Based on this framework, we use the six English interrogatives (why, what, when, who, how, where) as seed categories for analysis [11]. Feller and Fitzgerald [10] showed how these map to the categories of the Zachman framework [12,13] and Checkland's Soft Systems Methodology (SSM) [14]. As such the framework is well grounded in established IS literature. Table 1 summarizes the adapted analytical framework with corresponding question that guided the analysis.

Table 1. Boundary Resources Breakdown Analysis Framework, adapted from [10]

What. What was the BRB all about?
Why. Why did this breakdown happen? What could be possible reasons?
When and where. What are the temporal/structural conditions for the BRB?
How. How could the BRB and/or its implications have been mitigated?
Who. Which stakeholders were affected by the breakdown?

The final step of the analysis consisted of explicitly projecting the identified BRBs onto the BRM with the dual purpose of (a) informing the understanding of the breakdowns and (b) identifying possible limitations in the BRM itself as areas for theoretical development.

5   The Recommender Application

This section presents and analyzes the Recommender application. First, we describe the design process in general. Second, we discuss each breakdown in separate sections.

The Facebook application developed in this research is a music recommender application that automatically extracts information regarding user preferences through profile mining. The suggested playlist recommendations are based on the music preferences extracted from user profiles. Popular song videos are suggested and fetched from YouTube[3]. The user can see the music preferences of their friends who have set their privacy setting as 'public or friends' in the music preferences section. The music can therefore, be recommended according to their music taste as specified in their profiles. Social music recommendation enables people to discover music through a serendipitous process powered by human relationships and tastes, exploiting the user's social network to share cultural experiences. The user of the application will indicate successful music recommendations, which will strengthen the belief that music preferences listed in the users' profiles indicate their real taste for music. YouTube has been used to make random recommendations based on music preferences listed in the users' profiles. The reason for selecting YouTube is that users seem to prefer it because it has video accompanied with the song.

The recommendation problem is defined as given a pool of items; the subject selects an item that is relevant to them. The results of this approach are generated using a breadth first search. The speed and the amount of memory used by this searching algorithm were most productive in terms of this application. The application extracts music preferences of the top 20 friends of the user. The reason for this limit in number of users was that the users' preferences are extracted from Facebook in real time and

---

[3] http://www.youtube.com/

not from a separate database. Therefore, the server time limit to load a page hinders the extraction of all friends in the social network, which could be over a thousand, in some cases. The web user interface design was planned carefully focusing on user needs and tasks. It was a user-centered design process. The timeline of the BRBs as they occurred during the third party application development have been depicted in Fig. 3 and explained one by one in detail below.

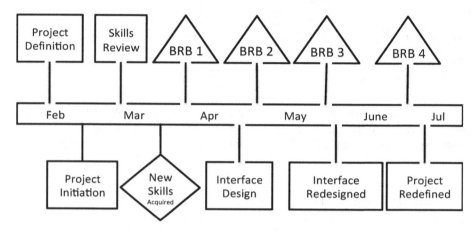

Fig. 3. Timeline of Breakdowns during 2011

5.1   BRB 1: Platform-Specific Language Deprecation

The project was initiated in the beginning of March 2011 and the Facebook application development was primarily done using the Facebook Markup Language (FBML) [15]. The beginning of the project considered of studies of the application development process on Facebook and one of the initial steps consisted of intensive study of FBML. Unfortunately, the acquired knowledge soon turned out to be obsolete due to the *platform-specific language deprecation breakdown*, as illustrated in the following analysis (Table 2).

Table 2. Breakdown #1 Analysis

What	By the end of March, Facebook announced to deprecate FBML on Facebook Platform.
Why	Facebook explains that FBML is replaced with more modern alternatives: "Over time, as Platform matured and embraced open standards, such as OAuth 2.0, HTML, and Javascript, the need for FBML has decreased"[4]
When and where	As per January 1, 2012, FBML is no longer supported. It is unclear whether there are other planned changes.

---

[4] http://developers.facebook.com/blog/post/568/, (Accessed on December 7, 2012)

Table 2. (*continued*)

How	The developer adapted to other technologies for the application development. A combination of HTML, PHP and JSON was sought as a solution.
Who	This breakdown affected the developers. At the same time, the move to more open standards rather than platform-specific tools should reduce the threshold for third-party developers to become more productive with familiar standardized tools.

5.2   BRB 2: Technological Backward Incompatibility

The *technological backward incompatibility breakdown* (see Table 3) is related to software updates in the platform environment. In order to deploy PHP code using Facebook API, secure certificates and CURL extension were required. These extensions required PHP version 5.3.7+. The university hosted the application, and their server was not upgraded since PHP 5.1.

Table 3. Breakdown #2 Analysis

What	The developers depended on the application server provider to meet the boundary resources of the platform host. The consequence was that the application was disconnected from the platform.
Why	It is reasonable to expect that a platform vendor updates their software to the latest version. Such updates are needed both to utilize the features of the APIs and to make sure that patches are installed (e.g. to improve security). However, the platform vendor could also provide backward compatibility or at least announce the changes in a clear manner to make developers aware of this type of technical requirement beforehand.
When and where	This boundary resource may change at any time to the latest version without backward compatibility, making the older versions unusable requiring many changes in the code.
How	The application developer needs to be certain that the application host upgrade their server software as soon as updates are available, and that they support the installation of custom extensions that may be required by the platform vendor (such as CURL).
Who	The affected stakeholders were both the application developers and the application host.

5.3   BRB 3: Interface Design Restrictions

The *interface design restrictions breakdown* (see Table 4) happened when the interface design, with associated design guidelines, was radically changed in about two weeks' time. Before the change, there used to be tabs for building applications. The tabs enabled smooth transitions between different views in the user interface.

Table 4. Breakdown #3 Analysis

What	The platform vendor decided to remove the possibility to create tabs in third-party application UIs.
Why	Apparently, the rationale was that "Functionality is limited in the Facebook Page tab because of FBML, which usually means anything robust will have to be developed as a full-blown Facebook application."[5]
When and where	The iframe window height value is fixed to 800px. Scrollbars appear if the iframe content is longer than 800px height in the iframe.
How	The developer had to redesign the application provided the new constraints for which the development tool was also changed (to Flash), for making the user experience more interactive. The main reason for using Flash was that the developer could not use PHP due to version problem as already explained earlier. Therefore, Flash was used for video streaming from YouTube.
Who	This breakdown affected the developers and the application interface. At the same time, the move to Flash brought some more benefits in terms of rendering time, etc.

The Graph API[6] provided by Facebook created some issues while connecting with the server and resulted in proxy errors. However, we have found that the time to retrieve the user queries became much more efficient with designing the application using Flash. Since, the data is fetched from Facebook in real time, the max execution time limit of 30 seconds in case of PHP was not sufficient. Therefore, the Flash time limit of 115 seconds was much more flexible, making the application more stable even if the user had more than one thousand friends. The limit to fetch music preferences for up to 20 users was considered reasonable, in order to save the application from crashing.

5.4   BRB 4: Abrupt Changes in Data Provision Policies

Facebook—as well as other social interaction platforms—keep track of large amounts of possibly sensitive information that needs to conform to privacy regulations, which led to the *abrupt changes in data provision policies* breakdown (see Table 5).

---

[5] http://sixrevisions.com/web-applications/new-facebook-page/ (Accessed on 30.11.12).

[6] According to Facebook: "The Graph API presents a simple, consistent view of the Facebook social graph, uniformly representing objects in the graph and the connections between them" Source: https://developers.facebook.com/docs/reference/apis/ (Accessed on 30.11.12).

Table 5. Breakdown #4 Analysis

What	A security patch was applied in late June, which stopped third-party apps from using the public data on which our recommender application was heavily relying upon.
Why	In May 2010, Symantec reported security flaws in Facebook applications [16]. There were indications that user information might have been compromised by third-party applications. It was feared that user information was handed over to advertising and tracking firms.
When and where	The publicly available data was made unavailable for certain period of time to the third-party application developers.
How	We looked for alternative ways to resolve this issue. As a solution, users own social network information was used. Actually, this was a crucial change for the project. In one way it seemed to be for the better, as we were interested in the music section of the user profile but most of the users were not displaying that information as public. The users profile on Facebook displays the type of music the users have liked on the platform, or mentioned explicitly by typing in manually; one can populate the most popular songs based on the band/musician/genre mentioned in the user profiles. Finally, the interest about Music Genre (techno, pop, rock et cetera) was extracted from the user profiles.
Who	This breakdown clearly affected the developers. On the other hand it concerned several stakeholders, including but not limited to the public and the platform vendor, as well as those seeking to exploit private information for commercial purposes.

6   Breaking Down the Breakdowns

Ghazawneh and Henfridsson pointed out the conflicting goals of third-party development [17] in a software platform context, namely *maintenance of platform control* and *transfer of design capability to third-party developers*. These seem to play a vital role in the breakdowns of the application development process. Nevertheless, the phenomena illustrated above in the Tables 2, 3, 4 and 5 cannot be fully explained using the BRM concepts, because the core concepts of BRM are developed based on the platform vendor's perspective whereas the breakdowns listed above require explanation from the developers' perspective, which is important in order to mitigate such breakdowns in the future. Terms such as resourcing, securing, etc. used in the context of the BRM, are helpful for the developer to investigate these issues but they fail ultimately to provide a profound understanding of the phenomenon. Therefore, BRM clearly requires another layer of understanding from a developer's point of view. The main problem identified in the current model of BRM is that there is no clear distinction between the different roles of the actors at the platform level. For example, it does not distinguish between the owners of the platform and developers involved in the development and maintenance of the platform, which makes it unclear if the platform owners and developers are two different roles with separate responsibilities. This is particularly important from the developer's perspective in order to sufficiently explain the lack of communication between the platform developers and third-party developers that can be attributed to the breakdowns stated above. The BRM assumes that:

"… third-party developer, on behalf of someone else, the platform owner, develops applications, services, or systems […] for satisfying end-users of the platform. Third-party development tends to be governed by arm's-length, contractually oriented, relationships" [17].

We disagree with this primary assumption that constitutes the BRM. Firstly, third-party developers do not necessarily need to act on behalf of someone else or the platform owner's behalf to develop applications, services, or systems for satisfying end-users of the platform. The third-party developers may simply utilize the platform to develop the apps, services or systems on the platform to facilitate end-users with services that they have been serving as an individual or firm anyway, through some other channels such as their own website, etc. However, we agree that the third-party developers are contractually bound with the platform in order to use it whereas the platform owner clearly states the publisher of the application or service provider explicitly. In, for example, the case of Facebook, there is a separate permission dialogue box that appears when the user attempts to access third-party applications, and the user is made aware that: "By proceeding, you agree to {third-party developer/publisher's} Terms of Service and Privacy Policy". Similarly, in the case of Apple's App Store, the developer of the application is explicitly mentioned. However, there is a great difference between the application rendering procedure on Facebook and Apple. Apple reviews[7] every application before it becomes available in the App Store whereas Facebook does not review every application in such detail and the application becomes available as soon as the third-party developer is launching it. Therefore, the platform owner declares and distinguishes itself from the third-party development and hence supporting our first argument, an extreme example of which is the case where Apple displays the Apple developed applications first on the iPhone webpage[8] and then proceeds to display further apps developed by third-party developers in the following page. The current BRM model stays close to the Apple context in which it was developed and therefore, in order to make the model more generalizable, one needs to compare it with other software platforms such as Facebook. Concluding from the above discussion, we would like to rephrase the assumption for third-party development as:

Third-party developers develop applications, services, or systems for satisfying end-users of the platform to leverage the large user base of the platform, governed by arm's-length, contractually-oriented, relationships. *Third-party applications remain an additional service and do not form an integral part of the platform.*

---

[7] https://developer.apple.com/appstore/guidelines.html
(Accessed on 11.01.2013).

[8] http://www.apple.com/iphone/from-the-app-store/
(Accessed on 25.02.2013).

It is interesting to note that in the context of the BRM [17] boundary resources are defined as the interface between the third-party developers and platform owners. We have above pointed out that the BRM suffers from inadequacy in terms of definitions of roles and associated responsibilities. The first breakdown, i.e. *deprecation of the platform-specific language*, is an example of lack of communication between the developers of the platform and third-party developers. If only the third-party developers were indicated earlier that the platform specific language (FBML in this case) was being deprecated, then the effort that went into learning and practicing a deprecating language could have saved the developer's time and the developer could have focused on other possible solutions. It is rarely the case that the platform abruptly decides to take such a crucial step without prior preparations. The developers involved at the software platform's development and maintenance must have known it well before the deprecation of FBML was officially announced. Facebook should have allowed them to disclose this upcoming change to the potential third-party developers at the Facebook's developers' forum[9]. Thus, lack of provision of timely information by the platform developers led to the first breakdown which can be mitigated in the future by filling the communication gap between the platform developers and third-party developers, which BRM does not address currently.

The second breakdown, i.e. *technological backward incompatibility*, is another example of the unexpected issues that may arise during a developer's transition from traditional web development to the development on propriety software platform. This problem would have not arisen if the software tool used for the development allowed backward compatibility. However, the second option would have been to upgrade the server software but it was not straightforward because this change would affect several already deployed applications on that server. It required several months of work to get the server upgraded. On the other hand, the problem could have been mitigated easily, if the proprietary software was not involved, the developer could code in whichever version she likes as in case of the traditional web. Looking back to the BRM [17], it doesn't actually help to analyze this problem because it does not address the dependency between the boundary resources and application server. So, there is a need for another layer between the boundary resources and third-party applications, i.e. the application server. A check for the compatibility between the software platform and the application server should also form a crucial step before proceeding with the development.

The third breakdown, i.e. *interface design restrictions*, put forth by the propriety software platform falls in a similar category as the second breakdown. It shows that the technological dependency on such propriety software platform is quite a challenge and the third-party developers must consider/address these problems beforehand. Otherwise, the changes may cost a lot of efforts in redesigning the application. Therefore, a carefully planned application development might save the developer from future problems that may arise due to ad-hoc development approaches. However, in order to achieve the former, the communication gap mentioned above needs to be addressed as well.

---

[9] https://developers.facebook.com [Available Online] (Accessed on 25.02.2013).

The fourth breakdown, i.e. *abrupt changes in data provision policies*, causes the most catastrophic effect among all the breakdowns identified. Due to the fact that if the propriety software platform decides to limit the access to the data by the third-party application, the third-party developer has no choice but to compromise on this and therefore, the application might never achieve what it was meant to achieve. For example, in case of a researcher who is mostly interested in collection of data using this platform, will not get the required data and therefore, the experiment will definitely fail since there is no way to go around that problem except to compromise on not having access to the data that was initially planned to be collected.

7   Discussion

In this paper, we have accounted for four software development process breakdowns related to boundary resources in third-party development for a software platform. These breakdowns reveal how developers depend on the platform vendor in the context of third-party application development. Due to the large number of applications developed for social media platforms, we argue that this problem is highly significant for software development practice. This paper contains some valuable contributions related to third-party application development. First, we recognize the problem from a third-party developer perspective by introducing the concept of *boundary resources dependency*, which we define as a phenomenon in which a third party application depends on boundary resources such that changes in the boundary resources directly affect the third party application development and maintenance, which in extreme cases can affect the implementation and/or working of the third party application and require major changes in the developed or developing product. Second, we have illustrated a set of implications of boundary resources dependency through a conceptualization of four types of breakdown that may occur due to platform vendor's changes to boundary resources. Third, we argue that knowledge about such breakdowns is valuable for third-party application developers. By maintaining an awareness of boundary resources dependency, we may potentially improve the capabilities to mitigate breakdowns or their implications.

In terms of implications for research, we consider the results to be a 'level 2' contribution, i.e. nascent design theory [19], regarding development of third-party applications in the context of software platforms. The boundary resources dependency concept and the associated concepts of breakdowns constitute an interpretation of the boundary resources model from a developer's perspective. The analysis leads to a set of design principles that can help mitigate these breakdowns. We refer to these as *the principle of technological independence, the principle of compatibility verification, the principle of change intimation* and *the principle of data accessibility*.

The principle of technological independence suggests that the software platform should embrace standardized boundary resources that are more likely to remain consistent over time (such as the open standards OAuth 2.0, HTML, and Javascript). This way developers do not have to learn new skills, such as platform-specific standards (e.g. FBML), which may deprecate over time and affect the application and the developers.

The principle of compatibility verification suggests that the compatibility between the software platform and the application server should be assessed by the developer before proceeding with development on proprietary software platforms. This is not usual practice in web development, as application servers are usually trusted to be up-to-date. But as seen in this study, this may not always be the case and cannot be taken for granted.

The principle of change intimation states that it is understandable that changes in the software platforms are inevitable due to the evolving nature of such platforms. Therefore, the platform owner should show courtesy to the developers and try to get the word out or start sending signals about the anticipated changes as soon as the changes are being planned rather than wait until the end and suddenly surprise the developers with an abrupt change. This would encourage third-party developers to embrace the change rather than causing problems and stimulating workarounds.

The principle of data accessibility means that the developers should not be re-stricted from accessing the data that they have originally been able to access at the time of application deployment at the software platform. However, if the restrictions on data access are inevitable (e.g. due to change in legal policies), then the third-party developers must be notified about the rationale behind such a radical change.

The principles of change intimation and data accessibility highlight the importance of timely communication between the developers of the platform and the developers of the third party application. However, even if the timely communication has been taken care of, in some cases changes will essentially require a lot of effort in rewriting the code and other significant changes, especially for those who have invested significant amount of time into learning obsolete platform-specific languages and tools. The principle of data accessibility signifies that developers should treat access to user data on the software platforms as a volatile privilege. Since, privacy concerns are a major threat to any third-party application based on a business model that is dependent on user data. Since, there are no readily available countermeasures against changes in data access policies, the business models should be designed considering this limitation.

8   Limitations

The principles stated above are based on a single case study, and therefore, findings are not generalizable in statistical sense. However, the importance of the principles stated above can be realized based on the additional environmental uncertainties that third-party application developers face by their lock-in to a particular platform, which emphasizes that the third-party developer should be aware that the platform parameters are volatile and subject to change at short notice. Concrete mitigation measures might then be derived to address this uncertainty: For example, checking in advance that the application server used, quickly updates to the latest version available might be a mitigation measure against.

Further rigor in this research area can be added by investigating the evolution of the data access policies of several platforms. In general, it is observed that the privacy concerns have the tendency to receive more public attention as the platform's popularity increases and therefore, gets more restrictive over time.

Future research on the BRM and boundary resources dependency could also include further exploration of the stakeholders involved (is there, for example, a need to distinguish between third-party application owners and third-party application developers?) and the impact of different types of software platform (for example, proprietary *vs.* open source).

9   Conclusion

In this paper, we have tapped into the existing knowledge base of platform boundary resources, and extrapolated further based on experiences from designing a Facebook music recommender application. We introduced the concept of boundary resources dependency, and a set of tentative design principles for both third-party application and boundary resources development. We hope that the paper will promote a reflective and responsible attitude towards development of third-party applications and towards the design of the boundary resources used in such development. Our hope is that the paper will promote a reflective and responsible attitude towards development of third-party applications and towards the design of the boundary resources used in such development. In terms of the theoretical contributions, we have scrutinized the developer's perspective in relation to the boundary resources model [17] by introducing the construct of 'boundary resources dependency'. The analysis of the empirical account shows the complexities faced by third party application developers. It also led to practical implications such as a set of tentative design principles.

Acknowledgments. This work has been supported by the Swedish Research Council Project 2011-6036 (What is the significance of economic incentives for the choice of university education?) and the Swedish Research School of Management and IT. We profoundly thank the reviewers for useful comments and suggestions for improvement.

References

1. O'Reilly, T.: What Is Web 2.0. O'Reilly Network: O'Reilly Media, Inc. (September 30, 2005), http://oreillynet.com/lpt/a/6228 (November 13, 2012)
2. Evans, D.S., Hagiu, A., Schmalensee, R.: Invisible Engines: How Software Platforms Drive Innovation and Transform Industries. MIT Press, Cambridge (2006)
3. Messerschmitt, D.G., Szyperski, C.: Software Ecosystem: Understanding an Indispensable Technology and Industry. MIT Press (2003)
4. Oinas-Kukkonen, H., Lyytinen, K., Yoo, Y.: Social Networks and Information Systems: Ongoing and Future Research Streams. Journal of the Association for Information Systems 11(2), 61–68 (2010)

5. Walsham, G.: Are we making a better world with ICTs? Reflections on a future agenda for the IS field. Journal of Information Technology 27(2), 87–93 (2012), http://dx.doi.org/10.1057/jit.2012.4 (retrieved)
6. Murugesan, S., Deshpande, Y., Hansen, S., Ginige, A.: Web Engineering: A New Discipline for Development of Web-Based Systems, pp. 3–13 (2001)
7. Kappel, G., Prýýll, B., Reich, S., Retschitzegger, W.: Web Engineering: The Discipline of Systematic Development of Web Applications. John Wiley & Sons ltd., CA (2006)
8. Star, S.L., Griesemer, J.: Institutional Ecology, 'Translations' and Boundary Objects: Amateurs and Professionals in Berkeley's Museum of Vertebrate Zoology, 1907-39. Social Studies of Science 19(3), 387–420 (1989)
9. Peffers, K., Tuunanen, T., Rothenberger, M.A., Chatterjee, S.: A Design Science Research Methodology for Information Systems Research. Journal of Management Information Systems 24(3), 45–77 (2007), doi:10.2753/MIS0742-1222240302
10. Feller, J., Fitzgerald, B.: A framework analysis of the open source software development paradigm. In: Proceedings of the Twenty First ICIS 2000, pp. 58–69 (2000)
11. Miles, M., Huberman, A.: Qualitative Data Analysis: A Sourcebook of New Methods. Sage, Beverley Hills (1994)
12. Zachman, J.: A Framework for IS Architecture. IBM Systems Journal 26(3), 276–292 (1987)
13. Sowa, J., Zachman, J.: Extending and Formalizing the Framework for IS Architecture. IBM Systems Journal 31(3), 590–616 (1992)
14. Checkland, P.: Systems Thinking, Systems Practice. Wiley, Chichester (1981)
15. Maver, J., Popp, C.: Essential Facebook Development: Build Successful Applications for the Facebook Platform, 1st edn. Addison-Wesley Professional (2010)
16. Houston, T.: Symantec: Facebook security flaw could have compromised user information (October 2011), http://www.huffingtonpost.com/2011/05/10/facebook-apps-flaw-leak-profile-access_n_860278.html
17. Ghazawneh, A., Henfridsson, O.: Balancing platform control and external contribution in third-party development: the boundary resources model. Information Systems Journal 23(2), 173–192 (2013), doi:10.1111/j.1365-2575.2012.00406.x
18. Sein, M.K., Henfridsson, O., Rossi, M.: Action Design Research. MIS Quarterly 35(1), 37–56 (2011), http://hdl.handle.net/2320/9888 (retrieved)
19. Gregor, S., Hevner, A.R.: Positioning and Presenting Design Science Research for Maximum Impact. MIS Quarterly 37(2), 337–355 (2013)

Organizational Design of Innovative Education – Insights from a Combined Design and Action Research Project

Olivera Marjanovic

The University of Sydney Business School
Sydney, NSW, 2006, Australia
olivera.marjanovic@sydney.edu.au

Abstract. This research aims to contribute to an emerging area of *organizational design research*, focusing on educational innovation. Our contribution comes in a form of an innovative organizational design solution for on-campus large lecture instruction, here named the Team Net Based Learning (TNBL) model, designed by the author and later independently adopted by other educators. The paper reports on a combined design and action research project of initiating, designing, implementing and evaluating the TNBL model (design research artifact), over a period of two years in a real-life setting, from a standpoint of a reflective practitioner/designer, engaged in action research in the context of her own practice. The model continues to be used to this day. Even though this project was implemented in the information systems domain, the main design artifact is discipline- and content- agnostic, and as such could be used in any other discipline. The outcomes of this research further strengthen the argument previously made by organization studies researchers that scholars researching organization systems and processes can use their knowledge and experience to organise and manage student activities.

Keywords: organizational design research, action research, innovative education, large lecture instruction.

1   Introduction

In spite of various educational and technological innovations, the practice of large on-campus lecture instruction remains in many university environments, especially in the first year undergraduate courses. The pedagogical aspects of this instruction model are well known and have been extensively studied by numerous educational researchers for many decades. Following a different idea that classrooms could be organized and managed as organizations, previously put forward by organization studies researchers such as Romme [1], this article focuses on organizational design of large lecture instruction. Although this research and its outcomes are envisaged to be relevant for any teaching discipline, the context of our research is the large foundation Information Systems (IS) course that is still predominantly a lecture course [2]. Widely known as Management Information Systems (MIS), this particular course continues to attract the attention of the international IS community [3-8], prompted by the

J. vom Brocke et al. (Eds.): DESRIST 2013, LNCS 7939, pp. 212–227, 2013.

world-wide "IS Enrollment Crisis" ([5], [7], [9-12]). *"If the discipline is to advance toward the implementation of effective strategies to combat declining enrolments, it is imperative to use a holistic approach that addresses the content, structure, resources and tone employed in the introductory MIS course"* ([3], p.18).

Confronted by the same challenge of improving student experience in the foundation IS course in our own environment, we observed that the innovation efforts reported in the relevant literature were mostly informed by education research. For example, various solutions proposed in the literature focus on innovative content, delivery methods, skills of teaching staff, assessment and technology used to support content delivery as well as various forms of student support through communities, student career camps, peer mentoring and industry links [9-14]. However, the *organizational design* of the key component of learning experience in this course - large lecture instruction - remains unchallenged.

Inspired by this important research gap, we focused on the challenge of large lecture instruction, inevitable in our environment, and approach it as an organizational design thinking challenge. This idea of looking at education from the perspective of organizational design, although novel in the IS field, is not new in organization studies, see for example [1], [15], [16].

This research aims to contribute to this line of emerging organizational design research, further strengthening the argument previously made by Romme [1] that scholars researching organizational systems and processes can use their knowledge and experience beyond educational content, in order to organize and manage student activities. Our contribution comes in a form of an innovative organizational design solution for large lecture instruction, here named the *Team Net Based Learning* (TNBL) model. TNBL is designed to combine two components: (i) an *innovative organizational structure* used to define different roles for all participants (students and staff) in a large classroom of any size, and (ii) a *set of interaction (coordination) patterns* designed to facilitate knowledge co-creation among these roles.

This paper reports on a combined design research (DR) and action research (AR) project of initiating, designing, implementing and evaluating the TNBL model. The perspective taken is that of a reflective practitioner/designer engaged in an action research in the context of her practice.

The TNBL model was designed and used by the author over two years (2008-2009), in four semesters, with more than 2500 students in total, and with up to 270 students in the same large lecture room. It was extensively evaluated both internally and externally, as reported in the paper. The same model was also subsequently and independently adopted by other IS colleagues in their own courses, who combined it with different content, learning activities and assessment methods and continued to refine it. The model continues to be used to this day. Even though the main outcome of this applied research (DR artifact) was implemented in the IS education domain, the TNBL model is discipline- and content- agnostic. As such it is suitable any other discipline.

2   Design Requirements

This project started from a challenge of keeping large lecture instruction, as an unavoidable constraint in our environment, leading to organizational design thinking to create a solution around it, aiming to leverage its positive aspects, in particular expert teaching and possibilities for small group interaction.

Based on the researcher's long-term experience of teaching large classes as well as an extensive literature review summarized below, we identified *four design requirements* for a new organizational model of large lecture instruction, as follows. This section offers a brief description of these requirements, explains their relevance in our context and justifies their importance using the related literature.

1. Design a more engaging model of face-to-face teaching/learning experience for students and their teachers in a large lecture environment of any size

The latest industry reports confirm that an even entry-level position in IS requires higher-level skills [7]. These skills include the ability to identify and solve problems, critically evaluate dynamic situations, deal with complexity and continuously innovate. The meta-learning skills of 'learning how to learn' are critical for future careers in IS and business in general, due to rapidly changing technology and information-intensive environments of tomorrow [17]. Development of these skills requires higher levels of engagement, ongoing feedback, challenging but highly supportive learning environment, and above all, expert teaching [18].

However, many years of educational research have confirmed that large lecture instruction is often focused on transmission of content and as such, does not help students to develop advanced learning skills, including critical thinking, problem solving and reflective skills [19]. While more experienced and engaging teachers would be able to engage a very large group by using, for example, some well-known strategies for teaching in large lectures, such as those described by Gibbs & Habeshaw, [20], most teachers will find the task of keeping whatever they perceive to be a large group of students engaged very challenging. This is especially the case with less experienced teachers [21]. *"Armed only with experiences gleaned from teachers they have had in the past, many novice teachers are left to swim to sink"* ([1], p. 697). Consequently they tend to adopt more traditional instructional methods, focusing on transmission of content.

2. Enable an immediate, meaningful, non-trivial feedback from every student to their teacher and from the teacher back to all students, regardless of a class size

Teacher's ability to understand students' learning needs and their current progress, in order to adjust their teaching accordingly, while teaching is in progress, is deemed crucial for development of higher-order learning skills [19] The key enabler of this adjustment is a meaningful, real-time, two-way feedback between a student and their teacher. This is very hard to achieve in large environments, even when students are organized in small groups. Even if class control is not an issue, a large number of small groups makes it is impossible for the teacher to meaningfully engage with each group, in order to provide an instant (rather than delayed), relevant and personalized feedback.

Equally important is the immediate feedback from students back to their teacher. However, it is very hard for the teacher to get an instant *non-trivial* feedback from most of their students, especially quiet ones in a large class, in order to adjust what they are doing in a real-time mode. Various technical solutions have been of a great help here (e.g. use of the so-called "clickers"), but only if students' feedback comes in a very simple and predefined form suitable for multiple-choice questions, rather than design tasks. However, in the IS field, even first year students are involved in design activities, such as design of a conceptual data base model or a model of an improved business process.

'We're a lot closer to the medical school than we are to the geology or physics departments...As graduates, our students need to solve problems – not to cure sick people, but to improve the business in which they work – increase competitive advantage, solve particular problems, improve decision making..... It's knowledge in action and not sinking with PowerPoint." ([8], pg. 1).

A very wide range of design solutions, both correct and incorrect, cannot be easily reduced to pre-defined choices to be used in multiple-choice questions, without compromising student's ability to design and improve through a meaningful feedback. In other words, in design-oriented problems, *recognizing a correct solution is not the same as designing a correct solution.* Therefore, the feedback exchanged during these design activities becomes quite complex and needs to be specific to student's particular solution, in order to be helpful.

3. *Prevent student isolation and anonymity in a large environment*

The main consequence for student learning in large environments focused on transmission of content is that they quickly turn into isolated and passive observers [19]. Students are able to hide behind anonymity, and as such, easily resist teacher's attempts to get them engaged. The related research in the area of situational leadership, confirms that the majority of first year students are highly dependent learners who require guidance, careful scaffolding of their activities and most of all, strong leadership [22]. The same literature also describes the experience of dependent followers not receiving guidance they need. "Lacking the ability to perform the task they tend to feel that the leader has little interest in their work and does not care about them personally" ([22], p.138). Consequently, students end up feeling even more isolated, especially the quiet ones.

4. *Ensure consistency of expert teaching across, and interaction with, all student groups, regardless of their number and size.*

The effective expert teaching is critical for the first year MIS course [3], [14]. While more interactivity is provided in a smaller tutorial environment, tutors (teaching assistants, instructors), are often less experienced teachers. They may have mastery of the content but not of the teaching methods. "For many higher education institutions, doctoral students or adjunct faculty teach the introductory IS courses, enabling tenure-track faculty to teach the more interesting and focused parts of the IS curriculum that come later in student's progression" ([3], p.21). Design of application-oriented learning activities, appropriate for developing students' higher-level cognitive skills, remains a major challenge because most teachers have traditionally focused the majority of their teaching on simply covering the content [21].

Another important problem is related to consistency and availability of expert teaching across a very large number of tutorials (for example, more than 30 tutorials per week), as it is increasingly hard to recruit equally committed and experienced IS tutors. This is because of declining numbers of IS recruits, in particular PhD students whose primary focus still remains on research and their doctoral studies, rather than teaching [23].

The above described key design requirements were addressed through design and implementation of an innovative organizational model of large room instruction called TNBL, described later in the paper. The next section introduces our research method.

3   Research Method

This practice-inspired research project followed the principles of Design Research (DR) [24-25] *combined* with Action Research (AR) [26-27]. Both DR and AR have been identified as research methods that could help the researchers to add to the existing theory while solving practical problems and making a research-based contribution to their practice. They both have a potential to increase practical relevance of scientific research, while providing rigorous method to guide and inform researchers/practitioners.

When used in the IS field, DR research method (also known as Design Science Research) is typically adopted to guide construction and evaluation of various technology artifacts i.e. software applications designed to solve practical problems. However, possible outcomes of DR are not only systems and could include constructs, models, methods and instantiations [25].

Furthermore, principles of DR continue to be used in other disciplines beyond IS. According to Simon [28], it is the process of design that distinguishes disciplines such as education, organization and management from natural sciences. However, "organization design science is still very early in its development" ([29], p.317). Our research aims to contribute to this emerging research direction as well as to DR in general.

The second component of our combined research method, Action Research (AR), uses an intervention into a problematic situation as a means to develop scientific knowledge. AR is a fundamentally "a change-oriented approach in which the central assumption is that complex social processes can be best studied by introducing change into these processes and observing the effects" ([26], p. 91). AR links theory and practice in a highly cyclic process where "the main intention is to create a synthesis with specific knowledge that provides actors in the situation, with the capability to act and the general knowledge that is suitable for similar situations" ([26], p.91). In general, an action research cycle consists of the following generic steps: diagnosing, action planning, action taking and specific learning. AR was determined to be highly suitable for this research project as complex social processes, including in-class learning processes (enabled by different interaction patterns) as well as in-class and between-classes knowledge sharing processes were studied when a complex change was introduced, and its effects were observed across several learning cycles.

The combined DR/AR method [30-31], adopted by this research was originally proposed by Cole, Rossi, Purao & Sein [30] with the following objectives: (1) to use scientific methods to solve a set of practical problems experienced by researcher/practitioner; (2) to contribute to the existing body of knowledge by creating new research artifacts. According to Cole et al. this integrated approach is required to stress the relevance, problem solving and intervening to learn, that are values inherent to both AR and DR [30]. The same core values are highly applicable to this research project and closely match its aims and objectives, both research and practical.

The combined DR/AR method was implemented in the following way. Looking from the DR perspective, the main research artifact of our project is the TNBL model. Design, implementation, evaluation and refinement of this DR research artifact were conducted over four AR circles. Each research cycle was designed to correspond to a single instance of course delivery, completed within 13-week semester. Furthermore, each cycle included a set of weekly "minicycles" that involved design and implementation of a new set of instructional design patterns, delivered in different lecture streams within the same week. The experience accumulated after each mini-cycle was then used in sub-sequent weeks to further improve the interaction patterns and find new ways of re-using them in order to design new activities.

Figure 1 shows the resulting research model with Design Research Circles by Hevner et.al, [24], extended to include an AR phase "Reflection and Learning", as suggested by Cole et al. [30-31]. This phase could be also described as "reflection-in-action" [32] with the author/researcher being the reflective practitioner initiating and implementing a major change in her own practice.

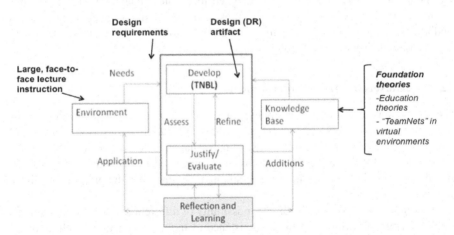

Fig. 1. A combined DR/AR research method used in this project

4   Foundation Theories - DR Knowledge Base

Design of the new model was inspired by a combination of experiences and insights that, *in reflection*, could be traced back to educational research and virtual environments. They are briefly described below.

4.1   Educational Research

From the educational perspective, design of the TNBL model was informed by an existing educational model of Team Based Learning (TBL) by Michaelsen et al [21]. The TBL model is a comprehensive group-based instructional format developed to facilitate active learning, even in large classes. The model is used worldwide in very diverse teaching disciplines such as management, economics and medicine. This approach enables an immediate in-class feedback to Multiple-choice questions (MCQ), facilitated via "scratch-it" cards given to students. By "scratching off" one of the four MCQ options, students could immediately determine if their selected answer is correct, by the presence or absence of an asterisk symbol (*). In this way, they receive an instant but simple feedback (i.e. solution is correct/incorrect).

A typical TBL class is run by an instructor. Each group engages in an active discussion to negotiate and determine their group's answer, getting the feedback/answer via scratch-it cards. Therefore, it is not vital for the TBL instructor to get to speak with every group. In fact, this role could be even taken by an administrative person in charge of distribution and collection of scratch-it cards.

Design of the TNBL model was inspired by the *main strength* of the TBL model, namely small groups of students working together in a large lecture environment. It was also informed by TBL's *perceived limitations* when used in an applied discipline such as IS. They include: the use of MCQs with pre-defined outcomes not suitable for IS design activities, a simple feedback communicated via "scratch-it" cards, limited role of the class facilitator and under utilization of his/her domain expertise and teaching skills. Our model of TNBL was designed to enable implementation of complex learning activities (including design activities) and provision of a much more complex feedback to all small groups, and most importantly, to every single student in a very large lecture environment, regardless of its size.

4.2   TeamNets in Virtual Environments

The second source of inspiration could be traced back to a very different field – virtual organisations. The so-called *TeamNets* have been used to describe networks of teams in dynamic virtual organizations, in particular their patterns of interaction and collaboration [33]. TeamNets' success is often attributed to boundary-crossing individuals who facilitate information flows among different teams helping to coordinate their activities [33].

The concept of TeamNets inspired a possibility of different patterns of interactions, within and across learning teams, the existence of multiple leaders, as well as boundary crossing roles and objects. However, compared to the virtual environments and TeamNets, our model of TNBL includes co-located teams - all working in the same environment, taking different roles, and engaging in different forms of interactions. This line of thinking opened up an opportunity to implement a completely different classroom design as described by the next section.

5   Design of the Team Net Based Learning (TNBL) Model - DR Build Phase

The innovative model of TNBL was designed with an idea to enable different patterns of knowledge sharing and co-creation, within and across different teams - all co-located in a large classroom environment. This section describes the two key components of TNBL: its organizational structure and its patterns of interactions.

5.1   Organizational Structure of TNBL

Figure 2 illustrates the organizational structure of our TNBL environment. As shown, students were organized in different small learning teams (LTs), depicted by circles. In our case, teams were self-selected but once formed had to remain together until the end of a semester. Each *LT* had one designated *tutor* and each tutor was allocated to a number of co-located LTs. Each LT had its own unique alphanumerical code that enabled us to track learning progress of each groups, and more importantly, the individual progress of each group member, thus every single person in a large class, as described later. In our case, LTs where also colour-coded to make it visually easier to match LTs and their allocated tutors (e.g. the activity sheets given to the same tutor's LTs were of the same colour, matching the colour of tutor's name badge). This was important for some learning activities, or in less-flexible environments, as illustrated later in the paper.

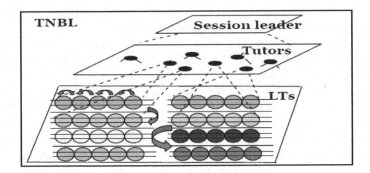

Fig. 2. The organizational structure of a TNBL and its implementation

Whenever possible, LTs allocated to the same tutor were physically co-located and asked to remain seated in the same area of the room for the whole semester, to facilitate easier access. While tutors assumed the leadership role for their LTs, each session was guided by one session leader responsible for the overall learning experience.

5.2   Patterns of Interactions

A very efficient system of horizontal and vertical information flows was designed to enable various communication and collaboration patterns. They in turn supported knowledge sharing and co-creation among all participants in the learning experience: (i) student-to-student within the same LT, or across different LTs via their tutor(s); (ii) LTs and their allocated tutor, (iii) between tutors and the session leader, (iv) LTs to LTs via their allocated tutor, (v) tutors to tutors, and finally, (vi) from the session leader to the whole class or a particular student, and back – all regardless of class size.

These horizontal and vertical information flows among the participants were then combined into six different interaction patterns. It is important to observe that these patterns were content-neutral and, as such, could be combined with different content and guided by different learning objectives. They were used as the basis for interactive learning activities, delivered in a very large class (in our case, the largest having 270 students in the same room). The interaction patterns are described as follows:

Pattern 1 This basic pattern captures a feedback loop between a tutor and his/her allocated LTs, enabling provision of a non-trivial feedback. Thus, irrespectively of the number of tutors and LTs, this pattern facilitates a provision of a personalized feedback to each and every student in a large class of any size. For example, while working on different problem solving activities (e.g. design of a conceptual data base model), each tutor would approach their allocated LTs, giving all team members an opportunity to ask questions and seek clarification. By observing the work of their allocated LTs, tutors could identify and observe both the types and causes of problems within and across their allocated groups - even those ones that their students could not even articulate. For example, rather than just focusing on a correct solution (design), tutors could observe an underlying cause of incorrect solutions, such as students' inability to differentiate between basic elements of a conceptual design.

Pattern 2 This is an extension of Pattern 1, designed to leverage the information flows between tutors and the session leader (SL). Thus, Pattern 2 was designed to facilitate an instant and closed feedback loop, originating from all LTs, going to their designated tutors and via them, all the way up to the SL and then back to individual tutors, their LTs and/or whole class. As in the previous example, a tutor may observe that a number of his/her LTs struggle to understand the same foundation concept, in spite of each LT having a different (incorrect) design. Rather than providing the same explanation to a number of LTs, the tutor would communicate this and any other cumulative feedback to the session leader, who could then immediately provide additional explanations, clarifications to the whole class, taking into account the issues reported across all groups or even using a LT's exemplary solution to better illustrate the problem. The session leader could provide real-time feedback to tutors who might seek some additional clarification. Most importantly, the session leader could immediately adjust the subsequent activities and instruct the tutors how to proceed.

Pattern 3 was designed to empower tutors to act as boundary spanners [36] between two or more of his/her allocated LTs, facilitating knowledge sharing and exchange between these teams. For example, via their tutors, two or more LTs could swap their group solutions and comment on another LT's work. If given a marking scheme, a LT could even (formatively) mark another LT's solution (another form of group work). Tutor's role is to help them to exchange their work, provide comments and guide students' marking efforts. Looking from the pedagogical perspective, this is a very important pattern, especially in the design-oriented fields such as IS. This is because students need to observe a number of different solutions, not only to learn from each other's mistakes but to understand and accept that IS activities often have more than one correct solution (such as different database designs). We found this to be a very important learning tool for students coming from other business fields such as finance and accounting, often expecting "the correct solution".

Pattern 4 was designed to enable a rapid selection process of the best solution(s) in the whole class, again regardless of its size. In the first step, tutors were asked to nominate one best solution, across their allocated LTs, and then together select the overall best solution in the class (e.g. by voting for the best three). Once the best solution was selected, tutors could immediately and easily locate the authors (i.e. LT) and ask them to present their work to the whole class. A variation of this pattern was used to enable competitions among different tutors via their allocated teams, looking for the most innovative solution, best team effort and so on.

Pattern 5 was designed to facilitate a wiki-like, paper-based co-creation among LTs allocated to the same tutor. Here each LT was asked to improve upon the cumulative effort of the previous teams. More precisely, each team needed to come up with a solution, and then starting from one team, their allocated tutor would pass this team's solution in a chain-like manner to the next LT, that could further improve it, before passing the cumulative effort to the next LT in line. This could be then easily combined with Pattern 4 and turned into an engaging competition, between color-coded teams and their tutors, as we often did.

Pattern 6 While previous five patterns illustrate knowledge sharing and co-creation among LTs co-located in the same room, Pattern 6 was designed to enable knowledge sharing between different lecture streams, again with tutors and session leaders acting as boundary spanners. For example, in our case the same group of tutors was working across different lecture streams. Therefore, they were able to share the accumulated feedback from their allocated LTs across different streams. This was very valuable not only to the LTs but also to different session leaders, as they were briefed in advance about possible problems with various concepts being covered and the solutions provided in the previous sessions. Some of this cumulative feedback was turned into learning activities in the subsequent weeks and/or posted online.

The above designed patterns of interaction, when combined with different content and learning objectives enabled design of weekly learning activities and their implementation with a very high level of student engagement.

6   TNBL Implementation – DR Implementation Phase

As already indicated, the TNBL model described in this paper was designed and used by the author over the four semesters (2008 and 2009) with the total enrolment of more than 2500 students. Each action learning cycle (e.g. each semester) introduced new challenges.

First of all, each semester brought a considerable increase in student enrolments, some quite unexpected. For example, within the first three of weeks of Semester 1, 2008 (the very first semester of this model's implementation), the enrolment number increased by more than 200 students and unexpectedly reached the total of 520 students. The course had to be organized in two streams, with 250 and 270 students in respective streams and per room. Both streams were led by the same session leader (the researcher) with the help of the same 6 tutors working across both streams. The trend continued, with over 600 students in both Semester 2, 2008 and Semester 1, 2009. In Semester 2, 2009, the enrollment reached over 700 students.

The increased student number led to the introduction of parallel teaching streams, creating the need for more session leaders in 2009. For example from two, then three teaching streams in 2008 all led by the same session leader, in 2009 the course was thought in six independent teaching streams, this time led by additional session leaders, completely new to TNBL. This in turn created the challenge of transfer of design artifact (TNBL), as discussed later in the paper.

7   TNBL Evaluation - DR Evaluation Phase

The research artifact (i.e. TNBL model) has been rigorously tested by a number of different stakeholders including students, tutors and IS and educational experts, both internal and external.

7.1   Addressing the Design Requirements

1. Design a more engaging model of face-to-face teaching/learning experience for students and their teachers in a large lecture environment of any size,

The previously described interactive patterns have enabled implementation of very engaging activities designed to promote active learning rather than passive observation, as in the traditional transmission model of teaching.

Most importantly, the whole teaching team was engaged in situated decision making that enabled real-time adjustment of the learning activities to meet students' learning needs. As one of the tutors commented: *"we interacted just like a NBA team, constantly observing the rest of the team and contributing to each others' activities, while helping our allocated LTs"* <a TNBL tutor>

2. Enable an immediate, meaningful, non-trivial feedback from every single student to their teacher and from the teacher back to all students, regardless of a class size

The previously described interaction patterns illustrate a direct and meaningful closed-loop and non-trivial feedback exchanged between students (even hundreds of them) and the session leader, facilitated by their designated tutors. The feedback provided to the session leader, went well beyond a simple choice (as in MCQ) that could be easily communicated by students via "clickers" or "scratch-it" cards. Tutors could communicate a cumulative feedback across their allocated LTs or, if needed, single out a particular LT. This feedback often included issues that students themselves, being novice learners, were not able to detect, let alone communicate.

Furthermore, tutors could easily provide personalized feedback to their allocated LTs in two forms: oral and written, all within the same session. Thus, while in session, tutors would collect group activity sheets and provide a quick written (formative) assessment to each group, returned to students within the same session.

3. Prevent student isolation and anonymity in a large environment

The underlying organizational structure of TNBL environment combined with the interaction patterns had enabled us to reach out to each student in a very large class, provide help but also to observe and assess their individual performance.

As in the conventional small group tutorials, tutors could observe the performance of all group members, even single out disruptive students by their name in a very large environment. This insight was not always welcome by students. As one pointed out: *"We cannot hide in the room full of people"*.

Furthermore, the practice of stating each group member's contribution to their respective LT's solution prevented freeloading and made student absenteeism highly visible. In this way, tutors could obtain a very deep insight into the performance of each team member in each LT, across the whole semester, as they would in typical tutorials. As non-performing or absent students could be easily detected quite early in the session, their allocated tutors were better placed to help them, but also help their fellow LT's members to manage their learning activities.

4. Ensure consistency of expert teaching across, and interaction with all student groups, regardless of their number and size

As one tutor pointed out, *"this model created an environment that is just like traditional tutorials but with "invisible" and transparent walls around our own LTs"*. Transparency enabled the highly experienced session leader to be present in "each tutorial" to support any tutor, answer any question and ensure that consistency is achieved across all tutors and their allocated LTs. This also meant that a single consistent message "version of truth" had been delivered to all students and reinforced by their tutors - all in the real-time mode. The session leader had an immediate/real-time insight into each tutor's work and could easily "team-up" and "shadow" less experienced team members. However, it is also important to point out that this transparency went both ways, as the teaching practices of session leaders also become highly visible to the team of their tutors. Unfortunately, this was not welcome by some session leaders, especially those in favor of the traditional transmission mode of teaching.

7.2   Other Forms of Evaluation

As per university policies, we performed both informal and formal course and teaching evaluations, both in weeks five and thirteen of each semester. However, we had to use the *generic evaluation instruments* designed for *traditional large lectures*. This meant that the outcomes of these evaluations *could not reliably used for the evaluation of the DR research artifact, as required by DR method*. However, they did provide interesting insights into students' perceptions and experiences.

For example, students' comments could be clearly divided into two groups - those who liked or did not like the experience for various reasons (e.g. "too much work", "have to work in lectures", "prefer to listen" etc.). Interestingly, in every semester a vast majority of students liked the in-class face-to-face group experience, but did not like working in groups (on their own) as required for their assignments.

In addition to continuously raising student numbers and successful outcomes in terms of student learning measured by the final exams and quality of their assignments (some receiving industry-sponsored awards), there were other key performance indicators. Looking from the financial perspective, the TNBL model turned out to be much more cost-efficient to run, in terms of its operating costs, in spite of parallel streams. For example the total cost of tutor-hours in all TNBL sessions per semester, with more students in total, was lower than the cost of running a very large number of tutor-led independent tutorials, we had in past.

The model and student learning experience, including the learning outcomes were also evaluated by the university academic board, acting upon a complaint by a non-performing student, not satisfied with the awarded in-class participation and assignment marks. They found the model to be "educationally sound" and confirmed that it was possible to trace this student's progress each week (even via group activity sheets), throughout the whole semester. The outcome of this independent evaluation was very encouraging and could be taken as a DR artifact evaluation by an independent group of (non-IS) educators.

However, the strongest confirmation of the design artifact, could be illustrated by the fact that the same model i.e. its organizational structure and some, if not all, design patterns were gradually and independently adopted in subsequent semesters by other colleagues who were not involved in the initial implementation of TNBL, without any deliberate attempt to propagate the model by any formal means. While the content and the learning and assessment activities they use are very different, the underling organizational model of a session leader supported by a number of tutors in charge of different LTs remains the same.

8   Learning and Reflection (AR phase)

There are many lessons learned in this project related to knowledge management, change management, educational research and situational leadership that continue to emerge even to this day. This section offers a brief overview of some important lessons related to design, implementation and transfer of design artifact (TNBL), relevant for design researchers.

While the author designed and implemented the original TNBL model, through reflection-in-action [32], the ongoing refinement of the model gradually took the form of "collective reflection-in-action" [34], shared with the very first group of tutors. The key enabler of this collective improvement of a design artifact could be attributed to its shared ownership.

Furthermore, the introduction of new parallel streams created a new challenge related to the transfer of the main design artifact and the associated "know-how" to new session leaders with various levels of teaching experience (some being novice teachers), and more importantly, different assumptions about teaching in large lecture environments ("just give me the slides"). This transfer of design artifact was facilitated by carefully designed and documented models of patterns of interactions and very detailed step-by-step description of learning activities. However, this was now sufficient for transfer of experiential knowledge. We found the key ingredient to be the sense of trust, especially among session leaders and their team of tutors. Trust takes time to be established and does not come with teaching allocations.

Successful implementation of this model requires strong situational leadership skills of the team leader, especially with very large groups. To some extent this could be offset by a strong and experienced team, or in the case of smaller groups this is not as critical. However, if the team leader is Stage 1-3 teacher, as classified by [35], i.e. focused on presentation of content or "survival" in front of the class, they are less likely to be accepted as leaders by the students or their teams. This is the *main limitation* of this model. Also, as Michaelson pointed out [22], many teachers are not trained or confident to lead interactive group activities so instead they focus on presentation of content.

Finally, in addition to being "boundary spanners"[36] among LTs, students and session leaders, the same core group of tutors became the boundary spanners from one semester to another, and later on, from this particular course to the other more advanced IS courses, that adopted the same TNBL model and employed some of the tutors. When adopted in the subsequent courses, the experiential knowledge of these tutors combined with their session leader's leadership, made the TNBL interaction patterns truly ubiquitous and "very easy to do", as commended by a new session leader without any previous experience with the TNBL model.

9   Conclusions and Future Work

This research aims to contribute to an emerging research stream organizational design research, focusing on the education domain. The paper describes a combined design research and action research project, resulting in an innovative model of Team Net Based Education (TNBL), with the researcher also being a reflective practitioner/designer. The model was designed and implemented in the author's own practice and extensively evaluated, both internally and externally, and later independently adopted by other IS educators.

The ongoing refinement of the TNBL model created many interesting opportunities for future research in the fields of process management (co-design of knowledge-intensive processes through boundary spanning), knowledge management (especially design and sharing of good practices across different streams and even different courses), management of educational innovations, change management as well as transformational leadership, organizational learning, organizational entrepreneurship and performance management in educational environments.

Finally, based on the experience gained in this project, we argue that in addition to contributing to teaching, our own teaching practices offer new opportunities for design-oriented 'mode 2 research' [37], in our own environments, that are often more challenging and complex to research and practice in, than any external organizations "out there". Educational design projects, such as the one described in this paper, illustrate new opportunities for "reinventing the future by adding design science to the repertoire of organization and management studies" [38], including new opportunities for reinventing the future of higher education.

References

1. Romme, A.G.L.: Organizing education by drawing on organization studies. Organization Studies 24, 697–720 (2003)
2. Holmes, J.D.: The introductory MIS course: using TQM to tame the widow-maker. Journal of Information Systems Education 14(3), 225–228 (2003)
3. Firth, D., Lawrence, C., Looney, C.A.: Addressing the IS enrollment crisis: a 12-Step program to bring about change though the introductory IS course. Communications of the AIS 23(2), 17–36 (2008)
4. Akbulut, A.Y., Looney, C.A., Motwani, J.: Combating the Decline in Information Systems Majors: The Role of Instrumental Assistance. Journal of Computer Information Systems 48(3), 84–93 (2008)
5. Granger, M.J., Dick, G., Luftman, J., Van Slyke, C., Watson, R.: Information systems enrollments: can they be increased? Communications of the AIS 20, 649–659 (2007)
6. Ives, B., Valacich, J., Watson, R.T., Zmud, R.: What every business student needs to know about information systems. Communications of the AIS 9, 467–477 (2002)
7. Benamati, J.H., Ozdemir, Z.D., Smith, H.J.: Aligning undergraduate IS curricula with industry needs. Communications of ACM 53(3), 152–156 (2010)
8. Kroenke, D.: The MISed opportunity. Teaching MIS Forum 10, 1–4 (2005)
9. Choudhury, V., Lopes, A.B., Arthur, D.: IT Careers camp: an early intervention strategy to increase IS enrollments. Information Systems Research 21(1), 1–14 (2010)
10. Street, C., Wade, M.: Reversing the downward trend: innovative approaches to IS/IT course development and delivery. In: Proc. of ICIS Conference, Montreal, Paper 123, pp. 1–5 (2007)
11. Koch, H., Slyke, C.V., Watson, R., et al.: Best practices for increasing IS enrollment: a program perspective. Communications of the AIS 26, 477–492 (2010)
12. Koch, H., Fuller, M.A., Slyke, C.V., Watson, R., Wilson, R.L.: Panel: attracting, retaining and placing IS students in an economic downturn. In: Proceedings of the American Information Systems Conference, Paper 354, pp. 1–4 (2009)
13. Grover, V., Straub, D., Galluch, E.: Editor's Comments: Turning the corner: the influence of positive thinking on the IS Field. MIS Quarterly 32(1), iii–viii (2009)
14. Looney, C.A., Akbulut, M.: Combating the IS enrollment crisis: the role of effective teachers in the introductory IS courses. Communications of the AIS 19, 781–805 (2007)
15. Banathy, B.H.: Systems thinking in higher education: learning comes to focus. Syst. Research 16, 133–145 (1999)
16. Lerner, L.: Making student groups work. Journal of Management Ed. 19, 123–125 (1995)

17. May, T.: The New Know: Innovation Powered by Analytics. John Wiley and Sons, Inc., Toronto (2010)
18. Ericcson, K.A., Prietula, M.J., Cokley, E.: The making of an expert. Harvard Business Review 85, 114–121 (2007)
19. Biggs, J.: Teaching for Quality Learning. Open University Press, Buckingham (1999)
20. Gibbs, G., Habeshaw, S.: 53 Interesting Things to Do in Your Lectures, 2nd edn. Technical & Educational Services Ltd., Sydney (1998)
21. Michaelsen, L.K., Knight, A.B., Fink, L.D.: Team-Based Learning. Stylus Publishing, Sterling (2004)
22. Grow, G.O.: Teaching learners to be self-directed. Adult Ed. Qtr. 41(3), 125–149 (1996)
23. George, J.F., Valacich, J.S., Valor, J.: Does IS still matter? -lessons for a maturing discipline. Communications of the AIS 16(8), 219–232 (2005)
24. Hevner, A.R., March, S.T., Park, J.: Design science in information systems research. MIS Quarterly 28(1), 75–105 (2004)
25. March, S.T., Smith, G.F.: Design and natural science research on information technology. Decision Support Systems 15(4), 251–266 (1995)
26. Baskerville, R.L., Wood-Harper, A.T.: Diversity in Information Systems action research methods. European Journal of Information Systems 7, 90–107 (1998)
27. Baskerville, R., Myers, M.D.: Special Issue on Action Research in Information Systems: Making IS Research Relevant to Practice – Foreword. MIS Quarterly 28(3), 329–335 (2004)
28. Simon, H.A.: The sciences of the artificial, 3rd edn. MIT Press, Cambridge (1996)
29. Jelininek, M.A., Romme, A.G.L., Boland, R.: Introduction to the special issue: organization studies as a science for design: creating collaborative artifacts and research. Organization Studies 29, 317–329 (2008)
30. Cole, R., Rossi, M., Purao, S., Sein, M.: Being proactive: where action research meets design research. In: Proceedings of the International Conference on Information Systems, pp. 325–336 (2005)
31. Sein, M.K., Henfridsson, O., Purao, S., Rossi, M., Lindgren, R.: Action Research Design. MIS Quarterly 35(1), 37–56 (2011)
32. Schon, D.A.: The Reflective Practitioner: How Professionals Think in Action. Basic Books, New York (1983)
33. Ibbot, C.J.: Global Networks. Palgrave Macmillan Palgrave, New York (2007)
34. Levina, N.: Collaborating on multiparty information systems development projects: a collective reflection-in-action view. Information Systems Research 16(2), 109–130 (2005)
35. Kugel, P.: How professors develop as teachers. Studies in Higher Education 18(3), 315–328 (1993)
36. Carlile, P.R.: Transferring, translating, and transforming: an integrative framework for managing knowledge across boundaries. Organization Science 15(5), 555–568 (2004)
37. van Aken, J.E.: Management research as a design science: articulating the research products of Mode 2 knowledge production in management. British Journal of Management 16, 19–36 (2005)
38. van Aken, J.E., Romme, G.: Reinventing the future: adding design science to the repertoire of organization and management studies. Organizational Management Journal 6, 5–12 (2009)

Don't Ignore the Iceberg: Timely Revelation of Justification in DSR

Dirk S. Hovorka[1] and Jan Pries-Heje[2]

[1] Department of Informatics, Bond University, Gold Coast, QLD AU
dhovorka@bond.edu.au
[2] Department of Communication, Business and Information Technologies,
Roskilde University Roskilde, DN
janph@ruc.dk

Abstract. Design theory is often an outcome of Design Science Research (DSR) and kernel theories provide explanatory justification of design principles. But like an iceberg, many of the design principles lie hidden under the surface or inadequately specified. Ascertaining the completeness of the design principles requires additional design process steps to surface underlying assumptions and to abstract design principles which emerge during secondary design. We follow the development of a project management decision support artifact and describe the primary design, based on literature on agile systems development, and the subsequent secondary design that took place in a financial company. Analysis reveals an "iceberg phenomenon"; only a partial design justification was initially apparent, and underlying design assumptions are only revealed through deeper reflection and analysis. We conclude by providing guidelines for making design justification more explicit in both the design and the evaluation phases.

Keywords: Design Theory, kernel theory, primary design, secondary design.

1 Introduction

In Design Science Research (DSR), design theories are an outcome of designing, building, and evaluating the artifact that provide a solution in a specified problem space. These theories provide an abstracted set of components/capabilities which fulfill an abstracted set of requirements to address a class of problems. Although the importance of kernel theories in DSR is a matter of debate (Peffers, Tuunanen, Rothenberger, & Chatterjee, 2007), the importance of the design justification is well supported in the literature. Indeed, attempts to apply "Occam's razor" to design theory (R. Baskerville & Pries-Heje, 2010) reveal that the ex-ante justification for a specific design instantiation involve causal inference that selected general components of a design (the meta-design) will fulfill the general outcome requirements (the meta-requirements) based upon knowledge from the natural sciences, behavioral sciences and/or design principles. The specific principles of a meta-design are

J. vom Brocke et al. (Eds.): DESRIST 2013, LNCS 7939, pp. 228–241, 2013.

extracted from the knowledge-base of behavioral science (Hevner, March, Park, & Ram, 2004) and the inferences that they will fulfill meta-requirements has been termed justificatory knowledge (Gregor & Jones, 2007) or kernel theory (Walls, Widmeyer, & El Saway, 1992). But in most cases, only a few principles are explicitly identified, thus rendering the set of design principles, or the design theory, incomplete.

Although frequently invoked, the function of kernel theory is underspecified. Kernel theories originate in the body of knowledge composed of behavioral theories, prior design theory, experience, hidden assumptions and beliefs, and creative intuitions; they are frequently identified as the rationale for specific design choices. A deeper analysis of this concept illuminates two critical aspects of DSR. First the kernel theories justify the selection of components included in an explanatory design theory through inference that the requirements for system functions are fulfilled. Kuechler and Vaishnavi (2008) suggest that kernel theory acts as a locus for abduction to transforming behavioral knowledge into design principles. But not all kernel theories are explicitly identified, suggesting that the design theory itself is incomplete. Surfacing a more complete justification for the design provides two important aspects of design theory. First, it allows for a more complete theoretical prescription. Second, a more complete set of design principles enables specific evaluations during both the design process and after implementation, serving to enhance the knowledge contribution of a DSR instance to the knowledge-base.

This research presents an ongoing instance of design science research. The primary design has been completed and evaluations have been initiated. But in light of a secondary redesign of the artifact by users, and further reflection on principles embedded in the design, a reevaluation of the essential components and requirements was initiated. The re-evaulation revealed some 'taken for granted' principles that had been carried over from prior design instances, and others which were only assumed to be relevant. Through examination of this instance of the design research process, we provide guidelines which inform the explicit surfacing of design principles and components.

This paper proceeds as follows. We first review the range of positions on the role and need for justification of design principles in design theory. We next describe the DSR project objectives and status before examining the secondary redesign which revealed the hidden assumptions. This is followed by a discussion of the interactions with the users during the evaluation phase. We conclude with guidelines for making design justification more explicit in both the ex-ante and post implementation evaluations.

2   Kernel Theory as Justification

One argument in the DSR literature is that kernel theory, or justificatory knowledge, provides functional explanation "by showing why a role or action of a system is necessary to bring about some goal" (Baskerville & Pries-Heje, 2010). This explanatory role pertains to both the interior and the exterior mode of a design (Gregor, 2009).

The kernel theories enable causal inference (Gregor & Hovorka, 2011) or abduction (Gregor, 2009) that the internal design of the system will work together as predicted and also that the functions of the overall design will create the phenomenon the system is intended to create. Others have argued that kernel theories are not necessary (Venables, 2010) but design principles which predict how the internal working of an artifact will have desired external effects and prescribe functions and components are necessary. Design theories frequently identify only a few kernel theories, or principles, and do not explicitly list assumed design principles. This suggests that design theories are underspecified and that design processes can be improved.

3   Research Method

The starting point for this primary design example was when a number of project managers approached one of the authors of this paper and asked: When should we use the traditional project management principles and when should we use agile? The author was teaching classic project management – understood as the nine knowledge areas defined by Project Management Institute (PMI, 2008) – and was also doing research on agile methods.

The easy first answer was: "If you need a lot of change and you need something fast then you should consider using agile." But upon reflection, this question and the context presented an opportunity to undertake a DSR project.

Hevner et al. (2004) presents a definition of DSR and outlines three key processes. First there is the relevance process whereby you should take your starting point in a relevant problem or an identified need. Here our starting point was the question of when to use agile and when to use plan-driven methods. The kernel theories underlying the answer to this question are classic systems development theory and project management theory on one hand, and newer theory on agile approaches on the other hand.

The second key process in DSR is the research process ("rigor"), where the input from the existing knowledge-base is obtained, and where the contributions to scientific knowledge that the design allows are reported. Whether the knowledge is in the form of theory, model, method, framework or something similar, it is the researchers' task to build upon existing knowledge while contributing back to the knowledge-base. In relation to this key process, we relied partly on a thorough literature search, and partly on earlier research and experience on agile approaches, systems development, and project management.

The third key process is the design itself, which is an iteration between building and evaluation. Here you build on the problem space identified and you "stand on the shoulders of others" to create an innovative design theory or set of principles that is believed to solve the problem identified. Hence DSR theories are both prescriptive, in that they suggest how to address a general problem space and they are explanatory/predictive in that design theories specify the explanatory mechanism embedded in an artifact that is predicted to create specific desirable outcomes. Therefore, design science differs from analytically oriented sciences, where the objective is to describe, explain and predict existing realities.

3.1   The Primary Design Phase

The search for literature on agile methods and approaches brought forward numerous papers. We focused on papers with empirical evidence as opposed to more conceptual or speculative papers. The literature study was synthesized into the following eleven dimensions that provide part of the answer to the research question:

1. Expected changes: agile approaches have been defined either as an approach focusing on delivering something useful at high speed (Ågerfalk, Fitzgerald, & Slaughter, 2009) or as an approach that can adapt to a continuously changing target or requirements (Conboy, 2009).
2. Project size: The Cockburn Scale (2001) categorizes project size in terms of the number of development staff. He uses an open-ended scale representing project size as: 1-6 for a very small project, followed by gradations 7-20, 21-40, 41-100, and 99-200, 201-500 and 500+ for very large projects.
3. Project clarity: An inability to pre-define system requirements – the scope - is the central, defining constraint of agile development (Baskerville, Pries-Heje, & Madsen, 2011). The specification of scope and the elicited requirements specification has traditionally been the heart of systems development. Hence, if the scope is unclear from the beginning and requirements are hard to define then an agile approach may be preferable because it will allow requirements to persist in near or full ambiguity
4. Stakeholder consensus and level of politics: This is related to both changes and scope. In one agile method called 'Scrum' the customer view is represented by a 'Product Owner'. If the product owner cannot obtain a mandate for unilateral decisions when questions arise, all development will slow as developers wait for stakeholders to resolve conflicts.
5. Team experience: This goes back to a field study of software projects where one of the three problems found was the "thin spread of domain knowledge" (Bill, Krasner, & Iscoe, 1988).
6. Sufficient calendar time: In the literature, first-to-market is the central, defining high-priority goal of agile development. Minimizing time-to-market from concept to customer is an all-consuming activity and achievement of this goal drives almost all other elements of being agile. Hence sufficient calendar time is a defining characteristic. Many have found this dimension to be important in business (Smith & Reinertsen, 1995) and in software development (Cusumano & Selby, 1995; Iansiti & McCormack, 1997)
7. Developer experience: This was shown to be of great importance in internet software engineering studies (Ramesh, Pries-Heje, & Baskerville, 2002).
8. Team members "nativeness": This builds on the well-established observation that new-comers to an organization are not as effective as people who have been in the organization for some time. They may have "high uncertainty regarding how to do their job, how their performance will be evaluated, what types of social behaviors are normative, and what personal relationships within the organization might be beneficial to them" (Flanagin & Waldeck, 2004).

9. Project team distribution: Refers to the geographic and temporal distribution of the team (Sutherland, Viktorov, Blount, & Puntikov, 2007).
10. Team motivation: Lack of motivation by single member of the project team can ruin a team (Hackman, 1987; Turner, 2000).
11. Criticality: Process criticality is defined as the worst probable effect of an un-remedied defect, with loss of life being the worst result of a defect (Cockburn, 2001).

Of these 11 dimensions, some are more related than others (e.g. there is clearly a group defined by the abilities of the team; no. 7, 8, 9 and 10. Likewise there is another grouping (3, 4, 5 and 6) that will add complexity. Categorizing with these groupings consolidates the 11 dimensions into five.

The design process knowledge base provided justification for a meta-design using five dimensions. A scoring algorithm was found in a paper looking at project dimen-sions and how to adapt a project to the situation at hand (Pries-Heje & Avison, 2009), and was trialed during an action research project. Following Boehm and Turner (2003) the scoring was shown in a radar diagram, where patterns of the scoring were given a distinct meaning (e.g. "Bombs" are patterns with a high score on every di-mension and "Suns" have low scores on all dimensions).

Analyzing the five dimensions in more detail revealed that none of them provided ultimate complete answer to the question "should you use agile or plan-driven me-thods?" Each dimension could indicate a situation where it would be advantageous to bring in agile methods. For example the dimensions of many expected changes (1), a small sized group (2), very experienced and knowledgeable team (7 and 8) all suggest that agile should be considered. On the other hand it is not a show-stopper if many changes are not expected. That would merely be a potential advantage of agile that would not be realizable with traditional methods.

Table 1. The design of the five dimensions

Dimension	Scoring descriptions
1. Requirements stability	1 = More than 1/3 of requirements change 2 = Between 10% and 1/3 3 = Less than 10% of requirements change
2. Project Size	1 = Under 10 persons 2 = More than 10, less than 50 3 = More than 50
3. Complexity	Instruction: Give 2/3 p. for each "yes". Round up to nearest number "1", "2" or "3" a. Scope is quite clear b. Stakeholders are in agreement or disagree and there is lot of politics c. Project team members have experience in the area d. Sufficient calendar time is available

Table 1. (*continued*)

4. Project Team	Instruction: Give 2/3 p. for each "yes". Round up to nearest number "1", "2" or "3" a. Team consist of experienced developers b. Team members have experience working in the organization c. Team is distributed over many locations / is not sitting together d. Some people in the team are not motivated
5. Criticality – What can a defect lead to?	1 = Unpleasantness – but everything can be fixed 2 = Organization suffers a severe financial loss 3 = People may die

In the first design, the dimensions were phrased as statements that could be answered with a binary yes or no. The answers were then rated on a scale from "1" to "3" where "1" suggests agile approaches are appropriate from this dimension, and where "3" suggests that a plan-driven approach is preferred. The in-between rating "2" meant that the problems in this dimension should be carefully considered before deciding for an agile (or plan-driven) approach.

For each of the five dimensions (when combining the original eleven into categories as explained above) the statements shown in Table 1 were formulated. An example of how a scoring could look is shown in Figure 1.

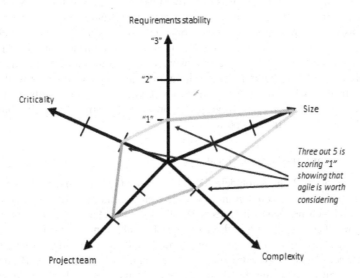

Fig. 1. An example scoring using the "Starfish" artifact

The scoring in Figure 1 shows a project that expects many requirements changes; has low complexity, has more than 50 participants, and where a defect in final IT-system will only cause unpleasantness. Hence you have to do something about that before you can consider using an agile method. The project team dimension scores "2". In this case a closer look at the four statements (categories) that goes into scoring the project team dimension is required to determine whether the potential problems identified can be alleviated.

This primary Starfish design, as presented here, was iteratively developed in multiple build and justify cycles. In 2011, the artifact was ready to be used for application in practice; i.e., for real project managers facing the decision about whether to use a plan-driven or an agile approach in their project. The implementation process associated with the Starfish was:

1. Present theory in general on agile methods
2. Present the five dimensions of the Starfish, relating it back to the underlying kernel theories on agile methods, plan-driven methods and systems development
3. Let the individual project manager answer to the statements and calculate whether each dimension is answered "1", "2" or 3"
4. Use the answer scores to draw the project-specific Starfish diagram
5. Conclude that if you have a majority of "1"s and no "3"s you should use agile methods. And if you have mainly "3"s then classic plan-driven project management is preferred

The first presentation of the design to project managers took place during a 3-day course in December 2010. Although minor wording changes of the dimensions were offered the participants evaluated the design positively and felt that it was understandable and the overall design was confirmed by the perceived utility. Subsequently, in the period from 2011-2013 about 100 project managers tried the "Starfish" exercise. It was presented as part of both an open course on general project management and during a specific one-day course for professionals. Participants in the courses were project managers and people that wanted to become project managers. There was a mixture of participants from public and private organizations as well as a mix of people from small and large organizations. Overall the participants evaluated the Starfish design artifact very positively; 4.6 on a scale from 1 to 5. No considerable changes were made during this period.

3.2   The Secondary Design Phase

In the autumn of 2012, the Almindelig Brand Insurance Company inquired about the Starfish. They wanted to embedded it in their project process model and make it a mandatory activity for all their projects. All projects, shortly after instantiation, would be analysed to determine whether an agile or plan-driven approach would be most beneficial.

We decided to hand over the primary design in a workshop. Together with a Project Director and a Project Portfolio Consultant from Almindelig Brand, we sat down and went over all the details of the Starfish including all the background material and design justifications and rationale. The experiences and knowledge-base from prior uses of the Starfish in numerous projects was also transferred.

Almindelig Brand did not adopt the primary design *as given* into use. They initiated an in-depth process whereby each and every dimension and category was discussed and scoring statements were re-phrased with terms and concepts suited to Almindelig Brand's specific context. In addition, a number of questions were added, pertaining to relationships to other projects, quality of the product, and whether the product of the project was projected to be used by many end-users. Furthermore, Almindelig Brand changed the weighting and ratings of some of the questions, (e.g. what constituted a "1" and a "2"). They also weighted selected statements, placing emphasis on some dimensions as being more important than others. Overall, Almindelig Brand created a Starfish secondary design quite different from the primary design. Differences between the primary design and the secondary design are highlighted with italics in Table 2.

Table 2. Secondary design by Almindelig Brand. Differences to Table 1 are shown in italics.

Dimension	Scoring description
How many requirements will change during project	*1 = Many* *2 = Half* *3 = Very few*
Size – How many work at the same time in project	*1 = Under 8 persons* *2 = More than 8, less than 13* *3 = More than 13*
Complexity	a. Scope is quite clear *(15%)* b. Stakeholders are in agreement or disagree and there is lot of politics *(15%)* c. Project team members have experience in the area *(30%)* d. Sufficient calendar time is available *(20%)* e. *Strong dependencies to other projects (20%)*
Project Team	a. Team consist of experienced developers *(20%)* b. Team members have experience working in the organization *(20%)* c. Team is distributed over many locations / is not sitting together *(20%)* d. *Part-time resources in project (20%)* e. Some people in the team are not motivated *(20%)*
Criticality	*40% based on what a defect can lead to:* 1 = Unpleasantness – but everything can be fixed *2 = Organization may suffer a loss* *3 = Organization suffers a severe loss of money* *30% based on high quality requirements are* *1 = Less than normal* *2 = Normally high* *3 = higher than normal* *20% based on whether delivery from project is to be used by end-user?* *1 = To a large degree* *2 = Partly* *3 = Limited*

In addition, Almindelig Brand re-envisioned the function of the design artifact with an increased emphasis on dialog and risk assessment. This is evidenced in the process document of the secondary design Starfish which states: "In the feasibility study phase it should be evaluated and recommended whether a project is to use SCRUM (agile) or V-model. The recommendation is made after a dialogue during the feasibility study where there is sufficient knowledge of the project's complexity, size and dependencies. See the section on feasibility study in the [Almindelig Brand] project management model. The dialogue is also used to identify the risks associated with the project and methodology. At the meeting it will be discussed how the project will ensure that these risks are minimized. The recommendation on whether to use agile or V-model is to be revisited to confirm / change when the project initiation phase."

In February 2013 the Starfish secondary design was evaluated by a project manager and his second through application to a real project. The project was a major Almindelig Brand initiative on a new Auto Insurance system for industry. The process was as follows:

1.   The Project Team was introduced to the core idea of the Starfish: decision support for selection between agile or plan-driven development life cycles.
2.   One by one the dimensions were presented and discussed. A spreadsheet was used to present the Starfish.
3.   The project manager provided answers to each question and responses were entered into the spreadsheet.
4.   After having been through all the dimensions the spreadsheet calculated and showed the resulting Starfish graphics.
5.   Based on the spreadsheet ratings it was concluded that the project at hand should not use agile but stay with plan-driven.

After the example project evaluation was completed, the Starfish artifact and the use process were evaluated. The project manager's overall conclusion after the evaluation was that the design artifact enabled "a very fruitful and valuable discussion". When asked about the spreadsheet and the scorings he responded that "the discussion was much more important than the spreadsheet" and that it was beneficial that "the discussion was facilitated" in that every dimension was explained before he (as project manager) had to take a stance on the statements for the specific dimension.

The Project Director, who was instrumental in the secondary design at Almindelig Brand, also evaluated the decision process. He was quite satisfied with the process and the spreadsheet-based implementation. In response to questions about next steps, he said that they would continue to align the Starfish artifact and process with the project process model at Almindelig Brand. The intention was to make the Starfish both a valuable and mandatory part of the project portfolio management process.

The Project Portfolio Consultant, the other Secondary designer at Almindelig Brand, also reflected on the scoring and weighting of statements within the dimensions and stated that "clearly some of these scorings needs to be discussed but we can work with it."

4   Avoiding Theorizing an Iceberg Pattern

An in-depth comparison of the primary design and the secondary design of the Starfish artifact reveals an "iceberg pattern" where the explicitly declared meta-design represents an incomplete design theory. Only a part of the design justification is initially revealed, and closer examination reveals important and necessary components in the design theory that should be surfaced to create a more complete theory. This research suggests three design process improvements:

First is designer reflection. In this case a discussion between the authors was initiated, which questioned the rationale for the specific primary design principles. As one example, the question was raised as to why only five dimensions were included in the Starfish rather than the original 11 dimensions which would better represent the complexity of the problem space. Upon reflection it was apparent that the primary design included an assumed principle of "simplicity" both in the number of dimensions and the limited values assigned to each dimension. Another of the unstated goals of the design was to provide a sense of used control. This was instantiated by enabling use of the artifact in a transparent and comprehensible manner using no more than a piece of paper and a pencil, with no reliance on hidden algorithms or complex computational analysis of inputs.

A second process improvement lies in the abstraction of specific design elements created by the users through secondary design processes. As the users worked with the primary design, they redesigned the artifact to fit their own specific tasks and context. This process of secondary design (Germonprez, Hovorka, & Callopy, 2007) reveals underlying assumptions and design principles which will improve the design theory. An example of the secondary design process is revealed in the changes the users made to weighting of the complexity and criticality dimensions. The primary design assumed weightings but implicitly assigned equivalent weightings to all dimensions thereby obscuring the design principle. The secondary design process revealed that the design theory should explicitly highlight the principle of dimension weightings. This highlighting will alert users that they may want to adjust the design with specific weightings which best fit their context.

A final process improvement echoes prior research (Baskerville et al. 2007) in suggesting that DSR artifacts should be field tested and have a lessons-learned step before the research process is considered complete. This would enable researchers to clearly specify what knowledge was added to the knowledge-base through design-build iterations and secondary design by users.

Applying these three design process steps will improve the theoretical contributions of DSR by demonstrating the potential knowledge contributions of seeing what happens when the design is implemented in practice. In the next section we demonstrate how these process steps were applying tour design case.

5   Justification Differences between Primary and Secondary Design

Analysis of the secondary design reveals additional design principles which strengthen the meta-design theory (Table 3). In the primary design, the choice of the radar representation was made to increase usability and ease-of-use. The principle of usability of a design was meant to increase the likeliness of adoption and use. In the secondary design at Almindelig Brand, the ease-of-use principle was maintained but was implemented through another mechanism, namely facilitation by specialists from the level above projects - the Project Portfolio Management. The rationale was that if you are a project manager just assigned to a project, it will be seen as a simple procedure to have facilitators come to you and facilitate the decision process using the dimensions of the Starfish. So the design principle was maintained, but the design means were changed.

In the primary design, a simple low-technology approach, completing a one-page paper form with a pen, was chosen primarily because it leaves the project manager with a sense of being in control of his own project. In the secondary design this principle was changed because Almindelig Brand wanted to use the Starfish in a facilitated process to initiate dialog instead. This principle of user control was lost in the evolved design due to an overall change in the functional purpose of the artifact. Instead of a simple low-technology artifact that could be implemented by any project manager, the goal was an artifact/process which could be uniformly implemented for the project managers across the company.

Table 3. Comparison of principles surfaced through modified design process

Design Principle	Primary Design	Evolved Design principles
Simplicity	Unstated (but assumed as limitation of short-term memory)	Stated as enacted by limited dimensions
Ease of use	Unstated (but assumed and enacted through specific visualization of results)	Stated as enacted by facilitator
Dimension weighting	Unstated (but assumed and enacted as all dimensions having equal weighting)	Stated and highlighted as variable by specific context
User Control	Low-technology artifact was explicitly designed to provide the user with transparency and a sense of control and understanding	Principle of user control eliminated as the functional purpose was redefined. Low-technology, transparency and user control were deemed less important than creation of a facilitated process which could be implemented for the project managers, not implemented by the mangers.
Functional purpose	The functional purpose of the artifact was to support a decision	The functional purpose of the artifact is to increase dialog and to provide points for discussion

6   Conclusion

Design theories provide prescriptive and explanatory/predictive knowledge by justifying problem solutions based, in part, on a broad knowledge-base of behavior and design science and on prior design experience. But justification for design principles is often focused on specific aspects of the problem space and important principles are not explicitly identified in the design theory. This "iceberg phenomena", in which explanatory justifications remain hidden under the surface raises two issues for design theorizing. First, if the meta-theory is under-specified, guidance for building specific instantiations is limited and comparison of designs across contexts may not recognize different underlying assumptions. Second, evaluations of the design theory are compromised as testing is less likely to examine the veracity of principles which are not stated in the theory. This limits the contribution of design evaluations to the knowledge base. To alleviate potential problems of theoretical incompleteness, evidence from this case example suggests three changes in the design theorizing process.

First, reflection by the designer or design team can reveal unstated assumptions and surface them in the design theory as principles or contingencies. For example, ease of use and simplicity are taken-for-granted components of design, but identifying how these principles are enacted in a design theory or instantiation highlights the principle for evaluation or replacement.

A second design process change is to compare the primary design principles with the principles and components realized after secondary design by the users. This process reveals assumptions, both correct and incorrect, which were embedded in the primary design. The comparison will also highlight aspects of the design that could be varied for specific instantiations (e.g. changing the weighting of dimensions.) As observed in our case, the principle of weighting the dimension is not changed, but the specific weightings are subject to adjustment and should be highlighted as a variable dimension.

Finally, the evaluation of the artifact *in situ* is a critical aspect of articulating contribution to the knowledge base. As user interpret principles embedded in the artifact, hidden and potentially unwarranted assumptions are revealed which may clarify, alter or support design principles.

The goal of these three design-theorizing process changes; surfacing 1) design principles, 2) identifying embedded assumptions, and 3) field testing and secondary design evaluation, is to enable researchers to develop and communicate more complete design theory. Comprehensively declaring the principles and components of design theory will enable a clearer comparison of the principles underlying design instantiations, and will strengthen the contribution of DSR to the knowledge-base of design.

References

1. Ågerfalk, P.J., Fitzgerald, B., Slaughter, S.: State of the Art and Research Challenges. Information Systems Research 20(3), 317–318 (2009)

2. Baskerville, R., Pries-Heje, J.: Explanatory Design Theory. Business & Information Systems Engineering 5, 271–282 (2010)
3. Baskerville, R., Pries-Heje, J., Madsen, S.: Post-Agility: What Follows a Decade of Agility. Information and Software Technology 53(5) (2011)
4. Baskerville, R., Pries-Heje, J., Venable, J.: Soft Design Science Research: Extending the Boundaries of Evaluation in Design Science Research. In: Proceedings of the 2nd International Conference on Design Science Research in Information Systems and Technology (DESRIST 2007), Pasadena, California, USA, May 13-15 (2007)
5. Bill, C., Krasner, H., Iscoe, N.: A Field Study of the Software Design Process for Large Systems. Communications of the ACM 31(11), 1268–1287 (1988)
6. Boehm, B., Turner, R.: Balancing Agility and Discipline: A Guide for the Perplexed. Addison-Wesley Professional, Boston (2003)
7. Cockburn, A.: Agile Software Development. Addison-Wesley Professional (2001)
8. Conboy, K.: Agility from First Principles: Reconstructing the Concept of Agility in Information Systems Development. Information Systems Research 20(3), 329–354 (2009)
9. Cusumano, M., Selby, R.: Microsoft Secrets: How the World's Most Powerful Company Creates Technology, Shapes Markets and Manages People. Free Press, New York (1995)
10. Flanagin, A.J., Waldeck, J.H.: Technology use and organizational newcomer socialization. Journal of Business Communication 41(2), 137–165 (2004)
11. Germonprez, M., Hovorka, D., Callopy, F.: A Theory of Tailorable Technology Design. Journal of the Association of Information Systems 8(6), 351–367 (2007)
12. Gregor, S.: Building Theory in the Sciences of the Artificial. Paper Presented at the DESRIST, Philadelphia (2009)
13. Gregor, S., Hovorka, D.S.: Causality: the Elephant in the Room in Information Systems Epistemology. Paper Presented at the European Conference on Information Systems (2011)
14. Gregor, S., Jones, D.: The Anatomy of a Design Theory. Journal of the Association of Information Systems 8(5), 312–335 (2007)
15. Hackman, J.R.: The design of work teams. In: Lorsch, J. (ed.) Handbook of Organizational Behaviour. Prentice-Hall, Englewood Cliffs (1987)
16. Hevner, A.R., March, S.T., Park, J., Ram, S.: Design Science in IS Research. MIS Quarterly 28(1), 75–106 (2004)
17. Iansiti, M., McCormack, A.: Developing Products on Internet time. Harvard Business Review 75(5), 108–117 (1997)
18. Kuechler, B., Vaishnavi, V.: On Theory Development in Design Science Research: Anatomy of a Research Project. European Journal of Information Systems 17(5), 489–504 (2008)
19. Peffers, K., Tuunanen, T., Rothenberger, M., Chatterjee, S.: A Design Science Research Methodology for Information Systems Research. J. Manage. Inf. Syst. 24(3), 45–77 (2007)
20. PMI. A Guide to the Project Management Body of Knowledge (PMBOK Guide), 4th edn. Project Management Institute, Newtown Square (2008)
21. Avison, D., Pries-Heje, J.: Flexible Information Systems Development: Designing an Appropriate Methodology for Different Situations. In: Filipe, J., Cordeiro, J., Cardoso, J. (eds.) ICEIS 2007. LNBIP, vol. 12, pp. 212–224. Springer, Heidelberg (2008)
22. Ramesh, B., Pries-Heje, J., Baskerville, R.: Internet Software Engineering: A different class of processes. Annals of Software Engineering 14, 169–195 (2002)
23. Smith, P.G., Reinertsen, D.G.: Developing Products in Half The Time, 2nd edn. Van Nostrand Reinhold, New York (1995)

24. Sutherland, J., Viktorov, A., Blount, J., Puntikov, N.: Distributed Scrum: Agile Project Management with Outsourced Development Teams. Paper Presented at the Proceedings of the 40th Hawaii International Conference on System Sciences (2007)
25. Turner, M.E.: Groups at Work: Theory and Research. Psychology Press (2000)
26. Venable, J.R.: Design Science Research Post Hevner et al.: Criteria, Standards, Guidelines, and Expectations. In: Winter, R., Zhao, J.L., Aier, S. (eds.) DESRIST 2010. LNCS, vol. 6105, pp. 109–123. Springer, Heidelberg (2010)
27. Walls, J.G., Widmeyer, G.R., El Saway, O.A.: Building an Information System Design Theory for Vigilant EIS. Information Systems Research 3(1), 36–59 (1992)

An Argumentative Approach of Conceptual Modelling and Model Validation through Theory Building

Sebastian Bittmann and Oliver Thomas

University Osnabrueck, Germany

Abstract. Conceptual modelling and theory building are tightly bundled together, since conceptual models are one way to express one's thoughts, assumptions, beliefs and convictions, respectively his theory referencing a domain. However, while theory building does account for a process of knowledge creation and the evolution of a theory, which is characterised by falsification and rebuttals, a conceptual model remains a vessel of expressing a current state of knowledge. A theory held in a person's mind might develop during gaining experiences and through discussions with others, usually held in natural language. A conceptual model, however, disregards these aspects of theory building. Therefore in this paper, we will introduce an approach of purposefully constructing and validating conceptual models by means of arguments. This approach will not just enable a validation of a conceptual model against the theory of the creator, but against all theories the respective stakeholders might have.

Keywords: Conceptual Modelling, Design Theory, Argumentative Modelling, Reasoning, Toulmin.

1 Introduction

Theory Building (TB) is an iterative process of describing and explaining phenomena in a certain domain as well as the validation of these descriptions and explanations [1,2]. Hence it enables the creation of understandings of domains. It is further grounded on the necessity for understanding, expressing and reflecting convictions and beliefs created in one's own mind as well as spread by others [2,3]. Moreover TB enables the generation of explanations based on theories for the development of new knowledge [1]. With an ongoing development of the own cognitive theories the development of the understanding about a certain domain can be depicted.

Conceptual Modelling has been developed to a sophisticated manner for expressing understandings and convictions about specific domains [4]. Hence, it enables the spreading of theories depicted by a conceptual model. However, conceptual models are mainly used for expressing own convictions and beliefs with the purpose of being discussed with others. These discussions then may result in new conceptual models, again only specified by one individual, which is capable of using a formal language [5,6]. While there is often the claim that a different, more familiar representation increases the understanding [5,7,8], we believe that the central component regarding the

J. vom Brocke et al. (Eds.): DESRIST 2013, LNCS 7939, pp. 242–257, 2013.

understanding of a conceptual model remains unconsidered, which is the process of knowledge creation. Nevertheless, TB considers the evolution of knowledge, because Theories, which were seen as granted, can be rebutted in the near future by other upcoming and completely new theories.

Whilst theories are often characterised by such an ongoing process of evolution, conceptual models seem to represent more or less a state of the art of knowledge in a domain. However, with the ongoing spread of a conceptual model certain aspects may be rebutted and certain theories of individuals are developed with respect to the conceptual model. Unfortunately, the evolution of theories results in the necessity for new conceptual models that embody upcoming and new theories. Furthermore, while a theory is constituted by justifications regarding beliefs and convictions, a conceptual model is not.

Although a conceptual model comes with the claim for expressing a theory, it lacks certain relevant aspects. First, conceptual modelling doesn't account for justifications. A conceptual model omits knowledge gained in its process specification, e.g. the falsification of knowledge, and embodies only the knowledge, which has been proofed as valid. Second, explanations regarding the conceptual model have to be expressed by certain other manners. These manners are often natural language or a further unrelated language. Third, conceptual model are the result of one individual applying a certain modelling language, whilst a theory builds up in multiple discussions considering multiple individuals.

In this paper we introduce an approach, which is capable of fully capturing a theory with conceptual modelling. This approach relies on the Theory of Argumentation offered by Toulmin [9]. In the next section TB and the relation towards conceptual modelling will be discussed in more detail. Within section 3 related work will be evaluated. Following, it will be introduced how a theory can be proposed in an argumentative approach, namely through the Argumentation Modelling Language. In the second last chapter 5 the approach will be illustrated by using it for validating theories proposed by means of ontologies. The paper ends with a conclusion.

2   Theory Building

2.1   Relation Towards Conceptual Modelling

TB is mainly considered with the creation of theories [1,2]. A theory in the sense of Ryle enables a person to succeed certain actions and further support these actions by explanations, justifications and responses to queries [10]. Thereby for the purposes of a theory, the constructs in a respective domain as well as their interrelations have to be identified. Furthermore a theory has to be falsifiable as this is a premise for an ongoing progress of an evolving theory [11].

Conceptual modelling can be regarded as an activity, which enables the creation of a theory and respective an understanding about a certain domain [12]. It is capable of spreading a theory by means of its considered constructs and the relationships among them. Furthermore conceptual model offer the possibility of falsifying theories through the identification of inconsistencies. [11]

The conceptual model can be used as a basis for discussions, where the conceptual model and the respective theory are presented to an audience [13]. Through a held discussion contradictions between the theory proposed by a conceptual model and the cognitive theories of the participants can be checked, whether they are able to be aligned or not. This process is depicted by figure 1. Hence, a conceptual model is a manner for expressing a cognitive held theory as well as a way for creating a cognitive theory by understanding the expressions offered through it.

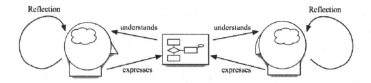

Fig. 1. Building of common theories

2.2   Problems with Theory Building in Conceptual Modelling

Although conceptual models offer a purposeful approach for depicting a theory, the support for a reasoning process among multiple individuals is far from sufficient. Respectively if a theory changes, the conceptual model, which embodies the theory has to change as well. However, while the change of a theory might be able to be depicted through new convictions and new beliefs, the evolution of a conceptual model might only be represented by descriptions given in natural language. Thereby the evolution of conceptual models can be followed from specification to specification, but without any given reasons for the embodiment of new and the omission of previous design decision.

More specifically for the validation of conceptual models regarding information systems, which requires accounting for the various views of the different stakeholders [14,15,16]. Accounting for these different perspectives requires intense communications and the understanding of the different reasons for requirements given by the various stakeholders. Unfortunately, reasons for design decision have to be explicitly illustrated for every stakeholder by means of natural language, since a conceptual model does simply not give any reasons. Next to the understanding of the requirements of the stakeholders by the modeller, it is necessary that the stakeholders are able to validate the conceptual model by means of their own requirements and therefore it requires their understanding of the modelling language. In general it must be said that although a conceptual model might depict a certain theory, the creation of a theory based on the conceptual model and namely the understanding of a conceptual model is not possible simply through the conceptual model. Further explanations are needed for stakeholders, which might be offered by the respective modeller in a discussion formed through arguments in natural language [17].

However, based on the increasing number of involved stakeholders and the raising complexity, it is doubtful that a certain 'expert' is available, who is able to explain the conceptual model. Furthermore the availability of all stakeholders in the several discussions with the goal of an alignment of the different requirements can't be expected. Therefore a conceptual model should provide explanations and the process of modelling shouldn't expect the availability of all stakeholders.

Moreover, in order to validate a conceptual model before the respective software system will be operated and certain organisational changes are applied to the enterprise, the respective stakeholders need to understand the conceptual model. Hence during conceptual modelling the theories that incorporate the respective domain knowledge have to be considered [14].

The cognitive-held theories are characterised by an ongoing process of invalidation, adaption and extension [18]. Based on the very first experiences the initial naïve theories of a human being will be refuted by its nature and extended or replaced by the theories created by others, respectively the society or the respective social system [19]. However, conceptual models only depict what is now regarded as true or what the current state of knowledge is. They do neglect any consideration of the process of TB and therefore only depict a small excerpt of the underlying theory. Furthermore their validity cannot be checked with respect to upcoming conceptual models and namely theories, due to the fact that the conceptual models are not integrated and the underlying theories are exposed mainly via natural language.

3   Related Work

Within literature there is a plethora of methods, paradigms and tools, which aim at the purposeful support for the specification of conceptual models. Procedural approaches, e.g. [20], which guide the act of modelling, only support the process of modelling and neglect problems that are rather domain specific. While certain phases of modelling are generally considered, e.g. requirements identification, support for domain specific and individual problems can't be included.

Ontological approaches, for example [21] and [22], try to represent domains through an ontology. The representation is undertaken by means of the most general classes existing, for example the class of a thing or a law. However, a representation by an ontological language is a representation of one specific perspective. Although this one perspective might be an aggregated one from a multitude of perspectives, still a single representation is an inhibitor of a discourse.

This mostly relates to the fact that an ontology doesn't come with explanations or even justifications for rebutting the embodied beliefs.

A general classification for conceptual models or more specifically for reference models was proposed by [23] and [17]. These approaches try to classify reference models for the adaptation of enterprise-specific solutions in order to justify their necessity and guide the identification of the appropriate domain. With such a classification frame the explanation of the purpose of a conceptual model is supported. However, with offering a frame the structures for explanations are fixed prior the need for an explanation. While different stakeholders require different arguments in order to be convinced, the space of arguments is restricted by those approaches.

Approaches, which focus more on arguments and therefore a consideration of a theory in an argumentative way, like [24,25,26], are often described formally and don't consider domain-specific knowledge. Furthermore the derivation of new knowledge, which is applicable on the respective domain, isn't possible as well.

Lastly, approaches were evaluated that try to tackle the previous describe problems with respect to natural language. On the one hand, approaches were introduced that try to formalise discussions held in natural language [5]. This is done by annotating certain nouns or verbs and associating them with a certain role. However with their lack of a previously defined vocabulary these approaches are rather imprecise. Actual queries or questions that are involved in the discussion can be usually specified with respect to a multitude of possibilities. So in order to prevent ambiguities, these approaches still rely on a higher schema, which forces the use of natural language to one specific structure. On the other hand, it was tried to use natural language and find a structure with the help of analyses between text passages [27]. Such a proceeding might support the understanding of the recipient of the arguments, but doesn't support the derivation of further insights, e.g. the participants must identify the contradictions between arguments manually. So, although an argument has been won, it is ought to recipient to properly interpret this argument and derive further implications.

4   Validation of Theories with the ArgML

4.1   The ArgML

The Argumentation Modelling Language (ArgML) was originally derived from Toulmin's Argumentation Model (TAM) [9]. According to Toulmin's Theory of Argumentation any claim is supported by a ground, a qualifier and a warrant. These concepts are already used during the application of modelling approaches. However, while the resulting models are constituted by the different claims, the other concepts of Toulmin's Theory are proposed through natural language. Hence, any argument given in a discussion regarding a model is constituted partly by the modelling language and the natural language. Thereby, the claims offered through a conceptual model are supplemented with specific semantics by the modelling languages, but the possible misinterpretation of the justifications of these claims is still high and serious, because of the use of natural language.

Therefore the main goal of the conceptualisation of an argumentative language was to reduce the level of possible misinterpretations without any compromises regarding the expressibility. ArgML refines the TAM by completely excluding the use of natural language. Hence, any concept, initially introduced in the TAM and refined by the ArgML, does not depend on the natural language for its specification. Regarding the exclusion of natural language, for the arguments formed by means of the ArgML specific domain-specific modelling languages (DSLs) and Object Constraint Language (OCL) were chosen as a substitute. Those languages offer an unambiguously interpretation. How the different concepts proposed by the ArgML is discussed in the latter. The specific concepts of the ArgML will be discussed in the following. Their specific relations are depicted by figure 2.

Claim. A claim comprises propositions, whose underlying knowledge is sought to be established. Hence, the discussion is primarily driven by the required justification of the claims with respect to the already established knowledge. Every claim is expressed through a model, which follows the syntax of the argument's associated language.

Argument. An argument is a container for a multitude of claims and their rebuttals. Hence a discussion is related to one specific argument. If the argument is settled, further claims may relate to the claims offered by the argument.

Rebuttal. A rebuttal is a statement that contradicts a claim. It is constituted by propositions, which can't be aligned with the rebutted claim. Therefore a rebuttal is a claim, which contrasts at least one further claim. Any rebuttal within one argument has to be aligned with the respective qualifiers in order to settle the argument.

Qualifier. Whenever a rebuttal exists regarding a claim, the validity is doubtful and it may only be valid for specific cases. Thereby the qualifier is in charge of aligning its qualifying claim towards those claims that rebut it. It defines the conditions for the claim to be granted as valid.

Language. A specific language is uniquely chosen to form the claims contained by one argument.

Concept. Any language, which is used in an argument, consists out of multiple concepts. The warrants and qualifiers can refer these concepts.

Model. Any model is an instance of the chosen language of an argument. It is an expression for representing the designated claims.

Ground. Contrasting to the claim, a ground embodies already established knowledge. Grounds illustrate the common knowledge, which could be used to justify the claims. Therefore a relation between the claim and its supporting grounds has to be revealed by means of the warrants and qualifiers.

Warrant. The relation between a claim and its supporting grounds is expressed through a warrant. Warrants describe the implication that leads from the ground to the claim, if the claim qualifies with respect to the qualifier. A warrant is mainly based on convictions and therefore requires the acceptance by the various participating stakeholders.

Both the concept of a warrant and qualifier are using the OCL as a basis for their specification [28]. They can be specified generally and are not restricted to a specific language, like the claims and grounds. The claims and grounds, however, are specified by a well-defined language, which is preferably constructed by means of a DSL that strictly follows a defined syntax and semantics [29]. By using DSLs and OCL for the specification of arguments it is possible to unambiguously interpret them.

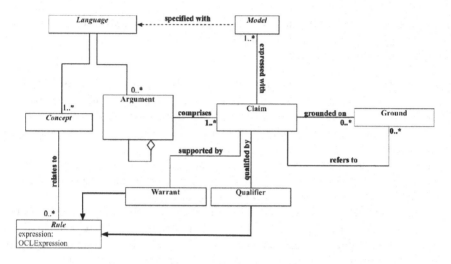

Fig. 2. Abstract Syntax of the Argumentation Modelling Language

Although the argumentative quality of the approach drastically relies on the respective modelling language, it still comes with some valuable benefits. Mainly, claims, which are not qualified to be formalised with the modelling language can't be introduced in the discussion. Hence, something that is per se invalid, will be identified before its introduction and any possible interpretation by others. However, with the possible need for certain expressions or models, the respective modelling language may also be the subject of an ongoing discussion held by means of the ArgML in order to extend the expressibility of the modelling language.

The purpose of the ArgML is the derivation of actual knowledge based from a held discussion. In terms of the ArgML it becomes possible to derive an actual conceptual model by consideration of all qualified claims. Hence those claims that have turned out to be valid will be integrated and represent the coherent and desired conceptual model. Based on the given arguments it can be assured that the claims do not stand in any conflict to each other and that the derived conceptual model is internally valid. A further derivation of a held discussion is a set of derivable rules, which are generated with respect to the given warrants and qualifiers. Any rule is an invariant, which have to be satisfied by the model. Hence if a qualifier of a given argument will be satisfied by means of the OCL and therefore is valid, the model has to satisfy the interrelated warrant of the argument as well. Thereby, from any argument an invariant, which takes the form of an implication, implying the warrant whenever the qualifier is satisfied, can be derived.

4.2   Construction of Theories

By means of the ArgML different parts of a respective theory may be expressed. First, it is possible to articulate statements of the respective domain by means of claims.

These may be both anticipated consequences and experiences of the respective individual. Second, it is possible to articulate rules or explanations that justify the proposed statements. These rules rely on agreed statements (grounds) and depict the evolution of knowledge that has led to the claim.

Based on the characteristic criteria for a theory specified in [11], the argumentative proposals of conceptual models can be regarded as a theory. With the ArgML the illustration of identified constructs is possible through the proposal of claims. Furthermore the relation between the constructs and justifications can be specified as well. Lastly it is possible to falsify the relations in an argumentative manner.

Furthermore with an argument as a container for multiple claims the different proposal can be checked regarding their alignment and the solving of contradictions. Thereby it is possible to validate different theories against each other, if those theories are expressed through the ArgML. Next to building a common understanding, the common understanding can be validated by means of the different theories.

4.3   Validation of Theories against Conceptual Models

Due to the ArgML, a participation in the modelling process by a multitude of different stakeholders becomes possible. Every participant is encouraged to provide arguments, regardless if the conceptual model has already been specified or its specification has just been initialized. These arguments are then included by the ongoing discussion about the conceptual model and are ought to be rebutted or its claim will be included by the conceptual model.

Furthermore each understanding of the stakeholders, namely their cognitive theories, has to be checked against the conceptual model in order to ensure the validity of it. The arguments depicting the different theories have to be first aligned to ensure the common understanding and second checked against the actual conceptual model. The process of validation by means of the ArgML supports the different stakeholders, since they are able to choose their required level of granularity for their arguments freely. However, the formalized approach ensures a validation of the conceptual model by means of the arguments in the current as well as in future discussions, for which current stakeholders may not be available. The rules that can be derived from an argument are mainly of interest in this process, because they form a basis for validating the conceptual model.

As depicted by figure 3, the ArgML supports the TB process. According to [30] the phases of a TB process are the phases of *building, evaluating, theorizing and justifying*. For each of the phases the ArgML comprises constructs, which are capable of supporting them. Furthermore, the ArgML not just supports the process based on its formalisation, it enables the participation of multiple individuals in a TB process. Following, it is described, which constructs support the different phases of the TB process, which is again depicted graphically with figure 3.

(1) Build through the creation of claims.
(2) Evaluate by reflecting claims and their recreation.
(3) Theorize by proposing more general statements, through qualifier and warrants.
(4) Justify by means of selecting grounds from which the proposed knowledge
   evolves from and by using the derived rules for other models, respective examples.

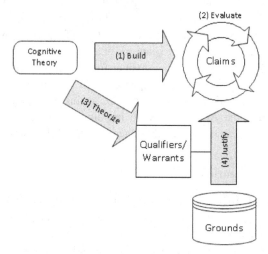

Fig. 3. Support of Theory Building by means of the ArgML

Hence a conceptual model can be regarded as valid, if it is aligned with all of the
contributing theories.

Furthermore, based on the formalisation of the ArgML, different criteria regarding
the quality of a theory, [15], do either correlate positively or are explicitly met.
Through the use of a modelling language for the specification of claims the internal
validity is ensured by the language's syntax. The external validity can be satisfied by
the consideration of the various stakeholders, which have proposed their theory
through arguments. Furthermore, the scope of the underlying theory is implicitly defined through the granularity of the different arguments and the aspect they address.
Lastly, the simplicity and the accuracy of a theory are promoted through the consideration of different views and the restriction towards the relevant views of the stakeholders. Additionally, the argumentative process supports the simplicity and accuracy
through the possible, but not required, stating of more detailed explanations by means
of arguments.

5   Theory Building in a Domain-Specific Context

5.1   Ontological Explorations

In order to evaluate the represented approach, it will be shown how the approach can
extend the expressive and argumentative power of ontologies. Ontologies are well

suited for expressing statements about a respective domain. However, an ontology is restricted to proposing claims about a domain and hence, offers only a very restrictive explanatory potential. An evaluation of the ArgML considered with ontologies will reveal this gap, lying within the relation between a statement and its justification. The evaluation will further show that obvious interrelations between parts of an ontology are yet unconsidered by ontological languages. Lastly, based on such on abstract view, which is constituted by the use of ontologies, it will be shown that modelling languages in general do not consider the prior described relations and interrelations. The ontological exploration undertaken in this example is on a rather high level, as it very generally discusses a certain concept. The example was chosen in order to illustrate the impact of the ArgML, not just on rather concrete modelling scenarios, but also on more abstract scenarios, e.g. the definition of modelling languages through meta-modelling.

An integration between an ontological language and the ArgML offers the possibility of ontological explorations. Starting with the most general assumptions, the ArgML supports the continuous evolution of knowledge embodied by the respective ontology. With an ongoing process of refutation, the knowledge embodied by the ontology will continuously evolve.

5.2   The Concepts of an Ontology

Ontologies can be used for purposefully exploring domains and their related concepts. One example is the Bunge-Wand-Weber Model (BWW), which is introduced in [21] and further specified through a meta model in [31]. The BWW defines concepts, which are especially designed with the purpose of understanding the structure and behaviour of information systems.

Although an ontology might depict a state of knowledge or more specifically a perception of a certain domain, no justifications are given solely by the ontology. This leads to problems of developing a common understanding about the concepts circumstanced in a domain. Since a specification of an ontology is only driven by one respective modeller, beliefs in behold by others remain unconsidered. However, it may be the case that discussions are held, prior to the act of modelling, but these discussions are often not documented and then only consolidated in one's mind. So the actual evolution of knowledge constituting a domain is missing.

Furthermore, it may be the case that between parts of a model an interrelation is identified [5]. This interrelation could be a causal one, e.g. due to a certain property of a thing, a further property is required. These interrelations are further not documented, so that during a change of a specific part the related parts remain unconsidered. A probable causality is the fact that conceptual model and even ontologies don't provide any explanations, e.g. examples for illustrating, regarding their proposals [5]. Ontologies do neither include any supplements for justifying their claims nor do they include any reference to other parts of the model in order to explain causality.

5.3   Ontology Based Discussions with the ArgML

The integration of the ArgML with the BWW enables the illustration of the process of TB for domains. Furthermore the different design decision doesn't have to rely on natural language for their justification. The justification can be given by means of the ArgML and therefore a direct linkage between the relevant parts of the model, the respective design decision dependent on, is possible. Additionally multiple individuals are able to participate in the process of modelling by stating their claims and justify them. The set of different claims will be the aligned for sakes of a common understanding and respectively a common theory.

Hence, every claim in such a discussion is an excerpt of the ontology. Beginning with the early assumptions the discussed ontology will be stepwise explored by stating claims about that ontology and justify them by already settled knowledge offered by grounds. Any claim contributes to a complete description of the respective ontology. However, through the use of the ArgML it is possible to just propose a small set of claims. Further, the claimants are continuously extendable for the contribution of new insights that are justified with a reference to the already settled knowledge.

5.4   Building a Common Understanding about Domains

In order to illustrate the developed approach, the used ontological concepts are restricted to the ontological concepts of a thing and property of a thing.

The discussed domain is business process management and hence it will be illustrated how the concept of an activity may be discussed by means of the ArgML. As illustrated with figure 4 the concept of an activity has a multitude of different properties, among them are required documents, related information systems and the required manual steps for its execution.

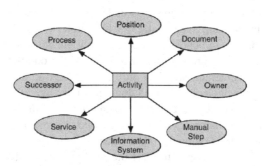

Fig. 4. Concept specification through an ontology

Whether the proposed ontological definition of the concept of an activity may be coherent with the respective literature or not, the actual design decisions for defining the concept in such a way are not given solely through the ontology. The chance for understanding other's implications is not possible through the ontology. So any reason regarding the proposed definition, which would enable the understanding of different beliefs, remains unconsidered by the ontology. Hence, even such a definition requires additional explanations. Furthermore if one doubts such a definition, it is required to judge his arguments against those that are already considered by the definition. Thereby the definition may be either coherent with one's cognitive theory or not, but the validity is not challenged based on the definition.

However by means of the ArgML it is possible to define arguments regarding the ontology. As depicted by figure 5, it is possible to claim certain properties about the concept of an activity and furthermore, justify them by means of grounds. Such a formulation of arguments will be discussed in detail. More specifically, any argument is an instantiation of the ArgML integrated with the ontological language. Such arguments should then be checked regarding their coherency or contradiction regarding the given definition. Furthermore, it has to be checked if arguments offer new insights and their relevance towards the definition.

Argument A of figure 5 justifies the relation towards of a position owned by the concept of an activity. It claims that the position, which is located within a respective company, is required because the execution of manual steps requires a human being. So the argument A is coherent with the given definition and doesn't contradict it. Any proposition offered by argument A is already considered, so that such an argument could also be used for a constructing dialogue, which defines the actual model. A further derivation of that argument would be a rule that states that every time a thing includes the property of "Manual Steps", then it has to include a "Position" as well. Therefore implications for future discussions are derivable.

However, argument B rebuts that an activity is related to a service, since an activity is already related to an information system, which may be or not already related to a service. Hence, there is a conceptual conflict regarding the validation of the conceptual model. The argument B contradicts the proposed definition. Therefore it is necessary to judge whether to rebut such an argument or to adapt the proposed definition of an activity.

The last argument C brings in a further perspective. It claims, that since an activity is related to a document, it should already be related to document permissions. The argument C doesn't contradict the proposed definition directly, but it offers further insights regarding the concept of an activity, which might be relevant. So different to argument B, this argument doesn't challenge the definition, but offers further aspects that may be considered by the ontological definition. So the definition is not required to be adapted, respectively invalidate former valid knowledge, but either has to be extended or the argument has to be challenged by refutations. For example it could be rebutted that an activity isn't related to document permissions, since a document is already related towards it's individual document permissions and hence that such a permission management is handled differently.

Therewith, such a formalised approach offers the opportunity to rebut not just arguments given by available stakeholders, but also stakeholders may participate remotely and in other periods of time.

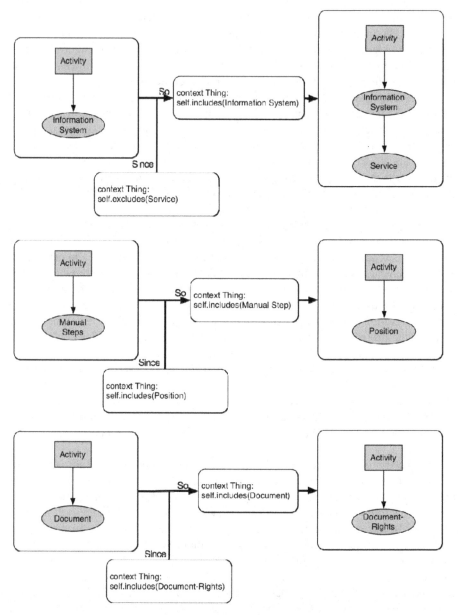

Fig. 5. Arguments regarding the concept "Activity"

6   Conclusion

In this paper it was shown, how conceptual models may be created and validated through an argumentative approach. Superior from previous modelling approaches, which mainly concentrate on the syntax and semantics of conceptual models, the presented approach does consider explanations. Furthermore, the given explanations can be interpreted without the use of natural language. So the interpretation of a conceptual model proposed with reference to the ArgML, can be understood solely by its specification. So, the theory captured by a conceptual model with reference to the ArgML is enriched in two ways. The theory will be increased in its explanative power as it uses arguments to explain design decisions. Additionally, the theory will be increased in its predictive power as it uses arguments to justify design decision based on valid knowledge included by the conceptual model [32]. Furthermore, we have shown how a discourse would be possible even with the exclusion of natural language and the complete focus on the specific modelling language.

However, such a discourse becomes only possible, if, and only if, the relevant stakeholders are able to propose their own perception and/or their requirements regarding a domain through a specific modelling language. Furthermore the process of justification has to be supplemented by the concepts of the ArgML.

The problem of translating natural language statements to modelling artefacts isn't completely excluded, but the translation from a cognitive theory to a conceptual model was shifted to a higher level of abstraction. This higher level of abstraction would only consider small excerpts of the complete model, which may be simpler and hence easier to understand. Therefore the validation effort would be decreased. Additionally reasons for design decision wouldn't get lost and documented externally, but would be embodied by the conceptual model.

The presented approach would also be a solid basis for software systems considered with collaborative modelling, because a direct discourse between the stakeholders isn't required and can be held through formalised arguments. Earlier design decisions can be rebutted by upcoming stakeholders and the conceptual model can be adapted, if the rebuttal was justified. Software systems for collaborative modelling that propose open models as in [33] could be extended in order to enable participants to contribute to conceptual models via sense making and in an argumentative way. A multitude of different experts could build conceptual models remotely, through their contribution of knowledge regarding a domain by proposing arguments. Next to the contribution, the evolution of knowledge within a domain through a conceptual model would be as well depicted. Such a depiction could then be a basis for further analyses.

However, we do see restrictions regarding the approach, which are mainly related to the use of language. Although the approach was derived from Toulmin's widely accepted theory, it has to be examined if arguments regarding modelling decisions do always follow the proposed structure. Furthermore, the expressibility of claims mainly relies on the used modelling language and therefore the set of possible proposition is restricted by the modelling language's syntax. Lastly, the OCL is a rather technical language and claimants might be unfamiliar using it for proposing warrants and qualifies.

References

1. Meredith, J.: Theory Building through Conceptual Methods. International Journal of Operations & Production Management 13(5), 3–11 (1993)

2. Lynham, S.A.: The General Method of Theory-Building Research in Applied Disciplines. Advances in Developing Human Resources 4(3), 221–241 (2002)
3. Killion, J.P., Todnem, G.R.: A Process for Personal Theory Building. Educational Leadership 48(6), 14–16 (1991)
4. Wand, Y., Monarchi, D.E., Parsons, J., Woo, C.C.: Theoretical foundations for conceptual modelling in information systems development. Decision Support Systems 15(4), 285–304 (1995)
5. Dalianis, H.: A method for validating a conceptual model by natural language discourse generation. In: Loucopoulos, P. (ed.) CAiSE 1992. LNCS, vol. 593, pp. 425–444. Springer, Heidelberg (1992)
6. Shanks, G., Tansley, E., Weber, R.: Using ontology to validate conceptual models. Communications of the ACM 46(10), 85–89 (2003)
7. Mylopoulos, J., Borgida, A., Jarke, M., Koubarakis, M.: Telos: representing knowledge about information systems. ACM Transactions on Information Systems 8(4), 325–362 (1990)
8. Rolland, C., Proix, C.: A natural language approach for Requirements Engineering. In: Loucopoulos, P. (ed.) CAiSE 1992. LNCS, vol. 593, pp. 257–277. Springer, Heidelberg (1992)
9. Toulmin, S.E.: The Uses of Argument. Cambridge University Press, Cambridge (2003)
10. Ryle, G.: The concept of mind (1949). Hutchinson, London (1949)
11. Doty, D.H., Glick, W.H.: Typologies as a Unique Form of Theory Building: Toward Improved Understanding and Modeling. Academy of Management Review 19(2), 230–251 (1994)
12. Barn, B., Clark, T.: Re-thinking software engineering approaches: a critical reflection on theory building (February 2011)
13. Lindland, O., Sindre, G., Solvberg, A.: Understanding quality in conceptual modeling. IEEE Software 11(2), 42–49 (1994)
14. Sargent, R.G.: Verification and validation of simulation models. In: Proceedings of the 37th Conference on Winter Simulation, pp. 130–143 (December 2005)
15. Aier, S., Fischer, C.: Criteria of progress for information systems design theories. Information Systems and e-Business Management 9(1), 133–172 (2010)
16. Rykiel, E.J.: Testing ecological models: the meaning of validation. Ecological Modelling 90(3), 229–244 (1996)
17. Thomas, O.: Management von Referenzmodellen: Entwurf und Realisierung eines Informations systems zur Entwicklung und Anwendung von Referenzmodellen. Logos, Berlin (2006)
18. Lynham, S.A.: The General Method of Theory-Building Research in Applied Disciplines. Advances in Developing Human Resources 4(3), 221–241 (2002)
19. Luckmann, T., Berger, P.L.: The Social Construction of Reality: A Treatise in the Sociology of Knowledge (Penguin Social Sciences). Penguin (1991)
20. Balzert, H.: Lehrbuch der Software-Technik: Software-Entwicklung, 2nd edn. Spektrum, Heidelberg (2001)
21. Wand, Y., Weber, R.: An Ontological Model of an Information System. IEEE Transactions on Software Engineering 16(11), 1282–1292 (1990)
22. Green, P., Rosemann, M.: Integrated process modeling: An ontological evaluation. Information Systems 25(2), 73–87 (2000)
23. Vom Brocke, J., Buddendick, C.: Reusable Conceptual Models-Requirements Based on the Design Science Research Paradigm. In: Proceedings of the 1st International Conference on Design Science Research in Information Systems and Technology (2006)

24. Dalianis, H., Johannesson, P.: Explaining Conceptual Models - Using Toulmin's argumentation model and RST. In: Third International Workshop on the Language Action Perspective on Communication Modelling, pp. 131–140 (1998)

25. Carbogim, D.V., Robertson, D., Lee, J.: Argument-based applications to knowledge engineering. The Knowledge Engineering Review 15(2), 119–149 (2000)

26. Wang, M., Wang, H., Vogel, D., Kumar, K., Chiu, D.K.: Agent-based negotiation and decision making for dynamic supply chain formation. Engineering Applications of Artificial Intelligence 22(7), 1046–1055 (2009)

27. Berente, N., Hansen, S., Pike, J.C., Bateman, P.J.: Arguing the value of virtual worlds: patterns of discursive sensemaking of an innovative technology. MIS Quarterly 35(3), 685–710 (2011)

28. Cabot, J., Gogolla, M.: Object Constraint Language (OCL): A Definitive Guide. In: Bernardo, M., Cortellessa, V., Pierantonio, A. (eds.) SFM 2012. LNCS, vol. 7320, pp. 58–90. Springer, Heidelberg (2012)

29. van Deursen, A., Klint, P., Visser, J.: Domain-specific languages: An annotated bibliography. ACM SIGPLAN Notices 35(6), 26–36 (2000)

30. March, S.T., Smith, G.F.: Design and natural science research on information technology. Decision Support Systems 15(4), 251–266 (1995)

31. Rosemann, M., Green, P.: Developing a meta model for the Bunge–Wand–Weber ontological constructs. Information Systems 27(2), 75–91 (2002)

32. Gregor, S.: The nature of theory in information systems. MIS Quarterly 30(3), 611–642 (2006)

33. Koch, S., Strecker, S., Frank, U.: Conceptual Modelling as a New Entry in the Bazaar: The Open Model Approach. In: Damiani, E., Fitzgerald, B., Scacchi, W., Scotto, M., Succi, G. (eds.) Open Source Systems. IFIP, vol. 203, pp. 9–20. Springer, Boston (2006)

BWW Ontology as a Lens on IS Design Theory: Extending the Design Science Research Roadmap

Ahmad Alturki, Guy G. Gable, and Wasana Bandara

Queensland University of Technology, Information Systems Discipline,
Brisbane, Queensland, Australia

Abstract. The Design Science Research Roadmap (DSR-Roadmap) [1] aims to give detailed methodological guidance to novice researchers in Information Systems (IS) DSR. Focus group evaluation, one phase of the overall study, of the evolving DSR-Roadmap revealed that a key difficulty faced by both novice and expert researchers in DSR, is abstracting design theory from design. This paper explores the extension of the DSR-Roadmap by employing IS deep structure ontology (BWW [2-4]) as a lens on IS design to firstly yield generalisable design theory, specifically 'IS Design Theory' (ISDT) elements [5]. Consideration is next given to the value of BWW in the application of the design theory by practitioners. Results of mapping BWW constructs to ISDT elements suggest that the BWW is promising as a common language between design researchers and practitioners, facilitating both design theory and design implementation.

Keywords: Design Theory, IS Ontology, Design Science Research Methodology, DSR-Roadmap, Design Ontology.

1 Introduction

Design Science Research (DSR) has become an accepted approach for research in the Information Systems (IS) discipline [6, 7], with dramatic recent growth in related literature [8]. However, there is a lack of consensus on DSR methodology [9, 10] and DSR outputs [11, 12], indicating that DSR in IS is still in its genesis [13, 14]. Views and prescriptions on the methodology of DSR appear disparate, e.g. [9, 15-21]. Evidences and observations have shown a lack of accepted, detailed guidance, and consequent methodological shortcomings in much DSR [10, 22-24]. Hence, there appears to be a need for a structured, detailed, comprehensive, integrated and validated DSR methodology in the IS discipline.

Prior work in this direction by Alturki et al. [1] resulted in the IS DSR-Roadmap (DSR-Roadmap), a structured and detailed methodology for conducting DSR, spanning the entire DSR lifecycle from the early 'spark' of a design idea through to final publication (see Figure 1).[1] It usefully inter-relates and harmonizes various otherwise

---

[1] It is compressed because of space limitations. For the readable version, please see Figure 1 in [1, 25].

J. vom Brocke et al. (Eds.): DESRIST 2013, LNCS 7939, pp. 258–277, 2013.

seemingly disparate, overlapping or conflicting advice and concepts reported in the literature. The DSR-Roadmap consists of the following four main interrelated components (explained in detail [1]): (A) Activities and Cycles; (B) Output, which adopts Gregor and Jones' IS Design Theory [5]; (C) Risk Management; and (D) the Central Design Repository (CDR). Component (A) incrementally populates as well as draws from component (D), which ultimately contributes to component (B). Component (C) and Component (A) are executed in parallel, both again using component (D). Consequently, Components (B) and (D) are the sources that contribute to both practice and knowledge base. The DSR-Roadmap continues to be validated and to evolve based on evaluation findings[2].

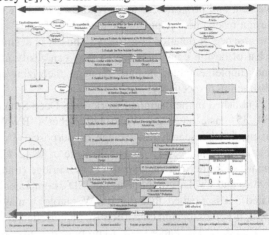

Fig. 1. The DSR-Roadmap

In achieving the principle objective, namely the DSR-Roadmap, the current study requires that the DSR-Roadmap presents all components in the DSR methodology. Although the DSR-Roadmap was evaluated and refined in different ways [39], it is still evolving. One aspect that it should have is the attributes or constructs that researchers must be aware of in DSR in order to describe their design; what things they need to describe and attain for the best design theory and instantiation.

Types of DSR outputs include: constructs, methods, models, instantiation, and design theory [5, 27-30]. Close attention to design definitions in DSR literature reveals that design in DSR can be viewed as a process or a product [27, 30]. These aspects on the design may justify the diversity in DSR outputs. DSR literature also reveals that few scholars focus on the design in terms of which general and detailed constructs should be considered, except for design requirements and functions. Walls et al. [30], Gregor and Jones [5], and Baskerville et al. [29] believe the design theory is the ultimate output of DSR in IS. They contribute to the design definition by proposing different structures of design theory. Others (e.g. Lee et al. [31] and Venable [32]) contribute to theorizing framework in DSR. Although these seminal efforts have proposed abstract representation of the abstracted design in the form of design theory, there is a need for general yet detailed constructs to describe the design.

More specifically to the DSR-Roadmap, the ISDT proposed by Gregor and Jones [5] is adopted as the primary output component in the DSR-Roadmap, because we believe it is the most comprehensive DSR output [1]. Nonetheless, we believe that in their abstract form, elements of the ISDT are not easy for design researchers to populate. Neither do the abstract elements readily facilitate practitioner construction of the

---

[2] See formative evaluations of the DSR-Roadmap reported in [25, 26].

intended system. Instead, researchers are required to transform instantiated knowledge into many forms until the abstract knowledge is developed and populated in the ISDT's elements, and then practitioners transform the abstract knowledge in the ISDT into many forms until the instantiation in specific context is developed, ready to implement and program (or to be read by a machine[3] [2-4]). The question here is: Can design researchers populate the elements of ISDT and then implement ISDT easily in the absence of detailed constructs? Thus, it is desirable for design researchers to have a list of design constructs which they can easily utilize to develop a comprehensive and implementable design theory; theorizing/abstracting and instantiation/de-abstraction respectively.

Published in their seminal work on IS Deep Structure[4] [2-4], and based on Bunge's [34, 35] basic ontology, Wand and Weber's 'BWW ontology' has been used extensively in IS research for a range of purposes [36]. Alturki et al. [37] describe the relationship between DSR and the core of IS [2-4]. Herein, BWW is considered for inclusion in the DSR-Roadmap [1] as a bridge (transition tool) between the DSR Activities and Cycles component, the ISDT component (abstracted), and artifact (instantiated). It is posited that the BWW ontology may provide design researchers with most, if not all, design constructs that are needed to describe their design.

Therefore, this paper seeks to propose design constructs for DSR in IS. This objective motivates the investigation of the applicability of the BWW ontology constructs for DSR in IS, specifically the inclusion of the BWW ontology in the DSR-Roadmap (DSR Methodology). This paper suggests the BWW ontology as a tool that allows researchers in DSR to produce design theory and convey their design to both academics and practitioners; hence, a tool to communicate design specifications of DSR in IS. This investigation is conducted by mapping between the BWW ontology constructs and Gregor and Jones' [5] ISDT elements.

The effort in this paper contributes to DSR by providing researchers in DSR with detailed design constructs (linked to ISDT elements) to promote a comprehensive yet parsimonious design, while also easing communication and implementation of their design. Researchers in DSR will benefit from these design constructs to guide them in design theory development. Articulating and specifying these design constructs constitutes sufficient base for design theory development. We believe these constructs to be a vehicle for developing a strong complete design and improving its quality, because design researchers will be aware of various detailed aspects of an imagined design solution. Similarly, Wand and Weber believe any representation tool, a design in essence, is not complete if the BWW ontological constructs are not considered [4]. Thus, the BWW ontology will explicitly strengthen the design of artefacts.

---

[3] From here onwards we use 'read by machine' so as to be consistent with Wand and Weber's terminology.

[4] Benbasat considers this work as one of the few ground-breaking efforts that challenge our thinking and lead to new exciting directions in research and teaching. We assume the reader is familiar with internal and external IS views proposed in [4, 33]. IS Deep structure, part of the internal view, describes the characteristics of the real-world phenomena that the IS is intended to represent, such as Entity Relationship Diagrams.

The remainder of the paper is organized as follows. First, we review the literature to provide an overview of the design nature in DSR and briefly explain the BWW ontology constructs. Then we justify why the BWW ontology is suitable for use in Design Research. In Section four, we illustrate and discuss the integration of the BWW ontology into the DSR-Roadmap through a mapping exercise between the BWW ontology constructs and ISDT's elements, showing the results of this mapping. We conclude by summarizing the paper's contributions and future work.

2   Literature Review

2.1   The Nature of "Design" in Information Systems Design Science Research

This section briefly presents an overview on the nature of the design definitions in DSR showing that these definitions range between design as process and design as product. In general, to design may be a verb referring to the performance of a design, a noun referring to the constructed artefact, or it can refer to the utility set in the artefact[5] [38]. Design is a constructive action that results in a product. Walls et al. [30] see design as both a noun and a verb, because it is a target object that will be constructed and an action (design) that fulfils design requirements. It describes the world as acted upon (processes) and the world as sensed (artefacts) [27]. Alexander (1969) cited in [30] distinguishes between scientists and designers. While the role of scientists is to discover the components of a system of interest, the role of designers is to shape those components. Synthesis is the essence of the design.

'Design' is "from the Latin désigñare, which means to point the way" [38]. Simon [39] sees design as creating options that are filtered and excluded until the design's requirements are fulfilled. Hevner et al. [27] believe design is a search activity that aims to find the best solution for important unsolved problems. Design includes creating new things, solving problems and moving to desired situations from less preferred situations [40]. The design is "[t]he use of scientific principles, technical information and imagination in the definition of a structure, machine or system to perform pre-specified functions with the maximum economy and efficiency" (Fielden cited in [30]). It involves building a solution intended to resolve a problem [9].

The design describes an artefact's organisation and functions [39]; yet few researchers describe this organization. In his seminal work Simon [39] describes an artefact as a meeting point – an interface – between the inner and outer environments. The inner environment is "the substance and organization of the artefact itself' [39]. The outer environment is "the surrounding in which the [artefact] operates". The artefact will achieve its anticipated objectives if the inner environment is suitable for the outer environment. The artefact's goals link the inner to the outer environment. The artifact's behaviour is forced by both its inner and outer environments; the artefact is 'structurally coupled' to its environment. The outer and inner environments are connected through the afferent (input) channel and efferent (output) channel. The former "receives information about the environment"; the latter "acts on the environment"

---

[5] In this paper we are interested in the first two meanings.

[39]. The 'bringing-to-be' of an artefact's components and organization, which interfaces in a desired manner with its outer environment, is the design activity [20]. Design is "shaping artefacts and events to create a more desirable future" (Boland cited in [17]).

Although most DSR methodological contributions mention 'design' as a key step in conducting DSR, e.g. [9, 17, 18, 20, 21], these methodologies have not focused on the design in terms of what attributes and constructs should be considered[6].

Scholars' definitions of design mentioned above are general and fluctuate between design as process and as product. They consider design as a creative process [27, 39] and for this reason, they may leave details to the creativity of design researchers. While we accept and value these high level definitions, we believe there is merit in exploring potential constructs and specification for design in general and specifically as product before (theorizing) and after (instantiation) it is theorized. It is advantageous to propose design constructs for IS DSR which allow design researchers to describe their design using limited constructs during the design process.

2.2   An Overview of IS Deep Structure Ontology Constructs

This section explains the BWW ontology constructs proposed by Wand and Weber [2-4, 33, 41] based on the seminal work of Bunge [34, 35]. Ontology is concerned of the structure of the real world; it is a school of thought that studies the existence of things. The BWW ontology defines the "set of constructs that are necessary and sufficient to describe the structure and behaviour of the real world" [33]. Since ontology concerns the structure of the real world, it is relevant to perceive IS from two points of view: 1) IS represents the real world; therefore, ontology provides the basic things in the real world that IS ought to be able to symbolize; 2) IS itself is an object in the real world because IS is also things in the real world; hence, ontology provides a basis for modelling [41]. Both views are important to our argument, but we are mainly concerned with the first view, because it directly enriches our discussion. This set of core ontological concepts can be used to illustrate the structure and behaviour of a designed IS which is representational of the real world [4].

Wand and Weber propose three models for IS deep structure: 1) representation model, 2) state track model, and 3) decomposition model. We believe the three models are relevant to the design product, but this paper focuses on the representation model. The representation model defines a set of constructs such as thing, state, properties, and transformation (see appendix A and Table 1 in [3]) which Wand and Weber believe is necessary and sufficient to describe the structure and behaviour of the real world in which IS operates. Wand and Weber believe these constructs have the ability to serve as the basis for any IS development (Routine Design explained later in the paper) uses representation language.

---

[6] We are aware of influential papers that describe the structure of the abstract design in the form of design theory [5, 29, 30].

3   The Rationale of Integrating the BWW Ontology with Design Research

Based on the preceding definitions and views of design, we argue that the ultimate objective of design in IS DSR is to design and develop an artefact (IS) in response to un/conceivable unsolved problems or to satisfy un/conceivable needs. This objective may include intermediate forms of artefact, such as method, before constructing a complete automated IS. In this section, we present our argument for the applicability and inclusion of BWW ontology by Wand and Weber [2-4, 33] to DSR in IS. The argument is based on: (1) IS consisting of Routine Design and Design Research; and (2) the integration between the DSR-Roadmap components, Activities and ISDT components.

For the first point, based on the distinction between Design Research and Design Science[7], Alturki et al. [37] argue that Design Research, as a type of DSR, is a part of the IS discipline. They propose that IS deep structure in Wand and Weber's view is divided into two parts: 1) Routine Design, and 2) Design Research[8]; see Figure 3 in Alturki et al. [37] for the relationship between the IS discipline (deep structure) and DSR in IS (Design Science and Design Research) and Routine Design.

Thus, based on the relationship between DSR and IS mentioned above, and using logical deductive reasoning, we argue that anything is applicable for IS deep structure as well as for Design Research and Routine Design. Consequently, we propose the ontology of IS deep structure developed by Wand and Weber [2, 3] and Weber [4] is applicable to Design Research as well.

For the second point, the DSR-Roadmap presented in [1, 25] proposes an integration between Activities and ISDT components. While the Activities component develops the design knowledge, the ISDT component codifies design knowledge in scientific structure and organization. In other words, the content of the ISDT component results from the Activities component. Piirainen and Briggs [42] believe that the DSR methodology mirrors the structure of the design theory. They "claim that the DSR methodology and DT [Design Theory] complement the DSR framework and give additional guidance" (p. 50). Furthermore, since the ISDT is a general representation of design knowledge and an intersection point practitioners, there is a need to make its construction and implementation much easier. Thus, there is a need to ease the transition (theorizing) from designed artefact to design theory and vice versa in (instantiation); which will enable direct and clearer interactions between them.

---

[7] There are two types of DSR: 1) "design research is aimed at creating solutions to specific classes of relevant problems by using a rigorous construction and evaluation process, [2)] design science reflects the design research process and aims at creating standards for its rigour" [10]. Kuechler and Vaishnavi [7] have a similar view, and see DSR in the IS field as research with design as either a topic or method of investigation; for more details see [37].

[8] Routine Design usually solves problems using current knowledge, state of practice, techniques and available components to produce a product without the creation of any additional knowledge. DSR, on other hand, produces new knowledge that yields value from a number of unknowns in the proposed design which were successfully overcome [20].

Consistent with the two design's views, of design as product and as process, Table 2 in [5] depicts the elements of ISDT. Focusing firstly on the design product, it is clear that core elements such as construct and principle of form and function are about the design as product. These elements are about the structure, properties, functions and requirements etcetera of an artefact. For the design process, the DSR-Roadmap has been developed to help design researchers conduct DSR. The Activities component includes determination of the artefact's functionality, architecture and properties, then building an instantiation which is the physical artefact [5, 8, 9, 27, 28, 30, 38, 43, 44]. The integration between the DSR-Roadmap's Activities and ISDT components provides consistency between the design as process and design as product results from DSR.

Since the two views of the design are two sides of the coin, the mapping between them is very advantageous. This association will work as a bridge between the Activity and ISDT components. On one hand, since ISDT, a formal representation (language) of the abstract design knowledge, is the output of IS DSR, this linkage using the BWW ontology works as a tool to achieve generalizability in ISDT theorizing. Thus, this mapping helps to easily populate and enrich the elements of ISDT. On the other hand, association helps to instantiate ISDT for a particular context for a specific problem. By using the BWW ontology constructs such as thing, state, and transformation [2-4, 41], researchers will have most of the needed constructs to produce a complete design theory and an artefact.

Although we justify integrating the BWW ontology into the DSR-Roadmap, it is difficult to assert the suitability of this inclusion without showing evidence to support this claim. The subsequent section explains how the BWW ontology is integrated into DSR in IS and linked with ISDT component presenting extended layers of ISDT.

4   The Integration between Information System Ontology and Design Science Research

This section is divided into three main subsections. In Subsection 4.1, we illustrate the role of the BWW ontology to DSR in IS. Next we explain the approach followed in the mapping between the BWW ontology and the ISDT elements to include the BWW ontology in DSR in IS, specifically in the DSR-Roadmap. The result of the mapping[9] exercise and its discussion are shown in Subsection 4.3.

4.1   The Role of Information System Ontology in Design Science Research

The role of the BWW ontology in IS DSR is explained diagrammatically in Figures 2 and Figure 3. The two figures relate to each other. Figure 3 is more detailed and can be considered as a lower level representation of Figure 2 which is relatively abstract.

---

[9] It must however be noted that the mapping activity is tentative.

The notions in these two figures[10] are developed based on the theoretical foundations in IS DSR works [5, 31, 38] and the BWW ontology in [2-4, 33].

Figures 3 and 4 are grounded on Purao's ontological view of DSR that an "artifact progresses from an idea to a 'thing in the world' ... [in]... several moves back and forth" [38]. Figures 3 and 4 are also based on Gregor and Jones [5] who believe that a "design theory instantiated would have a physical existence in the real world". These figures are consistent, and represent 'Design Theorizing Framework' [31] with details by employing the BWW ontology. Furthermore, Weber states "theories provide a representation of someone's perception of how a subset of real-world phenomena should be described. In this light, they can be conceived as specialized ontologies – instances of general ontology" [45]. Design Theory is no exception.

Firstly, Figure 2 depicts the use of the BWW ontology by researchers in design research (part of DSR) to represent and perceive the real world, their minds, or both for conceivable/unconceivable[11] problem/need, and then solution/innovation – see the box titled 'Part of DSR using BWW Ontology'[12]. Since DSR in IS is intended to be a representation of un/conceivable problem/needs and a solution [1] in the designers' minds and imagination, design researchers should have a group of constructs which are able to represent and symbolize these things, which leads to the design theory.

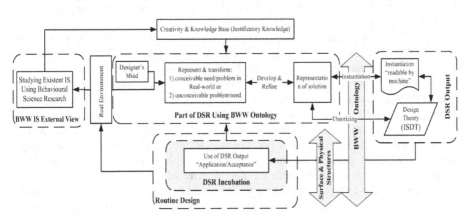

Fig. 2. The Role of BWW Ontology in IS DSR Lifecycle

The BWW ontology eases the construction of the ISDT by generalizing the content of the BWW ontological constructs. BWW ontological constructs can be used in the following DSR scenarios: 1) design researchers firstly develop abstract design knowledge (which includes an abstract problem and solution) and populate the elements of the ISDT. Then this abstract knowledge is tested and proved by developing an

---

[10] As the DSR-Roadmap is the principle aim of the study, Figures 3 and 4 will be considered and integrated in the DSR-Roadmap to complement its components.

[11] Conceivable means a design may target a problem/need that people experience; unconceivable means a design may target a problem/need that is not on the horizon. Unforeseeable/seeable might be equivalent to unconceivable/conceivable, respectively.

[12] Note: this box is part of DSR and other activities such as evaluation that are not represented in Figure 2 and 4.

instantiation, for instance solution and problem. 2) Design researchers firstly develop an artefact for instance solution and problem, and then they extract the abstract design knowledge, abstract problem and solution, to populate the elements of ISDT. 3) Design researchers develop the abstract design knowledge, abstract problem and solution, to populate the elements of ISDT, leaving the instantiation construction for others, or they just develop an artefact for instance solution and problem. In any scenarios, there are a number of iterations; emerging knowledge from instantiation construction can complete and amend the design theory (ISDT elements) and vice versa; see the arrows between the BWW ontology and output boxes.

Subsequently, successful instantiation and newly emerged design knowledge in ISDT become available to be implemented by practitioners and other design researchers in DSR incubation, and then in Routine Design. The knowledge in ISDT will be used through the BWW ontology in combination with surface and physical structures[13] [3, 4]. The BWW ontology facilitates specifying all aspects of ISDT to be used by designers in their contexts. Any required refinements emerged from DSR incubation, and Routine may spark DSR. Finally, a new artefact and possible phenomenon become part of the real world, which could be a subject for IS researchers to study from the IS external view through behavioural science research. Knowledge emerging from IS external view may again spark a new design idea, which initiates a new IS DSR cycle.

Figure 3 provides details to better explain the integration of the BWW ontology with IS DSR. The three axes in Figure 3 relate to: 1) Innovation (Y axis); 2) Reality (Y axis); and 3) Representation (X axis). The Y axis symbolizes both innovation and reality, with innovation ranging from low to high, and reality ranging from real systems to abstract systems. Representation is reflected on the X axis, with the degree of representation in IS construction increasing from left (low) to right (high). Figure 3 also combines the two main IS deep structural parts, as shown in Figure 2: Design Research and Routine Design. Any point of the Design Research and Routine Design can be described in terms of the three axes. For example, ISDT is more abstract than instantiation in terms of reality; both are high in terms of representation.

In order to grasp Figure 3, we start with Routine Design (blue area) as it represents the ordinary IS development. Routine Design starts with analysing a real system to convert it into different types of transformations using different language grammar tools such as ERD, flowchart etcetera until the last transformation is automated (code) which is readable by computers/machines [2-4]. The objective here is the automation by representing the real system in IS. Here there is no need to search the knowledge base to find a solution, or generate new knowledge from the solution. The used grammars in this transformation should have good consistency with IS ontological constructs, otherwise deficiencies may appear in IS as a result of inconsistency, e.g. two or more real objects are represented by one thing in IS [4]. The Routine Design takes the existing real system and converts it to another system called IS to represent the real situation to attain several benefits, such as quick reporting and simple observation. The reader should note that Routine Design only starts from the real world, as shown in Figure 3.

---

[13] We assume the reader is familiar with the surface and physical structures as part of Wand and Weber internal IS views proposed in [4, 33].

In contrast, Design Research (yellow area) could spark from two possible worlds: part of the real world and the virtual world.[14] For the former (see box titled 'Real World'), Design Research starts from the existent important unsolved but foreseen problem/need. The second sparks comes from the virtual world (see box titled 'Virtual World'); there is no existent problem/need in the current setting, but through the creativity of design researchers, an interested problem/need could be envisaged. In any case, design researchers should represent the problem/need for two main reasons: 1) to help them discover a design solution, and 2) to understand and emphasize the importance of a problem/need since it is unlikely a complete and good design will result if the design researchers' efforts are wasted in the wrong parts of the problem space [46]. Without representing all aspects of the interested problem/need in the IS DSR scope, design researchers may be unable to produce a comprehensive[15] designed solution. Yet it could happen serendipitously if they are really expert and lucky; they may represent unconsciously. The best problem/need representation the design researchers develop, the best design they may construct. For the second spark, the representation may be more important and essential than the representation in the former spark.

Subsequently, both sparks, part of the real world and the virtual world, have a similar problem solving process. Design researchers search for a solution for the interested problem/need, for which then they have two paths/options towards completion of DSR, namely the *'Red path and the Blue path'*. Designers can execute these two paths separately, complete one and then start the other, or alternately, execute them together in any combination. Consistent with the design theorizing framework [31], these two paths represent the *'Abstract Domain'* (arrows in the Red path) and *'Instance Domain'* (arrows in the Blue path) proposed in [31]. Most of the arrows in Figure 3 are bidirectional, which means designers can move forward and backwards inside one domain, or in between the domains representing the DSR's highly iterative characteristic. Furthermore, black arrows correspond to shifts alternating between these two domains, representing the instantiation process or the so-called de-abstraction [31] and theorizing process or the so-called abstraction [31], respectively[16].

Once the design in the Design Research area is instantiated successfully, ISDT (including abstract problem/need and design) become an existent part of the real world; it physicalizes what was in the designers' mind. In other words, the output of the Design Research becomes an input of Routine Design as depicted by the curved line between the yellow and blue areas in Figure 3. The different intermediate outputs such as models and methods could be developed during the Design Research progression.

---

[14] The real world and the virtual world contain a range of problems and needs that can be imagined or are beyond the imagination.

[15] We acknowledge Ciborra's [47] 'tinkering' concept as a very important, and perhaps the only, path to really innovative system designs. We agree with this concept yet though it is not totally congruent with our thinking, it is a valuable and effective in enhancement process when shortcomings discovered in design.

[16] In other efforts we find it empirically important to represent theorizing and instantiation in the DSR-Roadmap.

Although different types of transformation in DSR are applied, there are no common or acceptable constructs used that allow design researchers in IS DSR to specify their design entirely in order to help them to theorize design theory, ISDT structure, and then implement the design. In the next subsection, we address the following issue: Can design researchers populate the elements of ISDT and then implement ISDT easily?

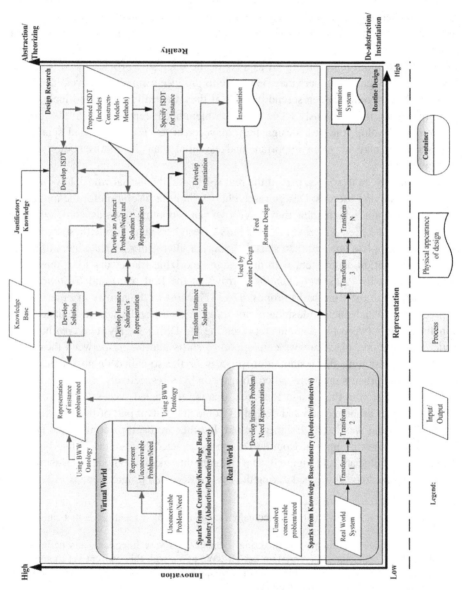

Fig. 3. Details of IS Ontology Role in IS DSR Lifecycle

4.2 The Approach of the BWW Ontology and Information System Design Theory Elements Mapping Exercise

In order to achieve rigorous results, we follow a similar approach to the procedural approach in [48]. This approach consists of three main steps; however, we split the first step into two steps, and due to single author coding, the last step in the procedure is marked for future work, as described below:

(1A) the process starts by distilling key aspects in each element of ISDT by breaking down each element of ISDT into micro building blocks. The objective here is to help the researcher in the mapping exercise to check the consistency between ISDT elements and the BWW ontology constructs and then he can conclude the applicability of the BWW ontology constructs to DSR. (1B) The researcher goes through the BWW ontology constructs one by one, listed in Appendix A, and has complete close readings to get sufficient understanding. 1a and 1b are relatively similar to work in [49]. (2) The researcher links the ISDT elements' micro building blocks with the BWW ontology constructs.

It is recognised that we may need additional new constructs for aspects that are particular to DSR such as kernel theory/justificatory knowledge, or un/conceivable problem/need. The main difference with these aspects is that they may be abstracted/virtualized as not being available in the real world; see Figure 1 in Gregor and Jones [5]. Three possible conclusions are expected (BWW ontology constructs fit totally into all ISDT elements, fit with deficits, or do not fit totally) as we envisage ISDT and the BWW ontology constructs in a master-details (parent-child) relationship.

4.3 Results from the Mapping Exercise between IS Deep Structure Ontology and Information System Design Theory Elements

Table 1 shows the results from the mapping exercise. The first two columns in Table 1 illustrate the micro building blocks for each element of ISDT. The third column shows the result of the mapping exercise between key aspects in each element of ISDT and BWW ontology constructs.

Table 1. The Result of BWW Ontology and ISDT Elements Mapping

Element	Key aspects in ISDT elements	IS ontology constructs
Purpose and scope	Design meta requirements. Design goals. Design Scope/Boundaries. Context/Environment in which the artefact is intended to operate.	System – system environment – input (component/state) - external event/transformation – output (component/state)
Constructs	Most basic level of ISDT. Represent physical phenomena. Represent abstract terms. Decomposition. Entities of interest.	Thing – attributes – property - state (stable/unstable) – system composition.

Table 1. (*continued*)

Principles of form and function	Principles define structure, organization, functioning. Functions. Properties. Features/attributes. "Blue print"/architecture. Relations.	Conceivable state space – lawful state space – Class – kind – coupling – system - subsystem – aggregate – system structure –system decomposition – level structure - internal event - transformation – lawful transformation – transfer function.
Artefact mutability	The degree of mutability of designed artefact. Changes in system state and changes that affect the basic form or shape of the artefact.	Equilibrium – History.
Testable proposition	Proposition: "if a system or method that follows certain principles is instantiated then it will work or etc" – heuristic propositions. Generality in terms of context and time.	Event – event space – lawful event space – transformation – lawful transformation – transfer function – well-defined event – poorly defined event.
Justificatory knowledge	Theories that link the mechanism for a number or all aspects of the designed theory/artefact. It may come from NS/SS/design theory/practitioner-in-use theory/evidence-based justification such as AR.	Law (natural and human) – state law
Principles of implementation	Process of how to build an artefact and bring it to reality How to implement it in practice.	NA
Expository instantiation	"A realistic implementation contributes to the identification of potential problems in a theorized design and in demonstrating that the design is worth considering". Instantiated afrtifacts are things in the physical world, while theory is an abstract expression of ideas about the phenomena in the real world.	NA

4.4   Results Discussion

This exercise proves that there is reasonably good mapping between the ISDT's elements as the high level specification, and BWW constructs as the detailed specification. Six elements have mapped to many constructs, which means the ISDT elements are more general than the BWW constructs. This confirms our initial expectations mentioned above. For instance, the element of principles of form and function is mapped to many IS constructs. Apparently, Table 1 confirms the high level specification of design knowledge of the design theory. Gregor and Jones [5] define a design theory as "something in an abstract world of man-made things, which also includes other abstract ideas such as algorithms".

Since ISDT proposed by Gregor and Jones [5] is abstract/ general representation, we believe there are two issues here. Firstly, ISDT direct applicability to the practice is not easy for practitioners to use it in building their intended system. Practitioners need to transform ISDT into many forms until it becomes ready to implement and read by machine as depicted in Figure 3 between ISDT and its instantiation. Secondly, developing/theorizing design theory is not straightforward in the absence of detailed design constructs. Therefore, the results of the mapping exercise proposes BWW constructs that can be used as a base of constructs collection that both researchers in DSR or practitioners use in theorizing and instantiation processes, respectively – see Figure 4. Researchers in DSR use the constructs collection, fully or partially, to define their design which are then used in extracting general design knowledge to build the design theory. Subsequently, practitioners use the design theory in conjunction with the defined design constructs by the design theory creator.

Unexpectedly, this exercise reveals that ISDT is not totally parsimony, because some BWW ontological constructs are under more than one of the ISDT's elements. This indicates some overlaps between the ISDT's elements. An issue can be raised Is ISDT parsimony (unambiguously specified)?

Interestingly, the last two optional elements of the ISDT, Principles of Implementation and Expository Instantiation, have not been mapped to any of the BWW constructs. Based on the ontological view of artifact and design theory discussed in [38] and [5], we may explain why we have this case. For the latter element, it is not surprising, because it represents the IS itself which is the result of constructs representation. For the former element, it is complex to justify. Deep thinking of this situation and based on what this element means and the authors' understanding of design as process and product, this element of ISDT could be pulled and stretched across the first six elements of ISDT. The rationale behind this is that all BWW constructs used in the mapping actually represent and specify this element. The BWW constructs and the relationships between them symbolize the design as process. Therefore, the ISDT can be divided into three separate layers, each of which: 1) contains the first six elements of ISDT, 2) contains the Principles of Implementation element of ISDT, and 3) contains the Expository Instantiation element of ISDT. Figure 4 demonstrates these three layers. Moving towards the third layer from the first corresponds to the instantiation/de-abstraction process; however, moving the opposite way stands for the theorizing/abstraction process. Design researchers can start from any layer and develop the other layers subsequently or interchangeably. Recently, Kuechler and Vaishnavi [50] propose 'A Framework for Theory Development in Design Science Research:

multiple perspectives'. Using this framework, we can find that the first and the third layers are located in this framework. The second layer which emerges from using the BWW ontology constructs may fit between the design theory and artefact components in their framework. Figure 4 may be injected into their framework.

Furthermore, we recognize that using the BWW ontology in DSR methodology (the DSR-Roadmap) provides interested design researchers or practitioners with traceability quality. Through this quality, they can trace the knowledge from their design to their design theory and vice versa. The traceability leads to apparent transparency which increases the credibility of the design.

Style is one of design's key aspects that affects the resultant product [39]. We believe the design style is a mirror of what represented inside the designed artifact/solution. Thus, in DSR using different BWW ontological constructs (any combinations), this influences delineating the design style making, it apparent to identify. Furthermore, Hevner et al. [27] suggest design style should be included in design evaluation. The BWW ontological constructs may simplify the evaluation of various designs. Since the combination of these constructs in the inner environment of the design represents the design style, this allows designers to predict the behaviour and effects of the design in response to the outer environment. Therefore, the BWW ontological constructs can be used to judge the quality of the design.

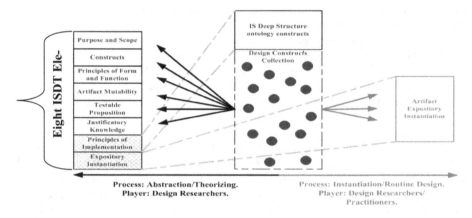

Fig. 4. The Three Layers of Information System Design Theory (ISDT)

Finally, the mapping exercise shows that there may be a need for some new ontological constructs for aspects that are particular to DSR in IS. This issue needs further careful investigation.

5   Conclusion

This essay has argued that design needs to be specified more and should be included in DSR methodology; it is motivated by observed methodological shortcomings. The purpose of the paper was to search for design constructs to help design researchers to specify their design. It has justified and investigated the applicability of using the BWW ontology in DSR to include it in the DSR-Roadmap.

This paper has shown that the BWW ontology can be integrated into the DSR methodology. The following contributions can be drawn from the paper:

- Using the BWW ontology simplifies and contributes to the ISDT construction and implementation in abstraction and instantiation processes. This may help to establish common language that allows design researchers to effectively communicate their design with researchers and practitioners.
- The BWW ontology will explicitly strengthen the design of artefacts and make them easier, because it provides most if not all constructs that researchers need in order to complete their design.
- There is good mapping between the ISDT's elements and the BWW ontological constructs. Although there is overlap in this mapping, this confirms the high level design in ISDT.
- The ISDT could be divided into three layers: 1) its first six elements, 2) the seventh element, and 3) the last element of ISDT. This allows researchers to trace the design and recognise its style.
- The mapping exercise shows potential needs for some new ontological constructs to satisfy the special nature of knowledge in DSR.

The obvious limitation lies in the fact that the mapping exercise is one author coded. For future work, further researchers need to conduct this mapping exercise, with other coders following the same procedure so as to support the results and resolve any conflicts. Another possible work to test the proposal in this paper would be to take an published ISDT and investigate the possibility of building its specification using the constructs of the BWW ontology. Furthermore, there might be the need to consider all three models (representation model, state track model, and decomposition model) proposed by Wand and Weber.

References

1. Alturki, A., Gable, G.G., Bandara, W.: A Design Science Research Roadmap. In: Jain, H., Sinha, A.P., Vitharana, P. (eds.) DESRIST 2011. LNCS, vol. 6629, pp. 107–123. Springer, Heidelberg (2011)
2. Wand, Y., Weber, R.: On the ontological expressiveness of information systems analysis and design grammars. Information Systems Journal 3(4), 217–237 (1993)
3. Wand, Y., Weber, R.: On the deep structure of information systems. Information Systems Journal 5(3), 203–223 (1995)
4. Weber, R.: Ontological foundations of information systems. Coopers & Lybrand, 212 (1997)
5. Gregor, S., Jones, D.: The anatomy of a design theory. Journal of the Association for Information Systems 8(5), 312–335 (2007)
6. Iivari, J.: A paradigmatic analysis of information systems as a design science. Scandinavian Journal of Information Systems 19(2), 39–64 (2007)
7. Kuechler, B., Vaishnavi, V.: The emergence of design research in information systems in North America. Journal of Design Research 7(1), 1–16 (2008)

8. Goldkuhl, G., Lind, M.: A Multi-Grounded Design Research Process. In: Winter, R., Zhao, J.L., Aier, S. (eds.) DESRIST 2010. LNCS, vol. 6105, pp. 45–60. Springer, Heidelberg (2010)

9. Peffers, K., et al.: A design science research methodology for information systems research. Journal of Management Information Systems 24(3), 45–77 (2007)

10. Winter, R.: Design science research in Europe. European Journal of Information Systems 17(5), 470–475 (2008)

11. Gregor, S., Hevner, A.: Introduction to the special issue on design science. Information Systems and E-Business Management 9(1), 1–9 (2010)

12. Offermann, P., Blom, S., Schönherr, M., Bub, U.: Artifact Types in Information Systems Design Science–A Literature Review. In: Winter, R., Zhao, J.L., Aier, S., et al. (eds.) DESRIST 2010. LNCS, vol. 6105, pp. 77–92. Springer, Heidelberg (2010)

13. Iivari, J., Venable, J.: Action research and design science research–seemingly sim-ilar but decisively dissimilar. In: 17th European Conference on Information Systems (2009)

14. Kuechler, B., Vaishnavi, V.: On theory development in design science research: anatomy of a research project. European Journal of Information Systems 17(5), 489–504 (2008)

15. Baskerville, R., Pries-Heje, J., Venable, J.: Soft design science methodology. In: DESRIST 2009. ACM, Malvern (2009)

16. Hevner, A.R.: A Three Cycle View of Design Science Research. Scandinavian Journal of Information Systems 19(2), 87–92 (2007)

17. March, S.T., Storey, V.C.: Design science in the information systems discipline: an introduction to the special issue on design science research. MIS Quarterly 32(4), 725–730 (2008)

18. Nunamaker Jr., J.F., Chen, M., Purdin, T.D.M.: Systems development in information systems research. Journal of Management Information Systems 7(3), 89–106 (1991)

19. Rossi, M., Sein, M.K.: Design research workshop: a proactive research approach. Presentation Delivered at IRIS 26, 9–12 (2003)

20. Vaishnavi, V., Kuechler, W.: Design research in information systems (February 20, 2004), http://www.isworld.org/Researchdesign/drisISworld.htm (cited January 10, 2010)

21. Venable, J.: A Framework for Design Science Research Activities. In: Information Resource Management Association Conference (CD). Idea Group Publishing, Washington, DC (2006)

22. Indulska, M., Recker, J.C.: Design science in IS research: a literature analysis. In: Proceedings 4th Biennial ANU Workshop on Information Systems Foundations, Canberra, Australia (2008)

23. Venable, J.R.: Design Science Research Post Hevner et al.: Criteria, Standards, Guidelines, and Expectations. In: Winter, R., Zhao, J.L., Aier, S. (eds.) DESRIST 2010. LNCS, vol. 6105, pp. 109–123. Springer, Heidelberg (2010)

24. Walls, J.G., Widmeyer, G.R., El Sawy, O.A.: Assessing information system design theory in perspective: How useful was our 1992 initial rendition. Journal of Information Technology Theory and Application 6(2), 43–58 (2004)

25. Alturki, A., et al.: Validating the Design Science Research Roadmap: Through the Lens of "The Idealised Model For Theory Development". In: Pacific Asia Conference on Information Systems (PACIS). Ho Chi Minh, Vietnam (2012)

26. Alturki, A., Gable, G., Bandara, W.: The Design Science Research Roadmap: in Progress Evaluation (2013) (Manuscript Submitted for Publication)

27. Hevner, A.R., et al.: Design science in information systems research. MIS Quarterly 28(1), 75–106 (2004)

28. March, S.T., Smith, G.F.: Design and natural science research on information technology. Decision Support Systems 15(4), 251–266 (1995)

29. Baskerville, R., Pries-Heje, J.: Explanatory design theory. Business & Information Systems Engineering 2(5), 271–282 (2010)
30. Walls, J.G., Widmeyer, G.R., El Sawy, O.A.: Building an information system de-sign theory for vigilant EIS. Information Systems Research 3(1), 36–59 (1992)
31. Lee, J.S., Pries-Heje, J., Baskerville, R.: Theorizing in design science research. In: Jain, H., Sinha, A.P., Vitharana, P. (eds.) DESRIST 2011. LNCS, vol. 6629, pp. 1–16. Springer, Heidelberg (2011)
32. Venable, J.: The role of theory and theorising in Design Science research. In: Proceedings of DESRIST, Claremont, CA (2006)
33. Wand, Y., Weber, R.: Toward A Theory of The Deep Structure of Information Systems. In: International Conference on Information Systems (1990)
34. Bunge, M.: Treatise on Basic Philosophy. Ontology I: The Furniture of the World, vol. 3. Reidel, Boston (1977)
35. Bunge, M.: Treatise on Basic Philosophy Reidel. Ontology II: A World of Systems, vol. 4. Reidel, Boston (1979)
36. Green, P., Rosemann, M.: Integrated process modeling: an ontological evaluation. Information Systems 25(2), 73–87 (2000)
37. Alturki, A., Bandara, W., Gable, G.G.: Design science research and the core of information systems. In: Peffers, K., Rothenberger, M., Kuechler, B. (eds.) DESRIST 2012. LNCS, vol. 7286, pp. 309–327. Springer, Heidelberg (2012)
38. Purao, S.: Design research in the technology of information systems: Truth or dare. In Unpublished Working Paper, Atlanta (2002)
39. Simon, H.A.: The sciences of the artificial, 3rd edn. The MIT Press, Cambridge (1996)
40. Goldkuhl, G.: Design theories in information systems-a need for multi-grounding. Journal of Information Technology Theory and Application 6(2), 59–72 (2004)
41. Wand, Y., Weber, R.: An ontological model of an information system. IEEE Transactions on Software Engineering 16(11), 1282–1292 (1990)
42. Piirainen, K.A., Briggs, R.O.: Design Theory in Practice – Making Design Science Research More Transparent. In: Jain, H., Sinha, A.P., Vitharana, P. (eds.) DESRIST 2011. LNCS, vol. 6629, pp. 47–61. Springer, Heidelberg (2011)
43. Järvinen, P.: Action research is similar to design science. Quality and Quantity 41(1), 37–54 (2007)
44. Orlikowski, W.J., Iacono, C.S.: Desperately seeking the 'IT' in IT research-a call to theorizing the IT artifact. Information Systems Research 12(2), 121–134 (2001)
45. Weber, R.: Evaluating and developing theories in the information systems discipline. Journal of the Association for Information Systems 13(1), 2 (2012)
46. Verschuren, P., Hartog, R.: Evaluation in design-oriented research. Quality & Quantity 39(6), 733–762 (2005)
47. Ciborra, C.: The grassroots of IT and strategy. In: Strategic Information Systems. John Wiley & Sons, Inc. (1994)
48. Rosemann, M., Green, P., Indulska, M.: A procedural model for ontological analyses. In: Information Systems Foundations: Constructing and Criticising. ANU E Press, Canberra (2005)
49. Rosemann, M., Recker, J., Indulska, M., Green, P.: A study of the evolution of the representational capabilities of process modeling grammars. In: Martinez, F.H., Pohl, K. (eds.) CAiSE 2006. LNCS, vol. 4001, pp. 447–461. Springer, Heidelberg (2006)
50. Kuechler, W., Vaishnavi, V.: A Framework for Theory Development in Design Science Research: Multiple Perspectives. Journal of the Association for Information Systems 13(6), 30 (2012)

Appendix A: IS Deep Structure Ontology Constructs (as described in [3])

Construct	Explanation
Thing	A thing is the elementary unit in the BWW ontological model. The real world is made up of things. Two or more things (composite or simple) can be associated into a composite thing.
Properties	Things possess properties; A property is modelled via a function that maps the thing into some value. A property of a composite thing that belongs to a component thing is called a hereditary property. Otherwise it is called an emergent property. Some properties are inherent properties of individual things called intrinsic. A property that is meaningful only in the context of two or more things is called a mutual or relational property. Attributes are the names that we use to represent properties of things.
State	The vector of values for all property functions of a thing.
Conceivable state space	The set of all states that the thing might ever assume.
State law	Restricts the values of the property function of a thing to a subset that is deemed lawful because of natural laws or human laws.
Lawful state space	The set of states of a thing that comply with the state law of the thing. It is usually a proper subset of a conceivable state space.
Event	A change of state of a thing. It is effected via a transformation.
Event space	The set of all possible events that can occur in the thing.
Transformation	A mapping from a domain comprising states to a co-domain comprising states.
Lawful transformation	Define which events in a thing are lawful.
Lawful event space	The set of all events in a thing that are lawful.
History	The chronological ordered states that a thing traverses.
Coupling	A thing acts on another thing if its existence affects the history of the other thing. The two things are said to be coupled or interact.
System	A set of things is a system if, for any bi-partitioning of the set, coupling exists among things in two subsets.
System composition	The things in the system.
System environment	Things that are not in the system but interact with things in the system.
System structure	The set of coupling that exist among things in the system and things in the environment of the system.
Subsystem	A system whose composition and structure are subsets of the composition and structure of another system.

System decomposition	A set of subsystems such that every component in the system is either one of the subsystem in the decomposition or is included in the composition of one of the subsystems in the decomposition.
Level structure	Defines a partial order over the subsystem in a decomposition to show which subsystems are component of other subsystems or the system itself.
Stable state	A state in which a thing, subsystem or system will remain unless forced to change by virtue of the action of a thing in the environment (an external event)
Unstable state	A state that will be changed into another state by virtue of the action of transformation in the system.
External event	An event that arises in a thing, subsystem or system by virtue of the action of some thing in the environment on the thing, subsystem or system. The before-state of an external event is always stable. The after-state may be stable or unstable.
Internal event	An event that arises in a thing, subsystem or system by virtue of lawful transformation in the thing, subsystem or system. The before-state of an internal event is always unstable. The after-state may be stable or unstable.
Well-defined event	An event in which the subsystem state can always be predicted given the prior state is known.
Poorly defined event	An event in which the subsequent state cannot be predicted given the prior state is known.
Class	A set of things that possess a common property.
Kind	A set of things that possess two or more common properties.

Towards an Innovative Service Development Process in the Electricity Industry

Yannic Domigall, Antonia Albani, and Robert Winter

Institute of Information Management
Müller-Friedberg-Strasse 8, 9000 St.Gallen, Switzerland
{yannic.domigall,antonia.albani,robert.winter}@unisg.ch

Abstract. The electricity industry is currently confronted with regulatory and technological change that leads to fundamental transformation of the value propositions and innovation processes of enterprises. New services are one possibility to compete in the new market environment. This paper proposes a service development process for the electricity industry that builds up on existing approaches. The process model was developed by means of an embedded research framework that combines qualitative and quantitative methods in a multi method approach. A first evaluation of the process was conducted with a partner of the electricity industry in Switzerland. Potential service areas resulting from literature research, expert interviews (N=19), and an Open Space event with lead customers (N=33) build the basis for a choice based conjoint study. Potential services could already be identified in a pretest study. The paper shows that co-creation with customers and experts, enables the service innovation process.

Keywords: Service Development, Electricity Industry, Conjoint Analysis.

1 Introduction

Despite the fact that about 70% of the world's gross value added can be attributed to the service sector, there is still an enormous need for research in this area to guide the service development process [1]. The structured and successful development of new and innovative services is a major task for companies and a critical success factor for enterprise profitability [2].

In contrast to the development of physical products, the development of new and innovative services is often executed ad hoc and not systematically [3]. However, knowing that new products that were launched during the last 5 years account for about 49% of the sales of innovative companies [4], the need for a systematical approach in the service development process becomes evident.

An industry where the need for new and innovative services is especially high is the electricity industry. Due to the fact that electricity may not be stored as easily and cost effective without bigger losses as other physical goods, the electricity industry has a special constellation of actors (e.g., network operators, electricity producers, power traders, service integrators, customers) that create value together. These actors

J. vom Brocke et al. (Eds.): DESRIST 2013, LNCS 7939, pp. 278–292, 2013.

need to ensure that supply and demand in the electricity market are always in perfect equilibrium. Due to this special situation, the customers have beside the economical relation to their service integrator a physical relation to the grid operator who delivers the electric current. This leads to the situation that many stakeholders have to be integrated into the service development process. Furthermore, new ways of electricity generation and smart grid technologies demand for new and innovative service types. Enablers are for example new tariff model options on the billing side or new opportunities in the load management area.

The aim of this research is to provide guidance for service innovation in the electricity industry by means of a systematic series of actions, summarized in the service innovation development process.

The basis for this research lies in the notion of service dominant logic (S-D logic) as a contrast to the classical goods dominant logic (G-D logic) [5-7]. S-D logic is a paradigm in service science research that puts a focus on the exchange of competences as a basis for co-creation instead of production and distribution in the goods dominant logic system. This shifts the production process from producers to a co-creation process of value [6, 8]. The important difference lies in the new understanding of value creation through competences and processes rather than value as a physical product [5, 6, 9]. Lusch et al. [10] argue that enterprises have to think about how to support customers in their resource integration and value co-creation activities. "All enterprises should strive to be an effective and efficient service support system for helping all stakeholders, beginning with the customer, become effective and efficient in value co-creation" [10]. According to Lusch et al. the S-D logic is very useful in a highly networked world. In the electricity industry – a highly networked industry – customer could e.g., become co-creators of the production of electricity [10].

Since the basic aim of this research lies in the development of new and innovative services for the electricity industry, service science builds the starting point for the derivation of our service innovation development process. Service science uses the dimensions "people", "organization" and "technology" to understand, categorize and explain a variety of existing service systems [7], and to analyze how service systems emerge and actors co-create value [7]. To derive at our service innovation development process we expand the generic service development model of [1, p.169] consisting of the five phases Service Identification, Service Exploration, Service Idea Generation, Service Prototyping and Service Evaluation and exemplarily apply it to the electricity industry. The focus of this paper lies on the second and third phases of the generic service model [1, p.169]. We propose to iterate the Service Exploration and the Idea Generation phases by using different methods for service innovation.

Our research follows the Design Science Research (DSR) approach according to [11-13] and executes the design science process steps (problem identification, objectives of a solution, design development, demonstration, evaluation and communication) as introduced by Peffers et al. [14]. This paper covers the first four steps. The artifact is not yet fully evaluated, but exemplary applied to the electricity industry.

The structure of the paper is as follows. In the Background Work section relevant process models for the development of services are presented and explained. We show what the advantages and disadvantages of the models are in respect to the development of innovative services for the electricity industry. The artifact – the service innovation development process – is presented in the section Service Innovation

Development Process. An exemplary application of the model is conducted in the section First Evaluation of the Service Development Process in the Electricity Industry. The section Conclusions and Future Work summarizes the results and shows further steps for future research.

2   Background Work

Aim of the service innovation process is to design the constituent parts of the future services. Input (Potential), Throughput (Process), Output (result) and the customer dimension [15]. In this section we give an overview over the existing process models for the support of service development and elaborate on their advantages and disadvantages.

We identified many different sources dealing with the generic development of services. Well established models such as the linear model of Edvardsson and Olsson [16] or the iterative service engineering model of Shostack [17] can be found in [18]. Some of these models reach back to 1989 and may be distinct into three different types of models: linear process models also called phase models, iterative process models and prototyping models [18].The most models we found are linear models, this might be, because they are easier to understand and apply [18]. Examples for this kind of models are the model of Edvardsson and Olsson [16], the model of Scheuing and Johnson [19], or the model of Ramaswamy [20].

The model of Edvardsson and Olsson [16] is mainly focused on the quality aspect of the service development. Aim of the model is to support the service engineering from the beginning to yield a higher service quality. Quality means in this context "satisfying the needs and meeting the expectations of three main groups: customers, staff and owners" [16]. In this model the service is seen as a customer process and value is jointly co-created with the customer [16]. Customer needs are differentiated between primary and secondary needs. Successful companies have, according to this paper [16], more and better supporting services. The results of the service engineering model according to Edvardsson and Olsson is structured in a hierarchical order with the components *concept development* in the top layer, *process development* in a middle layer and *system development* in the technical layer [16]. The model has been developed and evaluated in cooperation with a Swedish Telecom enterprise [16]. The Model of Edvardsson and Olsson is an approach to structure the service development process and include the customer into this process. A disadvantage of the model is that it gives virtually no advice about the exact methods and techniques that should be used to identify new services. Another disadvantage of the model is the lack of iterations that would improve the service development especially in an environment with many actors like the electricity industry.

The model of Scheuing and Johnson [19] is another example for a linear model. The major contribution of the proposed model is its aggregation of existing models and the empirical foundation. The authors consider already published service engineering models of that time and conduct an empirical study with 66 respondents [19]. The disadvantages of this model are the missing concreteness and the missing iterations. Concreteness means in this case that the model does not present methods or techniques that enable the service development. As in the model of Edvardsson and Olsson there are no iterations intended in this model. On the one side this makes it easier to understand the model, but on the other side this may lead to less grounded solutions.

The model of Ramaswamy [20] is a third example for a linear model. It consists of eight sequel steps that are differentiated between Design focused and Service Management focused. The Design focused steps conceptualize the new services that are then implemented in the management focused steps. The model is very competition oriented and may be used with an approach that maps requirements and minimal service standards of the newly developed services in dependence of the competitors services [20]. Beside the new service development part, this model focuses on the management and performance improvements by using controlling and measures and has therefore a more quantitative focus in the Service Management part. Even though the model gives more detailed information about the contents that shall be conducted as for example define design attributes or develop design details etc., there are no iterations between the different steps intended.

According to [1] and [3] the model of Shostack [17] is a representative of the iterative service engineering models. Shostack differentiates between product dominant and service dominant entities, where salt is an example of an extreme product dominant item and teaching is especially service dominant entity. The basic elements, the services and products that build up a value proposition should be modeled accurately by the use of methods as e.g., service blueprinting. The model of Shostack is primarily focused on a marketing view of the service development and the modeling of the services. Therefore the marketing mix components prize, promotion product and place (distribution strategy) play a major role in the developed artifact. Additionally, Shostack [17] gives no detailed advise on how to develop new services but presents only the service blueprinting and service modeling ideas.

An example for a prototyping model is the design thinking model [21]. It consists basically of two parts, the divergent and the convergent thinking part. The ambiguity, the number of ideas, is increasing in the first part and decreasing in the second part. The different stages are supported by specified methods and result documents [21]. From the authors perspective the major aim of the design thinking is the people enablement and not the process support or the further management of services.

Table 1. New Service Development Models compared

	Iterative steps	Empirically sound	The Model uses explicit Methods
Edvardsson`s and Olsson`s Model	X	(o)	X
Scheuing`s and Johnson`s Model	X	O	X
Ramaswamy`s Model	X	(o)	(o)
Shostack`s Model	O	(o)	X
Design Thinking Model	X	(o)	O

O = Yes   X = No   (o) = partially.

Table 1 summarizes the relevant approaches for service development known to the authors and mentioned above and shows that those models do not combine iterative service development with accurately explained methods in a structured process model. This is exactly where this paper contributes to the field.

3   Service Innovation Development Process

The aim of our Service Innovation Development Process is the integration of the co-creation of value idea into the service development process. As a basis, we follow the service design cycle according to [1, 3] and further extend the model by a detailed description of the interactions of the Service Exploration and the Service Idea Generation phases as highlighted in **Fig. 1**.

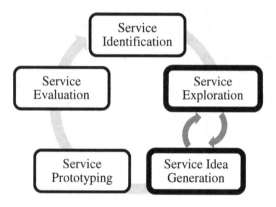

Fig. 1. Service Design Phases adapted from [1]

In the Service Identification phase, the targets of the service development have to be set. The aim of this phase is the identification of the basic conditions and the limiting factors for the development of services [1]. The Service Identification phase is the theoretical foundation for the following steps and therefore groundbreaking and of high importance for the right decisions in the next phases. In the Service Exploration phase, the customers with their needs and preferences stand at the forefront. The focus of the third phase, Service Idea Generation, lies in the development of new ideas to solve the problems previously defined in the Service Exploration phase. Some of the ideas are then implemented and pretested in the Service Prototyping phase. Central aim of the last phase is the evaluation of the user acceptance regarding the newly developed services. This happens in the fifth and last phase of the service design process. The repetition of the service design process potentially increases the quality of the developed services [1].

In this paper we concentrate on the Service Exploration and the Service Idea Generation phases and their interactions in order to support the process of service innovation (as highlighted in **Fig. 1**). To systematically identify potential topics for the innovation of services four dimensions of innovativeness can be differentiated: The structure dimension, the process dimension, the outcome dimension and the market dimension [1, 15]. According to [15] there are only few publications available that deal with the support of the four dimensions of service innovation through methods and techniques on a systematical and empirical basis. Here is where we contribute to the field, namely in defining a clear and structured process for service innovation in the electricity domain regarding all four dimensions. In this Service Exploration and Service Idea Generation phases the focus lies on the customer, his behavior and the development of new ideas for services [1]. The phases are separated in the process model of [1]. However, based on our experience we argue that this separation is artificial to a certain extend and claim that reciprocal effects between the two phases occur. To systematically identify the customer needs we integrate the customers from the beginning into our research approach and look at the two phases from a holistic point of view. We suggest to use multiple methods and follow therefore a strong pluralistic research approach as advocated by [22].The approach consists of a qualitative and quantitative part and six steps in total as shown in **Fig. 2**.

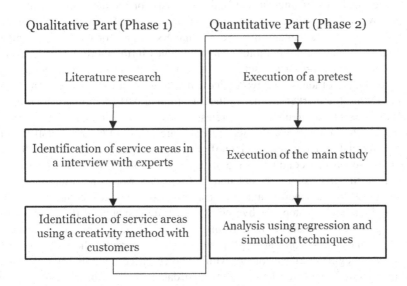

Qualitative Part (Phase 1)   Quantitative Part (Phase 2)

Literature research	Execution of a pretest
Identification of service areas in a interview with experts	Execution of the main study
Identification of service areas using a creativity method with customers	Analysis using regression and simulation techniques

Fig. 2. Research Approach following a multi-method approach according to [22]

The main purpose of the qualitative part (phase 1, shown left in **Fig. 2**) of our approach is to open up the mind for divergent thinking and to generate more ideas for potential services. The first step of the qualitative part consists of a structured literature research as presented in [23]. In a first step relevant journals and conference proceedings are identified. The literature is then electronically analyzed by using databases as for example EBSCOhost. The identified sources build a basis for the second step of the approach where potential service areas are identified by interviewing experts of related industries. The interests and ideas of customers are considered in the third step of the qualitative approach. To make sure that all ideas are optimally understood and controversially discussed, the use of a creativity method is useful. We suggest to use the Open Space method as explained in [24], since this method simplifies the structured creative working of the participants. The Open Space method works best if the following conditions are met [24]:

1. The topic is a real issue of concern
2. The topic is highly complex
3. Many skills and people are required to solve the problem
4. Very diverse stakeholder needs have to be addressed
5. A high urgency level

In the quantitative part (phase 2, shown right in **Fig. 2**), the focus lies on the selection of the most promising service ideas for the implementation. Therefore the used methods are focused on convergent thinking to decrease the number of ideas for potential services. The ideas for potential services that were identified in the qualitative phase are arranged in fields of interest that build the basis for the development of a questionnaire. We suggest to use a questionnaire that uses the choice based conjoint [25] design. This has the advantage that the willingness to pay for each service may be calculated. A survey with a conjoint analysis enables furthermore the evaluation and selection of the most promising services. A survey is therefore a good possibility to reduce the number of ideas for new services without using arbitrary selection mechanisms, but letting the market decide. In the quantitative part such a choice based conjoint study is executed, preceded by a pretest, to test the questionnaire. In the last step of the approach, the results of the questionnaire are analyzed by using statistical methods and simulation techniques to identify the most useful services that shall be implemented. We suggest conducting the analysis in two steps: In a first step the conjoint part-worth values should be calculated. These part-worths represent the customers preference for a specific attribute (in this case service) compared to other attributes. In a second step we hypothesize that fundamental differences between customer groups may occur. For the further analysis of the groups we suggest to use latent class analysis. According to [26] latent class is currently the best way to find homogeneous segments of customers within choice based conjoint data. A possible simulation scenario with the hereby generated data is for instance a ceteris paribus price increase in a market simulator. Furthermore we can calculate price sensitivities based on a broad basic population. The new service design steps we developed are shown in **Fig. 3**.

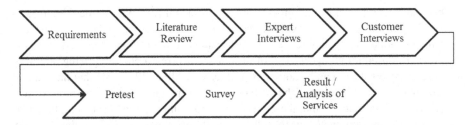

Fig. 3. Elements of the new service model

The requirements are the result of the *Service Identification* phase presented in Fig. 1. The following five steps: *Literature Review, Expert Interviews, Customer Interviews, Pretest, Survey* and *Result / Analysis of Services* are the core elements of the new service design procedure. As a last step the results are analyzed using for instance regression techniques. In **Fig. 4** we present our process model that includes the five information gathering steps (literature research, expert interviews, customer interviews, pretest and survey) as well as the analysis step (all introduced in in **Fig. 3**) by using the one cycle view of design science research as introduced by Winter and Albani [27].

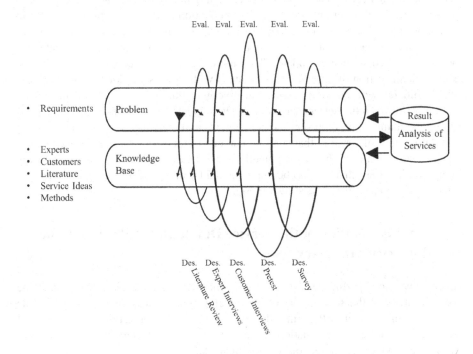

Fig. 4. Process Model for Service Innovation following the one cycle view of [27]

Inspired by the Spiral Model in software development [28] Winter and Albani [27] revisit Hevner's three cycle view [11] and argue that the design cycle of Hevner has rigor related and/or relevance related characteristics within each single iteration. They therefore proposed a one-cycle view of design science research, comprising alternating core activities design and evaluation. Winter and Albani [27] state that having the development and verification of the artifact not as a separate cycle in the Spiral Model underlined their conviction that the design, relevance and rigor cycles belong together and should not be separated. Further, having different types of artifacts that may be designed and evaluated in different cycles satisfied their need to restructure the design science Knowledge Base in order to better find the right means for each artifact type to derive at the desired ends.

As mentioned in [27], with every iteration, the understanding of the environment and the problem to be solved are enhanced. Additionally, every design iteration allows for revisiting the Knowledge Base in order to improve the problem solution. The cycle iterates until a sufficiently useful solution has been developed. When the iteration exits, a problem solving means has been developed and novel artifact components together with their related problem characteristics are added to the Knowledge Base. We apply the one cycle view of design science research in order to define the service innovation development process. Starting point for the development of innovative services are the requirements that were defined in the Service Identification phase shown in **Fig. 1**. These requirements build the starting state of the problem space. Relevant information for the service innovation development process stored in the Knowledge Base is the knowledge of the experts and customers, their methodological competencies, possible methods used to identify potential service candidates and the identified service candidates. The first three iterations consisting of literature review, identification of potential service areas with experts and identification of service candidates with customers represent divergent thinking that aims at increasing the number of potential service candidates. The two last cycles, consisting of the pretest and the main study, represent the convergent thinking, since they aim at reducing the total number of services that shall be pursued to the set of relevant service candidates. Having identified this set of potential services, the analysis allows for choosing the appropriate ones that need to be implemented by means of a prototype, as defined in the Service Prototype phase shown in **Fig. 1**.

4   First Evaluation of the Service Development Process in the Electricity Industry

Together with our partners in the electricity industry we have already executed the first four steps of the service innovation development process. This resulted in one exemplary service that will be introduced into the market prototypically in the first half of 2013. The service evaluation of the first service and the development of further innovative services are subject of our current work.

In this section we illustrate the steps executed to derive at potential service innovation candidates (see **Fig. 5**).

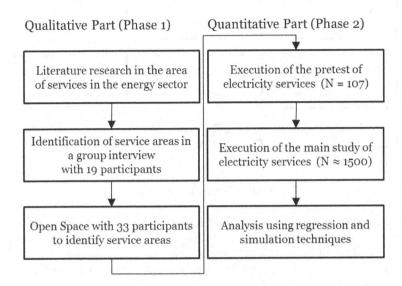

Fig. 5. Research Approach adapted from [22]

The literature review in the research approach shown in **Fig. 5** yielded only few publications considering electricity tariffs, product attributes or services. We discovered a gap between the need for new services and further growth in the electricity sector on the one side and the missing studies that evaluate the need for these services on the other side.

In the second step of our research approach we interviewed 19 electricity professionals from different parts of the electricity supply chain in Switzerland. The group consists of representatives of the electricity generation, distribution, marketing, electricity grid operators and electricity certificates trading. The participants were arranged in four groups for a group interview and had the main task to identify potential service areas in the field of energy consumption in households or the industry dependent on the group. The question was intentionally open formulated, since electricity can act as a substitute for energy of other sources.

The third and last step of the qualitative phase consisted of a group moderation session with 33 participants. In contrast to the first step, the attendees were this time customers and not professionals. The task was to identify interesting areas of electricity services from a customer perspective. The used creativity method was "Open Space" [24]. Due to the highly relevant topic and the active cooperation of the customers, interesting topics for future services have been identified.

From the expert and customer interviews seven relevant areas for innovative services and tariffing resulted. The areas are presented in **Fig. 6**.

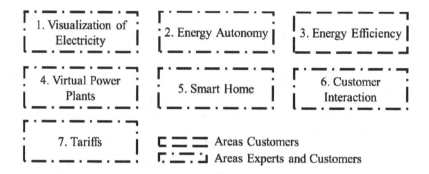

Fig. 6. Areas for potential new services

Service possibilities that we identified in the visualization of electricity area are services that visualize the consumed or produced electricity of customers to enable a proactive handling of the electricity consumption. The visualization may for example be executed via in home display; through a web portal or smartphone app. Ideas in the area of energy autonomy were for instance a container battery to compensate voltage fluctuation in the grid or to enable higher electricity autonomy of a building. The area energy efficiency was especially interesting for the customers. Potential services in this area are energy consulting and hints for reductions of the electricity consumed. Possible channels for such hints are web portals or the bill. The area virtual power plants, is a starting point for services that enable a further integration of renewable energy into the grid. In this area it is especially interesting to what extend customers are willing and able to let utilities control their electronic devices. In the area of smart home we identified potential services that enable a comfortable control of home appliances. The area customer interaction is basically the service channel via that the communication between customers and the enterprise happens. Classic channels are for example the phone or the service center a newer channel is the internet. The tariffs area influences the pricing possibilities and the customer interaction and is therefore of special interest for the service development.

The expert interviews showed us that many concerns that are often divergent have to be considered when developing services for the electricity domain. We included areas for the service innovation in our approach that deal with grid problems as well as marketing and sales issues. Furthermore we noticed that the ideas for potential services reached a higher maturity level and concreteness due to the discussion of experts from different divisions.

The major learning's from the Open Space were that customers are willing to participate in many ways, but are facing several knowledge barriers that make it difficult for them to calculate the expected savings or benefits. Services that deal with analytical data or the visualization of energy consumed seem especially interesting for the customers. The utility was often seen as a general partner for energy and not only as an electricity provider.

The identified service areas that are shown in **Fig. 6** build the basis for the fourth step of the multi method approach. In a first conjoint study with 107 respondents we tested service candidates for the main study. This shall preclude obviously unattractive services from being tested in the main study. Questions of every area are integrated in the study. Some questions e.g., questions regarding the customer interaction, are asked in every questionnaire, other questions like for example questions regarding the electronic appliance control are only asked if the customers are private property owners. Our aim is to identify the most wanted services through the main study, therefore we use the conjoint method. The data of the pretest is currently analyzed and used for the further development of the main study. The analysis of the pretest results is conducted in two steps. In a first step we calculate part-worth values of the Choice Based Conjoint (CBC) Analysis. These values represent the preference of a specific attribute compared to the other attributes in a conjoint study. In a second step we analyze the potential differences between homogeneous customer groups. This enables the identification of services that are only interesting for a certain customer group. To find such segments we use latent class, which is currently one of the best ways to find customer segments within choice based conjoint data [26].

In the fifth step we will conduct a large choice based conjoint analysis with the aim of about 1500 respondents. The results of the first four steps of the multi method approach all built the basis for this study, by delivering potentially interesting services that have already proven to be of interest for a smaller group that we addressed with our pretest. In **Fig. 7** we show a possibility of a choice-set that could be presented to the customers in the questionnaire of the main study. Every attribute is derived from a potential service area as presented in **Fig. 6**. As the pretest showed, all these attributes are important for the customer. The aim of the main study is to understand the exact importance of every attribute. The choice set presented in **Fig. 7** forces a tradeoff decision between the possible characteristics in every selection. From the selections chosen by a customer in the different choice sets we can identify the worth that a customer assigns to a specific attribute and its characteristics.

Attributes	Selection 1	Selection 2	Selection 3
Service channel	Internet only	Internet, phone and service center	Internet and phone
Presentation of the used electricity	Every Second	Every Second	Every Month
Services to enable energy savings	No Services	Efficiency portal	No Services
Price per person and month	40 CHF	70 CHF	50 CHF
	o	o	o

Fig. 7. Example of a choice-set

The sixth and last step of our research design consists of the deep analysis of the data that is generated by the main conjoint study. Central aim of the analysis is to show the exact impact of every attribute on the purchase decision of a customer.

In the Service Prototyping Phase (see **Fig. 1**), we plan to prototypically implement some services in the market. This enables a clearer valuation by the customers due to the concreteness of the offer [1]. The services used in this evaluation were developed by using the service areas shown in **Fig. 6** as a basis. Most services are tested with a questionnaire right now. One possible service that resulted already from the pretest will be implemented in the first half of 2013. It is a service that has been identified in the pretest. This tariff uses a variable tariffing approach and electricity visualization to incentivize customers to use the generated solar energy on their own instead of feed the energy into the public grid. This service shall prevent problems with peak load situations in the electric grid caused by solar panels.

The insufficient integration of customers into the service development process is according to Schneider et al. a major problem of many process models [3]. We took this into account and integrated the customers from the beginning of our service development into the process. The three formalized evaluation and exchange points with our customers are shown in **Fig. 5**: The Open Space with 33 customers, a questionnaire with 107 customers and a main study with a planned N of 1500. However, beside these feedback loops during the service development process a further evaluation of the newly developed services after their introduction into the market is crucial (see Service Evaluation Phase in **Fig. 1**). We plan to measure the customer acceptance after the market introduction of the product to evaluate its usefulness for customers.

The aim of this first evaluation of the proposed service development process was to test the ideas of co-creation in the innovation and the service delivery phases. We included the co-creation into the service innovation process through the use of expert interviews in an early stage and the further identification of potential service areas with lead customers through the structured method Open Space. The conduction of a pretest and the choice based conjoint study are two further elements that include co-creation aspects. Customers are not only included in the service innovation approach but additionally decide which services are implemented in the market through their answers in the questionnaire.

5   Conclusion and Future Work

Due to the deregulation and new technologies that enable innovative services in the electricity industry, the service aspects are becoming increasingly important in the next years. The transformation and innovation in the electricity industry can profit from structured approaches used by service science. This paper is a first step towards an industry specific process model for the development of new and innovative services and value propositions for customers in the electricity industry. The paper follows the five service development phases as introduced by [29] and refines the Service Exploration and Service Idea Generation phase by means of a multi method approach to derive at new and innovative services. With a partner of the electricity industry in

Switzerland we already tested our presented service innovation development process and went through the first four phases, Service Identification, Exploration, Idea Generation and Prototyping, in order to derive at new and innovative services that can be introduced into the market. One of the identified services will be introduce into the market in the first quarter of 2013. The fifth phase, the Service Evaluation is subject to our current research. For the future, our aim is to validate the presented service innovation development process with additional industry partners in Switzerland or abroad to proof its usefulness for the whole industry and not only for single players. The process should support service innovation through a structured approach. In this paper we focused on the service innovation in the electricity sector. To generalize the results, an application of the process model to other domains is necessary. From our perspective the service design procedures could be useful for other domains that use a physical grid or distribution facility for their business model. An example is for instance the gas distribution system. To use the model for the new service development in other industries the relevant expert groups for this specific situation have to be identified.

From our perspective, not only the development of services builds a value proposition for future co-creation but also the development process itself is subject to co-creation. Through a tight cooperation with customers we make sure that the developed artifact is both useful for the customers and also easy understandable.

Acknowledgments. This project is supported by the Swiss Commission for Technology and Innovation (CTI).

References

1. Leimeister, J.M.: Dienstleistungsengineering und -management. Springer, Berlin (2012)
2. Soukhoroukova, A., Spann, M.: New product development with Internet-based information markets: Theory and empirical application. In: Proceedings of the Thirteenth European Conference on Information Systems (ECIS) (2005)
3. Bullinger, H.-J., Scheer, A.-W.: Service Engineering - Entwicklung und Gestaltung innovativer Dienstleistungen. Springer, Berlin (2003)
4. Di Benedetto, A.C.: Identifying the Key Success Factors in New Product Launch. Journal of Product Innovation Management 16, 530–544 (1999)
5. Chesbrough, H., Spohrer, J.: A research manifesto for services science. Commun. ACM 49, 35–40 (2006)
6. Vargo, S.L., Lusch, R.F.: Service-dominant logic: continuing the evolution. Journal of Academy of Marketing Science 36, 1–10 (2007)
7. Maglio, P., Spohrer, J.: Fundamentals of service science. Journal of the Academy of Marketing Science 36, 18–20 (2008)
8. Wikström: The customer as co-producer. European Journal of Marketing 30, 6–19 (1996)
9. Spohrer, J., Vargo, S.L., Maglio, P.P., Caswell, N.: The Service System is the Basic Abstraction of Service Science. In: Hawaii International Conference on System Sciences (Year)
10. Lusch, R.F., Webster, F.E.: A Stakeholder-Unifying, Cocreation Philosophy for Marketing. Journal of Macromarketing 31, 129–134 (2011)

11. Hevner, A.R.: A Three Cycle View of Design Science Research. Scandinavian Journal of Information Systems 19, 87–92 (2007)
12. Hevner, A.R., Chatterjee, S.: Design Research in Information Systems: Theory and Practice. Springer, Heidelberg (2010)
13. Hevner, A.R., March, S.T., Park, J., Ram, S.: Design Science in Information Systems Research. MIS Quarterly 28, 75–105 (2004)
14. Peffers, K., Tuunanen, T., Gengler, C.E., Rossi, M., Hui, W., Virtanen, V., Bragge, J.: The Design Science Research Process: A Model for Producing and Presenting Information Systems Research. In: 1st International Conference on Design Science in Information Systems and Technology, pp. 83–106 (Year)
15. Bullinger, H.-J., Schreiner, P.: Service Engineering: Ein Rahmenkonzept für die systematische Entwicklung von Dienstleistungen. In: Bullinger, H.-J. (ed.) Service Engineering, pp. 53–84. Springer, Berlin (2006)
16. Edvardsson, B.: Quality in new service development: Key concepts and a frame of reference. International Journal of Production Economics 52, 31–46 (1997)
17. Shostack, L.G.: How to Design a Service. European Journal of Marketing 16, 49–63 (1982)
18. Schneider, K., Daun, C., Behrens, H., Wagner, D.: Vorgehensmodelle und Standards zur systematischen Entwicklung von Dienstleistungen. In: Bullinger, H.-J., Scheer, A.-W. (eds.) Service Engineering, pp. 113–138. Springer, Heidelberg (2006)
19. Scheuing, E.E., Johnson, E.M.: A Proposed Model for New Service Development. Journal of Services Marketing 3, 25–34 (1989)
20. Ramaswamy, R.: Design and management of service processes. Addison-Wesley Pub. Co. (1996)
21. Dym, C.L., Agogino, A.M., Eris, O., Frey, D.D., Leifer, L.J.: Engineering Design Thinking, Teaching, and Learning. Journal of Engineering Education, 103–120 (2005)
22. Mingers, J.: Combining IS research methods: towards a pluralistic methodology. Information Systems Research 12, 240–259 (2001)
23. vom Brocke, J., Simons, A., Niehaves, B., Riemer, K., Plattfaut, R., Cleven, A.: Reconstructing the Giant: On the Importance of Rigour in Documenting the Literature Search Process. In: 17th European Conference on Information Systems, pp. 2206–2217 (Year)
24. Owen, H.H.: Open Space Technology: A User's Guide. Read How You Want, San Francisco (2008)
25. Louviere, J.J.: Analyzing Decision Making: Metric Conjoint Analysis (Year)
26. Magidson, J., Eagle, T., Vermunt, J.K.: New Developments in Latent Class Choice Models. Sawtooth Software Conference Proceedings (2003)
27. Winter, R., Albani, A.: Restructuring the Design Science Research Knowledge Base - A One-Cycle View of Design Science Research and its Consequences for Understanding Organizational Design Problems. In: Baskerville, R., de Marco, M., Spagnoletti, P. (eds.) Designing Organizational Systems: An Interdisciplinary Discourse, pp. 63–81. Springer (2013)
28. Boehm, B.: A spiral model of software development and enhancement. SIGSOFT Softw. Eng. Notes 11, 14–24 (1986)
29. Bullinger, H.-J., Scheer, A.-W.: Service Engineering - Entwicklung und Gestaltung innovativer Dienstleistungen. Springer, Berlin (2006)

Design Science in Practice: Designing an Electricity Demand Response System

Philipp Bodenbenner[1,2], Stefan Feuerriegel[1], and Dirk Neumann[1]

[1] University of Freiburg, Freiburg, Germany
{philipp.bodenbenner,stefan.feuerriegel,
dirk.neumann}@is.uni-freiburg.de
[2] Detecon International GmbH, Cologne, Germany

Abstract. Information Systems play an important role in achieving sustainable solutions for the global economy. In particular, Information Systems are inevitable when it comes to the transition from the "current" to the "smart" power grid. This enables an improved balancing of both electricity supply and demand, by shifting load – based on the projected supply gap and electricity prices – on the demand side smartly. As this requires a specific Information System, namely a Demand Response system, we address the challenge of designing such a system by utilizing the design science approach: determining general requirements, deducing the corresponding information requirements, analyzing the information flow, designing a suitable Information System, demonstrating its capability, and, finally, evaluating the design. The design process is reiterated fully until a viable solution, i.e. an IS artifact, has been developed. This paper describes both the design process as such and the final IS artifact. Moreover, we summarize our lessons learnt from using and adopting the design science approach within this practical, bottom-up case study.

Keywords: Design Science Research, Green IS, IS-Architecture, Demand Response, Case Study.

1 Introduction

For a global economy, Information Systems (IS) play an important role in achieving sustainable solutions and, in particular, Green IS will facilitate to shape the power supply, transmission and consumption systems of the future. As a consequence, the IS research community has recently given significant attention to Green IS.

Until today, it was only possible to control the supply side in electricity markets, but Green IS introduces the power demand as an additional dimension subject to optimization. This degree of freedom is not entirely new, but *"affordable global communication infrastructure and embedded systems make it now relatively easy to add a certain portion of smart to the loads"* [1]. This so-called transition from current to smart power grids will lead to unexpected problems, unprecedented challenges and new opportunities – such as matching both power demand and supply. One possible path to balance power demand and supply is given by the concept of Demand

J. vom Brocke et al. (Eds.): DESRIST 2013, LNCS 7939, pp. 293–307, 2013.
© Springer-Verlag Berlin Heidelberg 2013

Response. Demand Response (DR) is defined by the U.S. Department of Energy [2] and the Federal Energy Regulatory Commission (FEDC) [3] as: *"Changes in electric usage by end-use customers from their normal consumption patterns in response to changes in the price of electricity over time, or to incentive payments designed to induce lower electricity use at times of high wholesale market prices or when system reliability is jeopardized."* In short, this implies shifting load to times when supply exceeds demand.

The purpose of this paper is to design a Demand Response system. We develop an IS artifact that enables retailers to minimize their expenditures on electricity by Demand Response. This problem is addressed by using the well-known design science research approach. Melville [4] states that *"design research is essential to developing innovative IS-enabled solutions to environmental problems and evaluating their effectiveness"*. This encompasses successive steps (compare Fig. 1) of determining requirements including the required information demand and flow, designing a suitable Information System, demonstrating its capability, and, finally, evaluating the design before starting off into the next iteration of the design process.

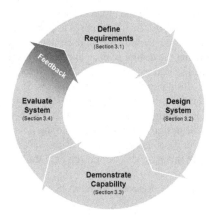

Fig. 1. Iterative Design Science Approach with a closed feedback loop based on Hevner et al. [5] and Simon [6]

As a main contribution to IS research, this paper describes not only the design of an Information System for Demand Response, but it also aims to evaluate the design science approach in practice. We will also share our experiences from applying the design science approach.

The remainder of this paper is structured as follows. In Section 2, related work on the IS perspective of Demand Response systems is reviewed. Subsequently, the Demand Response system (Section 3) is designed: First, we introduce general requirements. Then, we deduce the corresponding information requirements, analyze the information flow, list components matching the information requirements, and evaluate the design. Finally in Section 4, we revisit the design science approach according to the guidelines by Hevner et al. [5] and, in addition to that, we focus on what we have learnt from employing the design science approach in this case study.

2   Demand Response in IS Research

A recent literature review [7] shows that there are a small, but growing number of IS-related research papers on Demand Response. Our own literature research on these publications reveals that there are many studies demonstrating the responsiveness of residential, commercial and industrial customers to incentives and prices. However, we only came across few contributions dealing with the design of a Demand Response system. These publications have contributed to IS research:

- Corbett [8] claimed that a Demand Response system will increase the information processing requirements. As a consequence, the author argued that Demand Response systems will incur massive amounts of data and, thus, a Demand Response system poses an inherent IS problem.
- Several authors (e.g. Watson et al. [9]) advanced towards an IS-architecture. Tan et al. [10] designed an actual Demand Side Management decision supporting system, but the authors proposed a high-level structure only. Palensky and Dietrich [1] constructed a web-based energy Information System and named its typical components, while Law et al. [11] focused on tethering the end-consumer.
- Feuerriegel et al. [12, 13] integrated Demand Response into the Energy Informatics Framework and listed required components, but the authors lack a rigorous design science approach.

Since the above research papers have concentrated on partial examinations of either requirements or design, many questions have been left unanswered. All listed publications lack (i) a combination of design as well as requirements, and (ii) an in-depth evaluation of the proposed design. Consequently, a Demand Response system originating from a design science process still seems to be an open research questions. Therefore, we focus on a rigorous design science approach: First, we derive necessary requirements for a Demand Response system. Based on these requirements, we develop a system design, and evaluate this system design afterwards. However, we not only design the Demand Response system, but also give insights into the lessons learnt from iteratively developing the artifact.

3   Applying the Design Science Approach

The starting point for our research is the evaluation of financial benefits, which an electricity retailer can leverage by executing a Demand Response mechanism. As these benefits obviously do not come free, the cost perspective needs to be examined as well. Core prerequisite – and a major cost driver – for establishing Demand Response mechanisms is the setup of a broad Information System infrastructure. Therefore, we needed to gain an overview of both the required components and their relations. As there is no such system blueprint available (compare Section 2), we employ the design science methodology to conceptualize an Information System, which fits the set of defined requirements. Our approach is based on the multi-stage design science research methodology for IS research, which has been proposed by Peffers et al. [14]. According to Peffers et al. [14] our research intent requires the use of an *objective-centered approach*. An *objective-centered approach* is triggered by a research need that can be addressed by developing an artifact. Consequently, we start off with defining the objectives for the Demand Response system and subsequently pursue the previously described design science process (cp. Fig. 1).

3.1   Defining Requirements for the Information System

The objectives for the Demand Response system are deduced by transforming the overall problem description into functional and non-functional requirements. We also integrate knowledge about current solutions for Demand Response infrastructures and for other Smart Energy infrastructures into the definition of the requirements. This knowledge has been both extracted from literature (cp. Section 2) and expert interviews. For structuring and documentation of the requirements, we revert to the analytical level of the design science framework defined by Vahidov [15]. Hence, the salient features and properties of the system are described in a technology-independent and fairly descriptive fashion. The remaining section provides an excerpt of the overall set of requirements. First, we show the functional and non-functional requirements corresponding to category *structure* in Vahidov's framework. Second, we illustrate the corresponding information demand and flow in a dynamic representation (i.e. category *behavior*).

Functional and Non-functional Requirements

Implementation of a Demand Response mechanism requires substantial extensions of today's power networks. So far, power networks – on the distribution network level – have been mainly equipped with passive components and little to no Information Systems. Thus, Corbett [8] projects a strong future demand for increased information processing capabilities of the power networks to meet the challenges of the inevitable energy transformation. A core challenge is the matching process of fluctuating electricity supply and demand. The fluctuation increases – especially on the supply side – due to increased usage of renewable energy sources, such as wind and solar. Demand Response mechanisms form a viable solution to this issue. For determination and execution of an expedient load shifting and reduction scheme (i.e. the outcome of a Demand Response mechanism), the respective Information System has to satisfy a number of functional (RF) and non-functional (RN) requirements. We present the five most important requirements at a glance as follows:

- **Near-Time Access to Consumption Usage Data (RF1).** The determination and execution of an efficient Demand Response mechanism requires high quality forecasts of the electricity consumption for the next planning horizon (i.e. mostly the next 24 hours). Such a forecast quality can only be achieved by processing consumers' real-time resp. near-time consumption data [16]. Thus, the correspondent usage data record needs to be regularly transferred from the consumer to the electricity retailer's backend via a secure communication channel [17].

- **Centralized Remote Control of Connected Devices (RF2).** For realization of a Demand Response mechanism, the connected consumers need to support remote control of their devices [17, 18]. Based on the calculated load shifting scheme, the electricity retailer transmits control signals for shifting electricity load of the devices (cp. detailed Demand Response protocol description in Mohagheghi et al. [19]).

- **Easy Integration into Existing IS Environment of Retailer and Consumer (RN1).** The Information System needs to be developed with a *brownfield* approach as today's electricity retailers have a comprehensive IS landscape in place already [18]. The different Information Systems provide functionality for monitoring and controlling the complex power flow networks and connected components (e.g. distribution station) across different levels (i.e. transportation and distribution networks). The newly designed Information System, which brings additional *smartness* to the distribution networks, must fit into this legacy IS environment smoothly [20].

- **Openness to Implementation of Other Use Cases (RN2).** The Demand Response system must be shaped in an open and flexible manner. Additional use cases, apart from implementation of Demand Response mechanisms, should be enabled to use the deployed infrastructure and the collected data as much as possible. Faruqui et al. [21] state automated (monthly) billing based on usage data and improved customer service as possible use cases.

- **Cost Effectiveness (RN3).** Watson et al. [9] explain that *eco-efficiency* is a major sustainability goal. Thus, the Information System design should support both a cost-effective implementation and operation of the infrastructure.

Information Demand and Flow

We take the two functional requirements, namely (RF1) and (RF2), as basis for deducing the information demand and flow of the Demand Response system. For this, we make use of a sequence diagram similar to one of the UML method toolkit [22]. First, we define the involved actors, i.e. in our case the electricity retailer, the connected consumers, and external service providers. Subsequently, we work up use cases for these actors and convert the use cases into a sequence diagram, which is illustrated in Fig. 2. The sequence diagram shows the two-step approach of implementing a Demand Response mechanism: (i) forecasting of electricity load for the next cycle, and (ii) determination and execution of an appropriate load shifting scheme.

Load Forecasting. First, the electricity retailer determines the load forecast for the next optimization interval. This calculation is based on weather forecast data (A), electricity prices (B), historical (C), and current usage data (D). The electricity retailer retrieves weather data from specialized external service providers. Just as the weather data, electricity prices can be retrieved from external service providers, e.g. the EEX [23]. These two datasets are already available to and used by the electricity retailer for calculation of the load forecast today. In contrast, the usage data, both historical and current, needs to be more granular and dense compared to data available today (i.e. standardized load profiles). With the introduction of advanced communication infrastructures load profiles can be replaced by real-time usage data, which is retrieved regularly from the consumer.

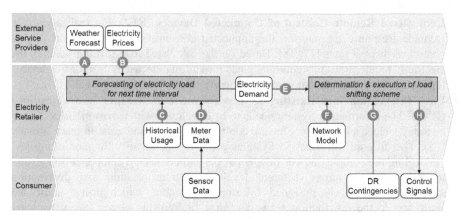

Fig. 2. Dynamic view of information flow in incentive-based Demand Response mechanisms

Load Shifting. If the load forecast algorithm detects a shortage in supply for the next optimization interval, a load shifting scheme needs to be calculated. There are three major variants of Demand Response mechanisms [19]: (i) incentive-based, (ii) rate-based, and (iii) consumer-induced. The different mechanisms entail different information requirements and communication protocols. We focus on incentive-based mechanisms in which consumer commit a-priori to electricity shifting and receive a monetary compensation in return as soon as a load shift took place. For calculating the optimal load shift the electricity retailer requires the projected electricity demand (E), the consumers' load contingencies (F) as well as the underlying network model (G). The electricity demand for the next optimization interval is retrieved as a result of the computed load forecast. The consumers regularly transmit their load contingencies and, thereby, communicate their maximum amount of shiftable power and maximum shift duration to the electricity retailer. The network model describes the detailed topology of the distribution network including the connected components and consumers. It is maintained within a repository of the electricity retailer. As soon as the electricity retailer has computed the optimal load shifting scheme, the required action is communicated towards the consumer. The consumer receives a series of control signals (H), which determine the shifting of electricity for the next optimization interval.

3.2 Designing the Information System

For developing the abstract, technology-independent system design, we rely on the synthetic level of Vahidov's framework [15]. As proposed by Hevner et al. [5], we utilize the knowledge base of reference disciplines and employ available frameworks, methods, and tools.

We start off with an evaluation of the current situation. Hence as a baseline model, we outline a typical Information System environment of today's electricity retailers on the distribution network level (e.g. [24]). The target model is being built on this baseline model and a series of available reference models. We proceed iteratively by starting from a generic view and refine the design towards a more specific solution.

The starting point is the Energy Informatics Framework [9], which provides the generic base structure of an Information System dealing with energy demand and supply. Watson et al. [9] divide an energy system into several building blocks: a central Information System, sensor networks, sensitized objects, flow networks, and related external stakeholders (cp. Fig. 3).

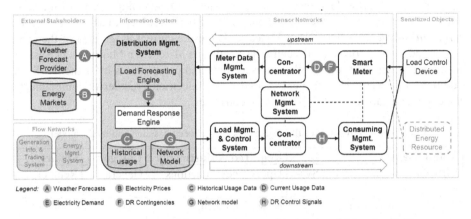

Fig. 3. System view on a Demand Response system with Advanced Metering Infrastructures based on Watson et al. [9], Simmhan et al. [17], Sui et al. [18] and Mohagheghi et al. [19]. Components of the baseline model are marked in gray.

We refine and reconfigure the Energy Informatics Framework based on the proposed architectures for Demand Response systems of Simmhan et al. [17], Sui et al. [18] and Mohagheghi et al. [19]. Furthermore, we consult reference architectures for Smart Metering infrastructures (e.g. [25, 26]).

For deriving the design characteristics of the Information System from the previously described requirements, we deploy the method of *quality function deployment* (QFD). We use an extended version of this method, which is adapted to the domain of IS [27]. This allows for matching requirements and solution proposals for Information Systems in a structured fashion. Moreover, the various design alternatives resp. reference architectures can be evaluated and compared with each other.

In the following paragraphs, we present an exemplary static view of the target model's Information System design, which corresponds to the category *structure* of Vahidov's framework. The overall Information System design is illustrated in Fig. 3.

The Distribution Management System (DMS) constitutes the core Information System in our setup. This type of Information System is already in operation at electricity retailers today. It features functionality for monitoring and controlling an entire distribution network [24]. Improving reliability and quality of service (e.g. reduction of outages, and maintaining frequency) are the key tasks of the DMS. The DMS communicates with external service providers, such as weather data providers and energy markets, via defined interfaces. Moreover, the DMS features interfaces for communication and data exchange with other neighboring parts of the power network (e.g. transportation network). For implementing Demand Response mechanisms, the DMS needs to be extended with a Demand Response Engine, which is responsible for computing the optimal load shifting scheme. The DMS is enhanced with a comprehensive communication infrastructure that needs to be established between the electricity retailer and the consumers. This setup of a real-time communication channel is essential for the implementation of a Demand Response mechanism. The communication path consists of two parts, namely an *upstream* and a *downstream* channel. The *upstream* channel transfers the current usage data and load contingencies of the consumer. This part contains the components that are being referred to as *Advanced Metering Infrastructures*. The Smart Meter reads out the current usage data of the consumer and sends it towards the central backend. The Meter Data Management System receives and aggregates the collected usage data and preprocesses it for the DMS. In addition, the *downstream* channel is used by the electricity retailer to communicate the control signals for load shifting to the consumer.

Table 1. Overview on results of gap analysis between baseline and target model

Component	Required Adjustments	Category	Owner
Distribution Management System (DMS)	Update, new functions	General	Retailer
Meter Data Management System (MDMS)	New component	AMI	Retailer
Concentrator	New component	AMI	Retailer
Smart Meter	New component	AMI	Retailer
Network Management System (NMS)	New component	AMI	Retailer
Load Management and Control System	New component	DR	Retailer
Consuming Management System	New component	DR	Retailer
Load Control Device	New component	DR	Consumer
External Interface: Weather Forecast Data	None	General	Retailer
External Interface: Electricity Prices	None	General	Retailer

Based on the defined baseline and target model, we have conducted a gap analysis to determine which adjustments and extension are required compared to today's Information Systems. The results are presented in Table 1.

3.3 Demonstrating Capability of the Information System

Based on the abstract Information System design, we have executed an exemplary instantiation of the Information System to gain first impressions on its capabilities and especially the cost structure. For the instantiation, we have defined the following setup that we used for conducting a computational simulation. As the implementation of Demand Response will be driven by electricity retailers, we assume an average

German electricity retailer serving 290,000 residents (i.e. 145,000 households) and 75,000 small industrial customers. These numbers correspond to around 220,000 smart meters that need to be connected to the distribution network. The remaining IS infrastructure is scaled accordingly.

3.4 Evaluating the Information System

In this section, we present a qualitative and quantitative evaluation of our proposed Information System design for implementing Demand Response mechanisms. Our evaluation effort is based on methods described in [5, 28]. We carry out both ex-ante (i.e. evaluation of the design) as well as ex-post (i.e. evaluation of an instantiation) assessments [28].

Functional Requirements [RF1 and RF2]. The evaluation of compliance and coverage of the proposed Information System design with the defined functional requirements is rather difficult on the level of abstraction that we have described in this paper. Nonetheless, we employed the QFD method to ensure a preferably high coverage of the defined requirements by the technical product specifications [27]. We applied the QFD method iteratively for increasing the level of detail of the resulting IS artifact. For example, for determination of the optimal transmission medium, we started off with comparing the various network types (cp. Fig. 4).

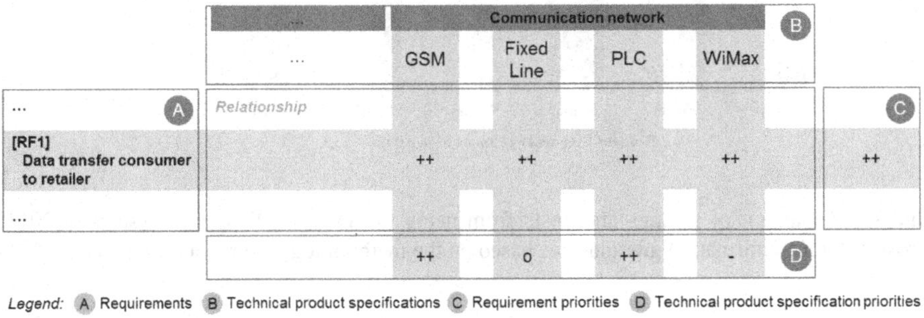

		Communication network				B
	...	GSM	Fixed Line	PLC	WiMax	
... (A)	Relationship					(C)
[RF1] Data transfer consumer to retailer		++	++	++	++	++
...						
		++	o	++	-	(D)

Legend: (A) Requirements (B) Technical product specifications (C) Requirement priorities (D) Technical product specification priorities

Fig. 4. Extract of the relationship matrix, which is the result of the first iteration of the quality function deployment method. Here, the relationship matrix illustrates the fit of certain communication technologies to a certain functional requirement in form of a rating (e.g. "++").

In a second iteration, we employed the QFD method to drill down into the communication network design. Therefore, we opposed the chosen transmission media, namely GSM and PLC, with a number of available reference models (e.g. [10]) in a relationship matrix to decide on the IS design. We conducted this method for the remaining requirements analogously. Summing up, we can assume that our Information System design fulfills the defined functional requirements.

Easy Integration into Existing IT Environment of Retailer and Consumer [RN1]. We try to minimize the integration effort by employing a brownfield approach. Thereby, the current IS environment is being defined as baseline model and, thus, it is being used as a basis for development of the target model.

Openness to Implementation of Other Use Cases [RN2]. Our Information System design is based on the reference model of Advanced Metering Infrastructures (cp. Section 3.2). In doing so, we ensure that additional use cases, which are built upon an Advanced Metering Infrastructure, can also be realized by using the proposed Information System design. In addition, the collected usage data is being stored in a repository within the central Information System, namely the DMS, which allows an easy, yet secure, access by other applications.

Cost Effectiveness [RN3]. We show that the designed Demand Response system works cost effectively (cf. Feuerriegel et al. [13] for details). Therefore, we calculate both costs and savings from using a DR mechanism using real-world data (cp. detailed description of simulation environment in Section 3.3). The individual cost components are given in Fig. 5. By varying the frequency of collecting usage data from the meters, we have designed four scenarios to evaluate our model across different information granularities. In short, we gain a positive annual surplus in the first scenario (60 minute intervals), but this negates with higher information granularities where the operating costs exceed the savings.

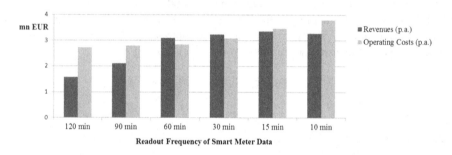

Fig. 5. Comparison of savings and costs from using the Demand Response system in 2011 across different information granularities based on the methodology from Feuerriegel et al. [13]

4   Revisiting the Design Science Approach

We look at the design science paradigm from two angles: First, we review the design science guidelines and check to what extent we have obeyed them. Second, we reflect how the design science approach supported us during the design process, and we discuss what we have learnt from our experiences.

4.1   Reviewing the Design Science Guidelines

The problem we tackled in our research was to develop a Demand Response system using a design science approach. Hevner et al. [5] states that *"in design science paradigm, knowledge and understanding of a problem domain and its solution are achieved in the building and application of the designed artifact"*. The successful application of design science research can be evaluated by examining the seven guidelines for good design science research by Hevner et al. [5]. In addition to that, we follow the suggestions by Brocke and Seidel [29] to consider the relevance of our research in matters of environmental sustainability for each guideline:

- **Problem Relevance.** The amount of interest and research (cp. Section 2) regarding the transition to the smart grid attests to the transition's relevance. Many countries face this transition as a major challenge (so-called *"Energiewende"*) to reduce electricity consumption and production. Without doubt, the energy transition is related to environmental sustainability.
- **Research Rigor.** Design science research relies on the application of rigorous methods for both the construction and for the evaluation of the design artifact. Our architectural design is based on the Energy Informatics Framework by Watson et al. [9]; the cost side is constituted in a mathematical model incorporating the components of the system; the realized savings are modeled through a linear optimization problem.
- **Design as a Search Process.** Implementation and iteration are central to design science research. We studied prototypes that, based on previous work from literature, instantiate posed or newly-learnt design prescriptions. Their use and impacts were observed, problems identified, solutions posed and implemented, and the cycle was then repeated until the status quo is acquired.
- **Design as an Artifact.** Design science research must produce a viable artifact in the form of e.g. a model; therefore we presented an architectural design for a Demand Response system in Section 3.2. According to Brocke and Seidel [29], this design artifact must contribute to the implementation of sustainable business processes. In fact, when implemented by an electricity retailer, this artifact can significantly contribute to environmental sustainability [12].
- **Design Evaluation.** The evaluation (cp. Sections 3.3 and 3.4) consists of a thorough review of the previously stated requirements. Although our model suggests that an average electricity retailer faces huge initial setup costs, we provide evidence that savings from load shifting exceed the running costs of the Information System significantly – by more than € 2 million per year. These savings ensure that the design artifact contributes to environmental sustainability as proposed by Brocke and Seidel [29].
- **Research Contributions.** The major contributions of this research are the proposed architecture for a DR system as the design artifact and the evaluation results in the form of real-world scenarios to gauge both costs and savings. These contributions advance our understanding of how Demand Response can help in the transition to the smart grid. As stated in Brocke and Seidel [29], this guarantees that our contributions are clear and verifiable.
- **Communication of Research.** In addition to the previously described design science process, Peffers et al. [14] outline a supplemental, final process step, namely communication. We address this demand by publishing this paper and additional versions (e.g. [13]) that also contain useful information for managerial audience (i.e. how Demand Response can be integrated as a business model). However, we must ensure that the results will be more accessible to an audience from energy

research in the future. On top of that, we showed how design science can be applied in practice in IS research and we presented our experience from using a design science approach.

4.2   Reflections on Design Science

Our experiences from designing the above Demand Response system have brought forth a number of practical concerns. The most important findings are listed below:

- It is difficult to plan design science research in advance. Our primary focus was on the financial benefits from using Demand Response mechanisms. However, we found out – during a later iteration – that both acquisition and operation of the corresponding infrastructure is tied to significant financial costs. Here, design science research with its iterative solving process allowed us to adjust and refine the focus of our research in an unconventional manner.
- While evaluating the quality of a design, we restricted our analysis not only to the requirements itself, but we also utilized the general guidelines [5] for reviewing the design process. As these guidelines are general in nature, we employed additional criteria [29–31] in our internal evaluation process to test each model against the requirements. In addition to that, we noticed the value of real-world simulations for evaluating design artifacts.
- However, we missed a standardized procedure to approach a design science problem for developing an Information System. Though guidelines and evaluation criteria assist to identify the necessary design steps, the steps themselves are unclear or ambiguous. This view is shared by various researchers (e.g. [32]) who point out the lack of a toolbox applicable to IS design. For us, this became particularly evident during translation of the requirements into a concrete system design draft. The UML toolkit does offer a help, although not completely as it does not provide full constructive support as required. Current IS research tries to close this gap (e.g. [33]). However, the IS community is still far away from the set of methods, which is available in e.g. the engineering domain (cp. [34]). All in all, we think that we could have benefited from support granted by tailored tools for representing IS artifacts.

Reflecting on our experience in designing the Demand Response system, we appreciate design science research as it assisted us in the search process to discover an effective solution to our problem.

5   Conclusion and Outlook

The challenge was to design a Demand Response system. We developed an IS artifact that enables electricity retailers to shift power demand and addressed this problem by using the well-known design science research approach. This approach encompasses successive steps of determining requirements including the required information demand and flow, designing a suitable Information System, demonstrating its capability and, finally, evaluating the design before advancing the next iteration of the design process.

Our IS artifact illustrates the electricity retailer's required infrastructure. For making a Demand Response mechanism work, substantial implementation effort is required on the consumers' premises as well. The consumers need to install both a powerful home area network (HAN) and devices that allow for remote control. In future work, we will focus on this consumer perspective to create a view of the overall system requirements and costs for implementing a Demand Response mechanism.

References

1. Palensky, P., Dietrich, D.: Demand Side Management: Demand Response, Intelligent Energy Systems, and Smart Loads. IEEE Trans. Ind. Inf. 7(3), 381–388 (2011)
2. U.S. Department of Energy: Benefits of Demand Response in Electricity Markets and Recommendations for Achieving Them. A Report to the Unit States Congress Pursuant to Section 1252 of the Energy Policy Act of 2005 (2006)
3. Federal Energy Regulatory Commission (FEDC): Assessment of Demand Response and Advanced Metering (2006)
4. Melville, N.P.: Information systems innovation for environmental sustainability. MIS Quarterly 34(1), 1–21 (2010)
5. Hevner, A.R., March, S.T., Park, J., Ram, S.: Design science in information systems research. MIS Quarterly 28(1), 75–105 (2004)
6. Simon, H.A.: The Sciences of the Artificial, 3rd edn. MIT Press, Cambridge (1996)
7. Strüker, J., van Dinther, C.: Demand Response in Smart Grids: Research Opportunities for the IS Discipline. In: Proceedings of 18th Americas Conference on Information Systems (2012)
8. Corbett, J.: Demand Management in the Smart Grid: An Information Processing Perspective. In: Proceedings of 17th Americas Conference on Information Systems (2011)
9. Watson, R.T., Boudreau, M.-C., Chen, A.J.: Information Systems and Environmentally Sustainable Development: Energy Informatics and New Directions for the IS-Community. MIS Quarterly 34(1), 23–36 (2010)
10. Tan, X., Shan, B., Hu, Z., Wu, S.: Study on Demand Side Management Decision Supporting System. In: 3rd Int. Conference on Software Engineering and Service Science, pp. 111–114 (2012)
11. Law, Y.W., Alpcan, T., Lee, V.C., Lo, A., et al.: Demand Response Architectures and Load Management Algorithms for Energy-Efficient Power Grids: A Survey. In: 2012 7th International Conference on Knowledge, Information and Creativity Support Systems (KICSS), pp. 134–141 (2012)
12. Feuerriegel, S., Strüker, J., Neumann, D.: Reducing Price Uncertainty Through Demand Side Management. In: George, J.F. (ed.) Proceedings of 33rd International Conference on Information Systems (ICIS). Association for Information Systems, Atlanta (2012)
13. Feuerriegel, S., Bodenbenner, P., Neumann, D.: Is More Information Better than Less? Understanding the Impact of Demand Response Mechanisms in Energy Markets. In: 21st European Conference on Information Systems (forthcoming, 2013)

14. Peffers, K., Tuunanen, T., Rothenberger, M.A., Chatterjee, S.: A Design Science Research Methodology for Information Systems Research. Journal of Management Information Systems 24(3), 45–77 (2007)
15. Vahidov, R.: Design Researcher's IS Artifact: a Representational Framework. In: International Conference on Design Science Research in Information Systems and Technology, Claremont, CA (2006)
16. Ziekow, H., Strüker, J., Goebel, C.: The Potential of Smart Home Sensors in Forecasting Household Electricity Demand. Working Paper. University of Freiburg (2012)
17. Simmhan, Y., Aman, S., Cao, B., Giakkoupis, M., et al.: An Informatics Approach to Demand Response Optimization in Smart Grids. University of Southern California
18. Sui, H., Sun, Y., Lee, W.-J.: A Demand Side Management Model Based on Advanced Metering Infrastructure. In: 4th International Conference on Electric Utility Deregulation and Restructuring and Power Technologies (DRPT), pp. 1586–1589 (2011)
19. Mohagheghi, S., Stoupis, J., Wang, Z., Li, Z., et al.: Demand Response Architecture. Integration into the Distribution Management System (2010)
20. Li, Z., Wang, Z., Tournier, J.-C., Peterson, W., et al.: A Unified Solution for Advanced Metering Infrastructure Integration with a Distribution Management System. In: 2010 First IEEE International Conference on Smart Grid Communications (SmartGridComm), pp. 501–506. IEEE (2010)
21. Faruqui, A., Harris, D., Hledik, R.: Unlocking the €53 billion savings from smart meters in the EU: How increasing the adoption of dynamic tariffs could make or break the EU's smart grid investment. Energy Policy 38(10), 6222–6231 (2010)
22. Object Management Group (OMG): OMG Unified Modeling Language, http://www.omg.org/spec/UML/2.5 (accessed Ferbuary 14, 2013)
23. European Energy Exchange (EEX): Market Data, http://www.eex.com/en/Market%20Data (accessed May 02, 2012)
24. Cassel, W.: Distribution management systems: functions and payback. IEEE Trans. Power Syst. 8(3), 796–801 (1993)
25. European Telecommunications Standards Institute (ETSI): Final Report on Standards for Smart Grids (2011)
26. OPEN Meter - D3.1 Design of the Overall System Architecture (2010)
27. Haag, S., Raja, M.K., Schkade, L.L.: Quality function deployment usage in software development. Commun. ACM 39(1), 41–49 (1996)
28. Venable, J., Pries-Heje, J., Baskerville, R.: A Comprehensive Framework for Evaluation in Design Science Research. In: Peffers, K., Rothenberger, M., Kuechler, B., et al. (eds.) DESRIST 2012. LNCS, vol. 7286, pp. 423–438. Springer, Heidelberg (2012)
29. vom Brocke, J., Seidel, S.: Environmental Sustainability in Design Science Research: Direct and Indirect Effects of Design Artifacts. In: Peffers, K., Rothenberger, M., Kuechler, B., et al. (eds.) DESRIST 2012. LNCS, vol. 7286, pp. 294–308. Springer, Heidelberg (2012)
30. March, S.T., Smith, G.F.: Design and natural science research on information technology. Decision Support Systems 15(4), 251–266 (1995)
31. Sonnenberg, C., vom Brocke, J.: Evaluations in the science of the artificial – reconsidering the build-evaluate pattern in design science research. In: Peffers, K., Rothenberger, M., Kuechler, B. (eds.) DESRIST 2012. LNCS, vol. 7286, pp. 381–397. Springer, Heidelberg (2012)

32. Offermann, P., Levina, O., Schönherr, M., Bub, U.: Outline of a Design Science Research Process. In: Proceedings of the 4th International Conference on Design Science Research in Information Systems and Technology. ACM, New York (2009)
33. Dromey, R.: From requirements to design: formalizing the key steps. In: Proceedings of First International Conference on Software Engineering and Formal Methods 2003, pp. 2–11. IEEE (2003)
34. Pahl, G., Beitz, W.: Engineering design. A systematic approach. Springer, London (1996)

A Decision Support Tool to Define Scope in IT Service Management Process Assessment and Improvement

Anup Shrestha, Aileen Cater-Steel, Mark Toleman, and Wui-Gee Tan

University of Southern Queensland , School of Information Systems,
Faculty of Business & Law, Toowoomba, Australia
{anup.shrestha,aileen.cater-steel,mark.toleman,
wui-gee.tan}@usq.edu.au

Abstract. Improvements in managing IT service management (ITSM) processes are continuously sought by IT organisations. However, resources are limited and the choice of processes for improvement is a critical decision point for the managers. In this paper, we report a process selection decision model developed with task-technology fit theory as the lens as the basis for our Design Science Research approach. The model is instantiated with an outcome of a decision support tool. The process selection decision model uses service perception factors from the Service Quality (SERV-QUAL) model and business drivers from the Balanced Scorecard (BSC) perspectives to ensure that the ITSM processes are prioritised based on the key business drivers that have the highest impact on the business. Responses to a service perception survey provided by the business stakeholders combined with workshops guided the tool development as did considering the BSC perspectives with business drivers rather than ITSM processes being ranked directly by stakeholder participants. Usefulness of the tool is then demonstrated in a case organisation. The main contribution of the study is to provide evidence-based decision support for IT service providers to select the most relevant service processes to improve. Future research includes longitudinal evaluation of the tool's output advice and the tool's use in other organisations.

Keywords: IT service management, decision support tool, design science research method, Balanced Scorecard, service quality, task-technology fit theory.

1 Introduction

The importance of process improvement in ITSM is clearly evident from the fact that the *de facto* ITSM framework, the Information Technology Infrastructure Library (ITIL®), has an entire volume dedicated to process-based continual service improvement [1]. Process improvement is also a requirement of the service management system in the international standard for ITSM ISO/IEC 20000 [2].

Maturity models can be used to target capability levels for improvement, for example the standard CMMI appraisal method for process improvement (SCAMPI) [3] and the measurement framework defined in the international standard for process

J. vom Brocke et al. (Eds.): DESRIST 2013, LNCS 7939, pp. 308–323, 2013.

assessment ISO/IEC 15504 [4]. A popular process assessment framework that combines ITIL and ISO/IEC 15504, Tudor's IT Process Assessment (TIPA) [5] suggests selecting ITSM processes to determine the scope of process assessments. While these models suggest the need to select the important ITSM processes to define a scope in ITSM process assessment, there is a lack of implementation guidelines on target processes to improve. Organisations seldom have budget, time, resources or requirements to assess all processes for improvement in a single project. Selecting the right processes to improve is therefore a crucial decision [6].

The problem identified provides motivation to develop an IT artefact as a decision support tool to help select ITSM processes for improvement. The objective of this paper is to describe the development of the artefact. The methodology that fits the proposed research approach is Design Science Research (DSR) [7]. We follow the six DSR Methodology (DSRM) steps suggested by Peffers et al. [8]: problem identification and motivation, objectives of a solution, design and development, demonstration, evaluation, and communication. We develop a decision support tool that provides evidence-based support in selecting IT service processes for assessment and improvement. The proposed tool can assist IT service managers when deciding on the scope of service improvement projects by providing a list of the processes that have the highest impact on business and that are perceived by key stakeholders as most important to improve.

This paper is structured as follows. In the literature review section, we explain how the task-technology fit (TTF) theory [9] integrates with the DSRM steps of our research project. We present the related work on the available guidelines for process selection and verify the rigour-relevance balance of the problem statement [10, 11]. The objectives of the proposed solution are then explained with the current business drivers and the service perception factors. The DSRM is then explained with sections on the artefact design and development, demonstration and evaluation. Finally the conclusion section provides the limitations and implications of the research and an agenda for future work.

2   Literature Review

Gregor [12] provides a taxonomy of five sets of theory in the field of Information Systems (IS): theory for analysing, theory for explaining, theory for predicting, theory for explaining and predicting, and theory for design and action. The fifth set, "theory for design and action" is essentially the output of design science research. The precise nature and role of theory in DSR is an evolving concept but the core of a DSR project is the development and evaluation of an IT artefact in the form of constructs, models, methods or instantiations [13]. Hevner et al. [7] support this centrality of the IT artefact in DSR projects to solve organizational problems. Theories can provide foundations to exert rigour in developing the artefact. Kernel theories are already established theories that are used in DSR projects to both inform and justify the steps of DSR [14, 15]. We present the TTF theory [9] as the kernel theory in our research to advise how the task requirements and technology characteristics fit together to articulate the artefact development and to demonstrate its utility. We integrate TTF with our design method and use it to explain the development of the artefact.

2.1 Task-Technology Fit and DSRM Phases

TTF theory holds that IT is more likely to have a positive impact on individual performance and be used if the capabilities of the IT match the tasks that the user must perform [9]. TTF deviates from self-reported user evaluations and looks at the "fit" between the technology features and the task requirements to be supported by the technology in the organisation [16]. While Goodhue and Thompson [9] developed TTF to examine the fit and its impact on individual performance, Zigurs and Buckland [17] verified the fit for the effectiveness of group support systems. Since then the theory has been applied to a diverse range of information systems. Fuller and Dennis [18] suggest while TTF theory predicts performance during first use of technology, it does not cater for performance as a result of repetitive tasks over time. The context of technology use in our project is to facilitate the selection of relevant ITSM processes in ITSM improvement projects. While improvement projects themselves tend to have repetitive and interactive tasks, defining the scope to select processes for improvement is a relatively isolated task and hence TTF theory provides a useful lens to study the use of technology to select processes.

The constructs of the TTF theory are operationalised from two aspects: context and process. In the context of the development of the decision support tool, we look at the requirements to make informed choice about selecting ITSM processes for improvements (*task requirements* from the problem space) and the features of the tool (*technology features* from the solution space). The solution space provides pointers to address the problem space using utility theories [15]. The utility theory here is represented by the *fit profile* which creates the "design" i.e. the ITSM process selection decision model. This is followed by the instantiation of the model to develop a decision support tool (the IT artefact) that prioritises the ITSM processes based on business drivers and service perception. Finally a case study is used to evaluate the usefulness of the tool in an organisation (*technology utility*) and eventually confirm whether using the tool has indeed contributed in defining a scope for ITSM process assessment and improvement (*performance improvements*).

TTF can be operationalised in terms of the research process mapped to the DSRM process model [8]. We deal with a decision task to define scope in ITSM process assessment and improvement by selecting processes that are relevant to the business and considered important by the stakeholders. This *task requirement* represents the first DSRM phase of *problem identification and motivation*.

Likewise, the three technology dimensions for Group Support Systems: communication support, process structuring and information processing proposed by Zigurs and Buckland [17] are applicable to the proposed decision support tool. The tool enables *communication* among all stakeholders to understand service perception factors. From the *process structuring* dimension, the tool facilitates a workflow of (a) understanding service perception, (b) selecting business drivers and (c) mapping business drivers and service perception to ITSM processes. Finally the tool uses a scoring metric to determine ranks for ITSM processes (*information processing* dimension). The second DSRM phase: ***objectives of a solution*** can therefore be defined by the three dimensions of the ***technology features*** proposed for the solution.

Ultimately the alignment between the task and technology is represented with an ideal fit profile that results in the design of the ITSM process selection decision model. The instantiation of the model is the resultant IT artefact, i.e. a decision support tool based on the model. The process of building the *fit profile* aligns with the ***design and development*** phase of DSRM. Similarly, a ***case study*** is conducted (***demonstration*** phase of DSRM) to determine the ***utility*** of the tool and to test the service improvement effects (***performance***) based on task-technology alignments (***evaluation*** phase of DSRM). Figure 1 demonstrates the mapping between the DSRM phases and the TTF theory in the context of our research.

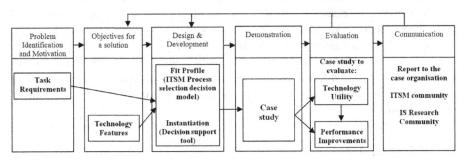

Fig. 1. Mapping of the DSRM phases and the TTF theory (adapted from [8] and [9])

2.2   Existing Studies on Process Selection for Improvement

A priori understanding and anecdotal observations of process improvement initiatives suggest that the processes that are selected for improvement should have the highest impact on business and be perceived by stakeholders as most in need of improvement. Many guidelines have been proposed based on this notion but decisions regarding which processes to choose for improvement have generally been complex [19] with little structure in the decision making process. At most, organisations tend to develop a checklist of factors to consider while selecting processes or ideal attributes of processes for improvement [20].

Firstly we discuss existing guidelines in the ITSM domain. Barafort et al. [21] suggest conducting pre-assessments to simplify process selection and experiment with Porter and Miller's Value Chain diagram [22] to identify the critical core processes that support business objectives. Hilbert and Renault [23] also provide an example of selecting processes aligned to the organisational strategic goals. Huxley [24] developed a ten-step targeted methodology to determine processes that are most critical. While these studies provide the linkage of business objectives to justify relevant process selection, they fail to incorporate the service perceptions of key stakeholders.

There are several business process management guidelines for selecting processes for improvement. The US Department of the Navy provided a handbook for basic process improvement [20] including a process selection worksheet that incorporates customer expectations and key attributes of processes that are ideal for inclusion. Hammer and Champy [25] suggested three attributes that make processes ideal for selection: dysfunctional (most problematic), important (highest impact), and feasible (likely to succeed). Likewise, Davenport and Short [26] suggested considering "redesign urgency" or "high-impact" to select important processes for redesign. Zellner et al. [27] posit a four-step approach in selecting critical processes for Six-Sigma projects: identify customer types and initial candidates for critical processes; analyse consistency of evaluation factors for selection; cross-check processes with evaluation factors; and finally prioritise processes based on the Analytical Hierarchy Process technique [28]. A similar four-step methodology has been proposed by Meade and Rogers [19]. These studies examined ideal process attributes for improvement or factors that associate processes with business goals. However for the ITSM model with its strong customer-oriented focus, it is risky to ignore how service beneficiaries and process performers alike prioritise the processes that need improvement. Moreover, there is a lack of a formal process selection methodology that can be implemented to select processes in ITSM. The IT service industry is seeking a structured process selection method with evidence-based decision support to effectively choose the key processes that are both critical to business objectives and perceived as important by key stakeholders.

3   Methodology

In our research, the objectives of the proposed solution in developing the artefact are twofold: (a) to determine the current business drivers that have the greatest impact on business; and (b) to obtain key stakeholders' perceptions of priorities in improving IT service processes. To achieve these two objectives, the decision support tool prioritises the ITSM processes for improvement in terms of two perspectives: business drivers and service perceptions. The Balanced Scorecard (BSC) [29] is used to identify the business drivers and the service quality model (SERV-QUAL) [30] is used to identify service perception factors. The use of these models in the tool is intended to ensure that the ITSM processes are prioritised based on the key business drivers that have the highest impact on the business and are endorsed by key stakeholders.

4   Design and Development of the Decision Support Tool

Based on the BSC perspectives and the SERV-QUAL model, we designed our model as shown in Figure 2 to prioritise ITSM processes for improvement based on the current business goals of the organisation and service perception of key stakeholders. The preliminary work on the development of the initial model of the tool has been previously reported [31]. Inputs comprise the current ITSM processes in the organisation, service perception factors and current business drivers. These three inputs are analysed to produce the final output: a list of prioritised ITSM processes for IT service improvement.

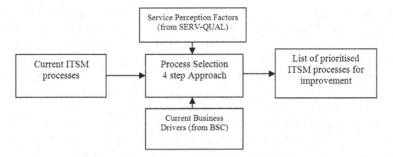

Fig. 2. ITSM Process Selection Decision Model

4.1 The Balanced Scorecard to Identify Business Drivers

We believe that the link between IT service processes and business objectives can be better explained with the concept of the BSC developed by Kaplan and Norton [29]. While other frameworks such as value chain analysis, cost/benefit analysis, critical success factors and risk assessments can also determine important processes that have the most crucial business impact, the choice of the BSC presents a more "balanced" analysis of organisations on a strategic level from four key perspectives: financial; customer; internal business; and innovation and learning [29]. Furthermore, the concept of BSC is well accepted in business as a core management tool [32].

Although the BSC is an overall strategic performance management tool, using this tool comprises breaking down business goals into objectives and specific performance measures at different levels of detail throughout the organisation. The evaluation of important performance measures, also known as "key performance indicators" in various versions of the BSC, answers the question "what is important to the business?" Such performance indicators that drive business forward are valuable intellectual capital of any organisation [33]. "Key performance indicators" and "business drivers" are often used interchangeably but we refer to the latter in our research to reinforce their impact on the performance of the business rather than the indication of performance measurement.

4.2 The Service Quality Model to Determine Service Perception Factors

Even though the customer perspective of the BSC produces business drivers to align IT service processes to business goals, the approach ignores the perception of the key stakeholders of IT services. In order to query key stakeholders in regards to their perception of quality service, we propose a service perception survey as an effective method. We refer to the SERV-QUAL model proposed by Parasuraman et al. [30] to organise our understanding of service perception factors.

The concept of service quality and its subsequent models originated from the marketing discipline. Based on Grönroos [34], there are three dimensions of service quality: *technical quality* refers to the outcome of the service; *functional quality* constitute the process of the service provision; and the corporate *image* built upon the technical and functional qualities. Since our research is concerned with the IT service processes, we are concerned with the functional quality aspects that are proven to work well when measured using the SERV-QUAL model [35]. In the context of IS however, the use of SERV-QUAL has attracted a deal of criticism [36, 37]. The objective of using the SERV-QUAL model in our research is not for measuring service quality but for gap analysis to determine service perception factors that shape stakeholders' understanding of their role and preferences in executing IT service processes. On this basis we determine that the SERV-QUAL model can provide an understanding of the service gap to determine service perception factors. Understanding the service gap can assist all key stakeholders to have a consistent and coherent view of their role and ultimately shape service perceptions that contribute to process selection.

4.3   Design of the Model for the Decision Support Tool

Our proposed process selection decision model includes four steps to prioritise the ITSM processes for service improvement: (i) service perception understanding, (ii) service perception confirmation, (iii) selection of business drivers, and (iv) selection of ITSM processes for improvement. Quantitative and qualitative methods are used to collect and analyse the inputs to the model and produce the intended output. The current portfolio of ITSM processes in the IT organisation is the unit of analysis. Steps (i) and (ii) provide service perception input while step (iii) comprises business driver input. Step (iv) then facilitates the output of the model. The workflow of ITSM process selection is illustrated in Figure 3.

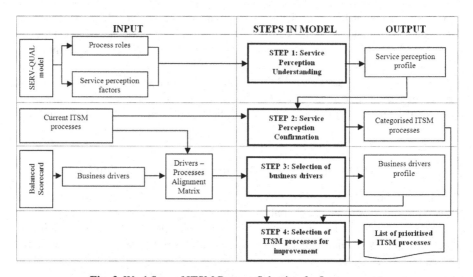

Fig. 3. Workflow of ITSM Process Selection for Improvement

(i) Service Perception Understanding. To begin, it is necessary that the key stakeholders of the IT services understand their role in the IT organisation. A service perception survey can be developed and conducted across the stakeholders to determine what they perceive in regards to their understanding of IT service provision. Based on the SERV-QUAL model for gap analysis, we firstly identified three distinct stakeholder groups related to IT service provision: service beneficiary (customers); service provider management (process managers); and service provider workforce (process performers). We call them "process roles".

We analysed the five service gaps regarding service quality perception proposed by Parasuraman et al. [30] in their SERVQUAL model to determine service perception factors. Gap 1, 2 and 5 from the SERVQUAL model dealt with expectation-perception gap between and among customers and service providers. Gap 3 was the deviation of the actual service delivery from the expected service. Likewise, Gap 4 dealt with communication issues. We therefore grouped the five service gaps in three major themes: expectation – perception gap; expectation – delivery gap; and communication gap. To address these three service gaps, we identified the three most common general factors in the ITSM model that underpin the service perception of stakeholders: value proposition; degree of confidence; and better communication. We then derive a total of nine specific service perception factors from the identified service gaps as listed in Table 1. A service perception survey is generated with questions for each of the identified service perception factors.

Table 1. Mapping of nine service perception factors to three ITSM service gaps

Service gaps (Problem Space)	General Perception factors (Solution Space)	Perspective	Service perception factors
Expectation – Perception Gap	Value proposition	Increasing benefits Decreasing costs Better partnership	Meeting expectations Budget spend effectiveness Importance as a partner
Expectation – Delivery Gap	Degree of confidence	Customer Staff Supplier	Customer focus Staff morale Supplier confidence
Communication gap (external and internal)	Better communication	Channel Understanding Knowledge	Communication channels Business understanding Process awareness

After conducting the service perception survey, the responses produce a consolidated service perception profile. The service perception profile provides an understanding of current service provision as perceived by key stakeholders and allows contrasts between the different stakeholders' views to highlight misalignment between the provider (management and staff) and receiver of services. No consideration of ITSM processes is made in this step since it relates only to high-level service perceptions. The reason to conduct this survey is to discuss the service perception profile with the stakeholders to help shape their overall understanding of service provision. This step will help the stakeholders to confirm their workshop responses in step (ii).

(ii) Service Perception Confirmation. After producing the service perception profile, an analysis is performed of the consistency of responses from different process roles. A workshop is organised with the key stakeholders to (a) confirm the service perception profile from step (i); and (b) categorise the processes based on their perceived importance to the business.

In this step, the service perception survey results are reviewed with the workshop attendees to obtain a full consensus. Since the workshop attendees comprising service provider management (process managers) would have completed the perception survey in step (i), this gives them an opportunity to revisit their understanding and compare and contrast with other stakeholder groups. This review is an important step for service managers to obtain an overall understanding of the service perception not only from their perspective but with insights from the customers and staff they manage. Such triangulation facilitates validation of data through cross-checking from three stakeholder group sources thereby promoting reliability and validity to determine regularities in service perceptions [38]. Finally, all workshop attendees are asked to allocate each of the current ITSM processes into one of five pre-defined categories in terms of their relative importance (critical, high importance, moderate importance, low importance and not important process categories) and a final consensus is reached on the categories.

(iii) Selection of Business Drivers. Using the ITSM concept that processes support the provision of services and these services support the business objectives and goals, we researched typical drivers across a variety of market sectors using different variants of the BSC [29] to generate a list of relevant business drivers for IT services. The business drivers are associated with IT service processes to assess the impact of the processes on the business goals – thus providing a measure to determine which processes are more important. We propose that the Customer perspective of the BSC can be split into Internal and External Customers to recognise that IT service providers generally deliver both internal- and external-facing services. This provides greater granularity in identifying the typical business drivers. A list of 25 business drivers was identified from the five perspectives of the BSC as illustrated in Figure 4.

After defining the common business drivers that underpin service management improvements we constructed a matrix that relates each of the drivers to the current ITSM processes in order to rank the processes that offer the greatest value in supporting each driver. This was done by cross referencing each process purpose and goals (derived from the ITIL framework and ITSM international standard ISO/IEC 20000) with each driver. A three-point rating scale was used with the score of one for low, two for medium and three for high importance of the process in contributing to the business driver. In order to finalise the list of business drivers and its mapping to ITSM processes, a Delphi technique in three rounds was applied. Input was received from five expert ITSM consultants with ITIL Expert level qualifications and a collective experience of 60 years within ITSM. A Delphi study is relevant in this context since it is a more democratic, inclusive and scientific method for development and evaluation of conceptual models [39].

A driver ranking survey is then conducted to shortlist the key business drivers from the list. This survey comprises two exercises: a ranking technique to shortlist ten important business drivers from the initial list of 25 business drivers; and a pairwise comparison technique widely applied in the Analytic Hierarchy Process [28] to compare the ten business drivers and produce the top five.

The reason for a driver ranking survey rather than ranking ITSM processes directly is that most managers struggle to comprehend their business in terms of processes [26] while business drivers derived from the BSC can provide a better alignment of process improvement initiatives with the business goals in mind.

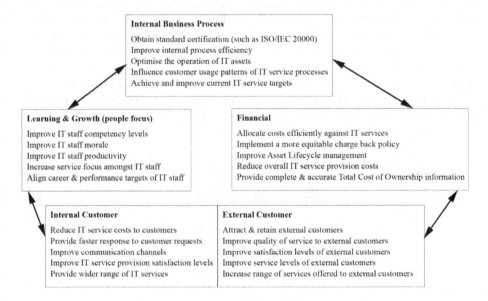

Fig. 4. BSC perspectives of 25 business drivers

(iv) Selection of ITSM Processes for Improvement. For each of the current ITSM processes, a weighting and summing activity yields the overall process score. The weights of the five business drivers are summed to calculate the process score. The maximum score possible for each process is 15 (i.e. score of 3 for all 5 drivers) and the minimum is 5 (i.e. 1 for each driver). Using this score and the score derived from the category of the process (1 to 5) from step (ii), a final process rank is derived for each process and then the prioritised list of processes is produced. This list of prioritised processes is ranked from the input of both business drivers (provided by driver ranking) and service perception (provided by process category). Hence, the ranking of the processes in terms of their importance for improvement is justified from the key stakeholders' service perceptions of improvement and the process's impact on the business goals. Finally, presentation of this prioritised ITSM process list provides an indication to the service improvement managers of which processes they should consider selecting for improvement.

4.4　Development of the Decision Support Tool

The steps discussed in section 4.3 regarding the design of the model for decision support tool are automated in the decision support tool developed as the IT artefact of the DSR project. The tool facilitates online surveys for service perception (step i); organises workshops to categorise processes (step ii); conducts online surveys for voting and pairwise comparison of business drivers (step iii); and calculates process scores to obtain the final prioritised ITSM process list for ITIL processes (step iv). The tool is developed in partnership with our industry research partner who provided us the software platform to implement our model. The online tool is developed using the Microsoft Azure® cloud platform [40] with features to automate online survey tracking and a facilitator console to manage the surveys and workshops. The tool also performs calculations of the process scores from the business drivers and service perception factors to generate the prioritised ITSM process list. Figure 5 is a screenshot of the decision support tool. This screenshot illustrates that a total of 26 ITIL processes are considered and categorised based on the perception workshop using the decision support tool.

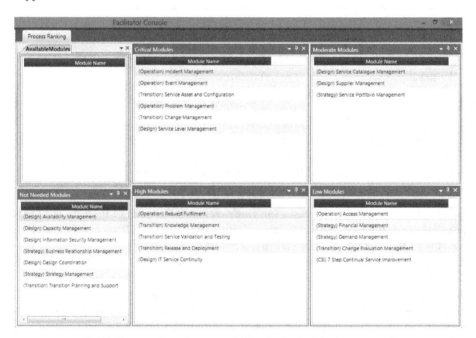

Fig. 5. A screenshot of process ranking in the decision support tool

5　Demonstration of the Decision Support Tool

We implemented the tool at one of our industry research partners: the IT service centre of Toowoomba Regional Council, a large local government authority in South Queensland region of Australia with over 50 IT staff servicing over 150,000 residents.

The online service perception survey was followed by the perception workshop and then the driver ranking survey. After the prioritised ITSM process list was generated by the software tool, it was presented to the organisation. The IT service managers selected six critical processes to define a scope of their ITSM improvement project: incident management, event management, service asset and configuration management, problem management, change management and service level management.

6   Evaluation of the Decision Support Tool

In order to conduct a thorough evaluation, we organise our work based on the framework of Pries-Heje et al. [41]. The use of established frameworks such as the BSC and SERV-QUAL models justifies the design of the artefact. This is an *ex-ante* artificial setting evaluation that continuously took place during the design process with several iterations of updates [42].

Moreover, we obtained the experience feedback from the workshop participants on the utility of the artefact (*technology utility* of TTF) and whether they agree with the final prioritised ITSM process list suggested by the tool (perception of *performance improvements*) using a post-implementation interview for qualitative analysis of the artefact. This evaluation has an *ex post* orientation as we evaluate our artefact after demonstration and lies in a naturalistic setting because the artefact is evaluated to determine its performance impacts on improvements in the real world scenario. This evaluation also confirms the service improvement effects of task-technology alignments.

The feedback from the service managers at the case organisation has been extremely positive on the utility of the tool and on their perceptions of performance improvements regarding the process of selecting the most pertinent processes to improve. The case organisation initiated their ITSM improvement project by selecting the top six processes suggested by the artefact.

The actual performance improvements however can only be evaluated after observing the end results of the ITSM improvement projects. This requires longitudinal data and is beyond the scope of our present study. It is also obvious that the actual performance of the ITSM improvement projects is dependent on a number of external organisational factors such as top management commitment, budget and priorities for undertaking improvement activities, effectiveness of the improvement plans and so forth. Nevertheless, it is certain that future evaluations of performance improvements can be undertaken in naturalistic settings since the DSR philosophy recognises the complexity in selecting appropriate evaluation methods of artefacts in the real world environment [43].

7   Communication

Regarding communication, the direct output of the artefact i.e. the prioritised ITSM process list is reported to the case organisation. This is the major deliverable of the research project. Likewise the research addresses a relevant industry problem in the

ITSM community: proposing an objective and transparent methodology and tool to select relevant ITSM processes to improve and hence provide a justifiable scope of any ITSM improvement project. We also intend to communicate our findings in the IS research community to elicit rigorous feedback on the development and application of the artefact. This will ultimately enable us to provide contextual and prescriptive contribution to the body of knowledge and further develop design theories from the DSR project.

8   Conclusion

In this work we confirm that the existing guidelines available to provide support on choosing IT service improvement processes lack a structured approach. To address this problem a process selection decision model was designed and then developed as a decision support tool to select processes for improvement. We chose a service perception perspective because it gives responses from the key stakeholders recommending ITSM processes for improvement. We chose the business drivers since they enable analysis of the relative importance of ITSM processes on the business goals.

A collaborative effort between academic researchers and industry practitioners has facilitated the development of the tool which was evaluated in a case organisation with positive results. Even though the proposed process selection decision model provides a structured set of activities to obtain the list of processes to improve, the ultimate decision to select processes is made by the service managers. Organisations can use the artefact as an evidence-based tool to support decisions on selecting important ITSM processes to improve. Process improvement projects can be disruptive in organisations and hence it is important to secure management buy-in early in the project [44]. We fulfilled the objective of this paper by describing the development and evaluation of the artefact. The application of the artefact provides informed choices to assure top management that a structured method is followed in selecting relevant processes for ITSM improvement. In terms of theoretical contribution, this research is the first to integrate TTF theory and DSR method in the context of ITSM improvements.

Despite the positive prospects of the artefact, it is necessary to conduct a full evaluation and consider the actual performance improvements from the ITSM improvement projects for further refinement of the artefact. To address construct validity, the service perception survey collected information from different stakeholder groups. Although the ITSM managers provided positive feedback and accepted the recommendations from the tool, there are no claims that can be made as to how well this artefact will contribute to actual service improvements since it has not yet been evaluated to that extent. This study evaluated the artefact in one case organisation. In future, to obtain a richer view of the effectiveness of the artefact, we intend to apply the tool in other organisations in order to generalise its applicability and effectiveness. The feedback cycle from several iterations of evaluation should lead to a robust artefact capable of defining a structure to guide decisions regarding selection of ITSM processes for improvement.

Note: ITIL® is a registered trademark of the HM Government Cabinet Office, UK.

Acknowledgements. This work is supported by an Australian Research Council Linkage Project. We thank Mr. Paul Collins, Chief Technology Officer of Assessment Portal and Mr Paul Fendley, Manager - Information, Communications & Technology of Toowoomba Regional Council for their involvement in the development and evaluation of the decision support tool.

References

1. Lloyd, V.: ITIL Continual Service Improvement. The Stationery Office London, UK (2011)
2. ISO/IEC: ISO/IEC 20000-1:2011 – Information Technology – Service Management – Part 1: Service Management System Requirements. International Organisation for Standardisation Geneva, Switzerland (2011)
3. CMMI: Standard CMMI® Appraisal Method for Process Improvement (SCAMPISM) A, Version 1.3: Method Definition Document. Software Engineering Institute, Carnegie Mellon University, MA, USA (2011)
4. ISO/IEC: ISO/IEC 15504-2:2004 – Information Technology – Process Assessment – Part 2: Performing an Assessment. International Organization for Standardization Geneva, Switzerland (2004)
5. Barafort, B., Betry, V., Cortina, S., Picard, M., St-Jean, M., Renault, A., Valdès, O.: ITSM Process Assessment Supporting ITIL. In: Tudor, P.R.C.H. (ed.). Van Haren Publishing Zaltbommel, Netherlands (2009)
6. Davenport, T.H.: Process Innovation: Reengineering Work Through Information Technology. Harvard Business School Press, MA (1993)
7. Hevner, A.R., March, S.T., Park, J., Ram, S.: Design Science in Information Systems Research. MIS Quarterly 28(1), 75–105 (2004)
8. Peffers, K., Tuunanen, T., Rothenberger, M.A., Chatterjee, S.: A Design Science Research Methodology for Information Systems Research. Journal of Management Information Systems 24(3), 45–77 (2007)
9. Goodhue, D.L., Thompson, R.L.: Task-Technology Fit and Individual Performance. MIS Quarterly 19(2), 213–236 (1995)
10. Hevner, A.R.: A Three Cycle View of Design Science Research. Scandinavian Journal of Information Systems 19(2), 87–92 (2007)
11. Kuechler, B., Vaishnavi, V.: Promoting Relevance in IS Research: An Informing System for Design Science Research. Informing Science: The International Journal of an Emerging Transdiscipline 14(1), 125–138 (2011)
12. Gregor, S.: The Nature of Theory in Information Systems. MIS Quarterly 30(3), 611–642 (2006)
13. March, S.T., Smith, G.F.: Design and Natural Science Research on Information Technology. Decision Support Systems 15(4), 251–266 (1995)
14. Gregor, S., Jones, D.: The Anatomy of a Design Theory. Journal of the Association for Information Systems 8(5), 312–335 (2007)
15. Venable, J.R.: The Role of Theory and Theorising in Design Science Research. In: 1st International Conference on Design Science Research in Information Systems and Technology. CGU, CA (2006)

16. Gebauer, J., Shaw, M.J., Gribbins, M.L.: Task-Technology Fit for Mobile Information Systems. Journal of Information Technology 25(3), 259–272 (2010)
17. Zigurs, I., Buckland, B.K.: A Theory of Task/Technology Fit and Group Support Systems Effectiveness. MIS Quarterly, 313–334 (1998)
18. Fuller, R.M., Dennis, A.R.: Does Fit Matter? The Impact of Task-Technology Fit and Appropriation on Team Performance in Repeated Tasks. Information Systems Research 20(1), 2–17 (2009)
19. Meade, L.M., Rogers, K.J.: Selecting Critical Business Processes: A Case Study. Engineering Management Journal 13(4), 41–46 (2001)
20. US-Navy: Handbook for Basic Process Improvement. The US Department of the Navy. The US Department of the Navy, USA (1996)
21. Barafort, B., Di Renzo, B., Merlan, O.: Benefits resulting from the combined use of ISO/IEC 15504 with the information technology infrastructure library (ITIL). In: Oivo, M., Komi-Sirviö, S. (eds.) PROFES 2002. LNCS, vol. 2559, pp. 314–325. Springer, Heidelberg (2002)
22. Porter, M.E., Millar, V.E.: How Information Gives You Competitive Advantage. Harvard Business Review 63(4), 149–160 (1985)
23. Hilbert, R., Renault, A.: Assessing IT Service Management Processes with AIDA–Experience Feedback. In: 14th European Conference for Software Process Improvement, Potsdam, Germany (2007)
24. Huxley, C.M.: An Improved Method to Identify Critical Processes. Faculty of Information Technology. Queensland University of Technology, Brisbane (2003)
25. Hammer, M., Champy, J.: Reengineering the Corporation: A Manifesto for Business Revolution. Harper Business Essentials Series. Harper Collins, NY (2003)
26. Davenport, T.H., Short, J.E.: The New Industrial Engineering: Information Technology and Business Process Redesign. Sloan Management Review 31(4), 11–27 (1990)
27. Zellner, G., Leist, S., Johannsen, F.: Selecting Critical Processes for a Six Sigma Project - Experiences from an Automotive Bank. In: 18th European Conference on Information Systems, Pretoria, South Africa (2010)
28. Saaty, T.L.: Relative Measurement and its Generalization in Decision Making. The Analytical Hierarchy/Network Process. RACSAM 102(2), 251–318 (2008)
29. Kaplan, R.S., Norton, D.P.: The Balanced Scorecard–Measures that Drive Performance. Harvard Business Review 70(1), 71–79 (1992)
30. Parasuraman, A., Zeithaml, V.A., Berry, L.L.: A Conceptual Model of Service Quality and its Implications for Future Research. Journal of Marketing 49(4), 41–50 (1985)
31. Shrestha, A., Cater-Steel, A., Tan, W.-G., Toleman, M.: A Model to Select Processes for IT Service Management Improvement. In: 23rd Australasian Conference on Information Systems, Geelong, Victoria (2012)
32. Rigby, D.K.: Management Tools 2011: An Executive's Guide. Bain & Company, Inc., MA (2011)
33. Marr, B., Schiuma, G., Neely, A.: Intellectual Capital–Defining Key Performance Indicators for Organizational Knowledge Assets. Business Process Management Journal 10(5), 551–569 (2004)
34. Grönroos, C.: Service Management and Marketing. Lexington Books, Lexington (1990)
35. Kang, G.-D., James, J.: Service Quality Dimensions: An Examination of Grönroos's Service Quality Model. Managing Service Quality 14(4), 266–277 (2004)
36. Dyke, T.P., Prybutok, V.R., Kappelman, L.A.: Cautions on the Use of the SERVQUAL Measure to Assess the Quality of Information Systems Services. Decision Sciences 30(3), 877–891 (1999)

37. Jiang, J.J., Klein, G., Carr, C.L.: Measuring Information System Service Quality: SERVQUAL from the Other Side. MIS Quarterly 26(2), 145–166 (2002)
38. O'Donoghue, T.A., Punch, K.: Qualitative Educational Research in Action: Doing and Reflecting. Routledge Falmer, London (2003)
39. Moody, D.L.: Theoretical and Practical Issues in Evaluating the Quality of Conceptual Models: Current State and Future Directions. Data & Knowledge Engineering 55(3), 243–276 (2005)
40. Microsoft. Windows Azure Features Overview (2013),
    http://www.windowsazure.com/en-us/home/features/overview (cited February 10, 2013)
41. Pries-Heje, J., Baskerville, R., Venable, J.R.: Strategies for Design Science Research Evaluation. In: 16th European Conference on Information Systems, Galway, Ireland (2008)
42. Vaishnavi, V., Kuechler, W.: Design Science Research in Information Systems (2004),
    http://www.desrist.org/design-research-in-information-systems (cited February 10, 2013)
43. Peffers, K., Rothenberger, M., Tuunanen, T., Vaezi, R.: Design Science Research Evaluation. In: Peffers, K., Rothenberger, M., Kuechler, B. (eds.) DESRIST 2012. LNCS, vol. 7286, pp. 398–410. Springer, Heidelberg (2012)
44. Hunsberger, K.: Giving Process its Due. PM Network. Project Management Institute, Inc., PA (2012)

Green IS for GHG Emission Reporting on Product-Level? An Action Design Research Project in the Meat Industry

Hendrik Hilpert[1], Christoph Beckers[2], Lutz M. Kolbe[2], and Matthias Schumann[1]

[1] Chair of application systems and E-Business, University of Göttingen, Germany
{hhilper,mschuma1}@uni-goettingen.de
[2] Chair of information management, University of Göttingen, Germany
{cbecker,lkolbe}@uni-goettingen.de

Abstract. Greenhouse gas emission reporting gained importance in the last years, due to societal and governmental pressure. However, this task is highly complex, especially in interdependent batch production processes and for reporting on the product-level. Green information systems, which collect, process and enhance the environmental information basis, are seen as a possible solution for this complex task, but only few Green IS accrued in IS research and practice. In this paper, we present initial results from an action design science research project. We studied three meat processing companies and developed a Green IS artifact that is capable to collect, process and report energy consumption and GHG emissions on product and process level. The evaluation for two sausage products shows that the artifact enhances the information basis with more detailed data towards average calculations, enabling more sustainable business processes. Finally, we propose design principles for the class of environmental accounting on product-level.

Keywords: Action Design Research, Design Science, Green IS, GHG emissions, meat industry, PCF, product carbon footprint.

1 Introduction

The global greenhouse gases (GHG) emitted due to human activities increased by more than 70 percent in the last three decades, whereby industrial processes account for 22.3 percent [1]. Especially the meat processing industry causes high environmental impacts [2]. Compared to products of vegetable origin, animal products result in 10 times higher GHG emissions [3]. For instance solely the livestock production contributes with 18 % of total GHG emissions, followed by further life-cycle stages of transportation, product processing and retailing [2].

Due to the increased environmental information demand by society, commercial chain partner policies or governmental regulations [4; 5], meat processing companies begin to disclose environmental performance information, using sustainability reports or product carbon footprints [6]. Nonetheless, disclosures about the underlying process of collection, processing and reporting are missing in actual company disclosures. Meat

J. vom Brocke et al. (Eds.): DESRIST 2013, LNCS 7939, pp. 324–339, 2013.

processing companies typically apply batch production systems due to raw materials of animal origin. As GHG emission accounting and reporting is already not easy for continuous material flows, batch systems increase the task complexity of accurate environmental accounting and reporting due to idle-times, reconfigurations and coincident processing of different batches at the same time [7]. Thus, we ask:

RQ 1: How do meat processing companies actually collect, process and report GHG emissions on product-level?

Recent research proposes that information systems (IS) can support and enable GHG emission accounting and reporting [8; 9; 5]. Coincident, studies showed that only few Green IS are adopted in practice and scholars only viewed Green IS from a "general utility perspective", rather than investigating actual IS-enabled eco-sustainability practices in organizations [10; 11]. We build on research question one and analyze if and how Green IS can support and enhance GHG emission and reporting tasks in the meat industry:

RQ 2: How can a Green IS support and enhance the GHG emission accounting and reporting in the meat industry?

The remainder of the paper is as follows: First, we provide related research on Green IS and environmental data. In section three, we explain the paradigm of action design research (ADR). Based on the ADR research process, we conducted case studies to capture the actual state of GHG emission accounting, reporting and its shortcomings in the meat industry. Section five draws on results of the case studies and explains the intervention, development and evaluation of a Green IS artifact to support and enhance the process of GHG emission accounting and reporting in the meat industry. Section six includes the discussion of results and we close with a brief conclusion (section seven).

2   Green IS

Green IS are information systems that contribute to sustainable business processes [12]. While Green IS cannot contribute directly to eco-sustainability, they can influence the "greenness" of business processes in organizations [4; 9], enabling sense-making about environmental impacts of business processes and in turn support decision-making and knowledge creation [5]. This leads to more sustainable business processes (Green IS) and causes medium- or long-term changes of behavior towards more eco-sustainability [11; 13]. The gained effect depends on the specific IS functionalities. Basically, Green IS collect and process data and are able to provide information about the environmental impact of an entity, whereby detailed functionalities of these IS reach from life-cycle assessment tools [14] and environmental reporting systems [15; 16] to complete environmental management accounting and information systems (EMIS) [17; 18; 19].

Green IS typically combines standard business data with environmental impact data [20]. Data about the environmental impact of business processes (e.g. energy consumption, GHG emission or water pollution) has to be collected separately by either direct measurement (water and energy meters or emission sensors) or by calculation. Environmental impact calculations use process activity data, reflecting "the quantitative measure of a level of activity" [21] (e.g. a physical resource amount used in a business process) and an environmental impact factor (EIF), providing the environmental impact per unit of activity data in a specific process (e.g. GHG emission factors). The necessary activity data is already present in current business IS[22; 14] but often remains unused, because enterprise IS target on classical economic goals [23]. Nonetheless, studies propose that Green IS should be integrated into the BIS environment, as activity data only need to be enriched by EIFs or sensor data [24]. Watson et al. [9] propose that Green IS need sensor network data (resource consumption and impacts) and flow network data (continuous material movements) to provide environmental impact sensitized objects, e.g. GHG emissions of a product, printed on a label.

Dependent on the source of business and environmental data, their quality can be classified in primary and secondary [21]. Primary data about the environmental impact is collected "from a specific process in the studies product's lifecycle" [21, p. 52], while secondary data is not specific to the analyzed product's life-cycle. Primary data is considered to have a higher quality than secondary data, which is only a proxy [21], leading to lower uncertainties in accounting in reporting processes [21; 9].

3   Action Design Research

The paradigm of design science research (DSR) becomes more and more accepted in the global IS research community [25]. DSR involves the construction of a wide-range of socio-technical artifacts that are used in organizations, influenced by business needs and applicable knowledge [25; 26].

Action design research (ADR) deploys action research into the DSR paradigm, involving researchers in organizational settings to solve problems and generate knowledge based on an organizational intervention [27]. ADR adapts this method and incorporates design science researchers in an organizational setting, addressing problem situations in a specific organizational context by intervening, developing and evaluating an IT artifact, generalizing findings to the class of problems [26]. The method is iterative with refining cycles in order to link theory and practice more comprehensively. The proposed method [26], the iterative cycle and the underlying principles are depicted in Fig. 1 and are explained briefly in the following.

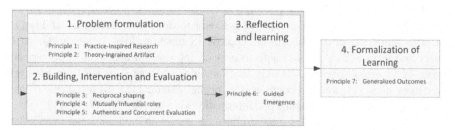

Fig. 1. Action Design Research (Source: [26], p. 41)

The ADR framework consists of three iterative stages. The first stage comprises a problem formulation, which addresses the perceived problem found in practice, providing knowledge-creation opportunities by applying generated knowledge of a case to the class of problems (principle 1). Furthermore, a design should be informed by theories (principle 2). Stage two is built upon the addressed problem in stage one to generate the initial design of the potential IT artifact. Sein et al. [26] propose to carry out this stage as an iterative process in the organization (principle 3), including the building, intervention and evaluating (BIE) of the generated artifact. In contrast to other DSR frameworks, ADR involves practitioners with first-hand experience of processes in the target setting and work practice while including theoretical knowledge by researchers (principle 4). The outcome is a realized artifact in its target environment, which is evaluated in this step and the target setting, influencing design decision-making and shaping of the artifact in further iterations (principle 5). Stage three is about reflecting and learning from intervention and artifact in the iterative and continuous process. The artifact is steadily shaped by organizational use, perspectives and participants (principle 6). Stage four includes the formalization of learning. This stage is about the casting of gained knowledge from a specific solution to a more general class of field problems, e.g. with design principles (principle 7).

We apply ADR to the field of meat processing companies. First, we conduct case studies (Section four), analyze the actual state of GHG emission reporting, which results in a problem formulation. Second, we build an initial artifact in two iteration cycles, encompassing interventions and evaluations within the companies (Section five). Based on this artifact, we generalize our findings to the class of problems and propose a set of generalized design principles (Section six).

4   Case Studies

Our action design research process starts with an analysis of how meat processing companies do account for GHG emissions and how this process is supported by IS. As Green IS is a nascent field in general [11] and accounting functionalities for GHG emissions in detail have not been studied comprehensively in the meat processing industry, we decided to conduct a multiple case study. Case study research is suitable for answering "how" and "why" questions and enables specific situation analysis in detail for analytical generalization purposes [28]. We choose three small and medium size (SME) meat processing companies, located in Germany and Austria, who indicate themselves as having a longterm sustainability strategy. Each company has disclosed various recent process improvements and is constantly redesigning products to enhance eco-sustainability of their company. To guarantee anonymity, the companies are further denoted as Company A, B and C.

We used multiple data sources to analyze the actual state within companies. The primary data sources are face-to-face interviews, which we conducted on site with all three companies that last around 60 to 90 minutes. The interview partners have been the CEO (chief executive officer) and the CIO (chief information officer) as well as the production manager (only Company A) and the sustainability manager (only

Company B). To ensure the reliability between cases, we used a half-structured interview protocol. Further, we reviewed the production processes on site and conducted a technology review of current IT/IS in the companies. Shorter telephone queries and email correspondence endorsed the collected data. Moreover, we gained access to energy consumption protocols, IS architecture and functionality description documents, which we used as secondary data sources.

Ongoing, we describe the results of actual state analysis in the companies A - C. Due to immense gathered data, we provide a brief company description and focus on the gate-to-gate process of sausage production, the actual IS/IT support and the actual state of accounting and reporting for GHG emissions.

4.1   Company A

Company A is a family-owned company located in Germany. The company has nearly 75 employees and a turnover of ~10 million € in 2012, producing approx. 100 different products that are processed on order. The complete batch production process flow is supported by a branch specific ERP (enterprise resource planning). The present ERP integrates a WMS (warehouse management system) module and a BIS (batch information system), which enables to track back a specific batch to animal production stage. As no PPS (production planning systems) and MES (manufacturing execution systems) modules are used, the production process is not automatized. Instead the processes are controlled manually, except for packaging. Therefore, process flow activity data is not available for any processes.

The energy consumptions and resulting GHG emissions are not collected and processed in detail at the moment. The company uses an external energy consumption monitoring system, which is hosted by their utility provider. The system is capable to display the total energy consumption of the production site in 15 minute intervals. Additionally, they have a load management system for their cooling warehouse, which is able to monitor the consumed energy in real-time. The other machines have no installed energy meters. Nevertheless, the production manager once collected energy consumption data manually, using a transportable energy meter. The oil consumption of the smokehouse is also known due to an oil level indicator, which is read off by hand daily. The quality of environmental data can be assessed as secondary for product-specific calculations, but is primary in the case of cold storage. The GHG emission accounting is done with Excel on stakeholder demand at present.

4.2   Company B

Company B is family-owned and located in Austria, having 1900 employees and an annual turnover of 195 million € in 2012. Their production portfolio enfolds ~ 300 products, including high quality bio beef and pork. Additional to meat processing, they also accomplish on-site slaughtering and retailing of their products. For this reason, finished batches are stored in their cold warehouse until retailing. Company B also uses a branch specific ERP system, which covers the complete sausage batch production process with a PPS, MES and WMS. Therefore, process flow activity data is available in ERP database for the complete production process. Whilst a BIS system with tracking and tracing functionalities, the company also developed "stand alone" supply chain management tools with own underlying databases to track information of origin related to their bio products.

Energy consumption and resulting GHG emissions within the production process are not monitored and reported automatically. On their request, the utility provider makes energy consumption tables available for a desired timeframe. The energy consumption is metered with one main meter on production site, other energy metering or resource consumption sensors are not used. The CIO mentioned that they calculated the energy consumption for their production process once, using estimations for an average production setting. Thus, the quality of environmental data is secondary. On request, they recalculate the amount of energy for their current production outputs using Excel and provide this data to their stakeholders.

4.3 Company C

Company C is family-owned, located in Germany, has 1700 employees and an annual turnover of 300 million € in 2012. The portfolio covers 700 different product types, which are mainly processed for large German commercial chains.

Company C uses a branch specific ERP system, which supports the batch production process, using a PPS, a WMS, and a BIS module. They also use a WPL (weight printing label) module for product-instance individual labeling. The WPL module is connected via an operating and machine data logging middleware (by field-bus protocol) to weight sensors and the label printer on the packaging machine. In the final packaging process, product-instances are weighted, the data is processed by the WPL module and the printer creates an individual label, which is glued on the package. Process flow activity data is available for the complete process, as single machines are controlled with MES. Additional to ERP, company C uses a "stand-alone" FMS (facility management system), which is used for building control and monitoring. The FMS system controls the cooling warehouse, the smokehouse and monitors single ma-chines for malfunctions in the production process. The system uses OLE (object linking and embedding) for process control (OPC) to communicate with sensor systems on machine and division level.

The energy consumption is monitored by the FMS system at least on division level. In terms of the cooling warehouse, the system is capable to monitor the energy consumption in real time. Machines are not monitored for energy consumption, but it is planned to upgrade them with energy meters. At the moment, the FMS can only provide energy consumption information for single production divisions, e.g. the packaging area in real-time. The consumed oil for smoking is monitored by the procurement system, in order to trigger reordering automatically. Nonetheless, the environmental data, which is monitored by the FMS, is on primary quality level. Company C does not provide reports about their environmental performance at the moment, but rather use the present data for production efficiency improvements. On request, they generate reports in their FMS about the energy consumption and work them up with Excel.

4.4   Comparison of Cases

The results of cases regarding the main production process control, availability of process flow data, the environmental sensor network and the actual state of GHG emission reporting is summarized in Tab. 1.

Table 1. Case study summary

Company / Characteristic	Company A	Company B	Company C
Batch process control modules	BIS, WMS and WPL	PPS, WMS, BIS	PPS, MES, WMS, BIS and WPL
Flow data availability	Storage process	Storage process	All process steps
Environmental sensor network coverage	Cold storage	Site-level with main meter	Cold storage and all single divisions.
Sensor network protocol	Field-bus	-	OPC network
Environmental data quality	Primary on cold storage division	Primary on site-level	Primary on division- level
Actual IS for GHG reporting	Excel	Excel	FMS and Excel

We found that the availability of process flow data mainly depends on the usage of PPS, MES and WMS. Only one company uses a MES, thus process flow data is available for all process steps. All companies use at least a WMS, resulting in process flow data for the cold storage process. Environmental sensors are available in the cold storage area (two companies), one company has a sensor network on division-level for all processes, using their FMS system and an OPC network protocol. In terms of environmental sensor network data, only company C collects environmental data on division level. The two other companies have only primary data on site-level, provided by energy meters from the utility provider. At present, the companies do not have IS that enable to account and report in detail about their environmental impact. Actually, they calculate energy consumption and subsequently GHG emissions of their products by dividing the total energy consumption by the total amount of production output. In result the meat processing companies in our case study do not collect, process or report GHG emission data on product-level comprehensively, answering our research question one.

In the interviews two companies mentioned that they plan to account and report on environmental impacts more detailed in future. Company A is forced to provide more detailed product-related GHG emission information to their commercial chain partners in future, thus actual methods will be insufficient. Company C strengthened that they also want to account on product batch level to reveal potentials for more eco-efficiency, e.g. reducing idle-times and broke material. Nevertheless, they are detained by the fact that current Green IS are not capable to collect and process data on product level for single product types or batches. Thus, a Green IS is needed that is capable to monitor and report GHG emissions on product type and batch-level (ADR principle 1: Practice-Inspired research).

5   Artifact Development: Resource Consumption Backpack

5.1   Calculation Methods and Basic Conceptual Design

The GHG emissions of a meat product occur due to resource consumptions of machines in the single processes it passes through. A product batch consists of a set of raw materials that are transformed to intermediate and finally finished products in the process. Guiding our initial conceptual design, we draw on Watson et al.'s [9] energy information framework as prescriptive design guidelines (theory type V, [29]). Thus each process needs to be analyzed for material flow and energy consumption to get detailed and differentiated GHG emission data on product type and even batch level (ADR: principle 2). Based on material flow and energy consumption, we found three different process types (machine processing, cooling, smoking), resulting in different calculation methods. The derivation of methods and a basic conceptual idea reflects the first iterative cycle (ADR: principle 3). The first type is machine processing, which occurs in the steps "grinding", "mixing", "filling", "finish closing", "cooking" and "packaging". In the cases, machines only process one material batch at the same time. In result, a batch causes the total energy consumption of a machine within processing time, wherefore the total energy consumption has to be allocated on the processed batch. Thus, the resource consumption of a material (identified with ID) on a specific machine (n) constitutes of the sum of energy consumption of the machine within the machine batch processing time ($t_{out} - t_{in}$), resulting in formula (1).

The second process type is cold storaging. In contrast to machine processing, a warehouse does not necessarily store only one batch at the same time. Rather different raw materials and batches are stored in the warehouse, wherefore the consumed resources have to be prorated on all batch materials that are in cold warehouse within a specific timeframe. The resource consumption for one material in cold storage have to be allocated by the total amount of materials in the warehouse for each timeframe where the total stored amount is stable. Every change in total stored amount requires reallocating the energy consumption of all stored materials. Thus, a consumption calculation is discrete only between two storage events (time $event_n$ and time $event_{n+1}$) and have to be fulfilled for each timeframe between two events, triggered by the last event of change. Moreover, partly outplacements need to be considered. In case of a partly outplacement of a material, e.g. 50 % of raw materials, it requires to allocate related consumed resources tracked so far to the partly outplacement. For instance, in case of 50 % outplacement these items are responsible for 50 % of the origin's material resource consumption. Formula (2) calculates the energy consumption for cold storage.

The third different process type is smoking. This process is mainly equal to cold storage, except for the consumed resources and a lead time before production processing. The smoking system combusts oil to generate smoke. The lead time oil consumption requires allocating the consumed oil within the lead time by similar shares to all materials that are processed subsequently. The resource consumption of a material in the smoking station constitutes of the allocated sum of combusted oil within two time stamps (time $event_n$ and time $event_{n+1}$), where the total stored amount is stable and a share of oil consumed in lead time (t_{lead_start} - t_{lead_end}) divided by total output of this day (Formula (3)).

$$RC_{ID,n} = \sum_{t=t_{In}}^{t_{out}} \text{Energy consumption of Machine (t)} \qquad (1)$$

$$RC_{ID,n} = \sum_{t=t_{event_n}}^{t_{event_{n+1}}} \left[\frac{Storage\ Amount_{ID}}{\sum Stored\ Amount} (\text{Energy Cons.}(t)) \right] \qquad (2)$$

$$RCB_{ID,n} = \sum_{t=t_{event_n}}^{t_{event_{n+1}}} \left[\frac{Material_{ID}}{\sum Materials} \text{Oil Cons.}(t) \right] + \sum_{t=t_{lead\_start}}^{t_{lead\_end}} \left[\frac{1}{\sum Output} \text{Oil Cons.}(t) \right] \qquad (3)$$

Therefore, the total resource consumption of a batch is the sum of all energy consumptions of raw and intermediate products caused in the complete production process, using the proposed methods. GHG emissions can be calculated by multiplying the resource consumption data with specific emission impact factors (e.g. CO_2-eqivalents). For this reason, we propose to develop a Green IS, which is capable to track the resource consumptions for each process step and every raw and intermediate material that belongs to a batch, thus accounting for the complete resource consumptions of a batch and a product from gate-to-gate. This detailed data basis enables to investigate single process steps and machines, regarding the energy consumption and the resulting GHG emissions. In contrast, the batch detail level also enables to provide product type mean values over time. As single batches can vary in terms of resource consumptions and in turn GHG emissions, they are representative for the batch instance but not necessarily for a product type. Therefore, it is reasonable to provide also an arithmetic mean over all batches of a specific product type, depending on the information demand. For instance, a PCF refers to product type, whereby batch instance data is useful for accounting purposes.

Conceptually, the artifact is realized by constructing a "resource consumption backpack" (RCB) for each processed material. The RCB stores information about every machine, cooling and smoking process step, regarding the GHG emissions of raw, intermediate and final products of a batch, using the proposed formulas (1) – (3). If raw or intermediate materials are transformed to a new material or product, the RCB of input materials plainly has to be committed to the new output material. After finishing the product, the collected information can be used to calculate GHG emissions. The concept is depicted in Fig. 2.

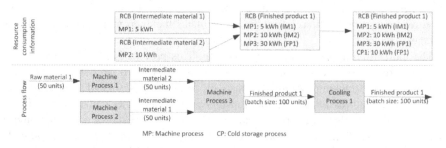

Fig. 2. Concept of Resource consumption backpack

We evaluated the basic conceptual design within the studied companies (ADR: principle 5). In a feedback round, they approved the utility of the basic design. Moreover, all three companies stated additional functional and non-functional requirements that they believe to be important for the proposed IS. The resulting requirements from companies A - C are depicted in Tab. 2.

Table 2. Green IS requirements from case studies

Requirement	Explanation	Companies
SC data exchange	Companies have the demand to include data from earlier stages and want to report resource consumption data to their commercial chain partners.	A and B
Compatibility	All three companies would only use a Green IS, if it is compatible to present IT/IS infrastructure.	A, B and C
Performance	The Green IS should be able to process real-time data, because they want to know the GHG emissions at the end of gate-to-gate process.	A, B and C

5.2   Instance Development

The second iterative cycle of our ADR research project includes the construction of an initial target instance prototype (ADR: principle 3), which is capable to track the resource consumption backpacks of single batches. Therefore, we draw on the requirements from the first evaluation cycle (ADR: principle 6) and on best available technology within the cases, using the IS/IT infrastructure of Company C, as they already have a sensor network at division level. The developed component architecture of our initial prototype is depicted in Fig. 3. and is explained in the following.

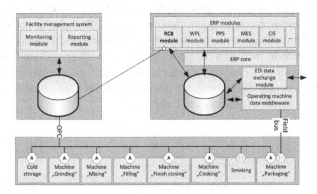

Fig. 3. Target state Green IS architecture

The target prototype includes a processing component that is located within the companies ERP environment and uses different data sources. Material flow data is derived from the ERP system and resource consumption data is derived from a sensor network via an interface. The material flow data include machine process cycle times (derived from MES), batch sizes, batch raw and intermediate material (derived from

PPS and BIS module) as well as storage amounts and storage timeframes (from WMS). The target prototype requires resource consumption data on machine/process-level. Therefore existing sensor networks needs to be extended to machine-level. The smoking machine requires an oil consumption sensor, while the other machines are equipped with energy meters. The sensors are connected to an OPC network, which transfers the data to a resource consumption sensor network database. In order to cope with the requirement of SC data integration, an EDI module is required (requirement one). The EDI module is used to gather data about the resource consumption of raw materials from suppliers, thus expand the scope from farm to gate, and to transmit the resource consumption of finished products to SC partners, e.g. commercial chains. The collected RCB data are stored in the existing ERP database, thus other ERP modules can use the environmental impact information (requirement two). For instance, the WPL module can use the environmental data to integrate a PCF on the product label. A simple additional method can gather the necessary data and enrich the existing product labels with a PCF.

The static structure of the RCB module consists of six classes (Fig. 4). The *ResourceConsumptionBackpack* class represents the main class. Everytime a new raw material enters the production process, a new RCB object is generated. It stores the related resource consumption from processes in a list of objects. Supplier resource consumption data that are available via EDI are imported by the *ImportBatchEDI* class. The list entries are derived from the *ResourceRecord* class, which provide data objects for the list entries. The *RCBConsumptionUpdater* class traces the production process and pulls process flow and energy consumption data from database, triggered by occurring MES events. The *RCBMerger* class is capable to combine the Resource Consumption lists from 1-to-n RCB objects in case of a transformation process. The *RCBVector* class is used to generate summarized resource consumption or environmental impact data, about single process steps, complete batches or single instances of a batch. The resource consumption data list in a RCB object is not stored persistently in the ERP database until the related batch production process is completed. This technical decision increases the performance, as cooling and smoking processes induce (re-) calculations with every event changing the total amount of materials and products in the process. Therefore, this design discharges the database and in turn increases the performance (requirement three).

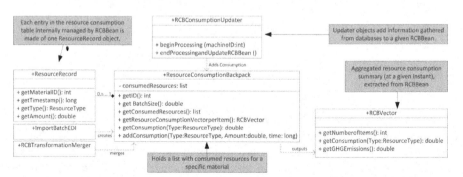

Fig. 4. UML-Class diagram of designed solution

Finally, we evaluated the implemented prototype regarding the proposed calculation methods, the model and its utility (ADR: principle 5). We acquired real material flow and resource consumption data for two batches of different sausage products (cooked and scalded sausages) from the production manager (ADR: principle 4), including the complete material flow, machine cycle times, cold and smoking movement events, energy consumption and batch size of a production day. This data has been processed by our artifact to calculate the GHG emissions of both product batches. Moreover, we acquired the total production output of the day and the total energy consumption (kWh from machines, cold storage and oil consumption from smoking) to calculate an averaged GHG emissions of the product batches on company-level, dividing the total resource consumption by total output. The calculated results by prototype are depicted in Table 3.

Table 3. GHG emissions of two sausage product batches, compared to daily avg. consumption

Cooked sausage (Batch size: 100 kg, EIF's: 1kWh=559 g CO_2, 1liter of oil=2.67 kg CO_2)								
Process	Cooling	Grinding	Mixing	Filling	Cooking	Smoking	Packaging	Sum
Processing Time (min)	7320	-	20	43	60	45	25	7513
CO_2 (kg)	34.784	-	0.671	4.024	10.598	34.309	3.012	87.398
CO_2 per kg =								0.874

Scalded sausage (Batch size: 200 kg, EIF's: 1kWh=559 g CO2, 1liter of oil=2,67 kg CO_2)								
Process	Cooling	Grinding	Mixing	Filling	Cooking	Smoking	Packaging	Sum
Processing Time (min)	14280	4	15	120	125	-	60	14600
CO_2 (kg)	78.696	3.913	0.363	13.975	22.080	-	17.217	136.224
CO_2 per kg =								0.681

Output of the day (2000 kg, EIF's: 1kWh=559 g CO_2, 1liter of oil=2.67 kg CO_2)				
	Machines	Cold storage	Smoking	Sum
Resource Consumption (ME)	1083,915 kWh	235 kWh	257 liters of Oil	
CO_2 emissions (kg)	605.908	131.365	686.190	1423.463
CO_2 per kg =				0.712

6   Discussion

In result, the calculation on product-level provides different data than the averaged calculation on company-level. While the GHG emissions of one kg of scalded sausages (0.681 kg CO_2) are nearly snapped by the average calculation of the day (0.712 kg CO_2), the GHG emissions of cooked sausage (0.874 kg CO_2) are more than 22 percent higher than in average. Additionally, the average calculation does not provide insights on causing processes and machines, while the resource consumption lists in RCB objects do (e.g. GHG emissions from cold storage). The artifact supports the analysis of different processes by comparisons to other batches and shows the energy consumption within different timeframes in detail. This in turn supports decision-making, e.g. optimizing the receipt for less energy consumption. In result, more eco-sustainable business processes are enabled. Due to our observations within the second evaluation cycle, we found major differences in energy consumptions between single products and days. For instance, the consumed electric power of the cooling warehouse varied between 200 and 650 kWh a day. This variation occurred due to seasonal weather conditions. As the cooling process is responsible for ~ 10 percent of gate-to-gate GHG, more detailed analysis should be encompassed. Additionally, such insights reinforce the utility of PCFs on product type and instance level to provide a better information basis for GHG emission accounting [7].

The outcome of this AD research project can be generalized to the class of problems of environmental data collection, processing and reporting on product-level in production processes (ADR: principle 7). In terms of problem generalization, the concept of RCB is suitable to other consumed resources in batch production processes. For instance, the water consumption of a batch can be tracked equally to GHG emissions, using the concept of RCB. Moreover, the proposed Green IS with the underlying calculation methods and RCB concept can be transferred to other industry branches with batch production processes.

The solution instance can be generalized too. We showed with our artifact that resource consumption data from sensor networks and material flow data is necessary to calculate the resource consumption of a product and in turn to calculate the resulting GHG emissions gate-to-gate. Further, we showed that an instance in the class of problems should include supply chain data to extend the scope of environmental information (e.g. gate-to-gate to farm-to-gate). These principles also guide the design of other solutions within the class of Green IS for environmental accounting and reporting on product-level. Green IS that obey these principles, will be able to solve the complex task of environmental accounting and reporting on product-level. Therefore, we propose three design principles that should be used for instances in the class of problems of environmental data collection, processing and reporting on product-level in production processes. The principles are summarized in Tab. 4.

Table 4. Design principles for Green IS

Design principle	Description
Primary data collection	A Green IS that accounts for environmental impacts in production processes should collect primary resource consumption data in the real process, using sensor networks.
Current IS compatibility	A Green IS that accounts for environmental impacts in production processes should be compatible to current business IS, because these IS holds activity flow data that can be used for environmental impact calculations.
SC data integration and exchange	A Green IS that accounts for environmental impacts in production processes should be able to integrate data from earlier SC stages and provide this data to later SC stages.

7   Conclusion

In this paper we applied action design research. We conducted a case study with three meat processing companies and analyzed the actual state of GHG emission collection, processing and reporting on product-level. In result, we found that the studied companies do not collect and process GHG emission data on product-level, but seek for IS-enhanced solutions that support environmental accounting and reporting tasks. Based on this problem formulation, we developed a Green IS artifact in the meat industry that is capable to collect, process and report GHG emissions on product-level in batch processes. We evaluated the artifact with real data from the studied companies showing its utility and generalize our findings to other environmental impacts, industry branches and Green IS, proposing design principles for the class of problems.

This paper however has limitations that also encourage for further research. First, the action design research project is not finished yet. The presented evaluation results are presented to the companies. An upcoming feedback round will turn out, if the increased environmental information basis is beneficial to the studied companies. If reasonable, we will implement the prototype in the studied setting, enabling to gather more detailed data on large amounts of different product batches and in turn increase knowledge about GHG emission causing factors. Additionally, the utility of sense-making, decision-making and knowledge creation and in turn the support of a more sustainable development in organizations have to be evaluated.

Second, our proposed artifact requires primary environmental data, wherefore environmental sensor networks are necessary. In the analyzed cases only company C has a sensor network on division level, leading to a target state Green IS based on their IS/IT architecture. Therefore, we have to consider in the upcoming feedback round that other companies, which are further apart from target state, are more likely not inclined to use the proposed Green IS. Thus, the willingness to adopt our artifact strongly depends on the actual state of automated environmental sensor networks in the companies. Finally, the resulting design principles are not evaluated yet. Further studies and instance implementations should be conducted in meat and other industries to prove the proposed Green IS design. While we generalized our findings analytical, a statistical evaluation with a larger sample is necessary.

References

1. European Union: CO_2 emissions by sector, http://ec.europa.eu/energy/publications/doc/statistics/ext_co2_emissions_by_sector.pdf
2. Food and Agriculture Organization of the United Nations: Livestock's Long Shadow—Environmental Issues and Options (2006), ftp://ftp.fao.org/docrep/fao/010/a0701e/a0701e.pdf
3. DEFRA: Environmental impact of food production consumption (2006), http://www.ifr.ac.uk/waste/Reports/DEFRA-Environmental%20Impacts%20of%20Food%20Production%20%20Consumption.pdf

4. Chen, A., Boudreau, M.C., Watson, R.T.: Information systems and ecological sustainability. Journal of Systems and Information Technology 10(3), 186–201 (2008)
5. Butler, T.: Compliance with institutional imperatives on environmental sustainability: Building theory on the role of Green IS. The Journal of Strategic Information Systems 20(1), 6–26 (2011)
6. Gerbens-Leenes, P.W., Moll, H.C., Schoot Uiterkamp, A.J.M.: Design and development of a measuring method for environmental sustainability in food production systems. Ecological Economics 46, 231–248 (2003)
7. Dada, A., Staake, T.: Carbon Footprints from enterprise to product instances: The potential of the EPC network. In: Ohlbach, H.J. (ed.) Betriebliche Informationssysteme vor dem Hintergrund des Klimawandels, Informatik 2008, München, pp. 873–878 (2008)
8. Elliot, S.: Environmentally Sustainable ICT: A Critical Topic for IS Research? In: Proceedings of PACIS 2007 (2007), http://aisel.aisnet.org/pacis2007/114
9. Watson, R.T., Boudreau, M., Chen, A.: Information Systems and Environmentally Sustainable Development: Energy Informatics and New Directions for the Is Community. MIS Quarterly 34(1), 23–38 (2010)
10. Ijab, M., Molla, A., Cooper, V.: Green Information Systems (Green IS) Practice in Organisation: Tracing its Emergence and Recurrent Use. In: Proceedings of AMCIS 2012, Paper 6 (2012)
11. vom Brocke, J., Seidel, S.: Environmental Sustainability in Design Science Research: Direct and Indirect Effects of Design Artifacts. In: Peffers, K., Rothenberger, M., Kuechler, B. (eds.) DESRIST 2012. LNCS, vol. 7286, pp. 294–308. Springer, Heidelberg (2012)
12. Boudreau, M.C., Chen, A.J., Huber, M.: Green IS: Building Sustainable Business practices. In: Watson, R.T. (ed.) Information Systems: A Global Text (2008)
13. Dedrick, J.: Green IS: concepts and issues for information systems research. Communications of the Association for Information Systems 27(1), 11–18 (2010)
14. Shaft, T.M., Sharfman, M.P., Swahn, M.: Using interorganizational information systems to support environmental management efforts at ASG. Journal of Industrial Ecology 5(4), 95–115 (2001)
15. Cranefield, S., Purevis, M.: Integrating environmental information: Incorporating metadata in a distributed information system's architecture. Advances in Environmental Research 5, 319–325 (2001)
16. Petrasch, R., Lang, C.V., Junker, H.: Environmental management information systems in the production-integrated environmental protection. In: Proceedings of EuroSustain 2002, Greece, pp. 59–65 (2002)
17. Teuteberg, F., Straßenburg, J.: State of the Art and Future Research in Environmental Management Information Systems – A systematic literature review. Information Technologies in Environmental Engineering, 64–77 (2009)
18. Carlson, R., Erixon, M., Forsberg, P., Palsson, A.-C.: System for integrated business environmental information management. Advances in Environmental Research 5, 369–375 (2001)
19. El-Gayar, O., Fritz, B.D.: Environmental Management Information Systems (EMIS) for Sustainable Development: A Conceptual Overview. Communications of the Association for Information Systems 17(1), Article 34 (2006)
20. Burrit, R.L., Schaltegger, S., Zvedov, D.: Carbon Management Accounting – Practice in Leading German Companies. Centre for Accounting, Governance and Sustainability Occasional Working Papers, No.2. University of South Australia, Adelaide (May 2010)

21. World Resource Institute: Product life cycle accounting and reporting standard, http://www.ghgprotocol.org/files/ghgp/Product%20Life%20Cycle %20Accounting%20and%20Reporting%20Standard.pdf
22. De la Pena, G.B., Gomez, J.M., Rautenstrauch, C.: Integrated material flow management and business information systems. In: Minier, P., Susini, A. (eds.) Proceedings of EnviroInfo 2004, Geneve, pp. 283–291 (2004)
23. Marx Gomez, J., Prötzsch, S., Rautenstrauch, C.: Data Defects in Material Flow Networks – Classification and Approaches. Cybernetics and Systems: An International Journal 35(5-6), 549–558 (2004)
24. Frysinger, S.P.: An integrated environmental information system (IEIS) for corporate environmental management. Advances in Environmental Research 5, 361–367 (2001)
25. Gregor, S., Hevner, A.R.: Positioning and presenting design science research for maximum impact. MIS Quarterly 37(2) (forthcoming, 2013)
26. Sein, M.K., Henfrisson, O., Purao, S., Lindgren, R.: Action Design Research. MIS Quarterly 35(1), 37–56 (2011)
27. Baskerville, R., Wood-Harper, A.T.: Diversity in Information systems action research methods. European Journal of Information Systems 7(2), 90–107 (1988)
28. Yin, R.K.: Case study research: design and methods. Sage, Thousand Oaks (2009)
29. Gregor, S.: The nature of theory in information systems. MIS Quarterly 30(3), 611–642 (2006)

Design Methodology for Construction of Mapping Applications

Olusola Samuel-Ojo[1], Lorne Olfman[1], Linda A. Reinen[2], Arjuna Flenner[1],
David D. Oglesby[3], and Gareth J. Funning[3]

[1] Claremont Graduate University, CA, USA
{olusola.samuel-ojo,lorne.olfman,arjuna.flenner}@cgu.edu
[2] Pomona College, CA, USA
lreinen@pomona.edu
[3] University of California, Riverside, CA, USA

Abstract. Geoscientists and engineers use anomalies which are parts of a profile that is above or below the surrounding average to infer subsurface targets (groundwater, ore and petroleum). Customarily, they are detected by processing field measurements including geological and geophysical data using methods such as stacking (averaging), Fourier analysis and filtering. The issue is these methods often result in partial detection because they perform partial separation of wanted from unwanted anomalies and the error in separation gets propagated into data layers and subsequent analyses, thereby resulting in less accurate spatial predictions. In order to understand and address this issue, we investigate whether the design methodology for construction of mapping applications for characterizing geospatial variables achieves logical consistency of data layers and improve mapping accuracy of groundwater flow. We present a design methodology as an artifact and evaluated it by applying it to hydrogeological and geodetic data acquired from the Santa Clara Valley, CA, USA. The result shows that data parts offer distinctive patterns of geometric features that are signatures of groundwater flow for sustainable groundwater management. The practical implications of the result can be applied by software developers and data modelers, information systems and operations managers to construct logically consistent and well-composed environmental information systems.

Keywords: environmental information system, mapping accuracy, logical consistency, spatio-temporal, error propagation, data layer, feature layer, spatial analysis, data part, groundwater flow, geospatial data pattern, surface curvature signature.

1   Introduction

For a sustainable environmental development of the groundwater system and monitoring, water managers need to track the inflow (recharge), distribution, and outflow (discharge) of groundwater on a continuous basis. They need to monitor the quantity and quality of surface flow and groundwater flow more accurately. Having a continuous

J. vom Brocke et al. (Eds.): DESRIST 2013, LNCS 7939, pp. 340–352, 2013.

and more accurate spatial data layer on groundwater is critical to studying different abstraction scenarios or remediation measures in terms of groundwater heads, flow lines, changes in recharge conditions, and chemical composition.

Spatial data always contain some errors (Bolstad, 2012; Blakemore, 1984) which impact the accuracy of the variable of interest. Errors are uncertainties in input data, parameters, methods or combined (Arbia, Griffith, & Haining, 1999). Errors result from how features of interest are conceptualized, methods of data collection and analysis, human error or outdated data. For an analysis that requires multiple stages, these errors get propagated through the stages to degrade the quality of the final output or model (Heuvelink, 1999).

Accuracy measure can be classified into four types namely: positional accuracy, attribute accuracy, logical consistency and completeness (Bolstad, 2012). Positional accuracy describes how close the location of a feature represented digitally is to the true location. Attribute accuracy describes how different the attribute values are from the true values. Logical consistency describes the presence or absence or frequency of inconsistent data. And completeness accuracy summarizes the how well the data set captures all the features it intended to represent.

Our study proposes a design methodology for construction of mapping applications for characterizing geospatial variables to improve the quality of spatial monitoring of groundwater flow by improving the logical consistency of data layers and mapping accuracy for sustainable groundwater management. The next section of this paper continues with the background, the methodology and conclude by summarizing the research and its evaluation, discussing possible implication and application areas in environmental information systems.

2   Background

The hydrogeological case, Santa Clara Valley (basin) was selected because of the availability of hydrogeological time series data. The valley includes the city of San Jose and numerous smaller cities with a population of 1.7 million people (USCB, 2011). The rock assemblage of the basin describes a complex sequence of Quaternary and Tertiary aged sediments (gravel, sand, fine-grained silt and clay) and impermeable serpentinites.

The valley is a fault-dissected alluvial basin, bounded by the Santa Cruz mountain to the southwest and the Diablo range to the northeast, an area of approximately 2 trillion square meters (Figure 1). The recharge flow occurs as natural areal precipitation infiltration. The discharge flow occurs as evapotranspiration, outflow to stream channels, subsurface flow to San Francisco Bay and pumpage from wells.

3   Literature Review

We reviewed relevant studies in data quality and groundwater monitoring problem and then elicited the research question. Geospatial data may be structured, semi-structured

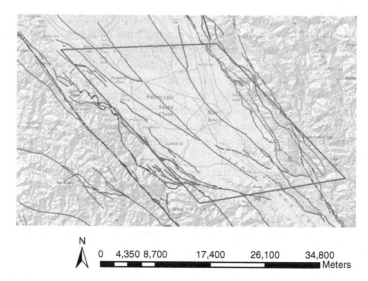

Fig. 1. Fault-dissected alluvial basin bounded by the mountains at the southwest and northeast sub-regions[1]. The area of interest, Santa Clara Valley, is bounded by the overlaid parallelogram. (A fault is a planar fracture or discontinuity in a volume of rock.)

or unstructured with the temperament of big data. They are voluminous, large in scale and scope, distributed and various (Pospiech & Felden, 2012). They come with data quality problem – noise. Geospatial data include those collected from field data loggers or sensors and those collected from geodetic equipment such as satellites which may be categorized as semi-structured and unstructured data respectively.

In the data quality research literature, there has been no consensus about the difference between data and information quality, however, data quality generally refers to technical issues while information quality refers to non-technical issues (Madnick, Lee, Wang, & Zhu, 2009). We found the characterizing framework of Madnick et al. (2009) useful, a two-dimensional matrix table consisting of topics and methods of data quality research dimensions. Since the purpose of this research is to address error propagation in data layers by improving the logical consistency of data layers and mapping accuracy through a design methodology, we situate our contribution within the data quality impact issue with focus on high accuracy performance. Next we examine groundwater monitoring literature.

Groundwater monitoring activities are organized activities for the continuous measurement of the dynamic state of the underground environment, often used for warning and control purposes (UNESCO, 1992). Monitoring activities might be complemented

---

[1] World Terrain base map courtesy of United State geological Survey (USGS) and others. Fault map courtesy of the California Geological Survey by United States Geoscience Information Network (USGIN) Initiative for the Geothermal Data Project and published as a web map service by Environmental Systems Research Institute (ESRI) and consumed by Arc-Map v10 educational release courtesy of ESRI.

by geophysical and remote sensing (geodetic) data collection methods. Remote sensing is defined as the collection and interpretation of information about a target without physical contact with the target (Sabins, 1986). Using remote sensing data (Synthetic Aperture Radar - SAR), Schmidt and Burgmann (2003) compute the 'incremental range change' between SAR scene in order to produce both the spatial and temporal pattern of uplift of Santa Clara Valley.

4   Methodology

We bring to bear design science research as the fundamental approach (Hevner, March, Park, & Ram, 2004) and information theory (Shannon, 1948) as the theoretical background, and synthesize mathematical modeling method, experiment and geological method (Fetter, 2001) to develop the design methodology as an artifact for improving the logical consistency of data layers and mapping accuracy of groundwater flow.

The philosophical underpinning of design science approach holds that the knowledge and understanding of a design problem space and its solution space are acquired in the building and application of an artifact (Hevner & Chatterjee, 2010; Hevner et al., 2004; Samuel-Ojo, Shimabukuro, Chatterjee, Muthui, Babineau, Prasertsilp, Ewais, and Young, 2010). We built a design methodology for construction of mapping applications for characterizing geospatial variables as an IT workflow artifact and applied it to disparate input datasets.

In geology, geophysics and cartographic studies, methods such as such as stacking (averaging), Fourier analysis and filtering are used to separate frequencies or wavelengths of signals and profiles (data). Fourier analysis by harmonics for example requires the whole signal or profile while filter needs only few succession readings that are in the 'window'. These methods often result in partial detection because they perform partial separation of wanted from unwanted anomalies and the error in separation gets propagated into data layers and subsequent analyses, thereby resulting in less accurate spatial predictions.

A cartographic visualization process, proposed by Wright, Brodlie, and Brown (1996) is mostly used to produce cartographic models and maps. This process consists of four main stages: data input (data collection, survey data or simulation), data filtering/enhancement, interpolation to grid and visualization technique (mapping), and display rendering. The process is based on Fourier analysis and filtering method and thus inherits the cons of these methods. It lacks the means of assuring data quality and preventing error in frequency separation from being propagated into the data layers and the subsequent models. Our proposed methodology, the design methodology for construction of mapping applications for characterizing geospatial variables, addresses these limitations.

The development of the design methodology evolves from one of our conference papers that focus on analysis (Samuel-Ojo, et al., 2013) but this paper is significantly different in that it is more than just analysis; it is a procedure or workflow that enables both the analysis and the synthesis of geospatial regionalized variables for construction of mapping applications.

The design methodology consists of three major phases: disaggregation, application and aggregation. The disaggregation phase separates input data into component data parts. It includes data acquisition and unification component, data reduction and quality component, and decomposition component as shown in the Figure 2.

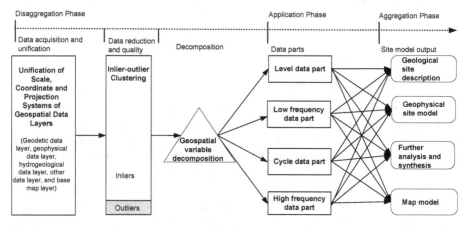

Fig. 2. Design methodology for construction of mapping applications for characterizing geospatial variables

The application phase, shown as data part component in the figure, puts into use the data part(s) such as removing certain parts whilst the aggregation phase shown as site model output component in the figure, assembles the modified data parts and maps the result.

4.1   Data Acquisition and Unification Component

This component takes a geospatial regionalized variable (Rev)[2] which is represented as a data layer and disaggregates it into its dimensions. In this study, the input datasets, the depth-to-water-level field data is recorded in feet in State Plane Coordinate Systems (SPCS CA zone 3), North American Datum of 1983 (NAD83). The coordinate and projection systems are harmonized for consistency and image registration alignment by projecting them into a geodetic parameter dataset of coordinate reference systems and transformations of European Petroleum Survey Group (EPSG).

4.2   Data Reduction and Quality Component

Data reduction ensures that relevant geophysical corrections (such as gravity and pore fluid pressure correction), migration (plumbing) and generic data conversion (scale normalization) are performed. Here, model quality is checked for stationarity (trending), precision, clarity, completeness, consistency and resolution.

---

[2]   A regionalized variable is a variable that is distributed in space, characterizing certain physical process.

Having made necessary corrections, the input datasets are grouped into two clusters: inliers and outliers using the BoxPlot statistics. The BoxPlot statistics summarize data into six quantities: sample minimum, lower quartile (Q1), median (Q2), upper quartile (Q3), sample maximum and outliers.

Inliers are data with relatively high probability of closeness to neighbors while outliers have low probability of closeness and high likelihood of noise. These two clusters are candidates for further exploration. Customarily, the inliers are processed for wanted anomaly detection while outliers are discarded. The inliers assure the logical consistency of data layers.

The inliers are logically grouped into 4D-elemental (XYZT) data and or feature classes (if geometric data are involved) and loaded into a database. While loading the data, data integrity check constraints are defined to achieve quality using primary and alternate keys. Primary or alternate keys are identifies, composed of one or more attributes that uniquely identifies a row in a relational database table. The constraints allow the prevention of occurrence of duplicate, incomplete or incorrect data.

The database is designed based on a star schema that models the relationship between a regionalized variable fact entity and its time and space entities (Chen, 2006). The entity relationship diagram and the fan illustration for geospatial repository pattern of database table for feature and data layers are shown in Figure 3.

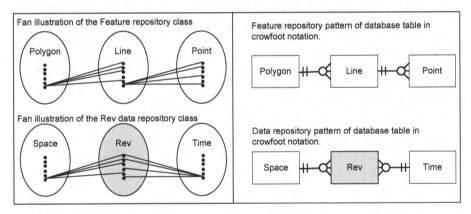

Fig. 3. Geospatial repository pattern of database table for feature and data layers

The fan illustration on the left of the Figure 3 indicates that feature layer pattern is hierarchical in that an instance of polygon contains many instances of lines and an instance of line contains many instances of points. Whilst data layer pattern of an XYZT Rev is not hierarchical; an instance of space or time contains many instances of Rev.

The geospatial repository pattern of object class for feature and data layers is shown in Figure 4. Each object class consists of public variables or properties (indicated by a prefix plus sign '+') and methods (functions). This pattern can serve as an interface class for each class object implementation.

Data repository class pattern in UML notation

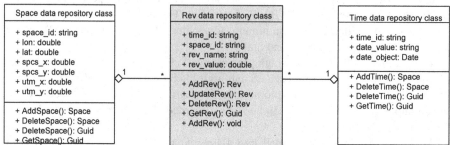

Fig. 4. The 4D (XYZT) repository database access objects for spatio-temporal problems using Unified Modeling Language (UML) for in software engineering

4.3   Decomposition Component

This component is illustrated by the geospatial variable decomposition prism. Much like how a physical prism splits white light into a rainbow of colors, the decomposer, which might be implemented by spectral, scale space, and matrix decomposition techniques, splits input data into data parts. The data parts offer potentials for richer descriptions of underlying geologic processes. The decomposition component is based on the premises that data might come from different processes, i.e., the observed attribute is a summary or average or sample of other attributes not observed.

Let a spatio-temporal data quantity h of a transaction (process) be described as a function of time t, h(t). In a frequency domain, let the process be described by its amplitude H as a function of frequency f, H(f) and angular velocity (2πf). Then the representation is given by:

$$H(f) = \int_{-\infty}^{\infty} h(t)e^{i2\pi ft}dt$$

$$h(t) = \int_{-\infty}^{\infty} H(f)e^{-i2\pi ft}df$$

Given an input function h(t), a mask function g(t) and their corresponding Fourier transform H(f) and G(f) with a mask lag τ, then the convolution of h(t) and g(t) is given by:

$$g * h \equiv \int_{-\infty}^{\infty} g(\tau)h(t - \tau)d\tau \equiv G(f) * H(f)$$

Thus, the Fourier decomposition of the convolution is just the product of the individual Fourier decompositions. The Fourier decomposer implements the Fast Fourier Transform algorithm for Averaging, Laplacian and Laplacian of Gaussian (LoG) filter. Filtering is a procedure that visits each element of the input data and replaces it with the filtered value. Filters apply a convolution tool. Convolution is the operation of replacing each element of an input with a scaled output functions. A 2-D averaging convolution of two signals f(x,y) and g(x,y) is expressed as:

$$z(x,y) = (f * g)(x,y) = \sum_{s=M_1}^{M_2} \sum_{t=N_1}^{N_2} f(x-s, y-t)g(s,t)$$

Where [M1 , M2] and [N1, N2] are the domains and (s, t) are the dimensions of the mask function in the discrete form.

A Gaussian filter implements first order differencing as shown.

$$\nabla g(x,y) = \frac{\partial g(x,y,\sigma)}{\partial x}U_x + \frac{\partial g(x,y,\sigma)}{\partial y}U_y$$

$$= -\frac{x}{\sigma^2}e^{\frac{-(x^2+y^2)}{2\sigma^2}}U_x - \frac{y}{\sigma^2}e^{\frac{-(x^2+y^2)}{2\sigma^2}}U_y$$

A Laplacian filter uses Laplacian operators and implements second order differencing on a Gaussian filter which is also called a Laplacian of Gaussian (LoG) filter. If P is a spatial data and if its coefficients are retained and derivatives are dropped, a 2-D (x, y) Laplacian of Gaussian (LoG) is expressed as:

$$\nabla(g(x,y) * P) = \nabla^2(g(x,y)) * P$$

The above expression is again estimated by convolving two Gaussian filters with difference variance (Marr and Hildreth, 1980). This estimation, known as a Difference of Gaussian (DoG) filter, is shown below,

$$\sigma\nabla^2 g(x,y,\sigma) = \frac{\partial}{\partial\sigma} \approx \frac{g(x,y,k\sigma) - g(x,y,\sigma)}{k\sigma - \sigma}$$

where g(x,y,σ) is a Gaussian function and k is a constant. The computational procedure for implementing these filters is detailed in the next section. The above expression is again estimated by convolving two Gaussian filters with difference variance (Marr & Hildreth, 1980). This estimation is known as the Difference of Gaussian (DoG) filter.

4.4   Data Part Component

The application phase comprises the data part components and other data operations required based on the objective in question. The data parts are: cycle, low frequency, level and high frequency. Cycle data describe seasonal short-term or long-term behavior, observable several times within the data. Low frequency data (trend) are changes in the data from one period to another. Levels are casted as edge points of contrast at different scales (of uniform intensity) or intercepts of regression lines. Edge point of contrast consistently defines regions of changing gradient depicting when an underlying physical process changed its operational level. High frequency data are local changes in data or variables that are not accounted for. These data parts allow us to answer different research questions.

4.5   Site Model Output Component

The site model output component defines the aggregation phase where we use the data parts directly or combine them. The outputs include geological site descriptions, site geophysical model, further analysis and synthesis, and map models.

5   Result and Interpretation

The digital elevation models (DEMs), constructed from triangular irregular network (TIN) of the median depth to water level shown in Figure 5, represent a water level surface, not the flow direction of the groundwater (which is typically shown by flow lines or potentiometric surface). The left map shows the median depth to water level readings before being decomposed into data parts while the right map shows the de-seasoned (after discounting seasonal mean) high frequency data part. As illustrated, there are more structures (curvature features) in the right map than that of the left.

From information entropy theory (Shannon, 1948), the more structure we have in a piece of data, the more information we are able to extract from the data. In Figure 5, we compare the patterns of geometric features (near straight lines following surface contrast) of the surface curvature in relation to faults mapped by United States Geoscience Information Network (USGIN) in color blue.

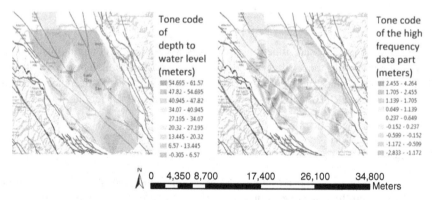

Fig. 5. Median depth to water level curvature of groundwater surface map. Left. Map of surface curvature of the median depth to water level data. Right. Map of surface curvature of the deseasoned high frequency data part of the same data. (Fault map courtesy of the United States Geoscience Information Network (USGIN), Water level data courtesy of the Records Management Unit, Santa Clara Valley Water District and Department of Earth Sciences, University of California, Riverside.)

The high frequency data part reveals more suggestive faults than that of the raw data. The left map of Figure 6 shows two major faults running from NW to SE, documented by the USGIN. The first fault runs through Stanford from the NW, then through Sunnyvale and Campbell toward Coyote in the SE. The new branching faults by Sunnyvale and Campbell are detectible directly from the well data. A fault was also detectible between the first and the second (Silver Creek fault) which runs through Alviso and Milpitas via San Jose toward Coyote.

By tracing the near straight line contrast on the surface curvature in the left map, the pattern supports the existence of the two major faults documented by USGIN. More interesting, new branching faults and fractures are suggested, dissecting the subregion between the two major faults that are not in the USGIN fault map.

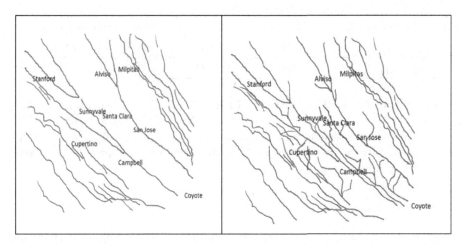

Fig. 6. Comparison of fault maps. Faults mapped by USGIN on the left versus Faults mapped by this study on the right.

The Kolmogorov-Smirnov non-parametric test of the high frequency data part yields a p-value of 2.2e-16 which is less than 0.05 indicating it is not random. The fault pattern mapped by the high frequency data part is detectable and can thus be construed as a signature. Faults are geologic forms that cause discontinuity of groundwater flow (Carr, 1995).Thus we established that data parts offer distinctive patterns of geometric features that are signatures, indicative of faults and fracture from the groundwater data.

6   Formative Evaluation by Unit Test

We achieved better data quality for modeling accuracy by extending the concept of unit test in test-driven development (TDD) paradigm (Beck, 2000; Hammond & Umphress, 2012). TDD is a software development method that allows fast feedback about whether a piece of code works. TDD can be employed to perform formative evaluation of the artifact by considering each phase of the proposed methodology as a unit and performing unit-level tests. We assessed the accuracy and predictive power of the decomposition unit of the methodology by implementing Fourier spectral technique and comparing it with the implementation of the wavelet scale space technique (Patton, 2008; Scriven, 1980). The accuracy and predictive power experiment utilizes Root Mean Square Error (RMSE) and Peak Signal-to-Noise Ratio (PSNR) evaluation statistics (Fgee, Phillips, & Robertson, 1999).

The accuracy and predictive power experiment is set up by reconstructing the original data from the decomposed four data parts (level, cycle, trend, high frequency), and by computing the RMSE and PSNR using the original time series data and the reconstructed data, and then by comparing their statistical values.

Table 1. Comparison of accuracy and predictive performance of Wavelet decomposition and Fourier decomposition

Regionalized Variable	Fourier Decomposition		Wavelet Decomposition	
	RMSE	PSNR	RMSE	PSNR
Depth to water level	1.45e-15	328.30	1.15e-11	250.32

The experimental results are shown in Table 1. The Fourier decomposition produces lower RMSE of an average of 1.45e-15 and higher PSNR of an average of 328.30 compared to Wavelet decomposition averages of 1.15e-11 and 250.32. Thus the accuracy and predictive power of the Fourier decomposition instantiation is taken to have lower error and a better signal to noise ratio.

7   Conclusion

We proposed the design methodology for construction of mapping applications for characterizing geospatial variables to improve quality spatial monitoring of groundwater flow for sustainable groundwater management. The design methodology is a three-phase method consisting of disaggregation, application, and aggregation. We applied the method to groundwater field data acquired from the Santa Clara Valley, CA, USA. We noted that the methodology aids in producing data components or data parts, suited to the construction of environmental information systems because of their inherent spatio-temporal characteristics.

Using these data parts, we built cartographic map models of different surface abstractions. In particular, we utilized the high frequency data part to produce an enhanced wanted anomaly. We confirmed those faults already documented and suggested new faults and fractures below the ground surface as well. Further research is required to produce signatures which might be used for predicting the behavior of groundwater in the region.

Resource managers and geoscientists might apply the inlier and outlier clustering to improve the fidelity of model building and enhance data and model quality for more accurate spatial prediction, interpretation, and better understanding of sweet spots or targets of rare geologic events for utility planning and placement. The results have practical implications useful for building well-composed environmental information systems.

References

1. Arbia, G., Griffith, D., Haining, R.: Error propagation and modeling in raster GIS: overlay operations. Int. Journal of Geographical Information Science 12, 145–167 (1999)
2. Ballou, D., Wang, R.Y., Pazer, H., Tayi, G.K.: Modeling information manufacturing systems to determine information product quality. Manag. Sci. 44(4), 484 (1998)
3. Beck, K.: Extreme Programming Explained: Embrace Change. Addison-Wesley, Readings (2000)
4. Blakemore, M.: Generalization and error in spatial data bases. Cartographica 21, 131–139 (1984)
5. Bolstad, P.: GIS Fundamentals: A first text on geographical information systems. Eider Press, White Bear Lake (2012)
6. Carr, J.R.: Numerical Analysis for the Geological Sciences. Prentice-Hall, Inc., Englewood Cliffs (1995)
7. Chen, P.P.-S.: Suggested research directions for a new frontier: Active conceptual modeling. Springer, Berlin (2006)
8. Fetter, C.W.: Applied Hydrogeology. Prentice-Hall, Inc. (2001)
9. Fgee, E.B., Phillips, W.J., Robertson, W.: Comparing Audio Compression Using Wavelets with Other Audio Compression Schemes. In: IEEE Canadian Conference on Electrical and Computer Engineering, vol. 2, pp. 698–701 (1999)
10. Hammond, S., Umphress, D.: Test driven development: the state of the practice. Paper Presented at the 50th Annual SE Regional Conf., Tuscaloosa, Alabama (2012)
11. Hevner, A.R., Chatterjee, S.: Design research in information systems:Theory and Practice. Springer publishing (2010)
12. Hevner, A.R., March, S.T., Park, J., Ram, S.: Design Science in Information Systems Research. MIS Quarterly 28(1) (2004)
13. Heuvelink, G.: Error Propagation in Environmental Modeling with GIS. Taylor and Francis, London (1999)
14. Lee, Y., Strong, D.M.: Knowing-Why about data processes and data quality. J. Manag. Inf. Syst. 20(3) (2004)
15. Madnick, S.E., Lee, Y.W., Wang, R.Y., Zhu, H.: Overview and framework for data and information quality research. ACM J. Data Inform. Quality 1(1), Article 2, 22 (2009)
16. Marr, D.C., Hildreth, E.: Theory of Edge Detection. Proc. R. Soc. B 207, 187–217 (1980)
17. Patton, M.Q.: Utilization Focused Evaluation. Sage, Thousand Oaks (2008)
18. Pospiech, M., Felden, C.: Big Data – A State-of-the-Art. Paper presented at the Proceedings of the Eighteenth Americas Conference on Information Systems, Seattle, Washington (2012)
19. Sabins, F.F.: Remote Sensing: Principles and Interpretation. W. H. Freeman & Co., New York (1986)
20. Samuel-Ojo, O., Olfman, L., Reinen, L.A., Flenner, A., Oglesby, D.D., Funning, G., Idemudia, E.C.: A Novel Business Intelligence Technique to Improve High Performance within an Organization Applying Insights from Hydrogeological Case. Paper Presented at the Proceedings of the 19th AMCIS Conference, Chicago (2013)
21. Samuel-Ojo, O., Shimabukuro, D., Chatterjee, S., Muthui, M., Babineau, T., Prasertsilp, P., Ewais, S., Young, M.: Meta-analysis of Design Science Research within the IS Community: Trends, Patterns, and Outcomes. In: Winter, R., Zhao, J.L., Aier, S. (eds.) DESRIST 2010. LNCS, vol. 6105, pp. 124–138. Springer, Heidelberg (2010)

22. Schmidt, D.A., Burgmann, R.: Time-dependent land uplift and subsidence in the Santa Clara valley, California, from a large Interferometric Synthetic Aperture Radar data set. Journal of Geophysical Research 108 (2003)
23. Scriven, M.: The Logic of Evaluation. Edgepress, Iverness (1980)
24. Shannon, C.E.: A Mathematical Theory of Communication. Bell System Technical Journal 27(3), 379–423 (1948)
25. UNESCO. International Glossary of Hydrology, Paris (1992)
26. USCB. Population 2009 Estimate of Santa Clara County, California (2011), http://quickfacts.census.gov/qfd/states/06/06085.html
27. Wright, H., Brodlie, K.W., Brown, M.: The dataflow visualization pipeline as a problem solving environment. In: Gobel, M., David, J., Slavik, P., van Wijk, J.J. (eds.) Virtual Environments and Scientific Visualization, pp. 267–276. Springer (1996)

Cherry Picking with Meta-Models:
A Systematic Approach for the Organization-Specific
Configuration of Maturity Models

Janusch Patas[1], Jens Pöppelbuß[2], and Matthias Goeken[1]

[1] Frankfurt School of Finance and Management, Frankfurt, Germany
{j.patas,m.goeken}@fs.de
[2] University of Bremen, Bremen, Germany
jepo@uni-bremen.de

Abstract. Information systems (IS) managers apply maturity models (MMs) to evaluate and enhance their organization's capabilities. Since the MM concept has become increasingly popular in research and practice over the past years, the number of similar or competing MMs has literally exploded. Despite their popularity, MMs are often criticized for being either too generic or too comprehensive. Therefore, prior to their application, organizations tend to adjust them according to their specific requirements. Unfortunately, IS management lacks methods to support this task systematically. In this article we intend to close this methodical gap as we develop a meta-model that supports a systematic configuration of MMs according to organization-specific requirements. We conduct a thorough literature analysis to construct this artifact, i.e., a maturity model meta-model (MMMM). Thereafter, we apply a tool-supported qualitative content analysis to extend, ground, and evaluate those components using a representative subset of 13 publicly available MMs. Finally, we identify four use cases and adapt configuration mechanisms from related research areas to illustrate and demonstrate our artifact's utility. Both IS practice and research benefit from our findings as we contribute a systematic meta-model-based approach that helps to analyze MMs and configure them to organization-specific requirements.

Keywords: Maturity models, maturity model components, meta-model, maturity model configuration, qualitative content analysis.

1   Introduction

Over the last two decades maturity models (MMs) have attracted increasing attention in information systems (IS) research and practice [1]. Tens or even hundreds of different MMs were identified in diverse literature reviews [2, 3]. Against this background, Pöppelbuß et al. [2] even observed "an inflation of maturity model research [in certain fields] that may call for integration and consolidation efforts in the future." The continuously growing number of MMs confronts IS management with the following challenges. First, they have to select a MM which is suited best to satisfy their

J. vom Brocke et al. (Eds.): DESRIST 2013, LNCS 7939, pp. 353–368, 2013.
© Springer-Verlag Berlin Heidelberg 2013

organization-specific requirements. Second, they may even see the need to synthesize or adjust existing ones to create a MM that fulfills their specific requirements sufficiently at all.

Apparently, developing and publishing additional MMs to meet every organization's requirements might not be considered as the first best and most effective answer to this management challenge. Instead, it seems more promising to allow for the situational configuration and augmentation of existing MMs according to organization-specific requirements [4]. Specifically for software development, first approaches for the meta-model-based configuration of maturity models and further methodologies have been suggested (e.g., ISO/IEC 24744, [5]). However, those approaches are domain-specific and they do not address the configuration of MMs in general. We believe that MMs are valuable management tools and their configuration should be supported beyond a specific application domain. For this reason, this piece of research at hand does not particularly focus on software development but on IS management in general.

In this paper, we therefore develop *a maturity model meta-model (MMMM) that supports IS management in configuring maturity models according to organization-specific requirements.* The objective of our solution is to enable the systematic design of tailored MMs based on components taken from existing MMs available in the IS domain.

Adhering to the design science research paradigm [6], we structure the paper as follows: Next, we present related work on MMs to identify the research gap and to motivate a solution (Sec. 2). Subsequently we describe the methodology (Sec. 3) before we identify MM components from literature to build a meta-model for maturity models (Sec. 4.1). In addition, we apply qualitative content analysis to ground and validate these components based on a representative subset of 13 MMs from the IS knowledge base (4.2). Next, we identify four use cases and adapt three configuration mechanisms from reference model research to operationalize our artifact and illustrate its utility (Sec. 5.1), followed by a demonstration of its application (Sec. 5.2). Finally, we conclude and provide avenues for future research (Sec. 6).

2   Related Work on Maturity Models and Motivation

MMs describe typical patterns in the development of organizational capabilities by means of a sequence of stages that mirrors a predictable, desired, or logical development path from an initial to a target maturity state [7]. They predefine a hardly reversible step-by-step progression of a capability which is assumed to be beneficial to an organization. They also provide criteria that are necessary to determine the status quo of a capability [8]. Organizations use MMs to evaluate, benchmark, or continuously improve their capabilities [1].

Over the last two decades, the IS discipline has witnessed a growing number of publications on the development, application, and evaluation of MMs [3]. In the late 1980s and in the 1990s, MM research in IS particularly focused on the Capability

Maturity Model (CMM) for software engineering (SE). Later on, the MM concept has been adapted to many fields apart from SE, both in research and practice. Apart from solely focusing on the MM development, more recent research explains and reflects on the MM concept. These contributions can be structured as follows:

- Descriptions of structures and components of MMs (e.g., [7, 9–13]).
- Procedure models for the systematic development of MMs (e.g.,[1, 4, 8, 10, 11, 14]).
- Criteria for evaluating the quality of MMs (e.g., [9, 13, 15, 16]).
- Reviews that outline the state-of-the-art of available MMs in research and practice (e.g., [2, 3, 8]).

Despite these considerable advancements in MM research, MMs have also been criticized for being static and for not satisfying organization-specific requirements [4, 11]. Most of the suggested procedure models (e.g., [1, 8, 14]) that ease and support the systematic development of MMs do not provide ways to cope with this criticism as they disregard the need for the organization-specific configuration of MMs.

Mettler and Rohner [4] (pp. 3) already emphasized the need to shift towards the development of situational (i.e., configurable) MMs: "Accordingly, it is crucial for maturity models with the intention of organizational engineering to clearly determine the situational characteristics where the deployment of the model is admissible (e.g. scope and level of analysis, audience) and/or to define configuration parameters to extend the focus of the maturity model." However, their recommendation only highlights the need to predefine configuration parameters during MM construction but they do not offer a mechanism for this purpose.

In this regard, Ahlemann et al. [9] have previously proposed a meta-model for both competence models and MMs. However, their meta-model simply describes that MMs comprise a list of maturity levels referring to requirements which are measured by criteria. This meta-model seems incomplete as, for instance, it neglects components as practices or resources that are present in almost every other MM [14]. Generally, components a MM should include, are often only theoretically discussed (e.g., [10, 11]) but not empirically grounded.

In order to close the identified research gaps, we apply ontological meta-modeling and qualitative research techniques to construct a more complete meta-model that constitutes the basis for configuration mechanisms that help to cater for organization-specific requirements.

3   Methodology

We structure the construction process of the generic meta-model for MMs (MMMM) into the following two phases (Table 1). In the first phase, we deductively construct the MMMM from literature that deals with the development of MMs in general, i.e., apart from the development of specific MMs. Taking the example of IT project management, Figure 1 illustrates the basic idea of meta-modeling. It depicts the distinct abstraction levels and illustrates the instantiation of the meta-model component Capability on M2 (meta-model level) which becomes the model component IT Project Management on M1 (model level) before it is instantiated as an organization-specific component, e.g., IT Project Management at Organization XY on M0 (reflecting an organization-specific maturity model, i.e., the capability as interpreted by the specific organization). We search the literature exclusively for meta-model components on M2 (MMMM components). This results in a preliminary MMMM that includes components and their relationships as present in pertinent literature.

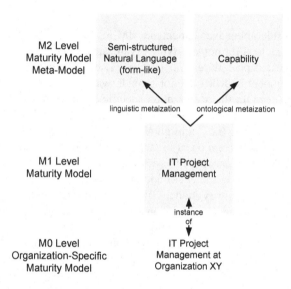

Fig. 1. Illustration of meta-modeling approaches adapted from [17].

In the second phase, we evaluate, substantiate, and extend the preliminary MMMM based on the analysis of popular MMs. This analysis is guided by qualitative research methods. We apply qualitative content analysis that postulates the utilization of "prior formulated, theoretical derived aspects of analysis" [18] and which supports a theory-driven analysis of text. We analyze prevalent MMs with respect to the occurrence and utilization of the MMMM components we have theoretically derived in phase 1. This way, our analysis in phase 2 can be interpreted as a grounding and evaluation of the MMMM and its meta-model components.

Basically, we apply two techniques to support our methodology and the creation of our results, i.e. ontological meta-modeling [19] and reciprocal translation [20]. Ontological meta-modeling, in contrast to linguistic meta-modeling (metaization), deals with the abstraction and classification of model components according to their content (Figure 1). Reciprocal translation analysis is a qualitative research technique that helps to merge identical or similar component into one another [21].

Table 1. Goals, activities, and results of our research process

| | Phase 1 (Sec. 4.1): Deductively constructing the MMMM | | Phase 2 (Sec. 4.2): Grounding and Evaluating the MMMM | |
	Step 1	Step 2	Step 3	Step 4
Level	Meta-model level (M2)	Meta-model level (M2)	Model-level (M1)	Model and meta-model level (M1; M2)
Goal	Identification of pertinent literature about the structure of MMs	Identification of generic MMMM-meta-model components	Representative selection of prevalent MMs	Evaluation of the MMMM Assigning model components to the MMMM
Activity	Literature Search I	Applying ontological meta-modeling and reciprocal translation analysis to the relevant literature (theoretical saturation)	Literature Search II	Qualitative Research: • Assigning excerpts of MM-descriptions to MMMM-components • Identification of further MMMM-components
Result	Relevant literature on MMs	MMMM	Set of MMs	Grounded and evaluated MMMM

4   Instantiating the Research Process

4.1   Phase 1: Deductively Constructing the Maturity Model Meta-Model

Step 1 (Meta-Model Level). For our first literature search, we referred to articles from the IS discipline which had recently been published in international IS journals (e.g., CAIS, BISE) and conference proceedings (e.g., AMCIS, ECIS) and which we knew prior to this research endeavor. From the reference lists of these pertinent papers we identified further relevant contributions that provide propositions about the meta-model components and structure of MMs. Existing literature reviews on MMs (as referenced in Sec. 2) were especially helpful as they yielded references to additionally relevant papers.

Step 2 (Meta-Model Level). We reviewed the relevant literature for MM components and their relationships and applied the aforementioned reciprocal translation. This research technique helped us to examine key components and to constantly compare them, and, furthermore, to derive and synthesize relevant components from prevalent approaches. We tracked the identified components in a list and documented their relationships in an entity-relationship-diagram. After the review of each individual paper we updated our list, i.e., we added new components, added synonyms for components, generalized components and revised their descriptions (Table 2). We updated and refined continuously the meta-model to consider all identified components and their relationships properly.

Step 1 and 2 were performed iteratively, i.e., the selection of new articles continued until no new meta-model components were identified and a theoretical saturation was achieved. In this context, the concept of theoretical saturation describes a state in which new conclusions cannot be obtained by adding further articles on maturity models [22]. In our case saturation was achieved having analyzed the references as given in Table 2.

The central meta-model component of the resulting MMMM is the capability, to which a maturity level is assigned during an MM assessment. A capability belongs to a domain that defines the general scope or subject of the MM (e.g., software development in the original CMM). De Bruin et al. [10] suggest to structure MMs hierarchically into multiple layers, i.e., the assessed capability should be detailed in a tree-like manner. Typically, the children of the overall capability (i.e., the root node of the tree) are further structured into different dimensions and areas (e.g., process or capability areas) which can be interpreted as sub-capabilities [7]. This leads to different levels of granularity [13]. We decided to depict this as a hierarchy of capabilities, i.e., sub-capabilities are capabilities which are the children of an overarching capability.

Another central feature of a MM is its set of maturity levels. These are ordered in a row, i.e., maturity level 2 is considered superior to maturity level 1 [11]. For each maturity level, it is typical to have a descriptor (ML Descriptor) and a generic description (ML Description) [7]. The number/ID of a maturity level and its descriptor refer to the overall capability, and mainly serves as identifiers.

The MM is populated by definitions of combinations of (sub-)capabilities and maturity levels. In a maturity grid, these would be the cells of the grid when having the maturity level as one axis and the capability (areas) as the other one [11]. Each combination is reflected by certain practices or activities which an organization should perform [7]. Practices, in turn, serve specific goals [12] and both meta-model components require different resources like assets or systems [2, 4, 14]. Assessment criteria intend to determine the maturity level of the organization and refer to goals and resources, i.e., the criteria measure whether the required resources are present and if or to which degree the goals have been achieved [9]. They can serve as benchmark variables [8].

4.2   Phase 2: Grounding and Evaluating the Maturity Model Meta-Model

Step 3 (Model Level). After we have constructed the MMMM as presented in Figure 2 (except for the gray shaded area), the goals of the next two steps were, first, to identify a representative and considerable number of well-established MMs and, second, to ground the theoretical MM meta-model components and to evaluate the deductively derived MMMM. To identify the MMs we searched GoogleScholar using "maturity

Table 2. Identified and synthesized maturity model meta-model components from literature

Component	Synonyms	Description	References
Assessment criterion	Characteristic, criterion, variable, benchmark variable, assessment item, measure	An indicator used to identify the maturity level of a capability.	[1–4, 8, 9, 12, 13]
Capability	Process, process area, dimension, domain component, domain sub-component, layers of detail, element, content, construct, maturity dimension, domain specific dimension, focus area, object, problem domain, dimensions of maturity	The capability in scope and its sub-elements which represent the core of and are evaluated by the maturity model; capability elements can be hierarchically structured into multiple layers of detail (levels of granularity)	[1–4, 7, 10, 11, 13, 14]
Domain	Scope, discipline, subject, focus, functional domain,	The subject area of the maturity model. The domain sometimes equals the root node of a capability.	[1, 2, 10–12, 14]
Goal	Target state, application target, objective	Goals explain to be achieved needs and thereby motivate the performance of practices and utilization of resources.	[2, 3, 11–13]
Maturity level (ML)	Stage, stage-of-growth, scale, state of completion	Levels of varying maturity, from low to high, typically 3-6 levels, which form the rating scale and the evolutionary path. The highest number represents high maturity as opposed to the lowest number.	[1–3, 7–12, 14]
ML Descriptor		Concise description of a maturity level, e.g., ad-hoc, initial, etc.	[2, 7]
ML Description		Description of the entire maturity level.	[7]
Practice	Key practice, activity, cell text, *intersection of process area and maturity level, process characteristics, work practice, guideline, responsibility*	Performed activities to deploy the capability under consideration.	[2, 7, 11, 12, 14]
Resource	Asset, system	Used to perform a practice and to support a goal.	[2, 4, 14]

model" as keyword. In detail, we defined the following three criteria with respect to relevant MMs: (1) Each MM must originate from the domain of IS (and not only software development), (2) has to be cited more than 50 times, and (3) must be digitally available since we use ATLAS.ti as our tool for the qualitative content analysis. Although our focus was not on software development, we decided to keep the original CMM within our sample as the structure of this particular MM has served as a blueprint for many other MMs in the IS domain [2]. The resulting set of 13 MMs that we used in this phase for our analysis is documented in Table 3.

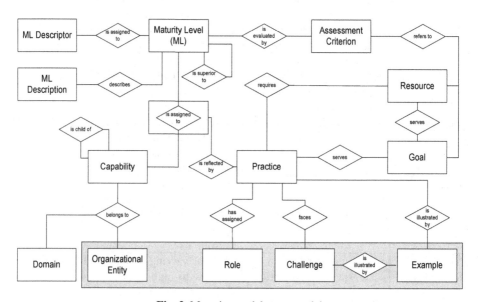

Fig. 2. Maturity model meta-model

Step 4 (Meta-Model and Model Level). For the qualitative analysis we used the MMMM illustrated in Figure 2 (except for the gray shaded area) and in particular the meta-model components described and presented in Table 2 as our preconception. Two researchers independently analyzed the MMs listed in Table 3. The first one conducted an extensive analysis in detail by interpreting and labeling text chunks using the predefined meta-model components (M2) to identify equivalent components on model level (M1). The second one went through the MMs with the goal to validate the results obtained by the first researcher. Text chunks that we could not label with one of our predefined meta-model components were regarded as a new component. Basically, we could identify four new meta-model components:

- *Challenge:* A challenge faced by an organization on a certain maturity level.
- *Example:* Provides an example for a challenge or practice.
- *Role:* A role is assigned to practice and represents a group of users who share some commonalities.

- *Organizational Entity:* An organizational entity is part of an organization and helps to restrict a maturity assessment to a relevant set of stakeholders within the organization.

As Table 3 illustrates, we found on model level (M1) the meta-model components (M2) role and organizational entity in almost every MM of our sample. These are new meta-model components that have not been discussed in theoretical MM research previously. The resulting MMMM is illustrated in Figure 2 (now including the gray shaded area).

Table 3. Maturity models and their components identified using qualitative contents analysis

Source	Meta-Model Component												
	Assess. Criterion	Capability	Challenge	Domain	Example	Goal	Mat. Level (ML)	ML Description	ML Descriptor	Organizational Entity	Practice	Resource	Role
[23]	✔	✔		✔		✔	✔	✔	✔		✔	✔	
[24]		✔		✔		✔	✔	✔	✔	✔	✔	✔	✔
[25]	✔	✔	✔	✔			✔	✔	✔	✔	✔	✔	✔
[26]	✔	✔		✔	✔	✔	✔	✔	✔	✔	✔	✔	✔
[27]	✔		✔	✔		✔	✔	✔	✔			✔	✔
[28]	✔	✔	✔	✔				✔	✔				✔
[29]		✔		✔		✔	✔	✔	✔		✔	✔	
[30]	✔	✔	✔	✔	✔	✔	✔	✔	✔	✔	✔	✔	✔
[31]	✔	✔		✔			✔	✔	✔	✔	✔	✔	✔
[32]	✔	✔		✔			✔	✔	✔		✔	✔	✔
[33]	✔	✔		✔	✔	✔	✔	✔	✔	✔	✔	✔	✔
[34]	✔	✔		✔		✔	✔		✔		✔	✔	✔
[35]	✔	✔		✔	✔		✔	✔	✔	✔	✔		✔
No. of MMs having the component	11	12	4	13	4	8	12	12	13	7	11	11	11

Nevertheless, although we have analyzed MMs for their meta-model components for the first time empirically, we do not claim our MMMM to be a universal and comprehensive representation of the structure of MMs. Our artifact rather intends to offer a "satisfactory solution" ([6] referring to H.A. Simon) for the abovementioned goals and applications, and must thus be regarded as provisional knowledge. For this reason, it is generally considered extendable. An extension can be meaningful for both empirical and conceptual reasons. If, for example, new components are found in MMs that we did not consider yet, the MMMM should be extended accordingly. A conceptually motivated extension might also be recommended if objectives behind the use of the MMMM change. After having developed the MMMM, we subsequently derive use cases and configuration mechanisms to demonstrate the operationalization of our artifact and thereby illustrate our artifact's utility.

5   Application of the Maturity Model Meta-Model

5.1   Four Use Cases and Configuration Mechanisms

In line with our research objective, we argue that our meta-model *supports the configuration of MMs according to organization-specific requirements*. To demonstrate the utility of our artifact, i.e., showing how it can be used to configure MMs, we subsequently discuss specific use cases that we found in literature and observed in practice. We believe that our MMMM has the utility to serve at least for the following four use cases (UC):

- *UC1 "MM Evaluation:"* When IS management has to select an appropriate MM for an organization-specific maturity assessment, it faces the challenge to choose the most suitable one from many available MMs (e.g., [2, 3]). Our MMMM can serve as an evaluation tool to determine the most 'mature' MM in terms of completeness which can be interpreted as the degree of MMMM components coverage.
- *UC2 "Cherry Picking:"* Organizations often use best-practice reference models as source of inspiration for "cherry picking" [36]. According to their requirements, they choose model components (e.g., goals in general on M1) from a selected MM to build their own MM. Our MMMM can serve as an analytical tool to systematically support this approach as it provides a set of the most important components to structure the model components of a MM.
- *UC3 "Synthesis and Extension:"* Often, none of the available MMs covers the entire set of an organization's specific requirements. In this case, the meta-model can serve as a tool for the synthesis of alternative models or for the extension with new components on meta-model (M2) and model level (M1) [20].
- *UC4 "MM Individualization:"* Since a MM usually provides rather generic descriptions [13] it does not necessarily comply with organization-specific goals, technical terms, etc. For this reason, components need to be adjusted and detailed mainly on the organization-specific level M0 [36].

Since MMs prescribe a development and maturation path for a certain capability, some IS researchers consider them as reference models, especially such popular MMs like the CMM [4]. Based on this perspective, we draw on existing research on best-practice reference model application [36]. Looso [36] applies three basic configuration mechanisms which we adapt to operationalize our four MMMM use cases.

In detail, these mechanisms are *selection, extension,* and *variation.* However, UC1 does not require a configuration mechanism because the MMMM already serves as the evaluation reference. Before we describe these mechanisms, it is important to mention the different effects that occur depending on the level where a certain mechanism is applied. Therefore, we distinguish between the organization-specific maturity model level (M0), maturity model level (M1), and the meta-model level (M2) as already illustrated in Figure 1.

Selection refers to the decision whether the organization requires all MMMM components or only a subset. The goal of applying the selection mechanism is to configure the MMMM in such a way that the MM will comprise only the relevant model components. For instance, if an organization's management does not plan to implement or evaluate goals, they may want to delete this component from the meta-model (M2). In consequence, all goals on model level and below will be also deleted (M1 and M0). In turn, if goals are deleted on M0 or M1, the corresponding component is not affected on the next upper level. The selection mechanism is typical for UC2, where the "cherries," i.e., the component on model level are picked to prepare an individual MM according to organization-specific needs. But it also supports UC3, in case those components on M2 or M1 are selected and synthesized from different MMs into a new one, and UC4, in case that a MM is individualized.

Extension refers to the addition of new components and relationships on either model (M1) or meta-model level (M2). If a new component is added on the meta-level it has to be connected to at least one another component on the same level. Additionally, it has to be instantiated to the model level or it represents a 'wildcard' on meta-level, which will be instantiated with the means of the variation mechanism on model level. For example, if management decides to split the component goal into IT and business goals, then a new 'is-a' relation has to be defined to connect these components. In particular, the extension mechanism is relevant for UC3, if the organization defines requirements that go beyond our current MMMM structure.

Variation refers to altering single or a set of components or instances mainly on the organization-specific MM level M0 can be also applied on M1. As opposed to the extension mechanism, variation does not create new components. According to Looso [36], tree sub-mechanisms are relevant for variation, i.e., *instantiation, specialization,* and *renaming. Instantiation* becomes relevant for M0 where the MM includes 'wildcards' on the model level. For instance, if the selected MM does not define specific goal instances but instead provides a wildcard for the components goal, then the wildcard has to be filled with specific organization's goals. *Specialization* refers to the adaptation of a model component to its context on instance level. For example, the MMMM component goal with its predefined components on model level should be detailed and specified to satisfy organization-specific requirements on instance level. In this case, a generally formulated goal may be transformed into an organization-specific goal. *Renaming* supports the adaption of model component to the M0 according to organization-specific technical terms. If a MM names a certain organizational entity IT department, it might be relabeled as technology department. To sum up, variation mechanisms are useful for UC3 and UC4.

5.2   Demonstrating the Artifact and Its Application

To demonstrate the artifact and the configuration mechanisms we randomly use one of the MMs provided by COBIT 4.1 [37]. The selected MM focuses on the IT governance *domain* 'plan and organize' and the *capability* 'defining a strategic IT plan.'

The first use case (UC1) covers the evaluation of the MM. Therefore, we used the MMMM as reference to analyze the COBIT 4.1 MM's content qualitatively with the help of the ATLAS.ti software (i.e., we imported the description of this MM into ATLAS.ti and coded it according to the MMMM components). Our evaluation provided the following results: The component *ML description* describes the *capability* comprehensively and contains the other components we were looking for. We found instances of the components *organizational entity, role, practice, goal,* and *resource* whereby the last two are referring to *assessment criteria.* However, our evaluation indicates incompleteness of the analyzed MM with regard to the MMMM as it does not define *challenges* or *examples.*

In the following, we demonstrate the operationalization of the MMMM for further UCs for maturity level 1 with the ML descriptor *initial/ad-hoc.* We describe and illustrate in Figure 3 the most important effects of the configuration mechanisms for UC2, UC3, and UC4 based on a fictive case.

Given that the MM is evaluated and all the instances are assigned to the components, the organization's management becomes only interested in the instances of the meta-model components *practice, resource,* and *goal* on model level M1 and thus selects this subset of the MMMM components on M2. Consequently, the other components disappear on M2 and also on the following lower levels (UC2, Figure 3). Moreover, management defines *outputs* as important work products of *practices.* Because the choose MM does not define *outputs* yet, they extend the MMMM and relate the component *output* to *practice* on M2. Now, those outputs represent 'wildcards' (illustrated in Figure 3 with '*') on M1 and must be instantiated (variation mechanism) as organization-specific outputs on M0. In our example, management defines the two *outputs* "O1: Basic IT Strategic Plan" and "O2: Adjusted IT Strategy to Business Needs". As for UC3, the organization's management applies the extension and variation mechanisms to arrive at a extend MM (UC3).

Finally, the organization's culture is coined by a set of technical terms that have evolved over the past years and management wants to be more precise regarding how those practices are formulated. In order to consider the technical terms and their management objectives, they apply the configuration mechanism variation to create an individualized version of the selected MM subset (UC4). First, to adjust the different technical terms according to their requirements, management renames the resources R1 and R2 from application and technology into soft- and hardware. The application of this variation mechanism has also direct implications for the formulation of the *goal* G2 (Figure 3, UC4). Management could be also more precise about those resources and instead renaming the resources R1 and R2 they could also instantiate those components into concrete technologies such as a governance, risk, and compliance (GRC) suit. Second, to specify the components *practice* according to their management objectives, they specify (specialization) the instances P1 and P2 on M0.

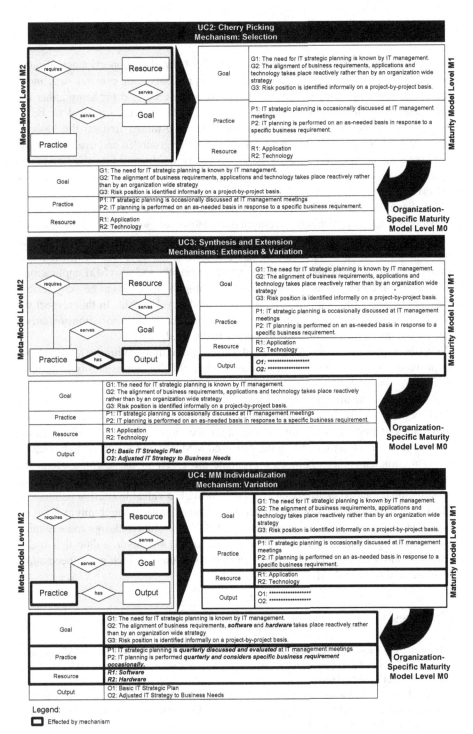

Fig. 3. Visualization of the configuration mechanisms and their effects on M2, M1, and M0

6   Conclusion and Avenues for Future Research

In this paper, we described the development of a MMMM that supports the configuration of MMs to satisfy organization-specific requirements. Our research was motivated by the growing number of MMs which are often criticized for being either too comprehensive or too generic. While constructing the artifact we tried to be as rigorous as possible. We therefore developed the meta-model first on the basis of theoretical MM components which we then empirically grounded and evaluated using qualitative content analysis. To demonstrate its utility we derived four uses cases and adapted three configuration mechanisms to operationalize and demonstrate the MMMM.

We believe that our artifact helps in configuring or developing more specific MMs that better satisfy organizations' requirements. However, we found during our research that MMs have been developed very unsystematically in the past and thus lack some of our identified components or just use them implicitly. Our MMMM might help to better structure future MM development endeavors and also MM applications. Moreover, the theoretical discussion about MM components seems to be very design-driven and neglects the empirical status quo in MM development. In this respect the application of the qualitative content analysis technique is a contribution towards a better grounding of the components that are actually used.

Nevertheless, this research is beset with certain limitations. With the MMMM, we only provide a tool for the systematic configuration of MMs but its ability to validate the utility of the resulting, i.e., organization-specifically configured, MM is limited. Although we assume that organizations will use the MMMM in a way that is beneficial to them, it would be generally possible that the outcome of selecting and reconfiguring components will not be useful to the organization. Therefore, future research should strive for extending the proposed MMMM and the presented mechanisms by a complementary approach to validate the utility of its outcome. Here, the aforementioned quality criteria for MMs (e.g., [9, 13, 16]) or assessment guidelines from situational method engineering [15] could provide a valuable starting point.

Besides eliminating the aforementioned limitations, future research might focus on a more fact-driven discussion about essential MM components to design more empirically grounded guidelines or rule for MM development. Moreover, a thorough analysis of more and different MMs could reveal new components which might necessitate an extension of our MMMM.

References

1. Becker, J., Knackstedt, R., Poeppelbuss, J.: Developing Maturity Models for IT Management – A Procedure Model and its Application. Business & Information Systems Engineering 1, 213–222 (2009)
2. Pöppelbuß, J., Niehaves, B., Simons, A., Becker, J.: Maturity Models in Information Systems Research: Literature Search and Analysis. Communications of the Association for Information Systems 29 (2011)

3. Wendler, R.: The maturity of maturity model research: A systematic mapping study. Inf. Softw. Technol. 54, 1317–1339 (2012)
4. Mettler, T., Rohner, P.: Situational maturity models as instrumental artifacts for organizational design. In: Proceedings of the 4th International Conference on Design Science Research in Information Systems and Technology. ACM, New York (2009)
5. Henderson-Sellers, B., Ralyté, J.: Situational method engineering: state-of-the-art review. Journal of Universal Computer Science 16, 424–478 (2010)
6. Hevner, A.R., March, S.T., Park, J., Ram, S.: Design science in information systems research. MIS Quarterly 28, 75–105 (2004)
7. Fraser, P., Moultrie, J., Gregory, M.: The use of maturity models/grids as a tool in assessing product development capability. In: IEEE International Engineering Management Conference, vol. 1, Cambridge, UK, pp. S.244–S.249 (2002)
8. Solli-Saether, H., Gottschalk, P.: The Modeling Process for Stage Models. Journal of Organizational Computing and Electronic Commerce 20, 279–293 (2010)
9. Ahlemann, F., Schroeder, C., Teuteberg, F.: Kompetenz- und Reifegradmodelle für das Projektmanagment - Grundlagen, Vergleich und Einsatz (2005), http://www.bow.uni-osnabrueck.de/reifegradmodelle.pdf
10. De Bruin, T., Freeze, R., Kaulkarni, U., Rosemann, M.: Understanding the main phases of developing a maturity assessment model. In: Australasian Conference on Information Systems, New South Wales, Sydney (2005)
11. Maier, A.M., Moultrie, J., Clarkson, P.J.: Assessing Organizational Capabilities: Reviewing and Guiding the Development of Maturity Grids. IEEE Transactions on Engineering Management 59, 138–159 (2012)
12. Ofner, M., Hühner, K., Otto, B.: Dealing with Complexity: A Method to adapt and implement a Maturity Model for Corporate Data Quality Management. In: Americas Conference on Information Systems, San Francisco, USA (2009)
13. Pöppelbuß, J., Röglinger, M.: What makes a useful maturity model? A framework of general design principles for maturity models and its demonstration in business process management. In: European Conference on Information Systems, Helsinki, Finland (2011)
14. Van Steenbergen, M., Bos, R., Brinkkemper, S., Van De Weerd, I., Bekkers, W.: The design of focus area maturity models. In: Design Science Research in Information Systems and Technologies, St.Gallen, Switzerland, pp. S.317–S.332 (2010)
15. McBride, T., Henderson-Sellers, B.: A Method Assessment Framework. In: Engineering Methods in the Service-Oriented Context, pp. S.64–S.76. Springer, Paris (2011)
16. Simonsson, M., Johnson, P., Wijkström, H.: Model-Based IT Governance Maturity Assessments with Cobit. In: European Conference on Information Systems, St.Gallen, Switzerland (2007)
17. Goeken, M., Alter, S.: Towards Conceptual Metamodeling of IT Governance Frameworks Approach - Use - Benefits. In: 42nd Hawaii International Conference on System Sciences, Hawaii, USA (2009)
18. Mayring, P.: Qualitative Content Analysis. Forum: Qualitative Social Research 1 (2000)
19. Atkinson, C., Kuhne, T.: Model-driven development: a metamodeling foundation. IEEE Software 20, 36–41 (2003)
20. Noblit, G.W., Hare, R.D.: Meta-ethnography: synthesising qualitative studies. Sage Publications Ltd., Newbury Park (1988)
21. Urquhart, C.: Metasynthesis of research on information seeking behaviour, http://informationr.net/ir/16-1/paper455.html
22. Bryant, A., Charmaz, K.: Hrsg: Discursive glossary of terms. In: The Sage Handbook of Grounded Theory, pp. S.603–S.612. Sage Publications Ltd., London (2010)

23. April, A., Huffman Hayes, J., Abran, A., Dumke, R.: Software Maintenance Maturity Model (SM^mm): the software maintenance process model. J. Softw. Maint. Evol. 17, 197–223 (2005)
24. Burnstein, I., Suwanassart, T., Carlson, R.: Developing a Testing Maturity Model for software test process evaluation and improvement. In: Proceedings International Test Conference, Piscataway, NJ, USA, pp. S.581–S.589 (1996)
25. Crawford, J.K.: The Project Management Maturity Model. Information Systems Management 23, 50–58 (2006)
26. Curtis, B., Hefley, B., Miller, S.: People Capability Maturity Model (P-CMM) (2009)
27. Fischer, D.M.: The Business Process Maturity Model: A Practical Approach for Identifying Opportunities for Optimization (2004), http://ww.w.bptrends.com/publicationfiles/10-04%20ART%20BP%20Maturity%20Model%20-%20Fisher.pdf
28. Gottschalk, P., Solli-Saether, H.: Maturity model for IT outsourcing relationships. Industrial Management & Data Systems 106, 200–212 (2006)
29. Kwak, Y.H., Ibbs, C.W.: Project Management Process Maturity (PM)² Model. Journal of Management in Engineering 18, 150–155 (2002)
30. Layne, K., Lee, J.: Developing fully functional E-government: A four stage model. Government Information Quarterly 18, 122–136 (2001)
31. Marshall, S., Mitchell, G.: Applying SPICE to e-learning: an e-learning maturity model? In: Proceedings of the Sixth Australasian Conference on Computing Education, pp. 185–191. Australian Computer Society, Inc., Darlinghurst (2004)
32. Niazi, M., Wilson, D., Zowghi, D.: A maturity model for the implementation of software process improvement: an empirical study. J. Syst. Softw. 74, 155–172 (2005)
33. Paulk, M., Curtis, B., Chrissis, M.B., Weber, C.V.: Capability Maturity Model for Software, Version 1.1 (1993), http://www.sei.cmu.edu/reports/93tr024.pdf
34. Paulzen, O., Doumi, M., Perc, P., Cereijo-Roibas, A.: A Maturity Model for Quality Improvement in Knowledge Management. In: Australasian Conference on Information Systems, Melbourne, Australia (2002)
35. Rosemann, M., de Bruin, T., Power, B.: A model to Measure BPM Maturity and Improve Performance. In: Jeston, J., Nelis, J. (eds.) Business Process Management: Practical Guidelines to Successful Implementations, pp. 299–315. Butterworth-Heinemann, Burlington (2006)
36. Looso, S.: Best-Practice-Referenzmodelle der IT-Governance. Struktur, Anwendung und Methoden (2011),
    http://www.frankfurt-school.de/dms/dissertations/Looso0/Looso.pdf
37. IT Governance Institute: COBIT 4.1 (2007), http://www.itgi.org

Towards a Domain-Specific Method for Multi-Perspective Hospital Modelling – Motivation and Requirements

Michael Heß

Research Group Information Systems and Enterprise Modelling
Institute for Computer Science and Business Information Systems
Faculty of Economics and Business Administration
University of Duisburg-Essen, Germany

Abstract. The paper motivates the design and development of a domain-specific method for Multi-Perspective Hospital Modelling and presents requirements the method should fulfil. The contribution follows the design science research process and the identified requirements serve as basis for evaluating related work from the medical informatics and information systems discipline. As out of all evaluated approaches, the Multi-Perspective Enterprise Modelling method fulfils the requirements to the greatest extent, it is to be extended towards the proposed Multi-Perspective Hospital Modelling method.

1 Motivation and Research Goal

The German public health, similarly to public health in other countries, is facing numerous challenges leading to an increased demand for high quality healthcare services and, in consequence, to increasing costs of the provision of medical care. However, while postulating higher quality of care, public health's stakeholders (e.g., patients, their relatives, insurers, government) demand more transparency in the medical care provision process as well as reducing the overall public health expenditures. Consequently, the German public health needs to meet the following, partly contradictory goals, namely to increase [1]: (1) quality of medical care, (2) transparency of the medical care provision process and of the resulting costs, and (3) its cost-effectiveness.

In order to increase the quality of medical care, medical care providers are expected to follow medical guidelines, i.e., "systematically developed statements to assist practitioner's and patient's decisions about the appropriate health care for specific clinical circumstances" [2, p. 38], which include information on the level of underlying evidence. In order to apply the knowledge provided by medical guidelines in hospitals, they need to be transformed into clinical pathways (CPs).

CP extends a guideline with institution-specific aspects (e.g., available resources, average costs per medical service, responsibilities), and is "a method for the patient-care management of a well-defined group of patients during a well-defined period of time. CP explicitly states the goals and key elements of care based on Evidence Based Medicine (EBM) guidelines, best practice and patient expectations by facilitating the communication, coordinating roles and sequencing the activities of the multidisciplinary care team, patients and their relatives; by documenting, monitoring and evaluating

J. vom Brocke et al. (Eds.): DESRIST 2013, LNCS 7939, pp. 369–385, 2013.

variances; and by providing the necessary resources and outcomes" [3]. Thus, CPs foster the increase of quality and transparency in medical care.

CPs can also support a pathway-oriented accounting, both on a type level and on a (patient-specific) instance level by supporting analyses on the resources used and the resulting costs; and by comparing those costs and the hospital's realised Diagnosis Related Groups (DRG) revenues. DRG, initially developed as a patient classification system, became a payment system based on the assumption that similar medical cases result in similar costs thus, all cases belonging to the same DRG result in a homogeneous payment. Consequently, the DRG-based payment system substituted the cost-recovery-principle's application in many countries' public health [4, p. 33], and CPs emerged as an adequate instrument to increase cost-effectiveness [5].

CP can be perceived analogously to a business process, which is "a recurring sequence of activities that conform to more or less rigid regulation patterns. It is goal-oriented and directly linked with the enterprise's market-oriented goods and services creation" [6, p. 18]. In turn, business process models serve as "purposeful abstraction of a business process type and are usually [...] represented in a graphical form" [6, p. 18]. CPs' graphical models could foster understandability and clarity of: medical knowledge, sequence of medical activities, and clinical decisions to be taken. However, the question appears whether it is sufficient to apply widely accepted techniques and methods of process modelling, to model CPs as hospitals' business processes.

The requirements analysis, presented in this paper, reveals that to allow for a full support of modelling and analysis of all CP's aspects, the development of a comprehensive modelling method is required. Such a comprehensive method has to support not only modelling and analysis of a clinical pathway itself. Aspects, such as: medical resources' usage, hospital's and IT infrastructure, hospital's strategic goals, information on costs and revenues, should be supported as well. Therefore, concepts have to be developed that provide adequate abstractions allowing to address specific needs of prospective users, and at the same time, in order to foster understandability and decrease learning efforts, correspond to their respective (professional) terminology.

To the best of our knowledge such a comprehensive approach allowing to include various perspectives and to model the entire hospital's action system, is not available. Consequently, a dedicated domain-specific modelling method (DSMM), which provides modelling concepts reconstructed from medical terminology, should be developed. "A modelling method [...] consists of at least one modelling language and at least one corresponding process model, which guides the construction and analysis of models, i.e., it guides the meaningful use of language concepts" [7, p. 5]. Such DSMM consisting of a set of modelling languages, each focusing on different aspects of the hospital's action and information systems, would support dedicated analysis tailored to the needs of different stakeholders supporting multiple perspectives.

The main goal of our research, which follows the pro-active research [8, 9, 10], is to design and develop a domain-specific method for Multi-Perspective Hospital Modelling. The main goal of this paper is to discuss the requirements such a modelling method should fulfil. The process of requirements identification was rigorously planned and the derived requirements result from the definition of CPs, challenges in the hospitals domain, interviews with stakeholders, and authors' experiences gathered in projects conducted in the public health domain. The resulting IT artefact [8], i.e., a requirements catalogue, serves as a basis for evaluation of existing approaches aiming at identifying, whether any of these approaches fulfils the identified requirements and whether one of them could become a basis for the development of the method.

This paper is organised as follows. First, the targeted method is outlined using an exemplary diagram. Then, the research approach followed is described. In Sect. 4 requirements towards the targeted method are presented. They serve as a basis for evaluation of existing approaches in the following section. The paper concludes with final remarks and outlook on upcoming research activities.

2   Outline of the Targeted Method

Nowadays, hospitals, analogously to traditional enterprises, have to be managed from an economical perspective. However, they incorporate a set of unique characteristics that justify the development of a corresponding domain-specific modelling method: the main goal of medical care processes, in opposition to traditional manufacturing processes, is to cure or at least relieve or palliate patients from their disease. A domain specific modelling method for hospitals, similarly to enterprise modelling, should allow to "comprise conceptual models of software systems, e.g., object or component models, that are integrated with conceptual models of the surrounding action systems, e.g., business process models or strategy models" [7, p. 2 f.]. One goal of enterprise models is to increase transparency of all relevant aspects of an enterprise. At the same time however, complexity of an enterprise represented in diagrams should be reduced, in order to avoid confusion and information overload. Consequently, adequate abstraction needs to be found that can help reduce model's complexity and simultaneously increase its understandability by reconstructing the domain-specific terminology. The abstraction can be supported by focussing on users' relevant perspectives while visualising enterprise models in corresponding diagrams.

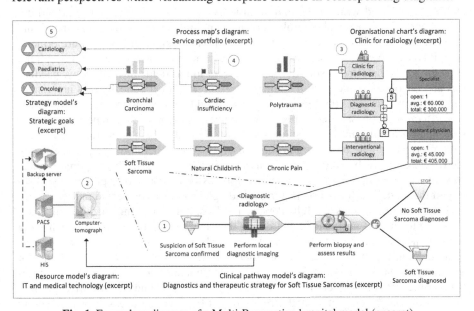

Fig. 1. Exemplary diagram of a Multi-Perspective hospital model (excerpt)

Taking above into account, a mock-up of a potential diagram of a hospital model has been prepared (Fig. 1). It presents the clinical pathway "Diagnostics and therapeutic strategy for Soft Tissue Sarcomas" ①, documented in a research project with the West German Sarcoma Centre at the West German Cancer Centre in Essen [11]. The CP model's diagram ① is integrated with elements from a resource model's diagram ② and an organisational chart of organisational structure model ③. Furthermore, concrete CP types are aggregated in the hospital's service portfolio diagram ④, which provides high-level information by visualising different KPIs' statuses as coloured bars and associates clinical pathway types with hospital's strategic goals in the corresponding diagram ⑤, to visualise their contribution to realising those goals.

The presented excerpt of a clinical pathway encompasses two processes "Perform local diagnostic imaging" and "Perform biopsy and asses results", represented respectively by the process types "Diagnostic Imaging" and "Cell and Tissue Diagnostics". The process body's blue colour indicates that they both represent diagnostic process types. Therapeutic process types would be represented by a green process body, in order to allow for an easier distinction between diagnostic and therapeutic concepts – two main categories of medical processes. In the process "Perform local diagnostic imaging" the resource type "Computertomograph" is used, which is modelled in the resource model of IT and medical technology ② and includes additional information on the usage of the hospital's information systems supporting medical processes. Diagnostic imaging is performed by one or more people from the department of Diagnostic Radiology, which is represented by associating this organisational unit ③ to the diagnostic imaging process. The organisational chart includes some of the department's KPIs, such as a number of different position types and its average position share. An aggregated view on each clinical pathway type can be represented in the service portfolio diagram ④, which allows for quickly assessing each KPI's current state (coloured bars) for each clinical pathway type included in the hospital's model and being analysed with corresponding instance data. In case of any unexpected developments, e.g., a medical controller can have a more detailed look at the underlying information and – if necessary – initiate appropriate counter measures. Furthermore, the CP types shown in the service portfolio diagram can be associated with hospital's strategic goals, here increasing the case numbers in the fields of cardiology, paediatrics and oncology, depicted in a strategy diagram ⑤. Direct contributions are visualised by arrows, whereas indirect ones are visualised by arrows with dotted lines.

By focussing on selected aspects, the diagram supports the perspective-specific presentation of relevant information – and consequently, the abstraction from irrelevant information – to avoid the information overload and therefore, supports reducing the risk of cognitively overloading the user's mind [12, p. 767]. This requires a corresponding modelling environment to allow for flexible, perspective-specific visualisation of the model's information in corresponding diagrams as presented in Fig. 1.

Therefore, the proposed Multi-Perspective Hospital Modelling method's primary goals are to support hospitals in addressing their current challenges by: (1) increasing transparency of the hospital's relevant aspects by providing corresponding models using domain-specific abstractions in order to foster clarity and understandability for all involved stakeholders; (2) serving as an instrument to foster communication between different stakeholders by providing concepts corresponding with their particular (professional) perspective and terminology; (3) providing a basis for conducting purposeful analyses in order to answer stakeholders' questions on the hospital's current state, e.g., from the medical, economical or technical perspective; (4) building a foundation for (re-)designing the hospital's action system, as well as its information systems to increase efficiency or respectively effectiveness.

3   Research Method

This contribution follows the pro-active research path based on the design oriented research paradigm [8], as well as the design science paradigm [9, 10]. The main goal of research activities, this paper contributes to, is to design and develop a domain-specific method for Multi-Perspective Hospital Modelling. In order to develop the postulated modelling method the main goal was divided into a number of sub-goals: (1) Identification of requirements towards a comprehensive domain-specific method for Multi-Perspective Hospital Modelling. (2) Development of a precise and complete (e.g., meta-model-based) specification of a domain-specific method for Multi-Perspective Hospital Modelling. (3) Prototypical development of the method as well as prototypical implementation into a corresponding modelling environment/modelling tool. (4) Evaluation of developed IT artefacts. This paper focuses on the first sub-goal only and aims at answering the question: *Which requirements have to be fulfilled by a comprehensive method for Multi-Perspective Hospital Modelling?*

The design-oriented information systems research follows the scientific principles of *abstraction, originality* and *justification*, and the resulting IT artefact has to provide at some point of time a *benefit* to stakeholders being directly or indirectly affected by it [8, p. 9]. Ideally, the research process consists of four phases: Analysis, Design, Evaluation and Diffusion [8, p. 9]. This research addresses the phases Analysis, Design, and Evaluation, as it proposes the design and development of a new domain-specific method for Multi-Perspective Hospital Modelling based on a brief, but comprehensive, analysis of the current situation and challenges in the hospital sector. The requirements catalogue serves not only as a foundation for designing and developing the targeted method, but also, in addition to a prototypical application in cooperation with hospitals, as an instrument to evaluate the resulting method. Furthermore, the requirements catalogue allows for a transparent and structured analysis of related work in Sect. 5. A prototypical application and publication of the proposed method contribute to the artefact's evaluation and diffusion in both, practice and research. Obtained feedback will initiate additional iterations of the analysis, design, and evaluation phase and contribute to the development and improvement of the method.

The proposed research design corresponds with the design science paradigm as defined by Hevner [9,10], which is constituted by three interdependent phases of Relevance Cycle, Rigor Cycle, and Design Cycle [10, p. 88]. The research relevance is shown by presenting current challenges of the German public health and its transferability to other countries' public health, and by outlining the targeted method. This allows for systematically deriving requirements based on the CP's definition, interviews with domain experts, authors' own experiences from previously conducted projects in the domain, as well as a thorough scientific and domain-specific literature study (which cannot be fully presented in this paper due to the space limitation), and in this way ensures the research process' rigorous foundation.

The constitution of the requirements catalogue is a part of the Design Cycle. Analogously to the design-oriented information systems research paradigm's iterative approach, the design science cycles have to be applied iteratively to integrate new findings from analysis and evaluation of the artefact into the Design Cycle and thereby, to contribute to the development and improvement of the proposed method.

4   Requirements Analysis and Definition

4.1   Requirements Analysis Process

As already stated, the requirements result from numerous research activities undertaken in the public health domain within last few years. The activities were targeted at verifying whether enterprise modelling can help to address the current challenges in the public health domain and were inspired by the observed reorganisation of social services based on principles of business administration.

One of the most important sources used for the needs of requirements analysis is a research project with the West German Cancer Centre in Essen established in order to evaluate commonalities and differences between public health institutions, in particular hospitals, and traditional enterprises. A number of experienced senior physicians and medical specialists working in different fields of oncology, such as surgical oncology, medical oncology, radio oncology, and pathology, were involved in the project. All of them were interviewed regarding their expectations towards the modelling approach to be applied in the public health domain. The knowledge gained during one-to-one and group interviews has been extended based on observations of different physicians during their daily working routines for a number of days in different departments, as well as observing multidisciplinary case conferences: here physicians from various medical disciplines jointly plan and control each patient's CP-based individual treatment plan. This allowed to gather additional data on the physicians' medical information demand, as well as on the information technology used to support physicians and nursing staff in the medical care provision process.

A next source used for the needs of requirements analysis is the *Hospital Engineering* research project focusing on selected processes performed in hospitals. Here, the main goal was to increase the transparency of material flow and usage, and resulting costs in non-medical and medical processes, as well as to reduce redundant processing of information during both, medical and materials management processes. Therefore, a comprehensive process analysis and documentation has been conducted in medical and materials management departments. The undertaken activities encompassed also analysis of information demand of different stakeholders within the hospital.

Both projects together, accompanied by additional research activities – literature reviews, analysis of CP definitions and current challenges hospitals need to deal with – provided a comprehensive insight into the hospital sector, which allowed to identify specific requirements towards the postulated method, as presented in the next section.

4.2   Requirements

As clinical pathways represent the hospitals' business processes, DSMM for Multi-Perspective Hospital Modelling should offer a dedicated DSML to create conceptual models of clinical pathways in order to increase clarity and understandability for prospective users because the medical concepts and terminology differ significantly from those in traditional enterprises (cf. [11, p. 215]).

Req. 1: DSMM for Multi-Perspective Hospital Modelling should provide a domain-specific modelling language for modelling clinical pathways.

As CPs aim at supporting medical decisions – primarily used by physicians, but also by patients and their relatives – modelling medical decisions (i.e., decision scenarios) should be supported [13, p. 273]. With respect to the prospective users, medical decision scenarios should be modelled in a structured, clear, and human understandable form [13, p. 274]. Concepts for modelling decisions should also provide information on underlying decision criteria, as well as values leading to different decision alternatives. In order to foster the reusability of modelled information on the possible decision scenarios, the information should be stored in a way that supports automated transformation into a computer-interpretable form, respectively the other way round [13, p. 275 f.]. Furthermore, it should be possible to model decision scenarios that cannot be described in a structured way, e.g., decisions under risk or uncertainty.

Req. 2: DSML for CP modelling should provide concepts supporting comprehensive modelling of medical decision scenarios including decision alternatives, decision criteria, and corresponding potential values of the decision criteria. It should be possible to represent the information both in a human-understandable and in a computer-interpretable form [13, p. 273 ff.].

In order to foster the decision support functionality of CPs, a corresponding method should support goal modelling as CP types may include goals, which can – but do not have to – be derived from medical guidelines, that should be achieved by medical activities [3, p. 553]. Furthermore, patient-specific goals should be taken into account within CP's patient-specific instantiations. Consequently, goals should be definable on both, a type and instance level. This would allow for supporting medical decision making, e.g., by comparing the medical activity's or CP's goal with patient-specific goals. Furthermore, a deviation analysis regarding the realised outcome of medical activities, respectively of CP, for each patient can be supported to allow for identifying required changes within the clinical pathway to improve the quality of care.

Req. 3: DSML for CP modelling should allow for specifying one or more goals for each medical activity based on both, (evidence based) medical knowledge and patient-specific preferences. Therefore, the integration of goal models needs to be supported on the CP's type and instance level.

CPs aim at streamlining the usage of scarce resources in hospitals. Therefore, the required resources for each medical activity have to be identified and specified. In order to support a comprehensive model based resource management, the hospital's available resources have to be inventoried and used to analyse the compliance of available and required resources based on the number of medical case types planned in a specified period of time. In order to associate medical resources to medical activities, corresponding concepts are required that allow for providing concrete information on the resources' usage both, on the type level (average usage) and on the instance level (patient-specific usage), e.g., quantity, time, costs of usage, as well as substitutability of resources, needs to be made available to support corresponding analyses [14, p. 74 f.]. As medical resources can be modelled independently from CPs as well, corresponding concepts do not have to be a part of DSML for modelling CPs, but a part of the comprehensive method for Multi-Perspective Hospital Modelling.

Req. 4: DSMM for Multi-Perspective Hospital Modelling should support modelling domain-specific medical resources that correspond to the medical domain's professional terminology. It should allow for defining the required quality, respectively qualification, of (human) medical resources. Furthermore, it should allow for allocating medical resources to each medical activity using various types of allocation (e.g., quantity-, time-, cost-based), as well as corresponding information.

Each medical activity – including the medical resources' usage – in CPs can be recommended based on evidence-based medical guidelines including information on its evidence level. Consequently, it should be possible to assign a level of evidence to each CP's medical activity originating from evidence based medical guidelines.

Req. 5: DSMM for Multi-Perspective Hospital Modelling should allow to add information on the underlying level of evidence to each medical activity modelled in clinical pathways derived from the evidence-based medical knowledge.

To each CP, a coordinating role [3] can be assigned in the sense of a process owner being responsible for a process. In case of multidisciplinary clinical pathways, the coordinating role can be filled in by more than one organisational unit. Each of these can be represented by one or more members of the multidisciplinary care team.

Req. 6: DSMM for Multi-Perspective Hospital Modelling should allow for assigning at least one coordinating role to each clinical pathway.

According to [15, p. 23] each clinical pathway includes information on both, responsibilities for conducting each medical activity and its results.

Req. 7: DSMM for Multi-Perspective Hospital Modelling should allow for assigning responsibilities to each clinical pathway's medical activity, differentiated into those for performing the medical activity, as well as those responsible for its outcome.

The model based analysis of medical care's cost-effectiveness requires hospital models to include information on costs. Therefore, corresponding concepts allowing for documenting average costs per medical activity, as well as providing information on how the overall costs result from resource usage based on the time and/or quantity of it, should exist. Furthermore, CP models should allow for the documentation of patient-specific costs on the instance level in order to allow for deviation analysis of planned, average costs on the type level and patient-specific costs. Based on this information, another economic analysis can be supported by comparing both, resulting costs on the type and instance level with the DRG revenue a hospital can realise for the corresponding medical case. If any deviations can be identified that require counter measures in order to improve cost-effectiveness, adequate measures can be chosen on a well-founded base of information.

Req. 8: DSMM for Multi-Perspective Hospital Modelling should allow for hospital model wide cost-based analyses. For clinical pathways it should allow for it, both on the type and the instance level, as well as the comparison of their resulting costs with correspondingly realised DRG revenues.

Serving as a risk reduction instrument [3, p. 553], requires CP models to comprehensively include potential risks for each medical activity, and CP itself. Therefore, a dedicated modelling concept should be provided that allows for documenting potential risks including its likelihood, both, factors increasing and decreasing the risk's occurrence likelihood, as well as potential counter measures to address occurred risks.

Req. 9: DSMM for Multi-Perspective Hospital Modelling should allow for modelling potential risks for each medical activity, as well as for the overall CP including the risk occurrence likelihood and factors influencing its increase and decrease. For the case of risk occurrence, appropriate counter measures should be provided.

In order to support the patient-specific medical documentation, CP's models should include generic information on the type level and patient-specific information on the instance level for each medical activity, which is relevant for documentation. Furthermore, the CP's type level model can be used to reduce the multidisciplinary care team's documentation efforts by following the "charting-by-exception" approach [16], which requires additional documentation only in the case of deviation from the pre-defined CP. Consequently, a deviation analysis of medical activities and its timespans should be supported to identify potential improvements in CP's performance.

Req. 10: DSMM for Multi-Perspective Hospital Modelling should allow for supporting patient-specific medical documentation and deviation analysis based on the defined (type level) and instantiated patient-specific clinical pathway by combining corresponding type and instance level information.

The portfolio of the hospital's clinical pathways can be represented in an aggregated overview realised analogously to a process map. Here, selected KPIs of each clinical pathway type can be integrated to support a high-level controlling perspective. In case of exceptional developments, a more detailed look into the CP type as well as into its instances has to be taken to identify the underlying cause. This should be supported analogously to a drill-down in data warehouses.

Req. 11: DSMM for Multi-Perspective Hospital Modelling should allow for providing an aggregated view on all CP types defined within the hospital in a medical service portfolio. This portfolio should support the visualisation of key performance indicators for each CP type in order to allow for a high-level controlling perspective.

Furthermore, the medical service portfolio can be integrated with the hospital's strategy to analyse how and which clinical pathway types contribute to realising the hospital's strategic goals – similar to an analysis of an enterprise's IT business alignment. Therefore, the possibility to model the hospital's strategy is required as well. The proposed controlling instrument can be seen analogously to a management dashboard, which provides highly aggregated information on a huge number of data and serves as an instrument for matters of controlling and managerial decision support.

Req. 12: DSMM for Multi-Perspective Hospital Modelling should support the analysis of the alignment of hospital's strategy and medical services.

From the perspective of Information Systems, the following requirements focussing on the use and integration of information technology in medical activities can be identified. Req. 4 can be complemented by modelling information technology used in CPs in order to document hardware (e.g., clinical workstations, servers hosting software), software (e.g., Hospital Information Systems, Picture Archiving Systems), and results of medical activities. Because of the advancing integration of medical resource types, such as, e.g., X-ray machines, into the hospital's information systems, corresponding interfaces for transferring and exchanging data should be incorporated in a corresponding IT infrastructure model. From the IT department's perspective, it should be possible to specify each IT component's Service Level Agreement to allow for a model based identification of critical IT resources. In general, allocating IT resources to medical activities increases transparency on their usage in medical activities and can point at its relevance to the fulfilment of the hospital's business activities. Such models can also support the definition of IT budgets and IT strategy.

Req. 13: DSMM for Multi-Perspective Hospital Modelling should allow for modelling relevant IT components used in the context of provision of medical care including data exchange protocols and Service Level Agreements.

In order to analyse the degree of information systems' integration both, system interfaces as well as data structures and data flows between information systems should be documented. A lack of integration can lead to media breaks in information processing, which may result in higher costs and can cause errors by manual data input respectively transfer. This may in the end lead to potential risks for each patient.

Req. 14: DSMM for Multi-Perspective Hospital Modelling should support modelling relevant data structures and data flows to allow for performing analyses regarding the flow and usage of data within medical activities and supporting information systems, as well as the degree of information systems' integration.

The graphical representation of domain-specific modelling concepts should correspond with the concepts it represents and therefore, optimally originate from the domain of discourse. The design of the concepts' graphical representations "is of considerable relevance for the comprehensibility, usability and productivity of DSML" [17, p. 49] and therefore, should follow a structured and well-defined procedure with clear rules, e.g., provided by [12].

Req. 15: DSMM for Multi-Perspective Hospital Modelling should provide a graphical representation of the modelling concepts, which illustrates the intended semantics in an easily accessible and understandable way for prospective users (domain experts) – at best at a glance (cf. [11, p. 215]). It has to be applied to all previously stated requirements resulting in creating domain-specific modelling concepts.

As hospital models include a variety of different information relevant for a number of stakeholders with specific perspectives either on the entire hospital or on selected aspects of the hospital only – depending on their role within the hospital – a corresponding modelling method should support multiple perspectives on the resulting hospital model. In this way, the method can foster reducing the model's complexity by purposeful and adequate conceptual abstractions and resulting views on the model's diagrams. This would actively support reducing the risk of cognitively overloading the user's mind [12], as already mentioned. Consequently, this requires a corresponding modelling environment (cf. Req. 19) to allow for flexible, perspective-specific visualisation of the model's information, as presented in Fig. 1.

Req. 16: A comprehensive method for Multi-Perspective Hospital Modelling should support the creation of corresponding diagrams tailored to the stakeholder's perspective-specific information needs.

Finally, some generic requirements applicable to modelling methods in general, are formulated. These requirements are valid for the modelling method and all its elements. "A precise and complete specification" [17], e.g., by one or more meta models, a grammar or an ontology, of all modelling languages is required to allow for identification of syntactically correct or incorrect models. Furthermore, it contributes to the method's implementation in a corresponding modelling environment (cf. Req. 19).

Req. 17: The syntax of DSMLs being a part of a domain-specific method for hospital modelling should be specified by "a precise and complete specification" [17].

In combination with Req. 17, a publicly and freely available method and language specification fosters an easy evaluation, as well as reuse and extension of the specified concepts, e.g., in case of method engineering based design and development of corresponding artefacts.

Req. 18: The specification of the entire DSMM as well as its incorporated DSMLs should be publicly and freely accessible.

The application of each modelling method significantly benefits from the availability of a corresponding modelling environment that guides the modelling process and avoids creation of syntactically incorrect models by automated syntax checks. It can also support automated functionalities facilitating analyses on created models. Furthermore, it can support perspective-specific views on the hospital model's diagrams (cf. Req. 16).

Req. 19: DSMM for hospital modelling should be supported by a modelling environment providing support in modelling, analysis and perspective creation.

The requirements presented here constitute a first solid foundation for the design of a Multi-Perspective Hospital Modelling method and for the related work's evaluation, as presented in the next section.

5   Related Work and Its Evaluation

Within this section, representative modelling approaches from the fields of medicine and medical informatics, as well as Computer Science and Information Systems that have been already applied in the medical domain, are evaluated. Although the scope of approaches not originating from the field of enterprise modelling does not equal the targeted method's scope, they are going to be analysed towards the requirements fulfilment, to check whether they can contribute to the targeted method's development by addressing some challenges. A short characteristic of approaches follows.

Clinical Algorithm (CA) was first used in 1968 by Tuddenham [18] in the context of teaching in radiology. It is based on logical flow charts and provides the following concepts [19]: Clinical State Box (representing the initial clinical problem to be addressed), Decision Box (explicating questions to be answered in the flow of the algorithm), Action Box (representing medical activities to be performed), and Link Box, (referring to other boxes or pages). The sequence of boxes is indicated by arrows.

Guideline Interchange Format (GLIF) was developed in the 1990ies to support the "exchange of clinical practice guidelines among institutions and computer-based guideline applications" [20]. It follows a best of breed approach by building "on the most useful features of other guideline models and [incorporating] standards that are used in healthcare" [21]. It provides concepts similar to CA, but supports nesting within CP models and provides a number of concepts for modelling (nested) structured decision scenarios, and concepts for branching and synchronising the control flow [22]. Additionally, external data can be integrated. The language specification is provided using UML class diagrams and the Object Constraint Language [22].

PRO*forma* was developed in the late 1990ies as process-oriented language for knowledge representation [23]. It provides concepts similar to the GLIF approach, but extends it for modelling sources of information, warning conditions and data items [23]. PRO*forma* allows for external data sources' integration in order to interpret this data during the patient-specific clinical pathway's execution by using interfaces.

The Sage project was initiated in 2002 by a consortium of Stanford University, University of Nebraska Medical Centre and software development companies working in public health and aims at advancing existing approaches for describing computer-interpretable guidelines by following a best of breed approach including the usage of standards (e.g., Health Level 7 Reference Information Model and SNOMED Clinical Terms ontology [24]). Sage basically provides similar concepts as GLIF, but it supports integration of various data from existing information systems [24].

Architecture of Integrated Information Systems (ARIS) was founded in 1992 [25] by introducing Event-driven Process Chains (EPC). Basic EPC modelling concepts are "function", "event", "organisational unit", "information object", and "process interface" [26]. Control flow is represented by arrows connecting events and functions. Branches and parallelisation can be realised by "AND"-, "OR"-, and "Exclusive-OR"-connectors. Organisational units and information objects can be associated to functions [26]. The ARIS method's modelling environment [27] provides integration of various approaches for conceptual modelling, e.g., Entity-Relationship-Model [28], UML [29], BPMN [30], and using balanced scorecards [31].

The primary goal of Business Process Model and Notation (BPMN) 2.0 [30] "is to provide a notation that is readily understandable by all [...], from the business analysts that create the initial drafts of the processes, to the technical developers responsible for implementing the technology that will perform those processes, and finally, to the business people who will manage and monitor those processes." [30, p. 1]. Basic BPMN concepts are "event" and "activity" [30]. Branching and parallelisation are realised by the concept "gateway". BPMN allows for differentiating between "Sequence Flow" and "Message Flow". "Information" and "Artefacts" are associated to activities by a directed and undirected "Association".

Multi-Perspective Enterprise Modelling (MEMO) method was developed in 1993 as a comprehensive method for modelling enterprises multi-perspectively [32] based on the assumption that within enterprises different stakeholder groups focus on different aspects of the enterprise [7]. Currently, the MEMO method provides DSMLs for: modelling of organizational structures and business processes [33, 34], the enterprise's strategy [35], its IT landscape [36], its resources [14], the design of performance indicator systems [37], and enterprise knowledge management [38]. The DSMLs' application is guided by corresponding methods [7] and all DSMLs are specified using the common MEMO Meta Modelling Language [39]. Selected languages have been prototypically implemented in the modelling tool MEMOCenterNG [40].

Unified Modeling Language (UML) Activity Diagrams are part of UML, which is maintained by OMG [29]. Activity Diagrams support the concepts "activity node" and "object node" [41, p. 95 ff.]. An arrow visualises a control flow between activities, a dashed arrow visualises an object. Branching and parallelisation are realised by fork and join nodes, the activity diagrams start with an initial node and end with final nodes, differentiating between end of activity, respectively of control flow.

The results of evaluation of each approach, based on the requirements formulated in Sect. 4, are summarised in Tab. 1. It shows that – as expected after the approaches' brief description – no approach is fulfilling all requirements. Obviously the medical (informatics) approaches fulfil the requirements to a lesser extent than the Computer Science and Information Systems approaches. Here, the approaches dedicated to enterprise modelling fulfil the requirements to a greater extent than the others.

Table 1. Evaluation results based on the defined requirements

Requirements (Key words)	Medicine and Medical Informatics				Computer Science and Information Systems discipline			
	Clinical Algorithm	GLIF (V3)	PROforma	Sage	ARIS method	BPMN	MEMO method	UML Activity Diagram
Req. 1: DSML for modelling clinical pathways	X	X	X	X	X	X	(✓)	X
Req. 2: Modelling decision scenarios in CP models	(✓)	✓	✓	✓	✓	✓	✓	(✓)
Req. 3: Modelling goals for CPs' medical activities	X	X	(✓)	✓	✓	X	✓	X
Req. 4: Modelling of domain-specific medical resources and allocation to CP's medical activities	X	X	X	X	(✓)	(✓)	(✓)	(✓)
Req. 5: Assigning information on the evidence level to each medical activity in clinical pathways	X	✓	(✓)	(✓)	X	X	✓	X
Req. 6: Assinging coordinating roles to each clinical pathway	X	X	(✓)	X	(✓)	(✓)	(✓)	(✓)
Req. 7: Assigning responsibilities to each medical activity in clinical pathways	X	X	(✓)	(✓)	(✓)	(✓)	(✓)	(✓)
Req. 8: Concepts for supporting cost-based analyses	X	X	X	X	✓	X	(✓)	X
Req. 9: Concepts for modelling risks and assigning them to medical activities in clinical pathways	X	(✓)	(✓)	(✓)	✓	(✓)	(✓)	X
Req. 10: Concepts for supporting patient-specific documentation based on clinical pathway models	X	(✓)	(✓)	(✓)	(✓)	(✓)	(✓)	X
Req. 11: Concepts for representing a medical service portfolio including aggregated KPIs	X	X	X	X	(✓)	X	(✓)	X
Req. 12: Concepts for supporting analysis of alignment of hospitals' strategy and medical services	X	X	X	X	✓	X	(✓)	X
Req. 13: Concepts for modelling IT artefacts	X	X	X	X	✓	(✓)	✓	(✓)
Req. 14: Concepts for analysing data structures, data flows and IT integration	X	(✓)	(✓)	(✓)	✓	✓	✓	✓
Req. 15: Complementing domain-specific modelling concepts with corresponding graphical representation	X	X	X	X	X	X	✓	X
Req. 16: Concepts for associating clinical pathways to hospital's strategy	X	X	X	X	(✓)	X	(✓)	X
Req. 17: Complete and precise method specification	(✓)	✓	(✓)	✓	(✓)	(✓)	✓	✓
Req. 18: Publicly and freely available method specification	(✓)	✓	(✓)	✓	(✓)	✓	✓	✓
Req. 19: Corresponding modelling environment available	✓	✓	✓	✓	✓	✓	✓	✓
Legend: ✓ Requirement fulfilled X Requirement not fulfilled (✓) Requirement partly fulfilled								

Clinical Algorithm fulfils the requirements least of all, as it was never intended to serve as an approach for conceptual modelling. The approaches aiming at computer-interpretable support of CPs fulfil the requirements almost to the same extent, even though PROforma and Sage a bit more extensively than GLIF. Their strengths are in the fields of modelling decision scenarios (Req. 2) and assigning information on the underlying scientific medical evidence to medical activities (Req. 5). They also may allow for an easy extension of existing concepts and interfaces to support modelling and assigning risks to medical activities (Req. 9), as well as a patient-specific medical documentation (Req. 10), as they already allow for processing patient-specific data imported from external data sources. Similar to that, results of decisions and performed medical activities could be exported to a medical documentation system. Because of the possibility to import external data, they may also allow to analyse underlying data structures and flows, as well as potentially the degree of information systems' integration (Req. 14). The specification is basically freely and publicly available (Req. 18). All approaches are supported by a dedicated modelling tool (Req. 19).

BPMN (partly) fulfils more requirements than UML Activity Diagrams. This is mainly because BPMN 2.0 supports the models' execution with a corresponding workflow engine, which can, e.g., be adapted for the needs of patient-specific documentation (Req. 10). Both approaches neither support cost-based analyses (Req. 8), nor a medical service portfolio's creation including KPIs (Req. 11), or the strategy modelling in general (Req. 12).

Both enterprise modelling approaches, ARIS and the MEMO method (partly) fulfil most of the requirements. Out of the ARIS method's design goal to serve as a general-purpose enterprise modelling method, its main shortcoming results: it does not provide DSML. Thus, it cannot fulfil requirements postulating domain-specific modelling. In contrast, the MEMO method is dedicated to support domain-specific and Multi-Perspective enterprise modelling, and as it was already extended towards modelling of CPs by providing a basic distinction into the types of medical process, diagnostic process and therapeutic process, which arises out of the medical domain and terminology itself [11], it (partly) fulfils Req. 1 and 5, as well as 15. Considering MEMO's already existing domain-specific modelling methods and languages, and integration possibility by using a common meta modelling language and specifying method-wide common language concepts, most of the requirements can be considered as being at least partly fulfilled. The MEMO method's entire specification is available publicly and freely in a precise form (Req. 17 and 18) as the method or DSMLs being part of it – including its specification – are presented in a multiplicity of scientific publications. In contrast to this, the authors were not able to find a complete and precise specification of the ARIS method in any form. Only selected parts of it can be found in scientific publications. Based on this, Req. 17 and Req. 18 are rated as only partly fulfilled.

In order to decide which approach is the most promising one to be extended, it is not sufficient to select the one with the most requirements being (partly) fulfilled. A critical success factor for extending an existing modelling approach is that its specification is both, precise and complete (Req. 17), as well as publicly and freely available (Req. 18). Regarding those two requirements the MEMO method is to be preferred over the ARIS method. In addition, MEMO method dedicatedly aims at domain-specific modelling, whereas ARIS is a general purpose enterprise modelling method.

6   Conclusions and Future Research

Following the design science paradigm, we have presented the motivation of a comprehensive method targeted at Multi-Perspective Hospital Modelling and defined high-level requirements it should fulfil. The requirements served to evaluate modelling approaches originating from both, medicine and medical informatics, as well as Computer Science and Information Systems. The evaluation reveals that MEMO method suits the proposed requirements at best. Therefore it is chosen to be extended in order to build a domain-specific method for Multi-Perspective Hospital Modelling.

Next research activities aim at addressing the second sub-goal – defining a precise and complete DSMM's specification. Within this, DSML for modelling CPs is going to be extended with additional domain-specific process types, conjointly with extending DSML for modelling resources with medical resource types. The DSMM's resulting parts would allow for a prototypical application and evaluation in practice. Subsequently, the remaining requirements can be addressed and additional research process iterations conducted to complete DSMM for Multi-Perspective Hospital Modelling.

References

1. Nagel, E. (ed.): Das Gesundheitswesen in Deutschland. Struktur, Leistungen, Weiterentwicklung, 5th edn. Deutscher Ärzte-Verlag, Köln (2013)
2. Field, M.J., Lohr, K.N.: Clinical Practice Guidelines: Directions for a New Program. The National Academies Press (1990)
3. de Bleser, L., Depreitere, R., De Waele, K., Vanhaecht, K., Vlayen, J., Sermeus, W.: Defining pathways. Journal of Nursing Management 14(7), 553–563 (2006)
4. Hsiao, W.C., Sapolsky, H.M., Dunn, D.L., Weiner, S.L.: Lessons of the New Jersey DRG payment system. Health Affairs 5(2), 32–45 (1986)
5. Rotter, T., Kinsman, L., James, E., et al.: Clinical pathways: effects on professional practice, patient outcomes, length of stay and hospital costs (review). Cochrane Database of Systematic Reviews 7(3) (2010)
6. Frank, U., van Laak, B.: Anforderungen an Sprachen zur Modellierung von Geschäftsprozessen. Tech Report 34, Universität Koblenz-Landau. Institut für Wirtschaftsinformatik, Koblenz (2003)
7. Frank, U.: Multi-Perspective enterprise modeling: Foundational concepts, prospects and future research challenges. Journal of Software and Systems Modelling (2012), doi:10.1007/s10270-012-0273-9.
8. Österle, H., Becker, J., Frank, U., Hess, T., Karagiannis, D., et al.: Memorandum on design-oriented information systems research. EJIS 20, 7–10 (2011)
9. Hevner, A.R., March, S.T., Park, J., Ram, S.: Design science in information systems research. Management Information Systems Quarterly 28(1), 75–106 (2004)
10. Hevner, A.R.: The three cycle view of design science research. SJIS 19(2), 87–92 (2007)
11. Heise, D., Heß, M., Strecker, S., Frank, U.: Rekonstruktion eines klinischen Behandlungspfads mithilfe domänenspezifischer Erweiterungen einer Geschäftsprozessmodellierungssprache: Anwendungsfall und Sprachkonzepte. In: Thomas, O., Nüttgens, M. (eds.) Dienstleistungsmodellierung 2010, pp. 210–227. Physica, Heidelberg (2010)
12. Moody, D.L.: The physics of notations: Toward a scientific basis for constructing visual notations in software engineering. IEEE TSE 35(6), 756–779 (2009)
13. Heß, M., Schlieter, H., Täger, G.: Modellierung komplexer Entscheidungssituationen in Prozessmodellen – Anwendung am Beispiel der Tumorklassifikation bei Weichteilsarkomen. In: Thomas, O., Nüttgens, M. (eds.) Dienstleistungsmodellierung 2012, pp. 268–290. Springer, Gabler (2012)

14. Jung, J.: Entwurf einer Sprache für die Modellierung von Ressourcen im Kontext der Geschäftsprozessmodellierung. Logos, Berlin (2007)
15. Küttner, T., Roeder, N.: Definition Klinischer Behandlungspfade. In: Roeder, N., Küttner, T. (eds.) Klinische Behandlungspfade. Mit Standards erfolgreicher arbeiten, pp. 19–27. Deutscher Ärzte-Verlag, Köln (2007)
16. Short, M.S.: Charting by Exception on a Clinical Pathway. Nursing Management 28(8), 45–46 (1997)
17. Frank, U.: Outline of a method for designing domain-specific modelling languages. ICB Research Report 42, University of Duisburg-Essen, Essen (2010)
18. Tuddenham, W.J.: The use of logical flow charts as an aid in teaching roentgen diagnosis. American Journal of Rentgenology 102(4), 797–803 (1968)
19. Society for Medical Decision Making: Proposal for Clinical Algorithm Standards. Medical Decision Making 12(2), 149–154 (1992)
20. Ohno-Machado, L., Gennari, J.H., Murphy, S., Jain, N.L., et al.: The guideline interchange format: A model for representing guidelines. JAMIA 5, 357–372 (1998)
21. Peleg, M., Tu, S., Bury, J., Ciccarese, P., et al.: Comparing Computer-interpretable Guideline Models: A Casestudy Approach. JAMIA 10(1), 52–68 (2003)
22. Peleg, M., Boxwala, A.A., Tu, S., Wang, D., Ogunyemi, O., Zeng, Q.: Guideline Interchange Format 3.5 Technical Specification (2004)
23. Sutton, D., et al.: Evaluation of PROforma as a language for implementing medical guidelines in a practical context. BMC Medical Informatics and Decision Making 6, 1–11 (2006)
24. Tu, S., Campbell, J.R., Glasgow, J., Nyman, M.A., et al.: The sage guideline model: Achievements and overview. JAMIA 14(5), 589–598 (2007)
25. Keller, G., Nüttgens, M., Scheer, A.W.: Semantische Prozeßmodellierung auf der Grundlage Ereignisgesteuerter Prozeketten (EPK). Heft 89, Universität des Saarlandes, Institut für Wirtschaftsinformatik, Saarbrücken (1992)
26. Staud, J.: Geschäftsprozessanalyse. Ereignisgesteuerte Prozessketten und objektorientierte Geschäftsprozessmodellung für Betriebswirtschaftliche Standardsoftware, 3rd edn. Springer, Berlin (2006)
27. Software AG: ARIS Method. ARIS Platform. Version 7.2, Darmstadt (2012)
28. Chen, P.P.S.: The Entity Relationship Model – Toward a Unified View of Data. ACM TODS 1(1), 9–36 (1976)
29. OMG: Unified Modeling Language Specification Version 2.3 (2011)
30. OMG: Business Process Model And Notation (BPMN). Version 2.0 (2011)
31. Kaplan, R.S., Norton, D.P.: The balanced scorecard – measures that drive performances. Harvard Business Review 70(1), 71–79 (1992)
32. Frank, U.: MEMO: Visual Languages for Enterprise Modelling. Tech Report 18, Universität Koblenz-Landau, Institut für Wirtschaftsinformatik, Koblenz (1999)
33. Frank, U.: MEMO Organisation Modelling Language (2): Focus on Business Processes. ICB Research Report 49, University of Duisburg-Essen, Essen (2011)
34. Frank, U.: MEMO Organisation Modelling Language (1): Focus on Organisational Structure. ICB-Research Report 48, University of Duisburg-Essen, Essen (2011)
35. Frank, U., Lange, C.: E-MEMO: A Method to support the Development of customized Electronic Commerce Systems. ISeB 5(2), 93–116 (2007)
36. Kirchner, L.: Eine Methode zur Unterstützung des IT-Managements im Rahmen der Unternehmensmodellierung. Logos, Berlin (2008)
37. Strecker, S., et al.: MetricM: A modeling method in support of the reflective design and use of performance measurement systems. ISeB 10(2), 241–276 (2012)

38. Schauer, H.: Unternehmensmodellierung für das Wissensmanagement – Eine multi-perspektivische Methode zur ganzheitlichen Analyse und Planung. VDM, Saarbrücken (2009)
39. Frank, U.: The MEMO Meta Modelling Language (MML) and Language Architecture, 2nd edn. ICB-Research Report 43, University of Duisburg-Essen (2011)
40. Gulden, J., Frank, U.: MEMOCenterNG. A full-featured modeling environment for organisation modeling and model-driven software development. In: Proceedings of the CAiSE 2010, Hammamet (2010)
41. Rumbaugh, J., et al.: The unified modeling language reference manual, 2nd edn. Addison-Wesley, Boston (2005)

The Service Meta Modeling Editor – Bottom-Up Integration of Service Models

Christoph Augenstein and André Ludwig

Information Systems Institute
University of Leipzig, Grimmaische Straße 12, D-04109 Leipzig
{augenstein,ludwig}@wifa.uni-leipzig.de

Abstract. The logistics service industry is characterized by a high level of collaboration between logistics customers and providers. In fact, sophisticated, knowledge-intense business models such as fourth party and lead logistics evolved in recent years that are responsible for planning, coordination, and monitoring entire supply chains across logistics companies. The Logistics Service Engineering and Management (LSEM) platform is a service-oriented infrastructure for the development and management of collaborative contract logistics enabling fourth party and lead logistics. The service modeling framework (SMF) is a central element of the LSEM-platform. It allows users of the platform to define, manage and combine logistics services from different providers and allows for an integrated view on complex services setups. In this paper, the Service Meta Modeling Editor is presented as an essential part of the SMF. It allows connecting and integrating various types of service models and avoids the need to define and maintain a complex, global service model. Instead a comprehensive service model is built bottom-up in that elements from different models are linked on a metamodel level.

Keywords: logistics, service modeling, metamodeling, service editor.

1 Principles of Collaborative Logistics

For recent years, companies outsource their logistics activities to specialized providers. Beginning with small, self-contained tasks such as transportation of packed goods, outsourcing of tasks became more complex in that planning and management tasks of supply chains are performed by specialized providers today. Surveys in recent years [1; 2] illustrate that these markets for so called value-added services, i.e. based on fourth party (4PL) and lead logistics provider business models [3; 4], are growing steadily (increase in use of outsourced logistics services and increase in outsourcing activities). Those specialist logistics providers are responsible for managing long and mid-term logistics contracts in terms of an entire supply chain for their customers. They aim at inheriting all tasks that belong to planning, coordination and monitoring of logistics services [5; 6]. Due to specific requirements each company has (amount of demanded services or integration level) and due to industry-specific requirements (security or tracking issues) each requested logistics service is individual in scope.

J. vom Brocke et al. (Eds.): DESRIST 2013, LNCS 7939, pp. 386–393, 2013.
© Springer-Verlag Berlin Heidelberg 2013

Thus, 4PL businesses need to provide highly individual service offerings to their clients and thus individuality is a main principle for 4PL business models.

As the primary focus of 4PL business models is on planning, coordination and monitoring, such providers utilize sophisticated, specialized logistics domain knowledge and primarily rely on IT-infrastructure instead of physical assets [7]. This lack of physical assets is substituted by involving multiple logistics providers, which have the capability to transport, store, and process the goods delivered. Consequentially, in this context further principles of the 4PL business model are collaboration and integration with senders and recipients of goods as well as with providers of logistics services. Within a network of affiliated logistics providers a 4PL selects matching providers according to the needed services and integrates them in order to meet customer's requirements. Moreover they govern the overall process and optimize it and as such act as a prime contractor for the customer. They are the main contact person, coordinate the involved logistics providers and have the responsibility for the overall process and its quality of service.

The Logistics Service Engineering and Management platform (LSEM-platform) is a service-oriented infrastructure for development and management of long and mid-term logistics contracts [8]. It is specifically tailored to the needs of logistics service integrators, like 4PLs and encompasses a number of integration, planning, coordination, and monitoring functions. It is designed to extensibility in that future planning tools can be integrated thereby ensuring that the overall planning, monitoring and controlling process for logistics services is kept efficient. The LSEM-platform utilizes service-oriented design paradigm principles, such as modularity and encapsulation to select adequate providers, as well as loose coupling and service composition to develop logistics contracts. On this basis, 4PL business becomes a service business with supply chains based upon service compositions. The challenge for the platform thus is the management of the provider network and the integration and collaborative management of provided services.

2 Research Rigor

The development of the Service Modeling Framework (SMF) as an essential part of the LSEM-platform and its components follows a constructivist approach following the framework and guidelines of Design Science research [9]. Following a constructivist approach, we built on a collaboration with and analysis of a network of logistics providers which are in a process of establishing a 4PL business in Germany[1]. Based on this empiric knowledge base, important insights were gained and led to the concept of a service-oriented approach in the framework. From a service modeling point of view, our approach of building service models bottom-up is novel. The reasons for this are twofold. On the one hand, we drew requirements from the network, mainly to be cost-efficient and small in matters of investment because of small margins within the logistics industry. Thus, we preferred a model-driven approach. On the other

---

[1] Ref. http://www.logistik-leipzig-halle.net/en/network.html

hand, in the design phase [10] we were unable to identify common elements in service models. Thus, in [11] we showed that identifying a certain point of culmination is troublesome. Because of elusiveness of services there are no objective criteria what a service model should consist of. In consequence, there are many service models with varying scope, purpose and used languages (standards). Each of them is well suited to represent a different aspect of services. This led to the approach of building a service model bottom-up. With our approach of specifying a base model and providing an editor to work with, we are able to allow users to work with standardized models in terms of languages. We preserve the independence of these models but are still able to interconnect models and model elements to form a comprehensive model. Using model-driven software development (MDSD) to realize SMF components, we chose an explorative prototyping method to be suited to our needs in that we can test feasibility and validity of concepts and build preliminary versions for enhancements and evaluation purposes. Following suggestions of [12] we performed a build (prototype) and an evaluation step alternately. In a build step a new version of the editor was generated and in the following evaluation step knowledge was derived from this version. For instance, we altered our approach in that we additionally involved a specific domain model (i.e. logistics domain) in the description of the interconnection between elements in order to have a more precise and self-explaining description for users.

3   The Service Modeling Framework

In order to work with different types of services on the LSEM-platform, appropriate information is needed regarding different aspects, for instance an interface or a process description, a service level agreement specification or specific characteristics in terms of runtime performance. Such pieces of information are persisted in individual models and hence modeled in different tools of the LSEM-platform workbench. The SMF is responsible of coping with these models, of integrating and storing them in order to ensure consistent engineering and management.

The overall approach of the SMF and hence the SMF editor is based on the concepts of model-driven engineering. In order to cope with the problems of overlapping information or multiple involved parties we foster the reuse of already modeled information and with this we are able to avoid the modeling of the same aspect in different manners. At present, the SMF comes with two components, a service repository described in [11] and the SMF editor described in this paper. The service repository is a first prototype and central feature for managing developed models and their metamodels respectively. A third component is to be developed which will handle information extraction from existing models and thus will heavily rely on the presented editor.

Common to all components of the SMF are few concepts which are essential to information reuse and uniform model handling on the LSEM-platform. As an initial assumption we take the fact that each planning tool on the platform uses a specific model and thus has a distinct metamodel as a formal base. Moreover we assume that the number of tools is limited but not restricted to a closed set and with this limited set of tools various model types are introduced to the platform which might be similar in scope and in contained modeling concepts but not necessarily have to. In order to reuse information in different models a suitable approach is to define rules for model transformations on metamodel level. However, model transformations are valuable and easy to perform if and only if both models (source and sink) cope with the same issue (e.g. transformation of a BPMN-model into a BPEL-model). Within the SMF, we have to cope with models which are totally different in scope and functionality though (e.g. processes, technical descriptions (WSDL), metrics or pricing models) and thus we need a more flexible way of dealing with information reuse.

A guidance to work with models on the LSEM-platform are reference modeling approaches and especially the configurative approach of [13]. Analogously to the configurative approach we subsume distinct service models as an aspect under a comprehensive model and thus we build a comprehensive model from bottom-up [11]. We further require that each service model to be used on the platform is compliant to a metamodel which in turn has to be compliant to Ecore (EMF)[2], an EMOF (Essential Meta Object Facility)[3]-based meta metamodel. We also specify a generic metamodel for the comprehensive model, the common service model (CSM, see Fig. 1). It contains all relevant modeling concepts used in the SMF and is the origin for several other related artifacts such as the SMF editor.

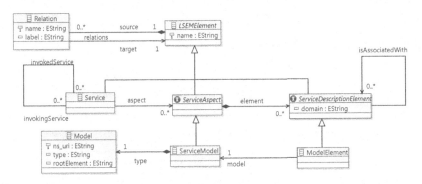

Fig. 1. Common service model (CSM)

With SMF we thus maintain the principles of collaborative logistics. We allow the use of individual models from different sources and avoid prescribing modeling languages in order to participate on the platform. We achieve collaboration within a network of logistics providers by integrating descriptions, i.e. models, from participants and by joining them in a more complex model. The SMF editor, presented in the following section, thereby represents a cornerstone for integrating models.

---

[2] Ref. http://www.eclipse.org/modeling/emf/?project=emf
[3] Ref. http://www.omg.org/mof/

4   Service Meta Modeling Editor

An extended version of the CSM is used to generate the structure of the SMF editor in a MDSD process and hence the editor allows creating only models which conform to the CSM. Implementation of the SMF editor is based on the Eclipse Graphiti[4] framework which supports model-driven development of editors as the framework itself is generated and offers integration into the top-level project Eclipse Modeling Framework (EMF). As we use a modified version of the CSM within the editor we are able to model only valid relationships between different entities like services and their models. From the service repository we can drag services and models into the editor and define relationships as depicted in Fig. 2. Because the CSM is the metamodel of the editor the resulting model is thus a version of the comprehensive service model for a certain service. We can later on also extend this version if new service models are added to the service or if requirements changed and dependencies between models have to be updated. The comprehensive model is then used as input for an information extraction step which takes the contained models and their elements respectively and sees to transfer information into the appropriate places.

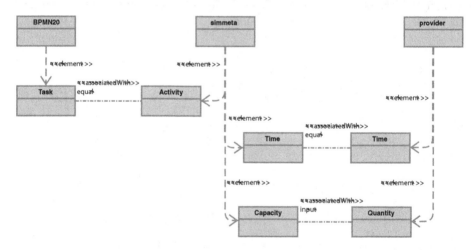

Fig. 2. Modeled example using SMF editor

In the following we present how and by whom the SMF editor should be used. Essential parties are a 4PL and a network with subsidiary providers; the LSEM-platform serves as an integration platform. Each logistics provider, willing to participate, has hence to register on the platform and to specify which kinds of services he is capable of and has to specify characteristics of these services. Beyond that, only employees of the 4PL work with the platform and make use of SMF components. The editor is intended for use by logistics domain experts. They are able to analyze logistics

---

[4] Ref. http://www.eclipse.org/graphiti/

processes and descriptions from subsidiary providers, to model information in logistics service models and therefore have deep knowledge about different model types on the platform. Logistics domain experts use the SMF editor in order to identify and mark model elements of different models which contain equal or similar information. A more concrete example will now serve as a showcase:

A tier one supplier in Germany is responsible for producing parts as well as for managing delivery of goods from lower tier suppliers to multiple OEM production sites. As the requirements for just-in-sequence delivery are high, planning of the supply chain is outsourced to the 4PL business network. There, an overall process has to be planned and appropriate logistics providers to be chosen in order to fulfill the contract. In order to model the process of such a complex service, the 4PL for instance uses the "Business Process Modeling and Notation" (BPMN) language. Furthermore, he wants to keep track of and choose providers due to specific characteristics for each of the involved logistics providers such as performance descriptions, availability, amount and categories of needed resources. And finally, the 4PL also wants to ensure the overall planning with the help of a simulation model which then has to incorporate the just described information.

During this process of planning, domain experts either create models (e.g. a BPMN process model containing necessary services from different providers) or select provider models created by providers when registering on the LSEM-platform. Thus, the planned logistics service for the tier one consists of various services by now whereas the underlying models might contain either disjoint or overlapping information in a sense that the same information is contained in multiple models (e.g. multiple provider models). In order to ensure the overall planning, i.e. the modeled process, meets customer's requirements, a simulation model is to be created which comprises process elements as well as provider specific elements. For this, domain experts use the SMF editor and model cross-model relationships (see Fig. 2). The result of this activity is a version of the comprehensive service model for the specific service and contains elements from three different models. As described earlier the comprehensive service model can now be used as input for the creation of the simulation model in an automated fashion as an information extraction step is performed afterwards. Hence, the editor is used to represent cross-model relationships in an intuitive and descriptive way and the serialized version of the comprehensive model, i.e. the textual representation, can still be processed further.

5   Adoption in 4PL Business Network

The German network of logistics service providers that we analyzed serves as an example for the evolution to collaborative 4PL businesses. Though, while new business models were developed, companies still experience a lack in an efficient handling of services from different providers as well as a lack in managing the underlying provider network. The LSEM-platform in general and the SMF and its components in particular offer possibilities to cope with this situation. While the overall platform enables the network to provide standardized functionality in terms of logistics services, SMF allows for a standardized handling of service descriptions and service models. With the help of the SMF editor, few 4PL domain specialists in the network can cope with different service descriptions without the need to remodel these descriptions in a specific, stipulated language. Especially, for an efficient planning and execution, services and their descriptions have to be handy in terms of analyzing and processing. The editor provides a flexible way of interconnecting models and model elements so that appropriate information is picked from the individual models and merged into a more complex service definition. For 4PL businesses, modeling relationships and a subsequent, automated interpretation of these relationships allows for a consistent and concise way of dealing with models and contained information. Only few logistics domain specialists are needed to deal with multiple languages and must know how elements from various modeling languages belong together in terms of logistics information. Planners and other users of the platform can focus on their core tasks and with this a separation of concerns is achieved.

6   Evaluation

Evaluation of the SMF editor was performed in two ways. On the one hand correctness and validity of produced model interconnection was tested in concrete scenarios on the platform and on the other hand usability of the editor was observed. The former was done within the planning process (example processes were taken from observed logistics companies, see section 3). For evaluation, the correct transformation was known in advance and then compared to the results of modeling dependencies between the involved models with the editor. Afterwards, an information extraction step was performed using the derived model of the editor. In the future, further evaluations will be executed with further interrelated models of the platform.

Testing usability was performed by two groups of users in a field experiment. Users where asked to test whether the editor was operable and whether the contained modeling concepts were self-explaining. Both groups had the task to identify necessary concepts in order to interconnect process, provider and simulation models. As a result, they had to build an extraction and transformation model as described in the first section. One group got the scenario description and an introduction into modeling services. Especially, they were introduced to important constraints on the LSEM-platform. A control group was taught in utilizing the editor in detail introducing to them the modeling concepts, the domain model and the models they had to interconnect. This experiment showed that using the SMF editor can be done intuitively, leading to valuable results in terms of identifying and connecting reasonable model elements. Additionally, there is a third test to be performed in the future. As we do not delimit our approach to the logistics domain, a further evaluation step is to replace the refining domain model and test if the final extraction and transformation step still yields to valuable results.

7   Prototype

An introduction to SMF and its components, i.e. the SMF editor, can be found at: http://lsem.de/SMF or at http://www.youtube.com/watch?v=joqOO9_Xfh0.

References

1. Terry, L.: 2010 Third-party logistics - The state of logistics outsourcing, Capgemini, the Georgia Institute of Technology, Panalpina and eyefortransport (2010)
2. Terry, L.: 2012 Third-party logistics - The state of logistics outsourcing, Capgemini, the Georgia Institute of Technology, Panalpina and eyefortransport (2012)
3. Schmitt, A.: 4PL-Providing-TM als strategische Option für Kontraktlogistikdienstleister: eine konzeptionell-empirische Betrachtung, Dt. Univ.-Verl, Wiesbaden (2006)
4. Nissen, V., Bothe, M.: Fourth Party Logistics - Ein Überblick. Logistik Management, 16–25 (2002)
5. Bamford, C.: The changing supply of logistics services - a UK perspective. In: Waters, C.D.J. (ed.) Global Logistics: New Directions in Supply Chain Management, Kogan Page, London (2010)
6. Blanchard, B.S.: Logistics as an Integrating System's Function. In: Taylor, D. (ed.) Logistics Engineering Handbook, CRC Press, Boca Raton (2008)
7. Kutlu, S.: Fourth Party Logistics: The future of supply chain outsourcing. Best Global Publishing Ltd., Brentwood (2007)
8. Klinkmüller, C., Kunkel, R., Ludwig, A., Franczyk, B.: The logistics service engineering and management platform: Features, architecture, implementation. In: Abramowicz, W. (ed.) BIS 2011. Lecture Notes in Business Information Processing, vol. 87, pp. 242–253. Springer, Heidelberg (2011)
9. Hevner, A.R., March, S.T., Park, J., Ram, S.: Design Science in Information Systems Research. MIS Quarterly 28, 75–105 (2004)
10. Otto, B., Österle, H.: Relevance through Consortium Research? Findings from an expert interview study. In: Winter, R., Zhao, J.L., Aier, S. (eds.) DESRIST 2010. LNCS, vol. 6105, pp. 16–30. Springer, Heidelberg (2010)
11. Augenstein, C., Ludwig, A., Franczyk, B.: Integration of service models – preliminary results for consistent logistics service management. In: SRII Global Conference, pp. 100–109. IEEE, San Jose (2012)
12. March, S.T., Smith, G.F.: Design and natural science research on information technology. Decision Support Systems 15, 251–266 (1995)
13. Delfmann, P.: Adaptive Referenzmodellierung: Methodische Konzepte zur Konstruktion und Anwendung wiederverwendungsorientierter Informationsmodelle. Logos-Verl., Berlin (2006)

Icebricks

Business Process Modeling on the Basis of Semantic Standardization

Jörg Becker, Nico Clever, Justus Holler, and Maria Shitkova

University of Muenster – European Research Center for Information Systems,
Leonardo-Campus 3, 48149 Muenster
{joerg.becker,nico.clever,justus.holler,
maria.shitkova}@ercis.uni-muenster.de

Abstract. Within this article the prototype icebricks is described by its main characteristics which are layers of abstraction, attribution, reference models and semantic standardization by the use of a glossary. The layers are predefined in order to enhance the clarity and comparability of the processes. Attribution is used – beside the layers of abstraction – as means to reduce the complexity of the models by shifting information to analyzable and easily maintainable attributes instead of sophisticated control flows within the process elements. The glossary is inspired by the idea of model conventions. Each business object within it is defined once and can be used with defined activities as process building blocks within all models with the same semantic meaning. Furthermore, reference models are incorporated into the prototype to enable modelers with the possibility to create or derive purposeful models in a short period of time. The prototype was thoroughly and very successfully evaluated in its web based version in two process modeling projects aiming for process reorganization for an ERP system change and for a complete documentation of the process landscape for knowledge management.

Keywords: Prototype, Modeling Tools, Business Process Management, Building Block based Modeling, Modeling Languages.

1 Introduction

Business Process Management (BPM) is a highly complex endeavor [1]. To overcome the complexity of a modeling effort, a model needs to abstract from the real world subject and focus on the relevant parts of the reality for the modeling purpose. The modeling tool presented in this article centers on creating and improving *transparency* within the process landscape of an organization with the help of semantically meaningful and comparable *process building blocks – icebricks*[1].

In the literature, there are numerous definitions of the term business process [2–6]. In this article, from an Information Systems point of view, a process is understood as

---

[1] http://presentation.icebricks.de/

J. vom Brocke et al. (Eds.): DESRIST 2013, LNCS 7939, pp. 394–399, 2013.

a "completely closed, timely and logical sequence of activities which are required to work on a process-oriented business object." [1]

2   Significance to Research

The icebricks artifact is inspired by guidelines of modeling [7, 8] to enable efficient and effective business process modeling. They encompass a layer concept, attribution, semantic standardization through a glossary and reference models as described in the following sub-sections.

2.1   Layers

To manage the complexity of process modeling undertakings, it is common practice to structure the processes into different layers of abstraction [1]. The challenge is to determine an adequate amount of layers accounting for the necessary process information delivered by the model with regard to readability and usability. This amount of layers depends highly on the purpose that is targeted in a modeling project. For example, a process modeling project targeted at a management audience usually requires a lower level of detail than a process modeling project preparing the introduction of a workflow management system.

In icebricks, the challenge of providing the modelers with a sufficient amount of layers for every modeling purpose is achieved by a four layer-architecture. Its four layers are a process framework, main processes, detail processes and so called process building blocks (PBB). This layer-architecture is depicted in Fig. 1. On the first layer, the process framework graphically fosters the general understanding of a modeling effort by providing a process overview respectively landscape consisting of all relevant main processes. This overview can be ordered by the modeler at their option, e. g. by functional areas. On the second layer, the steps which are usually carried out within a certain main process are depicted. This provides modelers as well as model users with a coarse overview of the necessary activities which are further specified on the detail process layer where all the atomic process activities are represented by PBB. These PBB provide the most detailed process information about singular atomic activities. On this layer, attachments like videos, documents, hyperlinks, wiki pages, etc. are supported. On the main process and detail process layers branching methods are provided by the tool to account for the handling of parallel activities. By this means the processes of the company can be easily found by simply navigating from the main process area to the desired process and the accompanying information.

2.2   Attribution

In addition to the layer-architecture, icebricks puts attribution at the disposal of the modeler. Thereby, detailed in-depth information can be assigned to every process model element on every layer. Hence, the need for more sophisticated branching methods in terms of the control flow is reduced to a minimum since relevant information

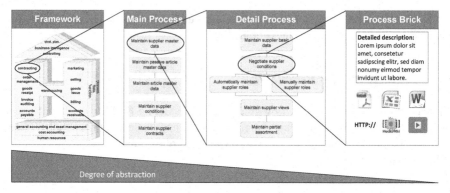

Fig. 1. Layer-architecture to handle the modeling complexity

is stored within the attributes. Therefore, the concept of attribution further reduces the complexity of the resulting process models and widens the area of utilization by providing the modeler with the possibility to enhance process information on any level via attribute attachment. The attributes can be specified by the tool administrators and, hence, allow for a utilization in any business domain and enterprise. Attribute types cover numeric, textual and hierarchical attributes as well as hyperlinks, attached documents up to entire HTML[2] pages.

2.3   Semantic Standardization through Glossary

BPM techniques often allow for a high degree of freedom, in syntax as well as in semantics. For example, modelers using the Event-driven Process Chain or Business Process Model and Notation are able to arbitrarily label elements like events and functions. Studies have shown, that the terms used in different modeling efforts can differ to a great extent [9], especially in timely, personally and regionally distributed projects [10]. These naming conflicts result mainly from synonyms and phrase structures [11]. Studies have shown, for example, that even when the number of words to be used as labels is limited to two, there are over 20 different phrase structures used by modelers [12]. This hinders the re-use of the models due to an increased complexity and resulting problems in understanding on the model users' side. Furthermore, an automated analysis and processing of the models is not possible.

To prevent naming conflicts, standardization of the possible choice of words and phrase structures is the key to success [1, 12]. This has to be done before starting to model and has to be enforced during a modeling effort. Proven scientifically, activity-object phrase structures are better understandable than any other phrase structure [13]. Therefore, icebricks provides a glossary, which is composed of business objects for certain domains. Beside the business objects, activities are maintained which can be combined with the business objects. By providing the administrators with the possibility to freely define allowed business object-activity combinations, customized modeling in

---

[2] Hypertext Markup Language is a text-based markup language for the description of texts, pictures and hyperlinks and forms the basis of the world-wide web.

any domain and organization is enabled. Every process framework has to be related to a single glossary which enforces the semantic standardization. All process elements are then labeled with one business object-activity combination specified within this glossary. Thereby, compliance with modeling conventions is guaranteed which renders refinements or corrections irrelevant and fosters the re-use of process models.

2.4   Reference Models

Within icebricks, the utilization of reference models is integrated to enhance model creation even further by providing an easy and efficient way to adapt existing reference models to the needs of specific modeling endeavors. Due to their established best or common practice character, models of high quality are created.

3   Design of the Artifact

According to the aforementioned rationales, icebricks is realized as a web-based tool to ensure the greatest possible availability. Due to its web-based nature, access to the tool is given anywhere where access to the internet is given. The tool is based on the Ruby on Rails-Framework which is a prominent model-view-controller framework encapsulating the business logic, data management and presentation. Due to its modular nature, additions to the tool are easily realizable. Moreover, the usage of JavaScript[3] in various aspects of the presentation layer, arranges for an efficient and effective utilization of the tool. For example, irritating and time-consuming reloads of web pages are contained with the asynchronous loading incorporated in JavaScript.

The targeted user group of the tool is, in the first place, consultants carrying out modeling projects. The tool was developed in close cooperation with a corporate consultancy. Thus, the specific needs of modeling undertakings directly influenced the development of the tool. In Fig. 2, an exemplary process inside the tool is depicted.

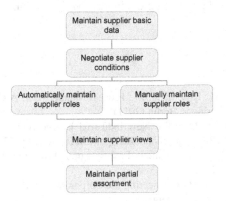

Fig. 2. Exemplary detail process "Maintain supplier master data" inside the icebricks tool

---

[3] JavaScript is a script language for the enhancement of user interactions with the web browser.

In addition to the integration of the abovementioned rationales, the tool provides a simple yet for the modeling purpose useful reporting component. Basic reports on the attributes allow for an analysis of the processes. For example, summation of a numeric attribute or the identification of affected hierarchical attributes in terms of changing conditions is enabled by the tool.

4   Significance to Practice and Evaluation of the Artifact

As stated in the previous section, the tool was developed in close cooperation with a corporate consultancy. In two projects so far 3 frameworks, 25 main processes, 104 detail processes and 301 process building blocks were created. In both projects direct modeling during interviews and workshops within the organizations was time efficient. Furthermore, a later enhancement of the process models in terms of additional information to existing process elements as well as more detailed modeling on a more detailed layer was possible and an effective way for complete process documentation.

The guidelines of modeling [8] are met by the tool. The semantic standardization helps to lower the costs of any business process modeling effort since the enhanced effectiveness and efficiency compared to non-standardized modeling methodologies leads to shorter modeling projects. Moreover, through the usage of attribution, the models are tailored to the modeling purpose resulting in a high clarity, correctness and comparability based on a systematic design.

5   Outlook

In the short run, an improvement of the user experience and the further development of the reporting component of the tool are desired. Building on a market analysis which is carried out at the time of this article, different usability features will be incorporated in the tool. Furthermore, founding on the results of a project carried out at the time of this article, the reporting component will be enhanced enabling more sophisticated analyses.

References

1. Becker, J., Kugeler, M., Rosemann, M.: Process Management: A Guide for the Design of Business Processes. Springer, Berlin (2011)
2. Davenport, T.H., Short, J.E.: The New Industrial Engineering: Information Technology and Business Process Redesign. Sloan Management Review, 11–27 (1990)
3. Hagen, C.R., Stucky, W.: Business-Process- und Workflow-Management. Teubner, Wiesbaden (2004)
4. Hammer, M., Champy, J.: Reengineering the Corporation: a Manifesto for business Revolution. HarperCollins, London (1993)
5. Melão, N., Pidd, M.: A conceptual framework for understanding business processes and business process modelling. Information Systems Journal 10, 105–129 (2000)

6. Gou, H., Huang, B., Liu, W., Li, X.: A framework for virtual enterprise operation management. Computers in Industry 50, 333–352 (2003)

7. Mendling, J., Reijers, H., Van der Aalst, W.M.P.: Seven Process Modeling Guidelines (7PMG). Information and Software Technology 52, 127–136 (2008)

8. Becker, J., Rosemann, M., Von Uthmann, C.: Guidelines of Business Process Modeling. In: van der Aalst, W., Desel, J., Overweis, A. (eds.) Business Process Management: Models, Techniques and Empirical Studies, pp. 30–49. Springer, Berlin (2000)

9. Hadar, I., Soffer, P.: Variations in conceptual modeling: classification and ontological analysis. Journal of AIS 7, 568–592 (2006)

10. Hadar, I., Soffer, P.: Variations in conceptual modeling: classification and ontological analysis. Journal of AIS 7, 568–592 (2006)

11. Batini, C., Lenzerini, M., Navathe, S.B.: A Comparative Analysis of Methodologies for Database Schema Integration. ACM Computing Surveys 18, 323–364 (1986)

12. Delfmann, P., Herwig, S., Lis, L.: Unified Enterprise Knowledge Representation with Conceptual Models - Capturing Corporate Language in Naming Conventions. In: 30th International Conference on Information Systems (ICIS 2009), Phoenix, Arizona, USA (2009)

13. Mendling, J., Reijers, H.A., Recker, J.: Activity labeling in process modeling: Empirical insights and recommendations. Information Systems 35, 467–482 (2010)

Estimating Operating System Process Energy Consumption in Real Time

Kaushik Dutta[1], Vivek Kumar Singh[1], and Debra VanderMeer[2]

[1] National University of Singapore, Singapore
{duttak,disvks}@nus.edu.sg
[2] Florida International University, USA
debra.vandermeer@fiu.edu

Abstract. The power consumption in data centers due to Information and Communication Technologies (ICT) is significant across the globe. With recent developments in Service Oriented Architecture (SOA), we notice a paradigm shift in computing. Desktops (PCs) and laptops are being replaced by smart phones and tablets. A major impact of this architecture is a shift of computing resources from personal desktops and laptops to centralized server farms. This implies increases in power consumption in the large-scale servers used in these infrastructures. In such a scenario, optimizing the IT resources for power consumption is a necessity. The first step of such an optimization at the application level is the knowledge of how much energy the application is consuming. A major challenge in this domain is to develop a software-based energy metering tool that can measure the energy consumptions at the OS process level. We have developed an OS process-level power metering tool that can accurately estimate the energy usage based on system resource usages, and demonstrated that our tool provides energy measurement for complex e-business applications with greater than 95% accuracy.

Keywords: Energy, Power Meter, SVM Model, Operating Systems.

1 Introduction

IT power consumption is a significant concern [1]. The issue of energy efficiency is receiving substantial attention along multiple fronts, from data center design [2, 3], to hardware design [4, 5], among others. These solutions impact the IT infrastructure, but do not consider the workload subjected to it, i.e., they do not address the scope of the workload generated by the software that runs on it. Recently, the Information Systems community has called for a broad research focus on improving IT energy efficiency. In line with that agenda, in addition to hardware, energy efficiency needs to be addressed in the software systems as well [6].

Measurement of the power for software processes and applications is an important step towards meeting this objective. As per [6], the major goals in achieving energy efficient IT systems include: (1) identification and operationalization of proxy metrics for computational complexity and thermodynamic depth of specific software

J. vom Brocke et al. (Eds.): DESRIST 2013, LNCS 7939, pp. 400–404, 2013.

applications; (2) implementation of a tool that measures these metrics; and (3) measurement of actual power consumption. In this research, we propose a method for measuring operating system (OS) energy consumption on a per-process basis, and describe a software tool that implements the method.

The task of measuring energy consumption for OS processes may sound similar to measuring memory and CPU utilization, and so may seem simple; however, OS kernel APIs do not provide energy consumption information. In the absence of a direct measurement from the OS, researchers have resorted to other approaches. In one approach [6], researchers attached a CPU clamp and a watt-meter to a CPU to directly measure CPU usage. While this does measure energy consumption, it involves cumbersome hardware enhancement and measures only CPU energy consumption. In another approach [7], researchers created a mathematical model of the energy consumption of a CPU, which still does not capture energy usage for all hardware components. In this research, we propose and develop a tool to measure process-level energy consumption that incorporates all OS process activities, including CPU, memory, I/O, and network communication.

2   Solution Approach

The energy consumed by the hardware in a server is an effect of the software or process stack running on top of the hardware stack. OS processes share the hardware resources through the OS. The OS captures this usage, and makes it available in terms of usage parameters. For example, in Linux, *Procfs* [8] filesystem can provide the details of the resource usage by a process such as usage of disk, CPU, memory and network. The energy usage of an OS process p is a function of these resource usages by the process. So we have,

$$Energy_p = (cpu_p, disk_p, network_p, memory_p) \qquad (1)$$

where, $Energy_p$ is the energy consumed by p, which is a function of CPU usage (cpu_p), disk usage $(disk_p)$, network usage $(network_p)$ and memory usage $(memory_p)$ of p.

To identify F, we collect OS level energy utilization $(Energy_o)$ using a watt-meter along with OS level overall cpu (cpu_o), disk $(disk_o)$ network $(network_o)$ and memory utilization $(memory_p)$ data. Thus for OS level we will have following equation, $$Energy_o = (cpu_o, disk_o, network_o, memory_o) \qquad (2)$$

From Equation 2, using the OS level energy and OS level resource utilization data (e.g., as provided by *procfs* in Linux) we derive the model F, which is then used in Equation 1 to estimate the process-level energy consumption from the process level resource utilization data.

We begin with a data collection phase, during which we collect OS process-level resource usage and total energy consumption at various system loads. Figure *1* depicts the architecture used for data collection phase. The target machine is the server. We installed the RUBiS [9] benchmark auction in the server, and the *JMeter* load testing tool on a laptop on the same local network as the server. Using JMeter, we simulated multiple simultaneous users on the RUBiS application. By varying the number of simultaneous users in JMeter, we can vary the server load. The server is connected to the power outlet through a watt-meter, which monitors energy usage by the server and periodically logs the data on the laptop via USB cable. At each server work load (measured by number of simultaneous JMeter users), we periodically log the resource usage using *procfs* system. A simple server program captured and logged the server resource usage data.

The above data collection exercise results in a set of OS level resource usage data (i.e. $cpu_o, disk_0, network_o$ and $memory_p$) along with the corresponding energy usages ($Energy_o$) by the computer at varying energy consumption level. This data is then used to model the function F using Equation 2.

As the relationship of energy usage with CPU, disk, network and memory usage is complex (i.e. non-linear) for real life applications like RUBiS, we felt the linear regression model, as followed in past research will be inapplicable. So, we used support vector machine (SVM) based regression modeling using R statistical tool. Specifically, we used epsilon regression of SVR with non-linear "radial" kernel. The output of the SVM regression is the trained model, which represents the function F.

For each data points we also captured the process level resource usage data - $cpu_p, disk_p, network_p, memory_p$, which is then used in Equation 1 along with the derived model F to estimate the process level energy consumptions.

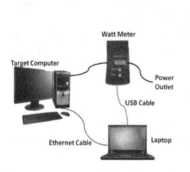

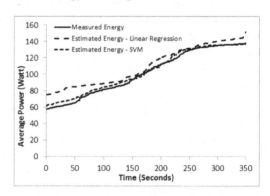

Fig. 1. Data Collection Architecture

Fig. 2. Comparison of actual vs. estimated energy measurement for SVM vs. Linear Modeling

In this approach, we need the watt-meter only in the calibration stage, in order to create the model *F*. Once F has been determined from the OS level data, the process level energy estimation can be done online on the server itself using the process level resource usage data - $cpu_p, disk_p, network_p, memory_p$. Calibration is required only once for a particular configuration of hardware and OS. If two machines have similar configurations both at the hardware and the OS level, the model F will remain unchanged and the model derived from one computer can be utilized for process level energy estimating in the other machine.

3   Experimental Result

We implemented our approach on a Linux-based enterprise operating system (CentOS release 6.3) running on a quad-core Intel Xeon processor machine with 8 GB RAM. To accurately capture the total power usage of the server, we extended the open source *PowerStat* tool for server based Linux system. This tool is integrated with the *WattsUp PRO* watt-meter and has been released in the open source community [10]. It periodically captures the total energy usage by the computer from the watt-meter and time-stamps it with the server's time. In parallel, we ran a program to collect the process-level resource usage data with the server's time stamp (one second interval). This approach allows the energy data to be synchronized with the resource usage data.

To emulate varied energy usage level in the server, we ran the RUBiS benchmark application in the server and varied the workload of the RUBiS benchmark using simulated users from JMeter. We varied the total number of simulated simultaneous users in JMeter from 10 to 1500, and this caused the total power consumption of the server to vary from 58 watts to 130 watts. We ran this experiment for 1 hour and collected 3600 data points.

We divided this data points to two random sets – training and testing. The training data set contains 20% of the data points (i.e., 720 data points) and the testing data set contains rest of the data points (i.e., 2880 data points). The training data set has been used to model the server's energy usage as a function of server's total resource usages. The model is used on the resource usage data in the testing data set to estimate both the process and server level total energy consumption.

Next, we compared the process level energy estimation. There is no readily available tool at present to measure the process level energy consumptions. So we resort to an indirect way of computing the accuracy. For each test data point, we computed the process level energy consumption for each process and then summed it over all processes running in the server at the same time to compute the server's total energy consumption. This computed total energy is compared with the actual energy consumed by the server as measured by the watt-meter (shown in Figure 2). As can be seen from the Figure 2, the total computed energy using the process level energy estimation by SVM modeling matches closely with the actual energy consumption across a wide range of the total energy consumption of server. The overall average error-percentage of our process level energy estimation is 4%. Additionally, for the sake of comparison with other modeling techniques (compared to SVM) we also plotted the estimated total energy based on linear regression modeling. The linear regression model performs worse than the SVM model. The linear regression modeling has an average error value of 15% compared to 4% for SVM based modeling. Additionally, we also notice that the linear regression model has higher deviation from the actual energy value at higher and lower total energy consumptions of the system – at the middle level of energy consumption by the computer system, the linear regression model performs slightly better though it is still worse than the SVM modeling. Thus we can conclude our approach provides a very accurate measurement of process level energy consumptions at a wide energy consumption range.

4   Conclusion

In this work, we have described an approach and tool to measure the process level energy consumption of any Linux based server. Our approach has high accuracy (over 95%). It also has several advantages. First, it does not require any watt-meter or additional hardware changes for online measurement. The requirement of the watt-meter is for the calibration only. Second, it relies on resource usages across all resources in a server providing energy measurement that is highly accurate. Third and finally, it relies on SVM based non-linear modeling than linear regression model as has been mostly followed in previous literature, resulting in very low error rate even for complex multi-tier e-business applications like RUBiS. In future work, we intend to do a wide variety of experiments and thorough analysis on a wide range of applications and hardware to find the robustness of our approach.

Acknowledgement. This project was partially funded by National University of Singapore Grant R-253-000-087-133.

References

[1] Koomey, J.G.: Worldwide electricity used in data centers. Environmental Research Letters 3, 1–8 (2008)

[2] Open Compute Project, Hacking Conventional Computing Infrastructure (2011)

[3] Google, Efficient Data Centers (2011)

[4] Childers, B.R., Tang, H., Melhem, R.: Adapting Processor Supply Voltage to Instruction-Level Parallelism. In: Proceedings of the Kool Chips Workshop (in Conjunction with MICRO33), Monterey, California, pp. 78–81 (2000)

[5] Kin, J., Gupta, M., Mangione-Smith, W.H.: The filter cache: an energy efficient memory structure. In: Proceedings of the 30th Annual ACM/IEEE International Symposium on Microarchitecture, pp. 184–193. Research Triangle Park, North Carolina (1997)

[6] Eugenio, C., Francesco, M.: Green IT: Everything starts from the software. Presented at the ECIS 2009 Proceedings (2009)

[7] Tan, T.K., Raghunathan, A., Lakshminarayana, G., Jha, N.K.: High-level software energy macro-modeling. In: Proceedings of the 2001 Design Automation Conference, pp. 605–610 (2001)

[8] Bowden, T., Bauer, B., Nerin, J., Feng, S., Seibold, S.: The/proc filesystem. Linux Kernel Documentation (2000)

[9] Open Web 2 Consortium. RUBiS: Rice University Bidding System (August 6, 2012), http://rubis.ow2.org/

[10] Dutta, K., Singh, V.: PowerStat for Server (2012), http://greenit.comp.nus.edu.sg/?q=node/3

Cross-Platform Development of Business Apps with MD^2

Henning Heitkötter and Tim A. Majchrzak

Department of Information Systems
University of Münster, Münster, Germany
{heitkoetter,tima}@ercis.de

Abstract. MD^2 is a framework for cross-platform model-driven mobile development. It consists of a domain-specific language for describing business apps concisely and of generators that automatically create complete iOS and Android apps from this specification.

Designers. MD^2 has been created as a research prototype at the Department of Information Systems, University of Münster. Henning Heitkötter and Tim A. Majchrzak, both interested in cross-platform approaches and mobile applications in general, supervised the implementation, which was mainly carried out by master students Sören Evers, Klaus Fleerkötter, Daniel Kemper, Sandro Mesterheide, and Jannis Strodtkötter.

Keywords: Business apps, mobile, cross-platform development, model-driven, domain-specific language, MDSD.

1 Introduction

Due to the rise of smartphones and tablets, more and more businesses are looking into mobile applications for their customers, employees, or business partners. The development of these so-called *apps* is a complex task of its own, as developers have to study a new environment and its unique capabilities. The heterogeneity of the mobile market further complicates app development. Most businesses target at least the two leading mobile platforms, i. e., iOS and Android (cf., e. g., [2]). Each platform increases development costs almost linearly due to profound differences in programming model, languages, and frameworks.

Cross-platform development approaches emerged to relieve developers from developing the same app repeatedly for different platforms. They allow implementing an app once and supplying several platforms from this common code base. A study by the authors [3] showed that existing approaches and solutions work well for certain situations. However, they do not achieve a truly native look & feel that resembles unique characteristics of each platform. This is often desired of high-quality apps or even a precondition for an app's functionality.

Our framework MD^2 employs a model-driven approach to cross-platform development of business apps. Developers specify an app using MD^2's domain-specific language (DSL). Generators transform this textual model to source code of iOS and Android apps. Our work makes several contributions to IS research:

J. vom Brocke et al. (Eds.): DESRIST 2013, LNCS 7939, pp. 405–411, 2013.
© Springer-Verlag Berlin Heidelberg 2013

MD^2 is a novel, model-driven method for cross-platform app development. Its DSL represents an innovative set of constructs for specifying business apps.

Section 2 describes MD^2's design, i.e., the overall method and the set of constructs that forms the DSL. Its significance to research and to practice is analyzed in Section 3. Results from evaluating MD^2 are presented in Section 4, before Section 5 concludes with a short discussion and an outlook.

2   Design of the Artifact

MD^2 has been conceived and designed to address the lack of cross-platform solutions that produce apps with a native look & feel. App users and, consequently, businesses commissioning apps often desire a native appearance, as it matches the user interface (UI) of other applications on the device. Besides giving a more professional impression, such apps also integrate more closely with the respective platform. At the same time, MD^2 should considerably simplify the development of apps by increasing the abstraction level compared to programming languages such as Java or Objective-C. Section 3 illustrates the relevance of our goals.

MD^2 focuses on data-driven business apps. They are defined as mobile applications that serve a specific business purpose and mainly deal with form-based input, processing, and display of data. In contrast to, for example, mobile games, they mainly use standard UI elements and layouts. They retrieve, modify, and store structured data that may reside on the device or on remote servers. Their application logic needs to control the UI, validate input, and access device features such as GPS. Advanced calculations, however, are assumed to take place on servers. This set of requirements has been collected through close cooperation with industry partners and a previous industry survey [7] in order to ensure relevancy. It served as basis for deriving constructs needed to describe apps.

A model-driven approach fits well with the problem outlined above. Model-driven software development (MDSD) aims to make models a first-class artifact in the development process, from which lower-level representations, e.g., source code, can automatically be generated. These models can exhibit a higher level of abstraction, because subsequent transformations can introduce necessary detail when translating the constructs used in models into the target environment. Thanks to the specifically designed DSL, MD^2 models are concise, expressive, and easy to understand. Developers using MD^2 do not need in-depth knowledge of developing for iOS or Android. In particular, no knowledge of Objective-C or Java is required. They need to accustom themselves with MD^2's DSL, a task facilitated by its intuitive concepts and well-structured components.

Details on the implementation of MD^2 can be found in a separate paper [4]. Furthermore, MD^2's DSL has been described in detail as well [5]. In the following, we describe the architecture and features of MD^2 as they apply in an IS environment. They are the foundation for MD^2's contributions (see Section 3).

Development of an app with MD^2 (see Figure 1) may start with an initial idea of the app's software design. The app is described in a textual model using MD^2's DSL (phase 1). The DSL provides constructs for describing data model,

user interface, and control logic of an app in a declarative manner. These three
parts are defined separately, but connected, as prescribed by the Model-View-
Controller (MVC) pattern.

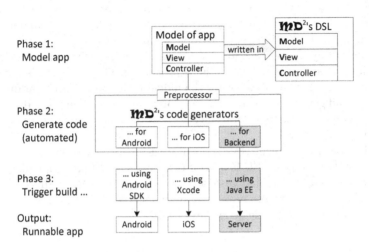

Fig. 1. Workflow and architecture of MD^2

The model part provides concepts such as entities with primitive-valued attributes and references to other entities. The modeler of an app instantiates these
concepts to describe the app's data model. MD^2's view part includes standard
UI elements such as text input fields, buttons, and labels. They can be arranged
using nestable layouts, e. g., a tabbed navigation with several individual tabs.
Modelers may define own styles and apply them to UI elements. The concept of
an automatic generator inserts a default representation of an entity type and its
properties.

The controller part of a model integrates model and view and specifies the
behavior of the app. The integration is described using data mappings between
UI elements and specific data stores. Essential behavioral constructs are events
and actions, as apps built with MD^2 follow an event-based interaction model.
In the controller model, custom actions are registered for certain events. Events
range from simple user interactions, e. g., touching a button, to changes of the
app's global state. For example, an action could be executed as soon as a certain
condition involving data and UI state is true. Actions may consist of different
kinds of predefined actions and also call other custom actions. There are predefined actions for event binding, data mapping, data operations, UI modification,
and accessing device features. Additionally, MD^2 supports workflows for defining and restricting the navigation paths within the app. Implicit and explicit
validators allow checking user input, for example, to ensure a particular format.

After the app – or a first version thereof – has been specified as a model,
MD^2 invokes a preprocessor and, eventually, the code generators (phase 2). Each

generator inspects the model and creates native source code and additional files for its respective platform, i.e., Android or iOS. The resulting project can directly be compiled without modifying the generated code (phase 3). The thus created native app can then be installed and executed on a suitable mobile device. Since each app directly uses the native source development kit of the respective mobile platform and native UI elements, generated apps are tightly integrated into their respective platform and inherently exhibit a native appearance.

Developers may change the model at any time and have the generators create a new version of the app following the same procedure. This enables a fast iterative development, as all phases except for the modeling are automated. Additionally, MD^2's backend generator creates a server application out of an app's data model, which provides apps with an interface for storing and retrieving data from a database.

MD^2 has been implemented as a set of plug-ins for the popular development environment Eclipse. Its DSL has been defined using Xtext, a language development environment [10] that also served to create powerful editors for MD^2 models. The code generators have been implemented in Xtend, a programming language with advanced code generation facilities [9].

3   Significance to Research and Practice

MD^2 is significant for both research and practice in that it is useful for practitioners yet addresses challenges in terms of fundamental and applied research.

While MDSD is well understood for developing desktop and server applications, its application to apps is rather new. In particular, understanding business needs for app development, identifying a set of requirements, and developing a corresponding DSL is no trivial task. Therefore, we provide not only a novel method for developing apps but also a set of constructs for describing apps as models. Developing such a DSL also fosters understanding of the domain. Our DSL highlights typical requirements and challenges of business apps.

The instantiation of our main artifact in form of a product connects the significance for research and practice. From a research perspective it proves the feasibility of our approach and the soundness of the underlying ideas. From a practical perspective it is the transfer of knowledge back from theory to practice.

Before work on our framework started, we participated in a project with regional companies that analyzed the status quo of app development and current challenges, especially regarding cross-platform development. Its results [7] showed the relevance of finding an adequate solution to tackle platform and device fragmentation and gave us insights into business needs. Additionally, we kept close contact with an IT consulting company that provided a pilot case for the first main prototype (see next section). In conclusion, MD^2 is highly significant and industry cooperation ensured its usefulness.

A multitude of cross-platform solutions, both from research and industry, also highlights the relevance of this topic. As demonstrated in a comparative study [3], existing approaches such as mobile web apps or hybrid apps – web apps packaged with a native runtime environment – are useful in *some* scenarios. However, their very nature makes it difficult to develop apps with a native look & feel, because these approaches do not resort to native elements only. Instead, the look & feel of such Web-based apps resembles that of Web sites, which is undesirable if requirements demand a close native integration or a high-quality user experience.

As a model-driven approach promises to overcome these shortcomings, other solutions take this route as well. For example, *applause* [1] provides a DSL for apps and generates iOS, Android, and Windows Phone apps. However, in contrast to MD^2, applause is limited to displaying data. *AXIOM* [6] is another model-driven solution, but not fully automated, as the transformation requires manual intervention and mappings for each app. *Modagile Mobile* [8] uses a graphical DSL to describe data model and UI of apps and requires manual code for control logic.

4 Evaluation of the Artifact

We have evaluated MD^2 by applying it to real-world scenarios. Throughout development, an insurance tariff calculator served as a guiding example. It represents a typical form-based business app that implements a workflow. As the app uses a variety of UI elements and relies on a back end to provide data and perform calculations[1], it was well-suited as a pilot case. It even utilizes device features such as GPS to propose a location for a customer. Our industry partner, who supplied us with this case based on an actual project of theirs, also discussed requirements of business apps in general with us. To complete our set of apps for evaluating MD^2, we also used MD^2 to implement a number of smaller apps such as an e-commerce shop and a library front end.

For the current release, ease-of-use of MD^2 had to be assessed and resulting apps had to be evaluated. Due to the compactness and expressiveness of the language, it is relatively easy to implement apps using MD^2. The learning curve was found to be steep; no experience with model-driven approaches was necessary to use it. We believe that a good documentation will enable domain experts to understand and use our DSL. Regarding the actual apps, we got very positive feedback from our industry partner. Apps indeed have a native appeal and the desired functionality could be realized. This is particularly noticeable since some characteristics of apps have to be implemented quite differently on Android and iOS. We are confident that extending MD^2 to further platforms will not pose major technical difficulties.

We also evaluated MD^2 from a quantitative point of view. Lines of code (LOC) required for implementing apps are an adequate metric. 709 LOC in MD^2's DSL specified the tariff calculator. This lead to 10 110 LOC Java and 2 263 LOC XML for Android, 3 270 LOC Objective-C and 64 LOC XML for iOS, and 1 923 LOC Java and 57 LOC XML for the back end. Figures for other sample apps are

---

[1] Insurance companies typically do not want to expose their calculations and hence strive to keep as much logic on their (secured) servers as possible.

similar [4]. Since generated code resembles code as it would have to be written manually, the savings are more than notable.

The set of criteria expected from cross-platform approaches that has been established in a separate publication [3] can also be consulted to evaluate MD^2. MD^2 scores well with respect to most development criteria: It is accompanied by mature tooling such as an DSL editor; supports clearly structured, modularized, and concise models; and speeds up development in general. Regarding infrastructure criteria, it fulfills the requirements of a native look & feel, good performance, and access to platform-specific features. So far, only the two most popular mobile platforms are supported.

5 Conclusion

We have presented MD^2, our novel framework for cross-platform app development based on model-driven techniques. MD^2 is significant from a research perspective, as the way we apply a MDSD approach is new and the domain of business apps raises both technical and economic questions. At the same time, it is highly relevant. While first evaluation results are promising and most data-driven business apps can already be implemented, MD^2 is currently still limited with respect to certain functionality, for example advanced device features. Our work on MD^2 continues with refining it, extending it, and applying it to additional scenarios.

In parallel, we will continue to monitor the market of cross-platform development solutions. Future improvements of Web-based approaches, for example, in connection with the upcoming HTML 5 standard, might require a reevaluation of their potential regarding native integration. However, corresponding progress will most likely be limited to accessing more platform-specific functionality, but not extend to the look & feel.

Materials

MD^2's Web site (http://wwu-pi.github.com/md2-web/) provides access to the set of Eclipse plug-ins, MD^2's documentation and screencasts.

Acknowledgments. We gratefully acknowledge the work done by Sören Evers, Klaus Fleerkötter, Daniel Kemper, Sandro Mesterheide, and Jannis Strodtkötter, who implemented MD^2. Furthermore, we would like to thank viadee Unternehmensberatung GmbH for their support.

References

1. Behrens, H.: MDSD for the iPhone. In: Proc. of SPLASH (2010)
2. Gartner Press Release: Gartner Says Worldwide Mobile Phone Sales Declined 1.7 Percent in 2012 (February 2013), http://www.gartner.com/newsroom/id/2335616

3. Heitkötter, H., Hanschke, S., Majchrzak, T.A.: Evaluating cross-platform development approaches for mobile applications. In: Cordeiro, J., Krempels, K.-H. (eds.) WEBIST 2012. LNBIP, vol. 140, pp. 120–138. Springer, Heidelberg (2013)

4. Heitkötter, H., Majchrzak, T.A., Kuchen, H.: Cross-platform model-driven development of mobile applications with MD^2. In: Proc. 28th SAC, ACM (2013)

5. Heitkötter, H., Majchrzak, T.A., Kuchen, H.: MD^2-DSL – eine domänenspezifische Sprache zur Beschreibung und Generierung mobiler Anwendungen. In: Proc. Der 6. Arbeitstagung Programmiersprachen (ATPS), GI. LNI, vol. 215 (2013)

6. Jia, X., Jones, C.: AXIOM: A model-driven approach to cross-platform application development. In: Proc. 7th ICSOFT (2012)

7. Majchrzak, T.A., Heitkötter, H.: Development of mobile applications in regional companies: Status quo and best practices. In: Proc. 9th WEBIST (2013)

8. Modagile Mobile (2013), http://www.modagile-mobile.de/

9. Xtend (2013), http://www.eclipse.org/xtend/

10. Xtext (2013), http://www.eclipse.org/Xtext/

Context-Awareness in the Car:
Prediction, Evaluation and Usage of Route Trajectories

Patrick Helmholz, Edgar Ziesmann, and Susanne Robra-Bissantz

Chair Information Management, University of Braunschweig, Germany
{p.helmholz,e.ziesmann,s.robra-bissantz}@tu-bs.de

Abstract. A route trajectory is described as the upcoming course of the road in geographical terms as well as in terms of time. This enables the possibility of providing context-aware applications in modern vehicles. In order to generate such a trajectory with its context aware information, it is still necessary to enter a destination point into a navigation system. However, the most frequent commutations (drives, trips) are to known destinations and are therefore not performed with any active guidance system. This means that the prediction must be determined in a different manner. This paper presents a method, which predicts the route trajectory of a vehicle based on the travel history of its user. In addition to the traveled distance further context parameters are used for the prediction. These parameters include the current time of day, day of week and the route frequency, which indicates the number of times a particular route has already been traveled. Moreover, the developed prediction is evaluated in a volunteers study with about 500 rides and about 9.500 driven kilometers. The results show that in 80 percent of the cases the forward-lying path can be predicted correctly.

Keywords. Route trajectory, driving context, context-awareness.

1 Introduction

Due to a flood of information from various application areas, the ability to filter information based on the current context is becoming increasingly important in today's fast paced world. To determine a user's context, it is necessary to have sensors or other data sources such as inferences about time, current location, weather conditions or social relationships at a disposal [1]. Common smartphones already have such sensors integrated and provide appropriate applications with significant information in order to focus on the current situation and the user's needs. Further, the diffusion of these devices and their usage acceptance show their importance in all life circumstances [2]. This trend can also be perceived in the automotive industry. Current developments show that vehicles are increasingly being equipped with sophisticated sensors and a mobile Internet connection [3,4] enabling services like Facebook updates, tweets or Google Maps as an everyday commodity [5]. This leads to customers also demanding most of their (context-aware) smartphone-known applications as an in-car implementation [6]. For providing context-sensitive information on a smartphone it is

J. vom Brocke et al. (Eds.): DESRIST 2013, LNCS 7939, pp. 412–419, 2013.

necessary to know the current location of the user. For in-vehicle applications however, it is even more important to know the future position or the route ahead, because the current location is a thing of the past after a few seconds [7].

The route ahead of the current position is referred to as route trajectory in this paper. It describes the upcoming route both geographically and chronologically. Navigation systems basically provide the opportunity to generate the route trajectory based on an entered destination and the calculated route. This route trajectory can be provided to other in-car applications. However, trips to known destinations tend to take place without navigational aid. This can be explained by the fact that the driver is already fully aware of the road ahead and that he doesn't want to pay the cost of inputting the destination for such known trips [8]. In fact, it has already been shown that only 6 percent of the drivers use a navigation device for daily trips [9]. This leads to the cause that necessary context information is not available on daily trips and that it prevents an automated use of many context-aware applications. Therefore, the question arises on how to determine the route trajectory in the first place when navigation systems are not being used. For these cases the route trajectory has to be determined automatically, so that it can be used [8,10]. This paper presents a method and a prototype, which predicts and uses the route trajectory of a vehicle.

2   Prediction of the Route Trajectory

Schönfelder & Axhausen (2001) determined in their study that about 80 percent of all trips lead to only five different destinations [11]. Supposing such a homogeneous geographical driving habit, it is possible to develop a system, which anticipates the next destination and generates the associated route trajectory based on past (historical) trips. Most importantly this is achieved without any user interaction with the navigation system. However, the possibility of overlapping routes represents a significant problem in determining the route trajectory.

If a driver is on a system-known route, which only leads to a single previously recorded destination, the system can only anticipate this destination and generate the corresponding route trajectory. But if the driver is on a section that is part of several already known routes, it is more difficult to predict the correct route trajectory. However, other studies show that the driving behavior also has a temporal regularity in addition to a geographic one. Thus, on average, about half of all journeys that lead to a certain destination are driven at the same time [12,13]. For example, many people go to and from work at predictable times and use only a few routes [10]. Therefore, the quality of the route prediction can be improved with the aid of the context parameters of daytime and weekday. In addition to these parameters, the route frequency also plays an important role in determining the correct route trajectory, because it contains implicitly a reliable empirical value for the (user-specific) selection of a route: If a user has chosen a route more often than another in the past, it is likely that he will take the same route in the future. The influence of these parameters on the accuracy of the route prediction is the research focus of this study and prototype.

3   Related Works

The prediction of the driver's future location and the route trajectory of vehicles have already been studied and analyzed in several publications. Beside methods using GSM-network cell information, the more accurate methods record the paths taken by a driver using their GPS signal for the prediction [12,13,14,15,16,17]. In contrast to the other mentioned methods, Froehlich & Krumm's (2008) method allows for a relatively wide forecast, since the entire route ahead is predicted. The authors conclude, that there is a correlation between daytime and the choice of a particular route, but they do not use this knowledge in their model. The result of the prediction is only based on the best and longest topological correspondence of a route concerning the current drive. Froehlich & Krumm (2008) finally suspect that this accuracy could be improved by using temporal context parameters. [12]

All publications, except [12], just consider the prediction accuracy for the next route segment. A statement about the accuracy for the entire course of the road ahead to the destination is not given.

The driver can benefit from such a system on everyday journeys, when the navigation device is not used. During these journeys it is necessary for many context-sensitive services to predict the entire road ahead and especially the destination. The specifically developed model presented in the next section deals with the prediction accuracy of the entire road ahead, checking the influence of different context parameters. This shall also confirm the presumption of Froehlich & Krumm (2008) regarding the correlation between the use of temporal context parameters and the prediction accuracy.

4   Development of an Own Model

This paper's model is based on consecutive recorded GPS position reports. These reports contain longitude, latitude, a time stamp, the altitude, the inaccuracy radius and - if available - a geo-coded address. To compare trips with one another for the purpose of predicting the route trajectory, they are modeled as a directed acyclic graph as it is shown in the example scenario in Figure 1. The position reports are represented as nodes of the graph. The edges of the graph link the position reports in pairs, thus forming the course of the route implicitly, which was not directly recorded.

It is assumed that an average user has a geographic homogeneity in his driving habits. Therefore, it is considered that on a trip the upcoming road ahead of a user (route trajectory) is related to the distance already travelled. Accordingly, the distance already travelled has to be compared with all past trips (Already Driven Trips, ADTs) for topological congruence. This is done by using a variant of the Hausdorff metric, which compares the topological congruence of two trips as well as the driving direction. Is there an ADT with an identical course, it is assumed that the user will repeat exactly this ADT at his current trip (Currently Driven Trip, CDT). In the example scenario of Figure 1 gray nodes characterize the candidates and white nodes demonstrate ADTs, which for various reasons are not eligible as candidates.

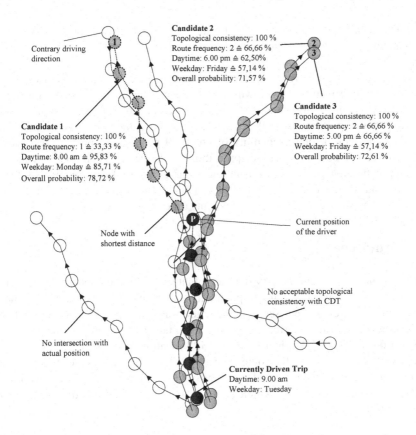

Fig. 1. Example scenario for generating the route prediction

It is probable that several ADTs come into consideration as candidates for the prediction of the route trajectory. In this case, all the candidates do have a high correlation with the CDT, but may have a different upcoming course of the road. To find the possibly correct candidate, the context parameters daytime, weekday and route frequency are considered in addition to the topological consistency. The context parameters time and day are very suitable as extended parameters for the prediction of the route trajectory, especially when assuming a temporal homogeneity in the average user's driving habits. Since it is assumed that repeated trips often begin at nearly the same time, the temporal context parameters are taken from the timestamp of the candidate's first position notification. These parameters are compared for their similarity with those of the CDT. For example, the daily hours 8.00 and 9.00 have a similarity of approximately 96 percent (= 100 - (100/24 • (9-8))) on a 24-hour scale. Equally, the weekdays Monday and Tuesday have a similarity of about 86 percent (= 100 - (100/7 • (2-1))) on a 7-day scale.

For driving habits that are not affected by a temporal homogeneity, the route frequency is a reliable parameter for a correct prediction of the route trajectory. It is considered in relation to the route frequency sum of all eligible journey destinations (candidates). In the example scenario of Figure 1, the probability for the left destination (candidate 1) is about 33 percent and for the right destination (candidate 2 and 3) about 67 percent.

The topological consistency and the different context parameters correspond to context-specific probabilities with which a user selects a specific route. In this regard, the overall probability of a candidate is crucial, calculated from the arithmetic mean of all the context parameters. In the example of Figure 1, the user drives the first candidate's route with a total probability of about 79 percent. To provide the relevant route trajectory to context-sensitive applications in the vehicle, that node of candidate 1's graph with the lowest distance from the actual position of the user (P) is selected. This one and all the following nodes of candidate 1's graph describe the probable driving path of the user and thus form his route trajectory.

5   Prototype

As part of the project and to carry out the volunteer study, the application "CARLA" (Context Aware Route Learning Application) was developed. Due to high demands on computing power, a client-server architecture was chosen. The CARLA client is an application for Android smartphones whose main task is to record journeys using the GPS sensor. The CARLA client sends its GPS location to the server throughout the entire journey and requests the route trajectory. The server determines this route trajectory with the described method and sends it to the client. A web application for CARLA[1] was also developed, which gives an overview of all recorded trips for the logged-in user (see Figure 2).

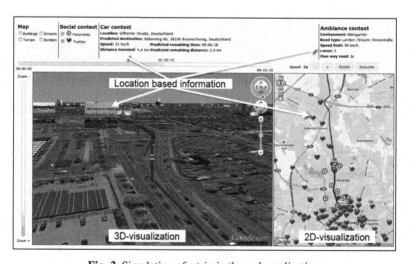

Fig. 2. Simulation of a trip in the web application

---

[1] Screencast of the web application: https://vimeo.com/61870664

Moreover, the user has the possibility to simulate all his trips in real-time, where the prediction of the route trajectory is shown. This is visualized in split view; on the right side as a two-dimensional view using Google Maps and on the left side as a three-dimensional view using Google Earth. The visualization is primarily for future development and testing of possible applications of the route trajectory. The first prototype uses the route trajectory to show location-based messages from Twitter and location-specific photos from Panoramio alongside the route. The inclusion of other location-based information services, like the rating platform Qype or location based music playback, are in progress. In the top area of the application, additional context information is shown: the predicted remaining driving time, the remaining distance, the destination, and relevant environment information. These information as well as the driving context of the user may be relevant for future in-car applications.

6 Volunteer Study and Evaluation

To make a first evaluation of the prediction method, a preliminary study was carried out. In this study five participants recorded a total of about 500 trips with about 9,500 kilometers total track length (see Figure 3). The evaluation was performed with a leave-one-out method, which means that exactly one drive of a user was simulated while the rest of the users trips were available as training data for the prediction. Though, a route trajectory was determined successively with every node of the simulated journey. Because the real upcoming course of the road was known, it could be compared to the determined route trajectory on topological correspondence ex post. The route trajectory was regarded as correct as long as the routes of the trajectory and the real upcoming course of the road diverged by not more than 50 m (Hausdorff distance). In order to show that the context parameters exert a positive influence on the prediction of the route trajectory, there have been two different evaluation runs: A first evaluation run, in which only the topological consistency of the ADTs with the CDT was used as a decision criterion for the prediction of the route trajectory and a second run, in which the three above-mentioned context parameters (CP) were included. The results of this evaluations can be found in Figure 3.

The results of the subjects A, B and E are relatively positive, as Figure 3 illustrates. Even without the use of additional context parameters, up to 72 percent of the road ahead can be predicted correctly. The high results for these subjects are mainly achieved due to their geographically homogeneous driving habits, since the rate of repeated trips is over 60 percent for them. The improvement of the results by considering additional context parameters suggests a temporal regularity in their driving habits. For the subjects C and D on average only up to 45 percent of the road ahead are predicted correctly. The usage of additional context parameters is not improving their results.

Since the prediction of the route trajectory is based on the travel history and the rate of repeated trips is comparably low for these subjects, it can be assumed that their driving habits are not yet completely captured, which may lead to a higher result.

Subject	Number of trips	Distance traveled [km]	Av. trip length [km]	Repeated trips [%]
A	49	442,1	9,0	61 %
B	199	2951,2	14,8	69 %
C	38	284,4	7,4	11 %
D	46	1369,2	29,7	9 %
E	162	4428,3	27,3	64 %

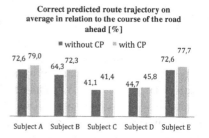

Fig. 3. Data from the study subjects and results of the study

7   Conclusion and Future Work

The present work demonstrates prototypically how context-sensitive automotive applications can be realized if a crucial basis is available: the route trajectory of the vehicle. There is still a lot of potential for improvement in this research field of predicting the route trajectory, but the project-related evaluation results show some noticeably good results. To verify the initial results of the study, a larger study with a larger number of participants over a longer period is required. It also has to be examined whether a different weighting of the used context parameters can lead to an improvement in the prediction accuracy. For example, it can be assumed that some of the common routes of a user are driven regularly at a certain time of day, while another part of the routes are driven at certain days of the week (and regardless of the time of the day). Therefore, a route-specific weighting of each context parameter as an extension of the presented approach seems reasonable and has to be examined.

In addition, detailed map data combined with a highly exact position sensor could enhance the prediction of the route trajectory, while the map data holds information about turning lanes. Thus, based on the traffic lane unlikely candidates could be excluded for the prediction of the route trajectory. The position of the direction-indicator control and the speed of the vehicle can be used as additional context parameters at intersection situations in order to improve the reliability of the prediction. Another potential problem is the possible (temporary) loss of the GPS signal. Besides a failure of the system, it also means that the recorded drive has a gap. Thus, the distance traveled is not represented optimally. If this incomplete drive is qualified as a prediction candidate for the route trajectory, it could have a negative impact on applications that use the route trajectory as a decision-making basis for the provision of services and content. To solve this problem, alternative technologies such as the triangulation over Wireless Local Area Networks (WLAN) can be used to determine the position. These improvements lead to a more extensive proposition of automotive services with the need of high position accuracy.

References

1. Abowd, G.D., Dey, A.K.: Towards a better understanding of context and context-awareness. In: Gellersen, H.-W. (ed.) HUC 1999. LNCS, vol. 1707, pp. 304–307. Springer, Heidelberg (1999)
2. IDC: Worldwide Quarterly Mobile Phone Tracker (2013), http://www.idc.com/getdoc.jsp?containerId=prUS23916413
3. Gerla, M., Kleinrock, L.: Vehicular networks and the future of the mobile internet. Computer Networks 55(2), 457–469 (2011)
4. Zauner, A., Hoffmann, H., Leimeister, J.M., Krcmar, H.: Automotive Software and Service Engineering (ASSE) - an exploration of challenges and trends from industry experts' points of view. In: Multikonferenz Wirtschaftsinformatik (MKWI) 2010, Göttingen, Germany (2010)
5. Goggin, G.: Driving the Internet: Mobile Internets, Cars, and the Social. Future Internet 4(1), 306–321 (2012)
6. Hoffmann, H., Leimeister, J.M.: Evaluating Application Prototypes in the Automobile. IEEE Pervasive Computing 10(3), 43–51 (2011)
7. Di Lorenzo, G., Pinelli, F., Pereira, F.C., Biderman, A., Ratti, C., Lee, C.: An Affective Intelligent Driving Agent: Driver's Trajectory and Activities Prediction. In: 2009 IEEE 70th Vehicular Technology Conference Fall (VTC 2009-Fall), pp. 1–4 (2009)
8. Terada, T., Miyamae, M., Kishino, Y., Tanaka, K., Nishio, S., Nakagawa, T., Yamaguchi, Y.: Design of a Car Navigation System that Predicts User Destination. In: Proceedings of the 7th International Conference on Mobile Data Management (MDM 2006), pp. 145–150 (2006)
9. Statista: Nutzungshäufigkeit PKW-Navigationssysteme (2011), http://de.statista.com/statistik/daten/studie/180738/umfrage/nutzungshaeufigkeit-von-pkw-navigationssystemen-in-deutschland/
10. Brillingaite, A., Jensen, C.: Online Route Prediction for Automotive Applications. In: Proceedings of the Thirteenth World Congress & Exhibition on Intelligent Transport Systems and Services (2006)
11. Schönfelder, S., Axhausen, K.W.: Mobidrive - Längsschnitterhebungen zum individuellen Verkehrsverhalten: Perspektiven für raum-zeitliche Analysen. In: Proceedings of 6th Symposion on Information Technology in Urban- and Spatial Planning and Impacts of ICT on Physical Space, pp. 315–321. Wien (2001)
12. Froehlich, J., Krumm, J.: Route Prediction from Trip Observations. In: Society of Automotive Engineers (SAE) World Congress (2008)
13. Simmons, R., Browning, B., Zhang, Y., Sadekar, V.: Learning to Predict Driver Route and Destination Intent. In: IEEE Intelligent Transportation Systems Conference (ITSC 2006), pp. S.127–S.132 (2006)
14. Ashbrook, D., Starner, T.: Using GPS to learn significant locations and predict movement across multiple users. Journal of Personal and Ubiquitous Computing 7(5), 275–286 (2003)
15. Chen, L., Lv, M., Chen, G.: A system for destination and future route prediction based on trajectory mining. Journal of Pervasive and Mobile Computing 6(6), 657–676 (2010)
16. Liao, L., Patterson, D.J., Fox, D., Kautz, H.: Learning and Inferring Transportation Routines. Journal of Artificial Intelligence 5-6(171), 311–331 (2007)
17. Li, Z., Xue, G., Zhu, H.: Traffic-Known Urban Vehicular Route Prediction Based on Partial Mobility Patterns. In: Proceedings of the 15th International Conference on Parallel and Distributed Systems (ICPADS), Shenzhen, China, pp. 369–375 (2009)

Self-Service Management Support Systems—
There's an App for That

Bernhard Krönke[1], Alexa Reinecke[1], Jörg Hans Mayer[2], Gotthard Tischner[3],
Hannes Feistenauer[4], and Jörg Hauke[4]

[1] Continental AG, Corporate Controlling
Vahrenwalder Strasse 9, 30165 Hanover, Germany
{bernhard.kroenke,alexa.reinecke}@conti.de
[2] University of St.Gallen, Institute of Information Management
Müller-Friedberg-Strasse 8, 9000 St. Gallen, Switzerland
joerg.mayer@unisg.ch
[3] Cundus AG
Schifferstraße 190, 47059 Duisburg, Germany
gotthard.tischner@cundus.de
[4] Darmstadt, University of Technology
Hochschulstrasse 1, 64289 Darmstadt, Germany
{feistenauer,joerg.hauke}@stud.tu-darmstadt.de

1 Managers and Their IS Support

Management support systems (MSS) help managers to perform their jobs more productively and efficiently by serving as their central, hands-on, day-to-day source of information [1]. As an umbrella term, "MSS" represents a major class of information systems (IS) covering management information systems, decision support systems, executive information systems, and, more recently, knowledge management and business intelligence (BI) systems [2].

The present moment is favorable for redesigning MSS for two reasons: On the one hand, managers have to make decisions faster than they have in the past and they want *self-service MSS* to help them to do so [3]. On the other hand, the more companies become larger and dispersed, the more managers become mobile workers [4].

In parallel, technical progress has been made in recent years, so that managers should be able to operate MSS themselves—even when they are mobile. However, recent developments have been driven by the consumer market, when Apple launched the iPhone in 2007 and the iPad in 2010. Their multi-touch, direct-manipulation user interfaces have raised managers' expectations significantly towards easy-to-use *smart devices* (smartphones, tablets, hardware perspective) [5]. Furthermore, thanks to Apple's million-dollar slogan "There's an app for that" [6] managers' awareness of *apps* (small capsulated software programs) is growing (software perspective).

The objective of this article is to lay out an app to investigate the boundaries of self-service MSS. Taking Continental as an example, the prototype on hand complements their managers' paper-based management reporting working routines especially when they are mobile.

J. vom Brocke et al. (Eds.): DESRIST 2013, LNCS 7939, pp. 420–424, 2013.

2   The Continental Case

The Company and Project Objective: Continental is a large European automotive supplier with, as of December 31st, 2011, annual revenues of EUR 30.5 billion (USD 39.5 billion) and about 164,000 employees at 200 production sites [7]. Along with digital immigrants who learned to engage with IS, *digital natives* populate Continental's management [4]. These new-generation managers accept MSS more naturally, but also have higher expectations of how these IS should accommodate their user preferences.

The project "self-service MSS" aimed at aligning the upcoming requirements of their new-generation managers with "modern" IS capabilities in two respects (1) to deliver an *electronic version* of the "green report" which Continental managers can easily navigate themselves and (2) to complement it with *add-ons "beyond the financials"* to make managers' mobile MSS use easier. Complementing the financial reporting with other MSS domains such as risk and compliance management and project management will follow step-by-step in mid 2013.

The *green report* contains Continental's management reporting to Level 1 (group CxO) and Level 2 managers (group directors and heads of divisions) covering their balance sheet, P/L statement, calculated key performance indicators (KPIs) such as economic value added, working capital, and more detailed KPIs such as days sales outstanding (DSO), etc. The green report runs on Continental's "Financial Reporting" (FIRE) IT which consists of SAP ERP 6.0 as the enterprise resource planning system, BW 7.3 as the data warehouse, and SEM-BCS 6.34 as the business application. It is available to managers by insertion as a page-by-page pdf-tile in Lotus Notes and most often used as paper-based printouts.

Results: A two-person BI-team and two IS-researchers started a five month project in September 2012. Firstly, to complement the FIRE IT, they evaluated different *frontend applications* focusing on easy-to-use IS handling, compatibility with the upstream SAP Business Warehouse, and mobile capabilities on smart devices [8]. The attached prototype shows two management reports with SAP Design Studio 1.0 as their new frontend application.

Secondly, regarding the end-user device, Continental voted for *tablets* as its new MSS smart devices. One reason was that tablets are expected to exceed conventional notebooks in units shipped in 2013 [9]. Although Apple currently dominates the tablet market, Gartner expects tablets running Microsoft (MS) Windows 8 as their operating system to reach a 39% market share in 2016—even more in business scenarios [10]. Continental specifically appreciate the fact that the new MS Surface Pro runs a full Windows 8 version and can handle full-fledged Windows desktop applications. Thus, the new self-service MSS app we present in the prototype is a MS Windows-8-native app on the Surface Pro.

Thirdly, equipped with these new IT capabilities, the BI team worked interactively with the business department on the app design. To avoid inconsistencies, the green report in the portable document format (PDF) is the basic content of the new Continental MSS. Leveraging on MS' new design philosophy, *tiles* provide an intuitive, consistent navigation and—with cundus *cNews* as an add-in—Continental can simulate an active navigation between the different PDFs by means of hyperlinks. Furthermore, dynamic inlays enable multi-media content such as videos. An integrated web browser offers analyst managers interactive "drill-throughs" such as queries on the data warehouse or external data sources with which new-generation managers are familiar. Complementing links to business apps such as flight plans and "semi-business" apps such as a restaurant finder (see the prototype), increase the utility of the Continental app on hand—unexpectedly for both analyst and consumer managers.

3   Design Recommendations for Practice and Impact for Researchers

Practice can benefit from our findings by leveraging the following three value propositions of our attached MSS app design: Firstly, the bunch of management reports which typically exists in companies can easily be clustered through an electronic index and two types of information channels. That allows managers to compile and instantly adapt their individual management reporting by subscribing from the available channels the information channels that are most useful to them, such as financial reporting or board presentations (see the prototype)—instead of receiving a print-out and then selecting the currently most important reports and pages. Furthermore, hyperlinks between several reports can rebuild "typical" scenarios of analysis carried out in prior board meetings or address special issues for the next meeting.

Secondly, reworked reports with new annotations are automatically synchronized with a central server. This triggers an action on the server side and the reports are distributed to all devices using the Windows 8 push notification mechanism. This ensures that managers can access coherent, up-to-date information both mobile online and mobile offline. Annotations added offline (e.g., in a plane or a car with a driver) are automatically merged when the mobile device is back online.

Thirdly, private and public annotations can be made by users anywhere in the management reports, for example, to obtain details or to interact with support staff and manager colleagues. This feature includes a topic-specific, direct dialogue which outperforms communication by emailing in terms of time and convenience of handling. Emails continue to be offered for communication with recipients who do not have access to the Continental app.

Our case study enables researchers to better understand MSS design in a natural setting [11]. This should help them focusing on relevant topics within an IS domain of growing importance as follows: Firstly, native apps can handle managers' mobile offline challenge. In contradiction to the "typical" consumer user, the case study reveals that managers are often mobile offline. Native apps that cache content on mobile devices can handle such offline MSS use situations and, thus, do not suffer from poor internet connectivity as browser-based applications do. The possibility of losing a device was dealt with by Continental by encrypting all stored data.

Secondly, taking Continental as an example, tablets accessing MSS can create their own use case in three ways [12]: They serve as (a) an advanced PDF reader more efficiently than smartphones, (b) they are handier than notebooks, thus they serve as an electronic typewriter for complex emailing especially when office documents are attached, and (c) tablets are starting to become managers' preferred device for simple ad-hoc analysis "on the fly."

4   Avenues for Future Research

Embracing self-service MSS and managers' new mobility, this article discussed a new MSS native app running on MS Windows 8 and the MS Surface Pro. The Continental prototype can serve as a blueprint for investigating managers' boundaries of IS use. However, a next design cycle with a broader demonstration and evaluation should follow. From the content perspective, strategies towards a powerful and flexible app IS infrastructure is another avenue for future research. Regarding end-user device selection, it should not be too difficult to define a company-specific profile, but how to generalize patterns for making such a selection, while bearing in mind the different use situations should be particularly interesting.

References

1. Clark Jr., T.D., Jones, M.C., Armstrong, C.P.: The Dynamic Structure of Management Support Systems: Theory Development, Research, Focus, and Direction. MISQ Executive 31, 579–615 (2007)
2. Carlsson, S.A., Henningsson, S., Hrastinski, S., Keller, C.: An Approach for Designing Management Support Systems: The Design Science Research Process and its Outcomes. In: Vaishanvi, V., Baskerville, R., Purao, S. (eds.) Proceedings of the Fourth International Conference on Design Science Research in Information Systems and Technology, Philadelphia, USA, 1–10 (2009)
3. Stodder, D.: Achieving Greater Agility with Business Intelligence: Improving Speed and Flexibility for BI, Analytics, and Data Warehousing, TDWI report (2013)
4. Vodanovich, S., Sundaram, D., Myers, M.: Digital Natives and Ubiquitous IS. IS Research 21, 711–723 (2010)
5. Mayer, J.H.: Using The Kano Model To Identify Attractive User-Interface Software Components. In: George, J.F. (ed.) Proceedings of the 20th International Conference on Information Systems (ICIS), Orlando, USA, HCI: 314, 1–17 (2012)
6. Apple: iPhone 3G Commercial (2009),
   http://youtube.com/watch?v=szrsfeyLzyg (accessed December 15, 2012)
7. Continental AG, http://www.conti-online.com/generator/www/start/com/en/index_en.html(accessed December 15, 2012)
8. Hauke, J., Mayer, J.H., Quick, R.: New-Generation Managers' Business/IT Alignment Perspective for a More Business-Driven IS Design. Research paper, Darmstadt University of Technology and University of St.Gallen (2013)
9. NPD DisplaySearch: Quarterly Mobile PC Shipment and Forecast Report,
   http://www.displaysearch.com/cps/rde/xchg/displaysearch/hs.xsl/130107_tablet_pc_market_forecast_to_surpass_notebooks_in_2013.asp (accessed December 15, 2012)

10. Gartner, Inc., `https://www.gartner.com/it/page.jsp?id=2227215` (accessed December 15, 2012)
11. Benbasat, I., Goldstein, D.K., Melissa, M.: The Case Research Strategy in Studies of Information Systems. MIS Quarterly 11(3), 369–386 (1987)
12. Mayer, J.H.: Improving Mobile IS Acceptance: A Business Perspective. Research paper, University of St.Gallen (2013)

Designing a Web-Based Classroom Response System

Dennis Kundisch, Philipp Herrmann, Michael Whittaker, Jürgen Neumann,
Johannes Magenheim, Wolfgang Reinhardt, Marc Beutner, and Andrea Zoyke

Universität Paderborn, Warburger Straße 100, D-33098 Paderborn
dennis.kundisch@wiwi.uni-paderborn.de

Abstract. It is well-established in the literature that active participation vitalizes
and supports the students' learning process much better than a traditional lecture style. One way of fostering participation in lectures is through pedagogical
designs that stimulate cooperative activities among students, using classroom
response systems. In this paper we present a prototypical implementation of a
classroom response system called PINGO (Peer Instruction for very large
groups). PINGO is offered to all instructors worldwide as a hosted service free
of charge.

Keywords: Classroom Response System, Live Feedback, Teaching, Peer
Instruction, Class-wide Discussion, Three-Questions Sequence Approach,
Learner-centered Pedagogical Design.

1 Introduction

In the literature it is widely documented that traditional lecture-style courses contribute relatively little to students' grasp of central scientific concepts [2, 3, 9]. Students
develop complex reasoning skills most efficiently when they actively participate in
the subject matter [2, 6, 9]. Active participation vitalizes and supports the student
learning process much better than a traditional lecture style. One way of fostering
participation in lectures is through pedagogical designs that stimulate cooperative
activities among students, using classroom response systems (CRS) [3, 9]. A CRS is a
system used in face-to-face settings that enables polling students and gathering immediate feedback in response to questions posed by instructors. In different meta-
analyses several potential benefits of CRS have been documented [4, 6, 13]. These
benefits include an increase in student attendance ("Students go to class more") and
attention ("Students are more focused in class") as well as interaction ("Students interact more with peers to discuss ideas") and discussion ("Students actively discuss
misconceptions to build knowledge") [6].

CRS have been used in higher education classrooms since the 1960s, while com-
mercialized products have been available since the 1990s [5]. These products typically involved a set of physical clickers[1], a radio-frequency connection device for the

---

[1] "Clickers" are portable, handheld devices that allow students to vote or make a selection by
pressing a button.

J. vom Brocke et al. (Eds.): DESRIST 2013, LNCS 7939, pp. 425–431, 2013.

instructor's laptop, and software to be installed on the instructor's laptop. However, instructors have found these CRS products cumbersome to use, e.g., in terms of the administration effort involved, especially in classes with more than 100 students [7].

2   Design of the Artifact

2.1   Problem Statement

The identified need appears to be for a cost-efficient, easy to use, scalable in-class polling system to support pedagogical designs that can actively involve students during face-to-face lectures even in large classes. In particular, the following requirements have to be met by the system [7]:

- **Usability**: The artifact should be intuitively usable by both instructors and students. It should be flexible and responsive for easy and instant adaptation during the lecture, for instance, in terms of the format of spontaneous polls.
- **Scalability**: As enrollments in introductory courses can exceed 1,000 students, the system must be highly scalable.
- **Cost efficiency**: In view of increasing budget restrictions at universities, the system should be free for instructors and students.
- **Operating system**: The artifact should be usable independently from the operating systems of the instructors' and the students' devices.
- **Installation**: Students and instructors should not be required to install any software on their devices.
- **Question formats**: The system should provide for different question formats (e.g., single choice, multiple choice, matching questions, multimedia drag&drop question, guesstimation questions) that may be used to implement a variety of learner-centered pedagogical designs.
- **Devices**: Students and universities should not be required to buy clickers. Instead, a solution should integrate available web-based infrastructure ("Bring-your-own-Device").

2.2   Use Cases

The following figure illustrates important use cases of the system. The instructor chooses a learner-centered pedagogical approach for her lecture, for example, Peer Instruction [2, 9], Class-wide Discussions [3] or the Three-Questions Sequence approach [11].

All approaches typically involve students preparing to learn outside of class by doing pre-class readings. In class, the instructor engages students by posing prepared conceptual questions (so-called ConcepTests) that are based on (potential) student difficulties. Each approach makes use of a CRS, i.e., polling students and collecting answers. The difference of the approaches is the sequence of events [1].

In Peer Instruction the students usually respond to the ConcepTest individually, then they discuss their responses, and the underlying reasoning, in small groups (so-called Peer Discussion). In contrast, Class-wide Discussion begins with small group discussion of the ConcepTest, followed by an individual or group response. The students then engage in class-wide discussion facilitated by the teacher. In Peer Instruction it is quite common to repeat polling students and collection answers if the answers where largely incorrect in the first poll.[2] The share of correct answers in the initial poll and repeated poll with respect to the same ConcepTest is compared after the repeated poll. This comparison has to be supported by a CRS.

Rather than concentrating on one ConcepTest, the Three-Questions Sequence approach is focused on using specially designed sets of, typically, three related questions working together to develop understanding of one concept [11].

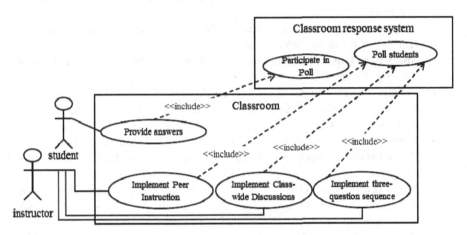

Fig. 1. Use case diagram

2.3 Intended User Groups

Instructors and students are the two main user groups of the artifact while being in a face-to-face teaching context.

Further potential user groups are high school teachers, researchers in e-learning, and corporations (for use in medium- to large-size meetings to get an anonymous, quick, aggregated opinion when choices have to be made).

2.4 Selected List of Features

- **Speed start**: Creates session and starts polling with two clicks.
- **Memory function**: Saves settings for question formats and answer options.
- **Spontaneous questions**: Starts polls within an open session spontaneously with just one click.

---

[2] On rare occasions this repetition of the original question is also applied in Class-wide Discussions.

- **Responsive design**: Functionality and design automatically adapt to the device and its capabilities.
- **Lecture feedback**: Collects feedback at the end of a lecture from students.
- **Visualization**: Collected answers are summarized in a table and a bar chart. If a poll is repeated, the answers are reported in comparison to the distribution of the initial poll.
- **Migration movement**: The migration of single students between an initial poll and a repeated poll are reported on an aggregated level in a contingency table.[3]
- **Different questions formats**: Dichotomous single choice questions (e. g. agree/disagree), single choice questions with several answer options, multiple choice, lecture feedback, different free text questions[*], guesstimmation questions[*].
- **Preparation and sharing function**[*]: Prepares and saves questions in the system and shares them with other instructors.
- **Math functions**[*]: Supports mathematical symbols in questions and answers (using TeX syntax).
- **Display questions/answer options on devices**[*]: If the questions and answers are prepared beforehand by the instructor, they can be displayed on the students' devices.
- **Language support**: German, English and Spanish[*] language version.[4]
- **Virtual tour**[*]: Interactively presents the most important features and usage of the system.
- **Video tutorials**: Introduce Peer Instruction as a learner-centered pedagogical approach and illustrate how a Peer Discussion should be conducted (available in German and English).
- **Backend**[*]: Usage of WebSockets for realtime communication and SPDY for ultrafast page loads (for Chrome or Android devices).

2.5   Design of the Artifact

The basic idea for the design of the artifact was to utilize the Internet-enabled devices that students already bring to lectures (e.g., laptop, smartphone, tablet). Surveys at different universities revealed that almost all students have access to such devices nowadays. By designing a web-based software-as-a-service solution, universities would not need to buy and administer large number of clickers, which would free up

---

[3] This is made possible by device tracking using a cookie. Device tracking also prevents students to vote twice with the *same* device. We have taken no precautions for the situation that a student uses *different* devices to vote more than once. As the tool is designed for anonymous participation and not for personal grading, the incentive to bring several devices and vote more than once should be small – particularly in larger classes. So far, we have not observed this behavior.

[4] To reduce configuration possibilities, the language is adapted automatically to the language that is set in the web browser on the respective device.

instructors from reserving, distributing and collecting clickers before, at the beginning and at the end of a lecture. Furthermore, no installation would be necessary on any device.

The developed artifact is called PINGO (Peer Instruction for very large groups). PINGO is implemented as a website building on the Ruby on Rails framework (www.rubyonrails.org). This open source framework was selected because of the availability of many standard web application features, which allows focusing on implementing core functionality. The goal to efficiently serve a large number of concurrent users in terms of response time and resource consumption led to an application design based on event-driven I/O. Using the document-oriented open source NoSQL database MongoDB (www.mongodb.org) avoids many multiple-table queries through the use of embedded object collections. Furthermore, MongoDB offers atomic promised operations, such as atomic increments and atomic pushes to arrays, which are used for tracking of votes and voters. Furthermore, a socket.io-module was integrated to support WebSocket communication with many concurrent clients. By running the PINGO application on top of this architecture, many concurrent users can be served efficiently and the application can be scaled, for example, using a computing cloud.

Earlier versions of the design have already been described, demonstrated and presented elsewhere [7, 8, 12]. New features to be demonstrated are marked with a "*" in 2.4.

3 Significance to Research and Practice

The developed artifact is significant to research for a number of reasons.

First, the design process focused on re-use instead of programming new functionalities from scratch. For instance, using the Ruby on Rails framework, a collection of so-called Gems – a couple of thousand small packages solving a particular problem – is already available for the Ruby platform. However, the right mix of re-used functionalities and newly implemented functionalities for high quality and economical software engineering remains an open issue.

Second, the artifact itself is designed for undertaking research as it allows researchers to conduct natural experiments in the area of teaching, learning, and technology use.

The artifact has been well received by practice, i.e., instructors at universities worldwide. From mid-October 2012 to the end of March 2013, over 250 instructors from more than 170 universities worldwide have piloted or used our artifact. These instructors have started over 1,600 polls – categorized in over 450 sessions – and collected over 17,000 votes from their students. During this time we have already received a bulk of emails both with positive feedback and wish lists for future development paths.

4   Evaluation of the Artifact

Over the last 2 years, the artifact has been evaluated ex ante and ex post by different means [10].

In an ex ante evaluation, we recognized that the costs of a physical clicker was around 30 Euros. As our university owned just around 100 clickers at that point in time and the main lecture hall accommodated around 700 students, the remaining clickers would have cost around 18,000 Euros. Furthermore, there are a lot of qualitative drawbacks using physical clickers, such as administration effort, exclusive use, necessary software installation etc. (see, e.g., [7]). A search for alternatives in 2011 revealed that there were no web-based service offerings that fulfilled all requirements.[5] In addition, the design of the artifact was discussed in several iterations with experts from the field in several meetings and workshops.

The first prototype was used in different course settings at the University of Paderborn in the winter term 2011/2012 and the summer term 2012. Amongst others, we tested the system in the following courses: Introduction to Business Information Systems (1,000 enrolled students), Teaching and Learning (250 students), Introduction to Information Management (100 students), and Teaching Methodological Concepts (20 students). Technology Acceptance Model and System Usability Scale evaluations were performed with an early version of the prototype [7, 8, 12].

Based on the feedback from these different settings, we further developed and improved the artifact. From October 2012 we started to offer PINGO to all instructors at the University of Paderborn as well as instructors worldwide.

5   Link to an Implementation of the Artifact

- **System**: PINGO can be accessed at https://pingo.upb.de.
- **Registration**: Instructors may register at https://pingo.upb.de/users/sign_up.
- **Project**: Information about the project can be found at http://www.upb.de/pingo (then choose "English" on the top left).

References

1. Boyle, J.T., Nicol, D.J.: Using classroom communication systems to support interaction and discussion in large class settings. Association for Learning Technology Journal 11, 43–57 (2003)
2. Crouch, C.H., Mazur, E.: Peer instruction: Ten years of experience and results. The Physics Teacher 69, 970–977 (2001)

---

[5] This has changed over the course of the last two years. Many suppliers of CRS have started to offer hosted web-based solutions. A list of available solutions can, for example, be found at http://www.educause.edu/library/clickers. A more detailed list of CRS suppliers as well as a discussion about how PINGO differentiates itself from other solutions can be found in [4].

3. Dufresne, R.J., Gerace, W.J., Leonard, W.J., Mestre, J.P., Wenk, L.: Classtalk: a classroom communication system for active learning. Journal of Computing in Higher Education 7, 3–47 (1996)
4. Fies, C., Marshall, J.: Classroom Response Systems: A Review of the Literature. Journal of Science Education and Technology 15, 101–109 (2006)
5. Judson, E., Sawada, D.: Learning from Past and Present: Electronic Response Systems in College Lecture Halls. Journal of Computers in Mathematics and Science Teaching 21, 167–181 (2002)
6. Kay, R., LeSage, A.: Examining the benefits and challenges of using audience response systems: A review of the literature. Computers & Education 53, 819–827 (2009)
7. Kundisch, D., Herrmann, P., Whittaker, M., Fels, G., Reinhardt, W., Sievers, M., Magenheim, J., Beutner, M., Zoyke, A.: Designing a web-based application to support Peer Instruction for very large Groups. In: Proceedings of the International Conference on Information Systems (ICIS), Orlando, USA (2012)
8. Magenheim, J., Reinhardt, W., Kundisch, D., Herrmann, P., Whittaker, M., Beutner, M., Zoyke, A.: Einsatz mobiler Endgeräte zur Verbesserung der Lehrqualität in universitären Großveranstaltungen. In: Proceedings of the E-Learning Symposium, Potsdam, Germany (2012)
9. Mazur, E.: Peer Instruction: A User's Manual. Prentice-Hall, Englewood Cliffs (1997)
10. Pries-Heje, J., Baskerville, R., Venable, J.R.: Strategies for Design Science Research Evaluation. In: Proceedings of the 16th European Conference on Information Systems (ECIS), Galway, Ireland (2008)
11. Reay, N.W., Bao, L., Li, P., Warnakulasooriya, R., Baugh, G.: Toward the effective use of voting machines in physics lectures. American Journal of Physics 73, 554–558 (2005)
12. Reinhardt, W., Sievers, M., Magenheim, J., Kundisch, D., Herrmann, P., Beutner, M., Zoyke, A.: PINGO: Peer Instruction for Very Large Groups. In: Proceedings of the Seventh European Conference on Technology Enhanced Learning (EC-TEL), Saarbrücken, Germany (2012)
13. Roschelle, J., Penuel, W.R., Abrahamson, L.: Classroom Response and Communication Systems: Research Review and Theory. In: Annual Meeting of the American Educational Research Association, San Diego, USA (2004)

New-Generation Managers and Their IS Support— Getting It Right with the Corporate Navigator

Jörg Hans Mayer and Robert Winter

University of St.Gallen, Institute of Information Management
Müller-Friedberg-Strasse 8, 9000 St.Gallen, Switzerland
{joerg.mayer,robert.winter}@unisg.ch

1 Design Problem

Companies today operate in an increasingly dynamic environment. Due to their over-all responsibility, managers are particularly affected by this situation. Information systems (IS) that aim at helping managers are known as management support systems (MSS). They are designed to serve as their central, hands-on, day-to-day source of information [1].

MSS design currently entails two interesting aspects. Taking the 2008/2009 economic crisis as our reference point, we firstly examine a new orientation of the corporate management task and its implications for the (functional) MSS design [2]. Secondly, digital natives increasingly populate organizations' management along with digital immigrants. The latter have learned to engage with IS and developed into MSS users over the years [3]. These new-generation managers more naturally accept MSS, but have higher (non-functional) expectations about how IS should accommodate their user preferences [4]. The objective of this article is to examine the changing IS requirements for a *new MSS architecture design*, implement and evaluate it with the prototype on hand.

2 Requirements Analyses

To specify a MSS architecture design for new-generation managers, we conducted a longitudinal study in the field. Since corporate management without IS has become impossible in large, international companies, the study targeted companies listed in the Financial Times "Europe 500" report on April 1st, 2008 and October 19th, 2009 with the following results [2].

More operational responsibility at headquarters: During the period of growth from 2003 to 2007, managers devoted most of their time to strategic leadership. According to our 2008 survey results, 23% of the managers said that they intervene frequently and extensively in operations—in parallel to their strategic management tasks. Another 8% characterized their involvement as very frequent and very extensive. This trend started 2008/2009 in the financial sector due to the economic crisis is now evident in the industrial sector as well: One third of the managers said their involvement in operations is frequent and extensive, another 10% specified that they intervene very

J. vom Brocke et al. (Eds.): DESRIST 2013, LNCS 7939, pp. 432–437, 2013.

frequently and very extensively. New-generation managers work more operationally than their predecessors. Thus, MSS have to increasingly provide operational information such as production rates, throughput times, quality information, and stock levels by incorporating drill-throughs into the underlying transaction systems.

More biased IS objectives: A second question examined new-generation managers' demand for flexibility. In 2008/2009, almost 50% answered that they are operating in an environment that is more aggressive than ever, and this situation continues in the 2009/2010 survey. While the earlier generation predominantly viewed IS as a "cost pool" [2], new-generation managers consider IS flexibility to be of similar importance in MSS architecture design (Fig. 1). Furthermore, managers have to make decisions faster than they have in the past and, thus, they want their MSS in a more self-service user mode [5].

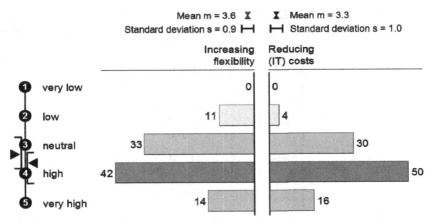

Fig. 1. New-generation managers' perspective on MSS architecture objectives [2]

3   Conceptual Design

Two characteristics distinguish the new MSS architecture[1] —we call it the "Corporate Navigator"—from its predecessors [7]: Firstly, it consistently integrates *four design layers* (strategic positioning, conceptual design, business/IT alignment, and IT components) to ensure that MSS can react flexibly to changing business requirements (Fig. 2, left side). The business/IT alignment layer[2] is structured by business domains, in a service-oriented architecture enterprise services, applications, and capabilities which align on different levels of granularity business requirements with IT capabilities. The remaining layers house the MSS software and data structures, as well as the IT infrastructure.

---

[1]   Architectures can be defined as "the fundamental organization of a system, embodied in its components, their relationships to each other and the environment, and the principles governing its design and evolution" [6].

[2]   The term business/IT alignment is used to indicate that the IS design is focused on business requirements and the business value of IS [8].

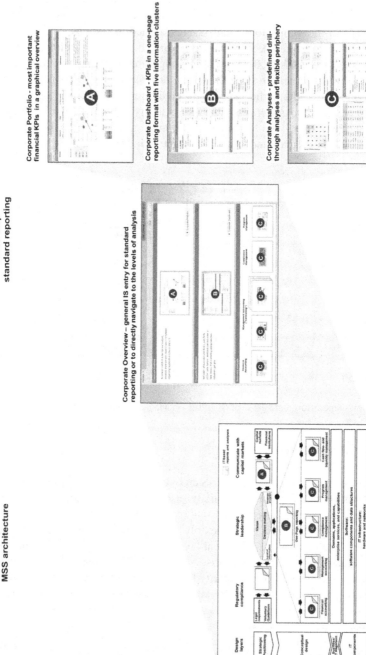

Fig. 2. Corporate Navigator-An integrative IS architecture with four design layers and a three-step standard reporting for new-generation EIS. Based on [2, 7].

Secondly, a *three-step standard reporting* ensures that information is synthesized hierarchically and presented in a condensed format for faster decision making with self-service MSS [9]. Easy-to-use IS handling supports navigation between the three steps of analysis. The corporate overview shows their interplay (Fig. 2, center): The *corporate portfolio* ("A") is the most aggregated level of analysis and provides a graphical overview of financial performance at the group, division, and business unit levels with just three KPIs: reward, risk, and relevance. The *corporate dashboard* ("B") is the second level of analysis and consists of a one-page report with more detailed KPIs structured in five information clusters: financial accounting, management accounting, compliance management, program management, and cash flow and liquidity management. Finally, *corporate analyses* ("C") enable deeper analyses with about ten standard analyses and a flexible periphery for ad-hoc reporting, non-routine information, and links to the underlying transaction systems.

4   Implementation and Evaluation

Implementing the Corporate Navigator at an automotive supplier with, as of December 31st, 2011, annual revenues of EUR 30.5 billion (USD 49.95 billion) and 164,000 employees at 200 production sites [10], has had two dimensions: modeling a more flexible MSS architecture and a revised group reporting for faster decision making leveraging self-service MSS.

The Financial Reporting (FIRE) navigator of the automotive supplier focuses on the accounting reports to Level 1 (group CxO) and Level 2 (group directors and heads of divisions), but other reporting domains are currently complemented step by step. The FIRE Navigator consists of SAP ERP 6.0 as the enterprise resource planning system, BW 7.3 as the business warehouse, SEM-BCS 6.34 as the business application, and Business Object (BO) dashboards as the frontend application. Fig. 2 shows the three-step standard reporting hierarchy and the attached click-demo presents further details.

For *research* purposes, the Corporate Navigator is a rigorous starting point. The architecture is driven by requirements that have been validated empirically from a business perspective and its modular design allows to integrate further results (Fig. 3). Environmental scanning systems—a Corporate Radar—complement our approach and enterprise services help to identify identical functionalities such as currency conversion applied in different solutions.

For *practice* purposes, the revised MSS architecture with an integrative multi-layer approach exposes essential artifacts for proper corporate management and is more flexible than the traditional MSS architecture in the early 1990s. Accommodating changing requirements, the Corporate Navigator increases the business value of performance data by presenting the most relevant KPIs in a content-wise comprehensive, but condensed, intuitive manner. Using a new frontend application makes MSS interfaces close to managers' "look&feel" needs.

Traditional MSS design (early 1990s)	Revised MSS architecture: Corporate Navigator
Requirements analysis: Business requirements often not aligned with IT capabilities	Requirements validated from a business perspective across companies listed in the FT "Europe 500" report
Design: Strategic leadership islands, often no integration with the downstream transaction systems	Integrative architecture with four design layers and three levels of analysis supporting "drill-throughs" into the underlying transaction systems
Prototyping: "One-size-fits-all" approach instead of flexible adaptation to different information needs and use situations	Modular design of financial and complementing non-financial reporting and adaptation mechanisms for different classes of similar user-group preferences

Fig. 3. "Corporate Navigator" compared to traditional MSS solution architecture [based on 7]

5   Avenues for Future Research

The more managers expand their role in day-to-day business and make decisions faster than in the past, the more a MSS architecture has to become integrative. The prototype on hand serves as a first demonstration for new-generation MSS. Thus, a next design cycle with a systematic, broader implementation and evaluation should follow.

Besides stationary MSS use, IS has to embrace managers' growing need to access MSS from mobile devices [11]. It should not be too difficult to define a company-specific profile to select appropriate devices and user-interface designs, but how to generalize patterns for such a selection, bearing different use situations in mind, should be another avenue for IS research.

References

1. Clark Jr., T.D., Jones, M.C., Armstrong, C.P.: The Dynamic Structure of Management Support Systems: Theory Development, Research, Focus, and Direction. MISQ Executive 31, 579–615 (2007)
2. Mayer, J.H.: Current Changes in Executive Work and How to Handle Them by Redesigning Executive Information Systems. In: Mancini, D., Vaassen, E., Dameri, R.P. (eds.) Accounting Information Systems for Decision Making, pp. 151–173. Springer, Heidelberg (2013)
3. Vodanovich, S., Sundaram, D., Myers, M.: Digital Natives and Ubiquitous IS. IS Research 21, 711–723 (2010)
4. Marchand, D.A., Peppard, J.: Designed to Fail: Why IT Projects Underachieve and What To Do about It. Research paper 2008-11. IMD International, Lausanne (2008)
5. Stodder, D.: Achieving Greater Agility with Business Intelligence: Improving Speed and Flexibility for BI, Analytics, and Data Warehousing, TDWI report (2013)
6. The Institute of Electrical and Electronics Engineers, Inc.: ANSI-IEEE 1471: Recommended Practice for Architectural Description of Software-Intensive Systems. IEEE Computer Society, New York (2000)

7. Winter, R., Mayer, J.H.: Systemarchitektur für Unternehmenssteuerungssysteme: Ein serviceorientierter Ansatz. In: Vom Brocke, J., Becker, J. (Hrsg.) Einfachheit in Wirtschaftsinformatik und Controlling, Festschrift für Heinz Lothar Grob, pp. 613–637, Vahlen, München (2010)

8. Henderson, J.C., Venkatraman, N.: Strategic Alignment: A Framework for Strategic IT Management. Center for ISR, Working Paper Nr. 190. MIT, Cambridge (1989 - reprint: IBM Systems Journal 38(2&3), 472–484 (1999)

9. Marx, F., Mayer, J.H., Winter, R.: Six Principles to Re-design Executive Information Systems – Findings of a Survey and Evaluation of a Prototype. ACM Transactions on Management Information Systems (ACM-TMIS) 2(4), article 26, 1–19 (2011)

10. Continental AG. Key Financials, http://www.conti-online.com/generator/www/start/com/en/index_en.html(accessed April 03, 2013)

11. Gartner: Worldwide PC, Tablet and Mobile Phone Combined Shipments to Reach 2.4 Billion Units in 2013: Traditional PC Market Predicted to Decline 7.6 Percent as Change in Consumers' Behavior Drives Transition to Tablets and Ultramobiles, http://www.gartner.com/newsroom/id/2408515 (accessed April 03, 2013)

MUSE: Implementation of a Design Theory for Systems that Support Convergent and Divergent Thinking

Oliver Müller, Stefan Debortoli, and Stefan Seidel

Institute of Information Systems, University of Liechtenstein, Vaduz,
Principality of Liechtenstein
{oliver.mueller,stefan.debortoli,stefan.seidel}@uni.li

Abstract. It has been asserted that information systems (IS) can both enhance and undermine creativity. Earlier, we have proposed an IS design theory for systems that support individual creativity through fostering convergent and divergent thinking. In this paper we outline how we have transformed this abstract blueprint into a running software prototype. We chose cooking – a familiar creative process – as an exemplary domain to illustrate the form and function of the prototype. In future work, the prototype and the underlying design theory will be empirically evaluated using focus groups and laboratory experiments.

Keywords: creativity, convergent thinking, divergent thinking, design theory, prototype, focus group, experiment.

1   Introduction

Creativity is typically understood as the production of novel and useful ideas, products, or services [1]. It has been asserted that information systems (IS) have the ability to both enhance and undermine creativity [2]. Examples of IS explicitly designed to support creativity include electronic brainstorming systems, open innovation platforms, computer-aided design tools, digital asset management systems, or knowledge management systems. In earlier work, grounded in theories of human cognition and creativity, we have proposed an IS design theory for systems that support creative work through knowledge provision [3]. The theory gives explicit prescriptions on how to design and develop creativity support systems by fostering two distinct but interrelated sub-processes: The *convergent process* of identifying and retrieving useful codified knowledge and the *divergent process* of discovering novel combinations of existing knowledge. We have developed a software prototype adhering to the abstract blueprint defined by the design theory. The prototype will be used in upcoming focus groups and laboratory experiments to collect empirical data that can be used to test and, subsequently, validate or refine the design theory.

J. vom Brocke et al. (Eds.): DESRIST 2013, LNCS 7939, pp. 438–445, 2013.

2   Design of the Artifact

2.1   The Design Theory

The design theory is grounded in the duality of processes of convergent and divergent thinking within creative problem solving [3]. Convergent thinking describes a mode of human cognition that strives for the deductive generation of single, concrete, accurate, and effective solution [4]. Divergent thinking, in contrast, describes the generation of multiple disparate answers to a given problem or task [4]. In combination, these two cognitive processes bear the potential to generate both novel and useful ideas [1]. Built upon these two basic cognitive processes, the design theory provides a set of design requirements for supporting convergent and divergent thinking, as well as a set of corresponding constructs (cf., Fig. 1) and principles of form and function (cf., Table 1). Together, these components constitute an abstract blueprint of an IT system (for further details see [3]).

Table 1. Principles of form and function of the design theory

Design requirements		Kernel theories	Selected principles of form and function
Supporting Convergent Thinking	C.1: Organize available knowledge taxonomically	Word-concepts theory [5, 6]	The system should comprise a repository for storing reusable explicit knowledge. The knowledge repository should be organized by taxonomic navigation structures (e.g., as in a biological taxonomy).
	C.2: Provide diverse perspectives on existing knowledge	Word-concepts theory [5, 6]	The system should comprise multiple parallel taxonomic structures providing different perspectives on the available knowledge (e.g., according to topic, time, place).
	C.3: Enable dynamic filtering of the knowledge base	Information processing theory [7]	The system should provide various filters that can be combined to dynamically restrict the set of displayed knowledge items.
Supporting Divergent Thinking	D.1: Provide explicit stimuli	Search for ideas in associative memory model [8]	The system should actively stimulate the user by pointing out latent associations between knowledge items (e.g., by using data mining algorithms).
	D.2: Provide different levels of stimuli	Search for ideas in associative memory model [8]	The system should provide both intra-domain stimuli (i.e., closely related knowledge items) and inter-domain stimuli (i.e., loosely related knowledge items).
	D.3: Stimulate both symbolic systems of human cognition	Dual coding theory [9]	The system should provide both verbal (e.g., text) and visual (e.g., images, videos) knowledge items.

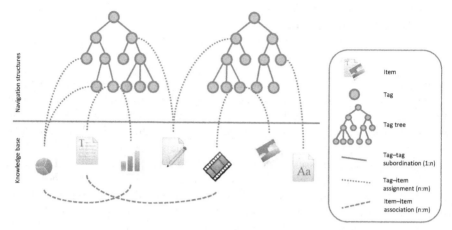

Fig. 1. Constructs of the design theory [3]

2.2 The MUSE Prototype

In the following we will present a concrete instantiation of the above described design theory, namely, the MUSE[1] prototype. We chose cooking as an exemplary domain to illustrate its form and function. Cooking is a process that is familiar to most of us and prior research on creativity has identified the "kitchen process" as a creative process [10, 11]. Consequently, the knowledge base of the prototype is filled with cooking recipes. These recipes are categorized via multiple tags which, in turn, are arranged in tree-like structures representing cooking-relevant taxonomies (e.g., ingredients, color, diet, ratings).

The prototype was built using the Microsoft ASP.NET MVC 4 web application framework, a framework implementing the model-view-controller pattern. Fig. 2 shows an excerpt of the data model of the application. As such, the data model is a transformation of the constructs of the design theory (cf., Fig. 2). The model also implements parts of the generic principles of form and function addressing design requirements C.1, C.2, and D.3 (cf., Table 1). Only the attributes of the item class had to be tailored to the specifics of the cooking domain.

Fig. 3 shows a screenshot of the graphical user interface of MUSE. The right-hand side shows the cooking recipes stored in the system and the left-hand side the different tag trees that can be used to navigate and filter the knowledge base. MUSE contains more than 25,000 recipes[2], categorized through more than 9,500 tags, which are organized in five tag trees (ingredients, diets, color, user ratings, source). Users can drill-down multiple tag trees in parallel (design requirements C.1 and C.2) and set and combine filters (design requirement C.3) to restrict the set of displayed items (e.g., "vegetarian" recipes with "goat cheese" and "olives" and a user rating of "4" or "5").

---

[1] In Greek mythology, poetry, and literature, the Muses are the goddesses of the inspiration of literature, science and the arts (Source: Wikipedia).

[2] The recipe data was acquired from Punchfork.com.

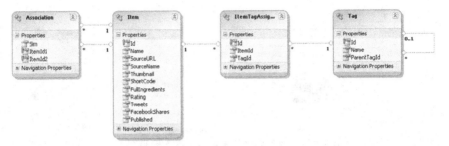

Fig. 2. Model of the MVC web application (Excerpt)

Fig. 3. Screenshot of MUSE (Knowledge base with recipes)

By clicking on a particular recipe the user can open a popup window (cf., Fig. 4) presenting additional visual and textual information (design requirement D.3), for instance, pictures, ingredients, preparation instructions, user ratings, tweets and Facebook shares. In addition, built-in recommendation algorithms display hidden associations between recipes (design requirement D.1). These associations represent intra-domain and inter-domain stimuli (design requirement D.2). Intra-domain stimuli are generated by using text mining techniques to retrieve recipes that are most similar to a recipe at hand. Inter-domain stimuli, in contrast, represent more loosely related associations. They are generated by randomly selecting a tag assigned to the recipe at hand and retrieving other recipes which are also marked with the same tag (e.g., other recipes with "tomatoes", other "vegan" recipes). By clicking on a recommendation, the user is directly forwarded to the corresponding recipe. This way, the user can rummage in the knowledge base and jump from recipe to recipe without using the taxonomic navigation structures.

Fig. 4. Screenshot of MUSE (Recipe details and recommendations)

3   Significance to Research

The theoretical importance of convergent and divergent thinking in creative work has already been recognized by researchers interested in the design of creativity support systems [2, 12, 13].

Still, prior research on actual prototypes of creativity support systems has focused almost exclusively on supporting the divergent aspects of idea generation. For instance, drawing from the metaphor of a Rubik's Cube Huang, Li, Wang and Change [14] developed a game-like collaborative brainstorming tool that offers features to stimulate creativity by shifting perspectives on a given creative problem. MacCrimmon and Wagner [15, 16] built the GENI (GENerating Ideas) system that implements a mechanism to help users make connections between different aspects of a problem as well as different aspects of emerging ideas. Young [17] proposed a relational database schema and an algebra for the automatic generation of metaphors, which constitute a recognized source of creative inspiration.

One of the few exceptions that also consider supporting convergent processes is the study of Cheung, Chau and Au [18]. These authors designed a creativity support system that implements elements of convergent thinking, namely support for knowledge reuse, and tested the effect of the system in laboratory experiments. The results suggest that individuals who engage in knowledge reuse perform less creatively than those who do not. Cheung et al. [18] argue that this effect is due to the nature of the applied IT system, which only provides knowledge without considering the potential negative effects of knowledge reuse (e.g., fixation on previous knowledge) in creative work.

Reviewing the above and other works, we can identify a lack of research on how to design IT systems that support both convergent *and* divergent thinking in creative work. Existing research focuses on IT systems that only cater for the support of divergent *or* convergent thinking. Due to the central role of both modes of creative cognition, and their intimate relationship in solving creative problems, we contend that our design theory and the here presented prototype are innovative artifacts that represent valuable additions to the scientific knowledge base.

4   Significance to Practice

The class of IT systems described by the proposed design theory and instantiated through the MUSE prototype are expected to support a wide range of creative tasks that can benefit from the reuse of digital, explicit knowledge. Systems that implement the constructs and principles of form and function put forward in the design theory, for instance, can assist product designers by offering and exploring a database of existing products, components, and materials in order to be inspired for new designs; assist visual effects producers in composing animated sequences by providing and exploring a repository of graphics, animations, and sound effects; or even inspire artists in creating new artwork by presenting and exploring a catalogue of paintings, graphics, and photographs.

5   Evaluation of the Artifact

We plan to use a tailored mix of qualitative and quantitative research methods to evaluate the developed prototype and its underlying design theory. Specifically, we aim to employ two main strategies.

First, we will use a series of explorative focus groups [19] to iteratively present the prototype to potential users, collect feedback, and subsequently improve its design. The main objective of the focus groups will be to (a) ensure that the features of the prototype are being perceived to foster convergent and divergent thinking in the context of creative problem solving, (b) resolve usability issues related to the user interface and system performance, and (c) pretest and refine creative tasks that will be used in later experimental studies.

Second, two-by-two factorial laboratory experiments will be conducted to quantitatively test the efficacy of the prototype. The design theory already provides a set of testable hypotheses that can be used to validate whether the use of IS that implement the proposed principles of form and function actually results in higher creative performance than using tools that do not implement these design principles. Specifically, it is hypothesized that:

— **H1 (Quantity of ideas):** The use of systems that support both convergent and divergent thinking will result in a greater number of ideas being produced for a given creative task than the use of systems that support only divergent thinking / the use of systems support only convergent thinking / the use of systems that neither support convergent nor divergent thinking.

— H2 (Creativity of ideas): The use of systems that support both convergent and divergent thinking will result in more creative ideas being produced for a given creative task than the use of systems that support only divergent thinking / the use of systems support only convergent thinking / the use of systems that neither support convergent nor divergent thinking.

The experimental treatments (independent variable) will be the IT support the subjects will use to accomplish a given creative task. The prototype will be used for all treatments in the experiments. As it supports both convergent and divergent thinking, four configurations of the tool are used: One that implements the full set of principles meant to address the design requirements for both divergent and convergent thinking, one that primarily implements the principles related to divergent thinking, one that focuses on the constructs and principles related to convergent thinking, and one that neither implements principles of convergent nor divergent thinking (control group). To measure the dependent variables (quantity and creativity of generated ideas) we will follow the procedures outlined in Dean et al. [20].

References

1. Woodman, R.W., Sawyer, J.E., Griffin, R.W.: Toward a Theory of Organizational Creativity. Academy of Management Review 18(2), 293–321 (1993)
2. Greene, S.L.: Characteristics of Applications that Support Creativity. Communications of the ACM 45(10), 100–104 (2002)
3. Müller-Wienbergen, F., Müller, O., Seidel, S., Becker, J.: Leaving the Beaten Tracks in Creative Work - A Design Theory for Systems that Support Convergent and Divergent Thinking. Journal of the AIS 12(11), 714–740 (2011)
4. Guilford, J.P.: The Nature of Human Intelligence. McGraw-Hill, New York (1967)
5. Quillian, M.R.: Word concepts: A theory and simulation of some basic semantic capabilities. Behavioral Science 12(5), 410–430 (1967)
6. Quillian, M.R.: The teachable language comprehender: a simulation program and theory of language. Communications of the ACM 12(8), 459–476 (1969)
7. Miller, G.A.: The Magical Number Seven, Plus or Minus Two: Some Limits on our Capacity for Processing Information. Psychological Review 63(2), 81–97 (1956)
8. Nijstad, B.A., Stroebe, W.: How the Group Affects the Mind: A Cognitive Model of Idea Generation in Groups. Personality and Social Psychology Review 10(3), 186–213 (2006)
9. Paivio, A., Lambert, W.: Dual Coding and Bilingual Memory. Journal of Verbal Learning and Verbal Behavior 20(5), 532–539 (1981)
10. Horng, J., Hu, M.-L.: The Creative Culinary Process: Constructing and Extending a Four-Component Model. Creativity Research Journal 21(4), 376–383 (2009)
11. Horng, J., Hu, M.-L.: The mystery in the kitchen: Culinary creativity. Creativity Research Journal 20(2), 221–230 (2008)
12. Shneiderman, B.: Creativity support tools. Communications of the ACM 45(10), 116–120 (2002)
13. Lubart, T.: How can computers be partners in the creative process: Classification and commentary on the Special Issue. International Journal of Human-Computer Studies 63(4-5), 365–369 (2005)

14. Huang, C.-C., Li, T.-Y., Wang, H.-C., Chang, C.-Y.: A Collaborative Support Tool for Creativity Learning: Idea Storming Cube. In: Proceedings of the IEEE International Conference on Advanced Learning Technologies, pp. 31–35. IEEE Press, Niigata (2007)
15. MacCrimmon, K.R., Wagner, C.: Stimulating Ideas through Creative Software. Management Science 40(11), 1514–1532 (1994)
16. MacCrimmon, K.R., Wagner, C.: The Architecture of an Information System for the Support of Alternative Generation. Journal of Management Information Systems 8(3), 49–67 (1991)
17. Young, L.: The metaphor machine: A database method for creativity support. Decision Support Systems 3(4), 309–317 (1987)
18. Cheung, P.-K., Chau, P.Y.K., Au, A.K.K.: Does knowledge reuse make a creative person more creative? Decision Support Systems 45(2), 219–227 (2008)
19. Tremblay, M., Hevner, A., Berndt, D.: Focus groups for artifact refinement and evaluation in design research. Communications of the AIS 26(1), 599–618 (2010)
20. Dean, D.L., Hender, J.M., Rodgers, T.L., Santanen, E.L.: Identifying quality, novel, and creative ideas: Constructs and scales for idea evaluation. Journal of the AIS 7(10), 646–699 (2006)

Mini Smart Grid @ Copenhagen Business School: Prototype Demonstration

Rasmus U. Pedersen[1], Szymon J. Furtak[1], Ivan Häuser[1],
Codrina Lauth[1], and Rob Van Kranenburg[2]

[1] Department of IT Management, Copenhagen Business School, Denmark
[2] Council IoT
theinternetofthings.eu

Project Smart Grid:
The Intelligent Electrical System Is the Way Forward

In 2012 Peter Møllgaard from Department of Economics and Rasmus Pedersen from Department of IT Management initiated a new project supported by CBS Sustainability Platform. The purpose of the project is to establish an understanding of microeconomic and IT challenges related to Smart Grid technology.

The mini-smart-grid project at Copenhagen Business School (MSC@CBS) project seeks to investigate the business opportunities and issues that arise from this new technology. The project revolves around the concepts of Smart Grids, Smart Meters and prosumers. Smart Grids are a new method of managing electricity and power supply. It has not reached its full potential yet, but it offers a more interactive platform for both the consumer and the main supplier e.g. Dong Energy. The Smart Grid will collect and control the behavior of consumers and suppliers in order to make the system more effective and sustainable. The consumers or suppliers will be able to control certain appliances in their homes so that they become a resource for the system. For example, the customer or supplier can choose to switch off the freezer for 30 minutes during the night to save energy.

What Is a Smart Meter?

A smart meter is an electrical meter and it records consumption of electric energy. One of the benefits of this new technology is that it enables two-way communication between the meter and the central system. This two-way communication gives rise to new business opportunities and consumer benefits. The centrals can offer lower rates at off-peak times and the consumers will have the possibility of selling back electricity to the central. Smart meters may be part of a smart grid, but does not constitute a smart grid. The concept of a prosumer is rather new, but it entails a consumer that strategically uses a commodity e.g. electricity. To give an example: when Smart Meters are implemented, the prosumer will be able to sit at work and check the prices of electricity and when it hits a low, the prosumer will e.g. turn on the washing machine or the dishwasher which are already loaded and thereby save money in comparison to starting it at 6pm when everybody else consumes electricity and the price is higher. One of the implications of this new consumer is outlined in the questions below.

J. vom Brocke et al. (Eds.): DESRIST 2013, LNCS 7939, pp. 446–447, 2013.
© Springer-Verlag Berlin Heidelberg 2013

The non-trivial and perhaps even more interesting effect of conducting a smart meter project is that we (CBS) can address some of the challenges that are associated with a new more dynamic electricity market:

• Possible ethical misbehavior: Mr. and Mrs. "Prosumer" try to "trick" smart meter consumers into buying electricity at the wrong times.
• Finance department: How do prices fluctuate in such a system where mass hysteria can make the electricity market very unstable? How to regulate it (optimally)?

The MSC@CBS Project

A budget of approximately 50.000 EURO has been allocated to complete the project. The project will through a constructed, yet realistic experiment, look into the different challenges that arise with implementing the new technology.

The experiment, which takes place centers on a large gas driven generator can produce enough electricity for 4-10 student "smart houses" (which may be tents for practical reasons). A main generator will supply the houses with electricity at one price pr. kW while the household would also supply electricity at another price pr. kW. We expect to experiment with various set ups in terms of gas generator supplied electricity and prices at which the students can either consume their own electricity or sell it back. The overall idea is to conduct research related to a scenario where each house is having a smart meter that can turn energy-intensive appliances on and off at home as electricity prices fluctuate.

The Sustainability Platform visited the experiment that was set up in front of Kilen on October 5th. Rasmus Ulslev Pedersen from the Department of IT Management presented the different components of the experiment; a gas run generator which can supply 6.5 kW and a "test suitcase" from Zensehomes with 4 plugs, an internet router and a control system. The students were able to control their virtual homes i.e. the test suitcase from their android phones. The experiment had three phases for selling and consuming electricity. In the first round of the project there was no restrictions for selling and buying electricity; in the second round, one group was the placebo group and the other an actual consumer; in the third round, there was time restrictions on selling and buying electricity. Through this exercise, the students become prosumers; buying the electricity at the best rates.

Acknowledgements. This prototype is supported by grants from Copenhagen Business School Sustainability Platform.

preCEP: Facilitating Predictive Event-Driven Process Analytics

Bernd Schwegmann[1], Martin Matzner[1], and Christian Janiesch[2]

[1] University of Münster, ERCIS, Muenster, Germany
bernd.schwegmann@uni-muenster.de,
martin.matzner@ercis.uni-muenster.de
[2] Karlsruhe Institute of Technology, AIFB, Karlsruhe, Germany
christian.janiesch@kit.edu

Abstract. The earlier critical decision can be made, the more business value can be retained or even earned. The goal of this research is to reduce a decision maker's action distance to the observation of critical events. We report on the development of the software tool preCEP that facilitates predictive event-driven process analytics (edPA). The tool enriches business activity monitoring with prediction capabilities. It is implemented by using complex event processing technology (CEP). The prediction component is trained with event log data of completed process instances. The knowledge obtained from this training, combined with event data of running process instances, allows for making predictions at intermediate execution stages on a currently running process instance's future behavior and on process metrics. preCEP comprises a learning component, a run-time environment as well as a modeling environment, and a visualization component of the predictions.

Keywords: Event-driven Process Analytics, Business Activity Monitoring, Complex Event Processing, Business Process Management, Operational Business Intelligence.

1 Introduction

Business value can be lost if a decision maker's action distance to the observation of a business event is too high. Action distance comprises the time needed to capture and process data as well as the time needed to decide which action to take. So far, two classes of information systems, which promise to assist decision makers, have only been discussed independently of each other: business intelligence systems, which query historic business event data in order to prepare predictions of future process behavior, and real-time monitoring systems such as business activity monitoring (BAM). We developed a method and implemented software which allows using real-time data for predictions in an event-driven approach. Our predictive event-driven process analytics (edPA) software preCEP brings together features of BAM and process intelligence with the intention to reduce action distance. In Section 2, we elaborate on the design of the prototypical artifact. Section 3 discusses the software's

J. vom Brocke et al. (Eds.): DESRIST 2013, LNCS 7939, pp. 448–455, 2013.

significance to research and practice. Section 4 discusses one of the steps undertaken to evaluate the usefulness of the tool.

2   Design of the Artifact

2.1   Problem Statement

The development of preCEP is motivated by two questions which rose while attempting to reduce action distance with current BAM approaches:

Question 1: "How can the BAM approach be further developed so that predictions of process instance behavior and estimations of process metrics are supported?"

We identified event-driven architecture to be a promising paradigm for exploiting event log data from historical process instances. By now, BAM systems report on the current situation of a process context only and therefore analyze events from running instances. In order to add prediction capability to BAM, it also needs to analyze event data from completed process instances so that it can learn about past process behavior (e.g., by using data mining models on historic data). However, data mining requires large data sets to form accurate prediction models and extensive data preparation is needed (such as a uniform format, variable selection, substitution techniques, etc.).

Question 2: "How can the dynamically increasing number of attributes of running instances be handled?" Data mining models typically require a set of predictors with a fixed length. In contrast, running processes dynamically generate new data.

Against this backdrop, we saw that there is currently no solution available for predictive edPA yet. Such a solution would include a *prediction runtime*, which analyzes runtime behavior of process instances, a *modeling component*, i.e. software support to specify the analytical approach to predicting process behavior and process metrics, and a *visualization component* which informs decision makers about predicted behavior and/ or process metrics.

2.2   Approach

In response to question 1, we developed a conceptual architecture for predictive edPA (A1) which uses CEP technology. In response to question 2, we developed a modeling approach for predictive edPA (A2). We chose to implement the architecture with standards of the shelf technology (S1) and developed a modeling environment for predictive edPA (S2).

Architecture (A1): The predictive edPA architecture comprises a CEP engine and a prediction runtime (cf. Fig. 1). Input adapters let the CEP engine tap into event data from persistent stores (historical events), events currently produced by operational systems (current events) or events with predicted values from the prediction runtime (predicted events). The CEP engine executes an event processing network (EPN) which transforms events into meaningful process or instance level key performance indicators (KPI) to assist detecting, analyzing, diagnosing, and resolving critical process behavior. The components are loosely coupled by publish and subscribe mechanisms for push-based exchange of the latest KPI or predictions. The prediction runtime can further pull KPI from historical events.

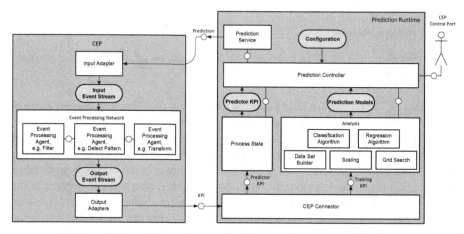

Fig. 1. preCEP architecture for integrating predictive analytics and CEP [1]

The prediction runtime is an event consumer of the CEP engine as it trains a prediction model with historic event data and as it makes predictions with current events. The CEP connector and the prediction service handle the cross-system event exchange while the prediction controller orchestrates the subcomponents internally. The analysis component calls a data set builder to link training KPI available in each execution stage with a response KPI. An execution stage holds a set of KPI available for a process at one point during its execution while a response stage holds a label for a set of training KPI in an execution stage. Both are modeled in the EPN and are accessible by the prediction runtime. The prepared data sets are scaled and a grid search for the best parameters of the algorithm compares measurements on the prediction quality of each model. Possible algorithms include support vector machines (SVM), decision trees and rule based techniques for classification and prediction of numeric values [2]. The classification accuracy and the mean square error (MSE) for numeric predictions are used as measures of the predictive power [3]. The prediction models are then stored for each execution stage. In case the prediction runtime consumes KPI from current events the process state component looks up the execution stage corresponding to the set of predictor KPI and executes the related prediction model with these values.

The prediction runtime also acts as event producer when making a prediction. Since the prediction is fed back into the CEP system, it is available for further processing such as providing context for the event, passing the prediction event to a dashboard or triggering an automated process improvement in a BPMS.

Modeling approach (A2): We organize metrics in execution stages to better handle the dynamically increasing number of KPI for running process instances – an idea that is adopted from process intelligence and process mining [2, 4–6]. In the EPN, events are processed by event processing agents (EPA) such as detect, filter, and transform. To find causalities or to derive complex events, EPAs may also relate single events to other events [7, 8]. We propose to model KPI through EPN (cf. Fig. 2). After events have been observed, they are transformed to numeric or categorical metrics which are related to an execution stage. Execution stages can be related to single activities, groups of activities or entire sub processes of the control flow structure. Next, the KPI are transferred from stage to stage so that at the end of the execution, the maximum data base is available. Execution stages refer to activities of a conceptual workflow model. Therefore, they may encounter abundance (e.g., loops) or incompleteness (e.g., XOR split) of related events. Such situations should be addressed by basic workflow patterns such as parallel split, synchronization, exclusive choice, simple merge, and iteration by means of data validation techniques such as elimination, inspection, identification, and substitution of incomplete records [9]. Only the KPI in the execution stages are needed to finally make a prediction. However, in order to train a prediction model, a dependent variable is needed which is made available in the response stage. All execution stages of an EPN can be related to the same response stage. It is also possible to assign them to different response stages. This enables more than one and also different predictions for each execution stage.

In contrast to instance metrics, process metrics constitute time series of values with the same general structure for each metric. Therefore, we propose to use the sliding input window feature of the EPA in order to define a time series of fixed length. This information is then used as input for process behavior prediction.

Implementation of the Architecture (S1): The presented architecture has been implemented on top of an internal release of a mayor software vendor's BPMS which also integrates CEP functionality [10]. We deliberately refrain from a detailed discussion of the flowchart of the prediction runtime and point only to some techniques that have not been described in the general architecture description so far.

In push based execution, the process state component receives predictor KPI always from the latest execution stage. In pull based execution, the execution stage is determined by first checking whether there is already a record in an execution stage for the instance of interest. Second, the process state component finds the latest predictor KPI by comparing all relevant execution stages timestamps. Independent of that, the prediction model is then applied for the predictor KPI received from the execution stage.

The analysis component of the prototype utilizes LIBSVM. LIBSVM is a popular library for support vector classification and support vector regression [11] which recommends scaling of the input data [12]. Therefore, all attributes are scaled to the range of -1 to 1. On the prepared data set, a grid search is conducted in order to find the optimal parameters for the SVM.

Modeling environment (S2): We built our modeling environment upon an existing design component for edPA that is an Eclipse based editor. It defines monitoring

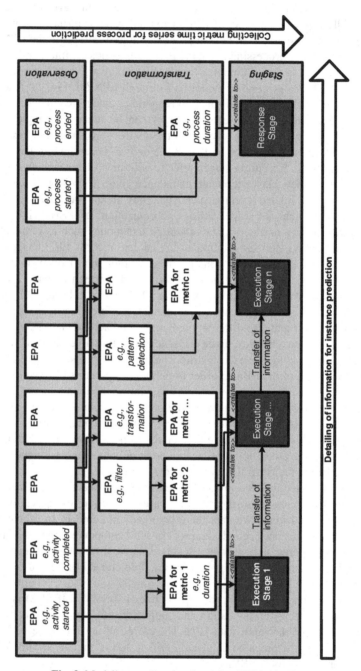

Fig. 2. Modeling predictor and training KPI in the EPN

models for conceptual workflow models. So far, its EPAs have not been used as representations for execution or response stages. Therefore, we introduce a new property section where the modeler can select the representation type and the prediction algorithm. This design information is stored in Java Script Object Notation (JSON) format.

Data mining procedures require extensive data preparation including data exploration and significance tests [13]. A design tool for predictive edPA should support this analysis by uploading historical event data to a preliminary EPN in order to investigate the KPI in the stages by statistical means. Due to limitations of our prototype this component is not implemented yet but could easily be added by using data mining libraries such as JDMP [14] or WEKA [15].

A user interface completes the prototype. Prediction results are either presented in the generic task user interface or as process visualization (along with the process model).

2.3   Use cases

The preCEP is intended to help decision makers in making better decisions faster in order to improve the operational performance of business processes. Examples include predictive maintenance of machinery, fraud detection in financials as well as route scheduling and optimization in logistics.

3   Significance of the Artifact

Significance for research: preCEP combines two areas of process analytics which so far had been studied separately only. Our software and the implemented method both outline, e.g., which data needs to be shared among monitoring components and prediction components in order to facilitate predictive edPA. Also with our approach, we offer a new perspective on how process-aware information systems can work together with analytical systems in near real-time. Future studies might directly take up and improve the IT artifacts suggested in this paper or test their application in enterprise contexts. They might also investigate problems, which occurred while designing and implementing our solution, such as the lack of a uniform event format for historical analysis as well as for the analysis of current events.

Significance for practice: The software prototype demonstrates how analytical systems and process aware IS can be coupled loosely via a CEP engine. This architecture allows for integrating several concrete software systems of each of the three system types. Design decisions such as the dual use of an EPN for historical and current events are made available to practitioners. Further, preCEP indicates options for refined development as regards, e.g., data exploration and visualization. The prototype not only adds to decision making on the operational and tactical level of an organization by providing predictions to business users but also allows for automated decision making in the CEP engine in a closed loop approach. Both ways, the tool supports proactive process performance management.

4   Evaluation of the Artifact

We analyzed the predictive edPA software tool's prediction quality with synthetic log data of a simple repair process which we obtained from [16]. Table 1 exhibits measurements on prediction quality. For numerical predictions, i.e. the overall duration, the mean square error (MSE) of the regression model of the predictive edPA solution is compared to the MSE of a simple arithmetic mean of the training data. Table 1 also depicts the classification accuracy. All values are related to the execution stages and the number of attributes used in the prediction model. This allows us to assess the relationship between the detail of data preparation in the EPN and the value gained in terms of prediction quality. While the arithmetic mean outperforms the proposed regression approach, the classification model works well. Only Execution Stage 3_1 does not perform. For classification and regression, additional attributes do not necessarily improve the predictive power. The classification accuracy does not increase after the first execution stage: A business user knows early in the process whether the instance will show exceptional behavior. A more detailed report on this analysis and further evaluation measures are given in [1].

Table 1. Prediction errors of edPA with synthetic log data [1]

Execution Stage	Number of Attributes	Regression (MSE)	Arithmetic Mean (MSE)	Classification (Accuracy)
1	7	378.407	377.9681	73.5
2	12	379.434	377.9681	73.5
3_1	16	361.6183	359.8436	49.41
3_2	16	409.2722	405.1011	86.18
4	28	378.791	377.9681	73.5

References

1. Schwegmann, B., Matzner, M., Janiesch, C.: A Method and Tool for Predictive Event-Driven Process Analytics. In: Proceedings of the 11th International Conference on Wirtschaftsinformatik, pp. 721–735. Leipzig, Germany (2013)
2. Castellanos, M., Casati, F., Dayal, U., Shan, M.C.: A comprehensive and automated approach to intelligent business processes execution analysis. Distributed and Parallel Databases 16(3), 239–273 (2004)
3. van der Aalst, W.M.P., Schonenberg, M.H., Song, M.: Time prediction based on process mining. Information Systems 36(2), 450–475 (2011)
4. van Dongen, B.F., Crooy, R.A., van der Aalst, W.M.P.: Cycle Time Prediction: When Will This Case Finally Be Finished? In: Meersman, R., Tari, Z. (eds.) OTM 2008, Part I. LNCS, vol. 5331, pp. 319–336. Springer, Heidelberg (2008)

5. Eder, J., Pichler, H.: Duration Histograms for Workflow Systems. In: Proceedings of the IFIP TC8 / WG 8.1 Working Conference, pp. 239–253 (2002)
6. Castellanos, M., Salazar, N., Casati, F., Dayal, U., Shan, M.-C.: Predictive business operations management. In: Bhalla, S. (ed.) DNIS 2005. LNCS, vol. 3433, pp. 1–14. Springer, Heidelberg (2005)
7. Etzion, O., Niblett, P.: Event Processing in Action. Manning Publications, Cincinnati (2010)
8. Eckert, M.: Complex Event Processing with XChange EQ: Language Design. In: Formal Semantics, and Incremental Evaluation for Querying Events (2008)
9. Shmueli, G., Koppius, O.R.: Predictive Analytics in Information Systems Research. MIS Quarterly 35(3), 553–572 (2011)
10. Janiesch, C., Matzner, M., Müller, O.: Beyond process monitoring: a proof-of-concept of event-driven business activity management. Business Process Management Journal 18(4), 625–643 (2012)
11. Chang, C.-C.C., Lin, C.-J.: LIBSVM: A library for support vector machines. ACM Transactions on Intelligent Systems and Technology 2(3) (2011)
12. Hsu, C.-W., Chang, C.-C., Lin, C.-J.: A Practical Guide to Support Vector Classification, http://www.csie.ntu.edu.tw/~cjlin/papers/guide/guide.pdf
13. Vercellis, C.: Business Intelligence: Data Mining and Optimization for Decision Making. John Wiley & Sons, West Sussex (2009)
14. Java Data Mining Package, http://sourceforge.net/projects/jdmp
15. Weka - Machine Learning Software in Java, http://sourceforge.net/projects/weka/
16. Process Mining Group: Process Mining Event logs, http://www.processmining.org/logs/start

Developing Creative Business Models – The OctoProz Tool

Matthias Voigt[1], Kevin Ortbach[1], Ralf Plattfaut[1], and Björn Niehaves[2]

[1] European Research Center for Information Systems, University of Münster, Germany
{matthias.voigt,kevin.ortbach,
ralf.plattfaut}@ercis.uni-muenster.de
[2] Hertie School of Governance
niehaves@hertie-school.org

Abstract. Business models are of great importance for business innovation. They can be understood as conceptual models that describe how organizations create and deliver value. Their creation is increasingly supported by information technology artifacts, as information technology facilitates information sharing, allows for continuous modification, and supports complex calculations. In this paper, we introduce a new prototype to create process-oriented business models: the OctoProz tool. We build up on creativity support system literature, present the design of the artifact, and discuss its significance for both research and practice. We close with an outlook on the evaluation of OctoProz.

Keywords: business modeling, prototype, OctoProz.

1 Introduction

Business models have gained significant attention in business strategy. "There has never been as much interest in business models as there is today" [1, p. 5]. We understand a business model as a scheme that describes how an organization creates and delivers economic, social, and other forms of value [2]. In our three-year research project KollaPro, funded by the German Ministry of Education and Research, we studied how business models are developed and deployed in practice and developed the collaborative, process-oriented business modeling method OctoProz [3].

In this article, we demonstrate how the method was technically implemented in form of the OctoProz tool. A tool implementation has several advantages over a pencil-and-paper application. First, the development of business models in virtual, dislocated teams is facilitated. Second, sharing of business models amongst different stakeholders is possible. Third, continuous modifications of business models can readily be made. Fourth, complex profitability assessments are supported. Last, the reuse of business models is facilitated by model export formats. We interpret business modeling as a creative process. Thus, business modeling tools shall support users in developing creative business models. We position OctoProz as a Creativity Support System (CSS), which "enable[s] more people to be more creative more often" [4].

J. vom Brocke et al. (Eds.): DESRIST 2013, LNCS 7939, pp. 456–462, 2013.

2   Design of the Artifact

The current prototype was created between March 2012 and February 2013 by a team of students and research assistants (21 developers) using the Ruby on Rails framework and other state-of-the-art technology. OctoProz supports the creation of process-oriented business models in a web browser using interactive controls and drag-and-drop functionality. The development of the OctoProz prototype was conducted with constant feedback from practitioners from multiple organizations (Section 5). The prototype (beta version) is accessible at http://OctoProz.de.

We see two general application scenarios of the OctoProz tool: First, a green-field approach, where a new business model is developed that creates a new customer solution as an independent business venture. This scenario may be relevant to entrepreneurs planning a new start-up. Second, OctoProz may also be used to analyze existent business models and redefine those models. This scenario calls for integrating multiple stakeholders, e.g. strategic decision makers or IT experts.

The functionality of OctoProz is clustered in *four components* that appear as separate screens. Each of the components has several associated *features and views*.

OctoProz allows for the management of multiple business models. In the *model management component*, the user can see all business models listed with their name, description, tag, the corresponding permission of the user, information on the date of the last update, and the rating. The user can *sort business models* with regards to all these categories and *search* for specific models. Business models are organized using tags. The model management component also allows for the *creation* of new business models and the *import* of business models from Microsoft Excel.

The *modeling component* of OctoProz is reachable from the model management component and depicted in Figure 1. In the center of the screen the modeler can create the business model using the methodology described in [3]. The top buttons allow the user to open a *wizard* (help) which guides the creation of a new business model. The *undo/redo*-buttons are used to correct mistakes in the modeling process. With the finance button the user can color all rows of the business model according to their costs or revenues. Activities with high costs are shown in dark red, those with high revenues in bright green. Thus, the modeler can easily *assess financially critical activities* in the business model. The copy button allows users to create personal copies of the model, in order to *create variants* of one business model. The export button enables users to *export the model* to PDF (e.g. for printing), Microsoft Excel (e.g. for further calculation and re-import), and to the ARIS Business Architect (e.g. for detailing of the process). The syntax check button opens the *syntax check view* on the right which indicates potential errors (e.g. resources without costs). The comments button opens the *comments view* on the right. Here, each model user with at least read rights can comment on the model in plain text. Last, the *currently online* button informs all users about other users currently watching the model. The model is locked by the first user with write or owner rights when opening the model. Only this user can edit the model. Her changes are pushed to the watching users in real time. The locking user can also transfer the lock to other users with the appropriate rights when clicking on the transfer lock button. In the upper left corner of the window, each user can also *rate the model* on a one to five star scale. The average rating is shown to all users.

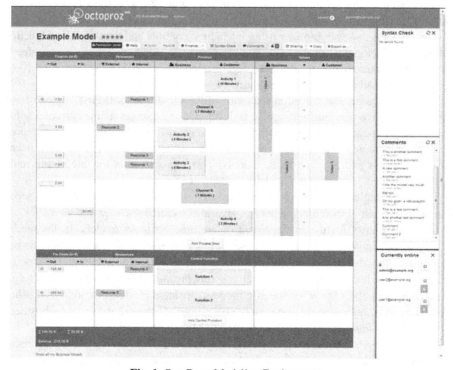

Fig. 1. OctoProz: Modeling Environment

As a second option to the finance button in the modeling component, the user can open a *financial analysis component* which allows an evaluation of the financials of the business model. The user is guided in a five-step calculation process for completing and analyzing the process-dependent financials, the central function financials, the process duration and iteration, the one-time investments, and the final calculations.

The sharing button leads to the *model rights management component*, allowing users to share the model with other users. Therefore, the owner of the business model has to enter a valid e-mail address and has to select between read, write, and owner rights. An invitation is sent to the collaborator.

3   Significance to Research

Creativity is commonly associated with the development of creative products which are both novel and useful. Both characteristics apply as quality criterion for business models: Created business models should be new to the market and provide customer value. Thus, business models created using OctoProz are creative products. CSS is an information system type which aims at supporting the development of creative products [4]. Group CSS (GCSS) are specifically tailored to the support collaborative creative processes [5]. We position OctoProz as a GCSS.

We contribute to design-oriented IS research on CSS design. We extend the notion of CSS as systems providing inspiration for generating ideas to systems for the design of complex creative products. OctoProz represents an instantiation of this extended notion of CSS. It provides for evaluations of the impact of design choices in CSS on, for example, the process of design, creative performance, and user satisfaction. From a business modeling research perspective, OctoProz is an artifact which incorporates collaborative, process-oriented business modeling. Thus, the artifact allows for the evaluation of this new business modeling approach, and its effect on, for example, the business modeling process or business model quality.

The notion of CSS as systems for the design of complex creative products is reflected in the architectural guidelines for GCSS [6]. OctoProz follows these architectural guidelines for GCSS, recommending six interrelated system components, referred to as components for collaborative idea development: Gathering and sharing of first, rough ideas is supported by the component *shared idea space,* representing an idea database which integrates all other components. The production and documentation of ideas is supported by the *shared idea editor*, which supports the creation of new ideas (e.g. text editor). Sharing and collaboratively editing ideas facilitates mutual inspiration of group members. The *communication component* facilitates communication during the generation of new ideas. Communication could be text based, audible, or audible-visual. The *individual inspiration component* provides stimuli to individuals and thereby enhances idea generation. This component is disregarded in our tool design, since it is not relevant to group applications. A *shared idea space visualizer* helps to organize and reduce the complexity of the ideas that have been generated and collected. Commonly, ideas can be organized in folder structures or mind maps. The assessment of ideas is supported by an *evaluation component* (e.g. voting or commenting). In Table 1, we relate the components and features of OctoProz to the GCSS components. OctoProz as a tool for the refinement of initial business ideas to complex business models has an emphasis on collaborative model design.

Table 1. Components of the GCSS architecture and their implementation in OctoProz

GCSS Architecture Component	OctoProz Component and Features
Shared idea editor (creation of ideas)	• Modeling component: collaborative model editing, view of users currently online, wizard for creating business models, assessment of financially critical process activities, syntax check, creation of variants, undo/redo of changes to the model • Financial analysis component: guided five-step calculation process for cost and revenue estimations
Shared idea space visualizer (organization of ideas)	• Model management component: sorting, searching, and grouping of related business models (including variants) • Print format export of business models, single business models may be exported to PDF

Table 1. (Continued)

Evaluation component (assessment of ideas)	• Comments: discussion of business model details (qualitative) • Model rating: assessing business models with five-star voting (quantitative) • Financial analysis component: Financial assessment of business models based on KPIs
Shared idea space (sharing of ideas)	• Model rights management component: management of user rights (model owner, read, write) for business models • Model export and import, multi-format (ARIS & Office) export and import of business models
Communication component (mutual inspiration and idea assessment)	• Comments: discussion of business model details

4   Significance to Practice

Collaboration can be considered an important aspect in business model creation, not only during idea creation but also within the structuring and refinement phases. Through several aspects such as sharing of models or real-time push of changes to watching users, the OctoProz prototype facilitates collaboration and is thus significant to practice. The comment functionality and star-based rating mechanism allows all users with the appropriate rights to assess business models. This allows managers to collect feedback from their employees for instance if different competing service ideas have been developed or if there are different models on a particular service idea.

In addition to these collaborative features, modelers and model users are supported individually. For instance, first time users benefit from both a step-by-step guide and a comprehensive syntax check that ensures validity of the model in terms of e.g. process structure and resource assignments. The tool provides a finance check which color-codes all process steps according to their financial requirements and outputs. This allows practitioners to quickly gain an overview of the most influential steps within a business model and therefore easily identify possible areas of improvement or refinement. Furthermore, financial experts are provided with a more advanced financial calculation and analysis module that seamlessly integrates with the basic modeling environment. Key figures (e.g. contribution margin, profit/loss, or return on invest) can be calculated using the financial information provided in the model.

After a particular business model is developed and structured by means of the OctoProz tool, further refinements, especially with respect to more advanced financial calculations are necessary. OctoProz opens up the possibility to export the process perspective of the created model in BPMN notation for the ARIS environment. Here, the process can be refined and expanded using the known ARIS toolset. In addition, OctoProz offers an Excel export which can be used for business casing.

5   Evaluation of the Artifact

The prototype was developed with constant feedback from industry partners (an office supply company, an SAP consulting company, and an IT consultancy). We allocated our tool development resources in accordance with their feature preferences. Seven project members participated in the feature voting: Business casing was the most important feature (seven votes), followed by Excel export (five votes), ARIS export (four votes), user management (three votes), and real-time collaboration (three votes). All features were implemented in the current release.

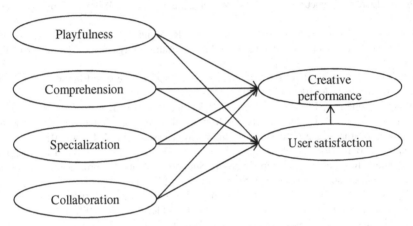

Fig. 2. Evaluation research model for OctoProz

From a research perspective, OctoProz should primarily be evaluated for its impact on the creative performance. In line with [7] we propose an evaluation research model (Figure 2): In a first step, OctoProz should be assessed with respect to the playfulness it allows for in business modeling, the degree of comprehension of the business model it facilitates, and the specific functionality of the tool for the context of business modeling. As a group specific evaluation criterion, collaboration support should be assessed. These four variables are hypothesized to influence user satisfaction and creative performance (while creative performance is also impacted by satisfaction). To test these hypotheses, corresponding components and features of OctoProz have to be identified activated or deactivated to separately control for the independent variables.

Moreover, OctoProz could also be evaluated against other business modeling tools such as Strategyzer by Business Model Foundry GmbH or Business Model Fiddle by Orbital Limited.

Acknowledgements. The OctoProz tool and this paper were developed in the context of the research project KollaPro (promotional reference 01FL10004) funded by the German Federal Ministry of Education and Research. The OctoProz tool has been implemented with the help of the following research assistants and undergraduate students: Andrea Malsbender, Jony Alam, Maurus Beck, Adrian Beheschti, Philipp Berg, Konrad Fögen, Steffen Höhenberger, David Ostendorf, Sören Reimler, Dennis Riehle, Lars Rüsenberg, Timo Schnieders, Victor Schönfelder, Shabdiz Ghasemivand, Christian Rest, Stefan Rocksch, Raimo Radczewski, and Jan Betzing.

References

1. Casadesus-Masanell, R., Ricart, J.E.: How to Design A Winning Business Model. Harvard Business Review (2011)
2. Osterwalder, A., Pigneur, Y.: Business Model Generation. John Wiley & Sons, New Jersey (2010)
3. Becker, J., Malsbender, A., Ortbach, K., Plattfaut, R., Voigt, M., Höhenberger, S., Niehaves, B.: zfo-Toolkit: Business Modeling. Zeitschrift Führung + Organisation 14 (under publication, 2013)
4. Shneiderman, B.: Creativity support tools: accelerating discovery and innovation. Communications of the ACM 50, 20–32 (2007)
5. Müller-Wienbergen, F., Müller, O., Seidel, S., Becker, J.: Leaving the Beaten Tracks in Creative Work – A Design Theory for Systems that Support Convergent and Divergent Thinking. Journal of the Association for Information Systems 12, 714–740 (2011)
6. Voigt, M., Bergener, K.: Enhancing Creativity in Groups – Proposition of an Integrated Framework for Designing Group Creativity Support Systems. In: Proceedings of the 46th Hawaii International Conference on System Sciences (2013)
7. Voigt, M., Niehaves, B., Becker, J.: Towards a Unified Design Theory for Creativity Support Systems. In: Peffers, K., Rothenberger, M., Kuechler, B. (eds.) DESRIST 2012. LNCS, vol. 7286, pp. 152–173. Springer, Heidelberg (2012)

Using Empirical Knowledge and Studies in the Frame of Design Science Research

Ilia Bider[1,2], Paul Johannesson[1], and Erik Perjons[1]

[1] DSV, Stockholm University, Stockholm, Forum 100, SE-16440 Kista, Sweden
[2] IbisSoft AB, Stockholm, Box 19567, SE-10432 Stockholm, Sweden
ilia@{ibissoft.se,dsv.su.se}, {pajo,perjons}@dsv.su.se

Abstract. The focus of this research in progress is relationships between Design Science Research (DSR) on one hand, and Empirical Research (ER) on the other. More specifically, it is devoted to investigating which tasks included in a DSR project should/could require conducting ER studies or using already existing ER knowledge. The paper presents a methodology for enumerating DSR tasks and gives examples of logical analysis of some of them to determine requirements or usability of ER studies or ER-related knowledge for completing these tasks. The enumeration of DSR tasks is done by considering possible trajectories of DSR projects in a specially constructed state space. The latter consists of two subspaces; one is the space of specific situations, problems and solutions, the other – of generic situations, problems and solutions. The first subspace represents test cases used for validating DSR hypotheses that the second subspace represents. In the terms of this space, DSR is considered to be a way of generating and testing hypotheses for future adoption. The project trajectory is identified via movements within and between subspaces. Examples of such movements are: generalization of a specific situation/problem, designing a generic solution, evaluating the results of implementing a solution in a specific situation.

Keywords: design science, empirical research.

1 Introduction

There is a substantial difference between qualitative and quantitative empirical research (ER) on one hand and design science research (DSR) on the other. The former [1] is aimed at investigating real life situations as-is, or as they were at some point in the past, in order to find commonalities between them that can give rise to a theory explaining the current or past state of affairs. DSR [2] is related to finding new generic solutions for problems known or unknown [3]. Following [4], we see DSR as a tool for generating and testing solutions for future adoption.

Despite the differences, both are needed for making progress in the field of Information Systems (IS). The goal of this paper is to investigate relationships and points of connection between DSR and ER. This work was inspired by S. Gregor's presentation

J. vom Brocke et al. (Eds.): DESRIST 2013, LNCS 7939, pp. 463–470, 2013.

at SIG Philosophy Workshop (at ICIS 2012) on the unification of design science and social science research [5] and the discussion that followed this presentation.

Roughly, [5] identifies three general points of connection between ER and DSR:

1. ER and/or results of previous ER studies are used when designing and testing a new solution/artifact.
2. DSR creates a new reality that can be investigated with ER methods. This happens after a solution/artifact designed in a DSR project has been adopted by practice.
3. DSR is used for creating tools/conducting experiments inside ER projects.

In this paper, we focus our attention on the first point of connection, i.e. using ER or/and ER-generated knowledge inside a DSR project. More specifically, we intend to present a methodology for investigating in which tasks of a DSR project ER can/should be used. The methodology is based on the view on a DSR project as a movement inside and between two different worlds: (a) the real world of specific situations, problems and solutions in local practices, and (b) the abstract world of generic situations, problems and solutions [4]. Some of these movements includes tasks that warrant employment of ER methods or, if available, results of previous ER studies.

The paper is structured in the following way. In section 2, we outline the model of DSR presented in [4]. In Section 3, we outline a methodology of identifying possible tasks in a DSR project and investigating the needs of using ER studies, or ER-based knowledge in these tasks. Section 4 discusses the results, and draws plans for the future. Due to the work-in-progress nature of this paper, it does not have a separate section on related works. So far, beside the already cited paper [5] we have found only one paper [6] that is strongly related to the question discussed in this paper. Thorough literature survey and related work analysis will be included in the full version of the paper.

2   Design Science as a Movement within and between Two Worlds

According to [4], DSR, as a way of generating and testing hypotheses for generic solutions, requires researchers to act in two different worlds: (a) the real world of specific problems and solutions in local practices, and (b) the abstract world of generic problems and solutions. The movements of researchers in these two worlds can be visualized as in Fig. 1.

The upper part of Figure 1 represents the real world as a specific situation-problem-solution space with three axes: (1) situation as-is, (2) problem, and (3) situation to-be (i.e. a possible solution) [1]. A problem is defined as a set of situations considered to be undesirable from some point of view. For example, the problem "a lack of communication

---

[1]   Using orthogonal spaces in Fig. 1 is a simplification made in order to use relatively simple pictures to illustrate the basic concepts. In reality, the spaces are neither orthogonal, nor do they have a real metric to measure the distance between the points. For details, see [4].

between the members of our project team" can be represented as a set of all possible ways of organizing our team that result in its members not exchanging important information between them in the frame of the project. The situation as-is in this case is "our team as of today". A possible solution - situation to-be - could be "our team using collaborative software for communication".

A point $<s, P, s'>$ in the upper space in Fig. 1 is called a test case. A test case represents a question whether problem P in situation s (i.e. $s \in P$) can be solved by transforming it into situation s' (i.e. $s' \notin P$). The answer to this question can be either negative – transforming s into s' has not solved the problem P (i.e. $s' \in P$), or positive – transforming s into s' has solved the problem P (i.e. $s' \notin P$). In the latter case, s' is considered to be a solution for problem P in situation s. The results of tests can be visualized in assigning the weight +1 to the point $<s, P, s'>$ if s' is a solution for P in s (see Fig. 1), and -1, otherwise.

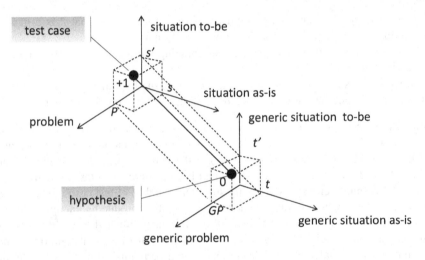

Fig. 1. Design science requires researchers to move between two worlds from [4]

The lower part of Figure 1 represents the abstract world as a generic situation-problem-solution space with three axes: (1) generic situation as-is, (2) generic problem, and (3) generic situation to-be, (i.e. a possible generic solution). We consider that a generic situation (as-is or to-be) is represented by some kind of a template that defines a set of similar situations; the template serving as an extension of this set. The generic problem is defined as a set of situations undesirable from some point of view. The generic problem, normally, encompasses larger number of situations than a specific problem from the real world. For example, if a specific problem P can be defined as a lack of communication between the members of a specific project team/department, the corresponding generic problem GP will be defined as lack of communication in project teams/departments of certain kind. The correspondence between P and GP can be defined through set inclusion: $P \subset GP$.

A point $<t, GP, t'>$ in the generic space is called a hypothesis and represents a question whether a problem P ($P \subset GP$) in a real world situation as-is s described by template t can be solved by transforming s into situation to-be s' according to template t'. Template t' constitutes what in design science literature is called an artifact.

The relationships between the two spaces in Figure 1 are of the type instantiation/generalization. If real situation s satisfies template t, then s is referred to as an instantiation of t. Alternatively, t is considered to be a generalization of s. Extending the notion of instantiation/generalization to the points in the two spaces, test case $<s, P, s'>$ in the specific space is considered to be an instantiation of hypothesis $<t, GP, t'>$ in the generic space if s is an instantiation of t, s' is an instantiation of t', and $P \subset GP$. Alternatively, hypothesis $<t, GP, t'>$ is called a generalization of test case $<s, P, s'>$.

The knowledge about hypotheses in the generic space can be visualized by assigning weights to the points of this space according to the following rule:

- +1 when there is a statistically valid proof (many test cases) that t' is a generic solution for generic problem GP in generic situation t.
- -1 when there is at least one test case instantiating the hypothesis with weights -1 assigned to it.
- 0 when there is at least one test case instantiating the hypothesis with weights +1 assigned to it, but the statistically valid proof has not been obtained so far.

In the term of the two spaces and weights introduced above, the primary goal of the DSR as a way of generating and testing new solutions for adoption could be defined as finding "blank" points (without weights) in the generic space and assigning them weights 0, or -1. Assigning weight +1, cannot be considered as a task of DSR, as research itself cannot generate statistically sufficient number of test cases. This assignment can be only made by practice adopting the solution producing enough cases for ER to investigate. Also, the efforts of DSR are primarily directed to find the generic solutions that work (weight 0), finding on the way that other potential solutions do not work but constitute valuable knowledge that should be published and marked on the map of Fig. 1.

3   Methodology Suggested

As followed from the introduction, our goal is to suggest a way of finding which tasks of DSR projects could/should use ER studies or ER-generated knowledge. This goal, naturally, can be split in two sub-goals: (1) compiling a list of possible tasks that can be completed in a DSR project, and (2) investigating each of them to see what kind of ER study/knowledge could be required for this task execution.

3.1   Identifying DSR Tasks

DSR does not impose a specific order of movement inside and between the two spaces introduced in section 2. For example, a researcher can start with a specific space and find an innovative solution for a problem in a specific situation, and then generalize the situation, problem and solution when moving to the generic space. In this case the initial solution will automatically serve as a test case of a generic hypothesis. Another possibility is starting with a specific situation and problem, then generalize them and try to invent a generic solution that can be tested to solve the initial specific problem in the initial situation. On the opposite side, the researcher can start with designing a generic solution for problem unknown, implement it in some specific situation, and then analyze whether it solves some specific problems, and whether this specific problem and situation as-is could be generalized.

Our suggestions for compiling the list of DSR tasks consist of considering all possible scenarios of movement between and inside the two spaces of Fig. 1. Below we present one such case to illustrate our approach, see Fig. 2. Fig. 2 represents a case of *generic problem solving* that arises from a specific problem in a specific situation. The process starts with *identifying* the situation and the problem in it that needs a solution – arrow 1. The next step is *generalizing* the situation and the problem – arrow 2. After that follows *design of a solution* – arrow 3, and *implementing* it in the original specific situation – arrow 4. The last task is *evaluating* whether the problem has been solved – arrow 5.

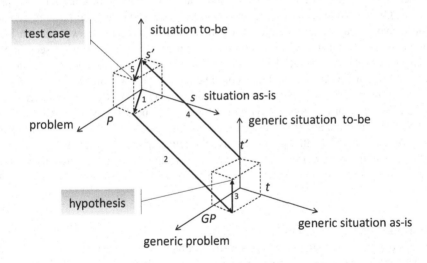

Fig. 2. Generic problem solving

Example –Developing A^3

To give an example of the research according to the *generic problem solving* scenario in Fig. 2, we present a short overview of a case from our own practice. In 2003-2006, we were engaged in a research project [7] aimed at investigating effects of the introduction of an integrated business process support and knowledge management system into operational practice of a non-profit interest organization. Soon after the first version of the system had been developed and put into operation, we discovered that very few used it, which made it impossible to investigate any effects.

The first analysis resulted in critique of the usability of the system, i.e. the system design was not sufficiently intuitive and user-friendly. The user interface was redesigned, but after some time it was obvious that still very few used the system. The second analysis resulted in critique towards the introduction process itself. Therefore, we tried to find a solution addressing systems introductions. However, our search for an existing solution in the literature gave no result. Solutions recommended for conducting an organizational change where related to planning it in the right way from the very beginning, and we were already in the middle of a not so successful system introduction that we could not "rewind". The only way to proceed for us was to design a solution ourselves.

A solution was designed as a general methodology called A^3 for conducting a system introduction process that was possible to apply even in the middle of unsuccessful introduction. The designed methodology was tested in the original situation with some success. We were able to substantially increase the usage of the system.

3.2   Finding the Needs for ER in a DSR Task

In section 3.1, we suggested enumerating possible scenarios of movement within and between specific and generic spaces to identify all tasks that can be completed in DSR projects. One possible scenario was presented in Fig. 2 and discussed in more details; other scenarios can be considered in a similar manner (see more examples in [4]). This gives a solution for the first sub-goal presented in the beginning of section 3 – finding tasks related to DSR. The other sub-goal is to investigate each task found to see what kind of ER study/knowledge could be required for its completion.

Identifying whether a specific DSR task from a specific DSR project scenario warrants an ER study or requires ER-based knowledge can be done by logical analysis of the task content. This analysis can be based on studying the literature or using experience of the analyst. In this paper, we use the latter approach, leaving the literature study for the future. In subsections below, we present analysis of three tasks from Fig. 2: *generalization* (arrow2), *designing a solution* (arrow 3), and *evaluation* (arrow 5).

Generalization (Arrow 2 in Fig. 2)
In terms of Fig. 1 generalization of a specific problem P that exists in a specific situation s consists in finding a corresponding generic problem GP that includes P and a generic situation t that generalizes s. Thus defined, the generalization is a purely formal act. However, to ensure that the generic solution to be designed will be valuable, assessment of whether there are other instances of the generic problem in local practices is required. Such assessment is aimed at investigating how spread the generic problem is that, naturally, warrants an ER study. If such study has already been conducted, the results are, possibly, to be found in the ER literature; otherwise, an ER study needs to be included in the frame of the DSR project.

In the scenario of Fig. 2, problem assessment can be done before trying to design a generic solution or after that. However, the latter approach includes two risks:

- Firstly, the generic problem may already have an acceptable solution. To mitigate this risk, available literature can be searched. If the problem has not been discovered before, there are sufficient chances that there is no solution for it.
- Secondly, there are no generic solution reported but the problem is not spread, and solution developed may not be requested more than once. This risk is, however, less important if there is a need to solve the problem, at least, in one particular case. In addition, if the problem has not been detected in the past there is a chance that this is a new kind of problems that might become spread in the future.

Returning to the *example of developing A³*, based on the study of ER literature in IT technology acceptance, and change management, we came to the conclusion that our problem was not unique and has its roots in that our system required change in the existing work practice. The problem thus was formulated as *introduction of an IT system that requires substantial organizational change*. During this search, we also found that there were no ready-made solutions for our situation - in the middle of a non-successful introduction.

Designing a Solution (Arrow 3 in Fig. 2)
A solution design does not need to be totally revolutionary, e.g. it may consist of a new combination of elements already known, or the ones that could be found in local practices. Both search of the current ER-based knowledge and conducting ER studies can help to discover components from which one can build a new solution.

Returning to the *example of developing A³*, when designing our solution, we used elements found in the literature. More specifically, we used recommendations and findings from three sources: (i) the approach to change management proposed by Kotter [8], (ii) institutional context changes found useful for IT introduction by Sharma and Yetton [9], (iii) findings of Unified Theory of Acceptance and Use of Technology [10]. The components from these works however where combined in a new way to solve the generic problem discovered in the course of the project.

Analyzing the Results of a Test Case (Arrow 5 in Fig. 2)
When a solution developed in the frame of a DSR project has been implemented in a test case, the results should be investigated. This requires an ER-study, e.g. conducting interviews, observations, surveys. In the case when the solution has been designed for solving an already identified problem, e.g. as in Fig. 2 (arrow 5) such an ER-study is aimed at establishing whether the solution has solved the problem or not.

Note that a solution that comes from a DSR project can, on its own, include a template for an ER-study, e.g. a new method of measuring organizational performance based on interviews and surveys. This was the case in *our example of developing A³*. Part of the solution that we developed included periodical assessment of the state of the introduction process. For this assessment, surveys and interview questions were designed. These were used during the implementation stage to conduct ER studies (mostly qualitative studies).

4   Concluding Remarks

Following [5], we believe that integration of DSR and ER would be beneficial for the development of information systems discipline. To reach this goal, a detailed analysis of how these two paradigms could benefit from each other is required. In this paper, we suggested a methodology of micro-level investigation of which DSR tasks can benefit or require ER studies or ER-based knowledge. We also demonstrated this methodology in use by: (a) considering a possible DSR project scenario and identifying tasks that can be completed in the frame of DSR projects that follow the scenario, and (b) analyzing several of these tasks to determine the needs to conduct ER studies or use ER-based knowledge in it.

The next stage of our research is to continue the work started in this paper by: (a) identifying other possible DSR projects scenarios, and DSR tasks included in them, and (b) analyzing connection of these tasks to ER studies, and/or ER-based knowledge, having the ultimate goal to compile an extensive manual that can be used by researchers and research students when completing DSR projects.

References

1. Neuman, W.L.: Social Research Methods. Qualitative and Quantitative Approaches. Pearson (2006)
2. Hevner, A.R., March, S.T., Park, J.: Design Science in Information Systems Research. MIS Quarterly 28(1), 75–105 (2004)
3. Anderson, J., Donnellan, B., Hevner, A.: Exploring the relationship between design science research and innovation: A case study of innovation at chevron. In: Helfert, M., Donnellan, B. (eds.) EDSS 2011. CCIS, vol. 286, pp. 116–131. Springer, Heidelberg (2012)
4. Bider, I., Johannesson, P., Perjons, E.: Design science research as movement between individual and generic situation-problem-solution spaces. In: Baskerville, R., De Marco, M., Spagnoletti, P. (eds.) Organizational Systems. An Interdisciplinary Discourse, pp. 35–61. Springer (2013)
5. Gregor, S., Baskerville, R.: The fusion of design science and social science research. In: Information Systems Foundation Workshop, Canberra, Australia, September 13-14 (2012)
6. Wieringa, R.J.: Design Science as Nested Problem Solving. In: Proceedings of the 4th International Conference on Design Science Research in Information Systems and Technology, pp. 1–12. ACM, Philadelphia (2009)
7. Bider, I., Johannesson, P., Perjons, E., Johansson, L.: Design Science in Action: Developing a Framework for Introducing IT Systems into Operational Practice. In: Joey, F.G. (ed.) Proceedings of the International Conference on Information Systems, ICIS 2012, December 16-19. Association for Information Systems, Orlando (2012)
8. Kotter, J.P.: Leading Change. Harvard Business School Press (1996)
9. Sharma, R., Yetton, P.: The Contingent Effects of Management Support and Task Interdependence on Successful Information Systems Implementation. MIS Quarterly 27(4), 535–555 (2003)
10. Venkatesh, V., Morris, M.G., Davis, G.B., Davis, F.D.: User Acceptance of Information Technology: Toward a Unified View. MIS Quarterly 27(3), 425–478 (2003)

Towards a Reference Model for a Productivity-Optimized Delivery of Technology Mediated Learning Services

Philipp Bitzer, Frank Weiß, and Jan Marco Leimeister

Kassel University, Information Systems, Kassel, Germany
{bitzer,leimeister}@uni-kassel.de, weiss@wi-kassel.de

Abstract. Technology mediated learning services (TMLS) play an important role for software on-the-job-training due to increasing cost pressure for on-the-job-training and increasing demand for mobile learning solutions. As there is no structured approach to systematically deliver productive TMLS this research study creates a holistic reference model of a productivity-optimized TMLS delivery process. This productivity-optimized model focuses on efficient use of resources at a constant or increasing TMLS outcome by a set of process models and design guidelines for TMLS providers. It is developed within a design research setting and derives existing knowledge from the literature and three in-depth-case studies with training providers for software applications. Consequently, we build a reference model that supports the following activities of technology oriented learning: training preparation, training delivery within the classroom, training delivery through internet and training evaluation under consideration of various stakeholders, such as the TMLS provider, trainer, TMLS participant and the participants company.

Keywords: technology mediated learning, service productivity, reference model, service delivery.

1 Introduction

Arthur et al. [1] and Gartner [2] identified the influence of technology in all learning scenarios referred to as technology-mediated learning as a major trend in education. Technology mediated learning services (TMLS) will gain more importance and will lead to innovative, more individual, more resource-preserving ways of learning, e.g. micro-learning at the workplace or location-independent cloud-based learning [3]. According to Wainhouse Research [4] the global market value of TML is expected to increase from $802.8 million in 2007 to $1.5 billion in 2011, for a compounded annual growth rate of 13%. Thereby, software trainings have the biggest share of trainings conducted in Germany [5].

Despite its many advantages, TMLS incite several fundamental challenges: First and foremost, it still remains challenging for TMLS designers to figure out, what the best combination of synchronous and asynchronous learning elements is for a specific TMLS participant groups and contents [6], [7]. The variety and heterogeneity of

J. vom Brocke et al. (Eds.): DESRIST 2013, LNCS 7939, pp. 471–478, 2013.

research results lead to an inconclusive database for a systematic productivity-optimized TMLS provision which fosters resource-saving aspects of IT use with potential learning success gains [6], [8]. The lack of transferable insights can be explained since many studies have used input-output research designs that ignore critical aspects of the learning method and process [7]. Consequently, without the consideration of the learning process perspective, including learning methods, the research done so far is not adequate to face the increasing use of technology in TMLS, and still is not sufficient for the dynamic development in practice [9], [10]. Therefore, a comprehensive view on TMLS is needed, which includes not only the input and output perspective but additionally the process perspective on TMLS. From a providers perspective, this is an important condition to systematically provide TMLS, supporting a productive respectively cost-efficient service delivery in terms of providers input and providers respectively customers output [11], [12].

The objective of this study is to develop a reference model that enables training providers for software applications ("software training providers") to deliver productive TMLS, i.e. with an efficient use of input factors during the provision process at a constant or improved output level for their customers. Provider and customer requirements are collected and a theory and practice based reference model for productivity-optimized TMLS delivery is derived.

Therefore, a reference model is built, comprising productivity-oriented TMLS delivery processes. The processes are developed through literature and case study analysis.

Accordingly, this paper aims to answer the following research question:

How must a reference model be conceptualized, in order to support the productive provision of TMLS in the context of technology mediated trainings teaching software application use.

In order to achieve our desired goal, the research in this paper is structured as follows in the ensuing sections. The related work, research method, case set up and respective information systems are introduced. Subsequently, the results are elaborated and discussed. Lastly, conclusions drawn on our part are summarized.

2   Foundation and Related Work

The term technology mediated learning services has many variations and is often a combination of the following learning modes: web-based or computer-based, asynchronous or synchronous, instructor-led or self-paced, individual-based or team-based [7]. More precisely, the goal of TMLS is to integrate the strengths of synchronous (face-to-face) and asynchronous (internet-based) learning activities [13]. According to this definition, we define technology mediated learning as teaching and learning activities which are conducted by means of traditional face-to-face training in combination with internet-based training activities.

Since the goal of this study is to develop a productivity-optimized reference model, we have to introduce the service productivity concept: In contrast to production productivity, service productivity has to consider not only quantitative aspects (e.g. number of participants) but also qualitative aspects (e.g. learning success) (McLaughlin and Coffey 1990). This implies that, although the efficient use of resources is in the focus of this study, i.e. the lowest possible use of resources such as working hours, also the effectiveness, i.e. the TMLS such as learning success or participant satisfaction, has to be considered for a productive TMLS delivery.

The challenge of a productive delivery of technology mediated learning services remains to deliver the right content in the right format to the right people at the right time, since learning requirements and preferences of each learner tend to be different [14]. The existing research shows various design recommendations for the efficient and effective delivery of TMLS in the context of software trainings [6]. Nevertheless there is no comprehensive approach to systematically deliver productive TMLS [7], integrating requirements like e.g. a holistic TMLS process perspective [7], [15]. Therefore, this study aims to develop a reference model incorporating findings from theory and practice, focusing on dimensions, roles, activities and processes.

3   Research Methodology

Despite the high need for supporting software training providers in the design of productivity-optimized TMLS, no corresponding reference model can be found in the literature. To close this gap, by the use of design science research, a process model and success factors for productive TMLS implementation are developed. According to Hevner et al. [16] a model uses constructs – language for the definition and communication of problems and solutions [17] – to present a real world design problem and to develop a concrete solution [18]. More concrete, a reference model is developed providing "best-practice processes for a domain, which can be adapted to aid companies in designing and operating their business [19 p.36]". Following this definition, reference models represent knowledge about a specific domain – in our case the knowledge to identify the business value of IT applications. The constructed model is set up to assist designers to reduce the time necessary to develop TMLS, reduce the development effort, incorporate new ideas best practices and minimize the risk of failure [20].

As described in Hevner et al. [16] design science focuses on "building and evaluation of artifacts designed to meet the identified business needs (p. 79-80)". To build artifacts by de-sign research Takeda et al. [21] propose a five-phased approach starting with creating awareness of the problem. In our study, following Ahlemann and Riempp [20], the problem domain was formulated through literature review. In addition to enrich the requirements respectively design goals found in literature three case studies with major German software training providers were conducted. Within the case studies,13 expert interviews and provided documents were analyzed and a training session was observed [22]. In accordance to Takeda et al. [21] in the next steps, based on the design goals derived, the artifact was developed. Insights complied from literature and workshops with TMLS providers and trainers were used to derive best practices. In a next step – to be conducted – the reference model will be evaluated

[21]. Conclusions drawn from the evaluation will be used to adapt and optimize the model [16].

4   Research Results

On the foundation of the three case studies (deductive) and the design requirements from the literature (inductive) a first version of the reference model was built. The following design goals, as shown in table 1, were derived and used for the model creation:

Table 1. Design goals for a reference model for a productivity-optimized TMLS delivery

Design goal	Description	Body of litera- ture	Derived from the case studies
Consideration of TMLS-productivity requirements	Resource-optimized TMLS delivery is the goal, evaluated by quantitative and qualitative input, process and output indicators	[23], [24]	yes
Holistic train-ings process orientation	The development of an end-user training program involves three consecutive dis-tinct phases: initiation, formal training & learning as well as post training	[25]	
Integration of multi-dimensional stakeholders	The following stakeholders are consid-ered: 1.) training provider, 2.) trainer, 3.) training participant and 4.) customer, i.e. the trainings' participant company	[26], [27]	yes
Learning goal oriented ser-vice delivery	The implementation of a training needs assessment is considered as a crucial initial step to training and is substantially influencing the overall effectiveness of training programs and serves as a fun-dament for design, development, deliv-ery and evaluation of training.	[1]	
Integration of configurable service ele-ments	Due to the great variety in customer demands and learning content, the inte-gration of configurable service elements is necessary.		yes

Table 1. *(Continued)*

Separation between process and learning units	The variability of service elements requires s separation between the process dimension, describing activities to support the actual learning units, i.e. a combination of learning methods.	[7]	
Integration of support processes	The integration of support processes such as providers administration, customer support		yes

4.1 The Reference Model Architecture

Various authors propose to develop reference model architectures to provide an overview of complex reference models [20], [28], [29]. Thereby, the overall problem domain can be decomposed into smaller manageable units to provide a high-level overview of the reference model [20].

The reference model architecture consists of eight layers, each of them comprising activities and modeled processes, using the Business Process Modeling Notation (BPMN), which were developed based on the derived design goals. Due to page limitations, only excerpts of the reference model are described in the following.

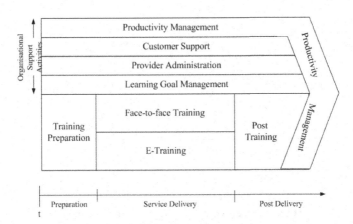

Fig. 1. Reference Model Architecture

Overall, the reference model comprises processes for every presented layer in order to deliver productivity-optimized TMLS. Thereby findings from service science, IS research, education and business science are integrated within the reference model. The processes which were modeled using the Business Process Management Notation (BPMN) include processes as well as productivity guidelines for the different layers describing actions which support a productive TMLS delivery in the context of soft-ware-trainings[1]. The reference model includes support activities as well as the service delivery activities. The support activities comprise the following layers: Within the productivity management layer measures for the productivity assessment are described, including a productivity measurement instrument, activities for the provider-specific customizing and measures to increase productivity. In the customer support layer activities for the support of the participants' company /companies (i.e. the customer(s)) are described, e.g. activities to integrate the learning content into the participants' working environment. The provider administration layer comprises activities for the organizational support of the participants and trainers before, during and after the service delivery process. Within the learning goal management layer activities concerning the identification, integration and accomplishment of learning goals are described.

The TMLS delivery process is separated into training preparation, including activities to train content before the actual training begins and to deliver additional, training related information, e.g. information about the training structure. The service delivery is further separated into face-to-face activities, comprising activities which are conducted within the training facilities, and E-Training activities, comprising activities which are computer-based and location-independent. Last, post training activities are presented within the Post Training layer. To illustrate the results, an example process, showing an excerpt of the face-to-face-training-process, is shown in figure 2.

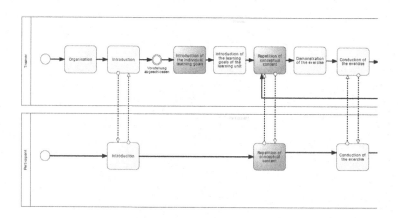

Fig. 2. Process excerpt of the face-to-face training

The yellow boxes depict the process components, derived within the case studies, the orange boxes were derived from the existing body of literature. Moreover, a detailed description and parameters for the customer-specific configuration of learning activities are included.

---

[1] In the following, the term "activities" describes processes as well as supporting measures.

5   Outlook and Expected Contribution

In the next step, the derived productivity-optimized reference model will be evaluated, in accordance with Ahlemann and Riempp [20], by means of expert workshops and the quantitative evaluation of the reference model within training sessions at a selected software training provider.

The expected contribution to theory comprises an empirically validated reference model for the productivity-optimized TMLS delivery in the context of trainings for software applications. Thereby the existing research gap of weaknesses in the systematic, theory-based delivery of TMLS is addressed. The expected contribution to practice comprises a reference model which enables software-training providers to design productivity-optimized TMLS.

References

1. Arthur, W.J., Bennett, W.J., Edens, P.S., Bell, S.T.: Effectiveness of training in organizations: A meta-analysis of design and evaluation features. Journal of Applied Psychology 88, 234 (2003)
2. Lowendahl, J.-M.: Hype Cycle for Education. Gartner, Stamford (2012)
3. MBB: Weiterbildung und Digitales Lernen heute und in drei Jahren: Mobile und vernetzte Szenarien im Aufwind (2011), http://www.wainhouse.com/images/reports/wrdistedelearnv1.pdf
4. AES: Weiterbildungsverhalten in Deutschland (2010)
5. Gupta, S., Bostrom, R.P., Huber, M.: End-user training methods: what we know, need to know. ACM SIGMIS Database 41, 9–39 (2008)
6. Gupta, S., Bostrom, R.P.: Technology-Mediated Learning: A Comprehensive Theoretical Model. Journal of the Association for Information Systems 10, 686–714 (2009)
7. Lehtinen, E., Hakkarainen, K., Lipponen, L., Rahikainen, M., Muukkonen, H.: Computer supported collaborative learning: A review. The JHGI Giesbers Reports on Education 10 (1999)
8. Alavi, M., Leidner, D.E.: Review: Knowledge management and knowledge management systems: Conceptual foundations and research issues. MIS Quarterly, 107–136 (2001)
9. Sasidharan, S., Santhanam, R.: Technology-based training. Human-computer interaction and management information systems: applications 6, 247 (2006)
10. Parasuraman, A.: Service quality and productivity: a synergistic perspective. Managing Service Quality 12, 6–9 (2002)
11. Grönroos, C., Ojasalo, K.: Service productivity: Towards a conceptualization of the transformation of inputs into economic results in services. Journal of Business Research 57, 414–423 (2004)
12. Garrison, D.R., Kanuka, H.: Blended learning: Uncovering its transformative potential in higher education. The Internet and Higher Education 7, 95–105 (2004)
13. Singh, H.: Building effective blended learning programs. Educational Technology 43, 51–54 (2003)
14. Compeau, D.R., Higgins, C.A.: Application of social cognitive theory to training for computer skills. Information Systems Research 6, 118–143 (1995)
15. Hevner, A.R., March, S.T., Park, J., Ram, S.: Design Science in Information Systems Research. MIS Quarterly 28, 75–105 (2004)

16. Schön, D.A.: The reflective practitioner: How professionals think in action. Basic Books (1984)
17. Simon, H.A.: The sciences of the artificial. The MIT Press (1996)
18. Becker, J., Schütte, R.: Handelsinformationssysteme. Verl. Moderne Industrie (1996)
19. Ahlemann, F., Riempp, G.: RefMod: A Conceptual Reference Model for Project Management Information Systems. Wirtschaftsinformatik 50, 88–97 (2008)
20. Takeda, H., Veerkamp, P., Yoshikawa, H.: Modeling design process. AI Magazine 11, 37 (1990)
21. Yin, R.K.: Case study research: Design and methods. Sage Publications, Inc. (2009)
22. McLaughlin, C.P., Coffey, S.: Measuring productivity in services. International Journal of Service Industry Management 1, 46–64 (1990)
23. Bitzer, P., Bittner, E.A., Leimeister, J.M.: Identifying a set of relevant input and output factors for a knowledge intensive service within a productivity model for educational services, Hamburg, Germany (2011)
24. Compeau, D.R., Higgins, C.A.: Computer self-efficacy: Development of a measure and initial test. Mis Quarterly, 189–211 (1995)
25. Fitzsimmons, J.A., Fitzsimmons, M.J.: Service management: Operations, strategy, and information technology. McGraw-Hill New York (2006)
26. Bitzer, P., Wegener, R., Leimeister, J.M.: Entwicklung eines Produktivitätsmodells zur Systematisierung von Lerndienstleistungen, Leipzig, Germany (2010)
27. Meise, V.: Ordnungsrahmen zur prozessorientierten Organisationsgestaltung. Kovač (2001)
28. Schlagheck, B.: Objektorientierte Referenzmodelle für das Prozess-und Projektcontrolling. Dt. Univ.-Verlag (2000)

A Framework for Classifying Design Research Methods

Dan Harnesk and Devinder Thapa

Division of Computer and Systems Science
Luleå Tekniska Universitet, Luleå
{dan.harnesk,devinder.thapa}@ltu.se

Abstract. Design Science Research (DSR) methods are much debated by the IS community with regard to outcome and research process. This debate creates ambiguity for the novice researchers in terms of selecting appropriate DSR methods. To address this ambiguity, this essay proposes a framework for classifying the DSR methods by providing conceptual clarity about DSR outcome and DSR research process. The proposed framework creates a taxonomy differentiating between outcomes as *a priori* formulated or *emergent* through contextual interaction, likewise, viewing the research process as *deductive* or *abductive*. The taxonomy provides guidance to the researchers before embarking any DSR projects. The essay contributes to the on-going discussion on utilization of the DSR methods in DSR projects.

Keywords: Design Science Research, Framework, Methods.

1   Introduction

While the IS design community agrees that IS design research methods are meant for developing scientific knowledge about artificial artifacts or processes but at the same time providing organizations with relevant practical solutions [1-5], the literature seems preoccupied with prescribing different intervention styles [6]. One type of intervention in design research typically proceeds along á priori defined software engineering approach comprising a set of activities to solve a known problem [3]. Other types of design research deals with a mixture of technical and organizational properties that dynamically and iteratively "emerge from design, use, and on-going refinement in context" [5] (p.38). Despite the difference in epistemology of these two views of design research both, however, seek to articulate generic design principles by generating prescriptive design knowledge [7].

While such instrumental goal is unquestionable, scholars have recognized the difficulty with methods in use. For example, proponents of design science research refer to the problem of differentiating between design research methods advocating that, "methodologies presents the researcher with choices for the structure of the research process and the presentation of the resulting solution" [8] (p.72). As design research involves the unfolding of changing ideas over time it is crucial for the researcher to be reflexive about his role and perspective when launching the study [9]. However, the

J. vom Brocke et al. (Eds.): DESRIST 2013, LNCS 7939, pp. 479–485, 2013.

question is how researchers go about turning implicit design research assumptions – unavailable to their conscious awareness – into explicit stance recognizing potential consequences of selecting a certain design research method. In line with the argument, this essay deals with how to distinguish between design research methods. We draw from seminal work in Design Science (DS) [3], Action Design Research (ADR) [5], Action Research (AR) [10], Dialogical Action Research (DAR) [11], and Engaged Scholarship [9] to identify and describe relevant dimensions that guide researchers to appropriate adoption of design research methods. Based on these seminal papers, we derived a framework that is described in the subsequent section.

2   Classification Framework

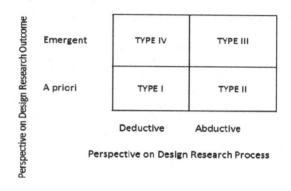

Fig. 1. A Framework to Classify DSR Methods

Two-dimensional typology diagrams are used in IS research to describe characteristics of a phenomenon. In particular, it is a representation of the assumptions about the nature of the phenomenon under study, see, e.g. [12, 13]. Given our review of the design research literature it is possible to adopt a similar characterization and viewing design research outcome from the two positions: à priori and emergent. Likewise, the design research process can be characterized as: deductive and abductive (figure 1), which are two common ways of reasoning about scientific knowledge discovery in IS DSR [14].

2.1   Type I Deductive – Á Priori

The type I design research methods, typically DS methods, represent a perspective that is firmly rooted in the positivistic research orientation, and thus contain informing elements suggesting ways to maintain control over design parameters [3]. Deductive-á priori oriented researchers assume the social world to be composed of stable empirical IT artefacts. In particular, they assume that an instance of an IT artefact is a proof of concept, and that the involvement of clients may, but not necessarily, have a positive effect on the outcome. Typical activities of type I methods are (a) classification and systematization of the instantiation, and (b) formalization. The purpose with classification is to create a class model that explains how the pre-defined problem should be solved. Systematization activities include specification of conditions controlling the events of the artefact and the variables that affect the artefact in use. Formalization is an approach for developing a conceptual scheme drawing on the consensus of the research team that further lead way into implementation activities. The researcher is also in control over evaluation of the artefact, which is conducted with experimental methods.

2.2   Type II Abductive – Á Priori

In this position the researcher adhere to the proof of concept idea through á priori designable artefacts. However, complexity of controlling changing contextual circumstances infers uncertainty about the nature of the problem. Although research methods, such as AR adhere to the regulative principles of positivism, they embody descriptions for analysing subjective opinions of the social world in which the IT artefact is situated [10, 11]. Using a type II method means that the researcher is reasoning about the real world problem to develop the richest possible descriptions so as to excel in design activities. Type II methods are used for both improvement actions and construction interventions, but has as [4] notes been used in studies of technology adoption rather that building technology. In cases where IT design has been in focus, evaluation of the IT artefact would, in contrast to type I methods, separate empirical tests from evaluation and learning.

2.3   Type III Abductive – Emergent

Access to clients is significant feature of type III design research methods. Research methods in this orientation oppose regulative steps and espouse creativity. With access to clients and hence their context researchers can draw from a broad spectrum of requirements to elaborate upon. Underlying type III methods rest the core notion that technology and organization interact during design in so far that design outcome is a result of emergent perspective on design, use, and refinement in context. Using Type III methods means formulating conjectures - that can be shaped into sharp propositions - rather than explicating hypothesis. ADR is a typical design research method representing the view of continuous stakeholder participation in the research project. Different stakeholders examine the propositions iteratively together with researchers to define and redefine options for the design.

2.4   Type IV Deductive – Emergent

Type IV research methods may seem unrealistic because of the mutual exclusive nature of the deductive – emergent position. However, design research are emerging where the researcher have control only over the meta-artefact and the research problem. An instance is released to audiences with control over empirical test and evaluation & learning. IT design under the flag of open innovation strongly emphasized in the so called Living Lab and 'crowd sourcing' research projects enable the emergence of concepts leading to innovative solutions involving users as co-creators [15]. As researchers consign test of the artefact to a community of which they have no control, the transferring of design data back and forth between researchers and the community is the critical passage point [16]. In essence, this will limit evaluation task, as pre-stated design hypothesis cannot be tested because of the dominance of summative evaluation before formal approaches.

3   Implications of the Proposed Framework

3.1   Implication for Problem Definition

While selecting DSR method, first and foremost criteria are to define the research problem. Defining or formulating the problem itself can be well structured or ill-structured where problem definition can emerge in interaction with the context [12]. As per the suggested framework, in Type I DSR method, problem is defined by researcher focusing on the existing 'gap of knowledge'. The gap can be understood through literature review, or understanding the practitioner's background. Likewise, in Type II, problem is defined by researcher together with practitioner in-situ. Empirical research such as case study can be conducted to understand and formulate the research problem. In Type III, the problem is defined in conjunction with contextual conditions like in type II, but in this type the problem itself can emerge with the progression of the research. The process goes through various discursive phases to check the relevance of the defined problem. In terms of Type IV DSR methods, the problem is defined like in Type I, however, the problem can emerge in a manner independent of primary researcher that can thus be one peculiar characteristic compare to Type I.

3.2   Implication for Evaluation

The evaluative or reflective approaches can be applied to construct the outcome. The evaluative in this context refers to evaluation of the outcome as the final undertaking of the research, whereas, reflective refers to evaluation as an iterative process of the research. As per suggested framework, design research of Type I, can be referred as artificial evaluative approach [17]. It produces planned outcomes that can be anticipated by reference to any a priori design. In this case, a researcher does not care to test the artefact in various contexts and reflect in the social settings. They typically take a distanced and outside perspective to maintain impartiality and legitimacy, or very controlled field evaluation.

Type II research methods uses naturalistic evaluation where research is conducted to evaluate artefacts (constructs, methods, policies, programs, or models) pre-set by designer's for solving practical problems. This kind of research focuses mainly on describing, explaining, and obtaining evidence-based knowledge of the practical problems that supposed to be solved. In terms of the engaged scholarship model [9], these decisions include the purpose of the evaluation study (problem formulation), the criteria and models used to evaluate the program in question (research design), and how study findings will be analysed, interpreted and used (problem solving). Type II suggests that engagement of stakeholders is important so that they have opportunities to influence and consent to those evaluation study decisions that may affect them. The outcome of these design research methods as a proof of concept can be useful in the field evaluation of conceptual artefact.

Design research methods of Type III use naturalistic [17] evaluation where criteria are adjustable. It produces outcome that may exhibit emergent features of numerous local actions (e.g. use, interpretation, negotiation and redesign), but these emergent features cannot be anticipated by reference to any a priori design. These kinds of research suggest that the researcher should engage with practitioner while making intervention in an organizational context. For example, action design research advocates that building of an artefact, intervention of the artefact, and evaluation of the artefact should be done as an iterative research process, but not as a final undertaking. The foundation of these methods is to learning through action and reflection in organizational settings. A researcher directly involves in context and utilizes their knowledge to formulate and solve the applied problems. However, this knowledge may not apply or may require substantial adaption to fit the ill-structured or context-specific nature of the client's problem. Furthermore, it is suggested that the only way to understand a social system is to change it through deliberate intervention and reflection through experiences. These kinds of methods may require intensive training, and consulting by the researcher with people in the client's setting.

Type IV, also uses naturalistic evaluation where the criteria is set by 'the users' on the fly. Evaluation of the artefact is done as an iterative research process but in a fuzzy environment (e.g. crowd sourcing and living lab). The foundation of these methods is to learning through action and reflection in natural-experimental settings. A researcher doesn't directly involve in context, rather users utilizes their knowledge to formulate and try to formulate the solutions to the emerging problems.

3.3   Implication for Theorizing

In this framework, design research of Type I and Type IV can apply deductive method that involves arriving at a 'result' based on applying a 'rule' or hypothesis to a case. These kinds of methods use variance model to make causal or conditional relationships among variables of units that are sampled, measured, and analysed. The outcome of this strategy will lead to meta-artefacts that can instantiated to context specific artefacts. Design science research method of Type II and Type III falls in the abductive (iterative cycle of deduction and induction) category, which is an inferential procedure in which we create a conjecture that, if it were correct, would contribute to the understanding of ill-structured problem of the world. Abduction entails creative insight that can combine the rigor and relevance to provide solution to the practical problems [14]. This strategy applies process model that seeks the answers to the questions like how things change and develop over time. The outcome of this strategy starts from instantiated artefacts that are gradually generalized to class of meta-artefacts. As suggested by [9], it requires longitudinal data because collecting primary data, building relationships with people in the field took long time.

4   Conclusions

Selection of an appropriate design science research method is vital before embarking any design research project; however, guidelines for selecting a DSR method need more attention. To address this need, the paper proposed a framework that characterizes the relationship between IS design research outcome: à priori and emergent, and IS design research process: deductive and abductive. Viewing through the two dimensional matric, the framework provides guidelines particularly to the beginners in the DSR research to make decision about which design research method to utilize in the DSR project. The research is still in progress; furthermore, more in-depth review of the seminal work as well as empirical research will be conducted to warrant the usefulness of the framework and development of key criteria for the selection of DSR method.

Acknowledgements. We kindly thank Professor Tero Päivärinta for his valuable input and feedback during the writing process.

References

1. March, S.T., Smith, G.F.: Design and natural science research on information technology. Decision Support Systems 15(4), 251–266 (1995)
2. Walls, J., Widmeyer, G., El Sawy, O.: Building an information systems theory for vigilant EIS. Information Systems Research 3(1), 36–59 (1992)
3. Hevner, A.R., et al.: Design Science in Information Systems Research. In: MIS Quarterly 2004. MIS Quarterly & The Society for Information Management, pp. 75–105 (2004)
4. Livari, J.: A Paradigmatic Analysis of Information Systems As a Design Science. Scandinavian Journal of Information Systems 19(2), 39–64 (2007)
5. Sein, M.K., et al.: Action Design Research. MIS Quarterly 35(1), 19 (2011)
6. Alturki, A., Gable, G., Bandara, W.: A design science research roadmap. Service-Oriented Perspectives in Design Science Research, 107–123 (2011)
7. Aanestad, M.: What If Design Is Something Else: The Challenges of Dealing with Interdependencies. In: Keller, C., Wiberg, M., Ågerfalk, P.J., Eriksson Lundström, J.S.Z., et al. (eds.) SCIS 2012. LNBIP, vol. 124, pp. 95–108. Springer, Heidelberg (2012)
8. Peffer, K., et al.: A Design Science Research Methodology for Information Systems Research. Journal of Management Information Systems 24(3), 45–77 (2007)
9. Van de Ven, A.: Engaged Scholarship: Creating Knowledge for Science and Practice. Oxford University Press, New York (2007)
10. Baskerville, R., Wood-Harper, A.T.: Diversity in Information Systems Research Methods. European Journal of Information Systems 7(2), 17 (1998)
11. Mårtensson, P., Lee, A.: Dialogical Action Research at Omega Corporation. MIS Quarterly 28(3), 29 (2004)
12. Pries-Heje, J., Baskerville, R., Venable, J.R.: Strategies for Design Science Research Evaluation. In: ECIS 2008 Proceedings (2008)
13. Hirschheim, R., Klein, H.K.: Four paradigms of information systems development. Communications of the ACM 32(10), 1199–1216 (1989)

14. Fischer, C., Gregor, S.: Forms of reasoning in the design science research process. In: Jain, H., Sinha, A.P., Vitharana, P. (eds.) DESRIST 2011. LNCS, vol. 6629, pp. 17–31. Springer, Heidelberg (2011)
15. Fölstad, A.: Towards a Living Lab For the Development of Online Community Services. The Electronic Journal for Virtual Organizations and Networks 10(Special Issue in Living Labs) (2008)
16. Bergvall-Kareborn, B., Hoist, M., Stahlbrost, A.: Concept Design with a Living Lab Approach. In: System Sciences, in 42nd Hawaii International Conference on HICSS 2009 (2009)
17. Venable, J., Pries-Heje, J., Baskerville, R.: A comprehensive framework for evaluation in design science research. In: Peffers, K., Rothenberger, M., Kuechler, B. (eds.) DESRIST 2012. LNCS, vol. 7286, pp. 423–438. Springer, Heidelberg (2012)

Constructing Software-Intensive Methods: A Design Science Research Process with Early Feedback Cycles

Robert Krawatzeck[1], Marcus Hofmann[1], Frieder Jacobi[1], and Barbara Dinter[2]

[1] Chemnitz University of Technology, Chemnitz, Germany
{robert.krawatzeck,marcus.hofmann,frieder.jacobi}
@wirtschaft.tu-chemnitz.de
[2] University of Erlangen-Nuremberg, Erlangen-Nuremberg, Germany
barbara.dinter@wiso.uni-erlangen.de

Abstract. Methods are a common artifact within design science research (DSR). In the context of a research project we faced the challenge to develop a method and a software artifact in parallel. However, existing work in DSR and method engineering does not explicitly address the simultaneous development of two interdependent artifacts. Therefore, we developed a DSR process that allows the construction of so-called software-intensive methods. It considers the interdependencies of both artifacts and optimizes common DSR processes by including early feedback cycles for intermediate results - allowing the identification of initial design weaknesses like missing or dispensable design elements, inappropriate element design and usability flaws. The process has been applied and its feasibility has been demonstrated in the research project.

Keywords: design science, research process, method engineering, software prototype, early feedback, generate-test cycle.

1 Motivation and Problem Statement

Methods are a major and approved means for organizational engineering in information systems research by providing detailed, goal-oriented descriptions of activities which have to be performed in order to solve a specific problem [1]. The construction is methodologically supported (amongst others) by generic design science research (DSR) processes, such as proposed by [2], and by method engineering [3]. Sometimes the application of a method requires extensive use of software artifacts. In such cases, the method should provide instructions describing the role of the software artifact within the method. If the required software artifact does not exist at the time of method construction, it should be developed simultaneously. We call such a method a software-intensive method (SIM). The construction of a SIM combines the disciplines of information systems research and software engineering (SE).

For two years we are working on a research project [4] in the context of IT system documentation. Throughout our research project aiming at constructing a SIM we

J. vom Brocke et al. (Eds.): DESRIST 2013, LNCS 7939, pp. 486–493, 2013.

realized that the simultaneous development of a method and a corresponding software artifact is not well covered by generic DSR processes. This observation resulted in the following research question: How can the construction of a SIM be supported by a DSR process that explicitly considers the simultaneous development of a method and of a software artifact?

In order to answer this question we have designed a SIM-specific DSR process by 'recursively' applying the generic DSR process as proposed in [2]. We have demonstrated its feasibility in the aforementioned research project. The remainder of the paper is organized as follows: After a short presentation of our research project we discuss the need for a SIM-specific research process in more detail (Section 2). By means of a generic DSR process we develop the SIM-specific DSR process in Section 3. Its demonstration in the context of our research project is presented in Section 4. Concluding, the findings are summarized and an outlook to further research is given (Section 5).

2   Situation and Project Presentation

The third party funded research project "Computer-Aided Data Warehouse Engineering" (CAWE) runs for three years (currently in its third year) with four researchers. The project aims at constructing a method for cost-efficient, high-quality, user-specific IT systems documentation, realized exemplarily for business intelligence (BI) systems [4]. Analyzing the state of the art has shown that no suitable software artifacts (tools) exist which cover the system documentation tasks comprehensively. Thus, the need to simultaneously develop such an artifact has emerged. A prototype has been implemented and presented to the scientific community [5] and practitioners. Currently, we construct the method for automated BI system documentation using the prototype.

We checked the domains of DSR, method engineering, and SE for adequate methodologies for SIM construction. However, existing DSR approaches [e.g. 2, 6] are of limited benefit, since they are too generic and do not address the simultaneous development of multiple artifacts as it is required for a SIM. Applying a generic DSR process would result in cycling the process (semi-)sequentially several times (in our case twice). In addition, the mutual and/or combined evaluation of the artifacts would be deferred to the final stages of the design and development process. If potential design weaknesses are not detected before the final evaluation, the adaptation of artifacts will be costly (in terms of time and money) since design, development, and evaluation activities have to be repeated.

Also, method engineering [3, 7] does not consider the interdependencies of a SIM and its corresponding software artifact. SE methods on the other hand describe in detail how to develop the software artifact but do not take into account how to construct the method. The missing support for the SIM construction in our concrete case and the observation that many projects in research and practice face the same problem have underlined the need for answering the research question as formulated in Section 1.

3   Design of a Research Process for the Construction of a SIM

We followed the DSR process as introduced by [2] to design a research process for the SIM construction. The steps are described briefly in the following.

3.1   Problem Identification and Motivation

The relevance of supporting the construction of SIMs has already been motivated in Sections 1 and 2. As previous contributions do not address the simultaneous development of artifacts (and of a method and a software artifact in particular) this research gap has to be closed.

3.2   Objectives of the Solution

Keeping in mind that costly steps should not be repeated during the construction of a SIM, and that early evidence about the SIM usability should be gained, evaluable intermediate results should be available as soon as possible. Those intermediate results aim at providing

- early information about initial design weaknesses like missing or dispensable design elements, inappropriate element design and usability flaws caused by design decisions (objective A) and
- insights, if the method will be superior compared to existing solutions (objective B).

Such information allows early, incremental adaptation instead of late and expensive changes. Consequently, the SIM research process should consider early intermediate results in the design and development process. A further objective is its applicability in other projects (both, in research and practice).

3.3   Design and Development

We are using the DSR process by Peffers et al. [2] not only to design and develop the research process for SIM construction. It also constitutes an appropriate starting point for our research question, i.e. we will modify this process by adding activities for the simultaneous development of a SIM and its supporting software artifact. Therefore, we adapt the activities as proposed by [2] and combine them with the "generate/test cycle" as proposed by [6]. The generate/test cycle allows early feedback cycles as also known from agile software development methods [8]. Those feedback cycles are necessary to ensure early information about initial design weaknesses and meet objective A.

Developing a method and the corresponding software being of use when applying the method can be supported by a model which describes and connects the business problem and software solution space [1]. Figure 1 exemplarily shows an extract of such a model which connects the domains *BI* and *Documentation*. Such a model can, for example, be specified using the Unified Modeling Language (UML) as known from SE. The model – in terms of a framework – can be used to develop the software prototype by instantiation and the method by construction. Since the model is a crucial part within the method development, its suitability and possible contribution should be proven early (objective B). According to [6], one option to evaluate artifacts is to compare the usefulness of the created artifacts against the usefulness of other existing artifacts which solve the same problem. If such other models are known and accessible, the evaluation can be performed at that time. Otherwise the evaluation has to be done indirectly via the model-based software prototype and the comparison with other software solutions. If the model is extensive, it might suffice to develop a vertical prototype which covers all model elements but not the whole business problem space.

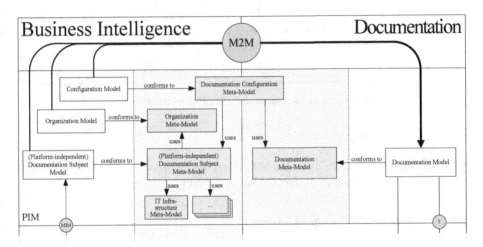

Fig. 1. Exemplary extract of a model which serves as the basis for software prototype development and method construction [4]

The considerations lead to the following SIM-specific DSR process (cf. Fig. 2). After the problem identification and motivation (1) objectives have to be defined (2). Thereafter, a model (3) has to be developed with regard to the objectives. This model describes the problem and solution spaces and connects them. In order to prove that the developed model is suitable, a software prototype will be instantiated based on the model (4). This prototype constitutes the basis for demonstrating the feasibility and serves as the starting point for the subsequent comparative evaluation (5). Positive evaluation results underline the suitability of the model as a basis for the method aimed at. The steps 3 to 5 should be repeated until the model suitability is proven (corresponds to the generate/test cycle as proposed by [6]). If so, the method based on this model can be constructed (6). This will be achieved by assigning all elements described in the model (e.g. the Configuration Model; cf. Fig. 1) to different stakeholder roles involved and formulating activities as well as necessary deliverables [3]. Finally, the method can be evaluated e.g. in form of case studies (7) which terminates the process if the result is positive. Otherwise, the process has to be repeated, starting from step 2, 3, or 6, depending on the weaknesses identified during the evaluation. The main modifications of the initial, generic DSR process by [2] refer to the steps 3 to 5.

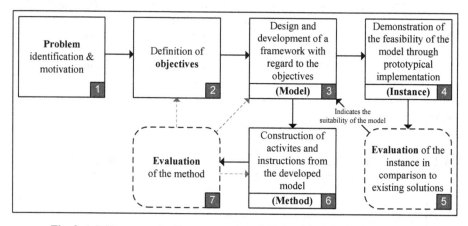

Fig. 2. A DSR process for the construction of SIMs with early feedback cycles

3.4   Demonstration

We demonstrate the feasibility of the SIM construction process in detail in Section 4 by applying it in the research project CAWE and therefore refer to this section.

3.5   Evaluation and Communication

Since this paper presents work-in-progress, not all research activities have been conducted at the time of writing. The research process will be evaluated by case studies and expert interviews. Communication will take place mainly by means of research papers, starting with this contribution.

4   Demonstration of the Feasibility through the Project CAWE

In this section a case study is presented to demonstrate the feasibility of the suggested research process. It is based on the research project introduced in Section 2.

Step 1: Problem Identification and Motivation. By means of an online survey, the CAWE project has identified three reasons why enterprises document the architecture components of BI systems insufficiently or not at all [4]: (I) The costs of the documentation creation are too high, (II) the durability of the documentation is too low, and (III) the lacking suitability of the structure and content of the documentation for different audiences. These shortcomings motivate the following research goal of the project [4]: Development of a method for BI system documentation.

An analysis of the software market has shown that no tool exists that can document BI systems comprehensively in an automated manner. Furthermore, existing software solutions for specific BI system layers document insufficiently [9]. Hence, not only a method but also a software artifact is needed to attain the research goal.

Step 2: Description of Objectives. In face of the aforementioned reasons why enterprises document their BI system architecture components insufficiently or not at all, the following objectives of a solution were defined [4]: The method aimed at should provide a possibility to generate documentation in a cost-efficient manner (objective I), being of high-quality (objective II), and user-specific (objective III).

Step 3: Design and Development of a Framework. Since previous studies have shown that the costs for the generation of documentation for multidimensional data structures – as one part of BI systems – using automated documentation processes can be reduced by up to 75% [10], an automated approach for meeting objective I has been chosen [4]. To meet objective II we decided to fulfill the eight criteria for high-quality documentation as suggested by Wallmüller [11]: changeability, up-to-dateness, clarity, identifiability, norm-conformity, comprehensibility, completeness and consistency. In order to consider different user needs (objective III), Wallmüller [11] further suggests to generate different instances of the documentation which are customized according to the interests of the audience. However, not all criteria of high-quality documentation are necessarily different for different audiences. Therefore, the criteria were divided into audience-dependent (called document criteria, such as completeness) and audience-independent criteria (so-called creation process criteria, such as changeability) [4]. The decision to use automation was applied to both criteria groups because the quality of the documentation as well as the user-specific content shall be achieved without high costs.

Subsequently, a model in form of a framework which describes the domains "BI systems" and "documentation" (cf. Fig. 1) has been designed and developed [4]. We decided to use the Model-driven Architecture (MDA) approach for automating the documentation process and for linking both domains.

By applying the automated generation of documentation directly on reverse-engineered BI application models, all creation process criteria are fulfilled. For generating audience-specific documentation, new models have been introduced to ensure the configuration ability. This configuration approach allows an audience-specific adjustment of the provided content [4].

Step 4: Demonstration of the Feasibility through a Software Prototype. In order to demonstrate the feasibility of the developed framework through a prototypical instantiation, the framework for the documentation has been limited to ETL (extraction, transformation, and loading) processes in BI systems [9]. This limitation allows the implementation of a vertical prototype, which covers all proposed model elements without the effort of implementing all BI system layers. Consequently, the vertical prototype can be used to gather practitioners' feedback and allows a comparative evaluation against existing ETL documentation tools.

Subsequently, a prototype for the automated generation of user-specific ETL documentation has been implemented and presented to the scientific community [5] and practitioners. Several shortcomings become obvious, resulting from practitioners' feedback and consolidated implementation experiences: a) It is not always possible to clearly assign a particular BI tool to a specific BI layer (inappropriate design), b) a central starting point, combining all available BI layer information, for analysis is missing (missing design element), and c) the proposed configuration can be implemented in general, but is too complex to be done by business users (usability problem of the design). These shortcomings have been considered within the early adoption of the initial designed framework, even before the method construction has been started.

Step 5: Comparative Evaluation. The prototype allows comparing the artifacts generated during the automated documentation against generated the ones by other documentation tools. The criteria for the comparison have been derived from the aforementioned objectives.

Different ETL modeling tools – namely the built-in documentation components of IBM DataStage and Talend Open Studio as well as the third-party tools SSIS Documenter and BI Documenter – were investigated with regard to their ability of automatically generating documentation [9]. Due to the restricted selection of automated solutions for documentation generation, all investigated tools, including our prototype, fulfill the objective for cost-efficiency (objective I) as well as the creation process criteria (first part of objective II). However, our prototype achieved significant improvements in the field of document criteria (second part of objective II) by means of meta-data analysis. Furthermore, our prototype is apparently the only tool providing the option for user-specific configuration (objective III).

Consequently, the former argumentation allowed us to conclude that the prototype is superior to other existing documentation solutions. Since the evaluated artifacts have been generated based on the developed framework, it is deducible that the framework itself provides additional benefit. Thus, it forms an adequate basis for the construction of the method for cost-efficient generation of BI system documentation.

Step 6 and 7: Method Construction & Final Evaluation. The project CAWE currently is in the phase of method construction. At the moment, the method covers activities required to fulfill objective III as formulated in Section 4.2, e.g. audiences should create and maintain their individual configuration models (cf. Fig. 1) before the automated documentation process can be started. The resulting method will be evaluated in form of case studies with industry partners who have already been involved in the research process. Finally, since the SIM-specific modification of the research process only affects steps 3 to 5, the steps 6 and 7 are conducted as described in [2].

5   Conclusion and Further Work

The paper suggests a DSR process for the construction of SIMs contributing to information systems research by enabling helpful feedback within early development stages. Thus, potential design mistakes become aware early and can be fixed with manageable effort and time, which leads to a more efficient but still rigorous design process and more suitable solutions in the field. The feasibility and advantages of the research process were demonstrated within a case study.

Since the presented work is in progress, further steps have to be performed. The demonstration will be enhanced by further case studies using similar research projects developing a SIM. In addition, the benefits of the suggested SIM research process in contrast to cycle generic DSR processes twice will be evaluated by expert interviews.

Acknowledgements. This research has been partly funded by the European Social Fund and the Federal State of Saxony, Germany.

References

1. March, S.T., Smith, G.F.: Design and Natural Science Research on Information Technology. Decision Support Systems 15(4), 251–266 (1995)
2. Peffers, K., Tuunanen, T., Rothenberger, M., Chatterjee, S.: A Design Science Research Methodology for Information Systems Research. J. of MIS 24(3), 45–77 (2007)
3. Brinkkemper, S.: Method Engineering: Engineering of Information Systems Development Methods and Tools. J. of Information and Software Technology 38(4), 275–280 (1996)
4. Krawatzeck, R., Jacobi, F., Müller, A., Hofmann, M.: Konzeption eines Frameworks zur automatisierten Erstellung nutzerspezifischer IT-Systemdokumentationen. In: Workshop Business Intelligence 2011 (WSBI 2011) der GI-Fachgruppe BI, pp. 15–26. CEUR (2011)
5. Krawatzeck, R., Jacobi, F., Hofmann, M.: CAWE DW Documenter: A Model-Driven Tool for Customizable ETL Documentation Generation. In: Castano, S., Vassiliadis, P., Lakshmanan, L.V., Lee, M.L. (eds.) ER 2012 Workshops 2012. LNCS, vol. 7518, pp. 400–403. Springer, Heidelberg (2012)
6. Hevner, A.R., March, S.T., Park, J., Ram, S.: Design Science in Information Systems Research. MIS Quarterly 28(1), 75–105 (2004)
7. Braun, C., Wortmann, F., Hafner, M., Winter, R.: Method Construction – A Core Approach to Organizational Engineering. In: 20th Annual ACM Symposium on Applied Computing (SAC 2005), pp. 1295–1299. ACM Press, New York (2005)
8. Jeffries, R., Jeffries, R.E., Anderson, A.: Extreme Programming Installed. Addison-Wesley, Amsterdam (2000)
9. Jacobi, F., Krawatzeck, R., Hofmann, M.: Meeting the Need for ETL Documentation: A Model-driven Framework for Customizable Documentation Generation. In: 18th Americas Conference on Information Systems (AMCIS 2012), Paper 23. AISeL (2012)
10. Gluchowski, P., Kurze, C.: Modellierung und Dokumentation von BI-Systemen. Controlling 22, 676–682 (2010)
11. Wallmüller, E.: Software-Qualitätsmanagement in der Praxis: Software-Qualität durch Führung und Verbesserung von Software-Prozessen, 2nd edn. Hanser Fachbuch, Munich (2001)

User Guidance for Document-Driven Processes in Enterprise Systems

Stefan Morana[1], Silvia Schacht[2], Ansgar Scherp[3], and Alexander Mädche[1,2]

[1] Institute for Enterprise Systems, University of Mannheim, Germany
morana@es.uni-mannheim.de
[2] Chair of Information Systems IV, Business School, University of Mannheim, Germany
{schacht,maedche}@es.uni-mannheim.de
[3] Research Group Data and Web Science, University of Mannheim, Germany
ansgar@informatik.uni-mannheim.de

Abstract. In practice up to 80% of the overall processed data is only available in an unstructured form, such as documents. The handling of documents within organizations is still an issue in both, research and practice. Employees perceive the way to handle business-relevant documents as high effort and struggle with handling documents compliant to organizational standards. As a result documents become decoupled from the defined business processes and scattered all over the organizations IT landscape. Understanding users and their needs in order to increase their intention to use Enterprise Systems consistent to organization-wide business processes is a gap in the existing literature. This paper presents a design science research project focusing on user guidance for document-driven processes in Enterprise Systems. Building on existing research in user guidance, we suggest to increase the user's individual awareness towards processing documents consistent to organizational processes. In addition to our research design, we present a preliminary artifact version based on the results of an exploratory interview study.

Keywords: Enterprise Systems, Enterprise Content Management, User Guidance, Intention to Use.

1 Introduction

Enterprise Systems (ES) offer a comprehensive set of functional modules that are generally based on industry best practices [1]. In contrast to traditional information systems (IS), ES target large-scale integration of data and business processes across a company's functional areas [2]. In the literature, the term ES is often used synonymously with Enterprise Resource Planning (ERP) application software focusing on streamlining business processes and the associated structured data. This rather transaction- and process-oriented perspective has been extended with packages targeting large-scale integration of structured and unstructured information and people. Accordingly, the term ES has grown to refer to all large organization-wide packaged applications, also including systems such as, Customer Relationship Management, Data

J. vom Brocke et al. (Eds.): DESRIST 2013, LNCS 7939, pp. 494–501, 2013.

Warehouses and Business Intelligence, Enterprise Content Management (ECM), Portals, Groupware, and application components of the software platform such as application servers or Business Process management engines on which these application systems are built [3].

In practice up to 80% of the overall processed data is only available in an unstructured form [4]. In particular, employees use, create and store different types of documents such as offers, invoices, contracts and others as part of their work practices. Ideally, the organization-wide defined business processes and the work practices should go hand in hand. However, due to complexity and lack in understanding of organization-wide business processes, a divergence can be observed in reality. Thus, documents are filed at many places, but often not at those locations where the organization intends them to be stored. Documents become decoupled from the defined business processes and scattered all over the organizations IT landscape. In order to prevent such scattering of documents containing information, which may be crucial for organizations [5], many companies have implemented technologies like Enterprise Content Management systems (ECMS) [6] supporting their employees in managing documents. ECM has also risen interested in research, subsuming studies on Content Management in general and Document Management in specific [7] . Some researchers also settle ECM into the field of Knowledge Management (KM), *"...since ECMSs can be used to capture and utilize content that contains explicit knowledge in repositories or to manage organizational knowledge resources"*[8], p. 2.

However, most existing research on ECM concentrates their work on the architecture of ECMS and their capabilities. Some researchers study the implementation of ECMS from a strategic perspective (e.g. [6]), while others like vom Brocke et al. [9] focus on a general business-process oriented approach to ECM or observe users' acceptance of ECMS (e.g. [10]) independent from business processes. An essential element that is missing in existing research is addressing the users and their needs in order to increase their intention to use ECMS, or more general ES for document handling, consistent to organization-wide defined business processes. We believe that this is an important factor to be investigated and suggest addressing the identified research gap by the following research question:

How to increase individuals' intention to use Enterprise Systems in order to decrease their effort in handling documents and being compliant to organizational process standards?

The remainder of this paper is structured as following: Section 2 presents the methodological foundations of our research following a design science research approach. In the subsequent section, we describe the identified problem. In Section 4, we sketch a preliminary solution proposal for the identified issues. Finally, we conclude the paper with a short summary and an outlook on future work.

2   Methodology

In order to answer our research question, we follow the design science research approach as described by [11]. Figure 1 shows the general design cycle taken from [11] and its adaption for the research project.

In the **first cycle**, we define and specify our overall research goal. Therefore, we plan to conduct both, a literature study and a case study in order to increase theoretical and practical relevance of our work. In doing so, we aim at getting a clear picture on the state of the art of existing studies and the issues of a case company related to document-handling. As a result of this first cycle, we intend to get an impression of a possible software solution to support users in the usage of ECMS, being compliant to organizational process standards, in the form of a mockup-based prototype. The **second cycle** focusses on the creation of a solution for the issues in document-handling. Through an intensive user study, we extract concrete design principles that may support individuals to use the ECMS in a business compliant manner with less effort. The artifact of the second cycle will be a testable software solution including instantiation of our discovered design principles. The **third and last cycle** serves for the evaluation and refinement of our design principles. An instantiation of our principles in form of a software artifact will be introduced in the case company and users' intention to use the ECMS and their satisfaction will be measured. We finalize our research work by developing a design theory on effective and efficient document-handling.

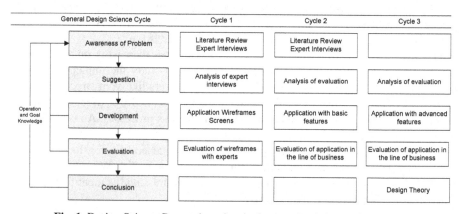

Fig. 1. Design Science Research project in three cycles (adopted from [12])

Our research is done in cooperation with a large manufacturing company. The company is a global supplier, development and service partner for customers of many various sectors such as automotive, civil aviation, and mechanical engineering. In 2011, the company had 12,630 employees in over 45 sites all over Europe and America and sales of more than 1.6 billion €. Since the company is aware of the document management challenges, a joint research project has been started. This enables us to observe individuals' usage behavior directly when using ECMS and triangulate data collection by document analysis and interviews [13]. Furthermore, in subsequent cycles of the design cycle we will have the opportunity to introduce and evaluate the artifact in a real-world environment.

3   Awareness of the Problem

We have conducted a series of informal, illustrative expert interviews with eight, selected users to gain an understanding of the issues on document handling in the case company. One researcher carefully selected the interviewees according to their job description and dependency on ECMS. All interviewees possess various functions in the corporate procurement department of the case company. We perceive the corporate procurement department as representative since many processes of this department highly depend on actual, consistent and complete information captured in documents. Compared to other departments, we assume a higher intention of individuals to use ECMS in order to meet user's requirements on work-related documents by avoiding scattered documents. The interviews were guided by the central question of current issues in handling relevant documents. On average, each interview lasted 15 minutes. With interviewees' consent, we have recorded the interviews that were subsequently transcribed. The resulting documents were coded by one researcher using MaxQDA – a software application for qualitative data analysis. In order to code the interviews, we implemented an inductive coding approach aiming to extract those statements of the interviewees that were mentioned frequently and thus, seemed to be a key issue of them [14]. These issues have been analyzed and aggregated to similar issues.

Within the interviewee series, three topics arose frequently. Most interviewees (six out of eight) perceive the scattering of documents as a main issue of company-wide document handling. Because the company is distributed in multiple sites over Europe and America, various ES are used to handle documents and are implemented in different departments. In order to exchange the documents between the departments, employees are forced to create media disruptions resulting in increased paper-based documents and inconsistent document filing. One interviewee said: *"Invoices are displayed in the system called WebCycle, but we need to print them [...]. Then, it has to be captured and edited in our SAP application. Finally, the paper-based document needs to be filed in our folders."*

Another challenge often mentioned by interviewees is the lack of guidance. The case company has implemented a bundle of ES and recommends using these systems. As stated in Grahlmann et al. [8], the case company's ECMS consist of multiple technological components. There is no clear guidance how the users have to handle the documents in which system(s). Thus, one interviewee called for some *"...guidance, claiming the system which needs to be used in a particular business process step."*

Even if employees know where to file their documents according to company's business processes at a particular point of time, new or modified processes due to changing requirements like governmental regularities also hamper a consistent document management. One interviewee substantiated this impediment by insufficient communication. She stated: *"Our main challenge is the currency of our documents. If there are some novelties, it is difficult to keep our documents up to date since the communication of such novelties tends to be zero. Often we realize such novelties only accidentally."*

All these issues result in an increased effort in handling relevant documents, which in turn leads to a higher reluctance of users to proceed daily work compliant to business processes. In order to reduce the effort of document handling, one interviewee summarized the requirements as following: "*A system needs to be user friendly and enable one to store the documents centrally. Furthermore, all departments should be able to access the documents – if they need to access them – via a consistent user interface. In consequence, all those who are accessing the documents are responsible to keep the documents up-to-date [...] using standards defining where to store which documents accordingly.*"

Summarizing, we realized three key issues discussed by the interviewees: (1) users perceive the way they need to handle business-relevant documents as high effort, (2) users are dissatisfied with the usability of company's ECMS, and (3) users do not know the processes they need to follow in order to handle documents compliant to organizational standards.

4 Solution Proposal

There are probably multiple solutions for the issues stated above. One possible solution was mentioned by an interviewee: guidance. User guidance supporting individuals in their decision of work-related actions has been intensively researched in the past. Scherp [15], for example, researches user guidance when using a highly-interactive, multimedia system called GenLab by providing a tutoring system. Others like Silver [16] study the phenomenon of decisional guidance. In his work, he provides an overview on situations when to implement decisional guidance, its opportunities, design and consequences. Building on this, Todd and Benbasat [17] research on influencing factors of individuals' decision behavior in order to manipulate their effort of decision making using guidance in Decision Support Systems.

Inspired by research in the field of decisional guidance, we belief that providing guidance to users increases the individual's awareness towards processing documents consistent to organizational processes. This increased process-awareness in turn may encourage users to handle documents more compliant to organization-wide defined business processes standards. Finally, the suggested guidance may lead to an increased intention to use of the ECMS and decrease scattering of documents. Building on this work, we propose that guiding employees can be a solution to the presented problem. Figure 2 sketches a preliminary view on the planned artifact. It is inspired by prior work on capturing and sharing best-practices in knowledge intensive activities and synchronizing them with the organizational business processes [18].

The principal goal of the artifact is the support of users in handling documents in their business processes compliant to organizational standards. The artifact builds on a set of preliminary meta-requirements (MRs) derived from the interviews and existing research. The first MR is the **visual depiction of business process steps with guiding information**. As shown in the left hand side of Figure 2, the software artifact provides information about the best-practices for executing a specific process, here the "purchase of raw iron". A process consists of a set of consecutive activities.

The current activity is highlighted, in our example the metal purchase request in SAP. Buttons and links connect the activity with the ES used for accomplishing the activity. This allows the software artifact to seamlessly connect the work practices of the individual knowledge workers to the IT-supported organization's processes. In our example, a specific SAP ERP transaction is required for the metal purchase. Finally, activities can consist of sub-activities. Sub-activities that are executed repeatedly within a specific activity are worth to be captured explicitly in our artifact.

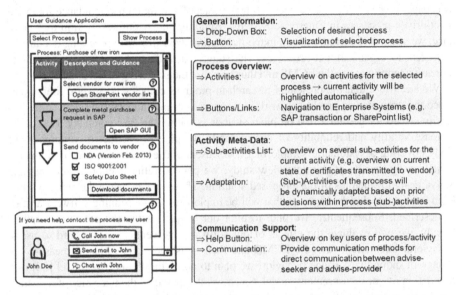

Fig. 2. Process guidance application (runs on user's desktop parallel to existing applications)

The second MR is the **possibility to communicate with key users of the process**. Individual activities can be connected with key users who can be contacted to obtain support for situations where the activity descriptions are not sufficient.

The third MR is the **capturing of individual (best) practices**. The users can arbitrarily modify the order of the activities in the processes. For example, when they experience a situation where the currently captured best-practice deviates from the actual process execution, e. g., when there are changes in the process flow due to legislative changes, updates of the ES, or just specific requirements of a customer. To modify the processes, the users can add new or change or delete existing activities. A key feature of our software artifact will be that such modifications during the execution of a process do not affect other concurrently executed processes [18]. Finally, the modifications made by the users can be incorporated again as best-practices and thus shared and communicated with the co-workers. This flexible management of processes, activities, and sub-activities in our software artifact is achieved by using a specific ontology-based, contextualized representation of the process executions and their models [19].

The implementation of the software artifact will be developed as standalone desktop application. This application will provide ES connectors for our case company. As depicted in Figure 2, the application follows a side panel approach. This enables the guidance application to be displayed next to the existing applications currently used by the employees. By this, context switches between different applications are minimized or even eliminated.

5   Conclusion

This paper presents a design science research project focusing on user guidance for document-driven processes in Enterprise Systems. Building on existing research in user guidance, we suggest to increase user's individual's awareness towards processing documents consistent to organizational processes. The suggested artifact of user guidance aims to increase intention to use the ECMS and thus decrease the scattering of documents.

We are aware that the presented research-in-progress comes with several limitations. Since the presented research is a work in progress, our preliminary interview study primarily served for getting a first problem awareness within the case company. In order to increase validity and reliability of our research, we plan to conduct a comprehensive study covering a systematic sample of ECMS users and experts of the case company. Based on the results of this interview study, we plan to refine meta-requirements and derive design principles of our proposed solution. These design principles will be translated in concrete design decisions that will be implemented in a running software artifact as described. Subsequently, we plan to pilot our artifact within the case organization. Finally, we will evaluate the effects of our software intervention with regard to users' behavioral intention to use the ECMS and their satisfaction. In order to measure the change of individuals' usage behavior, we plan to apply the IS success model [20] as a foundation of our measurement model. Since we also perceive the necessity of a distinction between individuals' attitudes about the system and their attitudes about using the system, we plan to adapt the extended IS success model by Wixom and Todd [21].

We are convinced that our research can contribute to both, theoretical and practical aspects in the context of providing user guidance for document-intensive processes. From a theoretical perspective, our research aims to increase the existing body of knowledge on ES design by studying the interplay between organization-wide business processes and individual practices in the context of document processing. In contrast to existing ECMS research, our work will focus on users, their requirements and satisfaction when using ECMS enriched with guidance. On the other hand, our work contributes to practice, since our design principles can provide guidance on how to design software solutions in order to enable individuals to handle documents compliant to company's processes.

References

1. Markus, M.L., Tanis, C., van Fenema, P.C.: Enterprise resource planning: multisite ERP implementations. Communications of the ACM 43, 42–46 (2000)
2. Devadoss, P.R., Pan, S.L.: Enterprise systems use: Towards a structurational analysis of enterprise systems induced organizational transformation. Communications of the Association for Information Systems 19, 352–385 (2007)

3. Seddon, P.B., Calvert, C., Yang, S.: A multi-project model of key factors affecting organizational benefits from enterprise systems. MIS Quarterly 34, 305–328 (2010)
4. Murthy, K., Deshpande, P.M., Dey, A., Halasipuram, R., Mohania, M., Deepak, P., Reed, J., Schumacher, S.: Exploiting Evidence from Unstructured Data to Enhance Master Data Management. Proceedings of the VLDB Endowment 5, 1862–1873 (2012)
5. Morschheuser, S., Raufer, H., Wargitsch, C.: Challenges and solutions of document and workflow management in a manufacturing enterprise: a case study. In: 29th Hawaii International Conference on System Sciences, vol. 5, pp. 4–12. IEEE (1996)
6. Nordheim, S., Päivärinta, T.: Implementing enterprise content management: from evolution through strategy to contradictions out-of-the-box. European Journal of Information Systems 15, 648–662 (2006)
7. O'Callaghan, R., Smits, M.: A strategy development process for enterprise content man-agement. In: ECIS 2005 Proceedings, pp. 1271–1282 (2005)
8. Grahlmann, K.R., Helms, R.W., Hilhorst, C., Brinkkemper, S., van Amerongen, S.: Reviewing Enterprise Content Management: a functional framework. European Journal of Information Systems 21, 268–286 (2011)
9. vom Brocke, J., Simons, A., Cleven, A.: Towards a business process-oriented approach to enterprise content management: the ECM-blueprinting framework. Information Systems and e-Business Management 9, 475–496 (2011)
10. Wiltzius, L., Simons, A., Seidel, S.: A Study on the Acceptance of ECM Systems. In: Wirtschaftinformatik Proceedings 2011 (2011)
11. Kuechler, B., Vaishnavi, V.: On theory development in design science research: anatomy of a research project. European Journal of Information Systems 17, 489–504 (2008)
12. Takeda, H., Veerkamp, P.: Modeling Design Processes. AI Magazine 11, 37–48 (1990)
13. Benbasat, I., Goldstein, D.K., Mead, M.: The Case Research Strategy in Studies of Information Systems. MIS Quarterly 11, 369–386 (1987)
14. Thomas, D.R.: A General Inductive Approach for Analyzing Qualitative Evaluation Data. American Journal of Evaluation 27, 237–246 (2006)
15. Scherp, A.: Software Development Process Model And Methodology For Virtual Laboratories. In: Proc. of the 20th IASTED Int. Multi-Conf. Applied Informatics, pp. 47–52 (2002)
16. Silver, M.S.: Decisional Guidance for Computer-Based Decision Support. MIS Quarterly 15, 105–122 (1991)
17. Todd, P., Benbasat, I.: Evaluating the Impact of DSS, Cognitive Effort, and Incentives on Strategy Selection. Information Systems Research 10, 356–374 (1999)
18. Scherp, A., Eißing, D., Staab, S.: strukt—A Pattern System for Integrating Individual and Organizational Knowledge Work. In: Aroyo, L., Welty, C., Alani, H., Taylor, J., Bernstein, A., Kagal, L., Noy, N., Blomqvist, E. (eds.) ISWC 2011, Part I. LNCS, vol. 7031, pp. 569–584. Springer, Heidelberg (2011)
19. Scherp, A., Staab, S.: Analysis and Comparison of Models for Individual and Organizational Knowledge Work. In: Proceeding of Mulitkonferenz Wirtschaftsinformatik (2012)
20. Delone, W.H., McLean, E.R.: The DeLone and McLean Model of Information Systems Success: A Ten-Year Update. Journal of Management Information Systems 19, 9–30 (2003)
21. Wixom, B.H., Todd, P.A.: A Theoretical Integration of User Satisfaction and Technology Acceptance. Information Systems Research 16, 85–102 (2005)

Cooperative Games and Their Effect on Group Collaboration

Maaz Nasir[1], Kelly Lyons[1], Rock Leung[2], and Ali Moradian[1]

[1] Department of Computer Science, University of Toronto, Toronto, Canada
{maaz.nasir,kelly.lyons}@utoronto.ca,
ali.moradian@mail.utoronto.ca
[2] SAP, Vancouver, Canada
rock.leung@sap.com

Abstract. The potential for multiplayer computer games to serve as activities that can help increase interaction, cooperative tendencies and harmony in groups has been the subject of past research. However, there is still a long way to go before we can understand how positive group behavior and team dynamics in multiplayer games can impact real world collaboration. In our research work, we investigate this relationship further through *Operation Sting*, a cooperative multiplayer game we have designed to serve as an ice-breaker. Our goal is to study how participation in such a game affects collaboration in subsequent group work.

Keywords: Multiplayer games, Collaboration, Ice-breaker, Cooperative work.

1 Introduction and Background

Many online multiplayer games today emphasize teamwork and cooperation. Massively Multiplayer Online Role Playing Games (MMORPG), such as *World of Warcraft*, include significant content that focuses on 'parties' of multiple individuals working together. Such cooperative content may either be in the form of group quests or the inclusion of high level bosses and enemies that can only be defeated when players work together. Several First Person Shooter (FPS) and Real Time Strategy (RTS) games include team-versus-team battle modes in which groups can work together to compete against other teams.

The shared virtual spaces at the core of such games provide a great medium for geographically distributed players to interact with one another and work together, particularly when face-to-face interaction is not feasible. Collaborative play in such environments has been the topic of prior research investigation [7, 12]. Furthermore, the use of game environments as collaborative workspaces for distributed teams to work together has been studied [1, 9, 16]. Ellis, et al. observe that games can be leveraged as team building activities which help mitigate problems associated with distributed teams, such as a lack of trust, low group cohesion and identification, and difficulties in communication [6].

J. vom Brocke et al. (Eds.): DESRIST 2013, LNCS 7939, pp. 502–510, 2013.

In our research, we are studying the use of a multiplayer game as an ice breaking activity that occurs before collaborative group work. Ice-breaking games have been shown to help groups work better together [6, 11]. We believe that a cooperative multiplayer game is a suitable ice-breaker because the cooperative elements in a multiplayer game can help develop more cohesive and productive teams, particularly when they have not worked together before. Working together to achieve a common objective in a game has been found to increase likeability among players [4].

There exist several examples of commercial multiplayer games that offer rich cooperative play and might be candidates for ice-breakers. However, many of these commercially available games are too involved for both gamers and non-gamers alike to quickly pick up and engage for a short duration (*World of Warcraft*, *Left4Dead*, *Little Big Planet*, *Starcraft* 2 etc.). At the same time, there also exist simpler games like *Rock Band* and *Rayman's Raving Rabids* (investigated in [11]), but these do not enforce cooperation amongst players beyond the accumulation of points. Many of the commercial games we surveyed did not cater to our unique needs and led us to the design our own ice-breaking game.

2   Game Design

The goal of our research is to investigate how participation in a cooperative ice-breaking game affects collaboration among teammates in subsequent group work. We hypothesize that playing a cooperative ice-breaking game will result in increased collaboration in subsequent group work as measured by improvements in each of three dimensions: I) Interaction among teammates; II) Level of individual participation; and III) Individual satisfaction with work outcomes and the group activity [3, 4, 10].

To our knowledge, no suitable co-operative ice-breaker game exists so we also sought to create such a game, leveraging the properties of cooperative multiplayer games. Such a game should allow participants to immerse themselves into the activity relatively quickly and accomplish a few well-defined objectives within a short timeframe (20-30 minutes). Our investigation leads us to the precise specification of the design requirements for an ice-breaking game (IBG, for short). We then use these requirements to design and implement our own game prototype *(Operation Sting)*.

Adopting an approach similar to the one used in the design of learning games [8, 14], we specify the desired characteristics for an IBG, using the properties of multiplayer games as identified in [8] & [17]. We divide these characteristics into two categories: *Game Play* and *Cooperative Play*.

Game Play:

- Moderate complexity
- Easy to use interface
- Moderately easy difficulty
- Appealing theme

Cooperative Play:

- Balanced individual participation
- Uniqueness of roles
- Need for social interaction
- Use of cooperative patterns
- Concurrent play

Moderate complexity: Complexity relates to the intricacy and details surrounding game objectives, the variety of choices a player can make, and the degree of control he/she has over the decisions made. The IBG should incorporate a moderate level of complexity, enough to mentally stimulate the players but not so much that the cognitive effort and time spent on the game has an adverse effect on performance in subsequent collaborative work.

Easy to use interface: The interface is the medium (both software and hardware) through which a player exercises control in the game. In an IBG, the interface should be easy to adapt to for people with varying levels of video game experience. Precise aiming and 3D navigation (as needed in FPS games like *Left4Dead*) or prior knowledge of unit micromanagement techniques (as in *Starcraft 2*) should not be a prerequisite to enjoy the game.

Moderately easy difficulty: Unlike complexity, difficulty relates to the skill, precision and likelihood of failure in carrying out a task, even if its nature and requirements may be explicitly clear [15]. We propose that an IBG should be moderately easy, so as to avoid frustration and allow steady team progress. We believe that this would help create a positive environment for subsequent collaborative work.

Appealing theme: The context of the story, the themes used, and the subject matter of the IBG should try to appeal to a wide variety of players so as to not marginalize certain individuals in the group. For example, games with a heavy emphasis on violence may deter certain players.

Balanced individual participation: The IBG should try to roughly allocate an equal amount of utility for each player to participate in the game, irrespective of their capabilities. It should also try to enforce a minimum level of participation for each player. In the subsequent collaborative group work, we would like to reduce problems such as *social loafing* and the *sucker effect* [13].

Uniqueness of roles: In the IBG, it would be desirable to give players different roles and yet have each player play a critical part in making progress for the group [18]. This would be analogous to real life work teams, where different individuals have different skills and expertise to contribute to the team work in different ways.

Need for social interaction: Actively encouraging players to communicate with each other is an important objective for ice-breaker games. For example, displaying selective information to specific players necessary for task completion may encourage increased communication with others [18]

Use of cooperative patterns: For a multiplayer game to be considered 'cooperative', it must include one or more cooperative gameplay patterns (or mechanisms). These patterns have been discussed in detail in [7]. Some examples include shared goals, shared puzzles, limited resources, and synergies between player abilities.

Concurrent play: A multiplayer game may be classified as *concurrent* (all players play simultaneously at same time), *synchronous* (all players play at the same time but take turns) or *asynchronous* (players make progress in the game without having to play at the same time) [17]. An asynchronous game would be inappropriate for a 20-30 minute IBG. Taking turns in a synchronous game may allow for better players to 'play for' their teammates while waiting for their turn and encourage *social loafing* in the group. Consequently, a concurrent IBG appears to be most appropriate.

3   Operation Sting – Overview and Implementation

Operation Sting is a 3- or 4-player cooperative game in which team members must work together to pull off a heist in an art museum. Each player is assigned a unique character with special abilities. The Conman character can use a lock pick to open padlocked doors and temporarily distract security guards. The Muscle is able to move around heavy objects and use items such as a crowbar to break down weak walls and windows. The Hacker can access sensitive information from computer terminals and disable cameras and laser detectors. Finally, the Executive has money that can be used to bribe certain individuals to overlook transgressions and is able to gain access to VIP areas of the museum. In the 3-player version, the role of the Executive is eliminated.

Fig. 1. All Characters: (From Left) Conman, Muscle, Hacker and Executive

The game consists of a single heist mission where the 4 characters infiltrate the museum, each from a different location. The players must navigate through areas on the map and overcome different obstacles. As in real project or collaborative work environments, players are put into situations where they need to rely on each other's individual abilities to move forward. For example, access to a padlocked door revealing a new area may be blocked with several wooden containers. The Muscle would need to first move these containers out of the way before the Conman may pick the locked door.

We have incorporated the IBG design considerations recommended in Section 2. *Operation Sting* is a moderately complex, obstacle-solving, concurrent 2D game with easy to use controls (directional arrow keys and spacebar on the keyboard) and easy gameplay. Furthermore, the group heist theme used in the game is quite common in popular culture and should hopefully be familiar to all players. The game assigns each of the players a unique role with special abilities and the levels are designed in a way that allows each player to make a roughly equal contribution to progressing through the mission. Finally, the special abilities granted, the unique information presented to specific players, and the use of shared obstacles require players to interact with one another in many situations to progress through the game.

Operation Sting is implemented in the style of a 2D overhead projected Role Playing Game (RPG). Multiplayer gaming is supported using a client-server architecture. The game client was developed using Adobe Flash and ActionScript 3 and can run on a Desktop computer using either Windows or OSX as the operating system. The server is a Windows executable which was written in C#. Communication between the client and the server relies on a 3rd party library (Player.IO) which makes use of the Transmission Control Protocol (TCP).

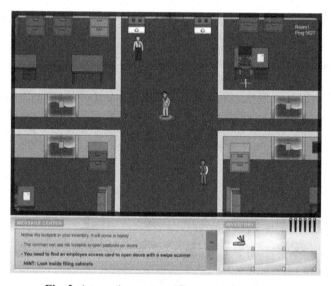

Fig. 2. A game in progress (Conman point of view)

4   Study and Evaluation

We designed and conducted a user study to evaluate if playing *Operation Sting* as a cooperative ice-breaking game improves collaboration in subsequent group work. To date, we have conducted an initial experiment in a classroom setting and are currently planning a second experiment in a work environment.

In the first experiment, we invited students enrolled in a project management course in the Faculty of Information at the University of Toronto to participate in our study. Students were assigned by the instructor to teams of 3-4 people to work on a course project. At the start of the course project, each team of students participated in a synchronous computer-mediated activity (for 40-60 minutes) in order to collaboratively identify projects that could implement an organizational strategy. The computer-mediated activity was carried out in two steps: a brainstorming step in which each team brainstormed project ideas; a project identification step in which each team selected a final list from the list of project ideas produced in the brainstorming step. The two-step activity was inspired by the Brainstorming and Fast Focus Thinklets of Briggs et al. [2].

For our study, the teams were randomly placed into 3 groups: a) Five teams (3 of size 3, 2 of size 4) played *Operation Sting* before participating in the computer-mediated project selection activity; b) Four teams (2 of size 3, 2 of size 4) participated in a generic ice-breaker game (Liar, Liar! [5]) before participating in the computer-mediated activity; and, c) Seven teams (4 of size 3, 2 of size 4, 1 of size 5) participated in the computer-mediated activity without first playing *Operation Sting* or the generic ice-breaker (i.e., control groups). Conversations during the computer-mediated project selection activity (Fast Focus) were recorded and analyzed quantitatively to measure Interaction (Dimension I) and Participation (Dimension II). Additionally, students were asked to complete a survey at the end of the activity to measure Individual Satisfaction (Dimension III). In the survey, students rated statements on a 5-point Likert scale such as, "I am glad that I was chosen to be part of this group and not another one", and "My group developed good and useful ideas".

5   Preliminary Results and Future Plans

Thus far, we have carried out a preliminary analysis of the data. In order to measure Interaction, we looked at the cumulative (per group) and individual (per person) number of ideas and comments submitted during the Brainstorming and Fast Focus steps respectively. These numbers are normalized by the time spent during each step. For the Brainstorming step, we normalize the number of ideas to a period of 10 minutes (i.e. {No. of ideas/brainstorming duration in minutes}×10). Similarly, in the Fast Focus step, we normalize the number of comments to a period of 60 minutes. In addition, the number of ideas and comments per group are normalized by group size. Error bars in Figures 3 and 4 indicate +/- 1 standard deviation.

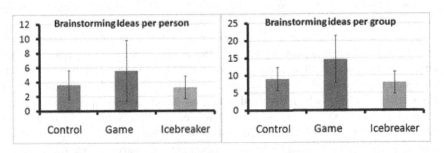

Fig. 3. Mean number of brainstorming ideas per person across each category (left), and mean number of brainstorming ideas per group (right)

For the mean normalized number of individual and total ideas (using a two-tailed t-test), we observe p-values of 0.08 and 0.14 respectively for the Game-Control comparison and 0.05 and 0.10 for the Game-Icebreaker comparison.

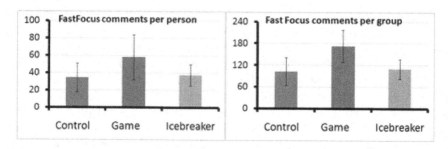

Fig. 4. Mean number of Fast Focus comments per person across each category (left), and mean number of Fast Focus ideas per group (right)

For the mean normalized number of individual and total comments, we observe p-values of 0.002 and 0.02 respectively for the Game-Control comparison and 0.008 and 0.04 respectively for the Game-Icebreaker comparison. Collectively, these results suggest increased Interaction in the Game category compared to the Control and Ice-breaker categories. We plan on having an independent reviewer rate each of the ideas and assign them a quality score which we will also take into consideration

Participation was measured by observing the contribution ratios (both Brainstorming ideas and Fast Focus comments) for each user in the group. A Participation Score for each group was calculated by taking the sum of $min(1/GS, N/NG)$ over all users in the group. Here, GS denotes the Group Size, N is the number of comments/ideas contributed by the user and NG is the total number of comments/ideas generated by the group. A higher Participation Score indicates balanced participation of all individuals in the group (with a maximum of 1 when all individuals in the group contribute equally) whereas a lower score indicates otherwise. To measure Individual Satisfaction, the average Likert scores (across individuals) for survey statements were compared for each of the 3 categories. Neither the analysis of the Participation Scores or the results from the survey indicated statistically significant differences.

We are currently planning a second experiment involving several teams of co-workers participating in a planning activity. In the first experiment we found that the game itself encouraged active discussion and dialogue between the players (who were seated side by side) but this model of interaction did not match the subsequent computer-mediated activity which involved typing on screen and no face-to-face interaction. In the second experiment, participants will engage in a face-to-face team-based activity following our ice-breaker video game. We will capture the interaction in the subsequent team activity using video and conduct content analysis of the discussion.

6   Conclusion

The goal of our research was to investigate the effects of using a cooperative ice-breaking game prior to team-based collaborative work. We developed a multiplayer video game designed to be used as a 20-30 minute ice-breaker for teams with mixed levels of gaming experience. We compared teams that carried out a collaborative activity after playing our game with those that did not participate in any ice-breaking activity and those that participated in a general ice-breaking activity. We found that teams which used our game prior to their group activity experienced increased inte-rac-tion but there were no significant changes measured in participation or satisfac-tion. A second experiment is planned to further evaluate the impact of the game on subsequent team based work.

References

1. Bartlett, K., Simpson, M.: Using Games as a Means of Collaboration. In: Proc. 2005 International Conference on Multi Media Modeling (MMM). IEEE Press (2005)
2. Briggs, R.O., De Vreede, G., Nunamaker, J.F.: Collaboration engineering with ThinkLets to pursue sustained success with group support systems. Journal of Management and Information Systems 19(4), 31–64 (2003)
3. Costa, A.C.: Work Team Trust and Effectiveness. Personnel Review 32(5), 605–622 (2003)
4. Dabbish, L.A.: Jumpstarting Relationships with Online Games: Evidence from a Laboratory Investigation. In: Proc. 2008 ACM Conference on Computer Supported Cooperative Work and Social Computing (CSCW), pp. 353–356. ACM Press (2008)
5. Dixon, J.S., Crooks, H., Henry, K.: Breaking the Ice: Supporting Collaboration and Development of Community Online. Canadian Journal of Learning and Technology 32(2) (2006)
6. Ellis, J.B., Luther, K., Bessiere, K., Kellogg, W.A.: Games for Virtual Team Building. In: Proc. 2008 ACM Conference on Designing Interactive Systems (DIS), pp. 25–27. ACM Press (2008)
7. El-Nasr, M., Aghabeigi, B., Milam, D., Erfani, M., Lameman, B., Maygoli, H., Mah, S.: Understanding and Evaluating Cooperative Games. In: Proc. 2010 ACM SIGCHI Conference on Human Factors in Computing Systems (CHI), pp. 253–262. ACM Press (2010)
8. Garris, R., Ahlers, R., Driskell, J.E.: Games, Motivation and Learning: A Research and Practice Model. Simulation and Gaming 33(4), 441–467 (2002)
9. Gurzick, D., White, K.F., Lutters, W.G., Landry, B.M., Dombrowski, C., Kim, J.Y.: Designing the Future of Collaborative Workplace Systems: Lessons Learned from Comparison with Alternate Reality Games. In: Proc. iConference 2011, pp. 174–180. ACM Press (2011)
10. Hathorn, L.G., Ingram, A.L.: Cooperation and Collaboration using Computer-Mediated Communication. Journal of Educational Computing Research 26(3), 325–347 (2002)
11. Lin, Q.T., Wu, J.: The Impact of Virtual Teamwork on Real-world collaboration. In: Proc. 2009 International Conference on Advances in Computer Entertainment Technology (ACE), pp. 44–51. ACM Press (2009)
12. Nardi, B., Harris, J.: Strangers and Friends: Collaborative Play in World of Warcraft. In: Proc. 2006 ACM Conference on Computer Supported Cooperative Work and Social Computing (CSCW), pp. 149–158. ACM Press (2006)
13. Piezon, S.L., Ferree, W.D.: Perceptions of Social Loafing in Online Learning Groups: A study of Public University and U.S. Naval War College students. The International Review of Research in Open and Distance Learning 9(2) (2008)
14. Reiber, P.: Seriously Considering Play: Designing Interactive Learning Environments Based on the Blend of Microworlds, Simulations and Games. Educational Technology Research and Development 4(2), 43–58 (1996)

15. Robinson, P.: Task Complexity, Task Difficulty, and Task Production: Exploring Interactions in a Componential Framework. Applied Linguistics 22(1), 27–57 (2001)
16. Sharma, G., Shroff, G., Dewan, P.: Workplace Collaboration in a 3D Virtual Office. In: Proc. 2011 International Symposium on Virtual Reality Innovation (ISVRI), pp. 3–10. IEEE Press (2011)
17. Zagal, J.P., Nussbaum, M., Rosas, R.: A Model to Support the Design of Multiplayer Games. Presence 9(5), 448–462 (2000)
18. Zagal, J.P., Rick, J., Hsi, I.: Collaborative games: Lessons learned from board games. Simulation and Gaming 37(24), 24–40 (2006)

Respondent Behavior Logging:
An Opportunity for Online Survey Design

Jonas Sjöström[1,2], Mohammad Hafijur Rahman[1,2], Asma Rafiq[1],
Ruth Lochan[1,2], and Pär J. Ågerfalk[1]

[1] Department of Informatics and Media, Uppsala University, Uppsala, Sweden
`{asma.rafiq,par.agerfalk}@im.uu.se`
[2] Department of Public Health and Caring Sciences, Uppsala University, Uppsala, Sweden
`{jonas.sjostrom,hafijur.rahman,ruth.lochan}@im.uu.se`

Abstract. This work-in-progress paper introduces the concept of Respondent Behavior Logging (RBL), consisting of static and dynamic models that conceptualize respondent behavior when filling in online questionnaires. It is argued that web-based survey design may benefit from logging as a technique for evaluation, since such data may prove useful during re-design of questionnaires. Although other aspects of online surveys have attracted considerable attention both in industry and in literature, how the Web may leverage new and innovative techniques to support survey design is still underexplored. Some preliminary results are reported in the paper, and issues are raised regarding how to appropriately evaluate and demonstrate the qualities of the RBL concept as a means for survey re-design.

Keywords: Questionnaire design, online surveys, evaluation, behavior logging.

1 Introduction

Research in information systems, as well as in other disciplines, often includes data collection through surveys [15, 17]. As stated by Krosnick & Presser [12, p. 263], "the heart of a survey is its questionnaire". The importance of well-designed questionnaires cannot be understated. Flaws in questionnaire design may lead to response errors [12] that may negatively impact the entire study.

There are several methodological guidelines to support questionnaire design. These can be divided into three broad categories [12]: (i) The design of questions and the options provided to answer the questions. Question design focuses on different types of open and closed questions, and how to appropriate suitable rating scales given the knowledge interest of the researcher. (ii) The structure of the questionnaire as a whole. Such guidelines address the order of questions, and various strategies to improve the interpretability of respondents' answers, e.g. through the use of vignette questions. (iii) Guidelines for the process of testing questionnaires formatively, as a means to prototype and improve the questionnaires before going live in a full-scale survey.

For online surveys, special design guidelines have been discussed [13]. In this paper, we argue that questionnaire evaluation has not yet exploited the potential of the

J. vom Brocke et al. (Eds.): DESRIST 2013, LNCS 7939, pp. 511–518, 2013.

online medium. We propose the novel concept of Respondent Behavior Logging (RBL) that allows us to scrutinize the respondents' process of answering questions. Through analysis of respondent behavior data we may be able to scrutinize and improve questionnaire design. Logged respondent behavior may also serve as an additional source of knowledge to interpret respondent answers.

Our work adds to the general knowledge base on questionnaire design and evaluation in the online context. This is especially important in order to support the evolution of commonly used instruments, such as the Hospital Anxiety and Depression Scale (HADS) in psychology. Respondent behavior logging - if used repeatedly in online research where common instruments are applied - supports fine-tuning of instruments over time, based on large data sets of respondent behavior.

The paper proceeds as follows. First, we provide an overview of existing knowledge and artifacts in the domain of online surveys. Second, we give a conceptual view of RBL, i.e. the focal design science artifact. Third, we present an instantiation of the artifact, along with insights from the design process and preliminary evaluation. Fourth, we briefly discuss the strategy for future naturalistic ex-post evaluation of RBL and the anticipated value of RBL as conceived at this stage.

2   Online Surveys—Existing Knowledge and Artifacts

There is no shortage of online tools and services to conduct online surveys. Several vendors (e.g. Google, SurveyGizmo and SurveyMonkey) provide features for designing questionnaires, collecting data and analyzing responses. Open source alternatives emerge, both in the form of software to power online surveys (e.g. LimeSurvey) and as open source schemas for describing and managing questionnaires (e.g. queXML and SUML). These emerging technologies and standards highlight various aspects of the complexities of conducting online surveys. In addition to questionnaire design, they support data collection and data analysis. As an example, SurveyGizmo provides the option to embed decision logic within questionnaires, and an application programming interface (API) for developers and social plug-ins for Facebook and Twitter. LimeSurvey supports multilingualism as well as 'skip logic' (e.g. showing question Y if and only if the user chose a specific optional answer for question X). As an additional example, there are typically features for data export/import to various formats, including CSV, PDF, SPSS, queXML and MS Excel. Third-party modules are available to, for example, connect LimeSurvey to Wordpress (SurveyPress) and Drupal (LimeSurvey Sync).

The existing tools and schemas include a variety of features to set up questionnaires, and to collect and analyze data. There is, however, little emphasis on the process of designing and evaluating questionnaires. Although guidelines for online questionnaire design exist [13], there is a lack of knowledge on how to design IT artifacts that support evaluation and re-design of questionnaires. Our ambition to develop such knowledge is so far influenced by two branches of literature, as outlined below.

First, our design builds on the philosophy of pragmatism, which leads us to seek an understanding of the world as an ongoing process of action [21]. The RBL concept is an attempt to understand the respondent's situation when filling in a questionnaire. Our view is based on Dewey's conception of a situation as a contextual whole [5], consisting of objects and events: "What is designated by the word 'situation' is not a single object or event or set of events. For we never experience nor form judgments about objects and events in isolation, but only in connection with a contextual whole. This latter is what is called a situation." We do not claim that we can get a full understanding of a 'contextual whole' through RBL, but our aim is to provide a concept that can bring us more understanding of the respondent's interpretation of the questionnaire by facilitating inquiry into the events through which their answers to the questionnaire emerged.

The pragmatic starting point has implications for conceptual modeling [1], a topic central to the IS field [3]. A common perspective in the literature is that information systems are symbolic representations of reality [20]. An alternative view, rooted in pragmatism, constitutes a critique to the representational view [1, 10, 11]. Drawing on the principles of pragmatism, language philosophers [8,16] have argued that language (and by extension also information systems) does not just represent the (state of the) world but also brings about change to the world. From such a pragmatic viewpoint, IT artifacts are instruments that are used in performance of action. From the pragmatic viewpoint, IT artifacts are instruments used to perform action [6, 18] and mediators of actors' intentions. In the case of RBL, we want to create a formalized representation of respondent behavior. That representation, however, must account for the actions the respondents have taken in the process of providing answers to a questionnaire. These actions reveal to us when the respondent hesitated, changed their mind, got tired of answering questions, *etc.*

Second, there is a general trend in web development to use data about user behavior to enable new types of application. This trend is clearly related to a pragmatist interest in human action. In the process of giving answers, users may 'give off' signs about their behavior that may be utilized in various ways by designers [2]. An example of this is the well-established use of 'clickstream' analysis on the World Wide Web, used (for instance) to tailor the display of ads on web pages [14]. Such tailoring is based on aggregated knowledge drawn from behavior of a large set of users in a community. The proposed RBL concept is analogical to other user behavior logging concepts. We thus conceive of RBL as an exaptation [7] of old questionnaire evaluation techniques ('prototyping') in combination with logging techniques, allowing us to design a new type of questionnaire evaluation technique in the online context. By measuring respondent behavior when filling in a questionnaire online, we mimic the established version of letting pilot respondents fill in paper-based questionnaires while observing them.

In essence, these two branches of literature (pragmatism and logging of web behavior), tells us to conceive of RBL as a concept to support keeping track of how respondents act while responding to a questionnaire. Further, we should be able to analyze respondent behavior for individual situations as well as aggregates. Such analysis should be useful to both (i) improve the questionnaire design and (ii) interpret the answers provided by respondents.

3   Method

The design of RBL is a part of a larger design research program in which a fairly complex piece of software[1] is built in the context of eHealth and eHealth research. The overarching project is a multi-disciplinary effort including researchers and practitioners from psychology, medicine, information systems, caring sciences, and economics. It aims a supporting people with potentially lethal somatic diseases to cope with their situation.

The integration of IS research into the multi-disciplinary context promotes the relevance of our research. The collaboration with senior researchers as well as practitioners in other fields than IS has been conceived as imperative in understanding the problem domain (psychosocial care) and the clinical needs. The multi-disciplinary approach influenced the discussions in the group. The representatives from academic traditions (e.g. caring sciences vs. economics) approach research from different angles, and different ideals are put into play both with regard to health issues and research issues. This environment tends to emphasize issues of relevance and rigor, since there is a continual need within the group to provide an agreed-upon rationale for design decisions.

The design process was set up in accordance with agile values [4], characterized by sprint reviews approximately every two weeks. The review meetings had several recurring members representing different professions and academic disciplines. In addition, external specialists and patient groups were invited to explore the software, followed by workshops in which they provided feedback to the design team. In total, 40+ design workshops have been organized, engaging a great variety of stakeholders. With respect to rigor, researchers from the included disciplines have contributed to the design process. IS researchers contributed with knowledge from the IS field and its sibling disciplines (primarily interaction design and software engineering). The IS input is based on a pragmatic stream of IS research, focusing social interaction through instrumental use of technology [1, 18]. The idea to log respondent behavior in the survey context as born in the larger context of logging user behaviors for research purposes, and to ensure accountability in the process of dealing with sensitive data. The software was equipped with extensive logging functionality to enable retrospective analyses of user actions.

4   The Concept of Respondent Behavior Logging

In this section, we present the RBL concept. First, we present a dynamic model to frame user actions related to filling in questionnaires. Second, we introduce a static model intended to keep records of these user actions.

---

[1] The complexity of the software is indicated by its size – it currently measures to approximately 40 000 lines of code and 100 database tables.

4.1   Dynamic Model of Respondent Behavior

A logical first step in development is to identify what user actions to log. During the design process, we identified a set of user actions that could be traced at the server side through the HTTP requests client browsers make to the web server. The flow-chart in Fig. 1 shows the dynamic model of user behavior.

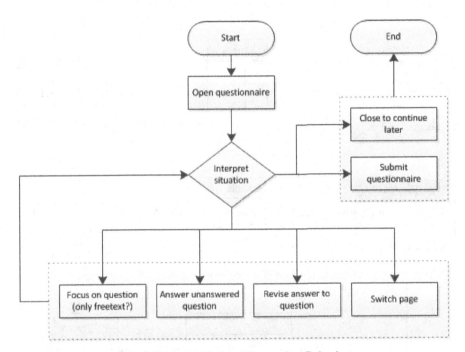

Fig. 1. Dynamic Model of Respondent Behavior

Seven action types are outlined in Fig. 1. All are possible to track in a web context. The action types 'open questionnaire', 'close to continue later' and 'submit question-naire' need no further explanation. The 'focus on question' action type means that there is some indication that a question is currently in the focus of the user, e.g. by hovering a question area with the mouse pointer or setting focus on a text field by clicking it. The 'answer unanswered question' occurs when a user answers a question that has not been previously answered, differentiating it from the 'revise answer to question' action type. It is also possible to track when users switch to another page in the questionnaire. The dynamic model, despite its simplicity, is an important concept to better understand what types of user actions we may trace in the context of online questionnaires. A main idea of tracking these actions is that a rich account of actions taken serves to indicate how the respondent interprets various situations when filling in a questionnaire.

4.2   Static Model of Respondent Behavior

The entity/relationship diagram (Fig. 2) shows a static model to keep track of user actions as shown in Figure 1. The purpose of the design is to allow traceability, i.e. that we are able to reconstruct the manner in which a respondent filled in a questionnaire. In addition, there is a need to keep track of the respondent's (user's) identity, to allow us to make queries related to a particular individual.

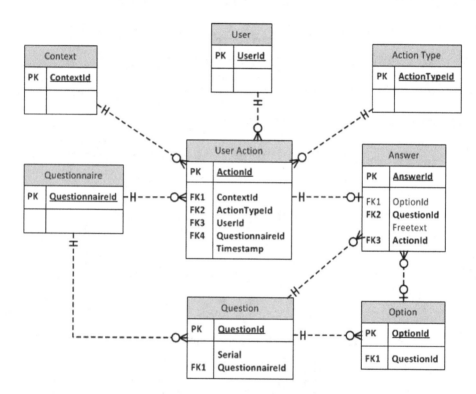

Fig. 2. Static Model of Respondent Behavior

'User Action' defines the actual log record. It shows how a user, at a certain point in time, performs an action of some type in relation to a specific questionnaire. This action may include an answer to a question, which may be free text, but it may also point out an optional answer to a question. Keeping track of context is imperative, since one questionnaire may be used at different times. This is the case in many randomized controlled trials where the same questionnaire is typically used repeatedly to measure the same construct (e.g. depression or anxiety) at different times in the study. By including action type, we facilitate queries of user behavior based on grouping by the type of action performed.

5   Evaluation Strategy and Concluding Discussion

So far, we have designed the RBL concept, on the basis of (i) existing artifacts, (ii) literature and (iii) a design process in the context of eHealth and eHealth research. The concept has been implemented in software (i.e. feasible to implement). Preliminary (artificial) evaluation results exist but only based on test data collected during beta-testing with non-authentic users. The remaining challenge is to convincingly investigate and demonstrate the qualities of RBL, as advocated in IS design science research methodology [9]. The research context will allow us to collect rather large amounts of data–around 1000 respondents are expected over a two-year period, each filling in more than ten questionnaires. This will allow us to query into a large amount of data collected using the RBL concept to conduct naturalistic ex-post evaluations [19]. We argue, however, that the logged data as such is not sufficient to evaluate whether or not RBL is a useful tool to improve questionnaires. The intention is to design a set of reports drawing on the collected RBL data, where respondent behavior is visualized. Various scholars will be invited to focus group workshops, with the purpose of discussing (i) the visualized respondent behavior, (ii) its implications for interpretation of collected data, and (iii) further implications for assessing and potentially re-designing the questionnaires. Through these measures, we should be able to assess the utility of RBL for questionnaire re-design, and thus demonstrate the qualities of our focal design science artifact (the RBL concept).

We do not consider RBL to be a substitute for other questionnaire design techniques, rather a complement that opens up novel possibilities for evaluation. While the implications of RBL at this stage are speculative, we find that it has good potential to become an important strategy for questionnaire evaluation and re-design. It is a new use of technology that may be integrated into the process of large-scale data collection online, supporting both the interpretation of collected data and the refinement of questionnaires.

Acknowledgements. This work was conducted as part of the Uppsala University Psychosocial Care Programme (U-CARE) at Uppsala University. U-CARE is a strategic research programme funded by the Swedish Government through the Swedish Research Council.

References

1. Ågerfalk, P.J.: Getting Pragmatic. European Journal of Information Systems 19(3), 251–256 (2010)
2. Ågerfalk, P.J., Sjöström, J.: Sowing the seeds of self: A socio- pragmatic penetration of the web artefact. In: Proceedings of the 2nd International Pragmatic Web Conference, Tilburg, The Netherlands (2007)
3. Wyssusek, B.: Ontological Foundations of Conceptual Modelling. Scandinavian Journal of Information Systems 18(1), 63–80 (2006)

4. Conboy, K.: Agility from first principles: Reconstructing the concept of agility in information systems development. Information Systems Research 20(3), 329–354 (2009)
5. Dewey, J.: Logic: The theory of inquiry. Henry Holt and Company, New York (1938)
6. Goldkuhl, G., Lyytinen, K.: A language action view of information systems. In: Ginzberg, M., Ross, C. (eds.) Proceedings of the 3rd International Conference on Information Systems (ICIS 1982), Ann Arbor, MI, pp. 13–29 (1982)
7. Gregor, S., Hevner, A.R.: Positioning and Presenting Design Science Research for Maximum Impact. To appear in forthcoming issue of Mis Quarterly (forthcoming)
8. Habermas, J.: The Theory of Communicative Action. Polity, Cambridge (1984)
9. Hevner, A.R., March, S.T., Park, J., Ram, S.: Design science in Information Systems research. Mis Quarterly 28(1), 75–105 (2004)
10. Hirschheim, R., Klein, H., Lyytinen, K.: Information Systems Development and Data Modeling: Conceptual Foundations and Philosophical Foundations. Cambridge University Press, Cambridge (1995)
11. Holm, P.: On the design and usage of information technology and the structuring of communication and work. Doctoral Dissertation, Stockholm University, Sweden (1996)
12. Krosnick, J.A., Presser, S.: Question and Questionnaire Design. In: Marsden, P.V., Wright, J.D. (eds.) Handbook of Survey Research, 2nd edn., pp. 263–313. Emerald Group Publishing Limited (2010)
13. Lumsden, J., Morgan, W.: Online-Questionnaire Design: Establishing Guidelines and Evaluating Existing Support. In: Proceedings of the 16th Annual International Conference of the Information Resources Management Organization (IRMA 2005), vol. 31 (2005)
14. Martin, D., Wu, H., Alsaid, A.: Hidden Surveillance by Web Sites: Web Bugs in Contemporary Use. Communications of the ACM 46(12) (December 2003)
15. Newsted, P.R., Huff, S.L., Munro, M.C.: Survey Instruments in Information Systems. MIS Quarterly 22(4), 553–554 (1998)
16. Searle, J.: Speech acts: An essay in the philosophy of language. Cambridge University Press, London (1969)
17. Sivo, S.A., Saunders, C., Chang, Q., Jiang, J.J.: How Low Should You Go? Low Response Rates and the Validity of Inference in IS Questionnaire Research. Journal of the Association for Information Systems 7(6), 35–414 (2006)
18. Sjöström, J.: Designing Information Systems – A pragmatic account. Doctoral Dissertation, Uppsala University, Sweden (2010) ISBN: 978-91-506-2149-5
19. Venable, J., Pries-Heje, J., Baskerville, R.: A Comprehensive Framework for Evaluation in Design Science Research. In: Peffers, K., Rothenberger, M., Kuechler, B. (eds.) DESRIST 2012. LNCS, vol. 7286, pp. 423–438. Springer, Heidelberg (2012)
20. Wand, Y., Wang, R.Y.: Anchoring data quality dimensions in ontological foundations. Communications of the ACM 39(11), 86–95 (1996)
21. Blumer, H.: Symbolic interactionism: Perspective and method. University of California Press (1969)

Towards Design Principles for Pharmacist-Patient Health Information Systems

Dirk Volland[1], Klaus Korak[2], David Brückner[2], and Tobias Kowatsch[1]

[1] University of St. Gallen, Dufourstrasse 40a, 9000 St. Gallen, Switzerland
{dirk.volland,tobias.kowatsch}@unisg.ch
[2] Konsortium Pilot AlphaStreams, Weinbergstr. 56/58, 8092 Zürich, Switzerland
{kk,db}@alphastreams.com

Abstract. A significant drawback of communications between patients and health professionals is their restriction to face-to-face encounters within healthcare institutions. This limits the support health professionals can provide to ensure patient adherence, which is a significant contributor to therapeutic outcome and overall healthcare expenses. Pharmacist-patient health information systems (PPHIS) have the potential to address existing non-adherence behaviors by enabling pharmacist-patient communication over the time of therapy. Due to the lack of prior research, design principles for PPHIS are derived from the information-, motivation-, and strategy model [4] and feedback from pharmacists in 21 Swiss pharmacies. To demonstrate the feasibility of the design principles, we implement and preliminarily evaluate a PPHIS.

Keywords: Pharmacist-Patient Health Information System, Design Principles, Mobile Information System, Prototype, Adherence, Communication.

1 Introduction

One of the key challenges in healthcare is to continuously balance access to and quality of care for individuals with associated costs for society. While most attempts focus on institutional efficiency and therapeutic progress, the patient herself has been described as healthcare's greatest untapped resource [6]. Patients however, are never simply isolated individuals, but are characterized by specific interactions and relationships with institutionalized health professionals. This provides an opportunity for healthcare information systems (HIS).

For patients and health professionals alike, relationships are still heavily influenced by a fundamental asymmetry of being on "the inside" or "the outside" of healthcare institutions such as pharmacies, physicians' practices, and hospitals. For the patient, leaving those institutions means leaving well-structured pathways where guidance and support is directly provided by health professionals. The absence of guidance outside institutions often has detrimental effects on patient adherence, and thus on therapy outcomes and associated costs. Adherence and non-adherence describe patients' behavior outside healthcare institutions, to either follow recommended guidance and treatment advice from health professionals, or not [4]. The underlying reasons for

J. vom Brocke et al. (Eds.): DESRIST 2013, LNCS 7939, pp. 519–526, 2013.

non-adherence are manifold. Targeting single factors often does not lead to a desired improvement [3]. Due to a pharmacy's unique position within the healthcare system, providing direct and cost-efficient access to medical experts, products, and services, as well as often being the last or sole care provider in personal contact with patients beginning their therapy, pharmacist-patient health information systems (PPHIS) have the potential to address non-adherence by allowing pharmacists to guide patients during therapy. However, to date no design principles exist that describe the generic design of such systems given the existing variety of medical diagnoses and therapies.

In response to these facts, the current work addresses the question of how PPHIS can overcome the spatial and temporal boundaries between patients and health professionals enabling a continuous and structured communication to improve patient adherence. To address this question, overall research follows an iterative design science methodology [5, 10]. That is, several build and evaluate loops are planned during the design of principles for PPHIS that support patient adherence. In particular, the current work first justifies its relevance by a literature review in Section 2. In Section 3, design principles for PPHIS are developed that support the communication between patients and health professionals with the overall goal to increase patient adherence in everyday situations outside healthcare institutions. These principles are informed by the information-, motivation-, and strategy (IMS) model [4] as a kernel theory for improving patient adherence and, from a practitioner's point of view, by feedback from pharmacists in 21 Swiss pharmacies. The PPHIS is prototypically implemented according to these principles and preliminary evaluated as described in Section 4. This work-in-progress concludes with a summary and an outlook on future research.

2   Literature Review

In order to identify existing work with a focus on design principles for HIS in general and PPHIS in particular, a search strategy of prior work was adopted [2, 11]. The list of journals of prior reviews was retained and enriched by articles from the DESRIST conferences and the journal Health Systems. The following three publications are the final result of an iterative search and subsequent rigorous analysis of publications between 2002 and 2013.[1]

The authors of the first article [7] propose an approach for designing an ubiquitous IS to reduce adverse drug events of patients by improving communication between health professionals and patients. Using the health promotion model as a kernel theory they derive five design principles. They specifically point to the difficulty of integrating the health promotion model into the design model and call for a deeper integration of kernel theories into the design process. The second publication describes the design and evaluation of a smart medication management system for improving medication adherence [14]. This paper also builds on the health promotion model. In the third paper, a framework is described that is designed to support the requirements of patient

---

[1] Exact search procedure, queries, and the resulting list of publications and applied criteria can be retrieved from https://dl.dropbox.com/u/2264855/2013-02-5-Literature-Review.xlsx

monitoring with a focus on emergency messages [13]. However, design principles for HIS with the goal to address adherence and communication situations when patients have left healthcare institutions were not found.

3   Design Principles for PPHIS

In the current work, the design principles for PPHIS are primarily derived from the IMS model as the kernel theory with a focus on health professional-patient communication and adherence. This model specifically focuses on the practical application of health behavior change. It builds upon multiple classic approaches to health behavior and incorporates elements from the entire range of healthcare professional-patient communication [4]. The authors offer three broad categories of achievement including goals, actions, and accomplishments to guide health professionals and patients towards adherence: (1) Information, (2) Motivation, and (3) Strategy. It is the task of health professionals to tailor the given categories to individual patients.

In addition to the IMS model, and given the importance of aligning human, organizational, and technological factors [15], the requirements derived from the IMS model are enriched and merged with findings from 21 semi-structured interviews in Swiss pharmacies, conducted in the last quarter of 2012, and 19 responses to a standardized questionnaires completed subsequent to the personal interviews. One to four pharmacists participated in these interviews. Personal interviews addressed the current situation of pharmacies, pharmacist-patient communication, the existence of after-care operations, methods to control, support, or identify adherence, and the requirements for a PPHIS to support patients subsequent to a pharmacy visit. The questionnaire aimed to quantify different themes surrounding topics of adherence and patient support by the pharmacist.[2] For the analysis of the interviews, themes were extracted by using conceptual and relationship codes [1]. Finally, as interactions between health professionals and patients are extended beyond sole face-to-face communications, emerging requirements of temporal and spatial dimensions are of central importance for the development of the design principles [8, 9]. In the following, five design principles are developed based on the IMS model and feedback from 21 pharmacies.

First, the IMS model originally targets face-to-face encounters, which are temporally and spatially limited to the pharmacy visit. Mobile computing has dramatically changed work practices and communication in a variety of domains, freeing users from the confines of fixed locations and time. Smartphones hold the potential to structure and influence the spatial and temporal arrangements of both actors and their actions beyond existing boundaries. The perspective of temporal structures that actors engage in as part of their everyday routines has been introduced by [9]. Examples of temporal structures are weekly meetings or project deadlines that can be "used by people to give rhythm and form to their everyday work practices" (ibid., p. 685). Likewise, these temporal structures can serve as powerful templates that may help to structure patients' therapies. These theoretical implications were also identified as

---

[2]   The interview guidelines and questionnaires can be requested from the authors.

the most prominent theme from the interview analysis. Pharmacists perceive it as a significant limitation that once the patient has stepped out, nothing is known about her progress and no further support can be provided. All participating pharmacists of the 21 pharmacies agreed that today no structured methods to follow up with patients exist. Six pharmacists ask patients in some cases to return to the pharmacy after a certain period of time (e.g. after 5 days) or meetings are set in advance. Telephone or e-mail support is possible as reported by four pharmacists, but is only applied in complex cases. Methods to check or control patients' adherence are limited to the face-to-face encounter, and in rare and complex cases to dosing and supporting systems. On average 5% of patients contact the pharmacy because of questions during therapy using phone or e-mail. By contrast, approximately 11% of patients return to the pharmacy during therapy. Based on the discussion of the IMS model and the findings from the pharmacies above, the first design principle is formulated as follows:

DP1: The PPHIS should allow a pharmacist to follow up with a patient and communicate with a patient during the time of therapy.

Second, the information construct of the IMS model highlights the importance of patients' knowledge and how information, effectively communicated, can influence adherence. When patients understand, interpret, and remember health information correctly, they are much more likely to be adherent. However, existing research shows that even when the right information is provided during the encounter, a majority of patients fails to recall it later [4]. Accordingly, the second theme identified in the interviews was the perceived need of patients (as seen by the pharmacists) to be supported over the time of therapy and the willingness and perceived competency of the pharmacists to provide that support. Asked about the number of questions pharmacists think their patients have after visiting the pharmacy, 14 pharmacists responded 1-2 and 5 pharmacists responded 3-4. Asked about the share of patients, who are able to follow their therapy as recommended, opinions of pharmacists diverged, ranging from 6% to 95%, with an average of 54%. Pharmacists strongly agree that continuous information about the therapeutical progress can improve the quality of therapy. A one-sample t-test was applied to check if the calculated average differs from the scale's medium of 3 (Mean = 4.47, SD = .70, p < .001) on a 5-item Likert scale from "strongly disagree" to "strongly agree". Following up with patients during their therapy could significantly improve therapy outcomes (Mean = 4.52, SD = .70, p < .001). At the same time, pharmacists acknowledge that they currently lack information about patients' therapy progress (Mean = 2.84, SD = .96, p > .25). However, providing information and receiving information is mutually dependent. Based on this discussion, the second design principle is stated:

DP2: The PPHIS should allow a pharmacist to provide health-information to a patient during the time of therapy and adjust and enrich that information depending on feedback from a patient.

Third, the motivation component of the IMS model refers to situations when patients only follow treatment recommendations they believe in. Consequently, it is important that health professionals help patients to trust the efficacy of treatment recommendations. Pharmacists need the ability to follow up with patients in case therapy does not progress as intended, the patients' confidence in treatment is low, or when the patient believes that she is not capable to adhere to the recommendations (as described above pharmacists estimate that only 54% of patients follow these recommendations). Based on the above, the third design principle is stated:

> **DP3:** The PPHIS should allow a pharmacist to motivate a patient e.g. by promoting the perception of efficacy during the time of therapy and adjust and enrich that motivation depending on feedback from a patient.

Fourth, the strategy component of the IMS model refers to situations where concrete barriers exist that prevent patients from following treatment recommendations. Hence, health professionals need to support patients in finding a workable strategy and provide concrete assistance [4]. This can include medication reminders, but also the structured informational and motivational support over time. Pharmacists strongly believe that they can increase patient adherence in everyday practices (Mean = 4.42, SD = 0.61, p < .001). Based on that, the fourth design principle is formulated:

> **DP4:** The PPHIS should allow a pharmacist to provide strategic support to a patient during the time of therapy and adjust and enrich that strategy depending on feedback from a patient.

Finally, because of the heterogeneity of informational, motivational, and strategic support needed by patients, it is essential that health professionals can configure follow-up content (DP2-4) and its temporal dimension (DP1) in the situation of face-to-face encounters. This corresponds to the third theme that emerged from the interviews regarding the need for seamless integration into existing pharmacists' workflows and the need for a low-investment solution. This is due to the limitations in personnel as well as workplace resources. So, on the basis of the given situation, pharmacists need the ability to situatively choose from a set of informational, motivational, and strategic elements and instantiate them at the point of patient contact. Depending on the configuration, the patient then receives adherence-supporting elements over the chosen follow-up window. Based on the above, the last design principle is stated:

> **DP5:** At the time of the face-to-face encounter with a patient in the pharmacy, the PPHIS should allow a pharmacist to choose from a given set of informational, motivational, and strategic elements and instantiate them for the given situation over a specified time pattern.

While DP2, DP3, and DP4 are design principles concerning the content of pharmacist-patient communication, DP1 and DP5 relate to the process of communication. During face-to-face encounters of pharmacist and patient, informational, motivational, and strategic elements are instantiated over a chosen period of time. When leaving the pharmacy, the patient automatically receives these elements following a predefined time pattern as configured by the pharmacist. These elements can inform the patient about her therapy in form of, for example, text or video. They can motivate the patient to ask questions or to document her therapy progress. They can provide strategic support, for example, by reminding the patient to take certain actions. Overall, it is a semi-automated process where pharmacists get involved depending on the actions of the patient, for example, when she asks a question or a photo is sent that documents the current state of therapy. The proposed design principles for PPHIS are flexible in that the respective elements are instantiated at the time of face-to-face encounters. They are dynamic in that the content itself (DP2-4), but also the structuring over time (DP1) and the instantiation (DP5) can be continuously improved, based on data generated through pharmacist-patient communication.

4   Application of the Design Principles

To demonstrate the feasibility and utility of the design principles, we implemented and preliminarily evaluated a PPHIS consisting of (1) a tangible code-element in form of a simple postcard, (2) a communication and monitoring interface for pharmacists tailored to a tablet-PC, and (3) a communication interface for patients in the form of a smartphone application.[3] Besides the ability to provide information to the patient and question and answer communication, several types of feedback are implemented that can be configured for a specific time pattern by the pharmacist such as (1) making a photo e.g. of affected skin, (2) reporting general therapy progress on a scale from "significantly worse" to "significantly better", or (3) reporting simple medical parameters such as blood pressure or pulse. Currently, the code-element (Fig. 1a) consists of eight digits in the format $xxxx-yy-zz$ that encapsulate a unique pharmacy and customer ID ($xxxx$), the structure of the content (yy), and the duration (zz) of the follow-up with a particular patient (DP1 and DP5). The handover of the code does not interrupt existing workflows and bridges the offline encounter in the pharmacy with the online interaction using the PPHIS. Several configurations of content and structure are currently predefined (e.g. the patient receives the invitation to ask questions on the second day, is asked about general progress on the third day, and is asked to provide a photo on the fifth day). Flexibility of code structure and code generation will be further improved in future prototypes.

When the patient first downloads the patient app, she is asked for the code and after entering it, she receives messages and notifications in a twitter-like main screen

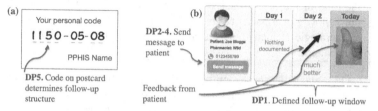

Fig. 1. Tangible code element (a) and particular patient record in iPad pharmacist app (b)

---

[3]   The primary target platforms were iPhone and iPad. However, the implementation was done in Titanium (http://appcelerator.com), consisting of an SDK that provides the necessary tools, compilers, and APIs to build for different target platforms.

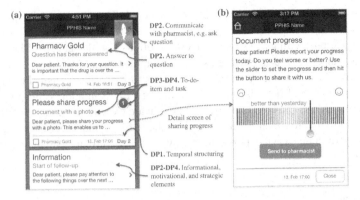

Fig. 2. Main screen (a) and screen of progress documentation (b) of iPhone patient app

(Fig. 2a). This process is automated over the specified duration and depends solely on the entered code. Informational elements that come into the stream provide health-related information, but other items require manual interactions such as when the patient is asked for her progress or if she has any questions related to her therapy (DP2-DP4). Further interaction or more detailed information is accessible when clicking on the messages in the main screen, for example, a screen to provide therapy progress (Fig. 2b). Only then, the pharmacist is notified in the pharmacist app and can view and respond to the feedback (Fig. 1b), or answer a question.

The PPHIS is currently pre-evaluated with 21 pharmacies. In each pharmacy, one pharmacist takes the role of the pharmacist while the other employees take patients' roles. So far, the implemented system has been tested by 21 pharmacists and more than 100 "internal patients". Log file analysis shows that the system has been extensively used (555 messages, 236 instantiations of follow-ups, and 183 documentations). Overall, qualitative feedback so far is positive, and pharmacists say that the PPHIS is easy and intuitive to use. The concept is seen as promising and pharmacies are eager to go live with their customers.

5   Conclusions and Further Research

In this work-in progress paper, we address the lack of prior research on design principles for PPHIS that enable pharmacist-patient communication beyond current face-to-face encounters to support patients' adherence. Accordingly, design principles for PPHIS are developed based on the IMS model and feedback from 21 pharmacies. They were finally applied during the design of a PPHIS that was pre-evaluated, too.

After the pre-evaluation of the PPHIS prototype within the pharmacies, qualitative feedback from all pharmacists will be collected once more to iterate again through the design cycle, and to proceed by testing the PPHIS including patients of participating pharmacies. To evaluate how the implemented PPHIS affects patients' adherence, a five-item self-report scale will be used as suggested in [4]. In addition to the qualitative feedback, valuable insights by analyzing PPHIS' log files and by "listening into" pharmacist-patient communication [12] are expected. The sample of 21 pharmacies with 50 to 500 patient encounters per day allows for a broad validation of the principles in different settings. Theoretical contributions for designing PPHIS are expected from analyzing usage patterns and communication contents by uncovering how patients can be optimally guided subsequent to a pharmacy visit. Practical contributions are expected regarding the feasibility of PPHIS in addressing population's adherence issues and thus reducing overall healthcare expenses. Finally, PPHIS might be a valuable tool for pharmacies enabling them to extend the range, value, and accessibility of their service portfolio by overcoming current spatial and temporal limitations.

References

1. Bradley, E.H., Curry, L.A., Devers, K.J.: Qualitative Data Analysis for Health Services Research: Developing Taxonomy, Themes, and Theory. Health Services Research 42(4), 1758–1772 (2007)
2. Chiasson, M.W., Davidson, E.: Pushing the contextual envelope: developing and diffusing IS theory for health information systems research. Information & Organization 14(3), 155–188 (2004)
3. DiMatteo, M.R., Giordani, P.J., Lepper, H.S., Croghan, T.W.: Patient adherence and medical treatment outcomes: a meta-analysis. Medical Care 40(9), 794–811 (2002)
4. DiMatteo, M.R., Haskard-Zolnierek, K.B., Martin, L.R.: Improving patient adherence: a three-factor model to guide practice. Health Psychology Review 6(1), 74–91 (2012)
5. Gregor, S., Jones, D.: The anatomy of a design theory. Journal of the Association for Information Systems 8(5), 312–335 (2007)
6. Kemper, D.W., Mettler, M.: Information Therapy: Prescribed Information as a Reimbursable Medical Service (2002)
7. Maass, W., Varshney, U.: Design and evaluation of Ubiquitous Information Systems and use in healthcare. Decision Support Systems 54(1), 597–609 (2012)
8. Martins, H.M.G.: Critical Concepts in M-Health Technology Development: Time, Space, and Mobility. In: Telemedicine and E-Health Services, Policies, and Applications, pp. 140–150 (2012)
9. Orlikowski, W.J., Yates, J.: It's about time: Temporal Structuring in Organizations. Organization Science 13(6), 684–700 (2002)
10. Peffers, K., Tuunanen, T., Rothenberger, M., Chatterjee, S.: A design science research methodology for information systems research. Information Systems 24(3), 45–77 (2007)
11. Romanow, D., Cho, S., Straub, D.: Riding the Wave: Past Trends and Future Directions for Health IT Research. MIS Quarterly 36(3), iii–A18 (2012)
12. Urban, G., Hauser, J.: "Listening In" to Find and Explore New Combinations of Customer Needs. Journal of Marketing 68(2), 72–87 (2004)
13. Varshney, U.: A framework for supporting emergency messages in wireless patient monitoring. Decision Support Systems 45, 981–996 (2008)
14. Varshney, U.: Smart medication management system and multiple interventions for medication adherence. Decision Support Systems (2012)
15. Yusof, M.M., Kuljis, J., Papazafeiropoulou, A., Stergioulas, L.K.: An evaluation framework for Health Information Systems: human, organization and technology-fit factors (HOT-fit). International Journal of Medical Informatics 77(6), 386–398 (2008)

Author Index

Ågerfalk, Pär J.   197, 511
Albani, Antonia   278
Almeida, Rafael   150
Alturki, Ahmad   258
Augenstein, Christoph   386

Bandara, Wasana   258
Becker, Jörg   394
Beckers, Christoph   324
Beutner, Marc   425
Bider, Ilia   464
Biegel, Harald   18
Bittmann, Sebastian   242
Bitzer, Philipp   471
Bodenbenner, Philipp   293
Brückner, David   519
Buckl, Sabine   73

Cater-Steel, Aileen   308
Clever, Nico   394

da Silva, Miguel Mira   150
Debortoli, Stefan   438
Dinter, Barbara   486
Domigall, Yannic   278
Dutta, Kaushik   400

Falk, Thomas   88
Feistenauer, Hannes   420
Feuerriegel, Stefan   293
Flenner, Arjuna   340
Funning, Gareth J.   340
Furtak, Szymon J.   446

Gable, Guy G.   258
Gaß, Oliver   18
Goeken, Matthias   353
Gonzalez, Rafael A.   59
Griesberger, Philipp   88

Harnesk, Dan   479
Hauke, Jörg   420
Häuser, Ivan   446
Heitkötter, Henning   405
Helmholz, Patrick   412

Herrmann, Philipp   425
Heß, Michael   369
Hilpert, Hendrik   324
Hofmann, Marcus   486
Holler, Justus   394
Hovorka, Dirk S.   228

Jacobi, Frieder   486
Janiesch, Christian   448
Johannesson, Paul   464

Kolbe, Lutz M.   324
Korak, Klaus   519
Kowatsch, Tobias   519
Krawatzeck, Robert   486
Krönke, Bernhard   420
Kundisch, Dennis   425

Lauth, Codrina   446
Leimeister, Jan Marco   471
Leist, Susanne   88
Leung, Rock   502
Li, Mahei   18
Lochan, Ruth   511
Ludwig, André   386
Lukyanenko, Roman   165
Lyons, Kelly   502

Mädche, Alexander   1, 18, 494
Magenheim, Johannes   425
Majchrzak, Tim A.   405
Marjanovic, Olivera   212
Matthes, Florian   73
Matzner, Martin   448
Mayer, Jörg Hans   420, 432
Moradian, Ali   502
Morana, Stefan   494
Mueller-Wickop, Niels   105
Müller, Oliver   438
Mustafa, Mudassir Imran   34

Nasir, Maaz   502
Neumann, Dirk   293
Neumann, Jürgen   425
Niehaves, Björn   456

Oglesby, David D.   340
Olfman, Lorne   340
Ortbach, Kevin   456

Parsons, Jeffrey   165
Patas, Janusch   353
Pedersen, Rasmus U.   446
Pereira, Rúben   150
Perjons, Erik   464
Piirainen, Kalle A.   59
Plattfaut, Ralf   456
Pöppelbuß, Jens   353
Pries-Heje, Jan   228

Rafiq, Asma   197, 511
Rahman, Mohammad Hafijur   511
Reinecke, Alexa   420
Reinen, Linda A.   340
Reinhardt, Wolfgang   425
Robra-Bissantz, Susanne   412
Rousi, Rebekah   181

Samuel-Ojo, Olusola   340
Schacht, Silvia   1, 494
Scherp, Ansgar   494
Schneider, Alexander W.   73
Schultz, Martin   105, 120
Schumann, Matthias   324

Schweda, Christian M.   73
Schwegmann, Bernd   448
Seidel, Stefan   438
Shitkova, Maria   394
Shrestha, Anup   308
Singh, Vivek Kumar   400
Sjöström, Jonas   34, 197, 511

Tan, Wui-Gee   308
Thapa, Devinder   479
Thomas, Oliver   242
Tischner, Gotthard   420
Toleman, Mark   308
Tremblay, Monica Chiarini   50

VanderMeer, Debra   50, 400
Van Kranenburg, Rob   446
Venable, John R.   136
Voigt, Matthias   456
Volland, Dirk   519

Weiß, Frank   471
Whittaker, Michael   425
Winter, Robert   278, 432

Ziesmann, Edgar   412
Zoyke, Andrea   425